The Official
OHIO STATE
Football Encyclopedia

JACK PARK

**Officially Endorsed and Licensed
by The Ohio State University**

Sports Publishing L.L.C.
www.SportsPublishingLLC.com

™

Director of Production: Susan M. Moyer
Interior Design: Michelle R. Dressen, Susan M. Moyer, Jennifer L. Polson
Dedication Design: Kenneth J. Higgerson
Cover Design: Christina Cary and Emily Washburn
Photo Insert Design: Christina Cary
Newspapers contributing graphic material:
 Columbus Dispatch
 Cleveland Plain Dealer
 Cincinnati Enquirer
 Dayton Daily News
 Akron Beacon Journal
 Scripps Howard

ISBN: 1-58261-006-1
Leatherbound edition: 1-58261-274-9

SPORTS PUBLISHING L.L.C.
www.SportsPublishingLLC.com

Printed in the United States

ontents ....

Accolades   *for The Official Ohio State Football Encyclopedia* iv

Introduction   *by Archie Griffin* vi

Foreword   *by Jim Herbstreit* viii

                       by Kirk Herbstreit ix

Reflection   *by Jim Houston* x

Preface   *by Jack and Sue Park* xii

Dedication   *to Coach Paul Brown and the 1942 Ohio State Buckeyes* xiv

Chapter 1   Jim Tressel: A New Beginning 1

Chapter 2   How It All Began (1890-1912) 9

Chapter 3   Joining the Big Ten (1913-1921) 51

Chapter 4   Creating Ohio Stadium (1922-1928) 85

Chapter 5   Football and the Great Depression (1929-1933) 117

Chapter 6   Francis Schmidt: Mr. Razzle Dazzle (1934-1940) 141

Chapter 7   Paul Brown: The Organization Man (1941-1943) 181

Chapter 8   Graveyard of Coaches (1944-1950) 217

Chapter 9   Woody Takes Command (1951-1960) 275

Chapter 10   The Turbulent '60s (1961-1970) 333

Chapter 11   Archie Arrives (1971-1978) 399

Chapter 12   The Earle Bruce Era (1979-1987) 473

Chapter 13   Cooper Takes Control (1988-1993) 541

Chapter 14   Cooper at the Helm (1994-2000) 583

Chapter 15   The Voice of the Buckeyes 637

Appendix   All-Time Records, Statistics, Honors,

                    Football Letterwinners 649

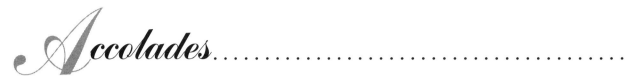

Accolades . . . .

The Official Ohio State Football Encyclopedia captures all of the great history of Ohio State football, and is an excellent tribute to the finest football program in the country. Dedicating it to an outstanding coach and gentleman, Paul Brown, and his 1942 national championship team is very appropriate because of their many achievements. Jack Park can be very proud of his work—it describes the essence of our great tradition. Every Buckeye should have a copy of Jack's book.

Coach Earle Bruce
Ohio State University

This book is a "must read" for any serious Ohio State football fan. Jack Park is the Dean of OSU football historians, and has done an outstanding job of capturing the dynamics of the Ohio State football experience.

Dave Van Stone, Vice President/General Manager
Sports Radio 1460 The Fan

The Official Ohio State Football Encyclopedia is an excellent history of Buckeye football. It is not only interesting and informative, but it is also amazingly accurate. It is a necessity for anyone who loves the Buckeyes. I can assure you it will settle any disagreements concerning Ohio State football.

Coach Lou Holtz
University of South Carolina

Save some space on your bookshelf. Everything you need to know about Ohio State football, its history and traditions, is right here from A (Albert Abbott who played in 1898) to Z (lineman Srecko Zizakovic, 1986-89).

Rusty Miller, Sports Editor
Ohio Associated Press

Jack Park is the unquestioned authority on Ohio State football history. But what really makes Park exceptional is his passion for OSU football. This allows him to capture the nuances that make Buckeye football such a unique experience with such a grand tradition. Any work by Park is far more than just a compilation of names, scores and numbers. It is a labor of love.

Frank Moskowitz, Publisher
Buckeye Sports Bulletin

Jack, keep up the good work. College football needs you.
Coach Joe Paterno
Penn State University

There is but one authority on the history of Ohio State football, and that is Jack Park. Only Jack could have written this book.
John Porentas, Editor
www.The-Ozone.net

Jack breathes life into the history of Ohio State football through his skillful profiling of the people and events that shaped the program.
Bob Scanlon, Vice President and General Manager
WJER Radio—Dover, Ohio

If you want to amaze your Buckeye buddies with your knowledge of Ohio State pigskin facts and figures, this is the book to have. In my 35 years of covering sports, I've never met anyone as familiar with a team's history, as Jack is with Ohio State football. Now, he shares it with you!
Mike Greene, Sports Director
WMFD-TV—Mansfield, Ohio

The tradition-laden Ohio State football program comes into sharp focus with Jack's new book. You won't truly bleed Scarlet and Gray until you have your copy. Go Bucks!
Tom Francis, Regional Sales Manager
WIMA Radio—Lima, Ohio

Jack Park scores again with *The Official Ohio State Football Encyclopedia*. Jack has demonstrated over the years that if you want the definitive word on Ohio State football, he is your source. Jack's Encyclopedia is predictably filled with facts, anecdotes, photos, and insight that bring this history to life.
Martin Rozenman, Editor
Suburban News Publications

Introduction . . . .

Ohio State football is extremely special, and Buckeye fans have played a major role in creating what is a fabulous tradition. People have very high expectations for the Ohio State program, but I wouldn't want it any other way. Those lofty goals simply show me how much our fans care about the success of Buckeye football.

I have been a very fortunate individual all of my life. It started with having a wonderful dad and mother who loved and cared for their children. Football has meant the world to me and my family. All of my brothers and I were able to obtain our college degrees because of our involvement in football. Jim played at Muskingum, Larry played at Louisville, and Daryle played at Kent State. Ray and Duncan were two of my Ohio State teammates, and Keith played at Miami of Florida. Our sister, Krystal, excelled at track-and-field.

Looking back, I am very happy that in 1972, Coach Woody Hayes convinced me to choose the Scarlet and Gray. I had offers from other schools, but things have really worked out well for me at Ohio State. Coach Hayes coveted a championship football program, but he wanted even more for his players—to graduate and become productive citizens. Today, as Associate Director of Athletics, I have the responsibility and opportunity to work directly with 13 of our 35 varsity sports.

Woody Hayes was a very wise man, and the many concepts we learned from him seem to be even more profound now than when he introduced them to us more than 25 years ago. Coach Hayes continually stressed teamwork and emphasized that each of us is better than we think we are when we are part of a strong team. This is so true! I never dreamed of capturing the Heisman Trophy, let alone winning it twice. But when placed in a team situation with other committed players, we all became better than we thought was possible. My Heisman Trophies reflect the excellent Ohio State teams of '74 and '75.

Coach Hayes truly cared about people, and he taught all of us the concept of "paying forward." It is not always feasible to pay back the many people who have helped us in the past, but it is always possible to provide support for those in the future. That's one reason my wife, Bonita, and I originated the Archie & Bonita Griffin Foundation Fund and the Archie Griffin Scholarship Fund. We intend to continue Coach Hayes' philosophy of "paying forward."

Jack Park and I first became acquainted in the summer of 1976, shortly before my first season with the Cincinnati Bengals. Paul Brown had just retired as head coach of the Bengals so he could concentrate solely on his responsibilities as the team's general manager. I would really like to have played at least one season under Coach Brown. It is very appropriate that *The Official Ohio State Football Encyclopedia* is dedicated to him and his 1942 squad, the first Ohio State team to capture a national title.

Jack has extensively covered every facet of OSU football, from the very first game at Ohio Wesleyan in 1890 through the hiring of Coach Jim Tressel in 2001. The *Encyclopedia* gives you a perfect seat at midfield to view all of those great Buckeye victories. Treasured memories have been dusted off and brought back to life through more than 200 short anecdotes, revealing many unusual, outstanding and humorous incidents.

I particularly enjoy reading about my varsity seasons of '72 through '75, when we captured four Big Ten titles and played in four Rose Bowls. Our three victories over Coach Bo Schembechler's Michigan Wolverines were three of the most exciting and intense in the long history of this great rivalry. Victories over Bo's teams were also Woody's favorites!

Some of my very talented teammates included Randy Gradishar, John Hicks, Kurt Schumacher, Steve Myers, Van DeCree, Neal Colzie, Pete Cusick, Tim Fox, Ted Smith, Cornelius Greene, Brian Baschnagel, Ken Kuhn, Tom Skladany, Pete Johnson, my brother Ray, and many others. You'll read about them all in this inspiring publication.

Enjoy *The Official Ohio State Football Encyclopedia,* and **Go Buckeyes!**

Archie Griffin
Associate Director of Athletics
Two-Time Heisman Trophy Winner
Three-Time All-American
Two-Time Captain and Team MVP

Foreword . . . .

My childhood ambition was to someday play football at Ohio State. In grade school I wrote an essay that described the 1949 Buckeyes' 17-14 Rose Bowl victory over California. Ohio State was the only school I seriously considered, and I have never had a second thought about this decision. The opportunity to develop close relationships with teammates and to learn from Coach Woody Hayes and his staff was an extremely rewarding experience.

As a 5-8 halfback who weighed 150 pounds, I was considered by some to be too small to compete at the major-college level. During my freshman season, I would often sit all alone in the south bleachers at Ohio Stadium and imagine the huge horseshoe filled with color and noise. I would envision myself someday walking to the center of the field as a Buckeye captain. The encouraging advice of Bob Richards, noted Olympic pole vaulter, to "dream a dream and make it happen" served me well.

Being elected a captain at Ohio State is a very precious honor. My captain's mug is my No. 1 keepsake, and it will always occupy a special place on our mantle. The thrills I experienced as a Buckeye captain were surpassed only by the joy I felt when Kirk called to tell me he, too, had been elected an Ohio State captain. It was a phenomenal feeling to realize that Kirk had become part of the captains' tradition that we both treasure dearly.

I clearly recall the excitement of attending my first annual "captains' breakfast." Some of the former captains I met were Jim Lincoln of the 1906 team, Honus Graf from 1914, and Mike Kabealo from 1938. There are only a handful of truly notable traditions in college football, and Ohio State is one of the finest. The challenge for today's Buckeye players and those of the future is to build upon these vast accomplishments.

Kirk and I are both very appreciative of the many opportunities afforded us through Ohio State football, both on and off the field. Through these experiences we have learned the importance of a strong work ethic and the value of perseverance. Intercollegiate athletics provide unique challenges for young people, and there is nothing old-fashioned about that.

Jack Park is a true authority on Ohio State football, and I have enjoyed his colorful radio spots for many seasons. *The Official Ohio State Football Encyclopedia* encompasses countless anecdotes—published for the first time. Enjoy a stroll through this great tradition, and **Go Bucks!**

Jim Herbstreit
Co-Captain 1960

Jim Herbstreit and son Kirk Herbstreit each served as a Buckeye co-captain.

ℱoreword . . . .

Playing football for the Scarlet and Gray was living out a childhood dream. There was never any doubt I was coming to Ohio State, and I was ready to commit in December of 1987, even before the announcement of John Cooper as OSU's new head coach later that month. The opportunity to be part of this great tradition is almost mythical. I have always been very appreciative of my dad leaving the decision to play at Ohio State completely up to me.

Growing up in Centerville, I clearly recall the thrill of autumn Saturdays. Our family would play records of the Ohio State Marching Band from early morning until kickoff. We would then listen to the play-by-play radio broadcast and often re-create the scoring plays in the front yard as the game continued. I often would pretend to be Archie Griffin or Cornelius Greene. It's amazing what your imagination can do for you. Saturday evening we watched a complete replay of the game on PBS-TV.

The transition from high school to college was difficult for me. I didn't play a lot during my early college years, and I even thought about quitting football and concentrating solely on baseball. Fortunately, I had the strong support of family and friends to help me get through the tough times. Through football, I learned a lot about life. When you get knocked down, you need to get back up and go again. In the end, it was very gratifying to be elected a captain and chosen the team's MVP my senior season.

My brother, John, and my sister, Teri, and I began going to the Ohio State games when we were very young. Dad would often take John and me inside the Ohio State locker room after the games. Woody Hayes would talk with me as I sat on his lap, and Archie Griffin would let us try on his helmet. I vividly remember those experiences as though they happened yesterday.

When my dad brought me to Columbus for my first fall practice at Ohio State, he told me that only six or seven of the 20 incoming freshmen would start for the Buckeyes during the next four or five years. He was right. I learned that hard work and perseverance truly help you prepare for the future. My roller-coaster college career has been very beneficial to my present position as an analyst with *ESPN's College Game Day* and *The Ohio State Football Radio Network*. It gives me a unique perspective to evaluate today's players and teams.

I first met Jack Park when I joined WBNS Radio in 1993. Each season his daily "Buckeye Flashback" commentaries bring the emotion and electrifying pageantry of college football to listeners throughout Ohio. Jack's meticulous research has made *The Official Ohio State Football Encyclopedia* one of the most complete accounts of this great heritage.

Kirk Herbstreit

Kirk Herbstreit
Co-Captain and Team MVP 1992

Reflection . . . .

It seems like only yesterday when I would visit with Coach Paul Brown, Otto Graham, Dante Lavelli, Lou Groza, Edgar "Special Delivery" Jones, Mac Speedie, and other members of that very first Cleveland Browns team in 1946. I was nine years old, and my brother Lin would take me inside the locker room after the games. It seemed almost unbelievable that in just 14 years I would be playing for the Browns, after being the No. 1 draft choice of the coach whom Lin and I so admired.

Lin had the rare distinction and opportunity to play under Paul Brown at Massillon High School, Ohio State University, and with the Cleveland Browns. He was an All-American guard for the Buckeyes' national champions in 1942. Lin and I had two brothers, Jack and Walt, who played at Purdue in the early 1950s under Coach Jack Mollenkopf. Mollenkopf had been a prominent coach at Toledo Waite High School. He actively supported Massillon's Paul Brown for the head coaching job at Ohio State in 1941.

Growing up in Massillon, I learned a lot about community pride at a very early age. The great Massillon tradition was created, at least in part, when Paul Brown transformed Tiger football into a nationally recognized high school program during the 1930s. Brown pioneered the concept of implementing his football system into the Massillon junior high schools, so that those players would be familiar with his methods when they entered high school. His emphasis on intelligence, physical conditioning, and an inner drive to excel is still part of the Massillon culture today.

We were state champions under Coach Chuck Mather in 1953 and Coach Tom Harp in 1954, my sophomore and junior seasons at Massillon. Both coaches were excellent at evaluating the strengths and weaknesses of our Tiger squads and those of our opponents. Much like Paul Brown, each was well organized and very articulate. Lee Tressel, Jim Tressel's father, followed Harp as head coach in 1956, two seasons before Lee became head coach at Baldwin-Wallace College.

At Ohio State, we won the Rose Bowl and captured the national title during my sophomore year of 1957. Our 17-13 victory over mighty Iowa that fall was truly a classic. Esco Sarkkinen was an excellent end coach who taught us many finite techniques, right down to foot position and angle of attack—tips that proved especially helpful against Iowa and in the Rose Bowl.

I noticed many similarities between Woody Hayes and Paul Brown. Both planned for everything to the "nth degree," and both prepared their players for success in life after football. They had the same intensity—Woody was more vocal, Paul was more reserved. Paul's practices were extremely well organized and never lasted longer than an hour and 30 minutes.

The Official Ohio State Football Encyclopedia is an unequaled portrayal of the great Buckeye tradition. Read about Archie Griffin's record-breaking afternoon against North Carolina in '72, find out why Ohio State became known as the "graveyard of coaches" in the 1940s, and learn more about the enormous Ohio State–Michigan rivalry. Relive some of the Buckeyes' greatest victories, including OSU's dramatic win over Wisconsin in '54, the '68 shutout of top-ranked Purdue, the '97 Rose Bowl win over Arizona State, and one of my personal favorites—our 38-28 triumph at Iowa in '58, the Hawkeyes' only setback that season.

Ohio State's loyal fans are a major part of the great Buckeye tradition, and Jack Park has included numerous anecdotes describing outstanding, humorous, and unusual fan activities. Jack has been one of OSU's most devoted analysts and radio commentators for the past 25 seasons. He has included remarkable stories and information unknown even to the most ardent Buckeye fan.

Enjoy *The Official Ohio State Football Encyclopedia*, an outstanding description of the long and glorious history of Ohio State football. It's the next best thing to being at Ohio Stadium on a Saturday afternoon!

Jim Houston

Jim Houston
Captain 1959
Two-Time All-American
Two-Time Team MVP

Preface . . . .

Ohio State's vast football heritage has been created through the leadership and accomplishments of many dedicated people for more than 11 decades. It is our pleasure to describe in *The Official Ohio State Football Encyclopedia* many of the proud achievements that symbolize this storied tradition.

The Official Ohio State Football Encyclopedia recalls many of the highlights, as well as a few of the disappointments, in the long and glorious history of Buckeye football. It also emphasizes the many humorous and unusual incidents that are so much a part of this grand legacy.

We are privileged to have the participation of Archie Griffin, Kirk Herbstreit, Jim Herbstreit, and Jim Houston. These Buckeye greats graciously shared many hours with us, providing treasured insights and memories from their careers. We appreciate their generous contributions, encouragement, and support.

The Official Ohio State Football Encyclopedia is proudly dedicated to Coach Paul Brown and his 1942 Ohio State team. This dedication is unique because of the cherished testimonies provided by this special group of people and their families. We offer special thank-yous to Mrs. Mary Brown for her encouragement, and to our good friend Gene Fekete, who eagerly helped us coordinate this inspiring project.

A sincere thank-you is extended to Dave Van Stone, Skip Mosic, Jeff Austin, and the many other fine people at Sports Radio 1460 The Fan (WBNS-AM) for having me as part of their football programming since 1979. We are grateful for the efforts of Brian Timm and former Executive Producer Ed Douglas, who in 1998 arranged for "The Buckeye Flashback with Jack Park" to be aired each season throughout Ohio on *The Ohio State Football Radio Network.* Additionally, some of the Ohio State memorabilia featured throughout this book were made available from Brian's vast collection.

We appreciate the support of Clarke Price, Joan McGloshen, Jim Hartley, and the fine membership of The Ohio Society of Certified Public Accountants, who each season sponsor The Buckeye Flashback commentary around the Buckeye state. Many of the stories first developed for the Flashback are included in the *Encyclopedia.* For many years, producer Bob Taylor of Sports Radio 1460 The Fan has played a major role in the creation of this feature.

Ohio State Assistant Athletic Director for Communications Steve Snapp and his talented staff have provided assistance and information for many years. Diana Sabau and Greg Aylsworth furnished numerous photographs and statistical files, and Dan Wallenberg coordinated many of our needs and requests.

We are grateful for the efforts and courtesies extended by Dr. Rai Goerler, Jana Drvota, and Bertha Ihnat of The Ohio State University Archives. Jana spent countless hours helping us select many of the photographs, and Bertha coordinated the selection of the football program covers, player rosters, and various graphics. Many of the action photos are from the outstanding work of Mr. Chance Brockway and his sons, who recently donated many of their pictures to the University Archives.

We appreciate the advice and fine services of photographers Ed Winters in Columbus and Greg Rajsich in Massillon, who took the photos for the back cover and elsewhere

throughout the book. Sheila Vent of Morton and White Photographers effectively coordinated the creation of the Buckeye collage for the front cover.

Trevor Parks, Director of Sports Information at Youngstown State University; Kevin Ruple, Director of Sports Information at Baldwin-Wallace College; and Coach Jim Tressel's mother, Eloise Tressel, all contributed significantly to the introductory chapter. Dave Martin arranged for the bronze bust of Woody Hayes, sculpted by Mike Major, to be available for the front cover. Vincent Margello contributed the Rose Bowl photo of Coach John Cooper and Joe Germaine. Assistant equipment manager Rob Lachey arranged for our use of the Ohio State football equipment and jerseys. Fred Stokes provided many of the programs, especially those from the Woody Hayes seasons.

We value the permission granted by the *Columbus Dispatch, Cleveland Plain Dealer, Cincinnati Enquirer, Dayton Daily News, Akron Beacon Journal,* and *Scripps Howard* to use selected headlines and illustrations from their past publications. These excellent materials help illustrate many of the important happenings in the 111 seasons of Ohio State football.

We are grateful for the efforts, patience, and guidance of Mike Pearson, Susan Moyer, and their fine staffs at Sports Publishing L.L.C. Our good friend Eric Kaelin of Sports Radio 1460 The Fan first introduced us to Mike Pearson in the fall of 1997. We also are very appreciative of the longtime encouragement of our close friends Jerry and Lenora Pausch, two of Ohio State's most ardent supporters.

Last, but maybe most important, we hope that our three wonderful children, Julie, Jane, and Jim, will find as much happiness and satisfaction throughout their lives as we have found being proud contributors to Ohio State football.

Jack and Sue Park reminisce with Jimmy Hague (left) and Dick Widdoes (above) at the 1949 team's 50th reunion. Widdoes held the ball, and Hague kicked the winning fourth-quarter field goal to defeat California, 17-14, in the January 2, 1950, Rose Bowl. Widdoes' father, Carroll Widdoes, was Ohio State's head coach in 1944 and 1945.

Jack and Sue Park

Coach Paul Brown

Dedication

The *Official Ohio State Football Encyclopedia* is dedicated to Coach Paul Brown and his 1942 Buckeyes, the first Ohio State team to capture the national title. Coach Brown and this special group of young men were national champions far beyond the playing field. Their career achievements, respect for each other, and contributions to society have created one of the most splendid chapters in all of college football.

Ohio State 1942 National Champions

Row one: Bill Durtchi (20), Bob Frye (36), Les Horvath (22), Tommy James (66), Lin Houston (96), Wib Schneider (12), Dick Palmer (62), Bill Hackett (28), Captain George Lynn (11), Martin Amling (92), Warren McDonald (24), Cy Lipaj (76), Loren Staker (32), Chuck Csuri (60), Paul Sarringhaus (88), Carmen Naples (86), Trainer Ernie Biggs.

Row two: Assistant Tippy Dye, Assistant Fritz Mackey, Assistant Carroll Widdoes, Hal Dean (84), Tom Antenucci (82), George Slusser (42), Tom Cleary (78), Paul Selby (54), Bill Vickroy (55), Jack Roe (74), Bob Jabbusch (72), Gordon Appleby (50), Robin Priday (30), Paul Matus (10), Bob McCormick (52), Phil Drake (68), Manager Chuck Diesem.

Row three: Head Coach Paul Brown, Assistant Hugh McGranahan, Assistant Paul Bixler, Cecil Souders (80), Ken Coleman (26), Jim Rees (90), Tom Taylor (64), Bill Willis (99), Bill Sedor (14), J.T. White (70), Ken Eichwald (48), Bob Shaw (40), Don McCafferty (98), Jack Dugger (94), Don Steinberg (46), Dante Lavelli (33), Gene Fekete (44).

The '42 national champions played their hearts out, and Paul always referred to the team as the finest he ever coached. He referred to them as "his guys." My husband insisted on high moral standards and left no doubt he was in charge at all times. He expected them to achieve in the classroom as well as on the field. Paul prepared them for life after football, to get their degrees, and to be successful in their chosen fields. He had the ability to bring out the very best in the young men he selected to make up his squads. Paul always thanked the players for their efforts.

Mrs. Mary Brown
Cincinnati, Ohio

Our 1942 team was in the best of shape, both physically and mentally. One evening Paul Brown told me that the coaches evaluated each player after each practice. I never forgot that, and have carried that practice over into my own business.

Martin Amling
Guard—Parma, Illinois

Tom remembered Paul Brown as a brilliant coach who often said the team had "steel," meaning a good ethnic mix. I remember the coach as a very kind gentleman who spoke to each member of the 1942 team, from the stars to the managers and all the wives. It became apparent to me that my husband's team was a group of very ordinary men who accomplished extraordinary feats in football, in war, with their families, and in their communities for many years.

Mrs. Betty Antenucci for Tom Antenucci
End—Niles, Ohio

It was quite an honor to be a member of the team which won the Big Ten and Ohio State's first national title. Paul Brown was a perfectionist and always a gentleman. You would run a play until you got it right, and you would remember that in later life with anything that you did.

Gordon Appleby
Team Most Valuable Player, 1943
Ohio State Captain, 1944
Center—Massillon, Ohio

*T*he coaches prepared the team for each game so that the idea of losing didn't exist. Paul Brown built an aura of success around the team. He blended great conditioning with a demand for perfect execution. Paul Brown truly wanted his team to be academically superior to the competition.

Ken Coleman
Center—Brooklyn, New York

*W*e worked well together and respected one another as people. Paul Brown taught us to be honest with ourselves and with other people. Paul had dignity, a sense of order, the ability to focus, and a sense of style as a human being.

Charles Csuri
All-American Tackle
Team Most Valuable Player
Ohio State Captain-Elect, 1943
Cleveland, Ohio

*O*ur team was successful because we did not have a singular star, but a group of Buckeyes who had pride in our university and the willingness to push ourselves to the limits of our abilities. Paul Brown taught us that you never have to be afraid of making a mistake as long as you have utilized all the information and skills available to you. I best remember him for the organization of his practices and his methods of teaching new skills.

Hal Dean
Guard—Wooster, Ohio

*G*reat men are recognized not for the awards and accolades, nor by the hype that is so common today, but by earning the respect of other great men. Such was the relationship between Paul Brown and his 1942 national championship football team. Brown was a teacher first and foremost. Winning or losing was secondary to completing the task at hand. My father remained loyal to Paul Brown throughout his life.

Robert Diesem for Charles Diesem
Manager—Columbus, Ohio

*M*y husband learned from Paul Brown the importance of priorities, discipline, and fairness in being successful at whatever you attempt, even through all the obstacles.

Mrs. Marilyn Drake for Phil Drake
Quarterback—Columbus, Ohio

*P*aul Brown was a fine judge of an athlete's ability, and he used his athletes accordingly. His team responded. From Paul Brown my husband learned organization skills, having the right man in the right place, and the importance of frequently showing interest in those who work for you. Paul Brown always spoke to you as an individual.

Mrs. Helen Dugger for Jack Dugger
Ohio State Captain, 1943
Big Ten Conference Top Scholar-Athlete, 1944
All-American End, 1944
Canton, Ohio

*T*he players all liked and respected Paul Brown. Brown's honesty and fairness with all his players brought out the best in all of them. Bill became a high school football coach. He practiced Paul's methods and had three undefeated teams.

Mrs. Betty Durtschi for Bill Durtschi
Halfback—Galion, Ohio

*P*aul Brown was very focused as a coach—everything was so well organized. We have had many great Ohio State teams, but in my humble opinion, none better than this outstanding team. There was great camaraderie, very much like a family. They played together so well.

Tippy Dye
Assistant Coach—Pomeroy, Ohio

*O*ur national title team had great cohesiveness and camaraderie. We are still very close to each other today. Coach Brown had tremendous pride in his profession and being successful in winning. He instilled in every player that everything revolved around the team! You play in a game like you practice.

Gene Fekete
All-American Fullback, 1942
Eighth in Heisman Trophy Voting during
Sophomore Season in 1942
Findlay, Ohio

It was such a thrill going out on the field at Ohio State. We were successful because of our determination to play to the best of our ability. Paul Brown was a remarkable man and a great organizer of his time. He had everything down to the minute. Perfection, discipline, respect, and he loved speed—everyone had to move and run.

Robert Frye
Halfback—Crestline, Ohio

My own development through the Paul Brown experience made me more dedicated to the building of complex systems, piece by piece, and it taught me the patience that goes with that long-term approach. Paul Brown's managerial ability has been the best I have had the occasion to study on a close-up basis. I think he could have done exceptionally well in many fields.

Campbell Graf
Assistant Freshman Coach—Columbus, Ohio

My dad had great memories of the '42 team. It was the start of his relationship with Paul Brown, a relationship that lasted over 40 years. My dad always spoke of Paul Brown as a strict disciplinarian who was both fair and honest with everyone. One of Dad's greatest accomplishments was the key part he played in bringing Paul Brown back into football in Cincinnati. I wish Dad were alive. He would be a great contributor to your book, Jack, and we sure miss him.

Bob Hackett for Bill Hackett
All-American Guard, 1944
Ohio State Captain-Elect, 1945
London, Ohio

Les really respected Paul Brown as a coach and enjoyed playing with all the teammates that he stayed friends with over the years. Paul helped Les later in life with his fiery approach and his winning attitude.

Mrs. Ruby Horvath for Les Horvath
All-American Quarterback/Halfback, 1944
Ohio State's First Heisman Trophy Winner, 1944
College Football Hall of Fame
Cleveland, Ohio

𝒫aul Brown was like a genius CEO in his organizational abilities with his motivational speeches and delegation of authority. He never seemed to get very close to any of the team's members, but he did give direct evaluations of performances both good and bad. He was an innovative leader, and his systems changed football at all levels and forced competition to follow suit.

Bob Jabbusch
Ohio State Captain, 1947
Big Ten Conference Top Scholar-Athlete, 1947
Guard—Elyria, Ohio

𝒥 had Paul Brown as my coach at Massillon High School, at Ohio State, and with the Cleveland Browns. He taught us to always strive to do better, set your goals high, and work hard to succeed. Paul Brown always stressed fundamentals, and he treated his players honestly and fairly.

Tommy James
Ohio State Captain-Elect, 1947
Halfback—Massillon, Ohio

𝓜y special memory of our 1942 national championship season is our continued camaraderie after graduation. We were successful because of our preparation, good players and coaches, and discipline. What I learned from Paul Brown that helped me later in life was to be responsible, have discipline, be on time, and work together.

Dante Lavelli
Pro Football Hall of Fame
End—Hudson, Ohio

𝒫aul Brown was a father figure for us, a gentleman, and a scholar. He had great influence on my life. Paul was very organized and wanted 100 percent effort in whatever we did, and he got it. He gave us qualities to make our character. I learned about all parts of the game of football from Paul Brown and also from Trevor Rees, who was on his staff and later gave me my first coaching job when he was head coach at Kent State.

George Lynn
Ohio State Captain, 1942
Quarterback—Niles, Ohio

Ohio State's 1942 national champions celebrated their 50th anniversary at Ohio Stadium on Saturday, October 10, 1992.

I remember playing Illinois at Cleveland Municipal Stadium. Having grown up in Cleveland, where I played football at Lakewood High School, it was a special homecoming to play at the stadium in front of family and friends—it was a day every boy dreams about. Paul Brown was a man of his word. He was a great motivator, very disciplined, and he helped me establish a winning attitude throughout my life. I went into high school coaching and tried to stay as close as possible to Paul Brown's philosophy, knowing that success only comes through hard work.

Cy Lipaj
Fullback—Lakewood, Ohio

I didn't know the meaning of the word "class" until Paul Brown showed us by example. He often repeated, "Always play the string out until the bitter end" and "You play like you practice." These two phrases I'll remember to my grave.

Bob McCormick
Tackle—Columbus, Ohio

I well remember our 1942 season because of our dedicated players and our great coach. We worked hard to attain the goals set out for us as a team. After the season, Paul Brown wrote a recommendation on my behalf to the Air Force, and he told me that if I ever "chickened out," I would hear from him. He taught us the importance of intelligence, speed, agility, intestinal fortitude, and desire.

Paul Matus
End—Wakeman, Ohio

I learned from Paul Brown that if you pay attention to the little things, the big things will fall in line. I remember his belief in what he was doing and his desire to be the best. And he would not ask the members of the team to do anything he would not do himself.

Bill Munro
Assistant Manager—Park Ridge, New Jersey

From Paul Brown I learned patience and honesty. Paul always said if you were honest with yourself you can be honest with anyone. He never forgot a person, and he was always considerate of people. Paul was a quiet man with such inner depth.

Carmen Naples
Guard—Youngstown, Ohio

Coach Brown was an excellent role model for his young players. His appearance and manner off the field as well as on the sidelines were exemplary. Paul Brown not only had a clear vision of how he wanted his team to perform, but he was an outstanding teacher. I learned from him that success in any endeavor requires sound planning, mastery of basic fundamentals, and a determination to follow through, regardless of adversity or temporary setbacks.

Robin Priday
Quarterback—West Jefferson, Ohio

Paul Brown taught us a systematic, methodical procedure of undertaking tasks to attain successful results in the face of unforeseeable, variable difficulties. He was a very intense, focused man who was an expert at discerning the essentials of what was necessary in order to develop effective teams.

Jim Rees
Tackle—Greenville, Ohio

My husband always said that Paul Brown made them want to give their all on the field. That team was so successful because it had an abundance of talent, a strong sense of camaraderie, and Paul Brown's superb coaching skills.

Mrs. Lillian Sarringhaus for Paul Sarringhaus
All-American Halfback
Hamilton, Ohio

The 1942 year was undoubtedly the most exciting year of my husband's life. After their Indiana victory, Wib ended up with the game ball signed by every member of the team. I still have the ball. Wib recognized that Paul Brown was a brilliant coach, and they loved him. Brown was a class act in every way, and we tried to be that in our lives and in the business we started together and passed on to our children.

Mrs. Helen Schneider for Wib Schneider
Guard—Gahanna, Ohio

*P*aul Brown taught us to do your best in any activity you are assigned. This team had an abundance of talent and a lot of good coaching.

Bill Sedor
End—Shadyside, Ohio

I remember most the feeling of belonging and the high regard I had for the quality of the players, whether star or benchwarmer, like myself. As Paul Brown himself told us years later at our reunions, he was proud of us as a championship team, but he was most proud of the successes we have had as citizens in every walk of life. I recall Paul Brown as a great football coach, but my most lasting recollection of him is that he was a most honorable man, a remarkable mentor, and a person for whom I have always held the highest regard and respect. Very often, almost daily in my professional life, that image of Paul Brown as mentor came into my consciousness.

Paul Selby
Quarterback—Columbus, Ohio

*O*ur team was made up of students first, then football players. Paul Brown taught us the value of hard work, planning, and not making excuses.

Cecil Souders
All-American End, 1946
Team Most Valuable Player, 1946
Bucyrus, Ohio

I became a high school, junior college, college, and professional coach, and the organizational system I learned from Paul Brown was always used with good results. He was a great role model with great discipline and a burning desire to win.

Bob Shaw
All-American End
Fremont, Ohio

*L*oren's team was so successful because of the players' attitudes, good moral values, pride in their school, and their growing team accomplishments. He was very proud of his association with Paul Brown, from whom he learned to always do his best and have respect for his fellow teammates.

Mrs. Marilyn Staker for Loren Staker
Halfback—Columbus, Ohio

I was never a self-made man. I truly believe that my life was guided by the rules and principles that Paul Brown laid down as our coach. Paul's insistence on love of family has made mine one of happiness and fulfillment. To be successful requires an education, a close relationship with other men and women, as in a team, and, above all, appreciation of our mentor—in this case, Paul Brown. He often repeated that 1942 was his favorite year in his years of coaching.

Don Steinberg
Big Ten Conference Top Scholar-Athlete, 1945
End—Toledo, Ohio

O ur '42 team had a complete dedication of each player, and the recognition that individual sacrifices were needed for success. As players, we had great respect for each other. Paul Brown was highly organized. He emphasized winning, but taught character and football fundamentals. From Brown I learned to set a good example for my family and to select football players for their character, mental ability, and speed—the aspects of the game can be learned.

Bill Vickroy
Big Ten Conference Top Scholar-Athlete, 1942
Center—Toledo, Ohio

W e had such great respect for Paul Brown, and he was the main reason I went into coaching. I'll never forget how well Brown knew each of us. Our team was so successful because we had great players, and we had great respect for each other both on and off the field.

J. T. White
End—River Rouge, Michigan

P aul Brown was a man of integrity. The lessons Paul taught in football served as a road map for successful living. He reinforced and stressed the need for self-discipline, determination, perseverance, teamwork, dependability, cooperation, and respect … respect for yourself, for authority, for your teammates, and for your fellowman. I also learned that one *plays* the game of life as he *practices* it … from day to day … to day.

Bill Willis
Two-Time All-American Tackle, 1943-44
College and Professional Football Halls of Fame
Columbus, Ohio

Author Jack Park described this book's special dedication at a luncheon for the Professional Football Hall of Fame Luncheon Club in Canton. Pictured are Danielle Turcola, professional speaking colleague and close friend of the Parks, who provided the concept to survey the team's members for the dedication; Hall of Fame Executive Director John Bankert; Sue Park; and Jack Park.

Courtesy of Gallery Studio

*T*he author appreciates the time, assistance, and information provided by the fine people in Massillon and Stark County who generously contributed to *The Official Ohio State Football Encyclopedia* and to this book's special Dedication: Greg and Michelle Rajsich of the Gallery Studio, who provided many excellent photos; former Ohio State center John Muhlbach, chairman of the Professional Football Hall of Fame's Board of Trustees; Gene Boerner and his talented Massillon Chamber of Commerce staff; Nick Navarra and his capable assistants at the Canton Regional Chamber of Commerce; and many wonderful people at both Massillon Washington High School and Canton McKinley High School who generously provided numerous records and materials.

A special thank-you is extended to John Bankert, Executive Director of the Professional Football Hall of Fame in Canton, who graciously shared information and arranged for us to speak at the Professional Football Hall of Fame Luncheon Club.

JIM TRESSEL
A NEW BEGINNING

**"I am so proud, so excited, and so humbled to
be your football coach at The Ohio State University.
I can assure you that you'll be proud of our young people—
in the classroom, in the community, and most especially
in 310 days in Ann Arbor, Michigan!"**

—Coach Jim Tressel

Jim Tressel became head coach of the Ohio State Buckeyes on January 18, 2001, and immediately emphasized his mission to build players' character, enhance classroom performance, and (naturally) defeat Michigan. Tressel seemed almost destined for the position. The son of Dr. Lee Tressel, a coaching legend and College Football Hall of Famer, he directed Youngstown State University to four Division I-AA national titles during the 1990s. The Ohio State selection committee was highly impressed with Tressel's active leadership roles in community projects throughout the Mahoning Valley and with his Youngstown players' classroom achievements.

When introduced as the school's 22nd football coach, Tressel related that three elements of the Ohio State community became very evident to him during the days leading up to his announcement—tradition, people, and excellence. He acknowledged his responsibility to uphold Ohio State's many great traditions and contribute to new ones, while guiding all people to reach their full potential.

Tressel named Ohio State football coach

Former Buckeye assistant will take reins today

Tressel is OSU's man

Ohio Stadium

Stately Ohio Stadium, one of the true citadels of college football, was dedicated in 1922. Funded largely through private donations, the original cost of the stadium was approximately $1.5 million. Following the 1998 season, a three-year project of preservation, renovation and expansion began. The complete project was ready for the 2001 season, and ensured the longevity of the unique horseshoe-shaped structure well into the 21st century.

Listed in the National Registry of Historic Places, Ohio Stadium has seen relatively few changes over the years. Some expansion was achieved with south stand bleachers and the field seats. In 1984, a large matrix-style scoreboard was erected. In 1971, a synthetic field replaced grass, only to see grass return in 1990 with Prescription Athletic Turf.

The 1998-2001 project lowered the playing field 14' 6". This necessitated removal of the track, which is now part of the beautiful new Jesse Owens Memorial Stadium located on Fred Taylor Drive. Ten new rows have been added to the lower region, creating "AA" Deck, and on the west side, a new "D" Deck has been added. There are 82 Hospitality Suites, and a new Press Box has been built.

The new playing surface is the latest technology Prescription Athletic Turf, with a massive pumping system capable of removing 10 inches of water per hour if necessary. A new scoreboard features a 30' x 90' video screen.

Now the capacity of Ohio Stadium is nearly 100,000. New locker rooms for the Buckeyes and the visitors are matched by new restroom facilities for the fans. There is a Stadium Club, which will be a wonderful gathering place throughout the year.

The cost of this project, nearly $200 million, will be financed through ticket surcharge, and the fees for the Hospitality Suites and 2,600 Club Seats. We have ensured the long life of our beloved Horseshoe and enhanced the experiences of Ohio State Football for years to come.

Enjoy the newly renovated Ohio Stadium, and **Go Bucks!**

Andy Geiger
Director of Athletics

Coach Jim Tressel, 2001 Spring Game

Tressel stressed the impact that excellence can make, and that leadership is striving for excellence on and off the football field.

At his January 18, 2001, press conference, Jim Tressel was accompanied by his wife, Ellen; daughters, Carlee and Whitney; and son, Eric. Their other son, Zak, a junior at Ohio State, was not with them because of a physics class. Tressel stressed that Zak's scholastic performance was a higher priority than the press conference. He related that his own dad had taught him that there was only one reason to miss a class, and that was because of a death in the family—your own!

The Buckeyes' new coach immediately emphasized the importance of the Ohio State-Michigan rivalry, explaining that during his first season at Youngstown State, the Penguins were scheduled to host the Akron

Zips on Saturday, November 22, 1986—the same afternoon the Buckeyes and Wolverines would be clashing at Ohio Stadium. Believing that no other college teams should play on the same day as the "Big Game," Tressel rescheduled his team's contest for Friday evening, November 21. Youngstown defeated Akron that night in a real thriller, 40-39.

Tressel's parents, Lee and Eloise Tressel, were close family friends with Lou and Jackie Groza, who lived near the Tressels in Berea, Ohio. Groza had been a freshman tackle and placekicker at Ohio State in the fall of 1942, when the Buckeyes captured their first national title. Tressel remembers the excitement during his childhood days, when he would hold the ball during practice for the Cleveland Browns' great placekicker and retrieve the ball following Groza's kicks.

Strong Family Ties

Jim Tressel graduated cum laude from Baldwin-Wallace College, where he earned four varsity letters at quarterback and received all-conference honors as a senior in 1974. Tressel's college coach was his highly respected father, Dr. Lee Tressel, who compiled an outstanding 23-season record of 155-

Baldwin-Wallace Coach Lee Tressel with his 1974 Co-Captains, Jim Tressel (7) and Mark Summers (42).

"Tressel Stole the Show!" — Paul Brown

As a high school recruit in the fall of 1942, Lee Tressel attended the 1942 Ohio State - Southern California game at Ohio Stadium. Soon after Jim Tressel became Ohio State's head coach, his mother gave him a program from that 1942 game that had been in the Tressel family belongings for nearly 59 years. The program contains Lee Tressel's handwriting of the game's attendance of 56,436. When relating this story, Jim envisioned how special it must have been for for his dad, a 17-year-old, to be invited by Ohio State to experience an afternoon at Ohio Stadium.

Lee Tressel enrolled at Ohio State in the spring of 1943 following graduation from Ada High School, where he was an All-Ohio halfback after leading Ada to an undefeated season his senior year. Tressel scored two touchdowns in the Buckeyes' 1943 spring intra-squad game at Ohio Stadium, prompting coach Paul Brown to comment, "Tressel stole the show!" Because of World War II, very few of those players that spring were still on campus playing football in the fall. Lee Tressel joined the Navy, where he earned the rank of Lieutenant Junior Grade.

Quarterback Jim Tressel directs the Yellow Jacket offense.

a three-year starter at quarterback and wingback under Lee Tressel in the mid-1960's. Terakedis, who was an all-conference selection his senior season, refers to Lee and his wife Eloise as surrogate parents who were very involved in the players' lives. "Eloise was B-W's number-one cheerleader, and we still keep in contact today," he recalled. Terakedis remembers Lee Tressel as a coach who took his football seriously, worked his team hard, but was most concerned about his players as people.

After Baldwin-Wallace, Jim Tressel earned his masters degree at the University of Akron, where he tutored the quarterbacks, receivers, and running backs through 1978. Tressel spent two seasons at Miami of Ohio as quarterbacks and receivers coach and two years as quarterbacks coach at Syracuse, before joining Earle Bruce's Ohio State staff in 1983. For three seasons he coached the Buckeyes' quarterbacks, receivers, and running backs, then moved to Youngstown State University as head coach in 1986.

52-6 at B-W from 1958 through 1980. Dr. Tressel earned his undergraduate degree at Baldwin-Wallace, his masters at Ohio State, and his doctorate at Indiana University. His B-W Yellow Jackets were NCAA Division III National Champions in 1978.

Lee's son, Dick, a 1970 B-W grad, coached Hamline University to 124 victories between 1978 and 2000. Dick remembers his father as an individual with a very even keel who was good at handling both joy and adversity. Dick's son Dave, who graduated from B-W in 1973, teaches in the Berea school system. Dave coached swimming at Berea High School for several years.

Columbus attorney John Terakedis was

Penguin Power

Under Tressel's leadership, the Youngstown State Penguins developed into one of the nation's most successful and respected

Youngstown State University—1994 National Champions

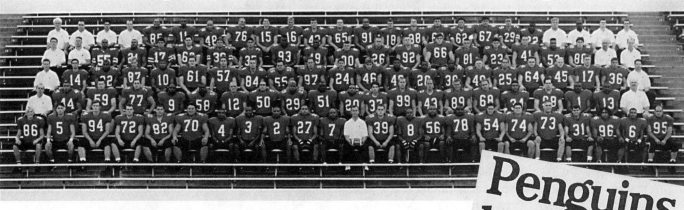

Coach Jim Tressel is pictured in the center of row one. Assistant Coaches Ken Conatser, far left in row two; and Mark Snyder, far left in row four; both joined Tressel as Assistant Coaches at Ohio State. Assistant Coach Jon Heacock, far left in row three, succeeded Tressel as Head Coach of the Penguins. Tressel also led Youngstown State to National Titles in 1991, 1993, and 1997.

Penguins building a dynasty
YSU tops Boise State for third I-AA crown

Cleveland Plain Dealer
Sunday, December 18, 1994

programs, capturing four Division 1-AA National Titles during the 1990s. Tressel was four times selected National Coach of the Year, while compiling a 15-year record of 135-57-2.

Mindy Drayer, a reporter at WCMH-TV in Columbus, covered Tressel and the Penguins when she worked at Youngstown's WYTV-TV during the late-1990s. "It was easy to see the compassion Coach Tressel felt for every one of his players," Drayer recalls. "His dedication, warmth, and sincerity were not only evident at YSU, but the entire community embraced him with respect and admiration. Coach Tressel's commitment to discipline, education, and the desire to win on and off the field made him the perfect choice as Ohio State's new head football coach."

Joe Malmisur, former Youngstown State Director of Athletics who hired Tressel in 1986, takes great pride in having had Tressel at YSU and seeing him move to Ohio State. Malmisur predicted the Buckeyes will prosper under Tressel's leadership. At Tressel's 2001 Spring Football Preview Luncheon, Pat Vivo, a community leader from Youngstown, related how valuable Tressel's contributions had been to her community. Jon Heacock, one of Tressel's YSU assistants who succeeded Tressel as head coach, remembers Tressel as a strong organizer who excelled at helping young people reach their potential.

Coaches Lee Tressel and Jim Tressel are the only father-son combination ever to capture NCAA National Championships.

Coach Earle Bruce and Bob Tucker, Director of Football Operations, at the 2001 Spring Game. Coach Bruce delivered the keynote address at Ohio State's Clinic for High School Coaches the previous morning. Bruce was Tucker's coach at Sandusky High School. Tucker later served as an Assistant Coach under Bruce at Iowa State and Ohio State.

Former Buckeye quarterback Jim Karsatos, sideline reporter for the Ohio State Football Radio Network, talks with quarterbacks (left to right) Steve Bellisari, Craig Krenzel, Rick McFadden, and Scott McMullen after the 2001 Spring Game.

Ohio State Football
2002 Coaching Staff

Jim Tressel
Head Coach

Jim Bollman
Offensive Coordinator/
Offensive Line

Bill Conley
Recruiting Coordinator/
Tight Ends

Joe Daniels
Quarterbacks
and Receivers

Mark Dantonio
Defensive Coordinator

Luke Fickell
Special Teams
Coordinator

Jim Heacock
Defensive Line

Mark Snyder
Linebackers

Tim Spencer
Running Backs

Dick Tressel
Associate Director of
Football Operations

Bob Tucker
Director of
Football Operations

Mel Tucker
Defensive Backs

HOW IT ALL BEGAN

Today's great spectacle of Ohio State football is a distinct contrast with its modest beginning. While national television audiences and Ohio Stadium crowds of approximately 100,000 now closely monitor every aspect of each play, Ohio State's first teams played before small, informal gatherings of people who were trying to understand this new game called "football."

The very first college game between Princeton and Rutgers was played on November 6, 1869, nearly four years before the Ohio Agricultural and Mechanical College opened its doors to approximately 24 students on September 17, 1873. Columbus, Ohio, was a bustling state capital with nearly 40,000 people. An isolated site some two miles north of the city limits was selected for the college's campus, so that the "happenings of the big city" would not interfere with the students' academic life. The student body rapidly increased in size, and the college's curriculum quickly expanded. In 1878, the Ohio legislature changed the college's name to The Ohio State University.

Baseball was the first recreational sport on campus, and several "intramural-type" teams were formed in the late 1870s. Sports were not as seasonal in the early years as they are today, and baseball was played in both the fall and spring. A baseball game between Ohio State and "Acme" was played on May 26, 1879, with Acme winning, 22-11. This contest is considered to be Ohio State's first athletic event with an "outside opponent."

As the student body grew, an Athletic Association made up of faculty was initiated

First Colors

Orange and Black were first chosen as Ohio State's colors in 1878, 12 years before the school fielded its first football team. When the selection committee learned that Princeton had already selected these colors, the committee picked Scarlet and Gray instead.

in early 1881 to create and administer an athletic program. Annual "Field Days," featuring races, jumping contests, and lawn tennis, were held on campus each spring.

There is evidence that a form of unorganized football was enjoyed in the evenings by male students at least as early as 1886. Footballs were usually homemade, and occasionally a student of substantial means might be able to provide a "purchased football." Most of the "jolly game" action took place on a large athletic field north of the "North Dorm" dormitory, which sat on the west side of Neil Avenue, near Eleventh Avenue. The athletic field ran downhill toward the Olentangy River, a situation that gave some advantage to the football team that occupied the higher ground. The field was located directly across from what is now Oxley Hall.

By 1890, football was already going strong in the East and portions of the Midwest. The first Harvard-Yale encounter took place in 1875, and Michigan fielded its first squad in 1879. Penn State's first game with an outside opponent was played in either 1881 or 1887, depending upon one's interpretation of a "first game."

In his book, *Ohio State Athletics,* published in 1959, Dr. James E. Pollard describes four stages of early competitive sports on the Ohio State campus:

1. From the late 1870s to the early 1880s sports were spontaneous and unorganized.
2. The 1880s saw the beginning of contests with outside teams, some college and some not.
3. The 1890s were marked by three developments: the organized scheduling of games, the emergence of a group of Ohio colleges that were natural competitors in what, after the turn of the century, became the "Big Six," and the appearance of hired seasonal coaches, particularly for football.

4. The last and most important phase, as far as Ohio State was concerned, began in 1912 with the University's formal admission to the Western Conference.

George N. Cole, class of '91, is credited with helping develop Ohio State's first official football team in 1890. Cole took up a collection among the students to purchase a "real" football, and he acquired a book of football rules from the Spaulding Athletic Supply Company. Cole persuaded his friend, Alexander S. Lilley, to be the team's coach without pay. In 1890, touchdowns counted four points, conversions after touchdowns were two points, field goals were worth five points, and safeties were two points (as they are today).

Cole and Lilley had gone to school together in Columbus, and Lilley later played football at Princeton. Lilley lived on East Main Street and rode an Indian pony to the campus for practice. Thus, from a very humble beginning, one of today's "elite of college football" was born. A plaque honoring Alexander S. Lilley hangs above the archway leading to the Ohio State dressing room in Ohio Stadium. Cole also arranged for K. L. "Snake" Ames, another of Cole's Columbus classmates and an early Princeton All-American, to demonstrate how to kick a football.

First Game at Delaware

Ohio State's first game was played at Delaware on Friday, May 3, against Ohio Wesleyan University before a very informal gathering of about 700. OSU won, 20-14, with quarterback Joseph H. Large scoring the school's first touchdown, which counted four points. The team left for Delaware at 6:00

Ohio State's first team in 1890. Coach Alexander Lilley is standing at the far left.

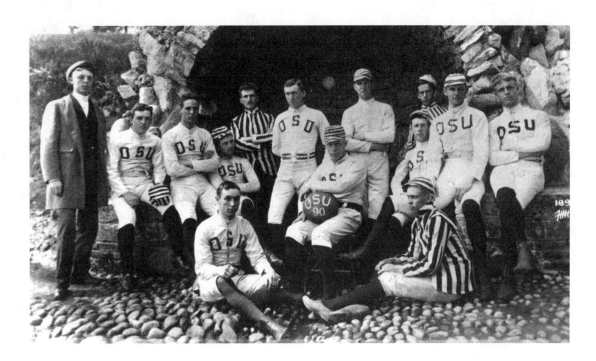

a.m., with the game starting around 9:30 a.m. "Center rusher" Jesse Jones and "first right" Paul Lincoln were Ohio State's first captains. No further games were played that spring, although there were plans for a return match with Ohio Wesleyan and a game with Denison University that never developed.

Football was resumed that fall, beginning with a game at Columbus' Recreation Park on Saturday, November 1, against Wooster College which fielded the first organized college football team in Ohio. Lilley did not return to coach the team. Instead, Jack Ryder, who had played football at Williams College, assumed the coaching duties. The first home game was simply no contest. Wooster won, 64-0. The November 3 *Columbus Dispatch* carried this account of the game:

Notwithstanding the raw, cold weather of last Saturday, a fair crowd went out to Recreation Park to see the first of the inter-collegiate football games, between the Ohio State University and Wooster

teams. A number of ladies were present and attempted to cheer the O.S.U. boys to victory, but it was of no avail, as there was not the remotest possibility of their winning, and the game closed with the score 64-0 in favor of Wooster. Several accidents happened during the game, the most serious of which was that to

PLANTED HERE ARE ELEVEN BUCKEYE TREES IN MEMORY OF OHIO STATE'S FIRST FOOTBALL TEAM SPRING OF 1890

JESSE JONES, CAPT.   JOHN B. HUGGINS
HAMILTON H. RICHARDSON   CHARLES W. FOULK
PAUL M. LINCOLN   WALTER H. MILLER
HERBERT L. JOHNSTON   JOSEPH H. LARGE
CHARLES B. MORREY   ARTHUR H. KENNEDY
DAVID S. HEGLER   FRANK W. RANE
HIRAM B. RUTAN   EDWARD D. MARTIN
RICHARD T. B. ELLIS, MGR.

Plaque honoring Ohio State's first team rests at the entrance to the Buckeye Grove, located east of Ohio Stadium.

O.S.U. TEAM SHUT OUT.

WOOSTER ELEVEN HAVE WALK-OVER AT FOOT BALL

Columbus Dispatch, Monday, November 3

Kennedy of the O.S.U. team. He was kicked in the chest and the calling of a physician was found necessary.

While he was injured so badly as to necessitate his being carried from the field it is not thought that any serious results will follow.

Ohio State lost at Denison, 14-0, on Friday, November 14, and was defeated at home by Kenyon, 18-10, on Thursday, November 27, Thanksgiving Day. This was the first of several Thanksgiving Day games against Kenyon, which often took on overtones of "society affairs."

Undergraduate student managers typically handled most of the administrative responsibilities for the early college teams in Ohio. This included scheduling of games, purchasing equipment, and making travel arrangements for away games. Otterbein College's student manager, B. V. Leas, twice sent letters to Ohio State in an attempt to schedule a game for the fall of 1890. It is not clear if Ohio State ever responded to either of Leas' proposals, and the two teams did not get together until 1893.

1890				
May 3	at Ohio Wesleyan	W	20	14
November 1	Wooster	L	0	64
November 14	at Denison	L	0	14
November 27	Kenyon	L	10	18
Total Points			30	110
	Season Record: 1-3			

Ohio State's first home games were played at Recreation Park, located on the south side of Columbus at the intersection of South High and Whittier Streets. Ohio State is shown in action against Denison University on November 28, 1891.

1891

A meeting of student delegates and managers from five colleges with similar interests in football was held on Saturday, October 24, at Kenyon College in Gambier. The five schools were Western Reserve (then called Adelbert), Denison, Akron (then called Buchtel), Ohio State, and Kenyon. Topics discussed included scheduling, selection procedures for umpires and referees, team expenses, and how ties would be played off. An "agreement" was developed, and an intercollegiate schedule was created. Wooster did not attend since its faculty had temporarily forbidden students to take part in intercollegiate sports.

Alexander Lilley returned as head coach that fall and led Ohio State to a record of 2-2. The football team petitioned the faculty to be excused from military drill so that they could devote that hour to football practice. The University trustees approved the request by a vote of three to two, on the condition that the practices be made subject to the same rules that governed the military drills.

O.S.U. played its first two games within a span of four days, losing badly at home to Western Reserve, 50-6, on Wednesday, November 11, and losing at Kenyon, 26-0, on Saturday, November 14. The team was very unhappy with the Kenyon trip, claiming that the playing field was in poor condition, and that the umpire provided by Kenyon was clearly unfair with his calls against Ohio State.

After some extended practices, Ohio State was able to defeat Denison University, 8-4, on Thanksgiving morning, November 26. The team finished the season with a 6-0 triumph at Akron on Saturday, December 5. The Akron victory was O.S.U.'s first shutout. It had been a formative season for Ohio State. Players had improved their skills, football was gaining popularity on campus, and "downtown papers" were beginning to devote more attention to the sport.

1891

November 11	Western Reserve	L	6	50
November 14	at Kenyon	L	0	26
November 28	Denison	W	8	4
December 5	at Akron	W	6	0
Total Points			20	80
	Season Record: 2-2			

1892

Popular Jack Ryder was back as "coacher," replacing Alexander Lilley as he had done in the fall of 1890. Ohio State expanded its schedule to eight games, and enjoyed its first winning season with five victories and three setbacks. A small set of spectator stands was constructed on the south side of the football field, located west of Neil Avenue. The new stands were also used for seating on the third base side of the baseball diamond.

Two-Time Leaders

There have been six two-time Captains during the first 112 years of Ohio State football. The first was halfback Richard T. Ellis in 1891-92. The other five are tailback Archie Griffin, 1974-75; linebacker Glenn Cobb, 1981-82; linebacker Thomas "Pepper" Johnson, 1984-85; linebacker Joe Cooper, 2000-01; and quarterback Steve Bellisari, 2000-01.

John W. Heisman was born at 2825 Bridge Avenue in Cleveland, Ohio, on October 3, 1869. Heisman led Oberlin College to a 40-0 win over Ohio State in his very first game as a head coach. He became one of football's most innovative and successful coaches. College football's most prestigious award, the Heisman Trophy, is named in his honor.

Historic Opener!

Ohio State opened the season Saturday, October 15, with a 40-0 loss at Oberlin. Interestingly, Oberlin had a new 23-year-old coach in 1892, and this victory over Ohio State was the very first game of his coaching career—his name was John W. Heisman. Over the next 36 seasons, Heisman would become one of the game's great innovators. College football's most prestigious award, the Heisman Trophy, is named in his honor. The October 16 *Ohio State Journal* carried this account of the game:

The Ohio State University team played at Oberlin Saturday. Though outplayed they fought a plucky up-hill game. The good play of Captain Ellis and of Haas is especially worthy of note.

In tackling the visiting team excelled their heavier opponents, though they were not so good at bucking the line and at intervening for the runner. The playing of Captain Williams and Savage of Oberlin is especially to be commended. Both teams played a good, clean game, though perhaps the Oberlin men played

VICTORIOUS OBERLIN.

Fifty to Nothing Was the Extent of State University's Defeat at Football

Ohio State Journal, Tuesday, November 8, 1892

a little roughly. Ohio State University is to be congratulated on her team. The score is as follows: Oberlin 40, O.S.U. 0.

Apparently Oberlin had a splendid team, since Ohio State was able to post shutouts in its next three games; 62-0 at Akron, 80-0 at home over Marietta, and 32-0 at Denison. But a return match against Oberlin in Columbus on Monday, November 7, was even worse than the opener. Heisman's team won again, 50-0. The *Ohio State Journal* carried the following description on November 8:

A good crowd gathered to witness the game, a large proportion of which were ladies. Oberlin has the strongest team in the state and has an unbroken record of victories. The whole game was clean and gentlemanly throughout, doing great credit to both teams and was a good exhibition of college football. The score, 50 to 0 in favor of Oberlin, does not indicate to any extent the hard playing that was indulged in, and in the second half the ball was in Oberlin territory most of the time.

Ohio State got back in the victory column with a 42-4 victory over the Dayton YMCA, then lost to Western Reserve for the second straight season, 40-18. The season finale at home on Thanksgiving afternoon drew a crowd of 1,200, the largest yet in Ohio State's first three seasons of organized foot-

ball. Kenyon was defeated for the first time, 26-10. The game had been planned for Thanksgiving morning, but the Kenyon squad decided to stay in Gambier to attend a Wednesday evening dance rather than travel to Columbus. This sudden postponement of the game from morning to afternoon disturbed many of the Ohio State fans, who had planned other activities for the holiday afternoon.

This was a significant victory for O.S.U., since Kenyon consistently fielded quality teams at that time. Ohio State's successful use of a new formation called the "Ryder wedge" was a key factor in the contest. The Thanksgiving-Day game also netted Ohio State a profit of $1,049, giving a big lift to the sagging athletic budget.

1892				
October 15	at Oberlin	L	0	40
October 22	at Akron	W	62	0
October 29	Marietta	W	80	0
November 5	at Denison	W	32	0
November 7	Oberlin	L	0	50
November 12	Dayton YMCA	W	42	4
November 19	at Western Reserve	L	18	40
November 24	Kenyon	W	26	10
Total Points			**260**	**144**

Season Record: 5-3

1893

Ohio State's schedule expanded to nine games in 1893, with the Scarlet and Gray winning four and losing five. Jack Ryder returned as coach, marking the first time O.S.U. benefited from having the same coach for consecutive seasons. Otterbein, Wittenberg, and Cincinnati were met for the first time. Ohio

Super Sleuth

A young lad enrolled at Ohio State in the fall of 1893 and came out for the football team just long enough to learn the plays. After a few weeks, he dropped out of sight, but he was later spotted with the Kenyon College team when Ohio State played Kenyon at Gambier on October 28. Years later when reminiscing about this game, Charles Wood, the Ohio State quarterback, recalled that "Kenyon just seemed to have all of our signals down pat." The final score was Kenyon 42, Ohio State 6.

1893

September 30	at Otterbein	L	16	22
October 14	Wittenberg	W	36	10
October 21	Oberlin	L	10	38
October 28	at Kenyon	L	6	42
November 4	Western Reserve	L	16	30
November 11	Akron	W	32	18
November 18	Cincinnati	W	38	0
November 25	Marietta	W	40	8
November 30	Kenyon	L	8	10
Total Points			202	178

Season Record: 4-5

1894

State lost its opener at Otterbein, 22-16, but defeated both Wittenberg (36-10) and Cincinnati (38-0). The other two wins came at the expense of Akron, 32-18, and Marietta, 40-8.

O.S.U. lost for the third straight season to Oberlin (38-10) and Western Reserve (30-16), and lost twice to Kenyon (42-6 and 10-8). A newly organized Ohio State band appeared at the Oberlin contest and gave a concert before the game. The second Kenyon game was the regular Thanksgiving Day event, which drew 4,000 fans. Ohio State led 4-0 at halftime, but when Kenyon went ahead in the second half, fans poured onto the field and tore down a portion of the fence surrounding the playing field. The game was halted until police were able to clear the field.

As the season came to a close, there were discussions in the Ohio Legislature aimed at either eliminating or radically changing football in the state. The sport was gaining an unfavorable reputation for its savageness, and there were many reports of players suffering broken limbs and occasionally even a fatality. Many teams used the "flying wedge," a mass momentum play, in which players slugged and elbowed the opposition as they stormed down the field in a "V formation."

With an increasing interest in football throughout the state, the Ohio State Board of Agriculture arranged for three games to be played at the 1894 Ohio State Fair. The primary objective was to introduce football to those fair visitors who had never attended a game. Ohio State played Akron on Wednesday, September 5, Denison faced Miami of Ohio on Thursday, September 6, and Ohio State met Wittenberg on Friday, September 7.

Akron defeated O.S.U. in the first contest, 12-6. The *Columbus Dispatch* of September 6 provided this account of the game:

The crowd at the football game yesterday afternoon was made up almost entirely of people who never saw a foot-

First Closed Practices

Ohio State's first closed practices were held in 1894 under the direction of coach Jack Ryder. University officials and the press were the only spectators permitted to attend.

ball contest before, and the great majority did not know which team was which. Plainer uniforms and a pennant distinguishing the part of the field belonging to each side would greatly help persons follow the game.

Wittenberg won over Ohio State in the Friday afternoon game, 6-0. Members of the winning team were given uniforms as prizes.

M. C. Lilley, a Yale Alumnus, began the year as coach, but resigned midway through the season because of the early losses and team dissension. Reliable Jack Ryder returned to complete the fall schedule with much better results, and the team finished the season at 6-5. Ohio State won four of its last five games, including a 20-4 triumph over rival Kenyon in the annual Thanksgiving Day game on Thursday, November 29.

AMONG THE SPORTS.

FOOT BALL TO BE A FEATURE OF THE STATE FAIR.

Something About the Game For the Benefit of the Uninitiated.

Columbus Dispatch, Monday, August 20, 1894

1894				
September 5	Akron*	L	6	12
September 7	Wittenberg*	L	0	6
October 6	Antioch	W	32	0
October 13	at Wittenberg	L	6	18
October 20	at Columbus Barricks	W	30	0
October 27	Western Reserve	L	4	24
November 3	Marietta	W	10	4
November 10	at Case	L	0	38
November 17	at Cincinnati	W	6	4
November 24	17th Regiment	W	46	4
November 29	Kenyon	W	20	4
Total Points			160	114
* Played at the Ohio State Fair				
Season Record: 6-5				

1895

Jack Ryder was back again as coach. Ohio State played its first games outside the state in 1895 and also incurred its first ties. O.S.U. was defeated at Otterbein on October 12, 14-6, but the players felt that the officiating favored the home team. Captain Renick Dunlay of Ohio State provided the following description, which was carried in the *Columbus Dispatch* on Monday, October 14:

The O.S.U. boys are very sore over the unfair treatment which they claimed they received in the football game with Otterbein. Captain Dunlap says that Referee Garst, an old Otterbein student, gave them the worst of it in the first half of the game despite all protests. In the last half, with a fair referee, O.S.U. held her own. Dunlap says Otterbein has a strong team and he does not claim O.S.U. would have won, but it would have been vastly more to Otterbein's credit to have won fairly. He characterized the game more as a slugging match than a foot-ball game. Otterbein refused to play O.S.U. a return game. This action is to be regretted, as it strengthens the oft-repeated assertion that Otterbein cannot win off her own grounds.

Ohio State lost at home to Oberlin the following Saturday, 12-6. A few days prior to the game, the O.S.U. band threatened to disband because it did not like the treatment it was receiving from the University's trustees. Apparently the band felt it was not receiving the proper support.

The team played back-to-back games against Kentucky in Lexington, and against Central Kentucky in Danville, on Friday, November 15, and Saturday, November 16.

Ohio State's 1895 team. Coach Jack Ryder, with necktie, is pictured in the center of the third row. Ryder was head coach three different times; the fall of 1890, 1892 through 1895, and 1898.

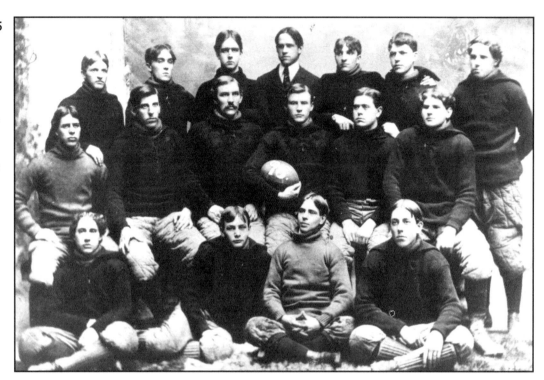

A squad of 16 players made the weekend trip. O.S.U. won over Kentucky, 8-6, but lost to Central Kentucky, 18-0. The *Ohio State Journal* reported that the Ohio State team "put up a game" on Friday, but was "physically weak" Saturday from playing two games in two days.

O.S.U. closed out the season with a 12-10 Thanksgiving Day victory over Kenyon on November 28. The following day's *Columbus Dispatch* carried this report:

VIVE LA O.S.U.

The Kenyon team was defeated yesterday afternoon upon the grounds of the Ohio State University by the latter team in a score of 12 to 10. The game was a hotly contested one and was won in an exciting finish. After the play the crowd went crazy and carried the winners off the field. Later in the evening the victors made the heaven ring with tin horns, a brass band, and a set of lusty voices that were trained to the hour. It was a great victory for O.S.U. and re-

flects much credit upon their able captain and manager, Mr. R. W. Dunlap.

O.S.U.'s first tie games were played against Denison (4-4) and Ohio Wesleyan (8-8). After six years of intercollegiate competition, Ohio State's accumulative record was exactly even at 22 wins, 22 losses, and two ties.

1895				
October 5	Akron	W	14	6
October 12	at Otterbein	L	6	14
October 19	Oberlin	L	6	12
October 26	at Dension	T	4	4
November 2	Ohio Wesleyan	T	8	8
November 9	at Cincinnati	W	4	0
November 15	at Kentucky	W	8	6
November 16	at Central Kentucky	L	0	18
November 23	at Marietta	L	0	24
November 28	Kenyon	W	12	10
Total Points			62	102

Season Record: 4-4-2

1896

Ohio State had not yet hired a regular coach when the 1896 season began, so Sid Farrer, a Starling Medical student and former player at Princeton, served as an interim coach. Farrer guided the team through its first few games until Charles A. Hickey was hired. Hickey had been captain at Williams College the previous season and brought a more complicated system of football to the Ohio State campus.

The October 17 Ohio State-Otterbein game was moved to Canton, Ohio, home of William McKinley, who was actively campaigning for the presidency. Having the contest as part of his crusade might have brought the famous "front porch" campaigner good luck. Ohio State won the game, 12-0, and McKinley won the presidency. The game had been scheduled for 2:30 p.m. However, the trains carrying some of the spectators from Columbus to Canton that morning were detained, causing the start of the game to be delayed until approximately 3:45 p.m. By mutual consent, the contest was called because of darkness with about six minutes remaining.

O.S.U. played four games within a span of ten days from Thursday, November 5, through Saturday, November 14, all at home. There were charges that Wittenberg used a "ringer" during its 24-6 win over Ohio State. Supposedly, Nicholas Dinkle, an 1895 Notre Dame graduate (where he played quarterback), had returned to his home in Springfield, Ohio, and was playing right tackle for Wittenberg.

A new feature this season was the sale of candy, popcorn, peanuts, and chrysanthemums at the grandstand. One of the team's co-captains was end Edward French, whose

OTTERBEIN DEFEATED.

State University Wins the Football Game at Canton by 12 to 0

Ohio State Journal, Sunday, October 18, 1896

brother, Professor Thomas French, would become a major force some 20 years later in the campaign to build Ohio Stadium. The team finished the season at 5-5-1, and Hickey was dismissed as coach after losing interest in the position.

Charles Hickey, head coach in 1896.

Beginning of The Big Ten

The seven charter members of the Western Conference in 1896 (later titled the Big Ten) were Chicago, Illinois, Michigan, Minnesota, Northwestern, Purdue, and Wisconsin. Wisconsin won the first league football title that season. Indiana and Iowa joined the conference in 1900, and Ohio State began play in 1913. Chicago dropped out after the 1939 season and was replaced by Michigan State in 1953. Penn State was admitted to membership in 1993.

1896

October 3	Ohio Medical	L	24	0
October 10	at Cincinnati	L	6	8
October 17	Otterbein*	W	12	0
October 24	at Oberlin	L	0	16
October 31	Case	W	30	10
November 5	Ohio Wesleyan	L	4	10
November 7	Columbus Barricks	W	10	2
November 11	Ohio Medical	T	0	0
November 14	Wittenberg	W	6	24
November 21	Ohio Medical	W	12	0
November 26	Kenyon	L	18	34

Total Points 122 104
* Played at Canton, Ohio

Season Record: 5-5-1

1897

Fielding Yost, player and coach at West Virginia and Ohio Wesleyan, made a trip to Columbus in February, 1897, seeking the Ohio State coaching position. Had it not been for Yost's exuberance, he might have been successful. After Yost demonstrated his physical competence on both a student and faculty member, instructions were given to "get that wild man off the campus." Yost, later nicknamed "Hurry Up," would become highly successful with his "point-a-minute" teams at Michigan, much to Ohio State's chagrin.

David Edwards, who had played halfback at Princeton the prior fall, was hired to replace Hickey as head coach, and the season developed into a total catastrophe. After opening October 6 with a 6-0 victory over Ohio Medical University (located in Columbus), Ohio State lost every remaining game, with the exception of a 12-12 tie with Otterbein, to finish the season at 1-7-1. To make matters worse, the win over Ohio Medical was somewhat suspect. The Medics were leading by one touchdown, but left the field after vigorously protesting an Ohio State touchdown. The referee awarded O.S.U. the victory by forfeit.

First Game with Michigan

Ohio State and Michigan met for the first time on October 16 at Regents Field in Ann Arbor, where Michigan won, 34-0. While O.S.U. was in its seventh year of intercollegiate football, Michigan had begun its program in 1879 and was fielding its 18th squad. All the scoring took place in the first half, and the outcome could have been much worse if Michigan coach Gustave Ferbert had wanted to run up a higher score. The game was called in the second half with approximately five minutes remaining.

Some of the home games were played at the stadium of the Columbus professional

State University Team Defeated by the University of Michigan Eleven.

OHIO BOYS' GOOD WORK.

Ohio State Journal, Sunday, October 17, 1897

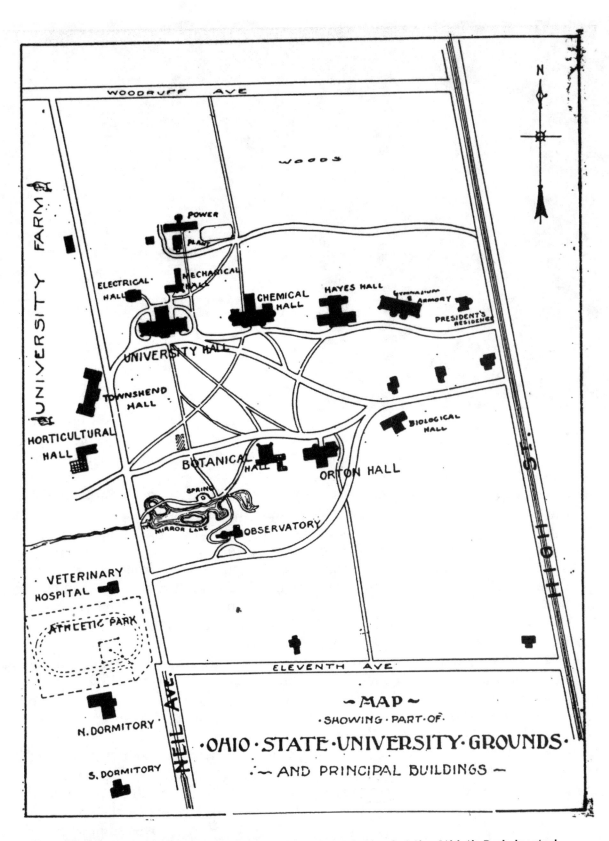

The Ohio State Campus in 1897. Home football games were played at the Athletic Park, located west of Neil Avenue and north of the North Dormitory.

David Edwards, head coach in 1897.

1897				
October 6	Ohio Medical	W	6	0
October 9	Case	L	0	14
October 16	at Michigan	L	0	34
October 23	Otterbein	T	12	12
October 26	Columbus Barricks	L	0	6
October 30	Oberlin	L	0	44
November 6	at West Virginia	L	0	28
November 13	at Cincinnati	L	0	24
November 25	Ohio Wesleyan	L	0	6
Total Points			18	168

Season Record: 1-7-1

1898

baseball team. The Athletic Association found itself in debt at the end of the season, partly because of low attendance caused by the team's poor play, and O.S.U. President James Canfield suspended athletics until the debt was retired. Various campus social events were staged, with the proceeds used to pay off the deficiency.

O.S.U. was shut out in each of its seven losses, and was outscored throughout the fall, 168-18. The 1897 season is the only year in history that Ohio State won only one game, and lost as many as seven. Edwards was let go at the end of the season.

Jack Ryder was hired for his third stint as head coach, and it was becoming evident that the football program lacked consistency. A new coach with a new system each season was making it more difficult for Ohio State to compete with schools who had more stable programs. With the brief Spanish-American War in effect, a portion of the proceeds from the November 19 game against Ohio Medical was donated to build a monument honoring the 4th Ohio Volunteer Infantry, a local unit that served in the conflict.

This season a new football field, running north and south, was developed on the west side of High Street and south of Woodruff Avenue, replacing the North Athletic Field which was located west of Neil Avenue. The new site carried the name "University Field" until it was renamed "Ohio Field" in 1908. The North Athletic Field's grandstand was relocated to the west side of University Field.

Ohio State improved somewhat over the '97 season, winning three and losing five. It was the Scarlet and Gray's last losing season until 1922 (the first year at Ohio Stadium).

Whose Side Are You On, Anyway?

Marietta College played at Ohio State on October 22, 1898. The Pioneers' traveling squad consisted of 12 players. Midway through the second half, two of the Marietta players were injured and unable to continue play. Not wanting to forfeit the game, Marietta coach C. M. Showalter asked Ohio State coach Jack Ryder if he could "borrow" one of Ryder's players to finish the game.

After pondering the situation for a few seconds, Ryder agreed, and signaled to his bench for a substitute to line up with Marietta. The player assigned to the Pioneers is believed to have been halfback Bob Hager.

Ryder and his entire team were stunned when Hager sprinted 67 yards around end for a Marietta touchdown on his very first carry—and Marietta won the game, 10-0. The Pioneers were ecstatic over their very first victory in Columbus, while Jack Ryder NEVER again loaned a player to one of his opponents.

O.S.U. and Heidelberg met for the first time in the season opener, won by Ohio State, 17-0. Ohio Wesleyan was the Thanksgiving Day opponent for the second straight season, as O.S.U. avenged the prior season's 6-0 loss with a 24-0 victory.

1899

Football fortunes for the Scarlet and Gray brightened considerably when John B. C. Eckstorm was hired as head coach in the spring of 1899. The new coach had been a star player and captain at Dartmouth College. Eckstorm, a good organizer and a student of physical fitness, met with the team in late May and encouraged them to practice on their own over the summer. He had been head coach at Kenyon in 1898, when his team defeated Ohio State, 29-0. Eckstorm truly enjoyed coaching, and it showed.

First Ohio Championship

The turnaround under Eckstorm was remarkable. Ohio State went 9-0-1 to capture its first championship of the Ohio colleges. O.S.U. outscored its 10 opponents, 184-5, for its best showing yet on the college gridiron. Its only blemish was a 5-5 tie at Case, as Ohio State shut out its other nine opponents. One of the season's biggest accomplishments was the school's very first victory over Oberlin, 6-0, on a very rainy October 28. The mud was six inches deep in some parts of the field. In six previous losses to Oberlin, Ohio State had been outscored, 200-10.

1898

October 1	Heidelberg	W	17	0
October 8	Ohio Medical	L	0	10
October 15	Denison	W	34	0
October 22	Marietta	L	0	10
November 5	at Western Reserve	L	0	49
November 12	Case	L	5	23
November 19	Kenyon	L	0	29
November 24	Ohio Wesleyan	W	24	0
Total Points			80	121
Season Record: 3-5				

CHAMPIONS

Of the Ohio Colleges.

O.S.U. Defeats the Kenyon Team

After Hard-Fought Game Of Ball

Columbus Citizen, Friday, December 1, 1899

The 1899 team, Ohio State's first champion of the Ohio colleges. Ohio State outscored its opposition, 184-5.

Left tackle Del Sayers ran 25 yards for the game's only touchdown after recovering an Oberlin fumble. The *Columbus Dispatch* of October 30 provided the following description of the game:

Smiling with perfect indifference in the face of rheumatism, pneumonia, and grip, the Ohio State University football team met the Oberlin aggregation in a quagmire Saturday afternoon, wallowed with this for 50 minutes in mud and rain, buried them under a decisive and crushing defeat, and waded proudly and victoriously from the field amid the deafening yells of 350 enthusiastic O.S.U. students who had cheered the varsity boys on to victory.

Two other significant victories were a 12-0 verdict over Ohio Medical University on November 18, and a close 5-0 Thanksgiving Day triumph over Kenyon before a crowd estimated at 6,000. John Eckstorm was immediately rehired by the Athletic Board for the next two years. The 1899 campaign was the first of 23 straight without a losing season (1889 through 1921).

First Special Train

Ohio State's first special train to an away game carried 300 rooters to Oberlin on October 28. The O.S.U. backers cheered their team to a 6-0 victory.

1899				
September 30	Otterbein	W	30	0
October 7	Wittenberg	W	28	0
October 14	at Case	T	5	5
October 21	Ohio University	W	41	0
October 28	at Oberlin	W	6	0
November 4	Western Reserve	W	6	0
November 11	Marietta	W	17	0
November 18	Ohio Medical	W	12	0
November 25	at Muskingum	W	34	0
November 30	Kenyon	W	5	0
Total Points			184	5

Season Record: 9-0-1

1900

Ohio State was highly successful during Eckstorm's second season, going 8-1-1 and outscoring its 10 opponents, 213-26. Both a scoreboard and additional bleachers were added to University Field. One of the team's fine freshmen was Lynn W. St. John, who would become Ohio State's Director of Athletics in 1912. The team began regular practice just four days before it opened September 29 with a 20-0 victory at home over Otterbein. Ohio University was defeated in Columbus by the same score the following Saturday. Ohio was added to Ohio State's schedule just that week, after Miami (Ohio) canceled its game with O.S.U. because of an "epidemic of fever" on the Miami campus.

Oberlin was defeated on October 27, 17-0, even though Ohio State felt the game's umpire was unfairly biased with his calls. The *Columbus Citizen* of October 29 provided the following account of the afternoon's officiating:

The game Saturday was one-sided, so far as the score went. It would have been more lop-sided than it was if umpire Young, whose selection the Oberlin management had made a condition of playing, had not been blindly partial to the visitors. At least two more touchdowns and probably three would have been scored by O.S.U. if it had not been for the uncalled-for penalties inflicted by Young, who will certainly never officiate another football game in this city unless he appears in disguise. Some of his penalties were inflicted for offenses of which no one knew anything at all, and even the Oberlin players were ashamed of the advantage he gave to them.*

On November 17, Ohio Medical University dealt Ohio State its only loss of the season, 11-6. The game had nearly been stricken from the Ohio State schedule. O.S.U. charged Ohio Medical with "professionalism," and the Athletic Board took action to prevent the contest. The issue was finally settled after Ohio Medical dropped one player from its squad.

The loss's disappointment was quickly forgotten after O.S.U. registered a "moral victory" with a scoreless tie at Michigan the following Sat-

John Eckstorm, head coach from 1899 through 1901.

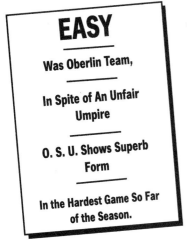

EASY

Was Oberlin Team,

In Spite of An Unfair Umpire

O. S. U. Shows Superb Form

In the Hardest Game So Far of the Season.

Columbus Dispatch,
Monday, October 29, 1900

urday. Approximately 900 rooters followed the team to Ann Arbor, the largest visiting crowd to ever attend a game at Regents Field. A driving snowstorm developed early in the afternoon, forcing the second half to be played in a sea of mud. One sign of steady progress in the O.S.U. football program was Michigan's willingness to play the following season's game in Columbus.

Ohio State closed out its season the following Thursday with a 23-5 Thanksgiving Day win over Kenyon. O.S.U. rented additional bleachers for the game from Sells Brothers Circus, expanding the seating capacity from 700 to 2,000, plus standing room. Total season attendance for eight home games was reported to be 13,000.

1901

During John Eckstorm's third and final season at Ohio State, his team won five, lost three, and tied one. After a scoreless tie with Otterbein in the September 28 season opener, Wittenberg and Ohio University were shut out, 30-0 and 17-0, respectively, on October 5 and 12. The following Thursday, October 17, the University of Cincinnati canceled its Saturday game against O.S.U. Manager George Rightmire immediately sent a telegram to Denison, Heidelberg, Marietta, Mt. Union, and Wooster, offering a game against Ohio State for Saturday afternoon if the school had the date open.

Marietta was the first to respond, and on Friday morning the Pioneers accepted Ohio State's offer to play in Columbus on Saturday afternoon, October 19. O.S.U. won the game, 24-0.

Remembering John Sigrist

Ohio State's 6-5 win at home over Western Reserve the following Saturday, October 26, was the first single-point decision in the first 12 seasons of Ohio State football. The victory was marred with a tragic injury to

1900

September 29	Otterbein	W	20	0
October 6	Ohio University	W	20	0
October 13	at Cincinnati	W	29	0
October 20	Ohio Wesleyan	W	47	0
October 27	Oberlin	W	17	0
November 3	West Virginia	W	27	0
November 10	Case	W	24	10
November 17	Ohio Medical	L	6	11
November 24	at Michigan	T	0	0
November 29	Kenyon	W	23	5
Total Points			213	26

Season Record: 8-1-1

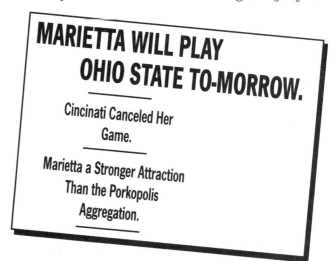

MARIETTA WILL PLAY OHIO STATE TO-MORROW.

Cincinati Canceled Her Game.

Marietta a Stronger Attraction Than the Porkopolis Aggregation.

Columbus Dispatch, Friday, October 18, 1901

DAMPENER

On Football Was Fatal Accident to Sigrist--Saturday's Games.

Columbus Citizen,
Monday, October 28, 1901

SIGRIST'S DEATH

Principal Topic of Conversation In Football Circles.

Columbus Citizen,
Tuesday, October 29, 1901

FUTURE OF FOOTBALL

At State University Will Be Decided Wednesday Afternoon.

Columbus Citizen,
Wednesday, October 30, 1901

OHIO STATE

Will Play Out the Schedule--Few Players Quit.

Columbus Citizen,
Thursday, October 31, 1901

Center John Sigrist died from an injury suffered October 26 against Western Reserve at University Field.

center John Sigrist, who suffered serious damage to his neck and died the following Monday at Grant Hospital.

Sigrist is the only player ever to lose his life from an injury suffered in an Ohio State football game.

A 27-year-old senior in the College of Agriculture, John Sigrist was described as "a very popular, modest, even-tempered young man, who was one of the best players ever seen on University Field." An extremely well-conditioned athlete from a family of 11 children, he worked his way through college with jobs each summer. Classes were canceled on Tuesday, October 29, and funeral services were held that morning in the University Chapel. Sigrist was buried in his hometown of Congress, Ohio, a small town in Wayne County located a few miles north of Wooster.

Football at the Crossroads

President William Oxley Thompson canceled the following Saturday's game with Ohio Wesleyan. A portion of the faculty and student body favored abolishing football at Ohio State, describing the sport as brutal and inhuman. It was decided that a vote of the Athletic Board and football team would be taken on Wednesday afternoon, October 30, to decide if football should be continued at the University. When it came time for the vote, the Athletic Board stepped aside and allowed the players to make the decision. The team endorsed the sport and decided that the Ohio Wesleyan game would be the only cancellation. Charles Sigrist, brother of the deceased and the football team's right tackle, strongly defended the game and urged that the sport be continued. It was felt that Charles Sigrist's attitude was a major factor in helping the team reach this judgment.

Some of the Ohio State faculty were strongly against the decision. At a November 4 faculty meeting, Professor N. W. Lord offered a resolution to cancel the remainder of the schedule. After a warm discussion, the resolution was defeated by a vote of 18 to eight.

Even with the decision to continue football, two players withdrew from the team at the request of their parents—quarterback Hardy and fullback Bulen.

Game No. 100

Play resumed with a 21-0 loss to Michigan in Columbus on November 9, followed by a 6-0 setback at Oberlin the following Saturday. The Michigan contest was O.S.U.'s 100th game since fielding its first football team in 1890. The school's all-time record stood at 52-41-7. Ohio State faced Indiana for the first time, with the Hoosiers winning, 18-6, at University Field on November 23. O.S.U. finished the season with an 11-6 win over Kenyon College on Thanksgiving Day.

Ohio State vs. Michigan
University Field - November 9, 1901
First Ohio State-Michigan Game in Columbus

After the season, John Eckstorm left Ohio State to become head football coach at Ohio Medical College. Eckstorm's resignation was a major disappointment for O.S.U. fans, since the well-liked coach had elevated the campus sport to its highest level of success and popularity. A coaching change would once again disrupt progress of the Ohio State football program. Eckstorm's successor would mark the seventh coaching change during the school's first 13 seasons.

1901				
September 28	Otterbein	T	0	0
October 5	Wittenberg	W	30	0
October 12	Ohio University	W	17	0
October 19	Marietta	W	24	0
October 26	Western Reserve	W	6	5
November 9	Michigan	L	0	21
November 16	at Oberlin	L	0	6
November 23	Indiana	L	6	18
November 28	Kenyon	W	11	6
Total Points			94	56
Season Record: 5-3-1				

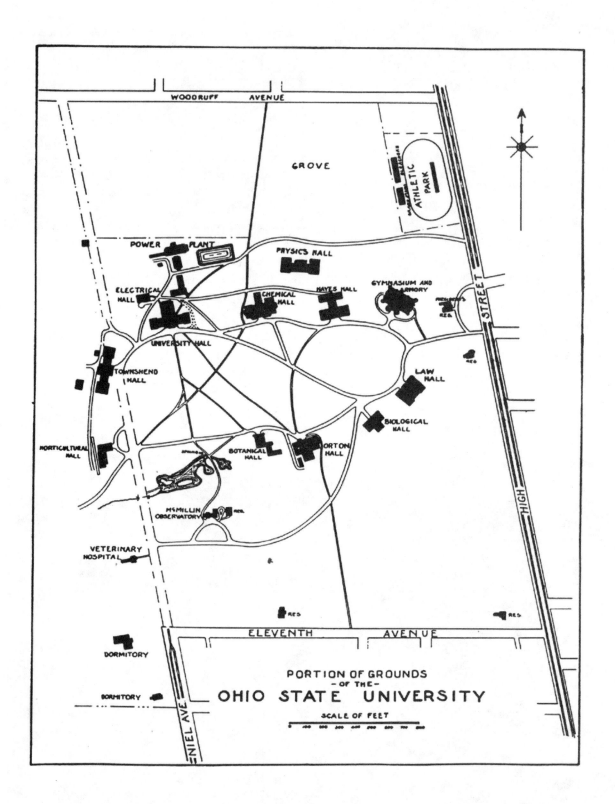

The Ohio State Campus in 1901. Home football games were played at what is labeled Athletic Park on North High Street near Woodruff Avenue. It was first known as University Field and later Ohio Field beginning in 1908.

1902

Perry Hale, a former star player at Yale, took over the coaching reins. Hale brought several new innovations to the program, including the fastening of "hand holds" on the halfbacks' belts to assist with the "flying wedge" formations. O.S.U. won its first four games by shutouts, outscoring Otterbein, Ohio University, West Virginia, Marietta, and Western Reserve, by a combined score of 86-0.

Ironically, Ohio State was thoroughly humiliated at Michigan, 86-0, in the season's fifth game on October 25. The score could

Never Again!

The Buckeyes' 86-0 setback at Michigan is the most lopsided loss in all of Ohio State football. The 86 points is also the highest combined score in an Ohio State-Michigan game, even though the Buckeyes did not score. The second highest is 70 points (Ohio State 50 - Michigan 20, 1961).

have been far worse had the officials not stopped the contest midway through the second half, simply because "the game was getting out of hand." Because the contest was so one-sided, there was concern that Michigan might not keep Ohio State on its schedule. Wolverine halfback Albert Herrnstein of

Football action in the early 1900s at University Field, renamed Ohio Field in 1908.

Chillicothe, Ohio, scored six touchdowns that afternoon, the most ever scored by one player in an Ohio State-Michigan game. Herrnstein became O.S.U.'s head coach four seasons later in 1906. On the train returning from Ann Arbor that evening, Fred A. Cornell wrote the lyrics to "Carmen Ohio," which became Ohio State's official alma mater.

Ohio State quickly bounced back with a 51-5 victory over Kenyon at University Field on November 1. That same afternoon Notre Dame edged Ohio Medical University at Columbus' Neil Park, 6-5. Ohio State's 51 points were the most O.S.U. had scored in one game since blasting Marietta 80-0 in 1892.

After a 23-12 loss to Case at home, Ohio State and highly-favored Illinois of the Western Conference (now the Big Ten) played to a scoreless tie at University Field on November 15. It was the first meeting between the two schools. The November 17 *Columbus Citizen* described Ohio State's play against Illinois as superior to any other game O.S.U. had played this season. Interestingly, the column describing the game action ended with the following prediction:

> *A few more of such contests will obtain for the local university universal recognition among the big Western colleges, and the organization will change its title to the "Big Ten."*

How true! Ohio State would begin play as the newest member of the conference just 11 seasons later in 1913.

Columbus Citizen, Saturday, November 1, 1902

O.S.U. finished the 1902 season with an exciting 17-16 win at Ohio Wesleyan, followed by a 6-6 Thanksgiving Day tie with Indiana. Coach Hale had proved to be a capable replacement for John Eckstorm, with his team finishing the year at 6-2-2.

1902				
September 27	Otterbein	W	5	0
October 4	Ohio University	W	17	0
October 11	West Virginia	W	30	0
October 18	Marietta	W	34	0
October 25	at Michigan	L	0	86
November 1	Kenyon	W	51	5
November 8	Case	L	12	23
November 15	Illinois	T	0	0
November 22	at Ohio Wesleyan	W	17	16
November 27	Indiana	T	6	6
Total Points			172	136

Season Record: 6-2-2

1903

Under Perry Hale's leadership, the 1903 Ohio State team compiled a fine record of 8-3, outscoring its 11 opponents, 265-87. Brutal play continued to characterize college football. The October 12 issue of the *Columbus Citizen* carried the following account of Ohio State's victory over Denison:

> *In a game replete with surprises and disappointments, the Ohio State eleven defeated the plucky team from Denison by a score of 24 to 5 on the "U" field Saturday afternoon. O.S.U.'s boasted defense was painfully lacking and the work of the team was a disappointment to the varsity rooters. Denison surprised*

OHIO STATE LOSES

To Indiana After an Exciting Game on Varsity Field.

Columbus Dispatch, Friday, November 27, 1903

whipped, doubtful tactics are used. Thrower (Ohio State right end) played so roughly that the officials were forced to throw him out.

all by the aggressiveness of her men, although they were poor on defense. The worst feature of the afternoon was the slugging and rough playing of Ohio State's men. It has become the rule now that when the Scarlet and Gray meets an opponent, aggressive and not easily

Muskingum College was defeated 30-0 at University Field on October 14, in a rare Wednesday afternoon game. Case whipped O.S.U. for the second straight season, 12-0, and Ohio State was again shut out at Michigan, this time by a score of 36-0. Indiana edged Ohio State, 17-16, on Thanksgiving Day, in one of the most exciting games ever staged in Columbus. O.S.U. scored three touchdowns, worth five points each, but missed two of the three extra-point kicks.

Ohio State's 1903 team. Coach Perry Hale, with necktie, is pictured at the far left in the third row.

Indiana scored only two touchdowns, but was successful on both conversion attempts. IU also kicked a field goal, which in 1903 was worth five points, the same as a touchdown. Perry Hale left after the season, and Ohio State was again searching for a new head coach.

1903				
September 26	Otterbein	W	18	0
October 3	Wittenberg	W	28	0
October 10	Denison	W	24	5
October 14	Muskingum	W	30	0
October 17	Kenyon	W	59	0
October 24	at Case	L	0	12
October 31	West Virginia	W	34	6
November 7	at Michigan	L	0	36
November 14	Oberlin	W	27	5
November 21	Ohio Wesleyan	W	29	6
November 26	Indiana	L	16	17
Total Points			**265**	**87**
	Season Record: 8-3			

1904

Ohio State's first all-year coach, E. R. Sweetland, was hired in the dual role to coach both the football and track teams. Sweetland had played football at the University of Chicago. The Ohio State Athletic Board decided not to sell season tickets,

STATE TO THE FORE

Decisive Defeat of Denison Saturday by 24 to 0 Puts Varsity in Lead.

Columbus Citizen, Monday, October 10, 1904

but instead to offer individual game tickets at varying prices, depending upon the opponent. Nine of the season's 11 games were at home. Tickets for Otterbein, Miami, Muskingum, and Denison were 25 cents, while the cost for the Case, Illinois, and Kenyon games was 50 cents. Tickets for the games against Michigan and the Carlisle Indians were priced at $1.00. An additional 1,500 bleacher seats were added to the east side of University Field.

Field goals were now worth four points instead of five, while touchdowns continued to count five points, conversions remained one point, and safeties still counted two points. Ohio State finished the season with a "so-so" record of 6-5, after outscoring its first four opponents, 184-0. Miami was scheduled for the first time, and the Muskingum game was again played on a Wednesday afternoon in early October.

Bill Marquardt Scores Against the Wolverines

Ohio State's 31-6 loss at home to Michigan on October 15 was almost a "moral victory." Both teams entered the game undefeated and unscored upon. With his team trailing 5-0 early in the second half, O.S.U. fullback Bill Marquardt picked up Frank Longman's fumble near midfield and raced the distance for Ohio State's first-ever score against Michigan. Ralph Hoyer booted the extra point, giving his team a 6-5 edge over the Wolverines as the highly partisan crowd of nearly 8,000 roared with approval. It was the first time Ohio State had ever been ahead of Michigan. It also marked the first time an opponent had scored against the Wolverines in their last 10 games, and just the second time in their last 17.

Coach Fielding Yost's Wolverines retaliated behind the running of their great halfback, Willie Heston, who scored three touchdowns to lead the comeback. The following day's *Detroit News* sports section carried the headline, OHIO SCORED ON MICHIGAN,

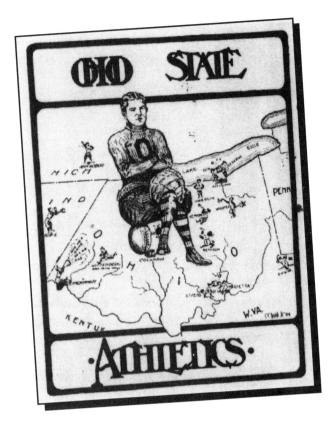

1904				
September 24	Otterbein	W	34	0
October 1	Miami	W	80	0
October 5	Muskingum	W	46	0
October 8	Denison	W	24	0
October 15	Michigan	L	6	31
October 22	Case	W	16	6
October, 29	at Indiana	L	0	8
November 5	Illinois	L	0	46
November 12	at Oberlin	L	2	4
November 19	Kenyon	W	11	5
November 24	Carlisle Indians	L	0	23
Total Points			219	123

Season Record: 6-5

implying that Ohio State's touchdown was more significant than Michigan's victory. Yost's Wolverines defeated West Virginia the next Saturday in Ann Arbor, 130-0.

Following the loss to Michigan, Ohio State lost four of its last six games, including a 23-0 setback to coach Pop Warner's Carlisle Indians on Thanksgiving Day. Apparently the efforts expended in the games against Michigan the past five years affected Ohio State's play the remainder of the season. From 1900 through 1904, O.S.U. had a record of 25-2-1 in games before facing the Wolverines, while in contests after the Michigan game, Ohio State's five-year record dipped to 7-10-2.

E. R. Sweetland, head coach in 1904 and 1905.

1905

E. R. Sweetland returned for his second season as head coach. For the first time in school history Ohio State played a 12-game schedule, winning eight, losing two and tying two. O.S.U. would not again play 12 games in one season until 69 seasons later in 1974.

After a 6-6 season-opening tie with Otterbein, Ohio State shut out its next four opponents, although only three of the games were actually played. For the third straight year, the Muskingum game was played on a Wednesday afternoon in early October.

Captains Debate Length of Halves

The game against Denison University was one of the most unusual in all of Ohio State football. O.S.U. came away with a 2-0 victory without running a single play from scrimmage. Relations between the two schools had become strained when Ohio State charged Denison with using two ineligible players on the grounds of professionalism. In an effort to save the game, this dispute was dropped, but another developed just prior to kick-off over the length of the halves.

Ohio State insisted upon playing 35-minute halves while Denison wanted the halves to be shorter. Section A of college football rule 12 stated: "The length of the game shall be 70 minutes, divided into two halves of 35 minutes each, exclusive of time taken out. There shall be a ten-minute intermission between the two halves. The game may be of shorter duration by mutual consent between the cap- tains of the contesting teams." When the Ohio State and Denison captains could not agree upon the length of the halves, the officials ruled in favor of Ohio State since there was not a mutual consent about the change. Denison refused to take the field! After a warning and a two-minute wait, the game was forfeited to Ohio State, 2-0.

The O.S.U. varsity stayed on the field and scrimmaged the second-stringers, but few of the 2,000-plus spectators stayed to watch. Most fans, while criticizing the handling of the entire affair, stood in line to receive a refund on their tickets. While Ohio State may have won the game, it lost at the gate. Ticket sales totaled $1,078 while the refunds amounted to $1,206—a loss of $128. Several children apparently sneaked inside University Field that afternoon, then stood in line and received their "refunds."

DePauw University was defeated, 32-6, in the only game ever played between the two schools. Ohio State's 15-0 win over Wooster marked their first meeting since Wooster registered a 64-0 victory in 1890, O.S.U.'s first season. Ohio State's two losses were shutouts by Michigan and Indiana, 40-0 and 11-0, respectively.

Ohio State athletics faced another financial crisis, partly because of the ticket refunds following the Denison forfeit. A financial report showed that a $2,022.50 "net deficit"

OHIO STATE GAME ENDS IN WRANGLE

Denison Loses Out on Forfeit by Referee Esterline.

A ROW OF HALVES.

Scarlet and Gray Sticks for Regulation Time—Criticism Flows Freely

Columbus Dispatch,
Sunday, October 15, 1905

First Booster Organization

Ohio State's first organized "rooters club" was formed in 1905 with Harry E. "Mother" Ewing as head cheerleader.

LICKED WOOSTER IN THE LAST HALF

Ohio State Team Found Itself in Trouble During First Part of of the Game.

Hoyer Kicks Goal from Placement and Barrington Runs 100 Yards for Touchdown.

Columbus Dispatch,
Sunday, November 26, 1905

had to be dealt with, otherwise the future of athletics was in doubt. Donations from faculty, students, and fans helped the cause, and a campus carnival raised nearly $1,000. Once again a financial dilemma was eased.

championship with an overall record of 8-1, while outscoring its nine opponents, 153-14. Ohio State was coached by the popular and successful Albert E. Herrnstein, a native of Chillicothe, Ohio, who was a graduate of the University of Michigan, where he had been a star halfback and end in 1900-01-02. Herrnstein was head coach at Purdue in 1905, leading the Boilermakers to a record of 6-1-1.

Herrnstein Scouts Alma Mater

O.S.U. had no trouble in its first two games, shutting out Otterbein and Wittenberg, 41-0 and 52-0, respectively. While his team was defeating Wittenberg on October 6, Herrnstein was in Ann Arbor scouting the Michigan Wolverines who defeated Case that afternoon, 28-0. O.S.U. defeated Muskingum, 16-0, in the rain and mud at University Field on Wednesday afternoon, October 10. Although the score was not as high as expected, Muskingum was not able to register a single first down and never advanced into O.S.U. territory.

Ohio State played only one game in the next three weeks, losing to Michigan, 6-0, in Columbus on October 20 for its only setback of the season. Herrnstein's advance scouting of the stalwart Wolverines obviously helped, but O.S.U. was unable to seriously penetrate the Michigan defense. The October 21 issue of the *Cleveland Plain Dealer* carried the following description of the game:

1905				
September 23	Otterbein	T	6	6
September 30	Heidelberg	W	28	0
October 4	Muskingum	W	40	0
October 7	Wittenberg	W	17	0
October 14	Denison	W	2	0
October 21	DePauw	W	32	6
October 28	Case	T	0	0
November 4	Kenyon	W	23	0
November 11	at Michigan	L	0	40
November 18	Oberlin	W	36	0
November 25	Wooster	W	15	0
November 30	Indiana	L	0	11
Total Points			199	63

Season Record: 8-2-2

1906

Ohio State fielded what was "the finest team yet" to represent the university. The 1906 squad was the first Ohio State team to play an entire season without giving up a single touchdown. O.S.U. won the Ohio state

First Opponent Scout

The first opponent scout to evaluate Ohio State at University Field was Frank Stewart, Kenyon's head coach. Stewart watched during Ohio State's 52-0 victory over Wittenberg on October 6, 1906. O.S.U. defeated Kenyon in Columbus on November 10, 6-0.

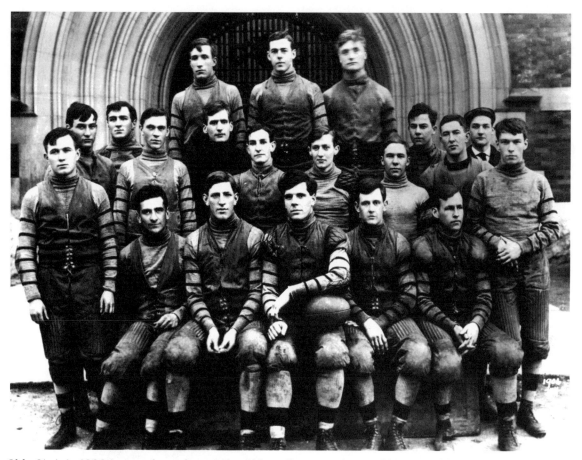

Ohio State's 1906 team, champion of the Ohio colleges, outscored its opposition, 153-14.

Michigan University's football team defeated Ohio State University 6 to 0, scoring on a field goal and a safety. The Ohio team, coached by Herrnstein, a former Michigan football star, put up a strong defense. Unable to carry the ball across Ohio's goal, and with but four minutes of the game remaining, Garrels made his fourth attempt to kick a goal from the field and was successful. After the next kick-off an exchange of punts gave Ohio the ball on her fifteen-yard line. A penalty put the ball back to five yards, and when Gibson dropped back to punt a bad pass sent the oval over his head and he was compelled to fall on it back of the goal line, giving Michigan two more points.

After victories at Oberlin and at home over Kenyon by identical 6-0 scores, Ohio State became the undisputed champion of the "Big Six" (Case, Kenyon, Oberlin, Ohio State, Ohio Wesleyan, Western Reserve), with a 9-0 triumph over powerful Case in Cleveland on November 17. In Columbus the following weekend, Wooster was dealt its first loss of the season, 9-0. It was the first game all season in which Wooster had given up a touchdown.

Ohio State captured the Ohio state championship Thanksgiving Day with a narrow

First Use of Forward Pass

Ohio State first used the forward pass in 1906. In O.S.U.'s 12-0 Ohio championship game victory over Wooster, end Harry Carr scored Ohio State's second touchdown on a 10-yard pass from quarterback Walter Barrington.

CAN HE CROSS THE LINE?

Case and Ohio State will meet at Cleveland Saturday in a game which will undoubtedly decide the "Big Six" Championship.

Columbus Citizen, Tuesday, November 13, 1906

11-8 verdict over Ohio Medical University, coached by John Eckstorm who had been quite successful at O.S.U. from 1899 through 1901. The November 30 *Columbus Citizen* ran the following portrayal of the game:

> For excitement, the game stands out as the strongest ever played at "U" field. Being a local game entirely, the two teams had plenty of sympathizers in the crowd, which numbered in the neighborhood of 6,000. The rooting forces of both schools did splendid work.
>
> State acted like a well-coached team throughout the game, and put up an excellent display of football knowledge and ability. It deserved to win. The interference shown was the best seen on "U"

field this year, and it never failed to carry the runner along for good gains. This was especially true of the quarterback runs in which Barrington distinguished himself until taken out of the line-up with injuries.

One individual came within a very small margin of defeating the football champions of Ohio Thanksgiving Day. That man was Jack Means, quarterback for the Ohio Medics, who in a splendid battle with Ohio State, kicked two field goals from placement and scored all of the 8 points of his team. One of Means' goals was a grand effort.

Standing 52 yards from the Ohio State goal he booted the pigskin over the bar in the first half.

WAHOO! STATE WINS FROM MEDICS: WAHOO!

Columbus Citizen, Friday, November 30, 1906

Wolverines Withdraw

Michigan withdrew from the Western Conference (now Big Ten) after the 1906 season, when the conference adopted a series of "far-reaching regulations." The Wolverines were particularly opposed to a limitation of five games, which would sever their strong ties with Eastern teams. Michigan rejoined the Western Conference effective November 20, 1917.

1906

September 29	Otterbein	W	41	0
October 6	Wittenberg	W	52	0
October 10	Muskingum	W	16	0
October 20	Michigan	L	0	6
November 3	at Oberlin	W	6	0
November 10	Kenyon	W	6	0
November 17	at Case	W	9	0
November 24	Wooster	W	12	0
November 29	Ohio Medical	W	11	8
Total Points			153	14

Season Record: 8-1

Ohio State deservedly won the game by piling up 11 points, but the Medic quarter gave the Scarlet and Gray supporters several attacks of heart failure in the second half when four times he shot the pigskin about the bar. He missed them all, but several of the tries fell shy of the coveted mark by the matter of only a few inches.

Fred Secrist, the Chillicothe lad, who played his second game for the Scarlet and Gray, was one of the sensations of the day. Every time he was given the ball, he made a gain and by his twisting and dashing playing, he was enabled to carry the ball over for both of State's touchdowns. With the winning of the Medic game, Ohio State closes her season the undisputed champion of Ohio.

"Signor Angelo," better known as Tony Aquila, joined The Ohio State University as a groundskeeper. Aquila would become a legendary campus figure over the next 41 years, providing expert care of University Field/Ohio Field and Ohio Stadium. The successful 1906 season also resulted in healthier gate receipts. A total of $18,650.60 was collected, while the season's expenses were $11,259.19, leaving a surplus of $7,391.41. Receipts from away games netted $1,871.38.

1907

Under coach Albert Herrnstein's direction, Ohio State fielded another strong team that put together a record of 7-2-1. Wooster played O.S.U. to a 6-6 tie in the season's fourth game at University Field on October 19. The Wooster squad was coached by Lynn W. St. John, who later would play a significant role in the development of athletics at Ohio State.

O.S.U. was still unable to defeat Michigan, losing to the Wolverines on October 26, 22-0, before an Ann Arbor crowd of approximately 7,000. This was the first OSU-UM

KENYON GOAL TWICE CROSSED BY STATE ON A MUDDY GRIDIRON

Ohio State 12, Kenyon 0

Otherwise Splendid Battle is Marred by Rough Work on Part of Two Visiting Players.

Bentley Removed From Game for Slugging — Slippery Ball Prevents Elevens From Showing Customary Speed.

Columbus Dispatch, Sunday, November 3, 1907

game to be played at Michigan's new Ferry Field. The Wolverines were beginning to effectively use the "forward pass," which was legalized as a part of college football in 1906. On this wet, cold and windy afternoon, Michigan completed seven of 10 passing attempts, including a 25-yard toss from William Wasmund to Paul Magoffin for the first touchdown pass in an Ohio State-Michigan game.

Kenyon was defeated at home the following Saturday, 12-0, in a game characterized by very rough play. The *Columbus Dispatch* of November 3 carried the following report:

Kenyon lost just a bit of Columbus esteem as a football force when Saturday afternoon a free fist or two on different occasions caused almost a general mix-up on the field. The heat of the battle was so intense that not even a mud-covered field and a driving rain could suffice to keep the minds of strenu-

ous athletes confined closely to the play. Kenyon in each instance (to tell the truth) was the initial offender. Pass that over, however, as an incident of the game and let that be as it may. Kenyon fought just as hard as she ever did and died just as hard before the big grinding force of the Ohio State football machine which represents the big university that sits supreme on its broad acres in the northern end of the capital city.

After a 22-10 win over Oberlin, Ohio State was defeated by Case, 11-9, in a game which prevented O.S.U. from repeating its championship of Ohio. Ohio State closed its season with a 23-0 victory over Heidelberg and a 16-0 Thanksgiving Day victory over Ohio Wesleyan.

Albert Herrnstein, a Michigan graduate, was Ohio State's head coach from 1906 through 1909.

1907				
September 28	Otterbein	W	28	0
September 5	Muskingum	W	16	0
October 12	Denison	W	28	0
October 19	Wooster	T	6	6
October 26	at Michigan	L	0	22
November 2	Kenyon	W	12	0
November 9	Oberlin	W	22	10
November 16	Case	L	9	11
November 23	Heidelberg	W	23	0
November 28	Ohio Wesleyan	W	16	0
Total Points			160	49

Season Record: 7-2-1

1908

Ohio State's record slipped to 6-4, with O.S.U. making its most powerful showings against the strongest opponents, yet losing to teams that were not expected to be very strong. New bleachers were added to the east side of the playing field, and a new scoreboard was installed to help spectators follow the play and keep track of the downs.

After starting the season at 2-2, Ohio State played extremely well while losing to Michigan, 10-6, on October 24. Fullback Millard Gibson's 75-yard touchdown run on a fake punt gave Ohio State a 6-4 halftime lead, but O.S.U. was unable to hold Michigan in the second half. This was the 10th game between Ohio State and Michigan, with the Wolverines holding a decided edge at 9-0-1.

The following weekend, Ohio State overcame a 5-4 halftime deficit to defeat Ohio Wesleyan, 20-9, before a crowd of 3,300. The Methodists (nickname changed to Battling Bishops in 1925) were coached by Branch Rickey, a former star athlete at Ohio Wesleyan, who later distinguished himself

as a major league baseball executive. Rickey broke baseball's color barrier with the Brooklyn Dodgers' signing of Jackie Robinson in 1947.

Ohio Wesleyan held a spirited pep rally Friday, with coach Rickey openly predicting "victory." A large cheering section accompanied the visitors to Columbus, including most of the male student body. Co-eds were not permitted to attend, since the faculty felt "it would not be proper" for them to leave the Ohio Wesleyan campus. The co-eds' petition to have this decision reversed was not accepted by the "relentless position of the faculty."

Using a wide-open attack, Ohio Wesleyan took a 5-0 lead midway through the

Harry E. "Mother" Ewing, popular "Yell Master." Ewing was awarded a Varsity "O", but declined the honor in the belief that such awards should go only to the players.

41

OHIO STATE WAS STRONG AT THE END

Wesleyan Suffers Defeat After Maintaining Lead Up to End of the First Half.

OHIO STATE 20—WESLEYAN 9

Wells and Secrist Prominent in Scoring Three Touchdowns— Barrington Kicks Field Goal.

Columbus Dispatch, Sunday, November 1, 1908

first half on a nine-yard touchdown pass from James Day to Leslie Stauffer. Near halftime, Walter Barrington booted a 23-yard field goal from a very difficult angle, to pull the Buckeyes within one at 5-4. The Buckeyes relied more on their rushing efforts. Ohio State sophomore halfback Leslie Wells scored three second-half touchdowns, all from inside the three yard line. Thomas Jones' conversion made it 20-5. Late in the game, the Methodists' Harrison Weaver kicked a 25-yard field goal to finalize the score at 20-9.

Victory No. 100

After losing the following Saturday at Case, 18-8, Ohio State defeated Vanderbilt at Nashville on November 14, 17-6. This triumph over "the champions of the south" was Ohio State's 100th football victory. O.S.U.'s all-time record now stood at 100-62-12.

University Field Renamed Ohio Field

Ohio State's University Field was officially dedicated as Ohio Field on November 21 during a 14-12 victory over Oberlin. Mrs. William Oxley Thompson, wife of the Ohio

State president, used a flask of water from a campus spring to christen the field with this statement: "In the name of clean athletics and manly support, I christen this 'Ohio Field'." O.S.U. closed out the season the following Thursday with a 19-9 triumph over Kenyon on Thanksgiving Day. At season end, Millard Gibson became the first Ohio State player to be recognized by writer Walter Camp, who each season selected an All-American team. Gibson was awarded an honorable mention.

1908			
September 26	Otterbein	W	18	0
October 3	Wooster	L	0	8
October 10	Denison	W	16	2
October 17	Western Reserve	L	0	18
October 24	Michigan	L	6	10
October 31	Ohio Wesleyan	W	20	9
November 7	at Case	L	8	18
November 14	at Vanderbilt	W	17	6
November 21	Oberlin	W	14	12
November 26	Kenyon	W	19	9
Total Points			118	92

Season Record: 6-4

THANKSGIVING DAY

OHIO STATE VERSVS KENYON

1909

Coach Albert Herrnstein guided Ohio State to seven wins and only three losses, but the setbacks were three of the season's "biggest games"—Michigan (33-6), Case (11-3), and Oberlin (26-6). Six of the seven victories were shutouts with a combined score of 183-0, and Ohio Wesleyan was defeated, 21-6. The Scarlet and Gray's 74-0 whitewash of Wooster was the most points O.S.U. had scored in one game since shellacking Miami of Ohio in 1904, 80-0. A crowd of 7,000 saw the game against Case, at the time the largest ever to attend an athletic event at Ohio State. Field goals were now worth three points instead of four, while touchdowns continued to count five points, conversions remained one point, and safeties still counted two points.

At Michigan on October 16, O.S.U. center Chelsea Boone scored his team's only touchdown by picking up a loose Ohio State punt near the UM goal line and running into the end zone. In 1909 a punt was an "alive ball." After O.S.U. punted, Wolverine fullback Charles Freeney allowed the ball to roll, apparently thinking it would bounce into the end zone for a touchback. Chelsea alertly grabbed the loose ball before it crossed the goal line, much to Freeney's surprise.

Scouting the Ohio State team at Michigan was Vanderbilt coach Dan McGugin, brother-in-law of Wolverine coach Fielding Yost. Four weeks later in Columbus, O.S.U. played one of its finest games of the season,

Ohio Field in 1909

SUBSTITUTE END PROTECTS STATE

Wright's Tackle Keeps Neely of Vanderbilt Away from Ohio Goal Line.

Jones and Hall Recover Kicked Ball, Giving Varsity Chance to Score Hatfield.

Ohio State Journal, Sunday, November 14, 1909

**Ohio State vs. Kenyon - Ohio Field
Thanksgiving Day - November 25, 1909**

defeating McGugin's powerful Commodores, 5-0. The November 14 *Ohio State Journal* described the intersectional clash as follows:

Ohio State passed out to Vanderbilt Saturday afternoon that which the Southerners dreaded to take, yet gamely received. Had it not been for Bill Wright, substitute end, State would have been unable to keep her goal line clear and might have been beaten. By one tackle Wright stopped Vanderbilt's greatest sweep, spoiled that eleven's best scoring chance and made Ohio's five points stand for victory.

Halfback Hatfield originated and completed the counting series of plays. He punted from near his own goal line. Captain Jones raced up the field ahead of his ends and recovered the free ball at midfield. Wells made an onside kick. Guard Hall recovered that and ran near the Vanderbilt goal. Two line plays and then a forward pass, Jones to Hatfield, took the ball over. Thirty-one minutes and 10 seconds of the first half elapsed before State swung ahead

Vanderbilt's comeback, one that turned into nothing more than an ad-

minister of fright, was late in the final half. Quarterback Neely received a punt deep in his own territory, received interference and clipped off yard after yard. He escaped both Jones and Wells and odds were in favor of his making the goal line. If that could be gained for a touchdown and a goal kicked thereafter, it would have been all off for Ohio State.

The 1909 season was the last for coach Albert Herrnstein, whose four-year record was an impressive 28-10-1. The 1909 campaign also marked the completion of O.S.U.'s second decade of football. Ohio State's 20-year all-time record stood at 109-65-11.

1909				
September 25	Otterbein	W	14	0
October 2	Wittenberg	W	39	0
October 9	Wooster	W	74	0
October 16	at Michigan	L	6	33
October 23	Denison	W	29	0
October 30	Ohio Wesleyan	W	21	6
November 6	Case	L	3	11
November 13	Vanderbilt	W	5	0
November 20	at Oberlin	L	6	26
November 25	Kenyon	W	22	0
Total Points			219	76

Season Record: 7-3

1910

A major change in college football was the allotment of a game's playing time into four 15-minute quarters rather than two 35-minute halves. Howard Jones, a former Yale All-American end, became Ohio State's new head coach. Jones was born in Excello, Ohio, a small community located in southwest Ohio between Dayton and Cincinnati. He played on the same Yale teams as his illustrious brother, Tad Jones, who became one of Yale's most successful coaches.

Howard Jones, who had been head coach at Syracuse in 1908 and Yale in 1909, brought the "Yale system" to Ohio State with much success. A gifted motivator, Jones gave full attention to perfecting the team's defensive capabilities before installing the squad's offense.

His team posted a record of 6-1-3, outscoring its ten opponents, 182-27. O.S.U. also had its first freshman coach, "Doc" Welch, who provided instructions for the first-year players.

After opening with four victories, Ohio State played Michigan to a 3-3 tie on October 22, before an Ohio Field crowd of 6,500.

Both teams kicked field goals in the second quarter. The Wolverines' Fred Conklin booted one from the OSU 23-yard line, and Ohio State retaliated with a three-pointer by Leslie Wells from the UM 25. Interestingly, both field goals were kicked on first down situations.

Case Wins Fourth Straight

Case handed O.S.U. its only loss of the season, 14-10, at Cleveland on November 5. The Ohio State-Case game had grown into one of the most fiercely contested each fall —it was Case's fourth consecutive victory in the series. O.S.U. protested the game, claiming Case deliberately selected game officials who favored the Cleveland school. Ohio State failed in its efforts to have the officials selected by someone independent of either team.

O.S.U. won a very close contest at home over Ohio Wesleyan the following Saturday, 6-0, before a crowd of 2,800. The November 13 edition of the *Columbus Dispatch* gave the following account of the action:

Ohio Wesleyan football cohorts, including a mighty good team and some 400 rooters, were turned back to the

WESLEYAN LOSER IN TIGHT BATTLE

Wells Smashes His Way to a Touchdown in Third Quarter, for Only Score.

STATE 6—WESLEYAN 0

Powell and Bachman Play Fine Football and Crush Most Attempts at End Runs.

Columbus Dispatch, Sunday, November 13, 1910

north country Saturday evening again beaten by Ohio State as they have been for each succeeding season since 1897. The battle Saturday was much closer than wanted and not until the third period was there enough ground yielded to permit the Scarlet and Gray backs to get across the line for the lone touchdown of the fray. Captain Leslie Wells made it and converted the play into a goal and 6 to 0 win.

Howard Jones resigned at the end of his first season, much to the disappointment of his players and the Ohio State fans. A strong believer in sound football fundamentals, Jones spent seven seasons as head coach at Iowa and 16 seasons at Southern California, enjoying great success at both schools. He led the Hawkeyes to their first two outright Big Ten titles with undefeated-untied seasons in 1921 (7-0) and 1922 (7-0). At Southern California, his teams compiled a 16-year mark of 121-38-13, including a "five-for-five" record in the Rose Bowl. Jones is a member of the College Football Hall of Fame.

Howard Jones, head coach in 1910.

1910				
September 24	Otterbein	W	14	5
October 1	Wittenberg	W	62	0
October 8	Cincinnati	W	23	0
October 15	Western Reserve	W	6	0
October 22	Michigan	T	3	3
October 29	Denison	T	5	5
November 5	at Case	L	10	14
November 12	Ohio Wesleyan	W	6	0
November 19	Oberlin	T	0	0
November 24	Kenyon	W	53	0
Total Points			**182**	**27**

Season Record: 6-1-3

1911

At the recommendation of Howard Jones, Ohio State turned the football program over to Harry Vaughn, another former player from Yale. Vaughn, who had no previous coaching experience, felt his players needed to have a good understanding of the game if they were to be successful. He displayed a poster which read: "To H _ _ _ with weight, it's BRAINS that counts in Football." Leslie Wells, last season's captain, helped Vaughn as an assistant coach.

Game No. 200

O.S.U. put together a "so-so" record of 5-3-2, with eight of the ten games being very close. With the exception of a 19-0 loss at Michigan and a 24-0 victory at home over Kenyon, no game was decided by more than nine points. The setback at Michigan on October 21 was Ohio State's 200th game of football (all-time record now 117-67-16). Case won over O.S.U. for the fifth straight season, 9-0, in Columbus on November 4. One of the cheerleaders accompanied the squad to

STATE DEFEATS CINCINNATI BY SCORE OF 11-6

Willaman Counts For State in Each of First Two Periods---Cincinnati Scores a Lucky Touchdown in the Third Quarter

Columbus Citizen, Friday, December 1, 1911

Left to right, Cheerleaders "Pink" Tenney, "Hub" Atkinson, and "Bob" Sigafoss. Atkinson was also a star basketball player and later served as an Ohio State University trustee.

Oberlin on November 18. It was the first time the Athletic Board had paid for a cheerleader's expenses to attend an away game. Ohio State played Syracuse for the first time, losing to the Orangemen in the season's last home game on November 25, 6-0.

This year's annual Thanksgiving Day game was played November 30 at Cincinnati, where O.S.U. defeated the Bearcats, 11-6. The following game recap was carried in the *Columbus Citizen* on Friday, December 1:

State won its final game of the season, defeating Cincinnati this morning, 11 to 6, in the presence of about 4,000 fans. The first part of the game looked like a runaway for State. Cincinnati took a big brace and badly outplayed Coach Vaughn's aggregation in the final two quarters of play.

State's first touchdown came in the first quarter, when Willaman intercepted a forward pass and ran 60 yards for a touchdown. State scored again in the second quarter and again it was Willaman who carried the ball over after a series of spectacular runs by himself and Foss, both of whom starred for State throughout. In the third quarter Vaughn sent in his second backfield. Early in the quarter Fenkner recovered a punt fumbled by Morrisey and ran 20 yards for a touchdown.

Harry Vaughn, head coach in 1911.

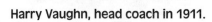

47

OFFICIAL PROGRAM
FOOT BALL, 1911
Saturday, Nov. 25th
Ohio State vs. Syracuse

1911				
September 30	Otterbein	W	6	0
October 7	Miami	W	3	0
October 14	Western Reserve	T	0	0
October 21	at Michigan	L	0	19
October 28	Ohio Wesleyan	W	3	0
November 4	Case	L	0	9
November 11	Kenyon	W	24	0
November 18	at Oberlin	T	0	0
November 25	Syracuse	L	0	6
November 30	at Cincinnati	W	11	6
Total Points			47	40

Season Record: 5-3-2

1912

Whilc Ohio Statc was playing in Cincinnati on Thanksgiving, Kenyon borrowed Ohio Field to host a game against Carnegie Institute of Technology (now Carnegie-Mellon University). Kenyon won, 6-0.

Harry Vaughn left O.S.U. after just one season to resume his law studies at Yale University, and Ohio State was left to search for its different head coach in just 23 seasons of organized football. There was sentiment at the university that Ohio State was playing too many small colleges from within the state, and that more state universities should be scheduled each fall besides Michigan. Mr. George W. Rightmire, graduate manager of athletics and a member of the school's law faculty, pointed out the desirability of applying for membership in the Western Conference, later known as the Big Ten.

The year of 1912 developed into one of the most significant in all of Ohio State athletics. The Athletic Board at a meeting on January 12, 1912, unanimously agreed to petition the Western Conference for admission, even though this would mean severing athletic relations with the University of Michigan. Ohio State felt that its annual game against the Wolverines was very good for the O.S.U. football program, even though Ohio State had been unable to register a single victory during the first 13 games in the series. However, since Michigan had withdrawn from the conference after the 1906 season, Western Conference policy now prohibited member schools from scheduling the Wolverines.

A committee of George Rightmire and Alonzo Tuttle, both law professors, and Carl Steeb, secretary of the University trustees, presented Ohio State's request at a conference meeting in Chicago on January 26. Rightmire made the actual presentation. Ohio State was elated to learn that the West-

STATE IS BEATEN AND LEAVES FIELD

Coach Richards Objects to Rough Tackling by Penn State.

Pennsylvanians Have No Trouble in Rolling Up the Score.

Cleveland Plain Dealer, Sunday, November 17, 1912

ern Conference voted favorably upon its membership request during an April 6, 1912, board meeting, and that O.S.U.'s first conference football games would be played in 1913.

In other developments in 1912, the Athletic Board was reorganized under faculty control, and there was a separation of the O.S.U. athletic program from the school's department of physical education. John R. Richards was hired as football coach and track coach, in addition to serving as the school's first Director of Athletics. Richards was a graduate of Wisconsin, where he won four letters in football from 1892 through 1895. He had been head coach at Wisconsin for one season, guiding the Badgers to a record of 5-1-1 in 1911. Touchdowns were now worth six points instead of five, conversions remained one point, field goals continued to count three points, and safeties still counted two points. This would be college football's last change in scoring until the two-point conversion option was introduced in 1958.

Richards was an innovator who was often described as a "driver with no sympathy for a loafer." As a result of Richards' doing away with secret practices, students and sup-

porters turned out in great numbers to watch the evening workouts, and enthusiasm for Ohio State football had reached a new high. Incandescent lights were used on the field so that the team could continue practice after sundown.

O.S.U. opened the season October 5 with a 55-0 blowout at Otterbein, the school's first road opener since losing 22-14 in 1893, also at Otterbein. This was the last of 18 games between Ohio State and Otterbein, with O.S.U. holding a record of 13-2-3. Otterbein was Ohio State's season-opening opponent 15 times, the most frequent opening opponent during O.S.U.'s first 111 seasons from 1890 through 2000. Ohio State defeated Denison in its home opener the following weekend, 34-0.

Michigan shut out O.S.U. at Ohio Field on October 19, 14-0, before an overflow crowd of 8,500, at the time the largest attendance in Ohio State history. Interestingly, each team entered the game at 2-0, with each having scored 89 points in their first two games. This was Fielding Yost's 100th game as head coach of the Wolverines. Yost's Michigan record now stood at a very impressive 86-7-7. This was the last game in the series for a few seasons, since O.S.U. would enter Western Conference competition the following fall. Ohio State and Michigan would next face each other in 1918, the year after Michigan rejoined the Western Conference.

After blasting Cincinnati, 47-7, O.S.U. broke a five-game losing streak with a 31-6 victory over Case in Cleveland on November 2. It was Case's most one-sided setback in "Big Six" competition in ten seasons. Ohio State's 23-17 win over Oberlin the next Saturday earned O.S.U. its first state title in six years.

Near the end of a November 16 game against eastern power Penn State the following weekend, coach Richards pulled his team from Ohio Field with nine minutes remaining, citing unsportsmanlike conduct by Penn State and a lackadaisical approach by the game officials in calling penalties. The *Cleve-*

land Plain Dealer described Richards' action in its November 17 edition:

Five minutes before the end of the game between Pennsylvania State University and Ohio State University, after the easterners had outplayed the local team by a score of 37 to 0, Coach Richards of Ohio State withdrew his men from the field because of alleged rough playing, and officials awarded Pennsylvania State the game by a score of 1 to 0.

Frequently during the game the Ohio coach objected to the "unnecessarily rough playing" of the visitors. When one of his men was tackled hard, Richards became angry and called the Ohio State team from the field and refused to allow the men to continue playing. Pennsylvania State played fast football and outplayed Ohio State in every point of the game, excepting along the line. Ohio State's line held so good that the eastern team had to make most of its gains around the end. The few gains that the local team did make were through Pennsylvania's line.

Ohio State players could not master the perfect interference of the visitors, who seemed to be able to score at will. Sixteen points were scored in the first quarter, none in the second, 14 in the third and 7 in the fourth, up till the time the game was forfeited.

After the game was called, an Ohio State freshman burned the Penn State colors on the goal post in view of Penn State President E. E. Sparks, an Ohio State alumnus. A group of students and alumni apologized to Dr. Sparks before he left Columbus, and a formal apology was sent to Penn State the following week. It would be 44 years before Ohio State and Penn State would again meet on the college gridiron.

O.S.U. defeated Ohio Wesleyan, 36-6, then faced the Michigan Aggies (now Michigan State) at Ohio Field on Thursday, November 28, in what was to be the last of the traditional Thanksgiving Day games. Before a crowd of approximately 3,000, the Aggies won, 35-20, after Ohio State led through three quarters, 20-14. The 35 points are the most Michigan State has ever been able to score against O.S.U. in a single game. Ohio State finished the season at 6-3.

Richards abruptly resigned shortly after the last game. This left Ohio State without a football and track coach and Director of Athletics, as preparations were underway to compete the following season in the Western Conference. Many far-lasting changes would be made in the next few months, and a much-needed "stability" would finally be attained by the Ohio State Department of Athletics. O.S.U. had finished its first 23 seasons of football with an all-time record of 126-72-17.

John Richards, head coach in 1912.

1912			
October 5	at Otterbein	W 55	0
October 12	Denison	W 34	0
October 19	Michigan	L 0	14
October 26	Cincinnati	W 47	7
November 2	at Case	W 31	6
November 9	Oberlin	W 23	17
November 16	Penn State	L 0	37
November 23	at Ohio Wesleyan	W 36	6
November 28	Michigan State	L 20	35
Total Points		246	122
	Season Record: 6-3		

JOINING THE BIG TEN

The year of 1913 was one of the most significant in all of Ohio State football. The school began play in the Western Conference, and John W. Wilce was hired as head football coach, bringing a much-needed stability to the position.

The Western Conference's official name is the Intercollegiate Conference of Faculty Representatives. It later became known as the Big Nine and the Big Ten. The seven charter members who competed for the league's first football championship in 1896 were Chicago, Illinois, Michigan, Minnesota, Northwestern, Purdue, and Wisconsin (Wisconsin won the '96 title). Indiana and Iowa joined the Western Conference in 1900. Michigan withdrew from the league after the 1906 season, then rejoined in 1917 after a 10-year absence. Chicago dropped out after the 1939 season and was replaced by Michigan State in 1953. Penn State began conference play in 1993.

In *Ohio State Athletics,* Dr. James E. Pollard explains that the 18-month period leading up to the fall of 1913 was marked by the following major developments:

1. The organization of the Athletic Board under faculty control.

2. The separation of athletics from the Department of Physical Education.
3. The hiring of year-round coaches with faculty status.
4. Joining the Western Conference and the scheduling of conference football games for the 1913 season.

Lynn W. St. John was hired in the fall of 1912 as Business Manager of Athletics, head coach of the basketball and baseball teams, and assistant football coach. St. John had been a freshman halfback at Ohio State in 1900 but was forced to drop out of school following his father's death. He graduated from Wooster College in 1906, and returned to Wooster to coach football, basketball, and baseball, following a one-year coaching stint at Fostoria High School.

St. John was planning to be a doctor. In 1909, he moved to Ohio Wesleyan in Delaware, replacing Branch Rickey who was unable to coach because of a temporary illness. In the mornings, St. John would study medicine at Starling Medical College in Columbus, then return to the Delaware campus on the interurban railroad to conduct football practice and attend to his duties as Director of Athletics.

St. John had been at Ohio State just a few months when John Richards resigned his positions of Director of Athletics and head football coach, following the 1912 season. On December 18, 1912, the Athletic Board appointed St. John as Ohio State's new Director of Athletics, and increased his annual salary to $2,500. Interestingly, St. John didn't even know he was being considered for the position until Professor Thomas French, President of the Athletic Board, told him of his appointment.

L. W. St. John's aspirations of a medical career quickly ended, and Ohio State had chosen a man who would lead its athletic program to national prominence. A talented administrator, St. John eventually became a nationally recognized leader in intercollegiate athletics, particularly with the NCAA. He remained Ohio State's Athletic Director until his retirement nearly 35 years later on July 1, 1947.

The Athletic Board also arranged in 1912 for the first permanent location of the Athletic Department. The Thomas House, one of the few remaining faculty houses on campus, was converted into an "Athletic House" with offices, shower rooms, lockers, and a training room. The facility was located on the west side of High Street near 16th Avenue, just south of Ohio Field. The Athletic House headquartered the Athletic Department until the department was moved to a new physical education building in 1931.

St. John's first major task was finding a new football coach to lead Ohio State in its first season of Western Conference (Big Ten)

competition. The position was first offered to Carl Rothgeb, coach at Colorado College, who had been a four-year letterman at Illinois in the early 1900s. Rothgeb declined the offer. John Schommer, a noted athlete from the University of Chicago, was next offered the position, but negotiations with Schommer did not work out. Eventually the position was awarded to John W. Wilce, a former three-sport letterman at Wisconsin, where he was an all-conference fullback and captain of the 1909 Badger football team. Following graduation from Wisconsin, Wilce had coached at La Crosse, Wisconsin, High School, and had been an assistant football coach and assistant professor of physical education at his alma mater.

Frank "Riley" Castleman, a former four-sport star athlete at Colgate, was hired from the University of Colorado to assist with football and coach the track team. The new coaching staff was set—Wilce was the new head coach, Castleman was an assistant in charge of backs, and St. John was an assistant to coach the line. The hiring of Wilce brought great stability and maturity to Ohio State football. Wilce coached 16 seasons with much success before retiring from his football position after the 1928 season. In comparison, there had been 11 different head coaches during the school's first 23 seasons from 1890 through 1912.

Ohio State opened its 1913 season with three Ohio opponents, defeating Ohio Wesleyan (58-0) and Western Reserve (14-8) and playing rugged Oberlin to a scoreless tie. After an open Saturday, OSU lost to Indiana on November 1, 7-6, in its very first Western Conference game. A "twilight rally" was staged at Ohio Field the Friday evening prior to the game, during which 800 students "snake danced" around a bonfire. Coach Wilce and Ohio State President William Oxley Thompson both spoke to the cheering crowd.

Indiana scored its touchdown by recovering an Ohio State fumble at the one-yard line. The November 2 *Columbus Dispatch* gave the following account of the action:

Ohio State football men—and men they were every inch of them—with their several thousand cheering hosts behind them were deprived of the fruits of a victory in their very first Western Conference game played Saturday afternoon at Ohio Field with Indiana University, as the foe, when all the greater yards gained on rushing the ball, all the finer tackling and sturdier defense, and most of all two stands for downs within their own five-yard line went for naught in the last two minutes of play, when a pass to Graf to punt got through him and dribbled to the one-yard line, where End Rush Krause, of Indiana, fell on it, rolled over twice, and made a touchdown. Decker converted the goal for the point that broke the tie and gave the Hoosiers the decision 7 to 6.

To add just the prescribed wormwool to make the defeat still more bitter, Captain Geissman had kicked the goal after Brigg's earned touchdown in the first period, but because Pickerel's finger was still under the ball when Geissman split the goal posts with the kick, that point was taken away by Referee Hackett on the technicality. Had it been allowed, the score would still have been a tie.

Even though it was OSU's first game as the newest member of the conference, the contest was the sixth between the two schools, with Indiana leading the series, 5-0-1.

The following weekend, Ohio State and Wisconsin met for the first time, with the Badgers winning at Madison, 12-0. Wilce's squad returned home November 15 to defeat Case, 18-0, and improve its record to 3-2-1. In the season's last game, Ohio State walloped Northwestern, 58-0. The *Columbus Dispatch* of November 23 carried the following story of OSU's very first Western Conference victory:

Ohio State opened the football season on October fourth by defeating Ohio Wesleyan 58 to 0, and closed it by sideswiping the Northwestern football special by another

NINE TIMES ACROSS NORTHWESTERN LINE

Ohio State's Eleven Does Some Runaway Stuff in Winding Up Its Season

One of the Touchdowns Made by Hobt in Minute—Three in Last Period

Ohio State Journal
Sunday, November 23, 1913

Senior Tackle

The first senior tackle was initiated by coach John Wilce during the last practice prior to the Northwestern game of 1913. All seniors who would be playing their last game for the Scarlet and Gray were recognized, as each took one last ceremonial hit on a tackling dummy. Senior tackle has continued through the years, and today is one of the oldest traditions in all of Ohio State football.

58 to 0 score. Hence it would appear that swamping Methodist teams is the specialty of the Scarlet and Gray boys. It was not a defeat that the Purple received Saturday afternoon. Defeats are recorded in scores where there is a comparison in points made, but when a roller travels over an opponent for march after march to the goal, it must be called a trouncing.

When Sam Willaman made the last offensive play of the game for Ohio State by bowling through a half dozen would-be tacklers for the last yards and a touchdown, he gloriously wound up the season at Ohio Field and with his teammates again earned the title of the "ever-coming" eleven.

League rules prohibited a member university from paying for the expenses of sending its band or cheerleaders to out-of-town games. OSU helped raise the necessary funds by "passing the hat" at the home games. There was also a stipulation that no more than 30 players could be taken to away games.

Conference regulations permitted its members to play only seven games. Ohio State was very successful in its first Western Conference season, finishing 4-2-1 overall and 1-2 in the league, and outscoring its seven opponents, 154-27. George Little, former captain at Ohio Wesleyan, helped with the coaching while doing graduate work at OSU. Little became head coach at Michigan in '24, and at Wisconsin in '25 and '26. Summer "Doc" Welch (with a salary of $100) coached the freshman team. John Wilce had proven to be a popular and competent coach in his first season, and enthusiasm among the students and fans was very high.

1913				
October 4	Ohio Wesleyan	W	58	0
October 11	Western Reserve	W	14	8
October 18	Oberlin	T	0	0
November 1	Indiana	L	6	7
November 8	at Wisconsin	L	0	12
November 15	Case	W	18	0
November 22	Northwestern	W	58	0
Total Points			154	27

Season Record: 4-2-1
Conference: 6th Place (Tie)

1914

Ohio State finished its second Big Ten season with a conference record of 2-2 and an overall mark of 5-2. OSU's 37-0 loss at Illinois on October 17 was the beginning of the longest uninterrupted series in all of Ohio State football (The two will meet in 2002 for the 89th consecutive season. This series will be interrupted in 2003 and 2004, then resume in 2005). OSU and Illinois also played in 1902 and 1904. Wisconsin played in Columbus for the first time, defeating John Wilce's squad, 7-6.

Ohio State registered its first victory over Indiana after six previously unsuccessful attempts, defeating the Hoosiers 13-3 at Bloomington. The November 8 *Ohio State Journal* explained how OSU's passing attack helped secure the victory:

FORWARD PASSING A BOON TO STATE

Quarterback Pickerel Shows His Hand Just at the Right Time to Score.

Indiana Gets a Three-Point Lead, but Loses it When Ohio Starts.

Ohio State Journal
Sunday, November 8, 1914

Ohio State's football eleven obtained this afternoon what it came over here to secure. Victory was taken by a score of 13 to 3 off the Indiana eleven and in such a way that nobody wanted to contend that the best team was on the short end. Five thousand people (including 300 from Ohio) saw the game, in which the Ohioans kept covered throughout the entire first half, that ended with the Hoosiers holding a three-nothing lead. In the final section of the game Indiana was swamped by the skillful forward passing system that the Ohio eleven brought into play.

There was a touchdown in each quarter of this last half. The first one came as a result of a majestic march from the kickoff that opened the third period. In a series of even plays, just 75 yards were gained and the Indiana goal line was crossed by Captain Graf on a second-down charge.

Harley Completes Brilliant Career at East High School

While Ohio State was winning 13-3 at Indiana on November 7, Columbus North High School defeated Columbus East High School that same afternoon at Ohio Field, 14-0, in the last game of the season for both teams. The East Tigers were led by an outstanding senior halfback, Charles W. "Chic" Harley, and this loss to the North Polar Bears was East's only defeat during Harley's three seasons with the Tigers. Ironically, that same pattern would later be repeated during Harley's three seasons at Ohio State.

In the fourth quarter, Sorensen fielded an onside kick at the middle of the gridiron and Ohio State started again. Holding by Whitacre gave the Columbus eleven 10 easy yards. Five plays, three of them being the forward-pass

Ohio State's 1914 team. Captain Campbell (Honus) Graf is in the center of the second row, holding the football. Head coach John Wilce is pictured wearing his Wisconsin letter sweater. All-American end Boyd Cherry is seated at the far right in the front row.

kind, got the ball back of the goal mark in Ginn's possession. Graf, who missed the first goal-kick, won in his second effort and gave his team its thirteenth point.

Senior end Boyd Cherry became OSU's first All-American and first All-Big Ten selection. Ohio State finished its 25th season of intercollegiate football with an all-time record of 135-76-18 (62.9%).

1914

Date	Opponent	Result		
October 3	Ohio Wesleyan	W	16	2
October 10	at Case	W	7	6
October 17	at Illinois	L	0	37
October 24	Wisconsin	L	6	7
November 7	at Indiana	W	13	3
November 14	Oberlin	W	39	0
November 21	Northwestern	W	27	0
Total Points			**108**	**55**

Season Record: 5-2
Conference: 4th Place (Tie)

1915

Excitement and support for Ohio State football continued to expand as John Wilce's third squad put together a fine overall record of 5-1-1 (2-1-1 league record). Many of the team's practices were now closed to the public. After starting the season with victories over Ohio Wesleyan and Case, OSU battled powerful Illinois to a 3-3 tie before a partisan crowd of 6,634 at Ohio Field. The deadlock was a "moral victory" over the defending National and Big Ten champions, who entered the game with a nine-game winning streak that stretched over two seasons.

Halfback Harold Winter's 33-yard field goal gave OSU a 3-0 lead with just over 11 minutes remaining in the fourth period. Ohio State had been held on downs at the Illinois two-yard line earlier in the half. Illini end Bart Macomber drop-kicked a 24-yard field goal very late in the game to tie the score. Illinois finished the season with a conference record of 3-0-2, good for second place behind Minnesota at 3-0-1.

After losing, 21-0, under a heavy snowfall at Wisconsin on October 23, Ohio State was idle the following Saturday. Coach John Wilce, Athletic Director L. W. St. John, and OSU captain Swink Boughton used the off weekend to scout Indiana, who played Washington & Lee to a 7-7 tie at Bloomington. The extra effort to prepare for the Hoosiers apparently paid off, as OSU was able to register its first home triumph over Indiana, 10-9. The November 7 *Columbus Dispatch* carried the following account of the victory:

MACOMBER SAVES TEAM FROM DEFEAT

He Matches 33-Yard Field Goal of "Fat" Winters by Drop-Kick in Last Few Minutes of Fourth Period.

Western Conference Champions Run Into a Greatly Improved Ohio Team and Are Outplayed in Most Departments.

Columbus Dispatch
Sunday, October 17, 1915

touchdown. They gave up the ball and it soon was booted safely out of harm's way, where it remained the remaining few minutes of play.

Ohio State finished the season very impressively with shutout victories over Oberlin (25-0) and Northwestern (34-0), but one of the school's first "great eras" was just around the corner. Fans were already anticipating the following season when freshman Charles W. "Chic" Harley would be eligible for varsity competition.

Indiana's jinx, which has roamed about Ohio Field for nearly a decade, was broken Saturday afternoon before 5,500 excited rooters, and at the end of a slashing game was left dead on the field. Ohio State won, 10-9, and for the first time since these two teams have met on Columbus turf was a victory purchased for the Scarlet and Gray.

There were folks present, plenty of them, who remembered how Indiana two years ago nosed out Ohio State 7 to 6, and most of them feared a repetition of something of the same sort at 4 o'clock Saturday afternoon when, with the score 10 to 9 in Ohio's favor, Indiana had a first down on the Scarlet and Gray six-yard line. No one would have offered a "dead kitten" for the game at this point, but the fighting crew from Ohio buckled to its business, and after four attempts the Indianas were still nine feet from a

1915				
October 2	Ohio Wesleyan	W	19	6
October 9	Case	W	14	0
October 16	Illinois	T	3	3
October 23	at Wisconsin	L	0	21
November 6	Indiana	W	10	9
November 13	Oberlin	W	25	0
November 20	at Northwestern	W	34	0
Total Points			105	39

Season Record: 5-1-1
Conference: 3rd Place (Tie)

1916

Ohio State had compiled a very satisfactory league record of 5-5-1 (14-5-2 over-

Action at Ohio Field in 1916.

all) during its first three years of Big Ten competition. But John Wilce's fourth team exceeded all expectations by going 7-0 to capture the 1916 Big Ten title. It was Ohio State's very first undefeated-untied season, as Wilce's squad outscored its seven opponents, 258-29.

The '16 OSU squad was led by sophomore Chic Harley, a 5'9", 150-pound halfback, who was almost impossible to bring down in the open field. Harley was also a superb passer, punter, placekicker, and defender. During his senior season of 1914 at Columbus East High School, the Tigers frequently drew more fans than Ohio State.

Chic Harley was born in Chicago and moved to Columbus at a young age with his family, which included three brothers and three sisters. After eight years in Columbus, the Harley family moved back to Chicago just when Chic was ready for his senior year at East High School. School principal John Harlor and John Vorys, captain of East's football squad, persuaded Chic's mother to allow him to remain in Columbus for his senior year. The Tigers won all but one game that autumn, falling to North High School in the season finale, 14-0. It was East's only loss during Harley's three seasons of varsity competition.

Campaign Opens with Back-to-Back Shutouts

OSU defeated Ohio Wesleyan in the October 7 season opener, 12-0, before an Ohio Field gathering of 4,000. On a very sultry afternoon, OWU's very solid line play allowed the visitors to impressively stop several OSU drives. Quarterback Howard Yerges scored both touchdowns, running three yards in the first period and nine yards in the third quarter. Four sophomores played well in their

Most One-Sided Triumph

The Scarlet and Gray's 128-0 drubbing of Oberlin College at Ohio Field on October 14, 1916, is the highest score and largest margin of victory in school history. It is the only time an Ohio State team has scored 100 or more points in a single game.

Ohio State's first Big Ten title team in 1916.

first varsity competition—Harley, center Ferdinand Holtcamp, guard Irwin Turner, and halfback Gordon Rhodes.

Led by Harley's running and passing the following Saturday, Ohio State posted an incredible 128-0 victory at home over perennial antagonist Oberlin. While everything seemed to click for OSU, nothing went right for the visitors. A crowd of 3,300 saw Wilce's squad score 19 touchdowns and 14 conversions, while amassing 1,140 yards in total offense.

Frosty Hurm and Harley scored touchdowns on Ohio State's first two offensive plays from scrimmage. OSU led in first downs, 43-2. The score read 102-0 after three periods of play. Following is the scoring by quarters:

	1	**2**	**3**	**4**	**Final**
Oberlin	**0**	**0**	**0**	**0**	**0**
Ohio State	**33**	**34**	**35**	**26**	**128**

Halfback Fred Norton scored five touchdowns, and fullback Dick Boesel tallied four times. OSU punted only twice, while Oberlin was forced to punt 16 times.

First Victory over Illinois Sets Tone for Season

Ohio State traveled to Champaign October 21 to open its conference schedule against powerful Illinois. The Illini were 17-3-3 since Bob Zuppke had become head coach in 1913, the same season John Wilce came to Ohio State. Illinois had not been toppled since a 19-9 loss at Minnesota in the last game of the 1913 season.

Before the game, the crafty Zuppke gave the OSU players a tour of the Illinois trophy room, which contained trophies and balls

OUR OWN CHIC SCORES ALL OF POINTS FOR WILCE MEN

East High Product Pulls Brilliant Run in Closing Chapter and then Calls for a New Shoe and Coolly Goes About Breaking 6 to 6 He Had Created.

Bart Macomber Puts His Illini Brethren to Fore Early in Game When He Twice Dropped Oval Across the Bars for Field Goals—Scarlett Defense Is Excellent.

Columbus Dispatch
Sunday, October 22, 1916

used during the Illini's big victories in all sports. Wilce's team was very impressed. It had rained all day in Champaign, and the playing surface was a sea of mud. With each team having trouble moving the ball, Illinois led 6-0 late in the game on field goals of 35 and 40 yards by captain Bart Macomber.

Late in the final quarter, Chic Harley passed his team to the Illini 12 with the clock showing just one minute and 10 seconds to play. Harley faded back to pass but found all his receivers covered. After faking the pass, Harley cut to his left, evaded three tacklers, then dove over the goal line at the northwest corner of the field to score the tying touchdown.

The modest Harley went to the sidelines and replaced his mud-covered shoes with a dry pair. In one of the most dramatic moments in all of Ohio State football, he calmly kicked the epic conversion to give his team the lead at 7-6. That ended the scoring and the 175 OSU fans among the crowd of 4,388 were delirious. Illinois had suffered its first conference loss at home in four years.

As the opposing players headed to their dressing rooms following the game, end Charles "Shifty" Bolen yelled, "Hey Zup, how would you like to have Harley's shoe for your trophy room?" A small squirmish was quickly broken up by the campus police. The famous shoes used by Harley to kick the winning extra point were given to him by his close friend, Joe Mulbarger, a former captain at Columbus East High School. The "block-toed" shoes had been made especially for kicking.

Thriller over Powerful Badgers Puts OSU in National Spotlight

Ohio State did not play the next weekend, giving John Wilce and his team two weeks to prepare for their November 4 encounter with powerful Wisconsin. Wilce, a Wisconsin graduate, had religiously drilled his squad until dark each evening in preparation for the Badgers. At a wild Friday evening pep rally, attended by more than 2,000 students and fans, the OSU coach seemed very confident about his team's chances.

On a beautiful homecoming afternoon, the Ohio Field crowd of 12,500 was (at the time) the largest ever to see a football game in the state of Ohio, surpassing the previous record of 8,200 for the Ohio State-Michigan game of 1902. Numerous mail requests for tickets had been returned unfilled, and scalpers were getting between $5 and $7 for their $2 seats. Both teams entered the encounter undefeated, Ohio State at 3-0 and Wisconsin at 4-0. The Badgers had outscored their four opponents, 91 to 10.

Wisconsin refused to wear numbered jerseys, so Wilce likewise had his team dressed in uniforms without numbers. It was the Badgers' first road game of the season, and coach Paul Withington apparently greatly underestimated the strength of Wilce's Buckeyes. Instead of accompanying his squad to Columbus, Withington put assistant Ed Soucy in command, while he traveled to Minneapolis to scout the Minnesota-Illinois game, two strong teams the Badgers would face in late November.

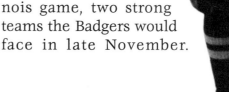

All-American tackle Bob Karch

Withington's absence in Columbus may have had a psychological effect on his players, who appeared to be overconfident. The Ohio State-Wisconsin contest would conclude much differently than Withington had anticipated.

OHIO STATE vs. WISCONSIN, NOV. 4

The visitors dominated play in the first quarter but were unable to score. Known for its crushing ground attack, Wisconsin also effectively passed much more than expected. Early in the second period, the Badgers drove 47 yards for the game's first touchdown, which came on a pass from Eber Simpson to captain Paulie Meyers. Simpson's conversion gave Wisconsin the lead, 7-0.

The Buckeyes came right back on their next possession to tie the game, with Harley scoring on the type of run that would soon make him a legend. With the ball at the Badger 27, Harley darted around his own right end and found a small hole after barely getting past the line of scrimmage. He then made a sharp turn to his left and headed for the far corner of the end zone. With only Glenn Taylor to beat, Harley veered back to his right, then crossed the goal line directly under the goal post. Harley kicked the extra point to make it 7-7 at the half.

The Buckeyes dominated play in a scoreless third period, leading in first downs, five to one. In the decisive fourth quarter, Harley made one of his most celebrated runs. Fielding a Taylor punt at his own 20, he

Ohio State's first victory over Wisconsin came at Ohio Field in 1916.

headed diagonally toward the east sideline and, after picking up a key block from end "Shifty" Bolen, sped 80 yards for the all-important go-ahead touchdown. Harley's conversion was his 14th point of the afternoon, as Ohio State had taken the lead for the first time with just eight minutes remaining.

Coach John Wilce called it the "perfect play" as Chic Harley gains yardage against Northwestern.

But the Badgers came right back. Taking over at the OSU 47, they moved to a fourth-and-goal at the one-yard line. The ball was given to Lou Kreuz, who butted across to reduce the margin to one. Two key factors in the drive were a 10-yard pass from Simpson to W. M. Kelly, and a 15-yard penalty against OSU. Wisconsin's critical conversion attempt was unsuccessful, however, leaving the score at 14-13.

Time expired after Wilce's team ran two plays, and Ohio State had accomplished its "biggest victory" in its first 27 years of intercollegiate football. Wisconsin was one of the seven charter members of the Big Ten in 1896 and had already captured four league titles before Ohio State joined the conference in 1913. This electrifying triumph brought national attention to the football program that was emerging in Columbus.

Chic Harley was carried off the field on the shoulders of exuberant students who had swarmed onto the playing surface by the thousands. Coach Wilce couldn't have been more elated, seeing his team defeat Wisconsin for the very first time after losses the three previous seasons. Wilce especially praised the sterling defensive play of guard Charlie Seddon, a 5'7" 150-pounder, who had started his very first game. Seddon went on to become an excellent lineman, and was affectionately known as the "watch charm" guard.

Ohio State had no trouble against Indiana at home the following Saturday, overwhelming the Hoosiers, 46-7. Harley played just the first eight minutes of the game, scoring touchdowns on runs of 33 and 43 yards. In Cleveland on November 18, OSU shut out the Case Roughriders on a field of snow and mud, 28-0. Ohio State was especially pleased with a new spirit of cooperation and support from the Cleveland newspapers.

Northwestern Game Decides Conference Championship

The season-ending encounter against Northwestern was likely the most significant ever staged between the two schools. Both teams were 6-0, and the winner would emerge with the school's first league title. A near-capacity crowd of 11,979 braved the bitter cold of wind-swept Ohio Field. For the first time, the Ohio State Board of Trustees attended a football game as a unit. The afternoon matched the Big Ten's two leading halfbacks, OSU's Chic Harley and Northwestern's John "Paddy" Driscoll.

JOINING THE BIG TEN (1913-1921)

In the opening quarter, Harley kicked a 34-yard field goal to give his team a slender 3-0 halftime lead. Northwestern had several good marches in the third period but simply couldn't score. The game's turning point came as Ohio State held the Wildcats on downs at the two-yard line. Early in the final quarter, the visitors tied the game, 3-3, when Driscoll drop-kicked a low bullet from the OSU 38 that just cleared the crossbar.

But the remainder of the afternoon belonged to Harley and his talented teammates. First he sent the crowd into an uproar with a 63-yard touchdown run around his own right end. The blocking was excellent, and coach John Wilce often referred to this run as "the perfect play." Harley scored again on a 15-yard sweep, and set up fullback Frank Sorensen's two-yard touchdown plunge with a 28-yard pass to Clarence MacDonald.

Ohio State won, 23-3, to capture its first Big Ten title. Northwestern had been held without a touchdown for the only time all season. The November 26 *Columbus Dispatch* carried the following account of the victory over the Wildcats:

November 25, 1916, will go down in athletic history as marking a new epoch in Ohio State football. Her place in Western Conference circles has been fixed, and it is a credit to have won from such a fine team as Northwestern placed on the field.

The Evanston eleven played wonderful football. Its men tackled fiercely;

Big Ten Conference Final Standings 1916 Season

	Conference			All Games		
	W	L	T	W	L	T
Ohio State	4	0	0	7	0	0
Northwestern	4	1	0	6	1	0
Minnesota	3	1	0	6	1	0
Chicago	3	3	0	3	4	0
Illinois	2	2	1	3	3	1
Wisconsin	1	2	1	4	2	1
Iowa	1	2	0	4	3	0
Indiana	1	3	1	2	4	1
Purdue	0	4	1	2	4	1

The Columbus Sunday Dispatch.

OHIO CHAMPS OF THE WEST.

Columbus Dispatch
Sunday, November 26, 1916

her speedy backs were great at forward passing and in returning punts and even her line gave the Ohio State forwards a real battle for three quarters of the way, but Ohio State had the final punch and the victory was just that much sweeter for having been snatched from a situation that at times was almost terrifying to loyal rooters.

Junior tackle Bob Karch and Chic Harley were selected All-American. Karch later helped develop the playing rules for the National Football League, and officiated NFL games for more than 40 seasons. He is enshrined in the referee's section of the Professional Football Hall of Fame. Harley was well on his way to one of the most celebrated careers in Big Ten history. A natural at every sport, he was the complete player, and his very modest and warm manner made him extremely popular with his teammates and fans alike.

1916

October 7	Ohio Wesleyan	W	12	0
October 14	Oberlin	W	128	0
October 21	at Illinois	W	7	6
November 4	Wisconsin (HC)	W	14	13
November 11	Indiana	W	46	7
November 18	at Case	W	28	0
November 25	Northwestern	W	23	3
Total Points			258	29

Season Record: 7-0
Big Ten Champion

If Ohio State's 1916 season could be described as "sensational," the 1917 campaign

Family Leaders

Ohio State's 1917 co-captains were brothers Harold and Howard Courtney of Columbus. It is the only season in which brothers have served as captains at the same time.

was "near-perfect." With Chic Harley and his proficient teammates exceeding almost all expectations, OSU went 8-0-1 to capture its second consecutive outright Big Ten Conference title. Coach Wilce's squad outscored its nine opponents, 292-6.

Many veterans returned for the Scarlet and Gray. Kelley Van Dyne replaced the departed Fritz Holtkamp at center, Bob Karch joined Charlie Seddon at guard, and brothers Harold and Howard Courtney manned the tackle spots. Charles "Shifty" Bolen and Dwight Peabody returned as the starting ends.

Talented Howard Yerges was the starting quarterback for the third consecutive season. Dick Boesel and Frank Willaman divided time at fullback, replacing Frank Sorensen, the '16 captain. Harley, now a junior, was joined at halfback by Gaylord "Pete" Stinchcomb, a very capable sophomore. Working with great precision, the '17 backfield would develop into one of the most effective in school history.

Midseason Form Displayed in Opener

Ohio State opened at home September 29, demolishing Case, 49-0. The offense scored on long runs around end and off tackle, while the defense held Case to a single first down. Harley was slightly injured and spent most of the afternoon on the sidelines.

The following Saturday, Wilce used 30 players in a 53-0 runaway victory over Ohio Wesleyan. Harley was the leading scorer with three touchdowns. OWU trailed only 14-0 at halftime, but simply ran out of gas in the final two quarters. Near halftime, Ohio

Starting line up for 1917 Big Ten champions. Line, left to right: Dwight Peabody, Howard Courtney, Charlie Seddon, Bob Karch, Kelley Van Dyne, Harold Courtney, Charles Bolen. Backfield, left to right: Dick Boesel, quarterback Howard Yerges, Chic Harley, Pete Stinchcomb.

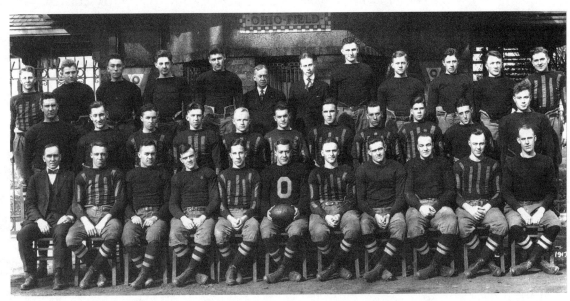

1917
Big Ten
Champions

Wesleyan moved the ball inside the OSU two-yard line after recovering an Ohio State fumble near midfield. But a quarterback sneak on fourth down was stopped short of the goal line. That was the closest any opponent would get to the Ohio State end zone all season.

Northwestern was humbled, 40-0, in the October 13 conference opener, as fan interest in Ohio State football continued to swell. The game was expected to be much closer, since the Wildcats had lost only once (to OSU) in their last eight games. Stinchcomb led the home team's attack with several long gainers and three touchdowns. Harley's crisp blocking paved the way for many of Stinchcomb's carries. After an off-Saturday, Wilce's well-coordinated scoring machine posted its fourth consecutive shutout, white-washing Denison at rain-soaked Ohio field, 67-0. The Big Red was back on the OSU schedule for the first time in five seasons, following strained athletic relations between the two schools.

Enemy Finally Scores

Ohio State and Indiana met November 3 at Indianapolis, which was close to Fort Benjamin Harrison where both schools had men in training for World War I. Players and fans were confused at times, since each team wore red. For some reason, Ohio State packed its red jerseys instead of the white ones normally worn by the visiting team.

The crowd of 11,000 on this gorgeous autumn afternoon included 1,000 OSU fans who cheered themselves hoarse during their team's 26-3 victory. Harley scored all 26 of his team's points with two conversions and four dazzling touchdowns on runs of 40, 8, 11, and 33 yards. The November 4 *Ohio State Journal* provided the following description of the game:

It's going to be the talk around Indianapolis for days to come that Harley alone whipped the big, burly fellows from Bloomington. That's not true in toto. "Chick" made all the points, but there was a line back of which he worked, and a line that, even before Harley got into the game, showed that the Indiana attack was something that could not be sustained.

Howard Courtney, as the Ohio right tackle, had a big job on his hands and filled the bill well. Let nobody fear in Columbus that Bolen and Peabody, the ends, did not deliver. Coach Wilce had a readjustment to make around the middle of the line and he also had Boesel and Willaman saw off at fullback. Indiana's Russell Hathaway booted a 27-yard field goal early in the fourth period for IU's only points. It was the first score against Ohio State this season.

Season's Toughest Challenge

OSU carried its 5-0 record to Madison the next Saturday to take on potent Wisconsin, who played the first ever game at new Camp Randall Stadium the previous weekend. The Badgers had celebrated their

homecoming that afternoon with a huge 10-7 upset over highly-touted Minnesota. Against Ohio State, Eber Simpson drop-kicked a 43-yard field goal to give Wisconsin a 3-0 first-quarter lead. It was the only time all season OSU would be behind.

When the Badgers' attacking defense limited Ohio State's rushing attempts, Harley got his team's offense going through the air. With the ball at the Wisconsin 44, Harley faked a kick, then passed to "Shifty" Bolen, who was tackled as he neared the goal line but was able to power his way across for OSU's first touchdown. Later Harley connected with Howard Courtney for 32 yards to the two, from where Yerges sneaked across for six points to make the score 13-3.

Harley booted a 40-yard field goal in the fourth period to make the final score, 16-3, much to the disappointment of the nearly 6,000 highly partisan fans. Ohio State had taken a major step to capture its second

Their Handling of Forward Passes, Flung by Harley, Gives the Ohioans Plenty of Points in Stiff Struggle Won From the Badgers at Madison.

Ohio State Journal
Sunday, November 11, 1917

Heated Competition

Emotions ran very high between the opposing coaches during the Ohio State-Wisconsin games of 1917, 1919, and 1920. Ohio State's John Wilce had played at Wisconsin and captained the Badgers' 1909 squad, while Wisconsin's John Richards had been Ohio State's head coach in 1912.

All-American center
Kelley Van Dyne

straight league championship. While few OSU fans were able to travel to Madison, several hundred congregated downtown outside *The Columbus Dispatch* office on Gay Street and along the Ohio Union building on campus. The game's play-by-play description was telegraphed back to Columbus, and an individual at each location used a megaphone to inform the gathered fans of the game's activity. "Grid-graf" scoreboards were also frequently used, enabling fans to follow the game's progress.

Illinois Tilt Settles Conference Title

After two weeks on the road, Ohio State returned home November 17 to face undefeated Illinois at homecoming. The Illini had not yet been scored upon this season. OSU could secure the league crown with a victory, while Illinois would need to beat Ohio State and also win at home over Minnesota the following weekend. Coach Zuppke's players were still smarting from their 7-6 loss to OSU at Champaign in '16.

In one of the hardest fought contests ever held on Ohio Field, coach Wilce's squad emerged with a 13-0 victory, although they led only 3-0 heading into the final quarter. Chic Harley was again the "man of the hour," booting field goals of 14 and 29 yards and passing 20 yards to Howard Courtney, who caught the ball as he was crossing the goal line for the game's only touchdown. Harley also added the extra point. The *Ohio State Journal* of November 18 carried the following portrayal of the game's atmosphere:

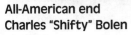
All-American end
Charles "Shifty" Bolen

All-American tackle and
captain Harold Courtney

With the possible fact that the weather was a trifle warm for the players, no power of nature could have supplied a better day. A dull November sun shown from the sky; there was a slight twang of autumn in the air and the gridiron, with its light barb of brown turf, offered a perfect footing for the players.

At 12 o'clock the immense homecoming throng began to assemble. At 2 o'clock when referee Magidsohn started play, every seat was taken and every aisle in the stands occupied, while trees and nearby buildings bore many anxious followers of Ohio State.

Ohio Field was surrounded with 15,000 human beings. The stands resembled a living, throbbing, nervous mass which lost all consciousness when Ohio State gained some slight advantage. It was an artistic crowd. Almost all the ladies wore great bobbing yellow or white chrysanthemums. Many men were decorated in a similar fashion. Everything was color.

Columbus Dispatch
Sunday, November 18, 1917

With the Big Ten championship now secure, Ohio State played two postseason games for the benefit of Ohio servicemen training for action in World War I.

On Saturday, November 24, OSU battled Auburn to a disappointing scoreless tie in Montgomery, Alabama, where numerous Ohioans were training at Camp Sheridan with the 37th division of the Ohio National Guard. Several players were out with injuries, and Ohio State simply lacked any type of offensive punch following its nerveracking win over Illinois. The following Thanksgiving afternoon, Camp Sherman from Chillicothe was defeated at Ohio Field, 28-0.

Harley was again chosen as an All-American as was end Charles "Shifty" Bolen, tackle Harold Courtney, and center Kelley Van Dyne. All four were also represented on the All-Big Ten team. The 1917 squad was one of the finest Ohio State teams ever assembled, and Ohio Field was filled beyond capacity for nearly every home game. Football fever was sweeping Columbus at a rapid pace, and Ohio State's program was gaining a national reputation.

Repeats!

Ohio State has twice captured consecutive outright Big Ten titles: 1916-1917 and 1954-1955.

1917				
September 29	Case	W	49	0
October 6	Ohio Wesleyan	W	53	0
October 13	Northwestern	W	40	0
October 27	Denison	W	67	0
November 3	at Indiana	W	26	3
November 10	at Wisconsin	W	16	3
November 17	Illinois (HC)	W	13	0
November 24	Auburn	T	0	0
November 29	Camp Sherman	W	28	0
Total Points			292	6

Season Record: 8-0-1
Big Ten Champion

1918

By the fall of 1918, the United States was intensely committed to the efforts of World War I in Europe. In September, the Big Ten Conference authorized the U.S. War Department to control all of the league's intercollegiate and intramural athletic activities. Freshmen became eligible when the War Department allowed any member of the Student Army Training Corps to participate in varsity competition.

Each school was allowed only one overnight trip during the season. Most of the underclassmen from Ohio State's 1917 Big Ten title team were serving in the military, including Chic Harley and Pete Stinchcomb. Only four members of that squad were still

Ohio State in 1918. In the center of the first row, holding the football, is Clarence MacDonald, team captain and All-America end.

in school in the fall of '18—quarterback Harold Wiper, guard J. A. Howenstein, tackle Fred Bell, and halfback Walter Metzger. None of the four were starters from '17, and only Wiper and Howenstein were available for the entire '18 season. Bell and Metzger entered the Army prior to the three conference games in late November.

One pleasant surprise was the addition of end Clarence MacDonald and halfback Roy Rife. Both were assigned by the Navy to continue their education on the Ohio State campus. MacDonald had been a letterman at OSU in 1916, and Rife had played at Ohio University in 1917. Coach John Wilce was inducted into the army but remained on campus to continue his study of medicine and to coach the football team.

Most conference teams played a shortened schedule that was somewhat unofficial. Ohio State's game with Northwestern was dropped from the schedule; OSU played only six games, three in the league and three against opponents from the Ohio Athletic Conference. In contrast, Indiana played only four games in '18, all outside the conference, while the University of Chicago played five games, all within the conference.

Widespread Influenza Dilemma

Another problem facing intercollegiate football this fall was an outbreak of the Span-

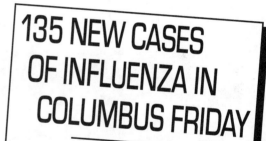

135 NEW CASES OF INFLUENZA IN COLUMBUS FRIDAY

Ban on Public Gatherings Will Not Be Lifted Next Week, Dr. Kahn Announces.

STORES NOT AFFECTED

Mayor Says Shorter Business Hours Unnecessary if Ventilation Is Thorough

NINE DEATHS REPORTED

Columbus Dispatch
Friday, October 18, 1918

Columbus Dispatch
Monday, November 11, 1918

ish influenza in many states. Approximately 20 of the 30 games scheduled to be played in the Midwest on October 12 were canceled because of the plague. Public gatherings were banned in many cities, and the Ohio State campus was closed for a few days following the widespread outbreak.

Ohio State opened with one-sided victories over Ohio Wesleyan (41-0) October 5 and Denison (34-0) October 12, then waited four weeks for its third game—a 56-0 triumph over Case on November 9. OSU lost all of its conference games the last three Saturdays of November against Illinois (13-0), Wisconsin (14-3), and Michigan (14-0). The setback at Illinois snapped OSU's unbeaten streak at 22 games. A far more significant occurrence was the end of World War I with the surrender of Germany on November 11. Several Ohio State students were lost during the war, including Fred Norton, a halfback in 1916, and Harold "Hap" Courtney, one of OSU's 1917 co-captains.

Captain Clarence MacDonald was chosen for the All-American and All-Big Ten teams. After a ten-year absence, Michigan officially rejoined the Big Ten on November 20, 1917, and was back on the Ohio State schedule for the first time since 1912. The two schools have played each season since 1918, with the series moved to the last game of the regular season in 1935.

Trainer E. G. "Doc" Gurney, coach John Wilce, and Athletic Director L. W. St. John. Wilce served in the Army in 1918 but was able to remain on campus to study medicine and to coach the football squad.

1918			
October 5	Ohio Wesleyan	W 41	0
October 12	Denison	W 34	0
November 9	Case	W 56	0
November 16	at Illinois	L 0	13
November 23	Wisconsin	L 3	14
November 30	Michigan	L 0	14
Total Points		**134**	**41**

Season Record: 3-3
Conference: 8th Place (Tie)

Ohio State was back in stride as coach John Wilce welcomed the return of many talented players from the war, including Chic Harley and Pete Stinchcomb. Cyril "Truck" Myers, Bill Slyker, and Jim Flowers saw most of the action at end, while Iolas Huffman and Bob Spiers started at tackle. Lloyd Pixley and Dean Trott manned the guard spots, and Ferdinand Holtcamp and Andrew Nemecek split time at center. Stinchcomb moved to quarterback after playing halfback in '17.

Harley, who was elected captain, was joined at halfback by Tom Davies, Harry Bliss, and Charles Taylor. Frank Willaman handled the fullback post. There were 30 players on the squad as compared with only 17 the previous season.

Ohio State opened October 4 with a 38-0 trouncing of Ohio Wesleyan before an Ohio Field record opening-day crowd of more than 7,200. Harley thrilled the fans when he zigzagged his way 35 yards for a touchdown on his first carry of the afternoon. OSU continued at home with routs over Cincinnati, 46-0, and Kentucky, 49-0.

They Finally Did It!

After 15 previously unsuccessful attempts, Ohio State merited its very first victory over Michigan, 13-3, at Ann Arbor on October 25. OSU entered the clash with 13 losses and two ties in the series, having been outscored by the Wolverines, 369-21, during these first 15 games. Among those first Michigan wins was an 86-0 drubbing of Ohio State in 1902, the most one-sided loss in school history.....and it could have been worse; touchdowns counted only five points in '02, and the game was stopped midway through the second half because of its one-sidedness.

Both teams entered the 1919 game undefeated and unscored-upon, OSU at 3-0 and UM at 2-0. Stinchcomb fumbled the open-

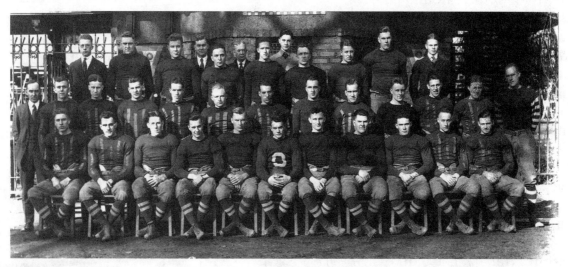

Ohio State in 1919

71

Following Ohio State's first victory over Michigan in 1919, the *Columbus Dispatch* of Sunday, October 26, predicted that Ohio State would also win 50 years later in 1969. Ironically, in 1969 Michigan dealt Ohio State one of its most devastating losses, 24-12. Bo Schembechler's Wolverines broke OSU's all-time winning streak at 22 and prevented Woody Hayes' Buckeyes from repeating as national champions.

ing kickoff, and Michigan's Archie Weston recovered at the OSU 20. But John Wilce's squad prevented early misery by holding UM without a score.

Late in the first quarter, tackle Iolas Huffman blocked a Wolverine punt, and end Jim Flowers recovered in the end zone for Ohio State's first touchdown. Harley's extra point made it 7-0. Michigan's Clifford Sparks connected with a 37-yard field goal late in the second quarter to narrow the margin to 7-3 at halftime.

The Buckeyes struck quickly midway through the third period after holding Michigan on downs at the OSU 34. First, Stinchcomb sped 24 yards to the Michigan 42. Harley then dashed around end, sidestepped two defenders, and outraced the rest for Ohio State's second touchdown and the game's final score.

After finding OSU's stronger line difficult to penetrate, Michigan took to the air. But Harley, in almost magical style, intercepted four of UM's 18 passes to erase any further threats. He also punted 11 times throughout the afternoon with a 42-yard average. Without question, Harley had come through with one of his most

brilliant efforts.

Michigan coach Fielding Yost seldom visited an opponent's locker room after a game. But this afternoon he toured the OSU dressing quarters, congratulating the victors for their brilliant play and excellent strategy. Ohio State coach John Wilce's long hours of preparation had paid off. The Ferry Field crowd of 25,000 included approximately

TWENTY-FIVE THOUSAND FANS WATCH OHIO STATE STALWARTS HUMBLE THEIR ANCIENT FOE

Captain "Chic" Gives Convincing Demonstration of Prowess That Has Placed Him at Pinnacle of Footballdom

PALS BACKED HIM SPLENDIDLY IN EARNED 13 TO 3 TRIUMPH

Coach of Vanquished Eleven, Even Though Feeling Sting of Defeat, Yields Unstinted Praise to Conquerors of His Pupils

Columbus Dispatch
Sunday, October 26, 1919

5,000 Buckeye fans, who had yelled themselves hoarse while watching their team do something no other Ohio State squad had ever done—beat Michigan!

After an off Saturday, Ohio State defeated Purdue at home November 8, 20-0, to extend its season record to 5-0. Harley raced 30 yards for one touchdown and passed 13 yards to Bill Slyker for another. It was OSU's first-ever clash with the Boilermakers. The next week's clash at Madison against powerful Wisconsin was far more difficult. The Badgers entered the game at 4-1. Harley dropkicked a 22-yard fourth-quarter field goal to provide his team a 3-0 victory.

Mammoth Disappointment

Everything was on the line for both Ohio State and Illinois in the November 22 season finale. Coach Bob Zuppke's squad traveled to Columbus with a record of 5-1, having lost only to Wisconsin (14-10) in the season's third contest. All of the Illini's seven games were against conference competition, while undefeated Ohio State played four league games. The winner would emerge with the outright Big Ten title.

Ticket demand was at an all-time high, especially since it was Chic Harley's last game in a Scarlet and Gray uniform. Nearly 20,000 jammed into the wooden grandstands at old Ohio Field, and Athletic Director L. W. St. John estimated nearly 60,000 tickets could have been sold. Upstairs windows on the south side of houses along Woodruff Avenue were crowded to capacity, while dozens more perched in trees looking down on the playing field. One family living on Woodruff

Getting In Was Half The Fun!

The late Reverend Ted Lilley, OSU '27, spent many successful years as a minister in Cedar Rapids, Iowa. As a youngster growing up in Columbus, Lilley and his friends devised creative ways of getting inside old Ohio Field to see Ohio State play football. Scaling the fences surrounding the field, known as "fencing," was the most popular method.

Another good routine was known as "blanketing." The players would run to Ohio Field from the old Athletic House near 16th and High, with their blankets either being carried or worn cape-like over their shoulders. As the players approached the gate, young fans would dart under a blanket and go through with one of the players.

A third method was called "gatecrashing." Timing was key, and Lilley learned that the best time to strike was near kickoff when impatient fans crowded through the turnstiles. Looking back, Lilley had pleasant memories of seeing Chic Harley, Pete Stinchcomb, and other great players of the time, but admits getting into old Ohio Field was half the fun.

Reverend Lilley's father's cousin was Alexander S. Lilley, Ohio State's first football coach in 1890.

erected a bleacher on the front lawn.

Illinois drew first blood, taking a 6-0 first-quarter lead when Ed Sternaman raced 50 yards around end for the game's first touchdown. The senior halfback stumbled and

"And there's nothing quite so thrilling from the first year to today, like the glory of the going when Chic Harley got away."
— James Thurber

Illinois Defeats Wilcemen When a Win Seems Assured

Zuppke's Ruse Enables Illini to Get on the Long End of a 9 to 7 Score -- State's Inability to Break Up Forward Passes Proves Fatal to Buckeyes.

Ohio State Journal
Sunday, November 23, 1919

Three-time All-American and captain Chic Harley. Harley lettered in football, basketball, baseball, and track, to become the first Ohio State athlete to win letters in four sports. In 1951, he became the first Ohio State player inducted into the College Football Hall of Fame.

and-nine, Harley passed 31 yards to Clarence MacDonald at the five. MacDonald, who made a sensational catch with an Illinois defender hanging around his neck, was finally brought down one yard short of the end zone. Harley dove over the Illini's left tackle for the touchdown. Pandemonium broke out when Harley's extra point put OSU ahead, 7-6. His kick barely made it, bouncing through the goal post after hitting the inside of the upright.

Both teams struggled throughout most of the final period, and it appeared that Ohio State would emerge with a single-point victory. Late in the game, Harley punted 47 yards for a touchback, giving the Illini possession at their own 20. Coach Zuppke instructed halfback Larry Walquist to throw on every down. Two long passes to end Chuck Carney carried the ball to the OSU 20. With eight seconds on the clock, sophomore Bobby Fletcher dropkicked a 25-yard field goal to hand Ohio State one of its most devastating defeats, 9-7. It was the first and only setback during Chic Harley's three seasons with the Scarlet and Gray.

Fletcher's brother, Ralph, was the regular kicker, and end Dick Reichle had also done some of the team's kicking, but both were injured. Bobby Fletcher's winning kick

nearly fell after he maneuvered to the outside, then followed almost perfect interference for the score. It was the first and only touchdown scored against Ohio State all season.

OSU finally got on the board late in the third period. After Harley returned a punt to the Illini 37, Wilce's squad netted only one yard on its first three carries. Facing a fourth-

was the first field-goal attempt of his career, and the victory earned Illinois the outright league title. Interestingly, the OSU student newspaper, *The Lantern,* had quickly assembled a "special edition issue" to be distributed immediately after the game with the headline stating that Ohio State had won, 7-6.

Harley became OSU's first three-time All-American, and Pete Stinchcomb was also selected to the All-America team. Ohio State fielded its first team in 1890, but many fans insist OSU football "really started during the days of Chic Harley." Interest had swelled, and suddenly old Ohio Field was too small to handle the crowds. This widespread enthusiasm sparked the drive to fund Ohio Stadium, which was dedicated in 1922. The giant horseshoe beside the Olentangy River has rightfully been named "the house that Harley built."

The Sunday, October 17, 1920, *Columbus Dispatch* supported the Ohio Stadium Fund Drive, which began the following day.

1919

October 4	Ohio Wesleyan	W	38	0
October 11	Cincinnati	W	46	0
October 18	Kentucky	W	49	0
October 25	at Michigan	W	13	3
November 8	Purdue	W	20	0
November 15	at Wisconsin	W	3	0
November 22	Illinois (HC)	L	7	9
Total Points			176	12

Season Record: 6-1
Conference: 2nd Place

1920

It was very obvious that John Wilce had proven to be a very effective college coach since taking over the reins at Ohio State. Wilce had not only compiled a fine seven-year record of 38-9-3 with two outright conference championships, but he was bringing a much-needed stability to the OSU program.

Until Wilce arrived in 1913, only one of the previous 11 head coaches had served as many as five seasons.

An abundance of talent returned in 1920, even with the graduation of Chic Harley. Cyril "Truck" Myers, Bill Slyker, and Noel "Dopey" Workman (also nicknamed "Sonny") logged most of the playing time at end. Captain Iolas Huffman, Bob Spiers, and Dean Trott were the tackles. John "Tarzan" Taylor and Bob Wieche handled the guard slots, and Andrew Nemecek started at center.

After one season at quarterback, Pete Stinchcomb moved back to halfback, and Harry "Hoge" Workman took over the signal-calling responsibility. Frank Willaman and Charles Taylor divided time at fullback, although Willaman's playing time was limited because of injuries. Howard Blair was the starter at the other halfback, with help from Harry Bliss, Dick Cott, Herbert Henderson, and Wilmer Isabel. For the first time, OSU would play as many as five conference games.

Ohio State opened the season at home October 2 by blasting outmanned Ohio Wesleyan, 55-0. "Hoge" Workman looked very comfortable in his first start at quarterback. The following week, Stinchcomb returned a kickoff 95 yards for a touchdown to pace OSU past Oberlin, 37-0. Willaman,

Stadium Campaign Initiated

An extensive drive to raise funds to build Ohio Stadium was launched on Monday, October 18. The timing was ideal, since OSU was undefeated and interest in Ohio State football had hit an all-time high.

THE OHIO STADIUM

OHIO FIELD
October 23, 1920

Wisconsin vs. Ohio State

The Monday, October 25, 1920, *Columbus Citizen* reflects change in a fan's mood after Workman's second touchdown pass to Stinchcomb defeats Wisconsin, 13-7, at Ohio Field.

who scored twice against Ohio Wesleyan, did not play against Oberlin because of an injury suffered in practice that week. On October 16, Wilce's squad posted its third straight shutout, beating Purdue 17-0 in the conference opener. Workman scored 10 of his squad's 17 points with a touchdown, a conversion, and a field goal.

Workman-to-Stinchcomb Gets It Done —Twice!

Ohio State faced always-tough Wisconsin in 80-degree weather the following Saturday before a packed Ohio Field crowd that exceeded 16,000. Among those in attendance was the noted Walter Camp, who at that time selected each season's All-America team. A minor controversy developed when the Badgers refused to wear numbered jerseys. This

game would eventually settle the outright league title.

The Badgers took a 7-0 halftime lead after driving 75 yards late in the second period. Harold Holmes scored from three yards out to complete a 75-yard drive. Ohio State finally scored midway through the final quarter with a 36-yard pass from Workman to Stinchcomb. But Stinchcomb's conversion attempt hit the upright and bounced back onto the field, leaving Wisconsin with a 7-6 lead.

Later that quarter, Ohio State took over at its own ten with just three minutes remaining. Operating against the clock, Workman directed his squad 90 yards for the winning score. With third-and-nine at the Badger 48 and only 50 seconds remaining, Workman sprinted to his right for what appeared to be

1920 Big Ten champions

an end sweep, then stopped and threw diagonally across the field. Stinchcomb had slipped behind Badger defender Edward Gibson at the southeast corner of the field, where he snagged Workman's pass on the dead run for the touchdown and a 13-7 victory.

Workman, who had played himself into a state of exhaustion, collapsed after throwing the winning pass. The star quarterback was so dazed that he didn't realize Stinchcomb had scored until he reached the dressing room after the game. Reserve Don Wiper replaced Workman for the contest's final seconds. It was Wisconsin's only loss that season.

In their book, *On Wisconsin,* authors Oliver Kuechle and Jim Mott describe this Badger loss as "one of the biggest heartbreaks in Wisconsin history." Because of some unfavorable remarks attributed to Wisconsin head coach John Richards, relations between the two universities became strained following the 1920 season. It would be ten years before Ohio State and Wisconsin would meet again.

Cliff-Hangers Become Habit Forming

Ohio State traveled to Chicago October 30 for its first-ever encounter with coach Amos Alonzo Stagg's University of Chicago Maroons. This battle between two unbeaten elevens drew a huge Stagg Stadium crowd in excess of 27,000. OSU again used some "fourth-quarter heroics" to pull out the victory. Down 6-0 in the final period, OSU drove 70 yards for a touchdown with fullback Charles Taylor plunging the final three yards for the score. "Hoge" Workman's extra point was the difference, as Ohio State narrowly escaped the windy city with a 7-6 victory.

THE WILCE PACKING COMPANY LOCATES IN CHICAGO

Columbus Dispatch, Sunday, October 31, 1920

THE OFFICIAL OHIO STATE FOOTBALL ENCYCLOPEDIA

MICHIGAN IS AGAIN LOSER TO BUCKEYES

Captain Huffman Once More Turns the Tide of Game to Ohio State in Desperate Battle.

21,000 ON HAND

Ohio State Journal
Sunday, November 7, 1920

Back home the next weekend, OSU made it two in a row over Michigan to run its season record to 6-0. Football fever was running rampant as a homecoming crowd of nearly 21,000 packed every available inch of Ohio Field. The Wolverines went ahead 7-0 in the second period, but it could have been worse. With UM facing a fourth-and-goal at the one-yard line, "Tarzan" Taylor prevented another score by stopping Edward Usher one foot from the end zone. Taylor was a very high-spirited tackle, who would occasionally toss his helmet to the sideline and play bareheaded for a few downs.

Late in the second quarter, Herbert Henderson's fourth-down plunge from the UM one capped a 34-yard match and knotted the score at 7-7. The drive's big gainer had been a 31-yard pass from Harry to brother Noel Workman. Early in the final period, Iolas Huffman stormed through to block Frank Steketee's punt, then fell on the bouncing pigskin for the second half's only score. Ohio State won, 14-7. Huffman had also blocked a punt that resulted in an OSU touchdown at Ann Arbor the previous year.

After three consecutive come-from-behind triumphs, OSU enjoyed an open Saturday on November 13. That afternoon, Wisconsin defeated favored Illinois at Madison, 14-9, handing the surprised Illini their first loss of the season. Undefeated Ohio State would need a victory at Illinois the following week to claim the outright league championship, since the Illini played six conference games compared to five for OSU and Wisconsin.

Could It Get Any Closer?

After World War I, The U. S. Army stored some of its trucks at the Ohio State Fairgrounds close to the OSU campus. Hundreds of creative Ohio State students "borrowed" some of these military vehicles, then formed a caravan to travel to Champaign for the all-important game against Illinois. The trucks were returned when the students got back to Columbus. The overflow crowd of 22,000 included approximately 4,000 fans from Ohio. This game also featured the very first college "Dad's Day" celebration.

It was a very cold, nerve-racking afternoon, with each team holding the other inside the one-yard line to keep the game scoreless. Ohio State had the ball at the Illini 37 with just four seconds remaining. Everyone expected OSU to attempt its highly successful passing combination of Workman-to-

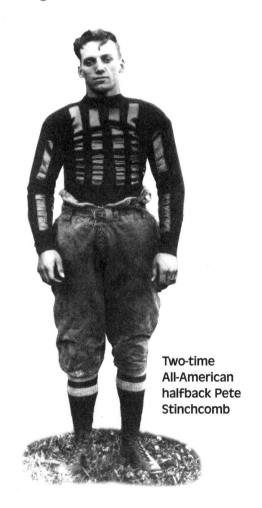

Two-time All-American halfback Pete Stinchcomb

Captain Iolas Huffman was a two-time All-American at guard and tackle.

Stinchcomb. As Workman dropped back to throw, the Illini covered Stinchcomb (who had lined up far to the left) like a blanket, leaving "Truck" Myers all alone. Workman side-stepped two defenders, then hurled the ball to Myers, who caught it in stride at the 17 and raced into the end zone untouched.

As Workman's pass was in the air, the time-keeper's whistle blew to signal that time had expired. Stinchcomb kicked the extra point, and Ohio State had pulled it out, 7-0, with one of the most dramatic finishes possible. With a regular-season record of 7-0, OSU claimed its third conference title in the last five seasons. Wisconsin finished in second place with an overall mark of 6-1 (4-1 in league play).

California Here
We Come!

An invitation to play in the Rose Bowl was immediately approved by university officials, but it required some compelling arguments by Athletic Director St. John before permission was granted by the Big Ten. For some reason, a few members felt that playing in the Pasadena game would lessen the conference's prestige. OSU was paired against the California Golden Bears, who were 8-0 and had outscored their opponents, 482-14. It was Ohio State's first game against an opponent west of the Mississippi River. The team traveled by train, making stops along the way for practice.

Wilce's squad was rated the favorite over coach Andy Smith's "wonder team," mainly because of what was considered stronger competition in the Big Ten. California won, 28-0, before a Tournament Park crowd of nearly 42,000, in what was a huge disappointment for Ohio State fans. The humid California weather with the temperature in the

ANOTHER WESTERN CHAMPIONSHIP FOR STATE; ILLINOIS DEFEATED IN LAST 4 SECONDS PLAY

The Ohio State Journal
Sunday, November 21, 1920

mid-80s definitely favored the home team, but in reality, the Golden Bears were superior at almost every facet of the game. OSU was weakened when Workman and later Stinchcomb were forced to the sideline with injuries.

California's second touchdown resulted from a spectacular pass from Harold "Brick" Muller to Brodie Stephens, which traveled a reported 53 yards in the air past OSU's stunned defense. It was first suggested that the pass traveled 70 yards, but later studies concluded that the distance was closer to 53. Muller, who became a unanimous All-American the following season, was a brilliant athlete who had captured second place in the high jump at the 1920 Olympic Games with a mark of 6' 3⅝."

Even with the Rose Bowl setback, Ohio State enjoyed a wonderful season. Stinchcomb and Huffman were both selected as All-American, the latter at guard, even though he played many games at tackle. OSU's record over its last six seasons stood at 36-6-2.

1921

Construction of Ohio Stadium began with an official ground-breaking ceremony on August 3, 1921. The massive project was scheduled to take 14 months. John Wilce gathered his squad to begin fall practice in September, realizing this would be Ohio State's last year at Ohio Field. The 1921 season would be quite successful, and it also developed into one of the most unusual in school history. OSU would complete the campaign with an overall record of 5-2, outscoring its seven opponents, 110-14. All five victories were shutouts, but the two losses were major upsets.

"Hoge" Workman was not in school and was replaced at quarterback by brother Noel (known as "Sonny" and "Dopey") and Richard Cott. After opening at home October 1 with a 28-0 triumph over Ohio Wesleyan, Ohio State suffered an enormously humili-

1920				
October 2	Ohio Wesleyan	W	55	0
October 9	Oberlin	W	37	0
October 16	Purdue	W	17	0
October 23	Wisconsin	W	13	7
October 30	at Chicago	W	7	6
November 6	Michigan (HC)	W	14	7
November 20	at Illinois	W	7	0
January 1	California*	L	0	28
Total Points			150	48
*Rose Bowl				
	Season Record: 7-1			
	Big Ten Champion			

Night Shift

Coach Wilce was so aggravated after his team's humiliating loss to Oberlin, that he ordered his team back onto the field for a hard practice immediately after the game. Search lights were brought in so that practice could continue past sunset. The strenuous scrimmages continued the following week and apparently had some effect — Ohio State won its next four games, all by shutouts.

Illustration by Tom Hayes

Ohio State Defeated by Oberlin 7-6

Ohio State Journal, Sunday, October 9, 1921

ating setback, losing to Oberlin College, 7-6. The Ohio Field crowd of 9,000 was in total disbelief. Down 6-0 in the third quarter, the Congregationalists drove 85 yards for the winning touchdown. The *Ohio State Journal* of October 9 provided the following reaction:

If Mars had dropped from its place in the solar system and bumped into Mother Earth yesterday, it wouldn't have caused any greater surprise in Columbus than that kicked up by little Oberlin when it licked Ohio State's football team 7 to 6 in the Buckeyes' own back yard. If the German Kaiser had stood at the corner of Broad and High Streets yesterday and said he was going to be the next President of the United States, he would have been believed as quickly as the man who said Oberlin would march 85 yards through Ohio State's line for a touchdown.

The real story of what happened is brief. The Buckeye eleven entered the contest confident that no matter what happened Ohio State would win. Oberlin licked the Buckeyes in a fair and square manner and deserved the victory. From the middle of the initial period until the close of the contest Oberlin outplayed Ohio State in every department of the game.

CAPT. MYERS, HERO OF HOUR, SCORES ONLY TOUCHDOWN

Inflicts First Defeat of Season upon Conquerors of Princeton Tigers.

OHIO ROOTERS GO WILD

Frenzied Demonstration by 3500 State Followers Continues to End of Game.

BOTH RESORT TO PASSING

Stuart Alone Stood Between His Mates and Disaster in Chicago's Forlorn Hope.

Columbus Dispatch Sunday, November 6, 1921

This was the last time OSU lost to an Ohio opponent. Wilce drilled his team especially hard until dark each evening the following week, and apparently it had an effect. In their first-ever game against Minnesota, the Buckeyes walloped the favored Golden Gophers on a muddy field, 27-0.

At Ann Arbor on October 22, Ohio State posted its

Captain Cyril "Truck" Myers, two-time All-American end

Ohio State University Athletic Association

PRESS TICKET

This Complimentary Ticket is for personal use. If presented by any person other than the one whose name appears on the face of this ticket it will be taken up at the gate and forfeited.

1921-22

M

Representing _Cleveland Plain Dealer_

No. _20_

Athletic Director

third straight victory over Fielding Yost's Michigan Wolverines, 14-0, before a disappointed homecoming gathering of 45,000. An enlarged Ferry Field was dedicated this afternoon, commemorating the expansion of the facility from the previous year's capacity of 25,000. OSU took advantage of UM's weak punting game to hand the Wolverines their only defeat of the season. John Stuart and Charles Taylor scored the Buckeye touchdowns.

After an open Saturday, Ohio State traveled to Chicago for the second straight season to face Amos Alonzo Stagg's undefeated

Maroons. A record standing-room-only crowd of 32,000 was jammed into every available inch of Stagg Field. Wilce's Buckeyes played brilliantly, handing Chicago its only loss of the year, 7-0. The November 6 *Ohio State Journal* described the victory:

Strategy and a little finer football sent the Buckeyes home today on the long end of one of the most memorable battles ever staged on Stagg Field. Coach Wilce offered only the simplest plays during the first half and then opened up with a series of puzzling passes, runs, and bucks, which swept the Maroons back to their goal three times.

The offense was finely handled by (Noel) Workman, who pulled one certain play at least half a dozen times until Chicago was convinced it had nothing more to fear from this formation. Then with the ball on the 12-yard line, the "comeback" play was staged. It found the Maroons unprepared and allowed Captain Myers to run almost untouched for 12 yards and what proved to be the winning score.

At Ohio Field, the Buckeyes won this mud battle over Purdue, 28-0.

All Chicago is sad tonight, but not a one of the rooters will not admit they were privileged to witness one of the greatest of gridiron classics and that the Ohio team, playing smarter, brainier football, earned its victory.

Back at home for the first time in four weeks, OSU shut out Purdue for the third straight season, this time 28-0. Only Illinois separated the Buckeyes from at least a share of the 1921 Big Ten championship. On November 19, Ohio State played its last game on Ohio Field, before an overflow crowd estimated to have been in excess of 20,000. Victory over the Illini was an almost certainty—but no one told coach Bob Zuppke. The "Dutchman" had other plans.

ILLINOIS PULLS THE "IMPOSSIBLE" BY BEATING BUCKEYES IN FINAL BIG TEN GAME TO BE PLAYED ON OHIO FIELD

Ohio State Journal
Sunday, November 20, 1921

"Fighting Illini" Originated in Columbus

Ohio State was an overwhelming favorite against the Illini. It was Homecoming, and the powerful Buckeyes entered the game 4-0 in league play, having shut out all four Big Ten opponents by a combined score of 76-0. Heavy underdog Illinois had lost all four of its league contests, having been outscored, 51-8. The Illini had not scored a touchdown in these four games and were in serious danger of not winning at least one conference game for the first time in 22 seasons.

Illinois accomplished the impossible that afternoon, shutting out the Buckeyes, 7-0. Zuppke, a master psychologist, used only 11 players the entire afternoon. His game plan contained several new schemes, including a "drop-back pass defense" to guard against the fine passing of Ohio State's "Sonny" Workman. Wilce used 33 players while attempting to wear down the inspired Illini.

Illinois scored in the second quarter on an extremely unusual play. With the ball at the Ohio State 35-yard line, Illini halfback Don Peden passed to end Dave Wilson. The ball escaped Wilson's grasp and bounced off the chest of Buckeye defender Cyril "Truck" Myers. Illini captain Laurie Walquist quickly snatched the ball and rambled into the end zone for the game's only touchdown. A few of the OSU players claimed the ball touched the ground before Walquist grabbed it, but the officials ruled

Harley's Rock marks the site of old Ohio Field on the west side of High Street and south of Woodruff Avenue.

otherwise.

The Buckeyes completely dominated the game's statistics, running 72 plays from scrimmage compared with the Illini's 49. Ohio State led in first downs, 14 to 5, and in total offense, 251 yards to 128. Ohio State had three excellent scoring opportunities deep in Illinois territory, but the Orange and Blue came through with timely defensive plays to preserve the shutout.

Sportswriter Harvey Woodruff, covering the game for the *Chicago Tribune,* was so impressed with the inspired play of the Illini, he referred to them in his Sunday column as the "Fighting Illini." The new nickname stuck, and the Illini have been known as the "Fighting Illini" ever since that monumental upset of Ohio State.

Tackle Iolas Huffman and end Cyril "Truck" Myers were both chosen as All-Americans. Myers and guard Dean Trott were also tabbed for the All-Big Ten team. Iowa captured its first Big Ten title with a perfect 7-0 record. The Hawkeyes were invited to play in the Rose Bowl, but the Big Ten refused permission, partly because of Ohio State's embarrassing loss the previous season. It would be 25 years before another Big Ten team would play in the Pasadena classic.

The curtain came down on Ohio Field, where the early Buckeye faithful had been thrilled for so many seasons by the development of Ohio State football. The program now enjoyed a national presence and a larger stadium had become a necessity. Since joining the Big Ten in 1913, the Scarlet and Gray had compiled a nine-year record of 50-12-3, and the roots of Ohio State's "Great Tradition" were now solidly in place.

1921

October 1	Ohio Wesleyan	W	28	0
October 8	Oberlin	L	6	7
October 15	Minnesota	W	27	0
October 22	at Michigan	W	14	0
November 5	at Chicago	W	7	0
November 12	Purdue	W	28	0
November 19	Illinois (HC)	L	0	7
Total Points			110	14

Season Record: 5-2
Conference: 2nd Place (Tie)

CREATING OHIO STADIUM

As the Buckeyes continued to draw increasingly larger crowds during their last seasons at Ohio Field, it became apparent that a larger stadium would soon be needed. Public interest in Ohio State football had reached unprecedented heights throughout the state. Additionally, the Ohio Field grounds along High Street were becoming too valuable for permanent athletic use.

College football had gained great popularity in the East, and in 1903 Harvard Stadium in Boston was completed with a seating capacity of nearly 45,000. It was the very first stadium to be constructed with reinforced concrete. The Yale Bowl at New Haven, Connecticut, was dedicated in 1913 and seated 70,000. Both stadiums were near large cities and drew grand crowds. Princeton's Palmer Stadium was completed in 1914.

French, Thompson, St. John, and Smith

Thomas French, an 1895 graduate of Ohio State and head of the Department of Engineering, was a true visionary who saw athletics playing a major role in the university's development. His brother, Ed-ward, played end and co-captained OSU's 1896 team. As Ohio State was growing, French chaired a committee that guided the expansion of Ohio Field from 6,000 to 10,000 in 1909.

Ohio State President William Oxley Thompson, an ordained minister, envisioned OSU becoming one of the nation's premiere institutions. Enrollment had doubled during the first decade of his presidency, and Thompson expected the university to provide expanded services to the state of Ohio. He appointed French chairman of the Athletic Board when Ohio State began Big Ten competition in 1913. Thompson, French, and Athletic Director L. W. St. John became the "driving forces" in the effort to build Ohio Stadium.

French and St. John agreed that Ohio State needed a much larger stadium. Writing for the *Ohio State Alumnae Magazine* in 1915, French predicted that Ohio Field's wooden bleachers would someday be transformed into a concrete stadium to rival those in the Ivy League. His article went almost unnoticed. In an address to the Columbus

Professor Thomas French, affectionately known as the "Father of Ohio Stadium," served as Ohio State's faculty representative to the Big Ten from 1913 until his death in 1944. The French Field House is named in his honor.

Ohio State President William Oxley Thompson was a visionary who understood the many benefits that Ohio Stadium would generate for the university.

Athletic Director Lynn W. St. John, a pioneer in intercollegiate athletics, played a major role in the building of Ohio Stadium and the development of the Ohio State football program. St. John Arena is named in his honor.

Architect Howard Dwight Smith won national acclaim for his design of Ohio Stadium. Smith designed over 40 campus buildings, including St. John Arena.

Chamber of Commerce, French predicted that OSU football crowds would one day number 50,000. French's prophesy met with a lot of skepticism, and opponents said it would never happen.

As Ohio State was capturing its first Big Ten championship in 1916, French took advantage of the growing interest in football and asked University Engineer Clyde Morris to prepare sketches for a new stadium. It would be oval in shape, seat about 40,000, and be built of concrete with an excavated playing field below ground level. The construction cost was estimated to be $300,000. The new stadium would be located in what was then a wooded area north of the oval and west of Ohio Field. With a height of 72 feet, it would be the tallest structure on campus.

The Board of Trustees approved the plan, but Thompson had concerns. The proposed stadium would be 10 feet taller than the library, the tallest campus building, giving the impression that athletics took precedence over academics. Also, with the growing use of automobiles, parking would be a problem at this location.

Thompson lobbied the board for a new proposal, and called upon University Architect Joseph Bradford to submit a second plan. This time the stadium would be located on the much larger flood plain of the Olentangy River. This structure would be horseshoe shaped with an open end to accommodate track and field events. It would seat 50,000 and cost approximately $500,000. Again, the board approved the design, but plans for the new stadium were temporarily delayed as the university focused on World War I.

In the summer of 1918, French asked 32-year-old Howard Dwight Smith, a 1907 Ohio State graduate and faculty member in the School of Architecture, to draw a new design for the stadium. Ten years earlier, Smith had spent a year in Europe studying the ancient ruins of the Roman and Greek empires. The Colosseum inspired his use of arches, and Smith had great admiration for the Pantheon's semi-circular dome. These characteristics would later become trademarks of Ohio Stadium.

Timing is Everything

With Chic Harley and his talented teammates back on campus after the war, Ohio State fielded another excellent team in 1919. When St. John estimated that as many as 60,000 tickets could have been sold for Harley's final game, French knew the time was right to push the trustees for a new stadium. Smith had been working on his new plans for nearly a year.

St. John felt the proposed 50,000-seat stadium was still not big enough, so French instructed Smith to include as many seats as possible as long as spectator comfort could be maintained. In an attempt to bring the fans as close as possible to the action, Smith planned a second deck (the first football stadium to be so designed). The sides of the stadium would be bowed and curved so that the spectators faced the center of the field. Rather than using brick, Smith preferred structural steel encased in concrete.

Great Idea But Who Will Pay?

Thomas French was devastated when he learned the university would not incur any cost in building the stadium. Since all funds would now have to come from private sources, it was decided to solicit donations from all alumnae and friends throughout the state. This would position the new stadium as "belonging not only to the university, but also to all of Ohio." The stadium's general design was publicized, but very little was said about the capacity and projected cost until it was known how much money could be raised.

French formed a Stadium Executive Committee to plan a civic campaign to raise $1 million. Mr. Sam Summer, a successful

Daily parades were a big part of the stadium fundraising activities in October, 1920.

Columbus businessman and OSU graduate, agreed to chair the committee. In an effort to contact every living Ohio State graduate (30,000 alums), volunteers from all 88 Ohio counties spent countless hours locating the graduates in each county.

The John Price Jones Corporation, a New York firm, was hired to develop and implement the fundraising plan. This program promoted several key concepts and reasons for giving:

1. A new stadium would bring prestige to Ohio State University and the city of Columbus.
2. It would be a "magnet" that would draw attention and put the city and state "on the map."
3. It would help young people get physically fit in anticipation of future wars.
4. Last, but not least, there was an emotional appeal. Ohio State had never before asked for help, and it would bc hard to say "no."

Stadium Week Huge Success

Mr. Simon Lazarus, head of family-owned F. & R. Lazarus Co., was in charge of publicity. On Saturday, October 16, 1920, a campus-wide ox roast and carnival kicked off a week-long celebration of Ohio State's 50th anniversary. Lazarus invited reporters from every newspaper in Ohio, and a model of the stadium was unveiled to the public. Lazarus even convinced a group of ministers to preach about the stadium on Sunday,

REACH GOAL OF $1,000,000 IN OHIO STADIUM CAMPAIGN

Columbus Dispatch, **Thursday, January 20, 1921**

October 17, and tout the stadium's benefits for the university and the city of Columbus.

On October 18, at 6 a.m., canon fire announced that the stadium campaign was officially under way. Almost 4,000 students (out of a student body of 7,000), dressed in athletic clothes, paraded down High Street to the Statehouse to publicize the new stadium. Lazarus wanted to capitalize on the importance people attributed to physical fitness following the war, and draw attention to the fact that Ohio State students were strong and fit.

Military Day was next. Over 1,000 members of the campus infantry and artillery units made the march down High Street. They then staged a "mock battle" along the Olentangy River to reinforce that the stadium site would also be used for military training. Another day's downtown parade was comprised of 51 floats representing campus organizations, fraternities, and sororities.

Daily at noon and 5 p.m., music, stunts, and peptalks kept the campaign alive in the hearts and minds of students and citizens alike. Signs promoting "Ohio Stadium—The Magnet" were everywhere, and ads appeared in newspapers and magazines. Volunteers in every county made their way throughout Ohio seeking donations, and students went door to door. Contributions poured in; nearly 12,000 individuals made pledges, and by January 20, 1921, the $1 million goal had been reached. Plaques honoring donors of $5,000 or more were later erected on individual stadium boxes.

But there was still one more high hurdle to get over. A battle was erupting within the Board of Trustees, who still needed to ap-

prove the stadium and its location. Physics Professor Thomas Mendenhall, an influential member of the board, was a vocal critic of the new plan.

In 1921, Mendenhall was the sole surviving member of Ohio State's original faculty of 1873. He cited a report that showed that Princeton University was already having problems with the cement structure of Palmer Stadium. Mendenhall strongly proposed that the board approve the construction of a brick stadium with a much smaller seating capacity.

The Board of Trustees met on May 24, 1921, to decide the fate of the new stadium. After a long meeting (and likely very heated discussions), the board voted six to one to build the stadium as Smith had designed it. President Thompson favored the larger concrete model, and it was felt that he may have influenced some of the trustees. Mendenhall cast the lone negative vote.

A formal groundbreaking was held August 3, 1921, with Governor Harry L. Davis turning the first shovel. A crowd reported between 1,000 and 2,500 marched to the stadium site to rejoice in the festivities and be entertained by the university regimental band. The schedule called for completion of the stadium in time for the 1922 season.

Personal Responsibility

When the lowest construction bid came in at $1.3 million, it was necessary for the Athletic Board to borrow nearly $400,000. The board believed that the athletic programs would generate more than enough funds to pay back loans, interest, and operating costs. However, there was a significant risk. If the

Ohio Stadium under construction

loan could not be repaid with athletic program proceeds, the Athletic Board members would be personally responsible for the debt.

Construction began in late August of 1921, giving workers 13 months to finish the project. Approximately 300 laborers worked on the stadium each day. The structural steel work went well throughout the winter, and by spring the workers began pouring 85,000 tons of concrete. The project was on schedule but not on budget. Because the site was subject to flooding from the Olentangy River, additional costs were incurred to provide an earth fill.

The Athletic Board was nearly out of money and, for the first time, was bitterly divided on how to proceed. One proposal was to temporarily leave off the north and south towers, then add the towers at a later date after the first loan was repaid. If the towers were to be built as planned, more funds would have to be borrowed. President Thompson cast the vote in favor of building the towers, and the board sank ever deeper in debt.

By the first week of October, 1922, most of the stadium construction was complete. Final construction costs totaled more than $1.5 million, and all loans were repaid within six years. At an Athletic Board meeting on November 1, 1928, L. W. St. John happily reported that "all notes outstanding on the stadium indebtedness had been paid." French, Thompson, St. John, and many others had put their reputations on the line—their dream had become a reality.

Ohio State christened its new stadium with a 5-0 victory over Ohio Wesleyan on

First Game in Ohio Stadium

Ohio State-Wesleyan Game Line-Up and Summary

Ohio State (5)	Pos.	(0) Ohio Wesleyan.
Schweinsberger	L. E.	Evans
Wasson	L. T.	Smith (C.)
Pixley (C.)	L. G.	Amrhein
Pauley	C.	Ballinger
Kutler	R. G.	MacCracken
Petcoff	R. T.	Thomson
Honaker	R. E.	Young
Workman	Q. B.	Sacksteder
Farcasin	L. H.	Snouffer
Isabel	R. H.	Winters
Hamilton	F. B.	Turney

SCORE BY PERIODS—
Ohio State 5   0   0   0—5
Ohio Wesleyan 0   0   0   0—0

Summary—Scoring: Ohio State, goal from field by Workman. Safety by Sacksteder of Wesleyan. Length of Periods 12½ minutes. Referee—Dr. Means, of Penn. Umpire—Mr. Swain, of Dickinson. Field judge—Mr. Thomas, of Ohio university. Head linesman—Mr. Hamm, of Kenyon.

Substitutions—Ohio State: Addison for Wasson, Wasson for Addison, Steele for Petcoff, Petcoff for Steele, Wilson for Schweinberger, Elgin for Wilson, Kyle for Elgin, Klein for Pauley, Fiorette for Honaker, Honaker for Fiorette, Blair for Farcasin, Klee for Isabel, Isabel for Klee, Harter for Isabel, Dunlap for Kutler, Michaels for Hamilton, Hamilton for Michaels, Blair for Hamilton. Wesleyan: Staten for Sacksteder, Elder for Smith, Smith for Elder, Knachel for Evans.

Columbus Dispatch, **Sunday, October 8, 1922**

Saturday, October 7, 1922. Although the crowd of 25,000 (including 1,000 from Ohio Wesleyan) was the largest ever to see a football game in the state of Ohio, athletic officials were concerned when more than half of Ohio Stadium was empty. The Buckeyes won the toss and chose to defend the south goal with a slight wind at their back. OSU scored a safety and a field goal in the first quarter.

Michigan Scouts Opener

Ohio State's five-point margin of victory was much smaller than expected, partly because Wilce may have been saving some of his offensive plays for the stadium dedication game two weeks later against Michigan. Scouting the Buckeyes was Michigan head coach Fielding Yost, while this same afternoon his Wolverine squad was at home defeating Case, 48-0. Interestingly, Michigan captain Paul Goebel and quarterback Irwin Uteritz were with their coach to scout the Buckeyes, rather than play against Case.

The Buckeyes of 1922, the first Ohio State team to play in Ohio Stadium.

OSU's 5-0 victory over OWU was the first Ohio State game to be broadcast by radio. The play-by-play report was transmitted by station WEAO from the Robinson Laboratory on the OSU campus, by the Department of Electrical Engineering. WEAO later became station WOSU. The Ohio State Marching band did not play in the stadium's first game, even though the visiting Ohio Wesleyan band made the trip from Delaware. Children were admitted at a special "kiddie program" price of ten cents.

Isabel Scores First Touchdown

Ohio State defeated Oberlin the following weekend, 14-0, before an even smaller Ohio Stadium crowd of 17,000. The Buckeyes scored both touchdowns in the third quarter. Halfback Wilmer Isabel had the honor of scoring the first touchdown in Ohio Stadium, plunging into the end zone on a fourth down call from inside the Oberlin one-yard line. Quarterback Hoge Workman scored the other six-pointer on a short plunge and also drop kicked both extra points.

The Ohio State and Oberlin bands both performed at halftime. Forty-two Buckeye freshman and junior varsity players attended the game as a group, then went through a short workout on the stadium field following the game. Michigan assistant coach George Little was on hand, scouting OSU in preparation for the following week's game.

Stadium Dedication

Ohio State dedicated its new stadium on Saturday, October 21, before the largest crowd ever to see a football game in the Midwest.

Renowned Drum Major Edwin "Tubby" Essington strutted his way into the hearts of Buckeye fans with his splendid high-stepping style. Essington was acclaimed by Walter Camp as the "All-American Drum Major" in 1922. His picture appeared on the cover of *Collier's* Magazine.

Ohio Stadium dedication ceremonies on October 21, 1922.

The overflow crowd was officially announced at 72,500, but no one knows for sure how many people made their way inside Ohio Stadium that afternoon. Many fans unable to secure tickets forced their way through a fence at the stadium's south end. Since the final stages of construction continued through the first two weeks of October, faculty, students, and even President Thompson spent the Friday before the game sweeping out the stadium.

The dedication game festivities were wonderful, and both the Ohio State and Michigan bands performed magnificently. The Buckeyes won the toss and chose to kickoff with the Wolverines defending the south goal. The only disappointment for Ohio State was the final score. The visitors won, 19-0, breaking OSU's three-game winning streak in the series.

Michigan scored in each quarter, with halfback Harry Kipke and end Paul Goebel scoring all the points. Kipke's "coffin corner" punting kept OSU deep in its own territory most of the afternoon. The Buckeyes had one excellent opportunity to score in the third quarter but lost the ball on downs at the Michigan four after driving 69 yards from its own 27.

Michigan assistant coach George Little played a bit part in the Wolverine victory. Little had been an assistant at OSU in 1914, and was very familiar with coach Wilce's forward pass offense and his defensive system. Little designed a defense that was very effective at stopping the Buckeyes' passing attack.

Thirty former OSU captains were seated together on the sidelines. Although Ohio State lost the game, French, Thompson, and

St. John felt vindicated about the size of the crowd. Fans, too, could share in the feeling of success, for their many donations had made it all possible.

The loss to the Wolverines was the first of four consecutive setbacks. The Buckeyes made their very first trip to Minnesota on October 28, losing to the Golden Gophers, 9-0. After an off Saturday, they suffered two narrow home losses to Chicago, 14-9, and Iowa, 12-9. It was the first time in 24 seasons that the Scarlet and Gray had dropped four in a row.

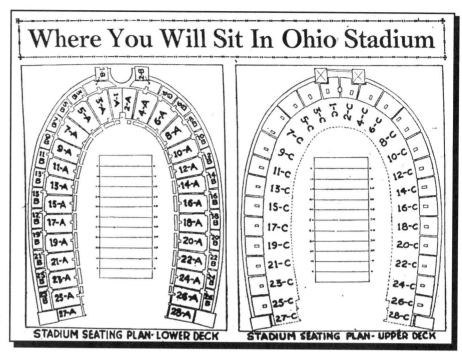

Diagrams of new Ohio Stadium
Columbus Citizen, Thursday, October 19, 1922

Losing Streak Snapped
at Illinois

Ohio State finally got back in the victory column with a 6-3 come-from-behind triumph at Illinois in the season finale. Halfback Ollie Klee fielded a punt on his own 30, then squirmed and hurtled his way 70 yards for the game's only touchdown, much to the delight of the 1,700 OSU fans among the crowd of 22,000. Coaches John Wilce and Bob Zuppke, who were both raised in Milwaukee, graciously chatted after the game and wished each other well.

The Buckeyes finished the 1922 campaign at 3-4, their first losing season since 1898. This initial year in Ohio Stadium was a stark contrast with the recent victorious seasons at Ohio Field. For the first time in seven years, no Ohio State player was chosen for All-American or All-Big Ten honors. Among the graduating seniors was captain Lloyd Pixley, an excellent four-year letterman at guard. In their first season at Ohio Stadium, the Buckeyes drew a total attendance of 162,500 in five home games for an average of 32,500. John Wilce had completed his tenth season as head coach with an overall record of 53-16-3.

94

1922

October 7	Ohio Wesleyan	W	5	0
October 14	Oberlin	W	14	0
October 21	Michigan*	L	0	19
October 28	at Minnesota	L	0	9
November 11	Chicago	L	9	14
November 18	Iowa	L	9	12
November 25	at Illinois	W	6	3
Total Points			43	57

*Dedication Ohio Stadium

Season Record: 3-4
Conference: 8th Place

1923

The Big Ten Conference allowed the expansion of football schedules from seven to eight games, and by 1924 all 10 members were playing a total of eight contests. There was still a difference in the number of league opponents scheduled by each team. In 1923, Northwestern played the most conference games with six, while Michigan, Minnesota, and Indiana scheduled only four within the league. There was also a shift from year-to-year to longer-range scheduling (three to five seasons in advance with some conference opponents).

Ohio State's record did not improve much in 1923. The Buckeyes went 3-4-1, which included a conference mark of just 1-4. For the ninth time in the last ten seasons, the Buckeyes opened at home against Ohio Wesleyan. Before an October 6 crowd of 24,283, OSU defeated the Methodists, 24-7. In the second period, Ohio State quarterback Ollie Klee sustained a shoulder injury which severely limited his playing time the next few games. Michigan coach Fielding Yost and assistant Ernie Vick were both in Columbus to scout the Buckeyes, while their Wolverines opened at home that same afternoon with a 36-0 triumph over Case.

Tie with Eastern Power Colgate

In the season's second game, Ohio State fought powerful Colgate to a 23-23 tie before an Ohio Stadium crowd of nearly 40,000. The skillful easterners, using a good blend of delayed passes and crisscross fakes, led 17-3 at halftime and 23-10 after three quarters. Hoge Workman scored the Buckeyes' last touchdown in the game's final two minutes, with a rugged 15-yard fourth-down run into the west corner of the south end zone. The Colgate defense was distracted on the play, when OSU end John Wilson raised his hands frantically to catch a pass that was never thrown. Workman's extra point tied the game.

The next two weekends were slightly embarrassing for John Wilce's team. Ohio

Ohio Victory Featured by Fight and Co-ordination Against Boilermakers

All-American quarterback
Harry "Hoge" Workman

Columbus Dispatch, Sunday, November 11, 1923

State lost at Michigan, 23-0, and was white-washed at home by the Iowa Hawkeyes, 20-0. In Columbus on November 3, the Buckeyes posted a much-needed non-conference victory over outmanned Denison, 42-0, to bring their record to 2-2-1.

The following Saturday, Ohio State displayed its best effort of the season with a 32-0 triumph at Purdue. It marked the first time the two schools had played at West Lafayette. The November 11 *Columbus Dispatch* carried the following story:

Every man in the game for Ohio, today, fought for all he was worth and played intelligent football. Only one stood out above the rest, he was Hoge Workman, who playing with a team like Ohio was today, is an All-American performer. His judgment of plays was nearly perfect, his passing accurate, his ability to carry the ball phenomenal, and his punting excellent.

On defense he was the same old Hoge, tackling deadly on every play coming around his end. He intercepted one forward pass. It was a great triumph for Hoge, for Dr. Wilce, for the other coaches, for the splendid team that finally showed its mettle, and for the handful of loyal fans.

Over 3,500 Buckeye fans made their way to Chicago the next weekend to see their team play well in a 17-3 loss to the Maroons. This was one of Amos Alonzo Stagg's finest teams, finishing the season at 7-1. Chicago had lost a heartbreaker at Illinois two weeks earlier, 7-0, in the first game ever played in the Illini's new Memorial Stadium.

The Buckeyes in action at Chicago

Wisconsin Wants Wilce

The University of Wisconsin made a strong appeal for John Wilce to return to his alma mater as head football coach, following the resignation of John Richards at the end of the 1923 season. Wilce was flattered but declined the offer, stating that he believed "thoroughly" in Ohio State's future.

Red Grange Scores Lone Touchdown

Ohio State again played well before losing to Illinois, 9-0, in the season's last game. The Ohio Stadium homecoming crowd of 39,877 witnessed an extremely physical battle that was scoreless heading into the final period. In the third quarter, OSU's Frank "Pete" Honaker appeared to have scored on a fourth-down plunge from the six-inch line, but referee Joe Magidsohn ruled otherwise. The strongly contested call prompted the November 26 *Columbus Dispatch* to report,

"Line is crossed once—Honaker puts ball over, but is pushed back before oval is declared dead."

Late in the game, sophomore halfback Harold "Red" Grange scored his team's only touchdown with a glittering 31-yard jaunt that completed a 10-play 82-yard march. Grange started off tackle, then cut back diagonally across the field and outraced all defenders for the score. He kept alive his record of having scored at least once in each game this season. Illinois and Michigan each finished the 1923 season at 8-0 and shared the national title.

Hoge Workman ended his brilliant career by making both the All-America and All-Big Team teams. In their second season at Ohio Stadium, the Buckeyes drew a total attendance of 148,113 in five home games for an average of 29,622. At 3-4-1, Wilce's team suffered its second consecutive losing campaign. Only once before had OSU endured back-to-back losing seasons—1887 (1-7-1) and 1898 (3-5).

1924

The 1924 season was not good for Ohio State football. Coach John Wilce's 12th Buckeye squad won only two of eight games, posting an overall record of 2-3-3. Ironically, OSU's first three years in Ohio Stadium became the only three consecutive losing seasons in school history, and Wilce was now

All-American end Harold "Cookie" Cunningham

1923

October 6	Ohio Wesleyan	W	24	7
October 13	Colgate	T	23	23
October 20	at Michigan	L	0	23
October 27	Iowa	L	0	20
November 3	Denison	W	42	0
November 10	at Purdue	W	32	0
November 17	at Chicago	L	3	17
November 24	Illinois (HC)	L	0	9
Total Points			124	99

Season Record: 3-4-1
Conference: 8th Place (Tie)

Groundskeeping legend Tony Aquila and his stadium sweeping crew. For 40 seasons, from 1907 through his retirement in 1947, he took great pride in the quality of the playing fields at old Ohio Field and Ohio Stadium. A real character, Aquila was very popular with athletic officials, players, and fans alike.

receiving some criticism from fans, alumni, and the "downtown coaches."

Ohio Stadium's First Big Ten Victory

The Buckeyes opened October 4 with a 7-0 victory over the Purdue Boilermakers before a crowd of nearly 30,000. The game's lone touchdown came on a 56-yard pass from halfback Bill Hunt to fullback Marty Karow on the first play of the second quarter. It was OSU's very first conference victory in Ohio Stadium, after a total of five league losses at home in '22 and '23. It also was Ohio State's first opening game against an opponent from outside of Ohio.

The following weekend, Ohio State made its initial trip to Iowa City, where the Buckeyes and Hawkeyes fought to a scoreless tie. Next, OSU defeated Ohio Wesleyan,

10-0, in the first of five straight games at Ohio Stadium. It was the 18th consecutive season the neighboring schools had met on the college gridiron.

Game No. 300

The Buckeyes were involved in tie games the following two weeks, battling Chicago to a 3-3 deadlock and being surprised by Wooster College, 7-7. The contest with Wooster was OSU's 300th all-time game (184-92-24). OSU's chances for a victory over Chicago were dampened when Marty Karow, OSU's fine fullback, was able to play only sparingly because of an injury suffered against Ohio Wesleyan.

The Buckeyes had many scoring opportunities against Wooster, but could get into the end zone only once—a seven-yard smash in the second quarter by sophomore halfback Myers Clark. The Wooster squad earned its tie with a late fourth-period touchdown, leaving Ohio State fans anything but impressed with the play of their Buckeyes.

Unforgettable Afternoon

October 18, 1924, is one of the most noteworthy dates in American football. While Ohio State was defeating Ohio Wesleyan, 10-0, Illinois' Harold "Red" Grange made football history by leading the Illini to a 39-14 win over Michigan in the official dedication of Memorial Stadium. In the game's first 12 minutes, Grange scored four touchdowns on runs from scrimmage of 67, 56, and 44 yards, and a kickoff return of 95 yards. The Wolverines had not lost in three years.

That same afternoon, Notre Dame defeated mighty Army, 13-7, at the Polo Grounds in New York City. Sportswriter Grantland Rice was so impressed with the play of coach Knute Rockne's backfield, he labeled them the "Four Horsemen."

Columbus Dispatch
Sunday, November 23, 1924

BUCKEYE LINE TORN TO SHREDS BY URBANA BACKS WHO FAIL TO BE EFFECTIVE WHEN NEAR GOAL

Wilcemen Ward Off Plunging Attack, Which in Five Drives Down the Gridiron Produces One Score—Another Touchdown Called Back Because of Off-Side.

SCARLETT AND GRAY LOSES TWO SCORING CHANCES

Zuppkemen Display Superior Brand of Football Throughout, Especially in Blocking—Lack of Punch When on Offensive Characterized Ohio's Play.

Things went from bad to worse as OSU lost each of its last three games. Indiana's 12-7 victory on November 8 was extremely disappointing. In the closing minutes of play, the Buckeyes drove 93 yards from their own four to the IU three, but time ran out before they could punch across what would have been the winning score. OSU's lone TD resulted from a short dive by Ollie Klee, while Lawrence Marks scored both Hoosier touchdowns, his second with a 55-yard run.

A packed Ohio Stadium crowd of 68,284 saw Michigan defeat Ohio State for the third straight season, 16-6. The Buckeyes vaulted to a 6-0 lead on the game's third play from scrimmage, when Bill Hunt passed to end Harold "Cookie" Cunningham for a 62-yard touchdown. The score stood until the Wolverines rallied for two TDs and a field goal in the game's final quarter. There were 11 interceptions this afternoon, six by Michigan and five by Ohio State. This was the first Ohio State–Michigan game to be broadcast, with Detroit's WWJ Radio describing the action.

Illibuck Initiated

The tradition of "Illibuck" was created in 1924. That fall, the men of Bucket and Dipper, Ohio State's junior honorary society, and their counterpart at Illinois, Sachem, decided that it would be desirable for the two schools to inaugurate a trophy that would rotate to the winner of each year's game. A turtle was agreed upon by both societies. Four members of Bucket and Dipper purchased a live turtle at a Columbus fish dealer, and took the reptile to Champaign for that season's game. The first Illibuck was 18 inches in diameter and weighed 16 pounds.

Illinois was victorious that year, 7-0, so Illibuck stayed in Champaign with Sachem. The original turtle died in the spring of 1927 and was replaced with a wooden replica. Beginning in 1925, representatives of the two honor societies have met at halftime of the annual Ohio State-Illinois game to smoke a peace pipe and present Illibuck to the previous fall's winning school.

Illini Victorious Without Grange

The Buckeyes closed the season November 22 with a 7-0 loss at Illinois, in a contest that was far more one-sided than indicated by the final score. It was a chilly overcast afternoon for the Memorial Stadium crowd of 27,378. Approximately 3,000 disappointed Buckeye fans had ventured to Champaign, including many students who had traveled all night on a "special train excursion" sponsored by the OSU Athletic Department.

Harold "Red" Grange, the Illini's splendid junior halfback, was unable to play, but it made little difference. Illinois dominated the day's action, running 66 plays from scrimmage compared with OSU's 27, and outgaining the Buckeyes in total offensive yards, 318 to 101. Chicago finished the season as the outright Big Ten champion with a conference record of 3-0-3 and overall mark of 4-1-3.

For the third consecutive season, Ohio State was able to win just one league game, and pressure was starting to build on the coaching staff. OSU end Harold Cunningham was selected as an All-American. The Buckeyes drew 196,072 fans for their six home games, an average of 32,678.

ever, when the Buckeyes were again able to win only one conference game. After a 10-3 victory over Ohio Wesleyan in the October 3 season-opener, Ohio State and Chicago played to a 3-3 tie for the second straight season. While the Buckeyes and Maroons slugged it out before 33,000 fans at Stagg Field in the Windy City, Capital University shifted its home game to Ohio Stadium and defeated Western Reserve, 9-0, on October 10.

Impressive Victory Over Eastern Power

Back in Columbus on October 17, Ohio State upset favored Columbia University, 9-0, in the first meeting between the two schools. At the time, Columbia was the largest university in the nation with a student enrollment of 15,000. The Lions featured a powerful rushing attack and were rated by most analysts as "the strongest team in the East." They had outscored their first three opponents (Haverford, Johns Hopkins, Wesleyan) by a combined score of 170-0. Columbia was coached by Charlie Crowley,

1924				
October 4	Purdue	W	7	0
October 11	at Iowa	T	0	0
October 18	Ohio Wesleyan	W	10	0
October 25	Chicago	T	3	3
November 1	Wooster	T	7	7
November 8	Indiana	L	7	12
November 15	Michigan (HC)	L	6	16
November 22	at Illinois	L	0	7
Total Points			40	45

Season Record: 2-3-3
Conference: 7th Place (Tie)

1925

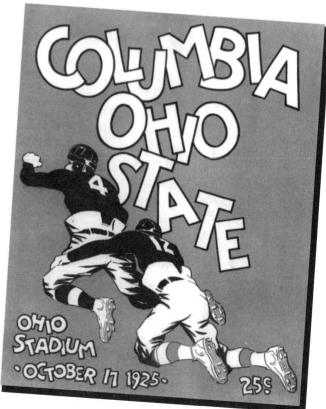

Thanks to three non-conference victories, Ohio State put together a winning record

Game day at Ohio Stadium in 1925

who in 1911-12 had paired with Knute Rockne as the starting ends at Notre Dame.

The Buckeyes started strongly and outplayed the stunned visitors at almost every phase of the game. Using a very intricate and well-balanced rushing and passing attack, Ohio State finally scored in the second quarter to lead 6-0 at halftime. The touchdown was scored by fullback Marty Karow, who in this game also called the offensive signals.

Early in the third period, tackle Leo Uridil kicked a 28-yard field goal to give Ohio State its nine-point advantage. Guard Ed Hess and end "Cookie" Cunningham blocked a Columbia punt to set-up the three-pointer. The Buckeyes dominated the game's statistics, leading in first downs, 12 to 7, and in total offensive yards, 247 to 156. OSU's fine

defensive effort was aided by the punting of halfback Elmer Marek, who averaged 46.8 yards on 10 kicks. His longest went 60 yards.

This was Ohio State's first "major" home victory since the opening of Ohio Stadium in 1922. Coach Wilce, normally quiet and reserved, loudly praised his team's gallant effort. He strongly complimented the passing of Marek and the defensive efforts of Hess and Karow, who led the shutout with many tackles behind the line of scrimmage.

Sportswriter Jim Harrison of the *New York Times* labeled OSU's passing attack, "the best I have seen in four years." Frank McCabe of the *New York World* reported "The open attack of Ohio State's Wilce proved to be too intricate for the Lions." Columbia finished the 1925 season at 6-3-1.

THE DISPATCH RECEIVES THE FULL REPORT OF THE ASSOCIATED PRESS

The Columbus Sunday Dispatch.

Always Better

COLUMBUS, OHIO, SUNDAY, OCTOBER 11, 1925.

VOL. LV. NO. 163. PRICE TEN CENTS

WEATHER—Warmer Sunday and Monday; increasing cloudiness.

In this Section
Local and Telegraph News.
Editorial Page.
Comment on Week's Events.

OHIO STATE AND CHICAGO BATTLE TO NO DECISION

Unfortunately, OSU could not sustain its momentum and was unable to defeat Iowa for the fourth straight season, losing at home, 15-0. After a 17-0 victory over Wooster, the Buckeyes defeated Indiana 7-0 to avenge their previous year's setback. Cunningham scored the game's lone touchdown on a second-quarter pass from sophomore halfback Freddie Grim to complete a 60-yard march. The contest was played in a "sea of mud" as depicted by the *Ohio State Journal* of November 8:

> *Mud, at some spots measuring over the ankle, and then ankle deep in the center of the field, made it impossible for the two teams to display their best form.*
>
> *The smallest crowd that ever witnessed two conference elevens in action here was present at yesterday's conflict.*
>
> *Only 13,500 persons were in the stands when the game began. Rain continued throughout the day in such a fashion that some folks were of the opinion that the game would be called off.*
>
> *Some radio station announced previous to game time that the contest had been called "on account of rain," which resulted in quite a few calls at the State Journal for information. Due to the inclement weather and conditions of the field, it was agreed upon by officials of both teams to shorten the final two quarters to 12 1/2 minutes each. The first two periods were 15 minutes each.*

Wilce's team lost its fourth straight to Michigan the following weekend, 10-0, in the last game between the two at UM's Ferry Field. The Wolverines dominated throughout the afternoon, while OSU was unable to mount a serious scoring threat. UM led in first downs, 15-1, and total offensive yards, 260-72. Ohio State now trailed in the series against Michigan, 3-17-2.

Grange's Last Game
Ohio Stadium "Classic"

The Buckeyes' season-ending homecoming clash with Illinois created an all-time demand for tickets and press box space. Sportswriters from all across the country flocked to Columbus for the final collegiate appearance of Illinois' Harold "Red" Grange, one of the game's all-time greats. Among the notables were Grantland Rice of the *New York Tribune* and Joe Corcornn of the *Chicago American*.

The Ohio Stadium paid attendance of 84,295 was (at the time) the largest crowd to attend a sporting event in this country. Over 100 fans unable to purchase tickets spent Friday evening in the stadium's amphitheater before being removed Saturday morning by watchmen. Approximately 40 boys cleared the fences using a homemade "rope ladder." Ohio State announced that 10,000 general admission tickets would go on sale one-half hour prior to kickoff—fans began assembling Friday evening, and by Saturday noon, five lines stretched from Ohio Stadium's southeast corner to Neil Avenue.

Since each team had already lost two conference games, neither was in contention

INDIANA OHIO

OHIO STADIUM NOVEMBER 7 ·1925·

PRICE TWENTY-FIVE CENTS

for the league title. Interestingly, the opposing captains, Grange and Cunningham, each wore jersey #77. The Buckeyes gave their finest effort of the season, but lost 14-9. Grange's all-around play definitely made the difference, as he electrified the crowd each time he touched the ball. His running set up a two-yard touchdown plunge by fullback Earl Britton to put the visitors on top, 7-0, early in the first quarter. Ohio State scored a second-quarter safety when Illini center Robert Reitsch missed a signal and centered the ball over his own goal. Later that quarter, Grange threw a 13-yard scoring toss to end Charles Kassel to complete a 60-yard drive, giving the Illini a 14-2 lead at intermission.

The Buckeyes really made a game of it in the second half. Quarterback Windy Wendler passed 22 yards to halfback Elmer Marek, who beautifully sidestepped two defenders and dove across the goal, to bring OSU within five late in the third period. But in the end, it was Grange's defensive play which made the difference. In the final quar-

Photo courtesy of Illinois Sports Information Office

Legendary Harold "Red" Grange with his famous #77 jersey following his final collegiate game in Columbus on November 21, 1925.

ter, the "Galloping Ghost" returned an intercepted pass 42 yards from his own 20 to end an Ohio threat. Two minutes later, Grange made another interception at midfield on the game's final play—it was a fitting conclusion to one of the most celebrated careers in all of college football.

Ohio State coach John Wilce was extremely proud of his team's play. His Buckeyes had given their best effort against one of the finest runners the sport has ever known. The following day, Grange signed a contract with coach George Halas to play the remaining six games of the 1925 season with the NFL's Chicago Bears. The professional league was struggling at the gate, but with Red Grange in the backfield, attendance at Bears' home and away games soared.

Wilce Under Pressure

With the downturn in Ohio State's football fortunes, criticism of John Wilce continued to mount. A portion of the conflict resulted from acute differences of opinion on the handling of the team between Wilce and some of his assistant coaches. Part of this disharmony was resolved when assistant line coach Grant P. Ward, one of Wilce's most vocal critics, resigned on December 21, 1925. Junior guard Ed Hess was chosen for the All-America and All-Big Ten teams. The Buck-

eyes drew 201,445 fans for their six home games, an average of 33,574.

1926

With an abundance of returning talent, the Buckeyes enjoyed one of their most outstanding years in school history. As a result, fan faultfinding with the Ohio State program and its head coach dwindled considerably. Only a single-point loss to Michigan spoiled what otherwise would have been an undefeated-untied season. Sam Willaman, fine fullback on OSU's first Big Ten team in 1913, joined Wilce's staff as an assistant coach. Willaman most recently had been head coach at Iowa State.

George W. Rightmire rose from Ohio State's first Graduate Manager of Athletics in 1893 to President of the University in 1926. The "Father of Ohio State Athletics" who played a very active role in the growth of athletics on the campus, Rightmire served as Ohio State's President until his retirement in 1938.

1925				
October 3	Ohio Wesleyan	W	10	3
October 10	at Chicago	T	3	3
October 17	Columbia	W	9	0
October 24	Iowa	L	0	15
October 31	Wooster	W	17	0
November 7	Indiana	W	7	0
November 14	at Michigan	L	0	10
November 21	Illinois (HC)	L	9	14
Total Points			55	45

Season Record: 4-3-1
Conference: 8th Place

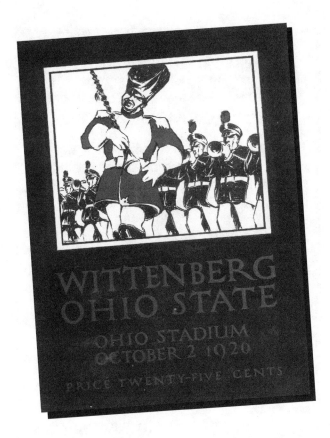

OSU had no trouble with its first two opponents, shutting out Wittenberg in the October 2 opener, 40-0, and following the same pattern with Ohio Wesleyan the next Saturday, 47-0. Wittenberg was coached by Ernie Godfrey, who would later distinguish himself as a long-time assistant coach with the Buckeyes. Sophomore halfback Byron Eby was impressive against Ohio Wesleyan with touchdown runs of 43 and 66 yards. The 47 points that afternoon was OSU's highest total since 1920, when the Buckeyes defeated Ohio Wesleyan 55-0 in that year's opener at old Ohio Field.

First Big Ten Team to Visit New York City

Ohio State posted its third victory of the season, 32-7, with an impressive showing against the Columbia Lions. The return match was played October 16 at New York's Polo Grounds before a rain-drenched crowd of nearly 30,000. The eastern fans were particularly impressed with the display of Ohio

State's 100-piece marching band. Speedy Freddy Grim scored three of his team's touchdowns, one with a 65-yard interception return. Lion coach Charlie Crowley praised the excellent line play of All-America guard Ed Hess and sophomore tackle Leo Raskowski.

Back at Ohio Stadium the following week in their Big Ten opener, the Buckeyes were finally able to defeat the Iowa Hawkeyes, 23-6, before an encouraging crowd of over 42,000. One of the game's highlights was a first-quarter 44-yard scoring toss from quarterback Robin Bell to Freddie Grim. On October 30, Wilce's squad scored six points in each of the

OHIO STATE A STEP NEARER BIG TEN GOAL

Coach Wilce's Buckeyes Gain Expected Victory Over Chicago by 18-0 Score.

45,000 SEE GAME

Ohio State Journal
Sunday, October 31, 1926

Two-time All-American guard Ed Hess

game's last three quarters to shut out Chicago, 18-0. The game drew a record attendance of 45,000 at newly enlarged Stagg Field. Guard Ed Hess led a tenacious defense with numerous tackles behind the line of scrimmage.

Wilce Watches Wolverines

The next Saturday, in the only game ever played between the two schools, Ohio State won over Wilmington College, 13-6. Assistant coach Jim Oberlander took charge of the

All-Time Low

Ohio State's victory over Wilmington College on November 6 was played before a crowd of 5,482, smallest in Ohio Stadium history.

The Queen that Mooed

The election of Maudine Ormsby as Ohio State's 1926 homecoming queen is one of the most remarkable college pranks of all time—Maudine was a pure-bred Holstein cow.

While the fraternities and sororities submitted the names of ten women candidates for queen, "Miss Ormsby" was sponsored by the College of Agriculture. A more crooked election was never held—Ohio State's enrollment was 9,300 students in '26, yet more than 13,000 ballots were cast. Election committee members were unable to unravel the ballot-stuffing problem, so they declared Maudine queen.

Maudine rode in the homecoming parade, but university officials refused to let the bovine attend the traditional dance held at the Crystal Slipper, which was located on the north side of Lane Avenue across from where the French Field House now stands.

The candidate who would have been queen, had it not been for Maudine, was Rosalind Morrison Strapp, OSU '27. In later years, Strapp laughed and joked about the event, agreeing that it really was her claim to fame. After graduation she attended every Ohio State homecoming until her death in 1986. Strapp often joked that her epitaph should read: "But for Maudine, here lies a queen."

Buckeye squad, while John Wilce and assistant Sam Willaman traveled to Ann Arbor to scout undefeated Michigan (UM won over Wisconsin, 37-0). OSU's third team played most of the game, while the second team saw limited action in the first half and fourth quarter. The Buckeye starters were

rested in preparation for their showdown against the Wolverines.

Thriller from Start to Finish

The Ohio State-Michigan homecoming game was one of the most memorable and electrifying in the series. The Buckeyes were undefeated at 6-0, while the Wolverines at 5-

1 had been beaten only by Navy (10-0) two weeks earlier. The Midshipmen's touchdown had been the only score against UM's defense so far this season. The opposing captains, OSU fullback Marty Karow and quarterback Bennie Friedman of Michigan, were both from Cleveland, Ohio.

The game was completely sold out in advance. Columbus hotels were bursting at the seams, forcing many out-of-town fans to stay in nearby towns. November 13 turned out to be a superb day in Columbus — warm temperature, clear sky, and bright sun. Approximately 2,000 general admission tickets went on sale the morning of the game for $2.00 each, but it is estimated at least another 15,000 could have been sold.

When the enormous demand for tickets could not be met,

WHO REMEMBERS THE MAN WHO SAID IT WOULD NEVER BE FILLED?

Columbus Dispatch, Saturday, November 13, 1926

many fans stormed the gates and surged inside. An estimated 10,000 fans who were unable to get through, remained outside and kept track of the action by listening to the stadium public address system. The official Ohio Stadium attendance was announced at 90,411, but no one knew for sure how many people actually were inside the horseshoe. Because of all these difficulties, standing room tickets were never again sold at Ohio Stadium.

Several youths suffered broken limbs trying to scale the stadium fences, while other spectators were struck by bottles dropped from the upper deck. As part of the pre-game festivities, aerial bombs were fired from a field south of the stadium. Unfortunately, one

Marty Karow, All-American fullback. Karow was Ohio State's baseball coach from 1951 through 1975.

bomb manfunctioned and exploded into the stadium's south stands, injuring two sisters. One was badly burned and spent some time in the hospital. The university covered her medical expenses and awarded her $5,000 for personal injuries. Ironically, the aerial bombs were fired under the direct supervision of OSU's Military Department.

Myers Clark put Ohio State in front early with a short field goal. Later in the first quarter, Karow bolted across to increase OSU's lead to 10-0. The touchdown, which was the first scored against the Wolverines by a Big Ten opponent in two seasons, was set up by a 40-yard pass from Robin Bell to Clark.

The second period belonged to Michigan. Friedman faked a field-goal attempt and passed 15 yards to Bennie Oosterbaan for a touchdown, then booted a 43-yard field goal just 10 seconds before the half to tie the game at 10-10. Friedman's field goal came from a very difficult angle near the west sideline.

The Wolverines went ahead 17-10 early in the fourth quarter, after the Buckeyes lost a fumble on a punt return deep in Ohio territory. The Buckeyes responded with a 69-yard scoring march, capped by Bryon Eby's sweep around left end for the final seven yards with just two minutes remaining. Myers Clark, a drop-kicker, was forced to hurry his extra-point attempt when Oosterbaan rapidly shot in from his left end position. The ball went between the uprights but below the crossbar, leaving Michigan with a single-point lead of 17-16, and that's how the game finished. The Buckeyes had suffered a real heartbreaker!

Clark's Extra Point Edges Illini

In the season's final outing, Ohio State nipped talented Illinois, 7-6. The crowd of 25,000 that braved the arctic blasts in Memorial Stadium that afternoon saw Byron Eby dash three yards around end for a second-quarter touchdown. Myers Clark's all-important drop-kick conversion put OSU up 7-0 at halftime.

Late in the game, the Illini drove 76 yards for a touchdown (a 10-yard pass from Dwight Stuessy to Russell Daugherity), but Forrest "Frosty" Peters missed the extra point, leaving Ohio State with the triumph. The Buckeyes all agreed that this single-point outcome was far more pleasant than the previous week's. The Illini ended the season at 6-2.

Michigan (7-1) and Northwestern (7-1) shared the Big Ten title with identical conference records of 5-0, followed by Ohio State (7-1) at 3-1. The Buckeyes outscored their eight opponents by 153 points (196-43). Interestingly, Michigan also outscored its eight opponents by 153 points (191-38). Ed Hess, Marty Karow, and Leo Raskowski were chosen for the All-America and All-Big Ten

HIS BOYS CLOSED SUCCESSFUL GRID SEASON SATURDAY

"JACK" WILCE

Columbus Dispatch, Sunday, November 21, 1926

teams. A total of 183,578 attended the five games in Ohio Stadium for an average crowd of 36,715.

1926				
October 2	Wittenberg	W	40	0
October 9	Ohio Wesleyan	W	47	0
October 16	at Columbia	W	32	7
October 23	Iowa	W	23	6
October 30	at Chicago	W	18	0
November 6	Wilmington	W	13	7
November 13	Michigan (HC)	L	16	17
November 20	at Illinois	W	7	6
Total Points			196	43

Season Record: 7-1
Conference: 3rd Place

1927

Ohio State's return to glory lasted only one year. The 1927 team dropped to a record of 4-4, three of the four losses were shutouts, and OSU could win only two of its five conference games.

One college football rule change mandated that the goal posts be moved back 10 yards from the goal line to the back of the end zone. The change was made partly be-cause of the injuries suffered during "goal line stands" when the posts were on the goal line.

After opening at home October 1 with an easy 31-0 victory over Wittenberg, the Buckeyes had their hands full with the Iowa Hawkeyes but won at Iowa City, 13-6. All scoring took place in the second half. The *Columbus Dispatch* of October 9 described the action:

Ohio State University's football Bucks defeated the Iowa Hawks here this afternoon 13 to 3. But, ladies and gentlemen, those Hawks didn't prove to be butterflies, and at the end of the hectic struggle on this parch of great western prarie, the husky birds were still battling like fighting cocks with only a few of their feathers missing. In other words, the Ohio State footballers are still conscious of the fact they were in a football game.

The whole thing in a nutshell is that Coach Bert Inwergsen of the Hawks slipped over a surprise. That line of his proved to

Two-time All-American
tackle Leo Raskowski

Buckeyes Shown Unsheathed Claws of Hawkeyes, Willingly Withdraw from Tall Corn State With 13 to 6 Win.

VICTIMIZED BY AERIAL ATTACK

Retrieved Fumble and Spectacular Run from Pass Give Ohio Hard-Earned Win. Green Team Proves to Be Red Hot.

Columbus Dispatch
Sunday, October 9, 1927

be more red hot than green. Be it strictly understood, however, that the Scarlet and Gray did earn every one of its 13 points. They came like lightening flashes out of a clear sky, making good the few opportunities to score.

In Columbus the following Saturday, Northwestern handed Ohio State its first loss of the season, 19-13. It was the first meeting between the two schools since OSU won at old Ohio Field, 40-0, in 1917. On October 22, the Buckeyes were given the honor of helping the Michigan Wolverines dedicate their new Michigan Stadium, but it was anything but a pleasant afternoon for Ohio State fans. Michigan won, 21-0, before a crowd of 84,401. UM's All-American end, Bennie Oosterbaan, shifted to the backfield and threw three scoring passes to halfback Louis Gilbert.

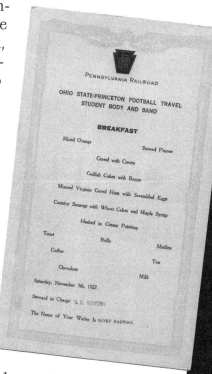

50-Yard Bell-to-Kriss Pass Trims Chicago

The Buckeyes defeated Chicago, 13-7, for their first conference victory before a Dads' Day gathering of 35,775 at Ohio Stadium. With the Maroons leading, 7-6, OSU quarterback Robin Bell heaved a 50-yard scoring toss to speedy halfback Howard Kriss for the victory.

Deb Rowan, who moved from end to fullback, played very well at his new position and scored Ohio State's first TD with a six-yard run. Chicago had a touchdown disallowed right before the half when one of the Maroon backs was signaled for an "in- motion" infraction. Time expired before Chicago could get off another play.

On November 5, the Buckeyes were humiliated by Princeton at rainy Palmer Stadium, 20-0. The Tigers set up two of their three touchdowns by blocking OSU punts deep in Ohio State territory. The game was a huge dis-

appointment for the many Buckeye enthusiasts who had traveled aboard the many Columbus Chamber of Commerce special trains. *Columbus Dispatch* writer W. F. McKinnon described the afternoon as, "a sorry spectacle and one of the lowest points in the coaching career of John Wilce." One bright spot was the sterling play of Leo Raskowski, who made the major portion of OSU's tackles.

Ohio State was home for its last games of the season, outclassing Denison, 61-6, before losing to Illinois, 13-0. The clash with Denison was the last between the Buckeyes and the Big Red. Illinois was able to capture the '27 league title with its win over OSU. The *Ohio State Journal* of November 20 gave this account of the Illini victory:

Fighting desperately in an attempt to throw a wrench into the championship machinery of Illinois, Ohio State was outpointed by the smoother working combination of the Illini gridders and forced to take the short end of a 13 to 0 score at the stadium Saturday. As a result of their victory, the undisputed Big Ten championship for 1927 is now securely in possession of the Zuppke Illini tribe.

Although the Indians outrushed, outgained, and outpunted the Buckeyes, it was their overhead attack that put them out in front and made their triumph possible.

Individually, Ohio looked as good as Illinois, and in the first half really had a shade on the visitors. Collectively, Zuppke's cohorts, in spite of the fact that they had to be more conservative than Ohio, looked much better than the Wilcemen.

Leo Raskowski repeated as an All-American and All-Big Ten tackle. The Buckeyes drew 188,776 fans for their five home games for an average of 37,755. Since moving to Ohio Stadium in 1922, the Buckeyes' six-year record was 23-19-5 overall but only 9-18-3 in Big Ten competition.

Criticism of John Wilce was now stronger than ever, and many of the "downtown coaches" were calling for his replacement, especially after six straight losses to Michigan. There was decided dissension among the players, and rumors were plentiful that Wilce would resign. The Toledo alumni club formally asked for Wilce's removal. This controversy would be resolved, once and for all, before the next season got underway.

1927			
October 1	Wittenberg	W	31	0
October 8	at Iowa	W	13	6
October 15	Northwestern	L	13	19
October 22	at Michigan	L	0	21
October 29	Chicago	W	13	7
November 5	at Princeton	L	0	20
November 12	Denison	W	61	6
November 19	Illinois (HC)	L	0	13
Total Points			131	92

Season Record: 4-4
Conference: 6th Place (Tie)

Complete Wire Reports of UNITED PRESS, the Greatest World-Wide News Service

The Columbus Citizen

HOME

VOL. 30.—No. 81.   COLUMBUS. OHIO, SATURDAY, JUNE 2, 1928.   Entered at Columbus Postoffice as Second Class Mail Matter.   PRICE TWO CENTS

WILCE RESIGNS AS BUCKEYE GRID COACH

1928

The strong contention surrounding John Wilce and his coaching methods came to a head when Wilce tendered his resignation on Saturday, June 3, 1928, effective at the end of the '28 season. Wilce, who received his medical degree from Ohio State in 1919, stated that he planned to enter the medical profession and remain on the campus to teach. His decision to leave his coaching position did not come as a complete surprise to many of Ohio State's ardent followers.

The Ohio State Board of Trustees accepted Wilce's resignation with "sincere regret." The board praised his lasting contribution to the development of the university and expressed complete support for Dr. Wilce to continue his university teaching relationships. Wilce expressed his full appreciation of the complete and cordial support of the board over his coaching period. Thomas French, Chairman of the Athletic Board, emphasized that Wilce would have complete control of the 1928 football team and not continue merely in an advisory capacity as some had speculated.

Halfback Byron Eby provided much of the Buckeyes' offensive punch from 1926 through 1928.

Victory No. 200 While Ohio Wesleyan Upends Michigan

The Buckeyes' season-opening 41-0 win over Wittenberg on October 6 was Ohio State's 200th all-time triumph (200-103-25). That same afternoon, Ohio Wesleyan embarrassed Michigan with a 17-7 surprise victory at Ann Arbor, marking the first time the Wolverines had lost an opening game in 46 seasons. The following Saturday, OSU, making its first trip to Evanston since 1915, defeated the Northwestern Wildcats, 10-0. The *Columbus Dispatch* of October 14 provided the following story of the game:

The score of the annual controversy between the Wildcat, which by the way was not so wild, and the peaceful Buckeye, was 10-0. But Ohio State legions, who tonight are hurrahing and seeking joy of different kinds are perhaps not taking into account how it was won—whether it was achieved by a finished football machine or scored through the weaknesses of an opposing team.

Ohio State defeated Northwestern Saturday afternoon because of several things. One was the absolute and wanton willingness of the Wildcats, who instead of roaring as is the want of Wildcats, did little more

WEAK MICHIGAN TEAM NOT EASILY DOWNED, HOWEVER, DESPITE 19 TO 7 SCORE

Colorful Crowd of 73,000 Experiences Thrills Aplenty at Annual Gridiron Meet of Buckeyes and Wolverines

OHIO OFFENSIVE IS UNCERTAIN

Freak Play Allows Michigan Score in Game in Which They Make But One First Down; Coffee and Eby Star.

Columbus Dispatch, Sunday, October 21, 1928

than meow in a plaintive heartbroken way. Northwestern did everything that an opposing eleven could be reasonably expected to do to help a rival. This redounds to the credit of the Buckeyes, for if they had not recognized the opportunity when it sauntered across their path, perhaps there would have been no Ohio State scoring.

Finally—Another Victory Over Michigan!

Back home on October 20, the Buckeyes broke a six-year losing streak to the Wolverines with a 19-7 victory. Playing before a crowd of 72,439, Ohio State defeated Michigan in Ohio Stadium for the very first time. Eight minutes into the game, quarterback Alan Holman passed 16 yards to end Wes Fesler, who stumbled at the three but was able to cross the Michigan goal for OSU's first touchdown. Fred Barratt's extra-point at-

tempt was wide, and the score remained 6-0. Holman and Fesler, both sophomores, had played very impressively in the first two games of the season.

Michigan went ahead, 7-6, on a very confusing and controversial play. Wolverine tackle Leo Draveling recovered a loose ball in the end zone for the touchdown. OSU's Charles Coffee had allowed a punt to roll, thinking it would bounce beyond the goal line for a touchback. But Coffee was blocked, causing his body to touch the ball before it rolled into the end zone. Officials ruled Draveling had possession of the ball long enough for the TD before the ball squirted out of the end zone. Ohio State players solidly disagreed, but to no avail.

Near halftime, the Buckeyes regained the lead, 12-7, after Byron Eby sped 21 yards untouched on a "naked reverse." Barratt's try for the extra point was blocked. After a scoreless third quarter, Holman passed perfectly to Coffee for a 21-yard touchdown midway through the final period. This time Barratt's kick was good, and Buckeye fans were ecstatic. Ohio State dominated the statistics, leading in first downs, 13-1, and in total offensive yards, 157-50.

The Buckeyes' defense continued to dominate the next week at Indiana. OSU intercepted four Hoosier passes en route to a shutout over the Hoosiers, 13-0. Ohio State now led the Big Ten with a conference record of 3-0.

113

Glorious Game Between
Two Unbeaten Powers

A sellout crowd of 72,496 watched Ohio State and Princeton struggle to a 6-6 tie in one of the most prominent non-conference games ever staged in Ohio Stadium. The Tigers, at 3-0-1, entered the game unscored upon, while the Buckeyes at 4-0 had given up only one touchdown. Princeton's great halfback, Al Wittmer, scored in the third period, while Bryon Eby tallied for the Buckeyes with less than three minutes to play. The Tigers' Trix Bennett and OSU's Fred Barratt each missed their extra-point attempts. The November 5 *Columbus Citizen* carried the following recap:

Ohio and Princeton supporters will never reach an agreement on who should have won the game. But they'll always be in accord on one point. It was one of the greatest games ever played anywhere by any two teams.

The crowd of more than 72,000, the rival bands, the Princeton and Ohio tradition, and the visiting celebrities, all added to the colorful scene. But they were dwarfed by the very magnitude of the football struggle out there on Tony Aquila's turf.

The game will go down with the Ohio-Michigan game of 1926, the Ohio-Wisconsin game of 1920, and the Ohio-

Columbus Citizen, Monday, November 5, 1928

Illinois game of 1919 among the annals of the most thrilling battles in Ohio grid history.

In another contest of two unbeaten teams, Iowa dealt the Buckeyes their first loss of the season, 14-7, before an Ohio Stadium gathering of more than 47,000. Powerful Hawkeye fullback Mayes McLain scored both Iowa touchdowns, the second in the last minute of play. One week later, on November 17, only 10,035 showed up to see Ohio State blast Muskingum, 39-0, in John Wilce's last game at Ohio Stadium.

The Buckeyes closed their season November 24 at Illinois with a chance to capture the conference championship, since Iowa lost to Wisconsin the previous week, 13-0. Unfortunately, OSU put on one of its poorest showings in many seasons, losing, 8-0. The players appeared to be trying too hard to send Wilce out a winner in his final game. It was the second straight season Illinois had shut out Ohio State. Michigan beat Iowa, 10-7, and Minnesota edged Wisconsin, 6-0, allowing the Illini to seize the outright league title with a conference mark of 4-1.

Sophomore end Wes Fesler had a superb season and was selected for both All-America and All-Big Ten honors. The Buckeyes averaged 46,451 fans per game by drawing a total of 232,256 for their five home dates. It was the first season Ohio State averaged more than 40,000 since moving to Ohio Stadium in 1922.

End of an Era

With the close of the 1928 season, John Wilce's 16-year coaching career reached its destination. More than anything else, Wilce was a "high achiever" who provided leadership and stability for the maturing Ohio State football program. He was a gentleman of impeccable integrity who at times appeared to be distant and reserved. A major figure in the growing popularity of American football, Wilce led the Buckeyes into the "big time" limelight with dignity and honor.

John Wilce's Ohio State teams compiled an impressive overall record of 78-33-9. During his reign, the Buckeyes captured three Big Ten championships and played in their first Rose Bowl. Sixteen different players were selected as All-Americans, including Chic Harley, the first Ohio State player to receive this honor three times. Wilce was later inducted into the College Football Hall of Fame.

Dr. John Wilce entered private medical practice in 1929. He taught many years in the OSU College of Medicine, and also specialized in the research and treatment of heart diseases. Dr. Wilce served as Director of Ohio State's Student Health Services until his retirement from the university in 1958.

Coach John W. Wilce

1928				
October 6	Wittenberg	W	41	0
October 13	at Northwestern	W	10	0
October 20	Michigan	W	19	7
October 27	at Indiana	W	13	0
November 3	Princeton (HC)	T	6	6
November 10	Iowa	L	7	14
November 17	Muskingum	W	39	0
November 24	at Illinois	L	0	8
Total Points			135	35

Season Record: 5-2-1
Conference: 4th Place (Tie)

FOOTBALL AND THE GREAT DEPRESSION

It was generally assumed that Sam Willaman would immediately be named Ohio State's new coach, following the close of Dr. John W. Wilce's last season in 1928. Willaman had been Wilce's top assistant for the last three years, and some Columbus newspapers spoke of Willaman's appointment as a "mere formality."

It also was taken for granted that the new coach would be named at a meeting of the Athletic Board on Friday, December 21, 1928. When the meeting lasted until midnight and was adjourned until the next afternoon, the Saturday, December 22, issue of the *Columbus Citizen* carried the following headline, "Appointment of Willaman Off till Today." However, when the Saturday meeting concluded without the naming of a new coach, there was then speculation that a new coach might not be named until the end of the 1929 season. One theory had Willaman as the "acting head coach" for one season, giving him the opportunity to demonstrate his ability before he was granted the position.

Knute Rockne to Ohio State?

Athletic Director L. W. St. John had told the board that he needed more time to evaluate the several candidates under consideration. St. John did not give the board a lot of specifics. It was later learned that, in early December, St. John had been notified by Big

John Wilce to Guide Nebraska?

While Ohio State fans were waiting for a new head coach to be announced in late December, 1928, it was rumored that John Wilce would be moving to the University of Nebraska as Head Football Coach and Director of the Physical Education Department. The Cornhuskers' head coach Ernest Bearg was leaving Nebraska to return to his alma mater, Washburn College.

However, Wilce devoted the rest of his career to the medical profession and never again coached football. Dana X. Bible replaced Bearg at Nebraska.

Ten Commissioner John Griffith that Notre Dame's Knute Rockne was interested in coaching in the Big Ten. Griffith told St. John that Rockne wanted to talk with St. John about the Ohio State opening. Rockne, who played at Notre Dame from 1910 through 1913, had been head coach of the Irish since 1918. He was 40 years old and had compiled an 11-year record of 86-12-5.

St. John and Rockne met at the American Football Coaches Association meeting in New Orleans in early January of 1929. Apparently the two reached an agreement for Rockne to become Ohio State's new coach, under the condition that Rockne could be released from his current contract. When Rockne returned to South Bend, however, he was convinced by Notre Dame officials to remain there. Rockne guided Notre Dame to a 9-0 record in 1929 and a 10-0 mark in 1930, before losing his life in a plane crash over Kansas on March 31, 1931.

Willaman Finally Appointed

With Rockne out of consideration, the Buckeyes turned to Sam Willaman. At St. John's recommendation, Willaman was appointed head coach at an Athletic Board meeting of January 16, 1929. At age 39, the trim and agile Willaman looked as if he could still carry the pigskin as he did during his OSU undergraduate days. The board also reported that other candidates receiving consideration included Andy Kerr of Washington and Jefferson, Harry Stuhldreher of Villanova, Charles Bachman of Florida, Al Wittmer of Princeton, Harry Kipke of Michigan State, and Russell Ashbaugh of Youngstown High School.

Willaman scored four touchdowns in his last college game in 1913, the season Ohio State joined the Big Ten. After graduation, he took charge of high school programs at Alliance and Cleveland East Tech. Willaman moved to Iowa State University as head coach in 1922, then returned to OSU in 1926 as an assistant to John Wilce. His four-year Iowa

Columbus Dispatch, **Thursday, January 17, 1929**

Columbus Citizen, **Thursday, January 17, 1929**

Ohio State 1929 coaching staff. Left to right: Jim Oberlander, Ernie Godfrey, Don Miller, Head Coach Sam Willaman, George Hauser.

State record was 14-15-3. Willaman was a strong fundamentalist who paid close attention to details and despised mistakes. He seldom raised his voice, and to many he appeared to be distant and reserved.

Hauser and Miller Boost Coaching Staff

Willaman immediately hired two fine nationally known assistants, line coach George Hauser and backfield coach Don Miller. Hauser, an All-American tackle and captain at Minnesota in 1917, had been line coach at Colgate for the last three seasons. He also had been line coach at Iowa State under Willaman in '24 and '25.

Miller, a native of Defiance, Ohio, gained fame as a member of Notre Dame's "Four Horsemen" backfield in 1924. He came to OSU after four seasons as backfield coach at Georgia Tech. Miller was elated with the Ohio State opportunity, partly because he was an attorney who practiced law in Cleveland during the off-seasons. Years later, Miller became a United States District Attorney for Northern Ohio.

Also joining Willaman's staff were Cyril Surington, who had lettered at end the last two seasons for OSU, and Ernie Godfrey, who had been head coach at Wittenberg University. Godfrey had earned a letter at OSU in 1914. He remained an able assistant for 33 seasons under seven different head coaches until his formal retirement from Ohio State following the 1961 season. Godfrey continued to work with the kickers for many seasons after his retirement.

1929

Ohio State opened at home October 5 with a 19-0 victory over Wittenberg before a crowd of 27,918. The Buckeyes looked "so-so" at best, making a lot of mistakes and scoring all 19 points in the second half. One bright spot was the distinguished play of All-American end Wes Fesler of Youngstown. Sportswriters covering the game were very pleased with a new press box at Ohio Stadium.

Two controversial calls fell in Ohio State's favor to help Willaman's squad slip past Iowa, 7-6, in Columbus, on October 12. Tackle Dick Larkins (later to become Director of Athletics) scored by recovering a blocked punt in the end zone, and center Fred Barratt kicked the all-important extra point. The *Columbus Dispatch* of October 13 provided the following account:

> *It was Columbus Day, so Columbus refused to be beaten by Iowa and knocked a lot of the whitewash off the black sheep of the conference and won, 7-6. The fact that Iowa was a slightly better ball club, playing slightly better football, gaining slightly more ground, and showing slightly more power failed to offset the fact that Ohio had slightly more generalship, much more luck and according to Iowa's team, much more from the officials in the way of decisions.*
>
> *Two decisions by officials turned the result upside down. The first, when an Ohio end seemed clearly off-side, and the officials did not call it, allowed Ohio to block a punt, recover the ball behind the line, and score its lone touchdown from which Barratt kicked a perfect goal. And on a later occasion, when (Oran) Pape, Iowa's brilliant smashing back, tore Ohio's left wing to shreds and broke through for a 40-yard run for a touchdown to have the ball called back because an Iowan was off side.*
>
> *It was not a satisfying victory to the forty thousand who came out in beautiful, warm, summer weather which*

Double Duty

In an effort to generate higher revenues, Michigan opened its 1929 season on September 28 with an extremely rare "doubleheader." The Wolverines defeated Albion in the opening game, 39-0, and outscored Mount Union in the second contest, 16-6. A crowd of 16,412 attended the two games at Michigan Stadium.

Michigan also scheduled doubleheaders to open its next two campaigns, defeating Denison (33-0) and Eastern Michigan (7-0) on September 27, 1930, and winning over Central Michigan (27-0) and Eastern Michigan (34-0) on October 3, 1931.

> *turned to rain before the end. But it was a sweet morsel for Coach Willaman and his helpers who revealed the fact that they have a team which, while weak in spots, is improving and will fight, and that there is at least the glimmer of hope that Ohio State may develop an offense.*

The following weekend Ohio State defeated Michigan, 7-0, to earn Willaman his first "big win" as head coach. An estimated 20,000 Buckeye fans were among the Michigan Stadium crowd of 85,088. On the eve of the game, the Ohio State band highlighted a huge torchlight parade and rally in Toledo. On the fourth play of the second period, quarterback Alan Holman heaved a perfect 22-yard scoring toss to Wes Fesler for the game's

only touchdown. Fred Barratt, 239-pound center from Lansing, Michigan, booted the extra point.

Defense Supreme

The OSU defense played a major role in securing Ohio State's second consecutive victory over the Wolverines. Near halftime, the Buckeyes held the Wolverines on downs at the OSU nine. The defenders became even more dominant in the second half, recovering a UM fumble at the OSU nine and holding the Wolverines on downs at the OSU 19. In the game's final minute, Willaman's invincibles still had just enough energy for one last gallant stand, stopping Michigan on a fourth-and-one at the OSU six-yard line.

Stock Market Crumbles

While Ohio State was preparing for its next game against Indiana, the national stock market dropped drastically on October 24, known as "Black Thursday." Major financial concern rapidly developed throughout the entire country. At Ohio Stadium on Saturday, October 26, the Buckeyes lost five fumbles and were forced to settle for a scoreless tie with the Hoosiers. The following Tuesday, October 29, stockholders panicked and sold a record 16,410,030 shares of stock, as many lost huge sums of money.

For most Americans, this was just the beginning of an historic tragedy that fully overshadowed their interest in college football. More than 5,000 banks in the United States closed between 1929 and 1933, wiping out the savings of millions of people.

During that five-year period, the value of goods and services produced annually in the United States fell from $104 billion to $56 billion. The unemployment rate soared to 25 percent by 1933, and many who kept or found jobs had to take a reduction in salary. Almost everything in America suffered, including attendance at college football games.

First Tangle with the Pitt Panthers

Undefeated Pittsburgh had little trouble with the Buckeyes, registering an easy 18-2 victory before a rain-soaked Pitt Stadium crowd of over 50,000 on November 2. Halfback Tony Uansa scored both touchdowns to spark the Pitt attack, his first a 73-yarder around OSU's left end in the first quarter. Coach Jock Sutherland's Panthers finished the season at 9-1, losing only to Southern California in the Rose bowl, 47-14.

Back in conference play the next week, Northwestern ruined Ohio State's Big Ten title hopes with an impressive 18-6 victory. Fullback Russell Bergherm was the chief cog in the Wildcat attack, handling the ball on almost every play while scoring two of his team's three touchdowns. The Buckeyes' lone score resulted from an extremely unusual play. Early in the second quarter, Northwestern had driven within a couple of feet of the Ohio State end zone. On fourth down, the snap from center bounced high into the air after hitting NU fullback Don Calderwood in the chest. Wes Fesler grabbed the ball in mid-air and sprinted 98 yards for a touchdown.

Navy Series Postponed

The Naval Academy was scheduled to play in Columbus on November 16, with the Buckeyes playing a return match in '30. But at the request of the Midshipmen, the two-game series was delayed one year until '30 and '31. Ohio State filled the open date with a 54-0 drubbing of Kenyon College. This was the final game between the two schools, who were heated rivals during the early days of Ohio State football. It also was their first clash since 1911.

Illinois scored at least once in each quarter to completely outclass OSU, 27-0, in the season's last game. The Illini had now shut out Ohio State each of the last three seasons. The Ohio Stadium crowd of 64,869 watched the Buckeyes endure their most one-sided

Halfback Bob Grady follows excellent blocking against Kenyon.

setback since the 37-0 loss at Illinois in 1914. Coach Bob Zuppke's squad led in first downs, 25-4, and in total offense, 350 yards to 81.

After starting the season with three victories, Ohio State won only once in its last five outings to complete the year at 4-3-1 (league record of 2-2-1). Buckeye fans were reasonably satisfied with Willaman's first season, especially since his team was victorious at Michigan. In six home games, OSU drew a total of 213,941 fans for an average crowd of 35,657. Wes Fesler, who played every minute of every game, was chosen All-American and All-Big Ten for the second consecutive season. Ohio State finished its 40th season of intercollegiate football with an all-time record of 208-108-27 (64.6%).

Holcolm was shifted from fullback to halfback. Sam Willaman spent considerable time installing Glenn "Pop" Warner's noted wingback system of offensive play. Floyd Stahl, a graduate of Illinois, joined the coaching staff, marking the beginning of a noted career in athletic administration that would continue until his retirement from Ohio State in 1970.

Before a crowd of 16,000, OSU rolled to a 59-0 victory over the Mt. Union Purple Raiders in the first September game ever played at Ohio Stadium. Fesler scored the season's first touchdown from his new fullback position. Altogether, eight different players scored nine touchdowns as Willaman used 53 substitutes throughout the afternoon.

Against much tougher competition the following Saturday, the Buckeyes scored 20 fourth-quarter points en route to a 23-0 tri-

1929

Date	Opponent	Result		
October 5	Wittenberg	W	19	0
October 12	Iowa	W	7	6
October 19	at Michigan	W	7	0
October 26	Indiana	T	0	0
November 2	at Pittsburgh	L	2	18
November 9	Northwestern	L	6	18
November 16	Kenyon	W	54	0
November 23	Illinois (HC)	L	0	27
Total Points			**95**	**69**

Season Record: 4-3-1
Conference: 5th Place (Tie)

1930

The Buckeyes made three principal position changes as they prepared for their September 27 opener against Mount Union College. Two-time All-America end Wes Fesler was shifted to fullback, senior Dick Larkins moved from tackle to end, and junior Stu

Wes Fesler, three-time All-American end and fullback

Ohio State Gridders Reveal Finishing Strength as They Batter Hoosiers to Win 23-0

Columbus Dispatch, Sunday, October 5, 1930

umph over Indiana. Fesler moved back to end midway through the first half, and senior Bob Horn took over at fullback. Errors dominated the first half, and the scoring was limited to left-footed Carl "Tubby" Ehrensberger's second-quarter field goal. OSU dominated the game's statistics, leading in first downs, 18-4, and total offense, 276 yards to 68. The Ohio Stadium attendance was 24,716.

Things changed radically at Evanston on October 11, where Northwestern scored all of its points in the first half to hand the Buckeyes their first setback of the season, 19-2. The *Columbus Dispatch* of October 12 carried the following account:

Today in this peculiar amphitheater given to Northwestern by a certain Mr. Dyche, the purpled herd Wildcats of Evanston won from the scarlet robed warriors of Ohio. The final tabulation was 19 to 2. Ohio's lone counter came in the fourth period by virtue of a punt which Sam Selby blocked behind Northwestern's goal line.

Ernest Rentner the punter recovered the ball but it went for a safety, thus affording Ohio a chance to escape a complete whitewashing, a feat in which there is some little satisfaction, little though it may be.

And here is a word or two of tribute in the direction of Lew Hinchman,

Wes Fesler back to punt against Wisconsin.

Ohio's brilliant sophomore pilot. He was the outstanding player of the day. Finally when he left the arena in the fourth period 40,000 persons rose as one and gave him a cheer that must have caused nearby Lake Michigan to ripple just a bit more than usual.

The next weekend, Ohio State fell to Michigan, 13-0, before a crowd of 68,459 at bitterly cold Ohio Stadium. Sophomore quarterback Harry Newman shredded the Buckeye defense with his pinpoint passing, and scored all 13 of his team's points. The game's final statistics were somewhat misleading, with OSU leading in first downs, 13-6, and total offensive yardage, 272-224. Michigan finished the season at 7-0-1, tying Northwestern for the Big Ten title with identical league records of 5-0.

After an open weekend, a homecoming gathering of only 40,488 was on hand to see Ohio State battle favored Wisconsin to a scoreless tie on November 1. Coach Willaman's cleverly conceived defense effectively stopped the Badgers, who had outscored their first five opponents, 148-13. For the first time in his brilliant career, Wes Fesler was injured slightly and was forced to leave the game early in the final quarter. The Buckeyes' season record was now 2-2-1.

Fast Finish

A fully recovered Wes Fesler played one of his finest games the following Saturday, leading OSU to a 27-0 victory over Navy at Baltimore. Fesler played both fullback and end, punted very effectively, was all over the field on defense, and threw a touchdown pass to Dick Larkins. Back home on November 15 in his last home game, Fesler led his team to a 16-7 victory over the Pitt Panthers, who entered the game at 5-1-1. Playing most of the game at fullback, Fesler completed eight of 11 passes and called the offensive signals. The Buckeye defense made four interceptions, which helped limit the potent Panthers to a single touchdown.

The News Unbiased and Unbossed

SUNDAY ☘ JOURNAL

MAIN Section

COLUMBUS, OHIO, SUNDAY, NOVEMBER 16, 1930.   EST. 1811.   VOL. CXX.   NO. 320.   PRICE TEN CENTS.

WEATHER: Occasional rain Sunday; colder Monday.

BUCKS TAME PITT PANTHERS, 16 TO 7

Lew Hinchman goes high for a pass against the Pitt Panthers.

In the season's final game, Ohio State broke a three-year losing streak to Illinois with a nail-biting 12-9 victory at Champaign. The memorial Stadium crowd totaled only 16,881. Fesler passed eight yards to Bob Grady, and Martin Varner plunged one yard for OSU's touchdowns, both in the first quarter, while the Fighting Illini scored all nine of their points in the second period. In his last college game, Fesler was a dynamo on defense with his timely tackling.

Wes Fesler Heisman Winner?

By closing the year strongly with three consecutive victories, Ohio State finished with a record of 5-2-1. The Buckeyes drew a total of 189,334 fans in their five home dates, for an average of 37,867. Indispensable Wes Fesler, one of the most talented athletes in conference history, was All-America for the third time. He was the first Ohio State player to be chosen the Big Ten's MVP. Sophomore quarterback Lew Hinchman was also chosen All-America. Fesler and Hinchman were also both All-Big Ten selections.

The Heisman Trophy, presented annually to college football's most outstanding player, was not initiated until five years later in 1935. Wes Fesler would clearly have acquired strong consideration for this honor, had the Heisman Trophy been awarded in 1930.

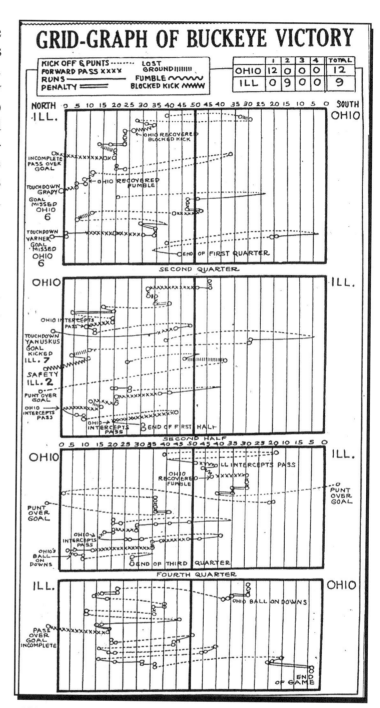

Ohio State Journal, Sunday, November 23, 1930

1930

September 27	Mt. Union	W	59	0
October 4	Indiana	W	23	0
October 11	at Northwestern	L	2	19
October 18	Michigan	L	0	13
November 1	Wisconsin (HC)	T	0	0
November 8	at Navy	W	27	0
November 15	Pittsburgh	W	16	7
November 22	at Illinois	W	12	9
Total Points			139	48

Season Record: 5-2-1
Conference: 4th Place (Tie)

The Ohio State football program continued to gain strength during Sam Willaman's third season. Junius Farrell and Sid Gillman manned the end positions, with extensive support from Bert Nasman, Fred Conrad, and Howard Rabenstein. Bob Haubrich and Bill Bell started most of the games at tackle, Martin Varner (halfback in '29) and Joe Gailus manned the guard positions, and Richard Smith was at center.

Lew Hinchman, last season's quarterback, joined captain Stu Holcomb at halfback, with frequent relief from Bill Carroll, Bob Grady, and Tom Keefe. Mickey Vuchinich took over at fullback and Carl Cramer was OSU's new quarterback. Holcomb became Purdue's head coach from 1947 through 1955, and was later President of the Chicago White Sox Baseball Club.

The Buckeyes' 67-6 victory over Cincinnati in the October 3 season opener was a total mismatch. Playing in midsummer temperatures before a home crowd of 15,699, Ohio State used basic straight-ahead power football to lead 40-0 at halftime. The Bearcats' only touchdown followed the recovery of a Buckeye fumble at the OSU seven in the third quarter. Even after substituting early and often, Ohio State still led in total offense, 468 yards to 32.

Vanderbilt handed the Buckeyes their first loss of the season, 26-21, after building up a 26-0 halftime lead. Fleet Bill Carroll accounted for two of OSU's three touchdowns,

> ## Developing Leaders
>
> Joining Sam Willaman's 1931 staff as assistant coaches were two of his fine seniors from the previous season, ends Wes Fesler and Dick Larkins. Fesler would later coach the Buckeyes from 1947 through 1950, leading OSU to its first Rose Bowl triumph at the end of the 1949 season. In 1947, Larkins would succeed L.W. St. John as Director of Athletics, a position he held until his retirement in 1970.

and appeared to have scored what would have been his third—but the officials spotted the ball just six inches short of the visitors' end zone. The *Ohio State Journal* of October 11 furnished the following account:

In a game that changed from an apparent rout to a thrilling struggle with a hair-raising finish, Vanderbilt defeated Ohio State, 26 to 21, at the Ohio Stadium Saturday afternoon.

This contest was replete with thrills and chills, good and bad football, brilliant and mediocre line play, terrible strategic mistakes and desperation football, loose and effective blocking, ragged and hard, smashing tackling, elusive and sloppy forward passing, inconsistent and hurried punting, mingled with

The Buckeyes of 1931

Bill "Blond Express" Carroll scores at Michigan.

intermittent spasms of flashy, speedy dashes by ball carriers, who at times rose almost to stardom.

It will be a long time before the spectators who witnessed the struggle between the Commodores and the Buckeyes, again will see a gridiron performance that had so much good and bad football in it from start to finish.

Huge Victory at Ann Arbor

Ohio State quickly got back on track with an impressive 20-7 upset at Michigan on October 17. The crowd of 58,026 was an excellent turnout considering the economic conditions of the 1930s. Michigan's second largest crowd that season was 37,251 for its 6-0 homecoming victory over Minnesota on November 21. Carroll scored twice with convincing runs of 10 and two yards, and Carl Cramer put the game away with a 45-yard punt return for the game's final touchdown.

Near halftime, Ivan William-son blocked an OSU punt

and recovered the loose ball in the end zone for the Wolverines' only score. Sam Willaman had won two of his first three in this heated rivalry. This was Michigan's only loss in 1931. Coach Harry Kipke's team shut out their last six opponents, 100 to 0, to finish the season at 8-1-1.

The Buckeyes played very well at home the next Saturday before losing to Northwestern, 10-0. The Wildcats, who scored all 10 of their points in the second half, repeated as conference co-champions for the second straight season. OSU fared better at Bloomington on October 31 with a 13-6 victory over Indiana. Ohio State intercepted five Hoosier passes. Carl Cramer scored both Buckeye touchdowns, the second with a 70-yard punt return in the final quarter. Tackle Bill Bell and end Sid Gillman both played very well on defense.

Lew Hinchman prepares to tackle Northwestern's Art Jens (#53) after Jens has received pass from Wildcat All-American Ernest Rentner.

Colorful Homecoming Crowd Of 60,000 Braves Sleet, Rain To See Ohio Sink Navy, 20-0

Columbus Dispatch, Sunday, November 8, 1931

60,640 See Buckeyes Sink Navy

Ohio State played fundamentally sound football to defeat the United States Naval Academy, 20-0, at homecoming on November 7. The weekend's top intersectional contest was attended by several key naval officials, including Admiral W. V. Pratt, Chief of Naval Operations. The Midshipmen were directed by coach Edgar "Rip" Miller, a former Notre Dame tackle who was one of coach Knute Rockne's "Seven Mules" that blocked for the "Four Horsemen" in 1924. Seven returning members of Ohio State's very first squad of 1890 were honored in a separate ceremony that morning.

Navy entered the game at 3-1-1. Playing in a constant downpour of rain and sleet, the Buckeyes used the "uncommon play" to score all three touchdowns. In the second period,

Halfback and captain Stu Holcomb

with the ball at the Navy 35, a pass from OSU's Carl Cramer was deflected by Navy end Larry Smith—the ball ended-up squarely in the hands of Sid Gillman, who raced to the end zone for touchdown number one. Near halftime Martin Varner blocked a Navy punt, which was returned 32 yards by Junius

Illustration by Tom Hayes.

Getting Navy's Goat

Navy's mascot goat, which was a somewhat dirty gray from all its travels, accompanied the Midshipmen to Columbus. During the night prior to the game, a group of mischievous Ohio State students found the animal in one of the campus agriculture buildings, and dyed a portion of the goat with Mercurochrome. Saturday morning the Navy plebes were stunned when first sighting their "Scarlet and Gray" mascot.

Ferrall for OSU's second score. Ferrall also scored the final TD with a 20-yard interception return in the third period.

The Midshipmen threatened five times behind the fine running and passing of halfback "Bullet Lou" Kirn, but simply couldn't cross the home team's goal. Interceptions by Stu Holcomb and Mickey Vuchinich killed Navy's last two drives inside the OSU 15. Navy's final record of 5-5-1 included a 17-7 season-ending loss to Army.

Ohio State moved back into conference competition with a 6-0 win at Wisconsin before a homecoming crowd of 35,000 at Camp Randall Stadium. The game was played in heavy fog on a very wet field. Late in the first quarter, two linemen accounted for the game's only touchdown. Martin Varner blocked a punt attempt by the Badgers' John Schneller, and tackle Bill Bell recovered in the end zone. Bob Haubrich's extra-point attempt was wide of the goal post.

The Buckeyes returned home November 14 to register their first triumph over Illinois in Ohio Stadium by the surprisingly high score of 40-0. It was the largest margin of defeat ever handed an Illini team during Bob Zuppke's 29 seasons as head coach, and it prevented Illinois from winning at least one conference game in 1931. The crowd of 20,642 saw Ohio State score 20 points in each half. Carl Cramer and Bill Carroll were sensational—either one or the other played a key role in each of OSU's six touchdowns.

Postseason Charity Games

With the country feeling the economic effects of the Great Depression, the Big Ten extended the season and staged three charity games on Saturday, November 28, between the conference's top six teams. Ohio State was scheduled at Minnesota. The net

Buckeyes Put End to Illini Jinx by Giving Zuppke Worst Beating Any Team of His Ever Had, 40-0

Ohio State Journal
Sunday, November 22, 1931

proceeds were donated to unemployment relief funds among the seven conference states. Approximately 25,000 fans braved the wind and cold of Minneapolis and contributed $46,000 to the Big Ten's fund for unemployment relief. The Golden Gophers won with unexpected ease, 19-7.

Ohio State simply couldn't control fullback Jack Manders, who ran for 121 yards and played a key role in each of his team's three long touchdown marches. Clearing a path for Manders was Minnesota's All-American guard, Clarence "Biggie" Munn. The Golden Gophers led in first downs, 19-7, and total offensive yards, 392 to 127. Munn and Minnesota head coach Fritz Crisler would one day be on opposite ends of one of

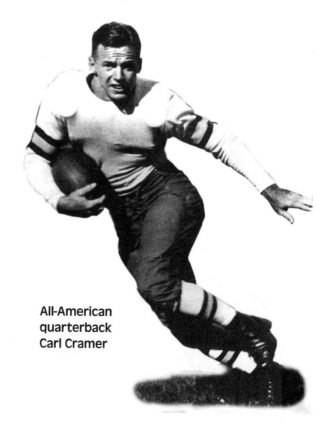

All-American quarterback Carl Cramer

Ohio Stadium in the early 1930s

football's strongest rivalries. Crisler would lead Michigan between 1938 and 1947, while Munn brought Michigan State into national prominence from 1947 through 1953.

While Minnesota was beating Ohio State, Michigan won at home over Wisconsin (16-0) and Purdue beat Northwestern at Soldiers Field in Chicago (7-0). These games counted in the league standings, allowing Purdue and Michigan to earn a share of the conference title with Northwestern (all three at 5-1). Otherwise, Northwestern would have been the outright champion with a league mark of 5-0.

In Willaman's third season, Ohio State finished at 6-3 overall and 4-2 in league action. The Buckeyes drew 163,356 fans for their five home games, an average of 32,671. Lew Hinchman repeated as an All-American and was joined on the select team by quarterback Carl Cramer. Both were also chosen for All-Big Ten honors. Tackle Bob Haubrich was selected Ohio State's MVP.

1931

Date	Opponent			
October 3	Cincinnati	W	67	6
October 10	Vanderbilt	L	21	26
October 17	at Michigan	W	20	7
October 24	Northwestern	L	0	10
October 31	at Indiana	W	13	0
November 7	Navy (HC)	W	20	0
November 14	at Wisconsin	W	6	0
November 21	Illinois	W	40	0
November 28	at Minnesota	L	7	19
Total Points			194	68

Season Record: 6-3
Conference: 4th Place

1932

With an abundance of experienced players returning, including Lew Hinchman, Bill

Carroll, and Carl Cramer, Ohio State was expected to make a strong run for the Big Ten title. But the season became an adventure in frustration when the Buckeyes "couldn't win their major games." With his team finishing the campaign at 4-1-3, coach Sam Willaman was really feeling the pressure from alumni, the school administration, and fans in general. Ohio State had not won a conference title since 1920. Willaman's strongest critics believed that his offense lacked imagination and that many players had vastly underachieved.

Assistant coach George Hauser received his medical degree from Ohio State in the spring of 1932. Dr. Hauser returned to the University of Minnesota to work in the Student Health Center and assist new Golden Gopher head coach Bernie Bierman. Hauser and Bierman had been teammates at Minnesota in 1915.

Final Encounter with First Opponent

Ohio State opened October 1 with a 34-7 triumph over Ohio Wesleyan before an Ohio Stadium crowd of 17,113. Bill "Blond Express" Carroll was the game's leading rusher with 115 yards. The Buckeyes' first stringers had little trouble against the Battling Bishops, but there was a noticeable change in talent when Willaman sent in his reserves.

Together Again

Often during the 1932 season, Lew Hinchman, Bill Carroll and Buzz Wetzel were in the Buckeye backfield together. All three had been teammates at Columbus North High School, located on Arcadia Avenue just north of the Ohio State campus.

This was the 29th and final meeting between these neighboring schools. Ohio State played its very first game at Ohio Wesleyan on May 3, 1890, and OWU provided the opposition for OSU's first contest at Ohio Stadium on October 7, 1922. The Buckeyes had a decided edge in the all-time series at 26-2-1.

Three of OSU's next four games ended in ties, causing Buckeye fans to become increasingly critical of the program. Ohio State's poor tackling and sluggish offensive attack helped underdog Indiana leave Columbus with a 7-7 deadlock. A gathering of only 17,183 watched IU's Fitzhugh Lyons miss a field goal attempt from the OSU 20, otherwise the Hoosiers would have pulled off a huge upset. Carroll scored OSU's touchdown with a five-yard sweep around left end in the second period. Indiana finished the season at 2-5-1.

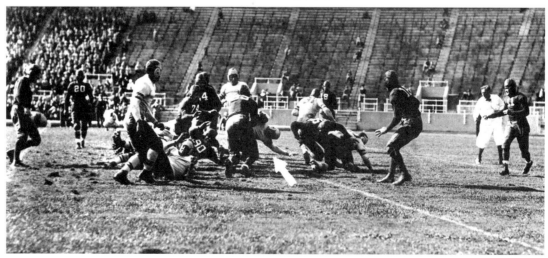

Bill "Blond Express" Carroll (arrow) scores Ohio State's lone touchdown against Indiana.

All-American tackle Ted Rosequist

Columbus Citizen
Saturday, October 29, 1932

Scoring Punch Conspicuously Absent

Michigan posted a 14-0 triumph the following Saturday before an Ohio Stadium crowd of 42,038—not a bad turnout considering the severe economics of the 1930s. Quarterback Harry Newman tossed two scoring passes in the first half and kicked both extra points. Ohio State effectively moved the ball most of the afternoon, but lacked the ability to score. Five times the Wolverines stopped the Buckeye offense inside the Michigan 10-yard line.

The following weekend at Pittsburgh, Ohio State delivered one of its most inspired efforts of the season, holding the highly favored Pitt Panthers to a scoreless tie. In the game's last minute of play, the Buckeyes fashioned one of the strongest defensive stands in school history. Pittsburgh had moved to a first down at the OSU one. The Buckeyes miraculously held on three con-secutive plunges, then batted down the Panthers' desperation pass on fourth down to preserve the tie.

Back home for Dad's Day on October 29, Ohio State had to settle for yet another tie, this one a 7-7 deadlock with Wisconsin. The Buckeyes scored in the first quarter as fullback Mickey Vuchinich bulled into the end zone for the final yard. Lew Hinchman's 29-yard pass to Sid Gillman on the previous play had advanced the ball to the Badger one. Wisconsin halfback Marvin Peterson tied the game with an elusive 70-yard punt return in the second period.

Lew Hinchman, three-time All-American quarterback and halfback

133

Script Ohio— The Rest of the Story

The Ohio State Marching Band performed its very first "Script Ohio" at halftime of the Pittsburgh game on October 10, 1936. But, according to George N. Hall, Michigan '35, the very FIRST Script Ohio was performed by the University of Michigan band four years earlier at the Ohio State-Michigan game of October 15, 1932. Hall, now retired and living in Ann Arbor, was a member of Michigan's band that season. He provided the accompanying picture and an article that appeared in the *Michigan Daily* on Sunday, October 16, 1932, describing Michigan script formation.

Reverend Joe Hotchkiss, a Michigan graduate and longtime recruiter for the Wolverines, now lives in Columbus. It is his understanding that the Ohio State Department of Music asked each visiting band in 1932 to do a salute to the Buckeyes as part of its halftime show, since that season Ohio State was celebrating the 10th anniversary of Ohio Stadium. Michigan came up with Script Ohio, then gave the band charts to OSU Band Director Eugene J. Weigel, since Michigan would no longer have a reason to use the formation.

There are strong differences of opinion, however, as to whether Michigan really performed a moving script formation. Hall loves to talk about the controversy. "I concede that Ohio people can both write and spell and that their brass band is reasonably good," he says, "but they weren't the first to do the script. We were!'

Michigan band performing "Script Ohio."

Ohioans Show Real Power In Major Victory

Hinchman, Oliphant And Rosequist Sparkle In Downing Northwestern.

PASS OFFENSE CLICKS

Ohio Displays Strength In Third Quarter; Purple Fumbles Costly.

Columbus Dispatch
Sunday, November 6, 1932

The October 30 *Columbus Dispatch* provided this description of the game:

Despite the fact that they outplayed Wisconsin in every department of the game and rolled up a tremendous margin in yardage from both straight running and aerial formations, Ohio State's football warriors suffered one fatal lapse Saturday afternoon and had to be content with a 7 to 7 tie.

Only 17,009 spectators, probably the smallest crowd that ever saw a Big Ten game in the stadium witnessed the final home conference encounter of the season. The deadlock with the Badgers marked the third stale-mate the Ohioans have encountered in five games and sent them into the November portion of their schedule still without a victory over a major opponent.

Led by the fine play of Lew Hinchman, Ohio State swept to its first significant victory of the season with a 20-6 triumph at Northwestern. The Buckeyes spoiled homecoming for a Dyche Stadium crowd of 30,000, by dominating play after the Wildcats had taken an early 6-0 lead. Marshall Oliphant was very effective at quarterback after Carl Cramer was sidelined with an injured ankle.

Wildcats and Quakers Are Apparently Buck's Favorite Dish

Columbus Citizen, Monday, November 14, 1932

1932				
October 1	Ohio Wesleyan	W	34	7
October 8	Indiana	T	7	7
October 15	Michigan	L	0	14
October 22	at Pittsburgh	T	0	0
October 29	Wisconsin	T	7	7
November 5	at Northwestern	W	20	6
November 12	Pennsylvania (HC)	W	19	0
November 19	at Illinois	W	3	0
Total Points			90	41

Season Record: 4-1-3
Conference: 4th Place

1933

The Buckeyes returned home November 12 for an impressive 19-0 homecoming win over Pennsylvania. Only 19,301 fans braved an afternoon of wintry blasts to see OSU take command of the game over a strong eastern opponent. Ohio State led in first downs, 17-7, and total offensive yards, 236-68.

Willaman's squad closed out its season with a 3-0 victory at Illinois, marking the first time Ohio State had been able to win three straight from the Fighting Illini. In the last two minutes of play, Mickey Vuchinich booted a muddy football through the uprights from the 17-yard line for the game's only points. The Memorial Stadium crowd of 6,718 was the smallest to see Ohio State play all season.

Lew Hinchman was named All-American for the third season and was also selected Ohio State's MVP. Sid Gillman, Joe Gailus and Ted Rosequist were also chosen All-America. All four were named All-Big Ten. The Buckeyes drew a total of 113,718 fans for their five home games for an average of 22,743, lowest in Ohio Stadium history.

Ohio State opened camp in the fall of 1933 with many returning veterans and several promising sophomores. Pressure was mounting on Sam Willaman, whose four-year record was 19-9-5 but only 10-7-4 in league

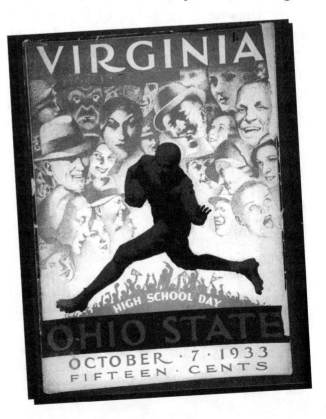

VIRGINIA

HIGH SCHOOL DAY

OHIO STATE

OCTOBER · 7 · 1933
FIFTEEN · CENTS

competition. Backfield coach Don Miller retired from football so he could devote more time to his promising law practice, and end coach Wes Fesler moved to Harvard as head basketball coach and assistant coach in football.

The Buckeyes scored at least twice in each quarter to demolish Virginia in the October 7 opener, 75-0. Nine different players scored 11 touchdowns. At the time it was OSU's fourth highest single game score, topped only by a 128-0 win over Oberlin in 1916, an 80-0 triumph against Miami in 1904, and an 80-0 victory over Marietta in 1892. The attendance of 42,001 was a season-opener record for Ohio Stadium. Nearly 30,000 of the fans were high school students from all parts of Ohio who were admitted free as guests of the university.

Ohio State's 20-0 home victory over Vanderbilt the following Saturday was more one-sided than indicated by the final score. Willaman's first team played sparingly after it scored two touchdowns in the game's first ten minutes. Vanderbilt never crossed the 50-yard line. Receiving one of the loudest rounds of applause from the crowd of 21,358 was Sam Drakulich, who returned a fourth-quarter interception to the Vanderbilt nine-yard line. Drakulich was a 145-pound senior quarterback from Salem, Ohio, who had seen little action during his first two seasons.

Season's Single Setback

The atmosphere changed radically at Ann Arbor on October 21 before a partisan Michigan Stadium crowd of 82,606. Playing in 80-degree temperatures, the Wolverines outplayed Ohio State in every phase of the game and won, 13-0. OSU's offense was able to register just three first downs. Sam Willaman's popularity with the press hardly improved when he refused to be interviewed following his team's disappointing effort. The October 22 *Columbus Dispatch* carried the following game description:

Michigan rose to the occasion here this afternoon and knocked Ohio State's challenge for Western Conference football honors to all parts of the gridiron. There was not a single department of the game in which Harry Kipke's championship squad demonstrated any weakness.

The double wing back formation as used by Ohio State is supposed to have its greatest strength from the trickery and deception that go with clever ball handling. However, Michigan with a modified punt formation, demonstrated that whirls, spinners, laterals, etc., mixed with straight offensive thrusts, are far more effective than anything the Buckeyes had to offer from the double wing back formation.

The Buckeyes recovered from the Michigan debacle by winning the remainder of their games, beginning at home with a 12-0 verdict over Northwestern before a home-

Legendary stars Pete Stinchcomb (left) and Chic Harley, who led Ohio State to national prominence during the Buckeyes' last seasons at old Ohio Field, got together at homecoming against Northwestern. Stinchcomb and Harley are both members of the College Football Hall of Fame.

The Buckeyes of 1933

coming crowd of 34,987. OSU's defense scored both touchdowns. In the first period, Stan Pincura recovered Harry Leeper's fumble in the end zone as Leeper struggled while trying to handle an Ohio State punt. Halfway through the second quarter, Sid Gillman grabbed Hugh Duvall's fumble in mid-air and raced 52 yards for his team's second six-pointer. Fullback John Kabealo of Youngstown kept the Wildcats deep in their own territory most of the afternoon, averaging 41 yards on 16 punts.

The legendary Chic Harley sat on the Ohio State bench to provide encouragement. For the first time in at least four seasons, Buckeye players did not wear long stockings. It was felt that the garments got very heavy from perspiration and impeded the players' speed. Northwestern led in first downs, 9 to 5, and total offensive yardage, 206 to 109. This was the Wildcats' first loss in Ohio Stadium.

Sophomores Shine

There were just 23,698 at the horseshoe November 4 to see the Buckeyes shut out Indiana, 21-0. Willaman's wing back formation worked well, as sophomores Dick Heekin, Stan Pincura, and John Kabealo each scored touchdowns. Particularly effective was a new "spinner play," which the coach had installed in his offense. The victory marked the first season in the 12-year history of Ohio Stadium that the Buckeyes had been able to win two conference games at home.

Ohio State continued its impressive play with a 20-7 victory at Pennsylvania before an Armistice Day crowd of 40,000. Buckeye

Columbus Citizen, Saturday, November 11, 1933

"Bad-Day-All-The-Way-Around"

Indiana's trip to Columbus was far from satisfactory for both the football team and the band. Bob Terry, IU's student band conductor in '33, recalled that the truck carrying the band instruments broke down and did not reach Ohio Stadium until late in the third quarter. The Indiana Marching Band performed its half-time show after the game.

tackle Ted Rosequist was one of the game's heroes with his outstanding defensive play against the Quakers. Approximately 1,000 OSU alums from all parts of the East had traveled to Philadelphia for the contest, including Bill Daugherty, composer of "Across the Field," who lived in New York. In the press box was noted coach Glenn "Pop" Warner.

Halfback Jack Smith's 55-yard touchdown sprint behind the excellent blocking of guard Joe Gailus, in the game's first three minutes of play, was all Ohio State needed to edge Wisconsin, 6-0. The November 18 crowd of approximately 10,000 was one of the smallest ever to attend a game at Camp Randall Stadium. The big story of the weekend came from Ann Arbor where Minnesota battled Michigan to a scoreless tie, breaking the Wolverines' three-year conference winning streak at 14 games.

"Twelfth Man" Benefits Buckeyes

Ohio State made it five straight with a thrilling 7-6 triumph over Illinois in the season's final game on November 25. The Buckeyes scored with a 42-yard third-quarter march, capped by Dick Heekin's sweep around left end for the final seven yards. Mickey Vuchinich's crucial extra-point kick was good, giving OSU the lead at 7-0. Illinois retaliated in the final period with a perfectly thrown 21-yard scoring toss from quarterback Jack Beynon to reserve end Bob Wright, who wrestled the ball from several OSU defenders. David Cook's placement attempt was partially blocked, leaving the score at 7-6. But the action was far from over.

Late in the game the Fighting Illini moved rapidly from their own 35 to the OSU 15. Beynon swept wide for two yards to the 13-yard line with approximately one minute remaining. A Buckeye fan who had a gun and was seated on the stadium's west side, fired a blank cartridge into the air that sounded exactly like an official's shot, sig-

BUCKEYES CLOSE CAMPAIGN WITH WIN OVER 'ILLINI'

Columbus Dispatch, Sunday, November 26, 1933

Changing Traditions

From 1919 through 1933, the Ohio State-Illinois contest was the last game of the regular season for both teams. The Buckeyes closed out their 1934 season against Iowa. Ohio State and Michigan began the tradition of meeting in the season's final game in 1935.

nalling the end of a game. Players from both teams swarmed onto the field, believing the game was over, and some fans headed for the exits.

After the officials were finally able to clear the field, Illinois lined up for Cook to attempt a field goal. Cook's concentration was obviously affected by all the confusion, and his short kick veered low and to the left of the goal post. OSU's "twelfth man" may have helped the Buckeyes preserve their single-point victory.

Ohio State finished Willaman's fifth campaign with a very fine record of 7-1, outscoring their eight opponents, 161-26. Five of their seven victories were shutouts. With a conference record of 4-1, the Buckeyes finished third in the Big Ten behind Michigan at 5-0-1 and Minnesota at 2-0-4. Joe Gailus repeated as an All-American and All-Big Ten selection, and Mickey Vuchinich was chosen the team's MVP. The Buckeyes drew 139,065 fans in their five home dates, for an average of 27,813.

Willaman Resigns

The Buckeyes' 1933 campaign was excellent by most standards, but there was substantial discontent among alumni groups, the "downtown" coaches, and even the Ohio State Athletic Department.

OSU had still not won a Big Ten title since 1920. The *Lantern,* OSU's student newspaper, openly called for a new coach. Sam Willaman's supporters called the attacks "unfair." To the surprise of few, Willaman officially resigned on January 30, 1934, 66 days after the season's last game. That same day, Western Reserve announced that Willaman had been hired as head football coach, and had been granted a full professorship of physical education.

Sam Willaman, who suffered from a chronic intestinal ailment, had decided several weeks earlier to leave his Ohio State post, but had delayed making his decision public until he had secured another position (it was

St. John Seeks New Coach As Willaman Quits

Others On Ohio State University Coaching Staff to Stay No Matter Who Is Selected As Successor, Says Director.

GOES TO WESTERN RESERVE

Football Mentor to Become Professor At Cleveland University; Receives Higher Salary Than at the State University.

Columbus Dispatch, Wednesday, January 31, 1934

revealed later that the Athletic Board knew of Willaman's plans prior to his public announcement). Those close to Willaman indicated that, after his resignation, he appeared to be "happy" for the first time in many weeks. Others revealed that he was looking forward to a "fresh start" at Western Reserve. Willaman's five-year Ohio State record was 26-10-5 (69.5%), which included a conference mark of 14-8-4 (61.5%).

Family Affairs

The Buckeyes' starting halfbacks, Dick Heekin and Jack Smith were the sons of Varsity "O" men. R. B. "Heinie" Heekin and Leonard Smith both won letters during their undergraduate days at Ohio State.

1933

October 7	Virginia	W	75	0
October 14	Vanderbilt	W	20	0
October 21	at Michigan	L	0	13
October 28	Northwestern (HC)	W	12	0
November 4	Indiana	W	21	0
November 11	at Pennsylvania	W	20	7
November 18	at Wisconsin	W	6	0
November 25	Illinois	W	7	6
Total Points			161	26

Season Record: 7-1
Conference: 3rd Place

All-America end Sid Gillman, coach Sam Willaman, and two-time All-America guard Joe Gailus. Gillman and Gailus were Ohio State's 1933 co-captains. Gillman became a distinguished college and professional coach and is a member of the Professional Football Hall of Fame.

FRANCIS SCHMIDT
MR. RAZZLE DAZZLE

"How about Michigan? They put their pants on one leg at a time, the same as we do!" Francis Albert Schmidt furnished that noted response to a sportswriter's question on March 2, 1934, the day he was introduced as the new football coach at Ohio State. Since the Buckeyes had lost nine of their last 12 games against Michigan, defeating the Wolverines was obviously one of Schmidt's primary objectives. Schmidt later formed the "Pants Club," awarding miniature metallic golden football pants to his players and coaches following each triumph over Michigan (a tradition that has continued since OSU's victory in 1934).

Francis Schmidt, 46, was Ohio State's 14th football coach and the first with a na-tional reputation. He moved to Ohio State from Texas Christian University, where his teams won two Southwest Conference titles in five seasons while posting a superb over-all record of 47-5-5 (86.8%). While Schmidt gained fame primarily for his offensive in-novations, his Horned Frogs also played su-perb defense, shutting out their opponents 34 times during his 57 games at the Fort Worth school. Schmidt enjoyed successful coaching stints at Arkansas and Tulsa before moving to TCU in 1929. He also guided Texas Christian to two SWC basketball titles.

The Buckeyes' new coach played college football at Nebraska, where he earned a law degree. During World War I, Schmidt served in Europe as a U.S. Army captain. Regarded as an offensive genius, Schmidt's 1916 Tulsa

SCHMIDT OFFICIALLY SELECTED

Ohio State Journal, Saturday, March 3, 1934

squad destroyed the Missouri School of Mines, 117-0, to complete the season with a perfect 10-0 record.

First Multi-Year Agreement

Schmidt was granted a three-year contract at an annual salary believed to be $7,500. It was the first time that an Ohio State coach had been under contract for a period of more than one year. The Athletic Department refused to reveal other candidates who may have been considered for the position. However, there were several unconfirmed reports that Clark Shaughnessy of Chicago had been contacted and that Detroit's Gus Dorais and Don Peden of Ohio University had been in the running.

Francis Schmidt's outgoing personality and wide-open style of football contrasted strongly with the routine of his predecessor, Sam Willaman. Schmidt was a tall, out-spoken, likable individual, whose entire life centered around football. He created a "razzle-dazzle" offense, in which each play was designed to go "all the way." Two or three laterals behind the line of scrimmage were very common, and his offensive system contained over 300 plays, which were run from seven different formations.

Schmidt's colorful explanations of his many offensive patterns were often preceded by his favorite expression, "Lookee here." He possessed an excessive passion for diagramming new plays and formations, and it was often suggested

that his abundant notes would fill several large trunks. An intense eccentric with unlimited energy, Schmidt spent 12 months a year formulating new strategies.

1934

Assistant coaches Ernie Godfrey, Dick Larkins, and Floyd Stahl were retained from Sam Willaman's 1933 group. George Staten was a new addition to Schmidt's first coaching staff.

Merle Wendt, Trevor Rees, and Sam Busich started most of the season at end. Charlie Hamrick, Gilbert Harre, and Lud Yards handled the tackles, captain Regis Mohahan and Inwood Smith were the guards, and Gomer Jones manned the center spot. Stan Pincura was the starting quarterback and recieved strong support from Frank Fisch and

Ohio State President George W. Rightmire, coach Francis Schmidt, and center Gomer Jones

Tippy Dye. Frank Boucher, Jack Smith, Dick Heekin, Dick Beltz, and Frank Antenucci all logged time at halfback, and Buzz Wetzel, John Bettridge, and John Kabealo provided great strength at fullback.

Impressive Inauguration

Ohio State opened October 6 with a powerful 33-0 triumph over Indiana. Like Schmidt, coach Bo McMillin was in his first year with the Hoosiers, who had opened the previous week with a 27-0 win over Ohio University. Fans were already fascinated with Schmidt's new brand of football, as evidenced by the attendance of 47,736, at the time the largest opening-day crowd in Ohio State history. Despite a number of fumbles and bad passes, the Buckeyes finished the afternoon impressively with three fourth-quarter touchdowns.

Ohio State used nearly every imaginable offensive alignment that afternoon, including the single wing, double wing, and short punt formations. In the first quarter, Frank Boucher brought the fans to their feet with a breathtaking 78-yard gallop for the season's first touchdown. The long-striding junior broke through the right side of IU's line on a fake reverse, then slid free to the east sideline and raced into the stadium's south end zone for the score.

McMillen's team used a very unconventional attack, which was questioned as to its legality. The Hoosiers broke from their huddle with six linemen and five players in the backfield—quarterback, two halfbacks, and two fullbacks. Before the ball was snapped, one of the backs would quickly shift up to the right guard position, giving IU the required seven players on the offensive line. The famed Pop Warner, head coach at Temple, visited with Schmidt after the game to congratulate him on his initial Ohio State victory. Warner was in Columbus to scout Indiana, Temple's opponent the following Saturday.

Year's Lone Loss

At Illinois, the Buckeyes were dealt their only setback of the season, 14-13, before an emotional Memorial Stadium crowd of 24,831. Down by 14 points heading into the final quarter, OSU rallied for two touchdowns, but Regis Monahan's all-important extra-point attempt following the first score was right of the goal post. Ohio State was unable to convert either of two other golden opportunities, being stopped at the Illini one in the second quarter and the 14 shortly after halftime.

Illinois scored its second touchdown with a new play known as the "flying trapeze," which was an outgrowth of coach Bob Zuppke's famed flea-flicker play. Five different players handled the ball on the trapeze play (hand-off, two laterals, forward pass), which went 36 yards for the score. Famed Illini halfback Red Grange was honored at halftime, commemorating his four-touchdown performance against Michigan ten years earlier in the stadium dedication game.

Totally Preoccupied

Coach Francis Schmidt concentrated solely on football 365 days a year. He was never without his 3 X 5 cards and stubby pencil, and he would continually make notes to himself as a new play came to mind.

One morning Schmidt and Athletic Director L. W. St. John decided to go hunting east of Columbus. Schmidt, who was driving, stopped for gasoline. St. John went inside to purchase some food, while Schmidt stayed in the car to work on some new plays for next season. When the service station attendant was through, Schmidt paid for the gasoline and drove away. He was several miles down the road before realizing he had left St. John (his boss) back at the station.

The Buckeyes rebounded to finish the season with six straight victories, beginning with a strenuous win over talented Colgate, 10-7, before 29,130 at Ohio Stadium on October 20. Coach Andy Kerr's squad had aspirations of playing in the Rose Bowl and winning the national title. OSU's 10 points represented the highest total against Colgate since the Red Raiders lost to New York University in 1931, 13-0. Jack Smith, playing with an injured knee which hampered his speed, plunged one yard for OSU's touchdown late in the fourth period. Monahan's second-quarter field goal from the 22-yard line was the eventual margin of victory.

While Ohio State was defeating Colgate, the "college game of the season" was staged at Pitt Stadium between two of the most powerful teams of the 1930s—Pittsburgh and Minnesota. The Golden Gophers won, 13-7, handing Jock Sutherland's Panthers their only setback of the season. Bernie Bierman's Minnesota squad finished the season with an overall mark of 8-0, to claim the school's first of six national titles.

At cold and windy Evanston, Ohio State survived George Potter's 90-yard touchdown

return of the opening kickoff to defeat Northwestern, 28-6. In a very physically tough game, the Buckeyes generated three third-quarter touchdowns to put the game out of reach, after failing to capitalize on three first-half scoring opportunities. OSU led in total offense, 317 yards to 59.

Ohio State scored 11 touchdowns, even after Francis Schmidt cleared his bench early in the second half, and completely outclassed Western Reserve, 76-0. The Buckeyes amassed 706 yards of total offense and scored

58 Seasons Between Ohio Opponents

Ohio State's 76-0 triumph over Western Reserve on November 3, 1934, was the Buckeyes' last encounter with an Ohio opponent until September 12, 1992, when OSU opened its season with a 17-6 victory over Bowling Green.

All-American guard and captain Regis Monahan

34-0 In '34

To the delight of 68,678 frenzied fans, Francis Schmidt's team buried Michigan at Ohio Stadium on November 17, 34-0. The glorious homecoming triumph was just OSU's seventh win over the Wolverines in 31 games, and the 34 points were by far the Buckeyes' largest margin of victory in the series. Ohio State's highest previous spread was 14 points in 1921 (OSU 14 - UM 0).

Unleashing a ground attack of bone-crushing ferocity, OSU scored in each of the first two quarters to lead 13-0 at halftime. Dick Heekin scored from the 1-yard line, ripping through a large hole with ridiculous ease, and Buzz Wetzel tallied from the 5-yard line. The Buckeyes really turned on the heat in the final period. Frank Antenucci scored by pouncing on Jack Smith's fumble just as the ball was bouncing into the end zone. Ohio State took to the airways for its final two touchdowns—Merle Wendt took a perfect pass from Frank Fisch to complete a 66-yard play, and Frank Cumiskey was on the receiving end of a 33-yarder from Tippy Dye.

The Buckeyes led in first downs, 24-3, and in total offense, 460 yards to 40. Fans tore down the goal posts for what was believed to have been the first time in Ohio State history. Michigan's Most Valuable Player in '34 was senior center Gerald R. Ford

on every possession except three. The game was played at Cleveland's old League Park before a gathering of approximately 11,000. The Redcats were led by former Ohio State coach Sam Willaman, who was in his only season as Western Reserve's head coach. Willaman suffered from an insistent stomach illness and passed away the following summer at the age of 45.

Back home on November 10 before an appreciative assemblage of 32,227, Ohio State's airtight defense paved the way for a 33-0 trouncing of Chicago. The Maroons played without Jay Berwanger, their ace halfback who was injured. It was the first meeting between the two since 1927.

The renowned Amos Alonzo Stagg had been forced to retire at age 70 following the 1932 season, as part of new President Robert Hutchins' decision to de-emphasize football. Clark Shaughnessy took over as Chicago coach in 1933, and remained with the Maroons until football was dropped as a varsity sport after the fall of 1939.

First Captains Breakfast

Former Ohio State captains gather for breakfast each fall on the Sunday following the homecoming game. The concept was initiated in 1934 by Columbus businessman Walter Jeffrey, who believed that Buckeye captains of the past should be so honored. Approximately 20 former captains and coaches attended the first breakfast, held at the Scioto Country Club. Each captain is presented with a mug bearing his name and season.

(jersey #48), a future President of the United States.

Ohio State closed out its season at home with a vicious 40-7 triumph over Iowa, as six different players scored touchdowns. The November 25 *Columbus Dispatch* provided the following description of the game and of the season:

> *Ohio State's mightiest football team in two decades, if not for all time, carved a secure niche in the Buckeye Hall of Fame Saturday. Taking to the air with a certainty that constituted first degree*

Three-time All-American end Merle Wendt

Halfback Dick Heekin

> *cruelty, the Buckeyes shot Iowa's hapless Hawkeyes completely out of the sky and then plucked the hapless creatures clear down to the pin feathers with a 40 to 7 victory.*
>
> *Call it sacrilegious if you will, you who hallow the memory of Ohio's great aggregations of 1916, 1917, 1919, 1920 and 1921—Ohio Saturday had a team which for sheer savagery, deception, speed, trickery and plain unvarnished power, knows no superior in Buckeye annals.*

While the Buckeyes were defeating Iowa, Minnesota swamped Wisconsin, 34-0, to capture the outright Big Ten title (5-0, 8-0). Ohio State finished second (5-1, 7-1), followed by Illinois (4-1, 7-1). End Merle Wendt and guard Regis Monahan were chosen for All-American and All-Big Ten honors, center Gomer Jones was selected the team MVP. Fans became attracted to Francis Schmidt's wide-open style of football. The five home games drew 205,095 fans for an average of 41,019, at the time the second highest in Ohio Stadium history.

1934

October 6	Indiana	W	33	0
October 13	at Illinois	L	13	14
October 20	Colgate	W	10	7
October 27	at Northwestern	W	28	6
November 3	at Western Reserve	W	76	0
November 10	Chicago	W	33	0
November 17	Michigan (HC)	W	34	0
November 24	Iowa	W	40	7
Total Points			267	34

Season Record: 7-1
Conference: 2nd Place

Columbus Citizen, Saturday, December 1, 1934

1935

There was strong optimism around the Ohio State campus as Francis Schmidt began preparations for his second campaign in Columbus. Returning at ends were regulars Trevor Rees of Dover and Merle Wendt of Middletown. Manning the tackle spots were huge Charley Hamrick of Gallipolis, Ernie Roush of Blacklick, and Gilbert Harre of Toledo.

Lining up at guard were returnee Inwood Smith from Mansfield and Jim Karcher of Forest, Ohio. Gust Zarnas, a fine sophomore from Youngstown, drew considerable playing time as the season progressed. At center was captain Gomer Jones of Cleveland, an outstanding lineman who rates as one of the finest in school history.

Talented Stan Pincura of Lorain returned at quarterback, with solid backup strength from Tippy Dye of Pomeroy and Nick Wasylik of Astoria, New York. Wasylik was the only out-of-stater among the 47 members of the '35 squad. Veterans Dick (Bull) Heekin of Cincinnati, John Bettridge of Toledo, and Frank Boucher of Kent provided plenty of speed and strength at halfback. Their play was supplemented by Dick Beltz of Findlay and "Jumping Joe" Williams, a speedy sophomore from Barberton.

Two veterans returned at fullback—John Kabealo of Youngstown and Frank Antenucci from Niles. Kabealo was an excellent punter and was one of four brothers to play for the Buckeyes during the 1930s. Sophomore Jim McDonald of Springfield also saw considerable action. Pete Stinchcomb, All-America in 1919-20, became an assistant coach, and Fritz Mackey, a three-year letterman tackle in 1924-25-26, joined Schmidt's staff as freshman coach.

The Buckeyes opened the season October 5 with a 19-6 victory over stubborn Kentucky. The attendance of 56,686 was, at the time, the largest opening-day crowd in Ohio

1935 Big Ten co-champions

Stadium history. OSU's offense played well in the first and fourth quarters, but stalled frequently during the middle of the game. Gomer Jones had a fine afternoon with two interceptions and a fumble recovery. Bettridge scored twice and Williams once, as the Buckeyes outgained the Wildcats in total offense, 331 yards to 159.

Ohio Stadium's Highest Score

The following Saturday Ohio State completely annihilated the Drake Bulldogs by the unbelievable score of 85-7. This game has appropriately been nicknamed the "Drake Relays." Schmidt used all 46 of his able-bodied players to accumulate 13 touchdowns and five conversions. His Buckeyes amassed 434 yards rushing, 236 by passing, and 241 on punt and kickoff returns. Ohio State led in first downs, 39-3. The 85 points is the highest single-game score in Ohio Stadium history.

The Buckeyes had little trouble with Northwestern in the season's first conference game, winning 28-7 at home on October 19. The following weekend at Bloomington, OSU overpowered Indiana 28-6 after spotting the Hoosiers an early 6-0 lead. At 4-0, the Buckeyes owned a 10-game winning streak that stretched over two seasons. They were ready for what would become one of the most famous afternoons in all of Ohio State athletics.

"The Game of the Century"

The Ohio State-Notre Dame encounter of November 2, 1935, is a game that will *"live in infamy in the annals of Ohio State football."* The Irish were 5-0 with wins over Kansas, Carnegie Tech, Wisconsin, Pittsburgh, and Navy. Notre Dame's captain and left tackle,

Joe Sullivan, had died of pneumonia the previous March. Instead of electing another captain, the team was dedicating each game to its missing teammate. Mild-mannered Elmer Layden, who in 1924 had been a member of ND's famed "Four Horsemen," guided Notre Dame. Taking a page from Knute Rockne's coaching manual, Layden waged psychological warfare by telling reporters his team would be lucky to hold the Buckeyes to five or six touchdowns.

Ticket demand for the Ohio Stadium affair was at an all-time high, even with the country submerged in the Great Depression. Athletic Director L. W. St. John estimated 200,000 tickets could have been sold. Scalpers scoffed at any ticket offer under $50. The game attracted record media coverage, including noted writers Grantland Rice, Paul Gallico, Damon Runyon, and Francis Wallace.

The Buckeyes struck early when fullback Frank Antenucci picked-off a Notre Dame pass at the OSU 25, advanced it 10 yards, then lateraled to halfback Frank Boucher who raced 65 yards for the game's first touchdown. Dick Beltz's conversion made it 7-0. The errant Irish pass had been thrown by halfback Mike Layden, younger brother of the coach.

Early in the second quarter, Stan Pincura seized another ND pass and returned it to midfield. The Buckeyes marched in for their second touchdown, with Joe Williams taking it across from the three. OSU held a 13-0 halftime lead, but had dominated the action much more than suggested by the score. The tenacious Buckeye defense had applied great pressure to the Irish passing attack, and had completely smothered the visitors' running efforts.

Layden surprised everyone by announcing his second-team "shock troops" would start the second half. The third quarter was scoreless, but the visitors began to gain momentum. The tide really turned on the third quarter's last play when Notre Dame half-

I Remember It Well!

Bo Gallo of O. P. Gallo Tailoring and Formal Wear in Columbus remembered an incident that occurred approximately 25 years after the famous Ohio State-Notre Dame game of 1935. One Saturday morning Gallo was getting ready to open his downtown store, when a man knocked at the front door and asked if he could have a button sewn on his coat.

Gallo took the man inside and personally began to sew on the button. Since it was a football Saturday, Gallo asked him if he was in town to see the Ohio State game. "Why, yes," he replied, "I'm one of the officials who will be working today's game at Ohio Stadium."

The two introduced themselves, with the man identifying himself as Mike Layden. Gallo asked him if he was related to the former Notre Dame football coach, Elmer Layden. "Yes, Elmer is my older brother," he said.

Gallo then recalled the '35 Ohio State-Notre Dame game, mentioning that his brother-in-law Frank Antenucci had been a Buckeye fullback who played against the Irish that afternoon. "Frank made a great interception, then lateraled to Frank Boucher who sped 65 yards for Ohio State's first touchdown," he remembered.

Gallo then asked Layden if he had seen this game. Layden laughed a little, then said he not only had seen the contest, but that he had played football under his brother at Notre Dame, and had been one of the starting halfbacks that afternoon. With that, Gallo said, "Do you remember Frank's interception?" Layden replied, "Mr. Gallo, I remember it very well—I'm the one who threw the pass!"

back Andy Pilney (remember the name) returned one of John Kabealo's booming punts 53 yards to the OSU 12.

The game's final 15 minutes were truly unbelievable. The Irish opened the quarter

Quarterback Tippy Dye (50) maneuvers around left end against Notre Dame. At far right is halfback Dick Heekin (6).

by going the needed 12 yards for their first touchdown. Pilney passed 10 yards to quarterback Frank Gaul, and fullback Steve Miller bolted the final two yards for the touchdown. Ken Stilley's extra point attempt hit the crossbar and wobbled back onto the field, leaving OSU with a 13-6 lead.

The Buckeyes were unable to move on the ensuing possession and again punted. Notre Dame quickly marched for what appeared to be another score, but Miller fumbled into the end zone from the one-yard line. Ohio State's Jim Karcher recovered for a touchback, and the Buckeyes' lead appeared to be secure.

After OSU was again forced to punt, the Irish took possession at their 20 with slightly over four minutes remaining. Behind beautiful protection, Pilney rapidly moved his team the needed 80 yards for Notre Dame's second touchdown (15-yard toss to Layden). Again the all-important conversion was missed, and the Buckeyes appeared to be in position to hold on at 13-12 with less than two minutes remaining.

Francis Schmidt had made a serious tactical error in the final quarter, pulling his starting backfield and replacing them with his shorter reserves. Under 1935 college rules, a player could not return in any quarter after being taken out in that same quarter. If a player left the game in the fourth quarter, he was finished for the afternoon.

As expected, Notre Dame tried an onside kick, but the Buckeyes recovered at their own 46. While trying to run out the clock, Ohio State fumbled out of bounds on second down. Again the rules of '35 became a significant factor—possession was awarded to the team that last TOUCHED the ball before it went out, rather than the last to have possession. Irish center Henry Pojman had brushed the ball on its way out, and Notre Dame was granted the ball on its own 49 with 55 seconds remaining.

Stout-hearted Andy Pilney again went to work. Finding his receivers covered, Pilney masterfully weaved his way 32 yards to the OSU 19 before sustaining a wrenched left knee on a very hard tackle. Pilney was

Interesting Connection

The student manager of Notre Dame's 1935 team was Woody Stillwagon, father of Ohio State's Jim Stillwagon, who captured both the Outland Trophy and Lombardi Award in 1970.

Who Caught The Pass?

The famous Red Barber broadcast all of Ohio State's games in 1935, including the Notre Dame encounter. Just as Bill Shakespeare completed the winning touchdown pass, the spotter covering Notre Dame for Barber became so ecstatic, he ran from the radio booth and headed for the playing field to join in the wild celebration.

Notre Dame wore numbers only on the backs of their jerseys, and Barber could not immediately identify the receiver. With his spotter gone, it took Barber several minutes to learn it had been Wayne Millner (#38) who caught Shakespeare's final throw.

dium carrying his uniform but was denied entrance until one of ND's student managers convinced a suspicious gate attendant that McKenna was a member of the squad. This was McKenna's first and only play in a Notre Dame varsity football game.

Following is the scoring by quarters:

	1	2	3	4	Final
Notre Dame	0	0	0	18	18
Ohio State	7	6	0	0	13

The Fighting Irish led in first downs, 13-10, and total offense, 286 yards to 111. Ohio State's offense completely disappeared in the second half—zero yards rushing and no completed passes. Elmer Layden's inspirational

Buckeyes Unable To Stave Off Final Rally

Columbus Dispatch, Sunday, November 3, 1935

carried off the field on a stretcher and was replaced by Bill Shakespeare.

Shakespeare's first pass, intended for halfback Vic Wojcihcovski, was in and out of the hands of a Buckeye defender for an incompletion.....Notre Dame still had life with 30 seconds remaining. Behind great protection, Shakespeare calmly hit big Wayne Millner in the end zone for what proved to be the winning touchdown. The extra-point attempt was again missed, but it didn't matter—the Irish had just staged one of the most amazing finishes in college history to win, 18-13.

Notre Dame's scoring play, an ends-crossing pattern, was carried into the game by fourth-team quarterback Jimmy McKenna. McKenna was not a member of the traveling squad but had managed to find a way to Columbus on his own. Saturday morning McKenna showed up at Ohio Sta-

Ronald Reagan Couldn't Believe Buckeyes Lost

Retired WCHM-TV4 Sports Anchor Jimmy Crum received the Sertoma International Service to Mankind Award in 1984, in recognition of his lifetime of service to others. As part of this honor, Jimmy and his wife, Miriam, visited President and Mrs. Reagan at the White House.

When the conversation turned to Ohio State football, Reagan recalled being in Iowa City in 1935 to broadcast the Iowa-Indiana game on the same Saturday Notre Dame was playing at Ohio State. At that time, scores of other games were provided by Western Union ticker tape.

The entire nation was interested in the outcome of the Ohio State-Notre Dame game, so Reagan had frequently been announcing the score. Aware that the Buckeyes had been leading 13-0 in the fourth quarter, Reagan received a tape showing the final score: Notre Dame 18, Ohio State 13. "I thought it was an error. I couldn't believe Notre Dame would have been able to score three touchdowns in so little time," Reagan told the Crums, "so I never announced the final score."

halftime talk led the way for his squad's monumental comeback. Many spectators were still sitting in their seats 30 minutes after time had expired, too stunned to leave.

Notre Dame fans frantically tore down the goal post at the stadium's south end and marched it downtown to the lobby of the Deshler Wallick hotel, where Irish fans celebrated long into the night. Classes at Notre Dame were dismissed early the first three days of the following week, allowing students more time to celebrate the victory.

Share Space with Wolverines? No Way!

At Stagg Field the following weekend, Chicago nearly pulled off one of the season's biggest upsets against the emotionally drained Buckeyes. The three-touchdown underdog Maroons led 13-0 midway through the third quarter. Ohio State finally put together three scoring drives to come away with a very fortunate 20-13 victory.

The Ohio State team left for Chicago by train following Thursday's practice. Two pep rallies that evening, one on campus and a second at Union Station, helped erase some of the squad's downhearted feelings following the loss to Notre Dame. The Buckeyes quartered at the Windemere Hotel near the University of Chicago campus. Michigan's squad, en route to a game against Illinois at Champaign, was also staying at the same hotel.

Francis Schmidt had scheduled a Friday afternoon workout for his Buckeyes at Stagg Field. Interestingly, Michigan had also planned a Friday afternoon practice at Stagg Field. Apparently Chicago's Athletic Department felt the two squads could share the facility, but did not inform either school of this arrangement. When Schmidt learned about the plan, he had his team work out at a public park rather than share Stagg Field with the Wolverines.

A steady Saturday morning rain left the playing field very slippery. Chicago started strongly, holding Ohio State on downs inside

the one during the first period. Warren Skoning scored the game's first touchdown in the second quarter to put Chicago ahead, 6-0. The Maroons recovered a blocked punt at the OSU nine to setup the score.

Early in the second half the Buckeyes were again stopped on downs, this time at the Maroon 15. On first down, Chicago's Jay Berwanger swept OSU's left end, reversed his field, and raced 85 yards for a touchdown. His conversion made it 13-0, and the home team was sensing the upset.

The First Heisman Trophy

Jay Berwanger's run rates with the greatest of all time. In his book, *Football: A College History,* author Tom Perrin describes it as "....the run which won the Heisman for Berwanger. He sliced through tackle at the

Courtesy of Downtown Athletic Club of New York

Chicago's Jay Berwanger was the recipient of the first Heisman Trophy in 1935. Berwanger's outstanding play against Ohio State helped him achieve this distinction.

All-American center and captain Gomer Jones

20-yard line, headed for the outside, then turned back toward center. At midfield, he was sandwiched between two defensive backs. He juked each one and ran between them. Once in the clear, he outran his pursuers for the touchdown."

Lew Byrer, veteran Sports Editor for the *Columbus Citizen,* described it as "as pretty a run as I have ever seen." Writer Russ Needham characterized Berwanger as "the best back I have seen in college football in the last ten years." At season end, Jay Berwanger became the very first winner of the coveted Heisman Trophy.

The stunned Buckeyes finally put matters together with scoring drives of 63, 43, and 57 yards. Halfback Dick Heekin got the first touchdown from the one, following a 24-yard pass reception from quarterback Stan Pincura. Early in the final quarter, Pincura combined with end Merle Wendt on a 30-yard scoring pass. Dick Beltz's conversion tied the score at 13. Later that period, Joe Williams raced 15 yards for the deciding touchdown.

Sam Busich kicked the extra point to conclude the scoring at 20-13.

Chicago mounted one last effort, but Tippy Dye intercepted a Berwanger pass at the OSU 25-yard line to end the threat. The Maroons had pushed Ohio State to the limit. With a devastating upset staring them in the face, the Buckeyes had risen to the occasion. Their superior depth was a key factor in the second half. OSU fans cheered wildly when it was announced that Northwestern had beaten Notre Dame,14-7, and Illinois had toppled Michigan, 3-0.

Looking back to November 9, 1935, Berwanger still vividly remembered that afternoon. "When the game started, there were probably no more than 5,000 people in attendance," he recalled, "but there were at least 25,000 in the stands when we came out to start the second half." Many students and nearby residents had headed for the stadium after becoming aware of the possible upset.

Francis Schmidt cited captain Gomer Jones for his standout effort. He also praised

Quarterback Stan Pincura

Against Illinois, Tippy Dye returns a punt for the game's only touchdown.

the play of sophomore full-back Jim McDonald, whose fine running helped keep alive the Buckeyes' three scoring drives. Chicago finished the year at 4-4 overall and 2-3 in the conference.

First Big Ten Title Since 1920

Heading into the season's final two games, Ohio State and Minnesota were tied for the Big Ten lead with 3-0 league records. The Buckeyes and Golden Gophers would not face each other this season.

Illinois was OSU's homecoming opponent on a cold and rainy November 16. The Buckeyes won, 6-0, as Tippy Dye returned an Illini first-quarter punt from midfield for the game's only touchdown. Minnesota kept pace with a 40-0 shellacking of Michigan.

Michigan Game Becomes Season Finale

In 1935, Ohio State began the tradition of meeting Michigan in the last game of the regular season. Before a November 23 Michigan Stadium gathering of 53,322, the Buckeyes scored six touchdowns (and had two more called back on penalties) to win, 38-0. This score stands today as OSU's widest margin of victory over Michigan. Ohio State led in first downs, 20-5, and total offensive yards, 447-85.

While OSU was manhandling the Wolverines, Minnesota whipped Wisconsin, 33-7. The Buckeyes and Golden Gophers shared the Big Ten championship with records of 5-0. It was Ohio State's first league crown since 1920.

Merle Wendt and Gomer Jones were each selected All-America and All-Big Ten, and Jones was chosen the team MVP for the second season. A total of 252,950 fans attended OSU's five home games for an aver-

Fullback and punter John Kabealo

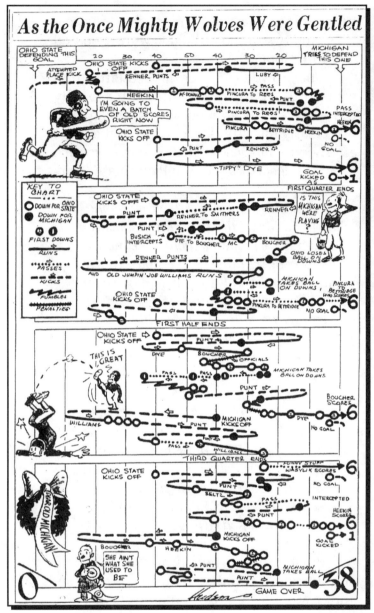

As the Once Mighty Wolves Were Gentled

Columbus Citizen, Monday, November 25, 1935

1935				
October 5	Kentucky	W	19	6
October 12	Drake	W	85	7
October 19	Northwestern	W	28	7
October 26	at Indiana	W	28	6
November 2	Notre Dame	L	13	18
November 9	at Chicago	W	20	13
November 16	Illinois (HC)	W	6	0
November 23	at Michigan	W	38	0
Total Points			237	57

Season Record: 7-1
Big Ten Co-Champion

1936

A record season-opening crowd of 72,948 showed up at Ohio Stadium October 3 to see Francis Schmidt's third Ohio State team smash New York University, 60-0. On the

age of 50,590 (highest during the first 14 seasons at Ohio Stadium). Francis Schmidt's two-season record of 14-2 included two shutout victories over Michigan. The 1935 Buckeyes were truly one of the most colorful and successful teams in all of Ohio State football.

155

Columbus Citizen, Saturday, October 3, 1936

times in their last 30 games over four seasons, and two of those defeats were executed by Minnesota.

The crowd of 71,711 watched Pittsburgh wait until late in the fourth quarter to tally the game's only touchdown, although Pitt was clearly the superior team throughout the afternoon. The October 11 *Columbus Dispatch* gave this description of the Panthers' 6-0 victory:

> *Harold Stebbins, Pittsburgh sophomore halfback, threw an extra shovel of coal into the boiler, watched the indicator on the Panther powerhouse move around to the "full steam" sign, gave an extra yank on the throttle and let nature take its course just five minutes before the Panther-Ohio State game reached the end of the allotted 60, Saturday, at the stadium.*
>
> *Running the famous Red Grange letter S play, Stebbins skirted Ohio's right end for 35 yards to cross the goal line standing up. The play was executed flawlessly. It is not a new maneuver and is in the notebook of all coaches, who credit Bob Zuppke of Illinois with devising it to break Red Grange into the open.*

Pittsburgh did not throw a single pass all afternoon. Neither team had a fumble, and it was the first time that an OSU team coached by Francis Schmidt had been shut out. Pitt led in first downs, 11 to five. The Panthers rushed for a net 243 yards, while Ohio State's offense totaled only 27 yards. Pittsburgh finished the season with an 8-1-1

game's very first play from scrimmage, Jim McDonald intercepted a Violet pass and brought it back 20 yards for the first of OSU's nine touchdowns. The Buckeye defense intercepted seven NYU passes that afternoon, the last being picked off by Nick Wasylik and returned 26 yards for the final score. *"Close the Gates of Mercy"* was the designation given to Schmidt by a sportswriter covering the assault. Apparently the writer felt the excessive scoring was not necessary, even though Ohio State used 41 substitutes. Schmidt would have liked to have saved some of those touchdowns for three of his team's next four games.

Weekend's Top Intersectional Clash

The following Saturday's competition was entirely different. Powerful Pittsburgh swept into Columbus with one of the most punishing running attacks the Buckeyes would face for many seasons. Coach Jock Sutherland's Panthers had lost only three

Initial *Script*

*S*cript Ohio, the trademark of the Ohio State Marching Band and one of the most famous formations in marching band history, was first performed at halftime of the Ohio State-Pittsburgh game on October 10, 1936.

All-American quarterback and co-captain Jim McDonald

Fundamentals Replace Razzle-Dazzle

Back home before a crowd of 44,410, Francis Schmidt reverted back to fundamental football and ground out a 7-0 victory over Indiana. By adding some "old plays" to the offense, Schmidt's razzle-dazzle element of deception was replaced by perfect execution of some old traditional plays—especially the off-tackle smash, the end run, and the simplified forward pass.

Using straight-ahead power football, Ohio State marched 60 yards in 10 plays for the game's only touchdown, midway through the second quarter. Behind perfect protection, Tippy Dye passed the final 15 yards to Merle Wendt, who cut in from the sideline and caught the ball almost directly in front of the goal post for the score. In the fourth quarter, the Buckeyes nearly scored again after driving 71 yards, but the march stalled on downs four yards short of the IU goal line.

Rules of the Game

A return match at Notre Dame on October 31 was every bit as nerve-racking as the '35 contest. The South Bend gathering of 50,017 (at the time, a Notre Dame Stadium record crowd) sat through an intense rain to see the Fighting Irish win, 7-2, after scoring on their only sustained drive of the afternoon. Coach Elmer Layden substituted frequently, particularly in the second half, and his fresh

All-American guard Inwood Smith

record, which included a 21-0 Rose Bowl victory over Washington.

On October 17, the Buckeyes finished on the short end of a 14-13 thriller at Northwestern before 35,000 "chilled to the bone" spectators. The two rivals created an afternoon of excitement from start to finish, with the lead changing hands four times. Ohio State passed for both of its touchdowns—Nick Wasylik to Mike Kabealo and Tippy Dye to Frank Cumiskey. But Merle Wendt's unsuccessful extra-point attempt following Kabealo's touchdown became the eventual margin of defeat.

Six Buckeye turnovers (three fumbles and three interceptions) greatly aided the Wildcat cause. It marked the first time Ohio State had lost consecutive games since 1930. The victory was especially sweet for Northwestern coach Lynn "Pappy" Waldorf who grew up in Cleveland.

Coach Francis Schmidt inserts some new offensive plays at halftime against Chicago. Schmidt has drawn up the plays on the blackboard pictured on his left.

Has The Shelbyville Score Been Announced?

This story was remembered by Dr. Chalmer Hixson, OSU '37, an expert on NCAA football rules and a former Professor of Physical Education at Ohio State. A group of Ohio State students who hung around together decided to attend Ohio State's game at Notre Dame. They left Columbus and headed for South Bend, Indiana, early Saturday morning. Unfortunately their car broke down near Shelbyville, Indiana, and they were forced to listen to the game on the radio while their car was being repaired.

While driving back to Columbus that evening, and not wanting to tell their friends exactly what had happened, the group decided it would be fun to tell everyone they had gone to the "Shelbyville University" game against "Snake Valley Normal." In addition to inventing Shelbyville U., one student composed lyrics to an "Oh Shelbyville" fight song.

The following season the group told their story to Leo Staley, Ohio Stadium public address announcer, and asked him to occasionally include Shelbyville when reporting other scores. Staley agreed, and once or twice a season for the next several years, he included the Shelbyville-Snake Valley Normal game when announcing scores from other games around the country. Shelbyville was usually a big winner—sometimes by as much as 55-0!

(Illustration by Tom Hayes)

troops played a big role in keeping Ohio State out of the end zone.

Meanwhile, the Buckeyes blew three golden opportunities and saw their season record slip to 2-3. Their most baffling experience was their final march in the game's last five minutes, when they drove from their 29-yard line to the ND 12. Darkness was descending in northern Indiana, making the opposing players barely visible from the sidelines.

On first down, Nick Wasylik's pass for Jumping Joe Williams was grounded in the end zone. His second-down pass also landed in the end zone incomplete, and Notre Dame was handed possession of the ball. The rules in 1936 stated that two consecutive incomplete passes into the end zone created a touchback, which awarded the ball to the defending team (this rule was later abolished). The Buckeye players argued that Wasylik's second pass struck the ground before it rolled into the end zone, but the officials didn't see it that way.

Quarterback Tippy Dye

Strong Finish

After three losses by a total of just 12 points, Ohio State closed solidly with three shutout victories. On November 7, the Buck-

Card Tricks

Coach Francis Schmidt was continually designing new plays for his offense. Quarterback Tippy Dye recalls that the Buckeyes had over 300 plays that were run from seven different formations. With such a complicated offense, the quarterbacks wrote the title of each play on 3 X 5 cards and carried these cards inside their helmets. During timeouts, they could quickly look through the cards to remind themselves of their many plays.

In the 1936 Michigan game, Dye was tackled very soundly, his helmet flew off, and his play cards all scattered across the playing field. The curious Michigan players immediately examined some of Dye's cards, but apparently they didn't learn much from them—Ohio State won the game, 21-0.

Ohio State Journal, Saturday, November 21, 1936

First *Associated Press* Poll

The weekly Associated Press college football rankings began in 1936. Minnesota (7-1) was selected the mythical national champion, followed by Louisiana State (9-0-1), Pittsburgh (8-1-1), Alabama (8-0-1), and Washington (7-2-1). Northwestern (7-1) was the only other Big Ten team to finish in the *AP's* final rankings, placing seventh. Ohio State was listed only once in any of the 1936 weekly standings, ranking 18th in the November 16 poll.

eyes steamrolled over Chicago, 44-0, before an Ohio Stadium crowd of 37,301. OSU scored six touchdowns and had four others called back because of infractions. Bill Booth added a 36-yard field goal in the second quarter. With his thoughts partially directed to

All-American tackle Charlie Hamrick

the next season, Francis Schmidt used 43 players throughout the afternoon, including 19 sophomores. The Scarlet and Gray intercepted five Chicago passes, most of them in enemy territory.

The following weekend, sophomore fullback Johnny Rabb pounded Illinois' defense for 144 yards to lead OSU over the Illini, 13-0, before a disappointed Dad's Day crowd of 19,465 at Champaign. Rabb sprinted 30 yards for his team's first touchdown midway through the third period. Bill Booth, a transfer from Illinois, scored the other six points on a five-yard Statue of Liberty play.

Game No. 400

Ohio State closed out its season with a convincing 21-0 triumph over Michigan before a thrilled homecoming crowd of 56,202. After a slow start that saw a Michigan drive stall at the OSU four, the Buckeyes relied on their passing skills to score in each of the final three quarters. Tippy Dye passed 14 yards to Frank Cumiskey to complete a 73-yard march for OSU's first touchdown. Rabb scored from 31 yards out on a lateral pass from Dye, and Nick Wasylik tallied the final touchdown with a 10-yard sweep around left end. Booth added a 23-yard field goal.

OSU dominated the game's statistics, leading in first downs, 18-5, and total offense, 341 yards to 117. Michigan did not cross the 50-yard line in the second half. This victory over the Wolverines was Ohio State's 400th all-time game (249-120-31).

Northwestern captured the outright league crown with a conference record of 6-0. Ohio State and Minnesota tied for second at 4-1. Even though OSU's overall record was only 5-3, the Buckeyes outscored their eight opponents, 160-27, giving up only four touchdowns all season. The team set a new Ohio Stadium attendance record, drawing 282,575 fans in five home dates for an average of 56,515.

End Merle Wendt repeated as an All-American, and was joined on the select team by tackle Charlie Hamrick and guard Inwood Smith. All three were chosen for All-Big Ten honors. Center Ralph Wolf was named the team's MVP.

1936				
October 3	New York University	W	60	0
October 10	Pittsburgh	L	0	6
October 17	at Northwestern	L	13	14
October 24	Indiana	W	7	0
October 31	at Notre Dame	L	2	7
November 7	Chicago	W	44	0
November 14	at Illinois	W	13	0
November 21	Michigan (HC)	W	21	0
Total Points			160	27

Season Record: 5-3
Conference: 2nd Place (Tie)

1937

The Buckeye faithful eagerly awaited the onset of Francis Schmidt's fourth campaign in Columbus. Schmidt's reputation was strong throughout the country, as evidenced by the University of Texas trying to entice Schmidt to take command of the Longhorn program. His OSU teams played an exciting style of football, put-

ting together a three-year record of 19-5.

The Ohio State football program was acquiring a "congenial personality" with which the public could relate. Even with the nation still suffering from the economic woes of the Great Depression, spectators still flocked to Ohio Stadium in record numbers. Fans took great pride in a respectable football program, especially when many of them were having great difficulty meeting their living expenses.

Beginning this season, college football players were required to wear numerals on both the front and back of their jerseys. Expectations for OSU were high this fall, despite the graduation of ends Merle Wendt and Frank Cumiskey, guard Inwood Smith, tackle Charlie Hamrick, halfbacks John Bettridge and Frank Antenucci, and quarterback Tippy Dye. Howard Blair joined Schmidt's staff as an assistant coach. The squad was saddened with the loss of halfback Bill Booth, who died in a late-summer automobile accident.

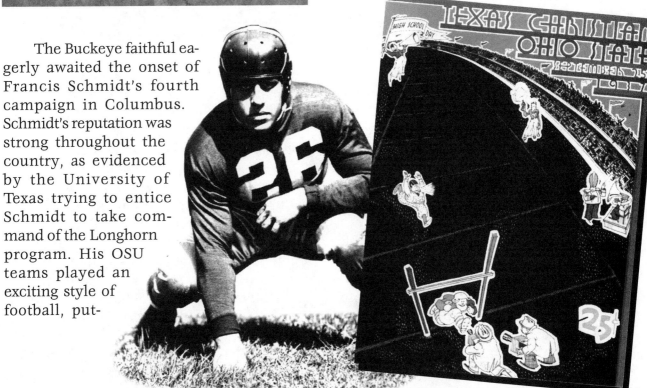

All-American guard Gust Zarnas

Southern California fullback William Sangster (in midair) is tackled by the Buckeyes. At left is Ohio State halfback Howard Wedebrook (14).

Ohio State opened September 25 with a lethargic 14-0 victory over Texas Christian. The Horned Frogs were coached by Dutch Meyer, a former Francis Schmidt assistant at TCU, who assumed the head coaching position when Schmidt came to Ohio State. One of Meyer's biggest challenges was finding a replacement for graduated quarterback slingin' Sammy Baugh, one of the finest passers and punters in Southwest Conference history. Meyer found his man, 150-pound Davey O'Brien, who in 1938 would capture the Heisman Trophy after leading the Horned Frogs to a perfect 11-0 record and the national championship.

The rain-drenched crowd of 68,291, largest in the nation this weekend, saw the conservative Buckeyes play solid, fundamental football. The wet playing surface hampered both offenses, and with many Big Ten scouts perched in the Ohio Stadium press box, Schmidt elected not to show a lot of his razzle-dazzle attack. Rabb scored with a three-yard power smash in the second period. In one of the afternoon's few long plays, halfback Jim Miller caught a 38-yard lob "picture pass" from Mike Kabealo for a third-quarter score at the stadium's south end.

Six Interceptions
Spark Second Triumph

Schmidt substituted frequently the following Saturday, using a total of 36 players to defeat Purdue, 13-0, before an Ohio Stadium crowd of 49,643. It was the first meeting between the two schools in 13 seasons. The Boilermakers were still mourning the loss of two teammates, Carl Dahlbeck and Tom McGannon, who died tragically the previous season in a locker room fire.

Two of the Buckeyes' six interceptions set up their second-half touchdowns. In the third period, halfback Dick Nardi brought back an interception 15 yards to near midfield, from where OSU marched for its first score. Nardi plunged one-yard through right guard for the touchdown. Halfback Frank Zadworney picked off a Boilermaker aerial in the final quarter, returning it 25 yards to the Purdue 20. Three plays later, halfback Mike Kabealo passed to end Fred Crow in the end zone for OSU's second score.

Another Single-Point Setback

The Buckeyes were nipped by Southern California, 13-12, on October 9 at the Los Angeles Coliseum. It was OSU's third one-point loss since Schmidt took control in 1934—all three resulted from failed extra-point attempts. Trojan halfback Ambrose Schindler, son of a British naval officer, almost single-handedly destroyed OSU with his lightning speed, imposing power, accurate punting, and clutch playmaking.

After Schindler's second-quarter touchdown plunge gave his team a 6-0 halftime lead, the Buckeyes retaliated in the third period when Jim McDonald (on his first carry of the season) made it into the end zone with a sharp two-yard stab inside tackle. Alex Schoenbaum missed the extra point, leaving the score tied at 6-6.

With seven minutes remaining in the final quarter, Kabealo passed 28 yards down the middle of the field to Nardi, who scored standing up to give OSU the lead at 12-6. The conversion attempt by Joe Aleskus was no

Co-captain Ralph Wolf, All-American center and team MVP

SiU — Ohio State's Friendliest Fraternity

The great tradition of Ohio State is exemplified by its non-fraternity fraternity, SiU, a group dating back to the deep depression days of the 1930s. "It all began as a gag to impress coeds," related the late Nate Fraher, OSU '37. "The name SiU was adopted from a wealthy fraternity at Kenyon College named Psi U. We hoped girls would assume we were from the same organization. Actually very few of the guys could afford to belong to a real fraternity. We all shared two circumstances—great friendship and an acute lack of money."

Smitty's Drug Store at 16th and High was a popular hangout for the football squads of the 30s. The basement was often used as a place to gather and socialize. Fraher was the store's soda jerk at the pretentious salary of 15 cents an hour. He jokingly referred to Smitty's as the international headquarters of OSU's sidewalk fraternity.

Some 20 years later, Fraher and a few others decided it would be great fun if everyone could get together again, so a banquet was scheduled for the evening of Friday, November 15, 1957, prior to that season's game with Iowa. The response was beyond belief as over 200 returned for the first reunion, and the group continued with a biannual get-together through the early-1990s.

Jim Smith, owner of Smitty's Drug Store, and Bob Hill of adjoining Hill Tailoring were honored at the first reunion as "SiU Men of the Year." The many other subsequent honorees included track star Jesse Owens, Governor James Rhodes, cartoonist Milton Caniff, quarterback Tippy Dye, coach Woody Hayes, and Mrs. Anne Hayes. All four of Ohio State's Heisman Trophy winners were on hand and honored at the 1985 banquet.

The SiU Motto tells it all: Never had a Charter, House, Pin, or Dues. Never had a Formal Dance, Ritual, or any Extra Money. ALL WE HAD WAS FRIENDSHIP.

How Extra Point Was Scored .. Referee Tells Why

This illustration of Ohio State's successful extra point against Northwestern appeared in the *Columbus Dispatch* of Sunday, October 24, 1937. Jim McDonald's kick was blocked by Northwestern's Bob Voights. Holder Mike Kabealo moved to his right, picked-up the bouncing ball, and tossed it to McDonald who ran around right end for the conversion.

many of the reserves playing a substantial portion of the second half. Chicago's once-proud gridiron heritage was clearly in decline, as the homecoming attendance at Stagg Field barely numbered 10,000. Heading into the season's last three weekends, Minnesota and Ohio State were the only undefeated teams in conference play.

Hoosiers Spoil Championship Dreams

Indiana handed the Buckeyes their first and only conference loss of the year, 10-0, before a disgruntled Ohio Stadium crowd of 47,056 on November 6. It was the Buckeyes' first conference shutout since Schmidt took over the coaching reins in 1934. OSU opened the game with an impressive 84-yard march to the IU one, where Mike Kabealo's first-down

good. Southern California brought the ensuing kickoff back to its own 41, then marched 59 yards for the equalizer. Schindler passed 37 yards to Bill Anderson for the touchdown, and Ralph Stanley booted the critical extra point to put USC ahead, 13-12. The Buckeyes tried three desperation passes in the closing seconds, but Schindler intercepted the last one to erase OSU's final threat.

After a well-deserved open week following the long trip to California, Ohio State shut out its next two opponents, Northwestern and Chicago. Early in the third period, the Buckeyes held the Wildcats at the OSU five. After two exchanges of possession, Schmidt's team marched 25 yards for the afternoon's only touchdown. Dick Nardi, who had now scored in each of OSU's first four games, smashed across from the three. Jim McDonald tallied the extra point with a run around right end after his placement attempt had been blocked. The final score was 7-0.

At Chicago on October 30, the Scarlet and Gray scored twice in each of the last three quarters to whitewash the Maroons, 39-0. Schmidt used a total of 36 players, with

Quarterback Nick Wasylik

The Columbus Sunday Dispatch

CENTRAL OHIO'S ONLY SUNDAY NEWSPAPER

THE WEATHER
Fair, continued cold, Sunday.
Somewhat warmer
Monday.

Wirephotos
Associated Press
and International
News Service

VOL. 67. NO. 144.　　Telephone—MAin 1234　　SUNDAY, NOVEMBER 21, 1937.　　98 PAGES　　PRICE TEN CENTS

BUCKEYE PASSES CRUSH MICHIGAN 21 TO 0

fumble was recovered by the Hoosiers. It ruined Ohio State's best scoring opportunity, and the game's momentum shifted sharply for the remainder of the afternoon.

The longest gainer on OSU's opening drive was a 57-yard pass from Gust Zarnas (normally a guard who had lined up in the backfield) to end Fred Crow, who had concealed himself in the flat near the sideline. Crow stumbled and momentarily lost his balance inside the IU 15, otherwise he likely would have scored standing up.

George "Sparky" Miller put Indiana on the board with a 27-yard field goal in the second period. In the third quarter, the Hoosiers completed a 78-yard march with a 12-yard touchdown toss from quarterback Frank Filchock to end Frank Petrick.

Ohio State rebounded with an imposing 19-0 homecoming victory over Illinois. Many of the crowd of 41,921 were barely seated when Nick Wasylik passed 54 yards "down the alley" to Jim McDonald to put OSU ahead 7-0 early in the first period. Dick Nardi scored the other two TDs on short plunges in the third and final quarters. This was the 26th game between Ohio State and Illinois, with the series all even at 12-12-2.

Michigan Again Held Scoreless

The Buckeyes repeated their previous year's tally of 21-0 to close out the season with their fourth consecutive shutout victory over Michigan. It was a cold, snowy day for the heavily bundled Ann Arbor crowd of 56,766, with the mercury hovering in the low-20s. Several OSU fans never reached Ann Arbor because of icy roads between Columbus and Toledo. Heavy snow late in the af-

ternoon made it difficult for the fans at Michigan Stadium to follow the action.

Ohio State was led by the passing of Nick Wasylik and the defensive heroics of center Ralph Wolf, end Charlie Ream, and guard Sol Maggied. Ream caught the Wolverines' Norm Purucker in the end zone for a safety on the first play of the second quarter. Senior halfback Jim Miller, who had played sparingly during his career, scored OSU's first two touchdowns, and Dick Nardi added the third. This was the last game for Michigan head coach Harry Kipke, who compiled a nine-year record of 46-26-4.

The Buckeyes finished the year very strongly at 6-2, placing 13th in the final Associated Press poll and outscoring their eight opponents, 125-23. All six victories were shutouts. Their league record of 5-1 placed them second in the final Big Ten standings behind Minnesota (5-0). Carl Kaplanoff, Jim McDonald, Ralph Wolf, and Gust Zarnas were selected as All-Americans and All-Big Ten

1937			
September 25	Texas Christian	W 14	0
October 2	Purdue	W 13	0
October 9	at Southern Cal	L 12	13
October 23	Northwestern	W 7	0
October 30	at Chicago	W 39	0
November 6	Indiana	L 0	10
November 13	Illinois (HC)	W 19	0
November 20	at Michigan	W 21	0
Total Points		125	23

Season Record: 6-2
Conference: 2nd Place

Players, while Esco Sarkkinen was also chosen for All-Big Ten honors. Wolf repeated as team MVP. Ohio State drew 274,432 fans for its five home games for an average of 54,886.

1938

Ohio State's fascination for Francis Schmidt and his exciting brand of football faded slightly this year, partly because his team's 4-3-1 overall record was the poorest since Schmidt had taken command in 1934. There was a growing disenchantment with some of Schmidt's coaching methods. His autocratic approach with long and difficult practices began to wear thin with some of the players. Schmidt did not delegate well, and the talents of his assistant coaches were not fully utilized. The administration also

warned him about his use of profanity, for which he was gaining a precarious reputation. Schmidt made three new additions to his coaching staff—former Buckeyes Gomer Jones and Sid Gillman and ex-Ohio Wesleyan star Eddie Blickle.

The Buckeyes were very fortunate to win over Indiana, 6-0, in the October 1 opener before an impressive Ohio Stadium crowd of 67,397. The Hoosiers won everything but the final score, outgaining OSU in offensive yards, 265 to 137. But the Hoosiers shattered a lot of their momentum by throwing four interceptions. Third-string fullback Tommy Welbaum made several key gains to spark OSU's 70-yard fourth-quarter scoring drive. Sophomore quarterback Jimmy Sexton passed 10 yards to sophomore halfback Don Scott for the touchdown.

The following week's contest against Southern California was a complete opposite of the Indiana opener. The Buckeyes dominated the game but came out on the short

This illustration from the *Columbus Citizen* of Saturday, October 8, 1938, indicated that Southern California's train trip to and from Ohio required an entire week.

NYU's Alexander Campanis plunges for first-quarter yardage against the Buckeyes at the Polo Grounds in New York City. Ohio State players include Keith Bliss (19), Steve Andrako (36), and co-captain Carl Kaplanoff (43).

end of a 14-7 score. Trojan quarterback Grenville Lansdell, who had been timed at 9.9 in the 100-yard dash, returned a punt 85 yards for USC's first score on the fourth play of the afternoon. In the second period, OSU's Keith Bliss blocked a USC punt, setting up sophomore fullback Jim Langhurst's touchdown plunge from the one. The Buckeyes led in first downs, 14-5, and total offense, 257 yards to 137. Southern California was coached by highly respected Howard Jones, who was born in Excello, Ohio, and had been Ohio State's head coach in 1910.

OSU and Northwestern struggled to a scoreless tie at Evanston on October 15, with both teams exposing obvious weaknesses. The high point of the afternoon for Buckeye partisans among the crowd of 35,000, was halfback Jim Strausbaugh's 59-yard gallop to the Wildcat 30. Three plays later, a lost fumble at the NW 12 ended the drive. It was Ohio State's first scoreless deadlock since a

Ohio State's 1938 co-captains, quarterback Mike Kabealo (16) and tackle Karl Kaplanoff (43). Kaplanoff was an All-American in 1937.

trip to Pittsburgh on October 22, 1932.

A crowd of 63,069 showed up at Ohio Stadium the next Saturday to watch the Buckeyes demolish ill-fated Chicago, 42-7, after leading 35-0 at halftime. Francis Schmidt began substituting early in the afternoon, using all 46 of his able-bodied players. Jim Langhurst scored three of his team's six touchdowns.

At New York's Polo Grounds on October 29, OSU enjoyed its second straight one-sided victory with a decisive 32-0 romp over New York University. On a gorgeous fall afternoon, the Coogan's Bluff gathering of 20,000 watched Schmidt's squad explode for four touchdowns in the second period to put the score out of reach. Ohio State's passing attack was the sharpest it had been all season. The Buckeyes' season record now stood at 3-1-1.

Purdue's Initial Victory

Back in Columbus before a Dad's Day gathering of 54,365, Purdue scored two fourth-quarter touchdowns to shut out OSU, 12-0. It was the Boilermakers' first victory over Ohio State after six previous losses. The November 6 *Columbus Dispatch* carried the following account of the game:

Machine-like precision, superior line and backfield speed, keener thinking, better choice and execution of plays and a better-rounded team were combined to produce a more cohesive organization and carry Purdue's black-shirted Boilermakers to a convincing 12 to 0 victory over Ohio State Saturday in the stadium.

Ohio State, although occasionally impressive, labored under a burden of its own mistakes, mechanical deficiencies and in a general air of confusion and uncertainty which first cost them their own scoring chances and then made them pliant victim to a sharp, forceful and straight punching offense which carried the visitors from Lafayette

Langhurst leads Buckeyes To 32-14 Win Over Illini

Columbus Citizen, Sunday, November 13, 1938

down the field like a squad of hard-riding cavalrymen in a last period surge which produced two touchdowns.

Ohio State made one of its finest showings of the season, defeating Illinois at Champaign on November 12, 32-14. The Buckeye line consistently outcharged the Illini on both offense and defense. Fullback Jim Langhurst scored three of his team's five touchdowns. That same afternoon, coach Amos Alonzo Stagg led his University of the Pacific team to a 32-0 drubbing of Chicago at the stadium which bore his name, Stagg Field. Six years earlier at age 70, Stagg had unwillingly retired from Chicago following the 1932 season.

Wolverines Too Strong

The season ended on a very sour note. Before a dejected Ohio Stadium homecoming crowd of 67,544, Michigan pounded the Buckeyes, 18-0, to claim its first victory in the series since 1933. The Wolverines were guided by first-year coach Fritz Crisler, who this season introduced the Michigan "winged helmet." Crisler brought the design from Princeton University, where he had been head coach six seasons before moving to Michigan.

Sophomore halfback Tom Harmon plunged one yard for UM's first touchdown, and passed 15 yards to end Ed Frutig for another. Fred Trosko, Harmon's back-up, put the game out of reach with a 38-yard gallop around OSU's right end for the final six-pointer. The Wolverines led in first downs,

10-9, and total offense, 269 yards to 109. It was the Buckeyes' most one-sided defeat since Schmidt took command of the program in 1934.

Spectators were somewhat confused by the Michigan band's halftime show. After spelling out BUCK in honor of Ohio State, the band converted this formation into BUICK in recognition of General Motors. The Detroit-based automobile giant had paid for the band's traveling expenses from Ann Arbor to Columbus. Several fights broke out after the game when Michigan fans attempted to tear down the goal posts.

For the first season since 1922, no Ohio State player was selected All-America. Sophomore fullback Jim Langhurst was chosen the team's MVP. A total of 314,893 fans attended OSU's five home games for an average of 62,978, at the time the highest in the history of Ohio Stadium.

1938

October 1	Indiana	W	6	0
October 8	Southern California	L	7	14
October 15	at Northwestern	T	0	0
October 22	Chicago	W	42	7
October 29	at N. Y. University	W	32	0
November 5	Purdue	L	0	12
November 12	at Illinois	W	32	14
November 19	Michigan (HC)	L	0	18
Total Points			119	65

Season Record: 4-3-1
Big Ten Finish: 6th Place

1939

It was strongly rumored throughout Ohio that Francis Schmidt's job was on the line as he assembled his squad for fall practice. Schmidt was in the last season of his second three-year contract. Captain Steve Andrako anchored the center position, Vic Marino and Bill Nosker were the starting guards. Several players divided time at tackle, including Charlie Maag, Jim Piccinini, Jim Daniell, Jack Stephenson, and Thornton Dixon. Esco Sarkkinen and Frank Clair were the starters at end.

Versatile Don Scott shifted from left halfback to the starting quarterback position. Frank Zadworney and Jim Strausbaugh handled the halfback spots, while Jim Langhurst returned as the starting fullback with strong support from Johnny Rabb. Sophomores who saw backfield action as the season progressed included Jack Graf, John Hallabrin, Dick Fisher, and Tom Kinkade.

Schmidt used a total of 51 players to score a convincing and generally satisfying 19-0 triumph over Missouri in the October 7 season opener before an Ohio Stadium crowd of 58,165. The Buckeyes' superb defense limited Tiger ace quarterback Paul Christman to eight completions for 80 yards, mostly in Missouri territory. The Tigers' starting ends

were identical twins Roland and Robert Orf. They looked so much alike, even coach Don Faurot had difficulty telling them apart.

The Buckeyes scored two fourth-quarter touchdowns to defeat Northwestern at home the following weekend, 13-0, in front

Ohio State's 1939 starting backfield: halfback Jim Strausbaugh (4), fullback Jim Langhurst (8), quarterback Don Scott (9), halfback Frank Zadworney (6).

JOHNSON, S.—MINN.

STRAUSBAUGH—O.

Halfback Jim Strausbaugh is forced out of bounds at Minnesota. Following the play at the right is Buckeye tackle Jack Stephenson (43).

of 55,622 fanatic fans. The Wildcats were unable to spring their fine halfback, Bill deCorrevont, around the ends, partly because Schmidt kept his players rested by rotating 14 different linemen throughout the afternoon. Don Scott really blossomed in just his second start at quarterback. He and Langhurst scored the touchdowns on short plunges.

Schmidt's Biggest Triumph

It likely was the most significant career victory for Francis Schmidt when his courageous Buckeyes twice came from behind to defeat powerful Minnesota, 23-20. The game was staged October 21 at Minneapolis before a stunned homecoming crowd of 55,000. Ohio State blended a splendid passing offense with excellent blocking and execution,

to overtake the Gophers' gallant rushing attack. The action-packed contest left both squads emotionally and physically exhausted.

The two schools had not met since 1931. It was just Minnesota's third loss in its last 33 conference games over seven seasons, and its first home conference defeat since a 3-0 shutout to Michigan in the final game of 1932. Coach Bernie Bierman's teams had compiled an overall record of 44-8-4 during his first seven seasons. His Gophers had been Big Ten champions four of the five previous seasons, and were National Champions in 1934, 1935, and 1936, and also in 1940 and 1941.

Minnesota won the toss and chose the west goal with the wind at its back—OSU elected to kick off. Midway through the first quarter, Ohio State's Jim Strausbaugh lost a

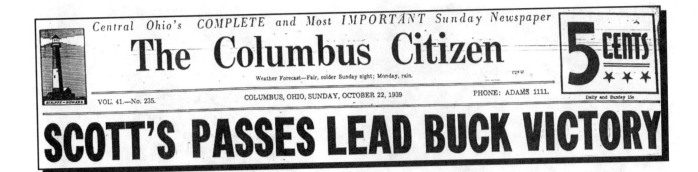

Central Ohio's COMPLETE and Most IMPORTANT Sunday Newspaper

The Columbus Citizen

Weather Forecast—Fair, colder Sunday night; Monday, rain.

VOL. 41.—No. 235.　　　COLUMBUS, OHIO, SUNDAY, OCTOBER 22, 1939　　　PHONE: ADAMS 1111.

5 CENTS ★★★
Daily and Sunday 15c

SCOTT'S PASSES LEAD BUCK VICTORY

fumbled punt on his own 13. Three plays later Joe Mernik slipped around OSU's left end for the game's first touchdown. Mernik's conversion gave Minnesota a 7-0 lead.

Six plays into the second quarter, quarterback Don Scott combined with end Esco Sarkkinen on a 31-yard touchdown pass to cap a 74-yard drive. Sarkkinen caught the ball at the seven and scampered into the end zone untouched. Scott's extra-point attempt was blocked, leaving Minnesota with a one-point lead.

After holding the Gophers on downs, Ohio State took over at the Minnesota 48. Four plays later at the 28, Scott completely fooled the Gopher secondary by floating a pass into the arms of fullback Jim Langhurst

for his second touchdown toss of the quarter. OSU had its first lead of the day at 13-7.

Minnesota retaliated with its patented running attack. George Franck returned Scott's kickoff 50 yards to the Ohio State 48 before Strausbaugh chased him out-of-bounds. On third-and-one, Harold VanEvery broke over left tackle, shook loose from two defenders, and raced 39 yards to paydirt. John Bartelt's extra point put the Gophers back on top, 14-13.

It was now the Buckeyes' turn. Near halftime, an Ohio State drive stalled at the Minnesota 14. On fourth down and from a difficult angle, tackle Charlie Maag booted an extremely important field goal from the 21, giving Schmidt's team a 16-14 lead at intermission.

1939 Big Ten Champions

All-American end Esco Sarkkinen

The Buckeye Grove on the east side of Ohio Stadium is comprised of memorial trees planted in honor of Ohio State's All-Americans.

The game became even more nerve-wracking in the second half. Five plays after receiving the kickoff, Minnesota's Martin Christiansen bolted through center for ten yards, then tried to lateral to VanEvery—his pitchout was wild and Langhurst recovered for Ohio State at the Gopher 45. After the ball was advanced to the 34, Scott again took to the air. After drifting back near the 50-yard line, he floated the ball perfectly into the hands of end Frank Clair, just as Clair was crossing the Minnesota goal. Scott's third touchdown pass and second conversion increased Ohio State's lead to 23-14.

Early in the final quarter a short punt gave Minnesota excellent field position at the OSU 39. On first down, VanEvery passed to Bruce Smith, who caught the ball at the three

and carried Scott across the goal line for the Gophers' third touchdown. Mernik's attempted conversion was blocked by Fritz Howard, leaving the score at 23-20.

After an exchange of punts, the Buckeyes took over at their own 19. On first down Langhurst bolted through right guard and raced 81 yards for an apparent touchdown, but the play was called back and OSU was penalized five yards for backfield-in-motion. Schmidt protested the call, but the penalty stood.

Langhurst lost a yard on first down from the Gopher 14. Dick Fisher then fumbled on an attempted end sweep, and Mernik recovered at the Ohio State 15 as the Gopher fans went wild. Schmidt again protested the call, claiming Fisher had been run out-of-bounds prior to the fumble.

After three rushing plays gained nine yards, Minnesota was penalized back to the OSU 21 for holding. Facing a fourth-and-16, the Golden Gophers lined up for a field goal. A complete silence fell over the huge crowd as Mernik's kick rose slowly, hit the crossbar, wobbled momentarily, then lazily fell back onto the playing field without going over. Ohio State partisans breathed a sigh of relief, but the game was still far from complete.

After Ohio State was unable to sustain a drive, Minnesota took over at its own 43 with less than a minute remaining. OSU's Jack Graf intercepted a VanEvery pass that was intended for Earl Ohlgin, but the Buckeyes were penalized for defensive holding, giving the ball back to the Gophers at the OSU 44. VanEvery intended his next long aerial for Franck, but Graf again intercepted at the five as the game came to a close.

Veteran *Columbus Citizen* sportswriter Lew Byrer called it "one of the greatest football games ever played anywhere by any two teams. I've never seen an Ohio State team show better blocking than the Buckeyes exhibited against the Gophers." Outstanding on the line were center Steve Andrako and guard Vic Marino, who played the most outstanding games of their careers. It was the first come-from-behind win for the Buckeyes since the Chicago game of 1935. A noisy crowd of 5,000 greeted the team train when it returned to Columbus Sunday evening.

#4 Versus #7

Ohio State moved up to fourth place in the weekly *Associated Press* poll and returned home October 28 to face seventh place Cornell. The Buckeyes jumped out to a 14-0 lead then watched helplessly as coach Carl Snavely's talented squad ran up 23 points in the game's final 39 minutes to win, 23-14. Reserve halfback Walter Scholl raced 79 yards through OSU's left tackle for the Big Red's first touchdown, then passed 62 yards to another reserve, halfback Jack Borhman, for his team's second six-pointer. The October 29 *Columbus Citizen* gave the following description:

Cornell's Ivy Leaguers put on one of the greatest come-from-behind battles ever seen on Ohio Stadium field yesterday afternoon to defeat Ohio State 23-to-14 in the first football battle in history between the two schools. Just how much Ohio State's grueling win over Minnesota a week ago had to do with it can't be accurately estimated.

The Cornell line, which had looked like a sieve at the start, was more like a stone wall in the closing minutes of play. The Cornell pass defense improved as the game went on. And the Cornell passing attack was something to marvel at. It was a great football game between two great teams. And the better team won.

The Ohio Stadium crowd totaled 49,583. The Buckeyes dropped to 14th in the weekly AP, while the Big Red advanced to third. Cornell finished the

Led by captain Steve Andrako (36), Vic Marino (50), and Bill Nosker (26), the Buckeyes take the field for their Dad's Day encounter against Indiana.

1939 season with a record of 8-0, good for fourth place in the final *AP* standings behind Texas A&M (10-0), Tennessee (10-0), and Southern California (7-0-2).

The Buckeyes bounced back with consecutive shutout triumphs over Indiana, Chicago, and Illinois. While OSU was flattening the Hoosiers at home on November 4, 24-0, Michigan was blasted at Illinois in one of the year's biggest upsets, 16-7. Iowa dealt Purdue its only conference setback of the season by the unusual score of 4-0, leaving Ohio State alone at the top of the Big Ten standings.

Chicago's Final Campaign

The Buckeyes won at Chicago, 61-0, against a school playing its last season of intercollegiate football. The Maroons had chosen to give up the sport and concentrate on academics. The Stagg Field crowd of 2,500 was one of the smallest to attend a Big Ten football game in many seasons. Chicago was yet to score a touchdown in league competition this year.

Back home on November 18, Ohio State trimmed Illinois 21-0 before a rain-swept homecoming crowd of 46,643. The victory assured the Buckeyes of at least a share of the Big Ten title. Jim Strausbaugh passed 32 yards to Don Scott for OSU's first touchdown. It was the first time Strausbaugh had thrown a pass in a Big Ten game, and Scott's switch from passer to the role of receiver caught Illinois entirely unprepared. Strausbaugh later broke away for a 19-yard touchdown through left tackle, and Scott passed 24 yards to Esco Sarkkinen for the third score.

Northwestern Lends Helping Hand

On November 25, an Ohio State victory at Michigan or an Iowa loss or tie at Northwestern would earn the Buckeyes the outright Big Ten championship. Fortunately, Northwestern played Iowa to a 7-7 tie. OSU was unable to maintain a 14-0 lead and lost

All-American guard Vic Marino

to the Wolverines, 21-14, before a frigid Michigan Stadium gathering of 78,815.

Ohio State capitalized on two early mistakes by Michigan's Fred Trosko—a lost fumble and an interception—to score two first-quarter touchdowns. Don Scott passed for both scores, heaving a five-yard toss to Vic Marino and an 18-yarder to Frank Clair. Marino, normally a guard, became an eligible receiver when an OSU shift at the line of scrimmage made Marino an end.

Wolverine star Tom Harmon led the Wolverine comeback, throwing a second-quarter five-yard TD toss to Forest Evashevski and racing around OSU's left end for a 16-yard score in the third period. Harmon kicked both extra points, and the score was tied at 14-14. Much like their performance four weeks earlier against Cornell, the Buckeyes couldn't generate any more points after scoring the game's first two TDs.

With 50 seconds remaining in the fourth quarter, Michigan had a fourth-down at the

Buckeyes Win Big Ten Title As Iowa's Tied

Last-Minute Fake Gives Michigan 21-14 Victory Over State in Finale

Columbus Citizen, Sunday, November 26, 1939

OSU 24. Tom Harmon lined up to apparently attempt a 41-yard field goal. Wolverine captain Archie Kodros centered the ball back to holder Fred Trosko, and Harmon stepped forward and swung his right leg. Trosko, however, tucked the ball under his arm, fell in behind Harmon and many other blue-shirted blockers, and flew around OSU's right end for a touchdown. The Buckeyes had been badly fooled, while Trosko felt vindicated since his two earlier mistakes led directly to OSU's scores. Harmon's extra point made the final score 21-14.

Even with the season-ending disappointment, the Buckeyes captured their first outright conference title since 1920. Francis Schmidt's job seemed to be safe, at least for another season. At 6-2, Ohio State finished 15th in the final *AP* standings. Don Scott, Esco Sarkkinen, and Vic Marino were selected as All-Americans and All-Big Ten Players. Steve Andrako was chosen the team MVP. The Buckeyes drew 250,885 in five home dates for an average of 50,177 per game.

Ohio State–Michigan Impact!

Ohio State and Michigan have each won an outright Big Ten title only once while losing to the other that same season. The Buckeyes were Big Ten champions in 1939, even with a season-ending 21-14 loss at Michigan. The Wolverines won the conference crown in 1982, but lost to Ohio State 24-14 in Columbus.

1939

October 7	Missouri	W	19	0
October 14	Northwestern	W	13	0
October 21	at Minnesota	W	23	20
October 28	Cornell	L	14	23
November 4	Indiana	W	24	0
November 11	at Chicago	W	61	0
November 18	Illinois (HC)	W	21	0
November 25	at Michigan	L	14	21
Total Points			189	64

Season Record: 6-2
Big Ten Champion

1940

The media experts' anticipation that Ohio State would enjoy another excellent season was buoyed by the return of Don Scott, Jim Strausbaugh, captain Jim Langhurst, and 18 other lettermen. *Collier's* magazine selected the Buckeyes sixth nationally in its preseason rankings, and most experts predicted another league title for the defending Big Ten champions (with Chicago dropping football, the conference was now called the Big Nine by some newspapers).

Ernie Godfrey (left) and Francis Schmidt intently view action in the season-opener against Pittsburgh.

ing 3-0 at halftime, thanks to Charlie Maag's 25-yard field goal, OSU exploded for three touchdowns in the third period. Several reserves saw considerable action, as Schmidt used a total of 34 players throughout the sultry afternoon.

Illegal Substitute Kicks Winning Field Goal

There was, however, a growing dissension within Francis Schmidt's coaching staff that had trickled down to the players. Some of the ill will was a direct result of Schmidt's very autocratic manner. Additionally, many opponents had devised ways to successfully confront his razzle-dazzle style of attack.

The Buckeyes opened September 28 with an easy 30-7 triumph over the once-powerful Pitt Panthers, before a sweltering Ohio Stadium gathering of 52,877. After lead-

Ohio State's 17-14 victory over Purdue on October 5 was seriously questioned the following week. OSU got off to a strong start and led 14-0 at the half on short scoring plunges by Dick Fisher and Jim Langhurst. But, the Boilermakers retaliated in the second half to tie the score, 14-14, with touchdowns by fullbacks John Petty and Bill Buffington.

Late in the final period, Ohio State advanced to a fourth down at the Purdue 12-

Placekicker Charlie Maag is hoisted by teammates after kicking the winning field goal against Purdue.

yard line with just 19 seconds remaining. Schmidt elected to send tackle Charlie Maag into the game to attempt a field goal. Maag's 29-yard kick at the north end of Ohio Stadium was perfect, and Ohio State won a real thriller, 17-14. Delirium swept through the spellbound crowd of 54,556.

The following week, sportswriter Wooly Holmes of the *Chillicothe News-Advertiser* reviewed a play-by-play account of the game and reported that, in his opinion, Charlie Maag had been an illegal substitution. Holmes indicated that Maag played the first part of the second quarter, then was replaced at tackle by Jack Stephenson. Before the end of the second quarter, Maag went back in and replaced Stephenson. College rules in 1940 prohibited a player from returning to play in any quarter once he had seen action in that quarter.

Holmes' column quoted the *Spalding Official Football Rules Guide,* rule 5, section 2, found on page 18 as follows: "A player may be substituted for another at any time, but a player may not return in the same period or intermission in which he was withdrawn. The penalty for this illegal entry is that the player shall be suspended from the game and his team penalized 15 yards."

When informed of the situation, Francis Schmidt acknowledged the violation and took full responsibility for the infraction. Schmidt was quoted in the *Columbus Citizen* as saying, "I made a sincere mistake, and I'm sorry. I honestly thought Charlie had not been substituted before in that period when I sent him back in late in that second quarter." Schmidt also absolved referee John Getchell from being responsible for not calling the infraction. According to Schmidt, the Big Ten coaches had a "gentlemen's agreement" that they would govern themselves on this regulation, and that they had promised not to violate the rule. Maag said, "I simply forgot I had been in the game earlier in the second quarter."

It was rumored that Ohio State may have contacted Purdue and offered to either forfeit the game or erase the field goal and allow the final score to remain at 14-14. If Ohio State did indeed make this offer, Purdue apparently declined the gesture. Both schools report the game in their press guides as an Ohio State victory of 17-14.

Schmidt Says Blame Is His For Violation

Columbus Citizen, Saturday, October 12, 1940

Season Crumbles

For the first time since Francis Schmidt took command of the OSU program in 1934, the Buckeyes lost three consecutive games. After dropping a heartbreaker at Northwestern, 6-3, Ohio State was defeated at home by seventh-rated Minnesota, 13-7. On October 26, top-ranked Cornell conquered the Buckeyes, 21-7, to increase its unbeaten streak to 16 games. The game was played at Cornell's Schoellkopf Stadium before a capacity crowd of 34,500.

Northwestern came from behind with the game's only touchdown late in the fourth quarter, after NU center Paul Helmenz intercepted Don Scott's pass to give the Wildcats great field position at the OSU 17. The Minnesota game was played in a steady rain before a crowd of 63,199. OSU recovered three Golden Gopher fumbles, but simply was unable to take advantage of its many opportunities. The Buckeyes led in total offensive yards, 346 to 231, but four times were unable to score after driving deep inside enemy territory.

Cornell's precision, power, poise, and versatility were more than the Buckeyes could handle. Schmidt's team drove 89 yards in 20 plays to lead, 7-0, the first time it had the ball. But Ohio State was intercepted five times, and only once got inside the Cornell 35 the rest of the afternoon. Athletic Director L. W. St. John accused Cornell coach Carl Snavely of coaching from the sideline by signaling plays to his quarterback—a practice that was against the rules in 1940. St. John also acknowledged that Snavely's poor sportsmanship played no major part in Ohio State's downfall.

Much Needed Victory

Back home November 2, the Buckeyes defeated Indiana, 21-6, much to the delight of a Dad's Day gathering of 56,667. While OSU was idle the next weekend, Minnesota nipped Michigan, 7-6, to hand the Wolverines their only setback of the season. After passing four yards to Forest Evashevski for Michigan's touchdown, Tom Harmon missed the extra-point attempt. The Golden Gophers went on to capture the national title with an overall record of 8-0.

At Illinois, a shivering Dad's Day crowd of just 15,571 braved an icy and capricious wind on November 16 to see the Illini go down in defeat to Ohio State for the sixth straight time. Don Scott scored both touchdowns and kicked both extra points, as the Buckeyes improved their record to 4-3 with their 14-6 victory. The conversions were his 19th and 20th over two seasons without a miss. The OSU defense intercepted four Illinois passes.

The following week, while Ohio State was preparing for its annual battle against Michigan, Cornell University initiated one of the finest acts of sportsmanship in college football history. On November 16, the Big

Prime Prognostication

On Friday evening, November 1, noted *Columbus Citizen* columnist Lew Byrer covered Massillon High School's 28-0 home victory over Toledo Waite. Byrer reported that a rain-soaked capacity crowd of 21,500 saw the Tigers extend their victory string to 31 games, while at least another 20,000 Massillon fans were turned away at the gate. The following two sentences appeared in Byrer's column:

One of these fine days you'll read where Paul Brown of Massillon has been named head coach of some big college football team. When you do, make a notation in your future book to watch that college go places in football.

Mr. Byrer had great intuition. The following season Paul Brown replaced Francis Schmidt at Ohio State. Brown led the Buckeyes to their first national title in 1942.

Red was credited with a very controversial victory at Dartmouth, 7-3. Cornell scored its touchdown with a six-yard pass on the very last play of the game.

Analysis of the Dartmouth-Cornell game films the following Sunday revealed that Referee Red Friesell had lost count of the downs and had mistakenly granted Cornell an additional "fifth down." Cornell used this extra down to score the game's only touchdown. On Monday, the Cornell team voted to concede the game that had rightfully been won by Dartmouth, 3-0. Coach Red Blake's Dartmouth squad graciously accepted the victory and saluted the entire Cornell team for its courage and integrity. It was the Big Red's first loss in 19 games, and it eliminated any chance Cornell may have had of capturing the 1940 national title.

Harmon One-Man Band

November 23 developed into one of Francis Schmidt's most embarrassing afternoons, as 73,648 rain-soaked homecoming fans watched Michigan disassemble the Buckeyes, 40-0. Captain Jim Langhurst won the coin toss, giving Langhurst a perfect record of calling the toss correctly for all five of Ohio State's home games. But that was about all that went right for the Buckeyes. The Wolverines dedicated this victory to Athletic Director Fielding "Hurry Up" Yost, who would retire after turning 70 the following April.

Michigan's Tom Harmon scored three touchdowns, passed for two more, kicked four extra points, rushed for 139 yards, passed for 151 yards, punted three times for a 50-yard average, returned three punts for 81 yards, and played excellent defense. After seeing nearly 59 minutes of action, Harmon received a standing ovation as he finished his last collegiate game. Even the Ohio State fans who were still on hand loudly

Two-time All-American quarterback Don Scott, coach Francis Schmidt, and fullback and captain Jim Langhurst.

acknowledged Harmon's accomplishments as he left the field. Harmon became the first Michigan player to capture the Heisman Trophy.

The Buckeyes finished the year at 4-4, being outscored by their eight opponents, 113-99. It was OSU's worst record since finishing 4-4 in 1927. It also was the first season a Schmidt-guided OSU team did not shut out at least one opponent. Don Scott repeated as an All-American and All-Big Ten selection.

Canton's municipal stadium is named in honor of Ohio State quarterback Don Scott, a graduate of Canton McKinley High School.

Center Claude White, who played several 60-minute games, was chosen the team's MVP. Ohio State drew 300,947 fans for their five home games for an average of 60,189.

Schmidt "Resigns"

There was an obvious dissatisfaction with the Ohio State football program, and speculation ran rampant following the loss to Michigan that Francis Schmidt had coached his last game in Columbus. Squad morale had fallen to a new low, as evidenced by the players' poor training habits and players simply not showing up for practice. In early December, the Athletic Board appointed a three-man committee to "examine the football situation." The committee quickly found the condition of the program to be "unfavorable."

Schmidt gave the impression he was oblivious to the entire dilemma, traveling to Los Angeles to scout the December 7 game between Southern California and Notre Dame. The Buckeyes and Trojans were scheduled to meet in the second game of 1941. When Schmidt returned from the west coast, he learned that his five assistant coaches had tendered their resignations.

On Monday, December 16, L. W. St. John reviewed the report with Schmidt. Later that day Schmidt resigned, apparently in lieu of being terminated. That evening, during a secret two-hour and 40-minute meeting at the Faculty Club, the Athletic Board unanimously accepted all resignations. The procedure followed by the board was obviously "cut and dried."

An embittered Schmidt told the press he did not attend the board meeting, stating somewhat sarcastically that "the board has everything from me that it needs. Mrs. Schmidt and I are going out to dinner."

Schmidt's seven-year record was 39-16-1, which included a league mark of 30-9-1. He was best known for his wide-open style of offense, but his teams also excelled defensively, registering 25 shutouts during his 56 games at Ohio State. In his publication, *The Big Nine*, author Howard Roberts reported that, "Schmidt brought with him the southwestern razzle-dazzle style of play to give the conference seven years of fancy offensive didoes. Planning new tricks of offense was his one great obsession."

Francis Schmidt moved to the University of Idaho in 1941, where he put together a two-year record of 7-11-1. Idaho was one of the more than 350 colleges and universities that suspended its football program in '43 and '44, because of a shortage of male students during World War II. Francis Schmidt, who had been in failing health for several months, passed away at age 58 on September 19, 1944.

1940				
September 28	Pittsburgh	W	30	7
October 5	Purdue	W	17	14
October 12	at Northwestern	L	3	6
October 19	Minnesota	L	7	13
October 26	at Cornell	L	7	21
November 2	Indiana	W	21	6
November 16	at Illinois	W	14	6
November 23	Michigan (HC)	L	0	40
Total Points			99	113

Season Record: 4-4
Conference: 4th Place (Tie)

Schmidt and All Aids Quit Posts; 11-Man Board to Name Successor

Columbus Citizen, Tuesday, December 17, 1940

PAUL BROWN
THE ORGANIZATION MAN

There could hardly have been a greater contrast in coaching style and philosophy than the change Ohio State experienced between 1940 and 1941. Francis Schmidt was succeeded by Paul Eugene Brown, a bold architect of organizational efficiency, who had transformed the Massillon Washington High School football program into a nationally recognized power. Many of his players had become football stars on college campuses across the nation. At age 32, the "Miracle Man from Massillon" was the Big Ten's youngest football coach, and one of the youngest in all of college football.

Paul Brown was truly the people's candidate for the Ohio State job. The *Massillon Independent* newspaper immediately trumpeted the qualifications of their hometown hero, and other publications around the state followed the "draft Brown" movement by recommending him through their columns and editorials. The Ohio High School Football Coaches Association mounted an organized campaign, with more than 500 of its members flooding the Ohio State Athletic

Board with written endorsements. In particular, Brown received very strong support from Jack Mollenkopf, the highly successful and influential coach at Toledo Waite High School, who later enjoyed a fine coaching stint at Purdue University. Even Governor John W. Bricker was brought into the picture, as fans urged him to intervene on Brown's behalf in the selection process.

After an intensive national search that linked at least a dozen prominent college coaches as candidates for the Ohio State job, the 11-man Athletic Board interviewed four candidates for the position. In addition to Brown, the Board talked with the following: Don Faurot, highly-successful coach at Missouri; Dr. George Hauser, line coach at the University of Minnesota who had been an Ohio State assistant from 1929 through 1931; and Alan Holman, an excellent head coach at Franklin and Marshall. Brown was the only candidate without college coaching experience, yet he was a unanimous choice of the Athletic Board for the football program's top spot. The selection of Paul Brown was made on Tuesday, January 14, 1941, and it would turn out to be one of the wisest decisions ever made by the Ohio State Department of Athletics.

Paul Brown was born the son of Lester and Ida Brown in Norwalk, Ohio, on September 11, 1908. The Browns had one daughter, Marian. Lester Brown was a very meticulous, serious-minded, highly disciplined gentleman, and those traits of precision would become the foundation for Paul Brown's coaching principles in the years to follow. Lester, a dispatcher for the Wheeling and Lake Erie Railroad, was transferred to Massillon when Paul was nine. Ida Brown was a very pleasant, outgoing woman, who enjoyed cooking for friends and relatives. Ida also loved contests of competition, particularly a good game of euchre or pinochle. Paul Brown often stated that some of his happiest times, even after he was grown and had moved from Massillon, were having Sunday dinner at home with his parents and family.

As a youth, Paul Brown played a lot of sandlot sports. One of his childhood heroes was Massillon's Harry Stuhldreher, who gained fame as the quarterback in coach Knute Rockne's "Four Horsemen" backfield at Notre Dame in 1924. Ironically, Brown and Stuhldreher would face each other in '41 and '42, when Stuhldreher was head coach at the University of Wisconsin.

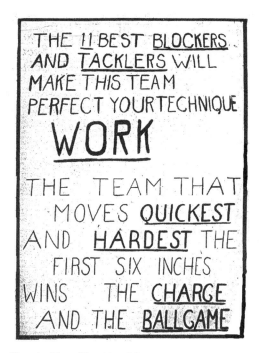

Sign in Massillon Washington High School dressing room. *Columbus Dispatch*, Tuesday, January 14, 1941

Brown became Massillon's starting quarterback by the time he was a high school junior in the fall of 1924. Although weighing just 135 pounds, he was an accurate passer, and a proven leader who directed the team with great self-confidence. After graduation in 1926, Brown enrolled at Ohio State, but transferred to Miami of Ohio after his first year in Columbus, realizing he was too small for Big Ten football at 145 pounds. He lost one year of eligibility because of his transfer, then had two fine seasons as Miami's quarterback under coach Chester Pittser, with whom Brown maintained a close friendship for many years. At the end of his junior season, Brown was chosen by the Associated Press for its All-Ohio small college second team.

Paul Brown married his high school sweetheart, Katy Kester, in the summer of 1929. After graduation from Miami in the spring of 1930, his high academic standing qualified him for a Rhodes Scholarship. He also considered attending law school, a move which would have greatly pleased his father. But with the nation now in the grips of the

Getting the Job

"I never even discussed money. I never asked them what the Ohio State job paid. I didn't care. I just wanted to go there and have the job. The only thing I really requested was a full professorship. I had just received my Master's Degree from Ohio State. I think the selection committee was pleased that I requested this, and I was made a full professor."

— Coach Paul Brown

Columbus Evening Dispatch
OHIO'S GREATEST HOME DAILY

Wirephotos
Associated Press
International
News Service

VOL. 70, NO. 198. ***—X   Telephone—MAin 1234   COLUMBUS, OHIO, TUESDAY, JANUARY 14, 1941.   26 PAGES   PRICE TWO CENTS

BROWN APPOINTED OHIO STATE'S COACH
Three-Year Agreement Made; Salary for First Year Is $6500

Great Depression, Brown opted for a coaching and teaching position at Severn Prep in Maryland, which was basically a prep school for the Naval Academy.

After two seasons at Severn, which saw his teams put together a record of 16-1-1, Brown received a huge break. At age 23, he graciously accepted an offer to become the head football coach of the Massillon Washington High School Tigers. Certainly neither the city of Massillon nor Brown, himself, could have envisioned the significance of his return to the community he so loved.

58-1-1

In the 1930s, Massillon thrived as a steel-producing city, even in the midst of the depression. A city of approximately 26,000, it had a healthy blue-collar work ethic. Located in Stark County in northeastern Ohio, the area is well-recognized throughout America as the cradle of American professional football. During Brown's nine seasons as head coach from 1932 through 1940, the Tigers put together an astonishing record of 80-8-2. His first three teams each lost to rival Canton McKinley by at least 15 points each game, but his last six squads all defeated the Bulldogs by a combined score of 112-18. The 1940 Massillon team outscored its 10 opponents, 477-6, with Canton McKinley being the only rival to score.

Brown's Massillon teams won six consecutive state titles from '35 through '40, and were declared national champions four of

those six seasons. Over that six-year period, Massillon was 58-1-1, outscoring its opposition, 2,393 points to 168. With an attendance of 116,000 for its seven home games in 1940, Massillon outdrew every college football program in the state of Ohio, except Ohio State.

How was this accomplished? For starters, Brown was a very intelligent individual who was extremely well organized at every phase of the game. Nothing was left to chance. Practice sessions were planned in advance down to the minute. Brown relied heavily on his assistant coaches (or position coaches as he called them), each with very specific duties for each practice. It was a system he developed after studying similar methods used by Dr. Jock Sutherland, highly successful coach at the University of Pittsburgh.

Brown and his staff had three basic criteria for selecting the players. Were they fast? He often used the phrase, "I like my players lean and hungry." Could they think? Intelligent players will make better decisions during the heat of action, and will be less likely to lose their poise, especially in tight contests. Do they like contact? Contact is what football is all about.

He stressed fundamentals and execution, earning him the nickname, "Precision Paul." Brown was a great teacher who emphasized not only the "how to," but also the "why." He believed that if players understood the reasons for their assignments, they would perform at a much higher level of achievement. He also installed his system in Massillon's junior high schools, where all the coaches would teach the same basic offensive and defensive plays and fundamentals. By the time the players reached high school, they were all well-schooled in Brown's highly effective Massillon system.

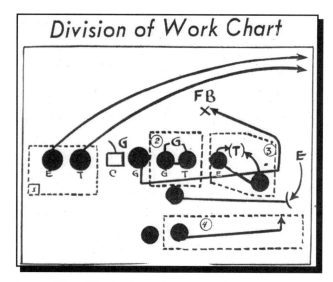

Dotted lines illustrate assistant coaches' position assignments in the Paul Brown system.
Columbus Citizen, Wednesday, January 15, 1941

1941

Brown's first Ohio State coaching staff included three assistants who accompanied him from Massillon Washington High School: Carroll Widdoes, Hugh McGranahan, and Fritz Heisler. From Francis Schmidt's 1940 staff, he retained Fritz Mackey, who had been Brown's dormitory roommate during Brown's year as an Ohio State freshman in 1926. His other two assistants were Trevor Rees, head coach at East Cleveland Shaw High School and a former Buckeye star end in 1933-34-35, and Paul Bixler, who had been an assistant coach at rival McKinley High School in Canton. To help his staff adjust to the col-

lege game, Brown and his assistants attended Northwestern's spring coaching clinic, directed by coach Lynn Waldorf. Ironically, Waldorf's Wildcats would be the only team to defeat Ohio State that fall.

There was a record crowd of 25,000 at the annual intra-squad spring game, mainly because of the extensive curiosity that had been building among fans since Brown's appointment in early January.

The '41 squad of 41 players reported to fall practice on Wednesday, September 10—13 seniors, 4 juniors, and 24 sophomores. While Francis Schmidt's offense contained more than 300 plays that were run from seven different formations, Brown's offense embodied fewer than 50 plays. It was an attack featuring power and precision rather than trickery—"execution" meant everything. Ohio State used the single wing formation

Coach Paul Brown and Ohio State's 1941 captain, tackle Jack Stephenson.

with an unbalanced line most of the time, and also ran a few plays from the T-formation.

The players used a notebook to record the various plays and instructions that the coaches would present at the team meetings preceding each practice. Each player had an assigned seat, and the squad moved to the practice field as a unit. One of Brown's strongest beliefs was that success came from unity, and he carried this out to the maximum. The intense and well-planned practices lasted no longer than one and one-half hours—Brown felt players lost their sense of concentration if the workouts were longer.

Ohio State had four seniors in its starting backfield—quarterback John Hallabrin, halfbacks Dick Fisher and Tom Kinkade, and fullback Jack Graf. Graf, a reserve quarterback the past two seasons, became one of the squad's strongest players after Brown moved him to fullback. Junior Bill Vickroy and sophomore John Rosen split time at center, sophomore Lin Houston manned the

Columbus Dispatch, Tuesday, January 14, 1941

right guard position, and seniors Fritz Howard and Ed Bruckner alternated at left guard. The starting tackles were seniors Jim Daniell and Jack Stephenson, the team cap-

Please Let Me In, That's My Team Inside!

When the bus carrying the team and coaches arrived outside Ohio Stadium for Paul Brown's first Ohio State game against Missouri, Brown stepped off to say hello to Tink Ulrich and other friends from Massillon while the stadium gates were being opened. By the time Brown attempted to enter the stadium, the bus and its police escort had pulled inside. The guard at the gate did not recognize the new coach and asked to see his ticket. "I don't have a ticket. I'm the new coach," Brown told him. "Is that right? Well, I'm President Roosevelt, but you must have a ticket if you want to see today's game," said the attendant.

Realizing the attendant was serious, Brown walked over to the stadium's southeast corner below the Ohio State locker room and began throwing stones against the windows. When one of the trainers finally peered down, Brown yelled, "Send someone out here who can get me through the gate!" The trainer ran down and explained that this gentleman really was the Buckeyes' new coach, and not an impostor trying to gain free admittance. Paul Brown was finally allowed to enter Ohio Stadium to coach his first Ohio State game.

Illustration by Tom Hayes

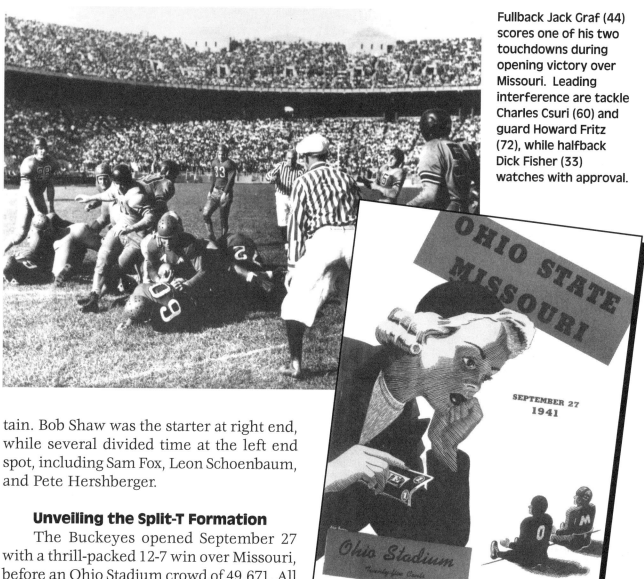

Fullback Jack Graf (44) scores one of his two touchdowns during opening victory over Missouri. Leading interference are tackle Charles Csuri (60) and guard Howard Fritz (72), while halfback Dick Fisher (33) watches with approval.

tain. Bob Shaw was the starter at right end, while several divided time at the left end spot, including Sam Fox, Leon Schoenbaum, and Pete Hershberger.

Unveiling the Split-T Formation

The Buckeyes opened September 27 with a thrill-packed 12-7 win over Missouri, before an Ohio Stadium crowd of 49,671. All men wearing uniforms of the United States armed services were admitted free. The game was far closer than expected. Missouri coach Don Faurot, who had been a finalist the previous winter for the Ohio State position, revealed a new formation he had invented—the split-T. Ohio State had prepared to defend against the Notre Dame box formation, which Missouri had used in previous seasons. The Tigers confused the Buckeyes with their new offense, particularly in the first quarter.

Jack Graf was outstanding at his new fullback position, scoring both touchdowns and playing tenacious defense. One of Graf's second-half punts traveled 72 yards, getting the Buckeyes out of a real hole. The team showed the effects of sound coaching in every department of play. There was deception to the attack, effective offensive blocking, and teeth-shattering tackling by the defense. Ohio State led in first downs, 15-7, while Missouri had a slight edge in total offensive yards, 204-194.

Don Faurot was impressed with Ohio State and predicted that the Buckeyes would do well against Big Ten competition. Faurot lamented his team's lost scoring opportunities, particularly early in the game. "If we should have won it, it should have been in the first quarter. That was when we had the real chances to score . . . but didn't," he said. Over in the Ohio State dressing room, Jack Graf was awarded the game ball for his outstanding play by captain Jack Stephenson. Graf also received proud congratulations from his father, Honus Graf, who played fullback on Ohio State's first Big Ten squad in 1913.

First West Coast Victory

The following Saturday, OSU scored one of the most smashing college upsets of many seasons, trouncing the favored Southern California Trojans, 33-0. The contest was played October 4 at the Los Angeles Coliseum before a stunned crowd of 65,000. This victory over USC was Ohio State's first triumph over a team from the west coast. It also was the first time Southern Cal had been shutout in 11 seasons, dating back to 1930 when Knute Rockne's Notre Dame team defeated them, 27-0.

The Buckeyes built up a 20-0 halftime lead with scoring drives of 83, 80, and 81 yards. Fullback Jack Graf scored the first touchdown on a two-yard smash through center. End Charlie Anderson made it into the end zone on a perfectly executed 17-yard triple-reverse, and Dick Fisher claimed the third six-pointer with a beautiful 29-yard scamper around his own right end.

In the third quarter, Graf threw a 48-yard touchdown pass to end Bob Shaw, and Fisher got his second six-pointer on a five-yard smash for Ohio State's last score. Quarterback John Hallabrin called a great game, mixing up his plays beautifully to keep the USC defense off balance the entire game. Brown substituted liberally in the scoreless fourth period. He used 11 different ball carriers to outgain USC 469 yards to 67 in total offense. OSU led in first downs, 18-5, and Dick Fisher was the game's leading runner with 134 yards.

In typical Paul Brown fashion, the Buck-

eyes were better conditioned, and simply beat the Trojans at almost every aspect of the game. West coast reporters stated that it had been years since they had seen a team block and tackle with the viciousness OSU displayed or run with the precision of the Buckeye backfield. It was apparent after just two games that Ohio State was developing into a cool, seasoned squad, and that their youthful new coach belonged in "big time" competition.

Buckeyes "Hang On" for Third Victory

The Ohio State squad returned from Los Angeles by train the following Wednesday, and was not scheduled to play the next weekend because of the long trip to California. Paul Brown and his players were amazed to be greeted at Union Station by an overflow screaming crowd, estimated at 20,000. Mrs. Brown was given 33 roses, and Captain Jack Stephenson thanked the massive gathering for its support.

The Buckeyes survived a second-half Purdue rally to narrowly edge the Boilermakers, 16-14, before a rain-drenched Ohio Stadium crowd of 66,074 on October 18. OSU piled up a 16-0 halftime lead, while Purdue made just four first downs and never advanced beyond the OSU 35. Midway through the first period, tackle Jim Daniell broke through the Purdue line and blocked Bob Hajzy's attempted punt. The ball rolled beyond the end zone for a safety, giving Ohio State the lead at 2-0. The two points didn't appear too significant at the time, but they would eventually become the narrow margin of victory.

Early in the second quarter, the Buckeyes used eight plays to systematically march 46 yards for their first touchdown. Jack Graf, Dick Fisher, and Les Horvath took turns picking up short yardage, with Graf plunging over from the one for the score. Later that quarter, Fisher recovered end Jim Rush's fumble at the Boilermaker 35-yard line. On first down, Fisher quickly connected with end

Charlie Anderson on a 35-yard touchdown pass. Leon Schoenbaum's second extra-point kick made the score 16-0, and it may have appeared that the only question to be answered was OSU's margin of victory.

Purdue coach Mal Edward, a 25-year coaching veteran who had been a teammate of Knute Rockne at Notre Dame, apparently gave his team a halftime pep talk that would have made Rockne proud. Spending almost the entire second half in Ohio State territory, the Boilermakers scored twice and nearly pulled off the upset. Purdue fullback John Petty accounted for both touchdowns on short runs. The Buckeyes were hindered when Dick Fisher's excellent 78-yard punt return for an apparent touchdown was nullified by a clipping penalty.

Season's Only Loss

Power-laden Northwestern blasted Ohio State from the unbeaten ranks on October 25, rolling over the Buckeyes, 14-7, before an Ohio Stadium crowd of 71,896. The Wildcat victory was clearly more convincing than indicated by the final score. Led by one of the finest and deepest backfields in NU history, the visitors simply packed too much of-

fensive punch for Ohio State to handle. Northwestern coach Lynn "Pappy" Waldorf had not won at Ohio Stadium in three previous tries. The OSU attack was weakened with fullback Jack Graf sidelined with a knee injury.

Play in the first half was relatively even. Running from the single wing attack, Northwestern took an early 7-0 lead on a 40-yard pass play from tailback Otto Graham to end Bud Hasse, who took Graham's toss at the

Discovering Otto Graham

During his team's 14-7 loss to Northwestern, Paul Brown marveled at the play of NU's sophomore tailback, Otto Graham, who passed for both of his team's touchdowns. Years later Brown remarked, "I never forgot Otto's tremendous peripheral vision and his ability to run to his left before throwing far across the field with such strength and accuracy. His fine running ability made his passing all the more effective, and he could quickly survey the field and pick out the correct receiver." Graham enrolled at Northwestern on a basketball scholarship and nearly gave up football following knee surgery his freshman season. He became an All-American in each sport.

After coaching a World War II service team two seasons at Great Lakes Naval Training Center in 1944-45, Brown accepted an offer from owner Art McBride to coach McBride's new franchise in professional football's All-American Conference—the Cleveland Browns. Realizing the importance of a skilled quarterback, Brown contacted Graham while Graham was completing flight training at Glenview Naval Air Station in North Carolina. They reached an agreement, and Otto Graham became the Cleveland Browns' first player.

Graham quarterbacked the Browns their first ten seasons from 1946 through 1955, taking them to the title game each year. Cleveland won seven league championships, and Graham was selected an All-Pro each season. The 1991 Ohio State-Northwestern game was very appropriately played in Cleveland on the 50th anniversary of their 1941 game, in the same stadium where Paul Brown and Otto Graham made professional football history.

Northwestern tailback Otto Graham

The 1941 Buckeyes, Coach Paul Brown's first Ohio State team.

three and dove into the end zone for the touchdown. The Buckeyes were suddenly behind for the first time all season. Ohio State retaliated late in the first quarter to tie the game, 7-7, with sophomore fullback Bob Hecklinger plunging over from the one to complete a 65-yard march.

The Wildcats' greater size and depth spelled the difference in the second half. In the game's final 30 minutes, Ohio State could advance no further than its own 47, while Northwestern drove inside the OSU 25 six times. Early in the third period, Graham tossed his second scoring pass of the afternoon, this one an 18-yarder to end Bob Motl who caught the pass without breaking stride.

The Wildcats finished the afternoon with a decided edge in game statistics, leading in first downs, 17-9, and total offensive yards, 368-175. Talented senior tailback Bill DeCorrevont netted 99 yards in just nine carries, even after spending most of the preceding week in an Evanston hospital with intestinal flu. Graham completed seven of 13 passes for 114 yards. Paul Brown took his first Ohio State defeat very graciously, simply stating, "We were beaten today by a much better team. Their backfield running had

great power. They were quick and strong. Even when tackled on the line of scrimmage they kept on coming. Our line had to fight for its life . . . and it did put up a grand fight."

The Buckeyes moved back into the victory column the following Saturday with an extremely hard-fought 21-14 triumph at Pittsburgh. Although the Panthers never led, they played a brand of never-say-die football that kept the outcome in doubt until the final whistle. It was difficult to understand how this same Pitt team had been shut out on successive October weekends by Michigan, 40-0, and Minnesota, 39-0. Jack Graf missed the game with an injury, but was ably replaced at fullback by Dick Burgett.

Dick Fisher played one of the finest games of his career for the Buckeyes, while Pitt's Edgar "Special Delivery" Jones helped keep the Panthers in the game with his superb passing, punting, and all-around defensive play. OSU went on top in the first quarter, 6-0, moving 35 yards in just two plays. Fisher picked up 33 yards around end, and Tom Kinkade sprinted the final two yards around the opposite end for the touchdown. In the second period, Burgett's two-yard scoring smash completed a four-play, 43-yard march, putting the Buckeyes on top, 12-0. Jones' fine running helped the Panthers score their first touchdown and tighten the score at halftime, 12-7.

Ohio State lengthened its lead to 19-7 early in the third period, marching 84 yards in just five plays. Fisher raced the final 35 yards, cutting back over tackle after faking an end sweep. Later that quarter, Jones returned an interception 44 yards for Pitt's second touchdown, and OSU's George Cheroke blocked a Pitt punt for a fourth-quarter safety. Fisher rushed for 174 yards in 25 carries. Ohio State's record now stood at 4-1.

Massillon Day at Ohio Stadium

The Buckeyes outlasted Wisconsin the following weekend, 46-34, in one of the wildest games ever played between the two schools. It was "Massillon Day" at Ohio Stadium. The Massillon Washington High School band spelled out PAUL and HARRY at halftime, honoring opposing coaches Paul Brown and Harry Stuhldreher, who had both grown up in the Stark County city. The Ohio State marching band's halftime show was a patriotic theme in honor of the following Tuesday's Armistice Day holiday.

A crowd of 58,519 braved the extremely cold afternoon to see the Buckeyes and Badgers collaborate for 12 touchdowns. The combined score of 80 points is the highest ever in the Ohio State-Wisconsin series. Also, the 34 points were the most the Badgers ever scored against Ohio State until 1999, when Wisconsin won in Columbus, 42-17. The Buckeyes led 20-7 after the first quarter, 20-14 at the half, and 33-20 at the end of three periods. Wisconsin led only once, 7-0, early in the game, but managed to tie the score early in the third quarter, 20-20.

Ohio State was strengthened with the return of fullback Jack Graf, who scored three touchdowns. Dick Fisher scored twice, and Tom Kinkade and Bob Shaw each tallied once. The Badgers were weakened when Pat Harder, their fine sophomore fullback and the Big Ten's leading scorer, was out of the game most of the second half with a leg injury. Wisconsin held a slight edge in first downs, 16-15, while Ohio State led in total offense, 439 yards to 375.

After the game, the Massillon High School Boosters Club staged a reception at the Deshler-Wallick Hotel in downtown Columbus, with both Brown and Stuhldreher in attendance. Also present was Dave Stewart, football coach at Sharon High School in Pennsylvania. Before moving to Sharon, Stewart had been head coach at Massillon from '21 through '25, where he became one of Paul Brown's strongest mentors. Stewart also helped Stuhldreher gain national fame at Kiski Prep, prior to Stuhldreher's playing days at Notre Dame.

Coach Paul Brown was a great teacher, and his team practices were well organized.

Columbus Citizen, Sunday, November 9, 1941

80 Points Made as Ohio Beats Wisconsin 46-34

Graf Crosses Badger Goal Three Times, Fisher Twice

1-2-3-4-(5)

During Ohio State's 46-34 win over Wisconsin, the Badgers' second touchdown came on a "fifth down" six-yard pass from Bud Seelinger to Tom Farris. After Farris failed to score from scrimmage on fourth down, the Badgers called timeout. Referee Jim Masker became confused and awarded Wisconsin an extra play. Coach Paul Brown protested vehemently following the official's miscount, but to no avail.

How the Ball Moved
Ohio State 46 - Wisconsin 34

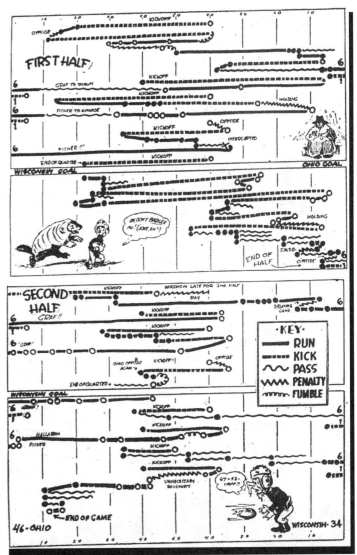

Columbus Dispatch, Sunday, November 9, 1941

Zuppke Engineers Near-Upset

The Buckeyes were very flat against Illinois November 15, in the season's last home game, but managed to survive, 12-7. The homecoming attendance of only 41,554 was Ohio State's smallest home crowd of the season. Illinois was in last place in the conference, having lost every league contest since 1939. The Fighting Illini scored first and led after one quarter, 7-0. In the second period, OSU got on the board with a 72-yard scoring pass from Dick Fisher to Bob Shaw. But Leon Schoenbaum's extra-point attempt was wide, leaving the Illini with a one-point lead at halftime.

Late in the third quarter, Jack Graf shot into the end zone from three yards out for the only score by either team in the second half. Schoenbaum's conversion attempt was again no good. The touchdown was set up when tackle Jim Daniell recovered an Illinois fumble at the OSU eight. The Buckeyes had possession of the ball most of the fourth quarter, but couldn't sustain a drive long enough to score a third touchdown. It was

Ohio State's seventh consecutive victory over Illinois.

This was the last of 29 seasons for the Illini's Bob Zuppke, one of college football's most innovative coaches. He is credited with creating the screen pass, the spiral snap from center, the huddle, and the "flea-flicker" play. Zuppke guided the school to seven conference championships between 1913 and 1941, while compiling a 29-year record of 131-81-13.

20-20

Ohio State and Michigan battled to a 20-20 tie before a Michigan Stadium crowd of 85,733, which included approximately 15,000 Buckeye fans. Each team began the cold and windy afternoon with a record of 6-1. Because of injuries, Brown had only 36 players in uniform. A total of 40 points were scored for the second straight year, but this time they were evenly divided, as opposed to UM's 40-0 win in 1940.

In one of the most exciting Big Ten games of the season, the score was tied 7-7 at halftime and 14-14 after three quarters. Each squad missed an extra-point attempt following a fourth-period touch-down. Jack Graf scored Ohio State's first two touchdowns on short plunges and connected with Dick Fisher on a 52-yard pass for the Buckeyes' third six-pointer. The Wolverines led in first downs, 19-15, and in total offense, 375 yards to 303.

Minnesota captured its second consecutive national title with an overall record of 8-0 and a Big Ten title mark of 5-0. Ohio State and Michigan finished next in the conference at 3-1-1 (6-1-1 overall), followed by Northwestern at 4-2 (6-2 overall). Michigan finished fifth in the final Associated Press poll, Northwestern was 11th, and Ohio State finished 13th. The 1941 season had been very successful for Paul Brown, who finished fourth in the national Coach of the Year poll behind Notre Dame's Frank Leahy, Minnesota's Bernie Bierman, and Earl Blake of Army. Fullback Jack Graf was selected the Big Ten's Most Valuable Player.

The 1941 Ohio State-Michigan game was played on Saturday afternoon, November 22. Just 15 days later, the United States was thrust into the thick of World War II following Japan's December 7 sneak attack on Pearl Harbor. For the next 45 months, the country would be immersed in an endeavor far more significant than any college football program.

1941			
September 27	Missouri	W	12	7
October 4	at Southern Cal	W	33	0
October 18	Purdue	W	16	14
October 25	Northwestern	L	7	14
November 1	at Pittsburgh	W	21	14
November 8	Wisconsin	W	46	34
November 15	Illinois (HC)	W	12	7
November 22	at Michigan	T	20	20
Total Points			167	110

Season Record: 6-1-1
Conference: 2nd Place (Tie)

Fullback Jack Graf, Big Ten MVP

1942

After the close of the 1941 season, the United States became totally involved in the World War II effort in both Europe and the Pacific. As most major universities immediately took an active part in training young men to serve as military officers, the status of college football was very much in question. Many military bases fielded football teams during the war to help promote morale: The Big Ten made two wartime changes; it allowed member schools to play ten games rather than the previous limit of eight and permitted the scheduling of contests with the service teams. Ohio State added Fort Knox and Iowa Pre-Flight (Iowa Seahawks) to its 1942 schedule.

Ohio State opened fall practice on September 11, Brown's 34th birthday. OSU's 43-man roster was composed of 24 sophomores,

16 juniors, and only three seniors. The Buckeyes had lost 18 lettermen from '41, including the entire starting backfield of quarterback John Hallabrin, halfbacks Dick Fisher and Tom Kinkade, and fullback Jack Graf. With only 11 lettermen returning, Brown's second OSU squad was picked for third or fourth place in the '42 conference race.

Ohio State operated primarily from the single-wing formation. The Buckeyes' starting line had the veteran Bob Shaw of Fremont and Don Steinberg of Toledo at the ends. Dante Lavelli of Hudson also contributed at end, although his playing time was reduced following an injury in the season's third game against Southern California. Bill Willis, a strong, quick athlete from Columbus, and Chuck Csuri of Cleveland were the tackles. Lin Houston of Massillon returned at one guard, and Hal Dean of Wooster occupied the other. Bill Vickroy of Toledo returned at center. Vickroy was a senior, Willis and Lavelli were sophomores, and the other five were juniors. A reserve tackle was senior Don McCafferty of Cleveland, later head coach of the NFL Baltimore Colts and Detroit Lions.

Captain George Lynn of Niles, a junior, was the starting quarterback. The halfback posts went to highly touted Paul Sarringhaus, a junior from Hamilton, and shifty Les Horvath of Cleveland, a senior. Sophomore Gene Fekete, a swift and powerful runner from Findlay, was the starter at fullback.

Four of the squad's 43 members had played their high school football under Paul Brown at Massillon. They were talented junior guard Lin Houston and three sophomores—halfback Tommy James, who especially excelled on defense; halfback George Slusser, who was one of the team's most accurate passers; and center Gordon Appleby, who became captain of Ohio State's unde-

Coach Paul Brown plans strategy with his starting backfield of (left to right) wingback Les Horvath, fullback Gene Fekete, quarterback George Lynn, and tailback Paul Sarringhaus.

feated national civilian championship team in 1944. Houston and James later played for Brown a third time as members of the newly formed Cleveland Browns.

Smooth Offense and Rugged Defense

Ohio State opened September 26 with a surprisingly easy 59-0 rout of the Fort Knox Army Base service team. Playing in the rain and mud, the well-conditioned Buckeyes completely outclassed their slower and heavier opponent. With the state of Ohio caught up in the war effort, a crowd of only 22,555 showed up at Ohio Stadium for the season opener. "Army Life" was the theme of the Ohio State Marching Band's halftime show. This season, all Big Ten schools donated ten percent of their gate receipts to the Army and Navy relief funds.

With seven players scoring nine touchdowns, OSU totaled 507 yards in total offense to minus-five for Fort Knox. Ohio State led in first downs, 15 to one. It was truly a team victory that featured excellent blocking and tackling and sound fundamentals. Ohio State had 38 players physically able to compete, with all of them seeing game action for at least five minutes. The second and third teams piled up 20 points in each of the third and fourth quarters.

Indication of Magnificent Season Ahead

The following week's competition was far stronger. Indiana invaded Columbus October 3 with one of its all-time greatest teams. Paul Brown described the Hoosiers as, "The finest personnel I've seen in the Big Ten in years." Coached by crafty veteran Bo McMillin (who had often visited Brown in Massillon to recruit high school players), Indiana featured two fine stars in triple-threat halfback Billy Hillenbrand and quarterback Lou Saban, who that season was the Hoosiers' MVP. Saban later played under Paul Brown with the Cleveland Browns, before spending many seasons as a coach in the college and professional ranks. The Hoosiers played the game without their captain, fullback Bob White, who spent the day in University Hospital with an infected arm.

With the lead changing hands five times, Ohio State outlasted the Hoosiers, 32-21, before an Ohio Stadium crowd of 48,277. Indiana led 21-19 after three quarters. But on this hot autumn afternoon, with the temperature in the low 90s, the Buckeyes' superior physical condition was the deciding factor in the final quarter.

Fullback Gene Fekete had a huge afternoon, scoring three of his team's five touchdowns and leading all runners with 132 yards in 23 carries. Paul Sarringhaus and George Lynn accounted for OSU's other two touchdowns.

George Lynn, quarterback and captain

FLASHY BUCKEYES SCORE 32-21 WIN OVER VALIANT HOOSIERS

Columbus Dispatch, Sunday, October 4, 1942

After using the single wing attack exclusively in the first two quarters, the Buckeyes surprised the Hoosiers by running many of their second-half plays from the T-formation. This change in strategy helped Ohio State outscore Indiana 13-0 in the final period. Halfback Tommy James was excellent on defense with two timely interceptions. Ohio State led in first downs, 19-10, and total offensive yards, 449-257. Coach Paul Brown called the contest, "The greatest game I ever saw." He substituted liberally because of the heat, and was extremely proud of his sec-

ond and third teams. Indiana finished the '42 season at 7-3.

Nation's Largest Crowd

Ohio State continued its winning pace with a 28-12 triumph over Southern California on October 10. On this bright and sunny autumn afternoon, the Ohio Stadium attendance of 56,436 was tops in the country for the second straight weekend. The Trojans were still smarting from their humiliating 33-0 loss to OSU in Los Angeles the previous fall. Assistant coach Tippy Dye watched

Grid-Graf Illustrates 28-12 Victory Over Southern California

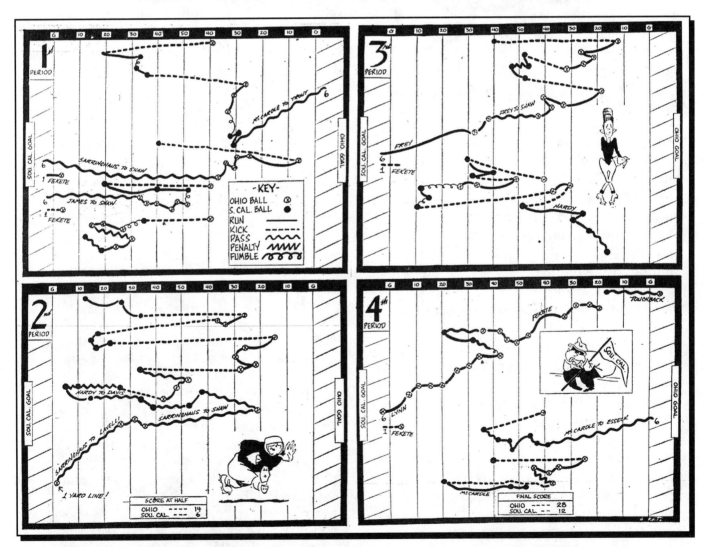

Columbus Dispatch, Sunday, October 11, 1942

Southern Cal's scoreless tie at Washington the previous week, but couldn't get back to Columbus with his scouting report until the following Tuesday night. Because of the war, a priority system on air traffic caused Dye to be bumped from his scheduled flight from Seattle. His forced switch to rail travel meant a long, three-day trip back to central Ohio.

After spotting USC an early first-quarter touchdown, the Buckeyes stormed back with 28 consecutive points. OSU's superior physical condition was again a factor, as Brown used many of his second and third team players throughout the game. Ohio State scored its first touchdown on a 64-yard pass play from Paul Sarringhaus to Bob Shaw, who caught the ball near the USC 37-yard line and raced the remaining distance after nearly swerving out of bounds. Later in the first period, Tommy James passed 40 yards to Shaw in the end zone for OSU's second touchdown and a 14-6 lead. Bob Frye rambled 37 yards early in the third period for OSU's third touchdown, and George Lynn tallied on an eight-yard sneak in the final quarter.

Gene Fekete kicked all four extra points and was the game's leading runner with 78 yards in 20 attempts. Sarringhaus gained 60 yards on the ground and went three-for-three for 137 yards through the air. Dante Lavelli injured his knee after catching a pass near the goal line late in the second period, and spent the second half on the sidelines in street clothes. New Southern Cal coach Jeff Cravath praised Paul Brown's squad, indicating Ohio State might not lose a game all season.

Number-One Ranking

Following their victory over USC, the unbeaten Buckeyes topped the weekly Associated Press poll. The Big Ten dominated the rankings with Michigan, third; Illinois, fifth; Wisconsin, seventh; Minnesota, 14th; and Iowa, 19th. Ohio State scored in each quarter to shut out Purdue the following Saturday, 26-0, before an Ohio Stadium crowd of 45,943, largest in the nation for the third consecutive week. While the attendance may seem low when compared with more recent seasons, it was extremely high for the war period when gasoline was scarce and civilian travel limited.

Fake Ticket Ring Smashed

Ten men were arrested outside Ohio Stadium for selling counterfeit general admission tickets to the Ohio State-Southern California game.

The bogus tickets, described as very close duplicates of the real thing, were sold for $1.10 as compared with the regular general admission price of $1.50. It was suspected that several hundred of the counterfeit tickets were sold, both for this game and for the previous week's home encounter against Indiana. There was less chance of discovery with false general admission tickets than with reserved seating.

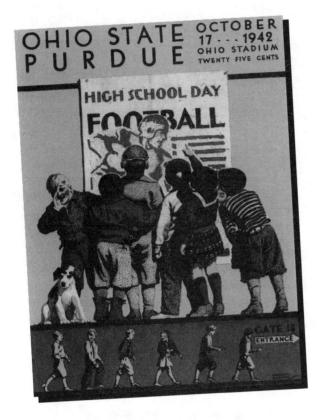

over tackle for the touchdown to complete a 53-yard drive, which was highlighted by Paul Sarringhaus' beautiful 38-yard open-field ramble. The Wildcats got as close as the OSU two and the OSU 21-yard lines, but both times were unable to score.

Ohio State used a relentless attack to score on sustained drives of 68, 43, 60, and 65 yards. Fullback Gene Fekete, who was magnificent on both offense and defense, scored his team's first two touchdowns on runs of three and eight yards. Paul Sarringhaus went two yards untouched around end for OSU's third six-pointer, and George Slusser bolted four yards over tackle for the final score. The afternoon was far more one-sided than suggested by the 26-point margin of victory. The Buckeyes led in first downs, 22-1, and total offensive yards, 341-14. Fekete netted 122 yards in 25 attempts.

After four straight victories at home, the nation's top-ranked team traveled to Evanston October 24 for a hard fought 20-6 win over Northwestern. It was NU's homecoming game, before a Dyche Stadium crowd of 46,000. The first half was extremely close, but the Buckeyes finally scored in the last 30 seconds of the second period to lead at halftime, 7-0. Gene Fekete plunged two yards

Ohio State 1942 Freshman Team

Player	Position	Hometown
Tony Adamle	Center	Cleveland
Charles Albright	Tackle	Van Wert
Warren Amling	Guard	Pana, Ill.
Pat Breese	Guard	Hamilton
Bob Brinkman	Guard	Huntington, W. Va.
Ed Burrus	Guard	Toledo
Wayne Caldwell	Center	Springfield
Jim Campbell	Center	Huron
Henry Carlton	Halfback	East Liverpool
Jack Chabek	Quarterback	Cleveland
John Colgrove	Center	Painsville
Bill Craig	Quarterback	Columbus
Joe DeMando	End	Massillon
Dick Dierker	Fullback	Columbus
Sam Dixon	End	Wyoming
Bill Doolittle	Quarterback	Mansfield
Jack Douda	Guard	Huntington, Ind.
Bob Droz	Center	Cambridge
Denver Duffey	Guard	Toledo
Dave Echols	Halfback	Columbus
Frank Garfield	Tackle	Canton
Sam Gordon	Tackle	Columbus
Lowell Gottfried	Tackle	Galion
Lou Groza	Tackle	Martins Ferry
Dick Havens	Halfback	Columbus
Louis Holzapfel	End	Greenville
Gordon Hobson	Halfback	Columbus
Talmadge Jackson	Halfback	Youngstown
Tom Jeffries	Halfback	Youngstown
Bill Johnson	Fullback	Logan
George Kessler	Guard	Springfield
Joe Kirkland	Tackle	Ft. Lauderdale
Dave Krashes	Center	Columbus
Gene Lillback	End	Painsville
Ed Montanus	Guard	Springfield
Jim Palmer	End	S. Vienna
Henry Parman	End	Dayton
Mike Perrotti	Tackle	Cleveland
Tom Phillips	Halfback	Berea
Len Puhalla	Halfback	Youngstown
Ken Ryan	Tackle	Cleveland
Ernest Savory	Halfback	Lynn, Mass.
Jim Shull	Halfback	Ashland
Charles Slemmer	End	Columbus
Dominic Stumpo	Fullback	Leetonia
Charles Stange	End	Mentor
Dave Templeton	Quarterback	Mansfield
Walt Weimer	Fullback	Mansfield
Joe Whisler	Fullback	Willard
Russ Wolf	Halfback	Upper Sandusky

Coach Paul Brown and his staff recruited one of the finest freshman classes in Ohio State history.

After a scoreless third quarter, the Buckeyes drove 68 yards for their second touchdown to lead, 13-0. Sarringhaus plunged over left tackle for the six points on a fourth-and-goal from the two. The drive was set up when Fekete intercepted an Otto Graham pass deep in Buckeye territory, and returned it to the OSU 32-yard line. Northwestern kept the pressure on with a 28-yard scoring toss from Graham to Nick Vodick, to bring NU within seven points at 13-6 with nine minutes remaining in the game.

All-American end Bob Shaw

Midway through the final period, Tommy James returned an interception 24 yards to the OSU 44. Four plays later, Sarringhaus slashed inside end for 15 yards and the game's final touchdown. The talented tailback, who was not expected to play because of an ankle injury, was the game's leading runner with 145 yards, and Fekete added 128. Otto Graham was the afternoon's top passer, completing eight of 16 attempts for 158 yards and NU's lone touchdown.

Paul Brown was extremely proud of his team, telling the press, "We've been waiting a year for this." He especially wanted this victory, since Northwestern was the only team to defeat Ohio State in '41. With a record of 5-0, Ohio State strengthened its hold on its No.1 AP ranking by collecting 80 of 123 first-place votes. Georgia was second with 25, followed by Alabama with six.

A Taste of Bad Water

The following weekend Ohio State headed for Madison for its biggest test of the fall, an October 31 showdown with sixth-ranked Wisconsin. Coach Harry Stuhldreher's Badgers, who entered the game at 5-0-1, had been pointing for Ohio State all season. The nationally spotlighted contest was billed as a re-match of the '41 clash between two of Massillon's favorite sons. It was Wisconsin's homecoming, with a record crowd of nearly 45,000 in attendance. The previous Camp Randall Stadium high had been 44,000 for a contest against Minnesota in 1938. The Buckeyes wore their white road jerseys for the first time this fall.

The game was broadcast to what was believed to be, at the time, the largest radio audience ever to hear a football game. Over 200 stations carried the contest throughout the United States and around the world to servicemen through stations in South America, Canada, Alaska, and Hawaii. The British Broadcasting Company relayed the game by short wave to all of England, Ireland, Australia, Africa, and India. Noted sportscaster Bill Stern voiced the play-by-play for NBC, while Bill Corley of WBNS and Wib Pettigrew of WOSU provided game coverage for central Ohio.

The Buckeyes suffered their only loss of the season, 17-7, and the weekend could hardly have been any worse. All first-class rail equipment had been appropriated to the war effort, forcing the team to travel in antiquated railroad coaches that had not been used for years. Old water was not drained from the coaches before fresh water was added, causing a massive attack of dysentery. By Friday evening the team was in a state of emergency, requiring medical help from the Madison community. Nearly half the squad was unable to play at full strength Saturday, causing Buckeye fans to label the loss the "bad-water game."

When playing at Wisconsin, the Ohio State squad normally spent Friday evening in the small town of Janesville, south of Madison. But with limited means of transportation, the team stayed at the Park Hotel in downtown Madison near the Wisconsin campus. The hotel's ancient elevators were not operating, forcing the players to climb six flights of steps. Pep rallies were held "until the wee hours" that night, allowing most of the team very little sleep. This Halloween weekend will long be a haunting memory in the annals of Ohio State football.

Fullback Pat Harder put Wisconsin ahead early in the second period, 7-0, with an eight-yard power play up the middle. Elroy Hirsch set up the score with a daring 59-yard open-field jaunt to the OSU 21. Harder added a 37-yard field goal later that quarter to put the Badgers in front at halftime, 10-0. Two lost fumbles prevented the Buckeyes from making any serious scoring threats in the third period.

Early in the final quarter, Ohio State cut the Badger lead to three points with an impressive 96-yard march for its lone touchdown, scored by Paul Sarringhaus. It ap-

All-American tailback Paul Sarringhaus

peared that OSU might be able to keep its winning streak alive, but Wisconsin retaliated with a 66-yard scoring drive to put the game out of reach. With the ball at the OSU 14, Hirsch faked a sweep before throwing to end Dave Schreiner for the game's final touchdown. The Badgers moved up to second place in the weekly Associated Press poll behind Georgia, and Ohio State fell to sixth.

Picture Brightens

Ohio State bounced back the following weekend to smother Pittsburgh, 59-19, before a Dad's Day crowd of 34,893. After OSU surged to a 41-0 halftime lead, Brown gave his entire squad an opportunity to contrib-

Fullback Gene Fekete, Big Ten Rushing and Scoring Leader. Fekete placed eighth in the 1942 Heisman Trophy balloting.

Buckeye Best

Fullback Gene Fekete's 89-yard touchdown gallop against Pittsburgh is the longest rush from scrimmage in all of Ohio State football.

ute. Twelve backs each carried the ball at least once for the Buckeyes, and six players each completed one or more passes. Eight different players scored the Buckeyes' nine touchdowns.

OSU had a decisive edge in first downs, 21-11, and in net offensive yards, 587-326. Gene Fekete was his team's leading runner with 139 yards in just three attempts, while George Slusser completed four of eight passes for 119 yards. Halfback Bill Dutton was a one-man show for Pittsburgh, rushing for 145 yards, passing for another 158, and tallying two of his team's three touchdowns. Dutton also handled the Panthers' punting duties.

The weekend's biggest shocker took place at Iowa City, where Dr. Eddie Anderson's Hawkeyes stunned favored Wisconsin, 6-0. Suddenly Ohio State, Illinois, and Iowa were all tied for the Big Ten's top spot with conference records of 3-1, followed

by Wisconsin and Michigan at 2-1. Ohio State and Iowa had each scheduled six league games, while Illinois, Wisconsin, and Michigan were all at a slight disadvantage with only five. The Buckeyes mysteriously slipped from sixth to tenth in the weekly AP, following their 40-point win over Pittsburgh, while Wisconsin dropped from second to seventh. Georgia and Georgia Tech now held the two top positions, Michigan was sixth.

Illinois Shifts Home Game to Ohio

Before 68,656 half-frozen fans at snow-covered Municipal Stadium in Cleveland, Ohio State registered a convincing 44-20 triumph over Illinois on November 14. The bitterly cold weather caused many fans to stay at home. Otherwise, Cleveland officials were hopeful that the attendance would exceed the stadium's all-time football record of 78,257, when Notre Dame defeated Navy 14-7 on October 21, 1939. With Iowa losing at Minnesota, 27-7, the Buckeyes were elevated to

Bucks Smash Illinois 44-20, Lead Big Ten

Victory in Cleveland Gives Ohio Half-Game Edge in Conference; Defeat of Wolves Will Win Title

Columbus Citizen, Sunday, November 15, 1942

undisputed first place in the Big Ten title chase.

The contest was an Illinois "home game." The Fighting Illini were suffering from poor attendance, so when Cleveland alumni of both Illinois and Ohio State urged that the game be transferred from Champaign to Cleveland, authorities from both schools consented. A combined Ohio State-Illinois alumni rally was held Friday evening, with Cleveland Indians shortstop Lou Boudreau, an Illinois graduate, serving as Master of Ceremonies. The Cleveland Shaw High School band provided the halftime show, since wartime travel restrictions prevented both universities from sending their bands.

Tommy James was outstanding, racing 76 and 33 yards for Ohio State's second and third touchdowns. The game was a fine homecoming for Les Horvath, who played at Cleveland Rhodes High School. The fine wingback scored twice, carried 12 times for 68 yards, and completed four passes for 109 yards. Paul Sarringhaus also tallied two touchdowns, the second on a 47-yard toss from Horvath, and Gene Fekete added a 25-yard field goal.

The 44 points were the most Ohio State ever scored against Illinois, until the Buckeyes defeated the Fighting Illini in 1962, 51-15. OSU led in first downs, 12-9, and total offense, 400 yards to 215. Ohio State (7-1) moved up to fifth in the weekly *AP* behind Georgia (9-0), Georgia Tech (8-0), Boston College (7-0), and Michigan (6-2). Wisconsin (7-1-1) remained seventh, Minnesota (5-3) advanced to 10th, and Indiana (5-3) was ranked 18th.

Mission Accomplished

Everything was on the line when fourth-ranked Michigan ventured south for one of the most significant Ohio State-Michigan games ever played. The well-balanced Wolverines at 6-2 had won impressively at Notre Dame the previous Saturday, 32-20. It was

Eventful Afternoon!

Ironically, the afternoon Ohio State captured the 1942 Big Ten title with a 21-7 victory over Michigan, November 21, Massillon High School lost its only game of the season to rival Canton McKinley, 35-0. While the Buckeyes were winning over the Wolverines for the first time in five years, Massillon suffered its first setback to McKinley in eight seasons.

the most points scored against the Fighting Irish in one game, since Notre Dame lost at Purdue in 1904, 36-0. Michigan had lost to Iowa Pre-Flight at home on October 10, 26-14, and at Minnesota, October 24, 16-14 (Golden Gophers' ninth consecutive victory over Michigan). The Wolverines' chief offensive threats were sophomore fullback Bob Wiese and junior halfback Tom Kuzma. Head

All-American guard Lin Houston

Paul Sarringhaus catches a 10-yard scoring toss from Les Horvath for Ohio State's first touchdown against Michigan. Pictured is end J. T. White (70).

coach Fritz Crisler entered the game with a record of 4-0 against the Buckeyes.

A rain-soaked Ohio Stadium crowd of 71,896 saw Ohio State use the forward pass to perfection to defeat Michigan, 21-7, and claim the outright Big Ten title. Even though extensive rains caused the crowd to fall slightly short of expectation, it was the second largest to see a football game in the country in 1942. At the time, it was the fourth largest in Ohio Stadium history. The contest was broadcast nationally by NBC's Bill Stern and Ted Husing of CBS. In Columbus, veteran Bill Corley called the play-by-play for WBNS Radio, and Joe Hill described the action for WCOL listeners. Ohio State was at a disadvantage with four of its halfbacks injured and unable to play—Tommy James, Bill Durtschi, Bob Frye, and Tom Cleary.

It was homecoming, but most student organizations did away with constructing their usual homecoming floats. Instead, the money normally used for these extensive decorations was donated to the war effort. Because of the heavy rain, the Ohio State Marching Band did not perform its normal pregame show. The band's spirited halftime program was dedicated to the 5,000 Ohio State students, staff, and alumni who were serving in their country's armed forces. Many service men attended the game as guests of the university.

The Buckeyes passed for touchdowns in each of the last three quarters—Les Horvath to Paul Sarringhaus for 10 yards, Sarringhaus to Bob Shaw for 60 yards, and Sarringhaus to Horvath for 32 yards. In pure Paul Brown fashion, it truly was a team victory in every

Central Ohio's COMPLETE and Most IMPORTANT Sunday Newspaper

The Columbus Citizen

Local Weather: Colder with showers today.

5 CENTS
★★★

VOL. 44.—No. 267 (Entered at Columbus, O., Post Office as second-class matter.)

COLUMBUS, OHIO, SUNDAY, NOVEMBER 22, 1942

PHONE: ADAMS 1111.   Daily and Sunday, 22 cents a Week

Bucks Roll Over Michigan 21 to 7
To Win Championship of Big Ten

manner possible. Early in the second quarter, tackle Charles Csuri blocked Kuzma's punt at the UM 35 to set up the Buckeyes' first scoring drive. Late that period, the Wolverines advanced to the Ohio State one-yard line as time expired at the end of the first half.

With less than five minutes remaining in the third quarter, Sarringhaus threw his scoring toss to Shaw to increase the Buckeyes' lead to 14-0. Shaw caught the ball at the UM 30, just a few feet from the east sideline, then raced the remaining distance for the six points. The Wolverines retaliated with a 64-yard, seven-play scoring drive, to tighten the game at 14-7. With only six seconds left in the third period, Bob Wiese plunged over from the one for Michigan's only touchdown.

Midway through the final period, Buckeye guard Bob Jabbusch recovered Paul White's fumble at the UM 32 (the Wolverine halfback was the brother of J. T. White, who played end for Ohio State). On first down with the rain pelting down, Sarringhaus passed perfectly to Horvath, who caught the ball at the five and stepped into the end zone for the game's final touchdown. Gene Fekete's third extra-point kick made the final score, 21-7. Later that quarter, Sarringhaus ended Michigan's final major effort with an interception at the OSU 23.

An almost speechless Paul Brown could not have been more proud of his players and staff. Brown gave much credit to his assis-

tants for their extensive game preparation. The inspirational Ohio State staff felt Michigan could be passed against, even with the slippery playing field and low ceilings. They were right! The Buckeyes' focus on perfection also played a big part in the outcome. OSU had no turnovers, while the Wolverines had two interceptions and lost three fumbles.

Ohio State's First National Title

With the conference title assured, the Buckeyes turned their attention to the

Charles Csuri, All-American tackle and team MVP

203

season's final game against the Iowa Pre-Flight Seahawks, and a possible shot at the national championship. While OSU was defeating Michigan, top-ranked Georgia was knocked from the unbeaten ranks by Auburn, 27-14, in the season's biggest upset. The Buckeyes, 8-1, moved from fifth to third in the national rankings behind number-one Boston College at 8-0 and second-place Georgia Tech at 9-0. Wisconsin (8-1-1) advanced from seventh to fourth and Georgia (9-1) fell to fifth. Michigan (6-3) dropped to ninth.

Ohio's Victory Over Seahawks Amazes Fans

Experts Rub Eyes At Great Exhibition Of Superiority

Columbus Citizen, Sunday, November 29, 1942

The Seahawks were a naval cadet service team comprised of former professional and college stars, and coached by legendary Bernie Bierman, who had guided Minnesota to five national titles from 1934 through 1941.

End Don Steinberg, Big Ten Scholar-Athlete 1945

Among their stars were quarterback Forest Evashevski of Michigan, All-American end Mal Kutner from Texas, Pitt quarterback John Michelosen, end Ray Kreick and fullback Eddie Jankowski of Wisconsin, and four excellent linemen from Bierman's former Golden Gopher squads—end Ray Antil, tackle Charles Schultz, guard Gene Flick, and center George Svendsen. The Seahawk starting line-up included three former OSU standouts—Jim Langhurst ('40 fullback and captain), Dick Fisher ('41 halfback), and Charlie Ream ('37 tackle).

Iowa Pre-Flight entered the November 28 game at 7-1, having suffered its only setback October 17 at Notre Dame, 28-0. The Seahawks, who outweighed Ohio State 20 pounds per player, were solid favorites. Showing no mental letdown after the Michigan victory, Ohio State crushed the Seahawks, 41-12, after jumping out to a 27-6 lead at halftime. The biggest difference in the two opponents this numbingly frigid afternoon was the Buckeyes' enormous speed.

Dante Lavelli, member of the Professional Football Hall of Fame. With the Cleveland Browns, Lavelli became one of the finest ends in NFL history.

Paul Sarringhaus led the OSU ground attack with 114 yards and two touchdowns, while ex-Buckeye Jim Langhurst was the Seahawk's leading runner with 108 yards. Senior wingback Les Horvath (who thought he was playing his last game in Ohio Stadium, but would be granted an additional year of eligibility in 1944 under relaxed war-time regulations) scored twice and contributed 39 yards. Gene Fekete and Tommy James accounted for Ohio State's other touchdowns, and Fekete kicked five extra points. James also completed passes of 52 yards to Fekete and 46 yards to Bob Shaw to set up his team's second and third touchdowns. The Buckeyes immensely helped their cause by intercepting five Seahawk passes, all thrown by former Ohio State halfback Dick Fisher.

While Ohio State was posting its colossal triumph in Columbus, Georgia smashed Georgia Tech, 34-0, at Sanford Field in Athens. But the totally inconceivable outcome came from Boston's Fenway Park, where unranked Holy Cross (who had won only four games all season under first-year coach Anthony Scanlon) crushed top-ranked Boston College, 55-12. It was the most one-sided game ever between these New England rivals, who were meeting for the 40th time.

The Boston College players were so distraught after the setback, that they canceled a celebration party that had been scheduled that evening at the fashionable Coconut Grove in anticipation of a national title. Their thrashing by Holy Cross became a blessing-in-disguise, when the Coconut Grove burned that night, killing 478 guests.

The Buckeyes had peaked at the right time. Riding the crest of a sensational sea-

Lou Groza, pictured kicking a field goal for the Cleveland Browns, was an Ohio State freshman in 1942 when freshmen were not eligible for varsity competition. With the Browns, Groza became one of professional football's premiere tackles and placekickers. Holding is former Michigan State quarterback Jim Ninowski. Groza is a member of the Professional Football Hall of Fame.

Center Bill Vickroy

son which finished with spectacular victories over Michigan and Iowa Pre-Flight, Ohio State captured its first national championship by a vote of 1,432 to 1,339 over second-place Georgia in the final Associated Press poll. Paul Brown was especially pleased with the manner in which his players rebounded after their mid-season setback at Wisconsin. At the team's appreciation banquet on Monday evening, November 30, Brown spoke very little about individual honors or championship titles, but instead praised the players and assistant coaches for their accomplishments as a team.

Bob Shaw, Chuck Csuri, and Lin Houston were selected as All-Americans, and Csuri was chosen as the team MVP. Gene Fekete became the first Ohio State player to finish in the top ten voting for the Heisman Trophy, placing eighth to winner Frank Sinkwich of Georgia (who was from Youngstown, Ohio). Fekete also led the Big Ten in both rushing and scoring with 550 yards and 52 points in six conference games.

Paul Brown was selected as one of the nation's ten "most outstanding young men."

Brown also was voted college football's coach of the year, but very graciously and secretly stepped aside so that the honor could go to Bill Alexander, head coach at Georgia Tech. Alexander, who had been one of college football's finest contributors for many seasons, was dying, and it was felt that this season might be the last opportunity for him to receive this tribute.

What Might Have Been

Paul Brown's 1942 freshman team was one of the finest in school history, and the future for Ohio State football was extremely promising. But with the nation in the midst of World War II, most of the players soon entered the armed services, where their talents were needed for a cause far greater than capturing a college football national title. A "college football dynasty in the making" was being terminated.

After the war, most of the team returned to campus to earn their college degrees. Many also resumed their football careers, either at Ohio State or other colleges, and a few joined the ranks of professional football. As the years passed, Ohio State's national champions of 1942 became ever greater performers in their own chosen professions. The great personal feeling they have for their

One Of College Football's Most Unique Careers

J. T. White has the distinction of not only earning a football letter at both Ohio State and Michigan, but also playing on a national championship team at each school. White played end on the Buckeyes' first national title squad in 1942. After returning from military service in World War II, White decided to finish his education at Michigan, where he was the starting center with the Wolverines' national champions of 1947. J. T. later served 20 seasons as a Penn State assistant under coaches Rip Engle and Joe Paterno.

1942

September 26	Fort Knox	W	59	0
October 3	Indiana	W	32	21
October 10	Southern California	W	28	12
October 17	Purdue	W	26	0
October 24	at Northwestern	W	20	6
October 31	at Wisconsin	L	7	17
November 7	Pittsburgh	W	59	19
November 14	Illinois#	W	44	20
November 21	Michigan (HC)	W	21	7
November 28	Iowa Pre-Flight	W	41	12

Total Points 337 114
at Cleveland

Season Record: 9-1
National Champion
Big Ten Champion

1942 National Rankings

Ohio State (9-1)
Georgia (10-1)
Wisconsin (8-1-1)
Tulsa (10-0)
Georgia Tech (9-1)
Notre Dame (7-2-1)
Tennessee (8-1-1)
Boston College (8-1)
Michigan (7-3)
Alabama (7-3)

BUCKS GRAB NO. 1 SPOT

Brown Admits Ohio Is Great Team

Columbus Dispatch
Sunday, November 29, 1942

Paul Brown with Ohio State's captain and three departing seniors at the annual football appreciation banquet. Left to right are Brown, Don McCafferty, Bill Vickroy, Captain George Lynn, and Les Horvath. Horvath was later granted an additional year of eligibility in 1944.

207

coach and for each other is still very apparent today, and the team continues to have 100% attendance at all of its reunions.

Dr. Don Steinberg authored a book, *Expanding Your Horizons*, detailing the notable lifetime accomplishments of his teammates and coaches. Steinberg's work was published in 1992 as part of his team's 50th anniversary celebration.

In his book, *PB The Paul Brown Story,* Brown described his three seasons at Ohio State as, "the only job I ever wanted." In 1989 he received the National Football Foundation's Gold Medal Award, in recognition of his quality contributions to college football. Brown's national champions were truly outstanding performers under very difficult circumstances. The Buckeyes of 1942 played a major role in creating "The Great Tradition of Ohio State Football."

1943

With the United States in the midst of World War II by 1943, most major universities had affiliated their programs with the military. Ohio State chose the army's ROTC program, as did Indiana, Iowa, and Pittsburgh. Others affiliated with the navy's V-12 program, including Michigan, Purdue, and Northwestern. College football was strongly affected by one BIG difference in the two military agendas. Trainees in the army programs were not allowed to participate in varsity sports. The navy programs, however, not only granted their enrollees eligibility, but also granted transfer players from other schools immediate athletic eligibility to. For example, Elroy Hirsch, one of Wisconsin's most outstanding players in 1942, moved to Michigan, where he was the starting left halfback for the Wolverines' Big Ten co-champi-

ons in 1943. Many college games pitted a "military team" against a "civilian team." The situation could hardly have been described as a "level playing field."

Most smaller Ohio colleges and universities could not field football teams in 1943 and 1944 because of a shortage of players. Major programs that were forced to drop football these seasons included Alabama, Auburn, Boston College, and Tennessee, among others. At one time it looked as if Ohio State might also have to give up football for the duration of the war.

In an effort to keep the sport active, particularly at schools with army ROTC programs, the Big Ten temporarily made freshmen eligible for varsity competition in all sports. The conference also allowed special summer football practices for these first-year players. Paul Brown and his staff held a four-week summer session, with nearly 50 17-year-old freshmen participating in at least a portion of the workouts.

By fall, Ohio State's squad of 44 players included only five from the previous season's national title team, all deferred from military obligations. The only returning starter was tackle Bill Willis, who had undergone surgery that summer for varicose veins. The other four were center Gordon Appleby, end Jack Dugger, guard Bill Hackett, and end Cecil Souders. Dugger was named team captain. Charles Csuri, who had been elected captain following the '42 season, was now

Back-to-Back

The Buckeyes have only once opened a season against the same opponent they faced in the final game of the previous year. Iowa Pre-Flight defeated Ohio State's "Baby Bucks" in the 1943 opener, 28-13. The Buckeyes had defeated Iowa Pre-Flight 48-12 in the final game of 1942.

serving in a fast-paced army engineering program in New Jersey.

The '43 team was affectionately named the "Baby Bucks." None of the 44 players weighed as much as 200 pounds, and the team equipment manager had trouble finding football pants small enough for many of the 17-year-old backfield players. Ohio State's five returnees (all linemen) were joined on the starting line by two freshmen, guard Bill Miller from Wapakoneta and tackle Russ Thomas of Charleston, West Virginia.

Freshmen comprised the entire backfield. Dean Sensenbaugher of Uhrichsville and Canton McKinley's Ernie Parks were the starting halfbacks, with Bobby McQuade from Columbus Aquinas also seeing considerable action. Glen Oliver (162 pounds) of University High School in Columbus and Canton McKinley's Matt Brown (also 162 pounds) split time at fullback. Albert Williams, also from Canton McKinley, was the starter at quarterback.

B-B Gun Versus 18-Inch Howitzer

The vastly undermanned Buckeyes began play September 25 against Iowa Pre-Flight, before a rain-soaked Ohio Stadium crowd of 23,946. The Seahawks won, 28-13, handing Ohio State its first opening-game setback in 49 seasons. OSU's last first-game defeat had been a 12-6 loss to Akron on September 5, 1894. Iowa Pre-Flight jumped out to a 28-0 lead, before OSU scored touchdowns in each of the third and fourth quarters. The final score could have been far more one-sided.

While the young Buckeyes gave it their best effort and went down fighting, the highly talented Seahawks were well stocked with former professional players, including 230-pound center Vince Banonis of the Detroit Lions, Washington Redskin tailback Dick Todd, end Perry Schwartz of the Brooklyn football Dodgers, and Chicago Bear halfback Frank Maznicki. Lieutenant Don Faurot, Seahawk coach while on leave from his head

Halfback Ernie Parks sprints 60 yards for one of his three touchdowns against Missouri.

Bucks Beat Missouri 27-6; Parks Scores Three Times

Columbus Citizen, Sunday, October 3, 1943

coaching duties at Missouri, was no stranger to Ohio Stadium. Faurot's Tigers had played in Columbus in '39 and '41.

After the game, Paul Brown thanked Faurot for holding down the score, telling Faurot, "You could have beaten us 100-0 if you had wanted." Brown compared the game to fighting a war with a B-B gun against an enemy who has an 18-inch howitzer. Iowa Pre-Flight finished second in the final Associated Press poll with a record of 9-1, losing only to top-ranked Notre Dame in the season's last game, 14-13.

Important Victory

At home the following Saturday, Ohio State rebounded to upend Missouri, 27-6, before a home attendance of 27,525. The victory was as important for team morale as it was for the win-loss column. For the first time this season, OSU ran some of its offense from the T-formation. Paul Brown told the press after the game, "It was very important that we won this one. The team needed to win and they did. It will have a fine effect on them." Parks, a former state high school dash champion, finished the afternoon with 186 yards on the ground, including touchdown sprints of 10, 26, and 60 yards. Sensenbaugher rushed for a net 152 yards, including a 27-yard dash for OSU's other score. Freshman Johnny Stungis kicked three extra points.

In their first road game of the season at Great Lakes Naval Training Center on October 9, the young Buckeyes played their hearts out before losing to the heavier and more experienced Bluejackets, 13-6. A crowd of 22,000 at Ross Field's bleacher-style stadium

saw the two battle to a scoreless tie at halftime. Jack Dugger scored OSU's only touchdown on a 24-yard pass from Gene Slough in the final quarter.

Midway through the third period following Great Lake's first touchdown, Dean Sensenbaugher made the play of the game, taking the kickoff five yards deep in the end zone and returning it 103 yards to the Bluejacket two. Tackle Bill Willis kept up with Sensenbaugher all the way, making a key block that made the long run possible. Unfortunately, the Buckeyes lost possession of the ball after four unsuccessful attempts at making the final two yards.

The Bluejackets finished sixth in the final *AP* poll with a record of 8-2. They handed national champion Notre Dame its only setback, beating the Fighting Irish at South Bend in their final game of the year, 19-14. Little did Paul Brown realize that he would replace Tony Hinkle as Great Lake's head coach the following season.

Purdue Game in Cleveland

With transportation shortages and gas rationing making it difficult for fans outside of the Columbus area to reach Ohio Stadium, Ohio State moved its October 16 conference opener against Purdue to Cleveland Municipal Stadium. A crowd of 55,000 was expected, but an all-day downpour kept the attendance at 41,509. Again the Baby Bucks gave it their best effort and led 7-0 at halftime. But the lack of depth and strength was too much to overcome in the second half, as the powerful Boilermakers rolled to a 30-7 victory.

Purdue strongly benefited from the transfer of many navy and marine trainees. Included in this group were guard Alex Agase, tackle John Genis, and fullback Tony Butkovich, who all played for Illinois in this stadium against Ohio State the previous season. These three fine experienced players were now wearing Purdue uniforms, further demonstrating the huge difference in player eligibility between the military and civilian programs. The Boilermakers finished the season at 9-0, good for fifth place in the final Associated Press poll.

Back home the following weekend before an Ohio Stadium crowd of 37,243, Northwestern handed the Buckeyes their third straight setback, 13-0. Tailback Otto Graham accounted for both Wildcat touchdowns, scoring the first on a six-yard run in the first period, and passing six yards to Lynne McNutt for the second TD early in the final period. It was the first (and only) time Ohio State had been shut out during Paul Brown's three seasons as head coach.

Even though they were again substantially outmanned, the scrappy Buckeyes made the game much closer than expected. Ohio State's undersized Baby Bucks were beginning to feel the effects of the season. With the injury list growing each week, Brown used only 19 players against the Wildcats, with only 14 of them playing any substantial length of time. NU coach Lynn "Pappy" Waldorf was able to play 31 differ-

HOOSIERS WIN 20-14 THRILLER

Columbus Dispatch, Sunday, October 31, 1943

ent members of his squad. Northwestern finished the campaign ranked ninth in the final Associated Press standings, with a record of 6-2.

Hoosier Heartbreaker

In one of the most thrilling games ever between the two schools, Indiana defeated Ohio State, 20-14, scoring its winning touchdown in the game's final 32 seconds. Led by

Arch Ward Impressed!

Covering the 1943 Ohio State-Northwestern battle from the Ohio Stadium press box was Mr. Arch Ward, prominent Sports Editor of the *Chicago Tribune*. After the game, Ward told *Columbus Dispatch* writer Paul Hornung, "My hat's off to Ohio State and its great young coach. Ohio State's sacrifice can bring only admiration from all sports lovers everywhere."

Arch Ward obviously was sincere when labeling Brown a great young coach. He later connected Brown with Mr. Arthur McBride, when McBride was searching for a coach for his new professional franchise in Cleveland. In Ward's Chicago office on Thursday, February 8, 1945, Brown signed a five-year contract with McBride as head coach and general manager of the team which soon would be named the Cleveland Browns.

Interestingly, the first player to sign with Cleveland was Northwestern's Otto Graham, who had played a major role in his team's 13-0 victory over Ohio State in that 1943 game.

the running and passing of Hunchy Hoernschemeyer, the Hoosiers led 13-0 at halftime and seemed to have the game under control. But the courageous Buckeye defense stiffened in the second half, and after Dean Sensenbaugher scored two fourth-quarter touchdowns, Ohio State was suddenly ahead, 14-13. There were nearly nine minutes remaining.

On its next possession, IU moved deep into OSU territory, where Bill Willis blocked John Tavener's field goal attempt from the OSU 26. It now appeared that the Buckeyes' single-point lead would be sufficient to earn OSU its first conference win of the season. Few of the Ohio Stadium crowd of 25,458 had departed.

After Ohio State was unable to sustain a drive on its next possession, Indiana took over at its own 43. Hoernschemeyer quickly

Planning for the Future

The Pitt Panthers gave Paul Brown his first real look at the modern T-formation with flankers and men in motion. Pittsburgh coach Clark Shaughnessy had created much of this offense when he coached Stanford to a 9-0 record in 1940. Brown took much of what he learned in Pittsburgh about this new offense and later assimilated it into his own system with the Cleveland Browns.

passed 24 yards to end Pete Pihos at the OSU 33. Bobby McQuade intercepted Hoernschemeyer's next pass, but the Buckeyes were penalized five yards for defensive holding, nullifying what would have been a game-saving interception. Hoernschemeyer

Outlining practice plans with coach Paul Brown are (standing left to right) assistant coaches Hugh McGranahan, Fritz Mackey, Ernie Godfrey, Paul Bixler, and Carroll Widdoes.

quickly threw 28 yards to John McDonnell for the winning touchdown, and the Hoosiers had pulled one out of the fire. With just 32 seconds on the clock, Ohio State had suffered one of its most disappointing setbacks in many seasons.

The Buckeyes broke their four-game losing streak, defeating the Pitt Panthers in the steel city, 46-6. Ohio State scored all its points in the first half, then played the second half with 13 players who had seen limited action during the season. On the Buckeyes' first play from scrimmage, halfback Ernie Parks raced 68 yards on a wide reverse for OSU's first of seven touchdowns.

For the first time this season, the Buckeyes wore their white game jerseys and scarlet pants. Pittsburgh, like Ohio State, was an army school, and the Pitt Stadium crowd of 30,000 included 2,000 uniformed army trainees. There was no halftime band show. Pitt began the season with a 45-piece marching band, but the unit was forced to dissolve in

NOT All in the Family

Freshman quarterback Howard Yerges Jr. could not finish the 1943 season after getting his orders to report to the Navy on November 1, but he had played enough during the season's first six games to earn an Ohio State letter. After World War II, Yerges enrolled at Michigan, where he earned three letters in 1945-46-47. He was the starting quarterback for the Wolverines' undefeated national title team in 1947. Yerges' father, Howard Yerges Sr., quarterbacked Ohio State to its first two Big Ten championships in 1916 and 1917.

late October after many of its members entered the armed services.

The "Fifth Quarter" Game

Ohio State faced Illinois on November 13 in the season's last home game. The homecoming contest developed into one of the most exciting games all season, with the lead changing hands four times. The afternoon also produced one of the most unusual finishes in college football history. The Fighting Illini scored their third touchdown late in the second period to lead at halftime, 19-13. Ohio State went back ahead, 26-19, with touchdowns in each of the third and fourth quarters. Illinois retaliated with its only points of the second half to tie the game, 26-26, with 6:50 remaining.

The Buckeyes received a huge break when Illini halfback Eddie McGovern fumbled, and Bobby McQuade recovered at the Illinois 23 with just 10 seconds on the clock. With time for just one play, McQuade fired a pass into the end zone, intended for halfback Ernie Parks, which fell incomplete. Field judge Irish Krieger fired his gun signaling that time had expired, and both teams headed for their dressing rooms. Many of the crowd of 36,331 left Ohio Stadium thinking that the game had ended in a 26-26 tie.

ILLINOIS OHIO STATE — NOVEMBER 13 — 25 CENTS

Johnny Stungis kicked a 33-yard field goal after time had expired to earn Ohio State a 29-26 "fifth quarter" victory over Illinois.

Illinois' left tackle, however, had been offside on the final down, but few had seen head linesman Paul Goebel signal the infraction, including the other game officials. After being informed of the infringement, the officials concurred that the game could not end on a defensive penalty. Referee Jim Masker made his way to the Ohio State dressing room, where he told Paul Brown that his team could have "one additional down." Krieger's task was much tougher—he delivered the same message to coach Ray Eliot in the Illinois dressing room.

Nearly 10 minutes after McQuade's pass had fallen dead in the end zone, both squads returned to the playing field for one final down. Many of the players needed a few extra seconds to get back into their equipment and uniforms. Johnny Stungis, a 17-year-old freshman from Powhatan Point, calmly booted a 33-yard field goal to earn Ohio State a 29-26 "fifth quarter" victory. The historic three-pointer, which oozed over the middle of the crossbar with little room to spare, was the first and only field goal attempt of his career.

Stungis had played tenor saxophone in the Powhatan Point High School band until his senior year, when the school's coach convinced him to play football instead of an instrument. He credited placekicking coach

Last Play of Hectic Battle Still Being Discussed by Fans

Columbus Citizen, Sunday, November 14, 1943

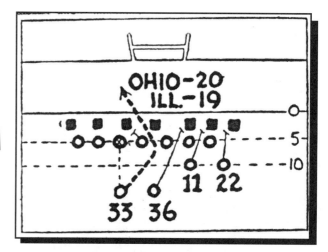

Dean Sensenbaugher scores Ohio State's third touchdown against Illinois with five-yard cutback.
Columbus Citizen, Sunday, November 14, 1943

Master And Protege Meet Again

In 1970, Coach Paul Brown led the Cincinnati Bengals to the NFL postseason playoffs in just their third season of play. Interestingly, the Bengals were defeated 17-0 in the first round by the Baltimore Colts, who were coached by Don McCafferty. McCafferty had been a tackle on Brown's 1942 Ohio State national title team. In 1970, McCafferty became the only first-year coach in NFL history to lead a team to the NFL title. The Colts defeated the Dallas Cowboys, 16-13, in Super Bowl V, played in Miami.

ing unbeatable odds most Saturdays, the team played the game to the best of its ability, and nothing more can ever be expected from anyone. Players were frequently physically outmatched by their older more-experienced opponents. Considering the circumstances, the team played extremely well.

Paul Brown was outspokenly proud of this young group, but he never completely forgave the Ohio State Athletic Department for not giving this team its normal appreciation banquet at the end of the season. Bill Willis was selected for the All-American team, and center Gordon Appleby was chosen the team MVP.

Following the 1943 season, Paul Brown, who was still young enough for the draft, was granted a Navy commission as a lieutenant, junior grade. On Monday, April 17, 1944, Brown reported to the Great Lakes Naval Training Center north of Chicago, where he soon was appointed head coach of the training center's Bluejacket football team.

After two seasons at Great Lakes, Brown joined the ranks of professional football, first as the founding coach of the Cleveland Browns who fielded their first team in 1946, and later in the same capacity with the Cincinnati Bengals in 1968. Paul Brown, the master creator, forever changed the game he so loved and respected with his many innovative contributions.

Ernie Godfrey for much of his newly developed kicking skills.

It was an extremely tough loss for Ray Eliot. His two fine halfbacks, Eddie Bray and Eddie McGovern, had combined for 249 yards rushing. Years later, when the coach was asked about this game by Cincinnati sportswriter Pat Harmon, Eliot stated, "If I had known what the official wanted when he knocked on the door, I would NEVER have let him in the dressing room to talk with us!"

The season's final game at Michigan on November 20 was another mismatch between a military team and a civilian team. The UM squad included 41 Navy and Marine trainees. Before a Michigan Stadium crowd of 39,139, the Wolverines won, 45-7, although the Buckeyes were able to hold UM to a 13-0 lead at halftime. Michigan placed third in the final *AP* poll with an overall record of 8-1. Its only setback was at home against Notre Dame, 35-12, on October 9. Purdue and Michigan shared the Big Ten title with identical league records of 6-0. Northwestern was next in the conference standings at 5-1.

Baby Bucks Special Team

Ohio State's 1943 team, a victim of World War II, was one of the most courageous ever to proudly wear the Scarlet and Gray. Fac-

1943				
September 25	Iowa Pre-Flight	L	13	28
October 2	Missouri	W	27	6
October 9	at Great Lakes	L	6	13
October 16	Purdue#	L	7	30
October 23	Northwestern	L	0	13
October 30	Indiana	L	14	20
November 6	at Pittsburgh	W	46	6
November 13	Illinois (HC)	W	29	26
November 20	at Michigan	L	7	45
Total Points			149	187
# at Cleveland				

Season Record: 3-6
Conference: 7th Place

GRAVEYARD OF COACHES

Coach Paul Brown was sworn in as a Navy lieutenant, junior grade, on Wednesday, April 12, 1944, and reported for duty at Great Lakes Naval Training Center the following Monday. While serving as head coach of the training center's Bluejacket football team, Brown remained Ohio State's head football coach "in absentia," expecting to return to the position at the end of World War II. To carry on the Ohio State program in his absence, Brown chose assistant coach Carroll Widdoes as his temporary successor. The Ohio State Athletic Board agreed with Brown's selection and appointed Widdoes as acting head coach on Friday, April 14. Widdoes's only other experience as a head coach had been at the junior high school level.

Carroll Widdoes was a soft-spoken, reserved individual, whose relaxed style of coaching contrasted sharply with Paul Brown's more dynamic approach. Widdoes was born in the Philippine Islands, the son of Dr. Howard W. Widdoes, a United Brethren missionary. At age 13, he moved to Lebanon, Pennsylvania, to live at the United Brethren Church Home, a facility maintained for children of missionaries. In 1922, Widdoes graduated from Lebanon High School, where he became a star member of the basketball, baseball, and track teams. Interestingly, Lebanon High School did not field a football team.

Widdoes became an excellent four-sport athlete at Otterbein College, where he played football for the first time. After graduation, he joined the faculty at Longfellow Junior High School in Massillon, where he coached

Paul Brown Sworn In As Navy Lieutenant

Columbus Citizen, **Thursday, April 13, 1944**

the football and basketball teams. In 1934, Widdoes became director of physical education in the public school system as well as an assistant high school coach in football and basketball. As an assistant to Brown, Widdoes became a great organizer and a fine fundamentalist, especially in blocking techniques. Widdoes came to Ohio State with Brown in 1941, after turning down the school board's very attractive offer to replace Brown as head coach of the Massillon Tigers.

1944

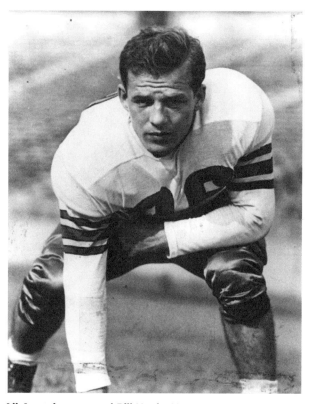

All-American guard Bill Hackett

With the war going strong in the South Pacific and Europe, transportation problems, gas rationing, and an acute shortage of players and coaches continued to create vital problems for college football in 1944. Most college teams were mostly made up of freshmen too young for the draft, and a few older players who did not meet military physical standards (4Fs). Nevertheless, continuing the game was highly encouraged for morale purposes by President Franklin D. Roosevelt.

Beginning in 1943, the Big Ten temporarily made freshmen eligible for varsity competition in all sports, and allowed a fourth year of eligibility for any player on campus working toward a graduate degree. Les Horvath, the fine senior wingback on OSU's national champions of 1942, was enrolled in Ohio State's School of Dentistry and was a member of the school's Army Specialized Training Program (ASTP), which did not permit participation in college athletics. Ohio State received a huge break in August of '44. The ASTP unit was discharged, and Horvath was returned to civilian status with one more year of eligibility. Despite a heavy study schedule with his dental school work, the 24-year-old Horvath elected to return to the playing field for one more season. Since

his first year of dental school had required so much time, Horvath had not attended all of Ohio State's home games in 1943.

The Buckeyes received two other fine breaks when guard Bill Hackett and guard-tackle Warren Amling were deferred from military service after they entered veterinary school. Hackett, from London, Ohio, had lettered in '42 and '43. Amling, a sophomore

Outstanding Accomplishment Under Trying Conditions

Few people realized the personal stress in Carroll Widdoes's life when the "acting head coach" began preparation for the 1944 season, not knowing if he would ever again see his parents. Widdoes's missionary parents had been captured by the Japanese and were being held as prisoners of war. Fortunately, both parents were found unharmed when rescued by U. S. Paratroopers in 1945.

from Pana, Illinois, had been a member of Paul Brown's outstanding 1942 freshman team.

Three Freshmen Join Horvath

Ohio State's 1944 squad of 44 players was made up of only five seniors, three juniors, five sophomores, and 31 freshmen. Widdoes continued much of Paul Brown's system, running the offense from both the single wing and T-formations. To make maximum use of Horvath's experience and abilities, Widdoes positioned him as the quarterback in the T and tailback in the single wing.

Horvath was joined in the backfield by three 17-year-old freshmen—Bob Brugge of Parma and Dick Flanagan of Sidney at the halfbacks, and fullback Ollie Cline from Fredericktown. Three other freshmen backs who saw considerable playing time were Bob Dove of Ashland, Gene Janecko of Campbell, and Tom Keane of Bellaire. Halfback Dean Sensenbaugher, who carried much of the offensive load in '43, had received an appointment to West Point.

Veterans Jack Dugger of Canton and Cy

Ohio State's 1944 coaching staff. Head coach Carroll Widdoes is fourth from the left with whistle and clipboard. On Widdoes' left is assistant coach Paul Bixler. Widdoes and Bixler would switch positions in 1946, with Bixler moving up to head coach and Widdoes becoming one of Bixler's assistants.

Souders of Bucyrus, both seniors, returned at ends. Souders entered the Navy after the fourth game, and was replaced by freshman Traian Dendiu from Campbell. The tackles were senior Bill Willis of Columbus, one of the finest linemen in Ohio State history, and sophomore Russ Thomas of Huntington, West Virginia. Joining Hackett at guard was freshman Tom Snyder from Upper Sandusky. Captain Gordon Appleby, a senior from Massillon, returned at center, and Amling

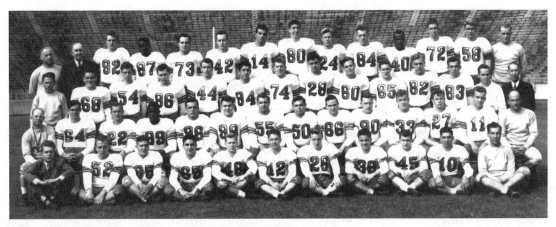

1944 National Civilian Champions, Big Ten Champions

219

saw considerable action at both guard and tackle.

Auspicious Debut

Ohio State opened September 30 with an impressive 54-0 win over the Missouri Tigers, before an Ohio Stadium crowd of 29,908. Behind Horvath's leadership and fine running, the Buckeyes built up a 34-0 lead at halftime. Brugge scored OSU's first of eight touchdowns on the seventh play of the afternoon, going 13 yards with a shovel pass around left end. Widdoes substituted liberally throughout the contest, using 16 different ball carriers. Horvath had a third-quarter 87-yard scoring run around right end nullified by a holding penalty. The Buckeyes led in total offense, 466 yards to 168.

Forty Buckeyes were in uniform, wearing white jerseys and scarlet helmets. Servicemen stationed in the area and military personnel home on leave were admitted free. Since the Ohio State marching band was still getting organized for the season, a 48-piece ASTP band played the national anthem and performed at halftime.

It was more of the same in the Big Ten

Two-time All-American tackle Bill Willis, member of the College and Professional Football Halls of Fame.

opener the following Saturday. Ohio State smothered Iowa, 34-0, much to the delight of a home crowd of 35,358. Horvath led the attack with 118 yards in 16 carries, including the Buckeyes' first touchdown on a nine-yard reverse. Five different players scored touchdowns, and Ollie Cline kicked three of his team's four extra points.

Widdoes was especially pleased with his team's overall speed, and its alertness while recovering five Hawkeye fumbles and intercepting three passes. OSU led in first downs, 12-5, and total offense, 348 yards to 98. The 100-member Ohio State Marching Band made its first appearance of the season under the direction of William McBride.

Major Victory at Madison

The Buckeyes faced their first real test of the season at Wisconsin on October 14. Coach Carroll Widdoes' squad was ranked eighth in the weekly Associated Press poll, while coach Harry Stuhldreher's team (2-0)

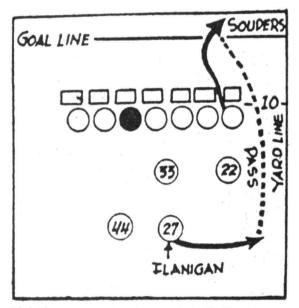

Dick Flanagan passes ten yards to Cy Souders for Ohio State's third touchdown against Iowa. *Columbus Citizen,* Sunday, October 8, 1944.

was 19th. Remembering the team's massive attack of dysentery at Madison in '42, the team this year brought its own supply of water.

The Badgers' acting captain was Bob Hecker, an Ohio State halfback the previous season, who was enrolled at Wisconsin as a V-6 naval radio trainee. The spirited contest, played in perfect weather before a Camp Randall homecoming crowd of 40,000, developed into an offensive duel between Ohio State's Les Horvath and Wisconsin's Earl "Jug" Girard.

The Buckeyes took the opening kickoff and drove 75 yards for the first half's only score—a one-yard plunge by Dick Flanagan, followed by Ollie Cline's extra point. The Badgers put together a 51-yard third-quarter drive to even the score at 7-7. The key play was a Girard-to-Ed Bahlow 35-yard completion to the OSU 16. Girard sliced over from the one for the touchdown, then kicked the extra point to tie the score.

In the fourth period, Bill Hackett partially blocked a Wisconsin punt, giving the Buckeyes the ball at the Wisconsin 32. From there, OSU drove for its second touchdown, with Bob Brugge getting the big yardage on a 27-yard reverse. Cline finally slammed his way across from the four to make it 13-7 with eight minutes and 55 seconds remaining. The Bucks' final six-pointer was set up when Horvath returned an interception to the Badger 14. Horvath scored the touchdown on a spinner play from the one with just 18 seconds remaining, and Ohio State had earned a big victory, 20-7.

Dr. John W. Wilce, OSU's retired coach and now Director of the Ohio State Student Medical Center, was with the Ohio State team in an unusual capacity. Wilce was filling in for Dr. Walter Duffee, team physician, who had gone duck hunting. Duffee was missing his first Ohio State game in 24 seasons. Wilce had been a rugged fullback at Wisconsin and was the Badger captain in 1909.

Ohio Stadium Overflows for Paul Brown's Homecoming

The season's fourth game, October 21, was one to remember—coach Paul Brown returned to Ohio Stadium, only this time he operated along the east sidelines, directing the visiting Bluejackets from Great Lakes Naval Training Center. Brown's service team included two former Buckeyes—Ernie Plank, an end in '43; and Jim Rees, a tackle from '42. Also on his squad was George Spencer, a quarterback fresh out of Bexley High School in Columbus, who would later play for the Buckeyes in '46 and '47. One of Brown's fullbacks was Ara Parseghian of Akron, who in 1951 would follow Woody Hayes as head coach at Miami (Ohio) before moving on to Northwestern and Notre Dame.

Ohio State, at 3-0, was ranked fourth nationally, while Great Lakes was rated sixth with a record of 4-0-1. This meeting between Widdoes and Brown drew considerable attention, and the crowd gave Brown a thunder-

Ohio State Whips Great Lakes 26-6; 73,477 See Brown's Sailors Beaten

Columbus Citizen, Sunday, October 22, 1944

ous ovation when he brought the Bluejackets onto the playing field to start the game. The action was broadcast nationally by NBC's Bill Stern and CBS's Ted Husing. The attendance of 73,477 was, at the time, the fifth largest crowd in Ohio Stadium history. Another 10,000 were turned away the day of the game.

After dominating play from the very start, Ohio State finally went ahead, 6-0, on Dick Flanagan's one-yard plunge with just 19 seconds remaining in the first quarter. It was the first time all season OSU had not scored on its first possession of the game. Great Lakes came to life in the third quarter, and tied the game at 6-6 heading into the final period. The fourth quarter belonged to the Buckeyes, as their superior strength and overall speed advantage began to show. Ohio State scored three touchdowns in the last period (two by Les Horvath) to win, 26-6, in a game somewhat closer than suggested by the final score.

The crowd was totally exhausted after watching Ohio State turn back one of the nation's leading teams. Brown was disappointed with his team's loss, but praised

Freshman quarterback Tom Keane (44) prepares to make a tackle against Great Lakes.

Widdoes and the Buckeyes for their outstanding play. Tackle Russ Thomas, who went the full 60 minutes, drew special attention for his efforts from both Widdoes and Brown. The two coaches had dinner with Athletic Director L. W. St. John that evening in Columbus.

The following Saturday, October 28, Ohio State defeated Minnesota, 34-14, before a home crowd of 43,563. Horvath played another excellent game, running for 90 yards, passing for another 113, and scoring two of his team's five touchdowns. After leading 20-0 at halftime, Widdoes substituted liberally throughout the second half.

The afternoon's big story came from Ann Arbor, where Michigan handed Purdue its first league setback of the season, 40-14. Ohio State (5-0 overall, 3-0 conference) suddenly found itself alone at the top of the Big Ten standings. The Buckeyes moved up to third in the weekly AP behind Army and Notre Dame, who also were both 5-0.

Brotherly Love

One of Ohio State's third-quarter drives was halted when Buckeye quarterback Tom Keane tried a short pass—it was intercepted by Keane's brother, Jim, a defender for the Great Lakes Bluejackets.

Indiana Big Hurdle

The competition was much stronger on November 4, when coach Bo McMillen's 15th-ranked Indiana Hoosiers brought their 5-1 record to Columbus for one of Ohio State's toughest tests of the season. The contest drew a Dad's Day crowd of 56,380, a significant number considering the wartime gas-rationing constraints. Widdoes' squad more than met the challenge, defeating the talented Hoosiers, 21-7. IU jumped out to a 7-0 first-quarter lead, marking the first time Ohio State had been behind this season. The Buckeyes methodically retaliated with touchdowns in each of the last three quarters.

Three factors that contributed to the Scarlet and Gray's sixth straight victory were its overall team speed, the penetrating work of its defensive line, and the brilliant offensive play of Les Horvath and Bob Brugge. Horvath passed 41 yards to Jack Dugger for OSU's first touchdown, and Brugge scored the last two on reverses of 13 and 22 yards. Horvath totaled 115 yards rushing on 20 carries, and Brugge added 78 more on 11 attempts. Indiana's Bob "Hunchy" Hoernschemeyer, a fine sophomore halfback from Cincinnati, stood out on both sides of the ball for the Hoosiers.

The flag at the stadium's south end flew at half mast in

Captain and center Gordon Appleby

memory of retired Professor Thomas E. French, affectionately known as "the father of Ohio Stadium," who died at age 72 the previous Thursday. Fullback Ollie Cline missed most of the game after suffering a severe shoulder bruise, but was ably replaced by understudy Matt Brown. The crafty McMillen accurately summed up the afternoon's action when he told the press that, "Ohio State simply had too many boys who were too fast for us." The 6-0 Buckeyes advanced to second in the *AP* standings, moving past Notre Dame who lost to sixth-ranked Navy, 32-13.

The following weekend, Ohio State overwhelmed the outmanned Pitt Panthers, 54-19, before a rain-drenched Ohio Stadium crowd of 26,566. Carroll Widdoes used his second and third teams most of the afternoon, otherwise the score would have been much more one-sided. Eight different Buckeyes scored touchdowns. OSU led 47-0 before Pitt finally registered its first touchdown in the third quarter. Widdoes was able to rest linemen Gordon Appleby and Bill Willis the entire afternoon, giving both of them extra time to recover from nagging injuries. The 7-0 Buckeyes were getting ready for two of their season's biggest tests—Illinois and Michigan.

Record Crowd in Cleveland

The Ohio State-Illinois game was played November 18 at Cleveland's Municipal Stadium, before a then-record attendance of 83,627, the largest crowd to see a football game anywhere in the country in 1944. Because of a printing error, some duplicate tickets were sold before the game, resulting in the sale of more tickets than seats available. Temporary

BUCKS WIN 8TH STRAIGHT BY TAKING ILLINOIS 26 TO 12

Columbus Dispatch, Sunday, November 19, 1944

seats were quickly set up near the sidelines to compensate for the error. The stadium's previous largest crowd had been 80,184, when the Cleveland Indians dedicated the stadium against the Philadelphia Athletics in 1932.

Coach Ray Eliot's Fighting Illini entered the game with a record of 4-3-1. Weather for the lake-front game was ideal, and scalpers were getting as much as $15.00 for box seats, which regularly sold for $4.50. A special radio booth was constructed for NBC's Bill Stern, who broadcast the game nationally and to servicemen overseas. The Lakewood High School band entertained fans before the game and at halftime. Representatives of the Army, Navy, Marines, and Coast guard participated in the flag-raising ceremonies.

Ohio State won a thriller, 26-12, after leading the Illini at halftime, 20-6. The game turned out to be a joyous homecoming for Les Horvath and Bob Brugge, who had grown up just two blocks from each other in suburban Parma. Brugge completely surprised Illinois when he unleashed his first collegiate pass, a 49-yard touchdown toss to Jack Dugger for the Buckeyes' second score. Brugge scored his team's third touchdown with a two-yard run inside Illinois' right end midway though the second period. Horvath, who scored OSU's other two touchdowns on short runs, was

the game's leading rusher with 116 yards on 24 carries.

The Ohio State defense held Illini speedster Buddy Young to just 61 yards in 10 carries. Tackle Bill Willis made one of the game's most exciting plays, catching Young from behind to prevent a touchdown. Bill Hackett was excellent on defense, making tackles all over the field. Carroll Widdoes played only 18 players throughout the afternoon, Eliot used 25. The stage was now set—Ohio State and Michigan would clash in Columbus for the 1944 Big Ten title.

A College Football Classic

Ohio State (8-0) advanced to third in the weekly Associated Press poll, Michigan at 8-1 was ranked sixth. The Wolverines were 5-1 in the conference, while Ohio State was 5-0.

Bob Brugge passes 49 yards to Jack Dugger for Ohio State's second touchdown against Illinois. *Columbus Citizen,* Sunday, November 19, 1944

All-American end Jack Dugger

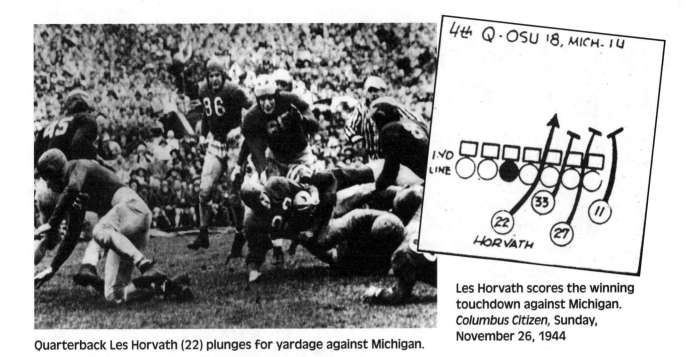

4th Q. OSU 18, MICH. 14

Les Horvath scores the winning touchdown against Michigan. *Columbus Citizen,* Sunday, November 26, 1944

Quarterback Les Horvath (22) plunges for yardage against Michigan.

Michigan could win the conference title with a win over Ohio State, since the Wolverines had scheduled seven league games compared with OSU's six. It was the first time in league history the winner of the Ohio State-Michigan game would be the outright conference champion.

Tickets were at a premium for the November 25 contest. Approximately 11,000 general admission passes were sold the Friday before the game, but quite a pushing and shoving disturbance developed among the many fans who had stood in line but were turned away after the last passes were sold.

By Saturday afternoon, the temperature had risen to the high-30s, with a stiff wind blowing from the northeast. The press box was bulging with 130 sportswriters and media representatives, at the time the second largest press contingent in Ohio Stadium history. Over 2,000 servicemen sat in the south end zone as guests of the university. At halftime, the Ohio State marching band created the formation, "13,149," honoring the 13,149 university students and staff who were away from campus to serve their country during the war.

Before a thrilled homecoming crowd of 71,958, the Buckeyes won a classic, 18-14. The lead changed hands after each of the game's five touchdowns. Ollie Cline's one-yard touchdown plunge climaxed a 56-yard drive, giving OSU a 6-0 lead with one minute and 42 seconds remaining in the first period. The drive's biggest play was Dick Flanagan's 20-yard sprint over right tackle to the UM 34. Jack Dugger's extra-point kick was blocked.

Michigan took its first lead, 7-6, on a one-yard bolt by Dick Culligan just 22 seconds before halftime. Wolverine halfback Ralph Chubb set up the touchdown, returning an interception 35 yards to the OSU 25. It was the first time Michigan had been inside Ohio State's 45.

Ohio State drove 23 yards to regain the lead midway through the third period, 12-7, following center Gordon Appleby's recovery of a Wolverine fumble. Les Horvath plunged over right tackle for the score from inside the one, but Tom Keane's conversion attempt was wide. Michigan retaliated with an 83-yard march in the final period to regain the lead, 14-12. Culligan scored his second touch-

225

18 to 14 Thriller Keeps 71,000 Fans Shouting All the Way

Great Comeback March By Ohio State in Last Few Minutes of Game Decides Tilt

Columbus Citizen, Sunday, November 26, 1944

down of the afternoon, plunging over right tackle from inside the one with 8:29 left to play.

Michigan's ensuing kickoff went just 12 yards, slicing out-of-bounds at the Ohio State 48. It appeared to be an intentional onside kick, but Michigan coach Fritz Crisler insisted otherwise. Crisler told the press, "It was just one of those things and was not planned that way." It turned out to be one of

the game's key moments. The Buckeyes used 14 plays to drive 52 yards for the season's biggest touchdown, scored by Horvath on a one-yard dive over center with three minutes and 16 seconds remaining. Horvath was like a "coach-on-the-field" during the drive, constantly encouraging the younger players. Dugger's extra-point kick was wide, but it didn't matter. Dick Flanagan stopped the Wolverines' final effort, when he intercepted Culligan's long pass at the OSU 33-yard line. The Buckeyes conservatively ran out the clock, securing one of the most meaningful victories in all of Ohio State football. The final score was 18-14.

The Buckeyes had gone 9-0 for just the second undefeated-untied season in school history. Widdoes stated, "We played our best game of the season, and Michigan was the toughest team we faced." He used

Cincinnati Enquirer, Saturday, November 25, 1944

1944 National Rankings

Army (9-0)
Ohio State (9-0)
Randolph Field (9-0)
Navy (6-3)
Bnbdg., Md. N. (10-0)
Iowa Pre-Flight (10-1)
Southern Cal (7-0-2)
Michigan (8-2)
Notre Dame (8-2)
Fourth Air Force (7-0-2)

THE ROSE BAWL

Columbus Citizen, **Monday, November 27, 1944**

only 16 players throughout the afternoon, with Horvath, Dugger, Hackett, and Flanagan going the entire 60 minutes. OSU led in first downs, 17-10, and total offensive yards, 225-190. Horvath was the game's leading runner with 106 yards, followed by Flanagan with 80.

Big Ten Says "No"

Ohio State was invited to meet Southern California in the Rose Bowl. At this time, however, the Big Ten did not allow postseason competition. A special vote of the schools was taken in Chicago on Sunday, November 26, but the member institutions voted against making an exception for Ohio State. OSU Athletic Director Lynn W. St. John was strongly disappointed, but agreed to abide by the conference's decision. With Ohio State unable to attend, the Rose Bowl picked Tennessee. The Volunteers incurred

their only setback of the season, losing to Southern California, 29-0.

First Heisman Trophy

The Buckeyes were declared the mythical "National Civilian Champions," and placed second to Army in the final Associated Press poll. Michigan (8-2) finished eighth; Illinois, 15th (5-4-1); and Great Lakes, 18th (8-2). Les Horvath became the first Ohio State player to capture the coveted Heisman Trophy, finishing ahead of sophomores Doc Blanchard and Glenn Davis of Army. Acting head coach Carroll Widdoes was named col-

Horvath Wins Heisman Award, Highest Honor for College Athlete

Columbus Citizen, **Friday, December 1, 1944**

lege football's Coach of the Year, the first Ohio State coach to receive this distinction.

Horvath, Jack Dugger, Bill Willis, and Bill Hackett were chosen All-Americans, and Horvath was also selected the Big Ten's MVP. Indiana's All-American center John Tavener edged Hackett by one vote as Big Ten Lineman of the Year. The 1944 season was truly one of the most magnificent accomplishments in Ohio State history, and Carroll Widdoes performed one of the finest coaching jobs in all of college football.

Bill Hackett, Carroll Widdoes, and Russ Thomas receive an explanation from a game official.

1944

September 30	Missouri	W	54	0
October 7	Iowa	W	34	0
October 14	at Wisconsin	W	20	7
October 21	Great Lakes	W	26	6
October 28	Minnesota	W	34	14
November 4	Indiana	W	21	7
November 11	Pittsburgh	W	54	19
November 18	Illinois#	W	26	12
November 25	Michigan (HC)	W	18	14
Total Points			287	79

at Cleveland

Season Record: 9-0
National Civilian Champion
Big Ten Champion

1945

Just 75 days after Ohio State's splendid 18-14 triumph over Michigan, the football world was stunned when Paul Brown agreed to become head coach of the Cleveland entry in professional football's new All-American Conference. The Cleveland franchise had been awarded to Arthur "Mickey" McBride, a wealthy Cleveland businessman, who developed a solid interest in football after his son, Arthur, Jr., enrolled at Notre Dame in the fall of 1940. McBride and Brown signed their contract on February 8, 1945, in the *Chicago Tribune* office of Sports Editor Arch Ward, who was the driving force behind this new professional football league. At the time, Brown's contract of $25,000 per year plus 15 percent of the team's profits was one of the highest ever offered a football coach. It was agreed that Brown would join McBride in Cleveland after Brown finished his military obligations at the end of the war.

Paul Brown's decision caused a major split among some of Ohio State's most ardent supporters. Many were counting on his return to the Buckeyes, even though Widdoes had done an admirable job as

Brown Quits OSU for Pro Field

the "acting head coach." Others criticized the young coach for his move into professional football, given the tremendous support he had received during his three seasons in Columbus. But with World War II still in progress, there were matters of far greater concern than who would guide the Ohio State football program.

Job Now Permanent

With the word "acting" now removed from his title, Carroll Widdoes officially became Ohio State's head coach on February 14, 1945. Between the end of the Buckeyes' spring workouts and the beginning of fall practice, the free world was blessed with Victory in Europe Day on May 8, and Victory over Japan Day on September 2.

Widdoes and his staff were saddled with a major rebuilding effort, since graduation and the draft had taken many players from the 1944 squad.

One significant challenge facing most college coaches was blending teenage freshmen and returning veterans, many in their mid-20s, into a cohesive team. Four veteran returnees who would play significant roles

this season were halfback Dick Fisher from '41; and quarterback Robin Priday, halfback Paul Sarringhaus, and end Don Steinberg from '42. The line was built around guard Warren Amling and tackle Russ Thomas. Captain-elect Bill Hackett could not play because of an injury suffered in an automobile accident during the off season.

Blazing Beginning

The Buckeyes appeared in midseason form, when they opened September 29 by crushing Missouri, 47-6, before an Ohio Stadium gathering of 41,299. Paul Sarringhaus scored four times, Ollie Cline bolted across for two touchdowns, and Don Steinberg returned a stolen lateral 15 yards for OSU's other touchdown. Widdoes, who was very pleased with how his team played as a unit, virtually cleared his bench in the second half.

In the conference opener the following weekend, Ohio State walloped Iowa, 42-0, after leading only 7-0 at the half. The weather was ideal for the Ohio Stadium crowd of 49,842. The Hawkeyes stymied OSU's rushing attack in the first two quar-

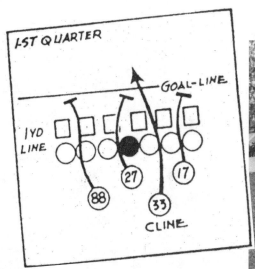

Fullback Ollie Cline powers over tackle for Ohio State's first touchdown against Iowa. *Columbus Citizen,* Sunday, October 7, 1945

Paul Sarringhaus (88) leads second-half surge against the Iowa Hawkeyes.

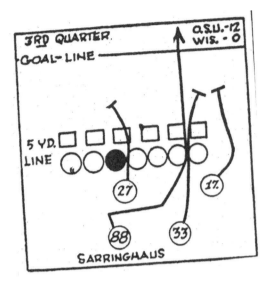

Tailback Paul Sarringhaus scores Ohio State's second touchdown at Wisconsin. *Columbus Citizen,* Sunday, October 14, 1945

ters, using what amounted to an eight-man defensive front with five linemen and three linebackers. Widdoes adjusted his offense at halftime to include more passing and sweeps to the outside—it resulted in five second-half touchdowns.

Wisconsin was a much stronger opponent on a very cold and windy October 13. The Buckeyes scored touchdowns in the second and third quarters to defeat the charged-up Badgers, 12-0, before a home crowd of 69,235. OSU's first touchdown was scored by freshman Tom Watson on a 10-yard pass from Dick Fisher, just one minute and 42 seconds before halftime. Paul Sarringhaus raced into the end zone from the five for Ohio State's second score, completing a 78-yard march at the beginning of the third period. The Ohio State Marching Band's halftime show paid tribute to all returning servicemen.

Winning Streak Snapped

In their fourth consecutive home game, the third-ranked Buckeyes were defeated convincingly by ninth-rated Purdue (4-0), 35-13, snapping OSU's victory string at 12. It

was Widdoes' first setback at Ohio State. The game was far more one-sided than indicated by the spread of 22 points. The Ohio Stadium contingent of 73,585 watched the Boilermakers build up a 28-0 lead before the Buckeyes scored their two touchdowns in the fourth period.

Coach Cecil Isbell's Purdue attack was spearheaded by the power running of Ed Cody and the razor sharp passing of quarterback Bob DeMoss. Cody weaved his way through the Buckeye defense for 146 yards and three of his team's five touchdowns, while DeMoss' 138 passing yards included two scoring tosses to Bill Canfield. OSU dropped to 12th in the weekly AP, and Purdue advanced to fourth.

The Buckeyes rebounded impressively to hand Minnesota its first setback of the season, 20-7, at Minneapolis on October 27. OSU's team spirit, very low after the Purdue ambush, was excellent. Ollie Cline, Dick Fisher, and end Bud Kessler scored touch-

Warren Amling, two-time All-American guard and tackle.

Field Goal In Last 2 Minutes Wins for OSU

Northwestern's 14-Point Lead Overcome by Battling Bucks In Thrill-Packed Contest

Columbus Citizen, Sunday, November 4, 1945

downs, and Max Schnittker was successful on two of three extra-point attempts.

This triumph at Minnesota was Ohio State's 300th football victory. The Buckeyes' all-time record now stood at 300-140-33. The surprise of the weekend came from Evanston, where Northwestern upset Purdue, 26-14, leaving Indiana alone on top of the league standings.

Fantastic Finish

Back home the following weekend, Ohio State ran its record to 5-1 with a heart-stopping 16-14 triumph over Northwestern. The Wildcats, who entered the game at 2-2-1, abruptly jumped out to a 14-0 first-quarter lead before a stunned Dad's Day crowd of 74,079. The Buckeye defense tightened, and Ollie Cline scored touchdowns on one-yard plunges in the second and fourth periods to pull the Buckeyes within one at 14-13.

Rushing Record Set

Against the Pitt Panthers, sophomore fullback Ollie Cline established an Ohio State single-game rushing record with 229 yards on 32 carries. Cline's record stood for 27 seasons until Archie Griffin ran for 239 yards against North Carolina in 1972.

With just one minute and 28 seconds remaining, 18-year-old freshman Max Schnittker calmly booted a 32-yard field goal to give Ohio State its first lead of the afternoon and a 16-14 victory. The winning kick was made at the closed end of Ohio Stadium from a very difficult angle, just 14 yards from the east sideline. William Schnittker, Max's father, raced onto the field immediately after the kick to join in the celebration. Afterwards, the elder Schnittker stated that, "I didn't realize where I was or what I was doing until I got out on the field." Cline had one of his finest games, rushing for 180 yards on 34 carries.

On November 10, the Buckeyes rallied for two touchdowns in the game's final eight minutes to defeat Pittsburgh, 14-0. Parts of ten Ohio State uniforms were stolen from the visitors' dressing room at Pitt Stadium Friday night, creating quite a challenge for OSU's equipment managers on Saturday morning. It was Pitt's 16th consecutive loss to a Big Ten opponent. Snow, sleet and rain

held the attendance to little more than 20,000. The Ohio State marching band made its first trip to an away game since 1941.

Superb Homecoming

Ohio State turned in one of its strongest games of the season, defeating Illinois, 27-2, before a homecoming crowd of 70,287. Playing in the cold and rain for the second straight Saturday, the Buckeyes used their superior line play to score 20 of their 27 points in the fourth quarter, and run their season record to 7-1. Ollie Cline again led the OSU ground attack with 122 yards and two of his team's four touchdowns. The other TDs came on an 11-yard bolt through right tackle by Hal Daugherty and a 15-yard toss from Paul Sarringhaus to fullback Chuck Gandee.

The Buckeyes advanced to seventh in the weekly AP, one spot ahead of their next opponent, the Michigan Wolverines (6-3). Heading into this last week of the regular season, Indiana was the only conference team still undefeated. The Buckeyes could

earn a share of the league title with a win over Michigan and a Purdue victory at Indiana. Neither happened. The Wolverines edged the favored Buckeyes, 7-3, while IU whitewashed the Boilermakers, 26-0.

Ohio State and Michigan staged a thrilling defensive battle, which could have gone either way. After a scoreless first half, OSU's Robin Priday intercepted Pete Elliott's pass at the OSU 30-yard line, setting up a march which went all the way to the UM 10. When the drive stalled, partly because an injury temporarily forced Ollie Cline out of the game, Max Schnittker booted a 27-yard field goal to put the Buckeyes in front, 3-0.

Midway through the fourth period, Michigan put together its only sustained drive of the afternoon, moving 44 yards in seven plays for the game's only touchdown to win, 7-3. Sophomore halfback Hank Fonde scored the TD

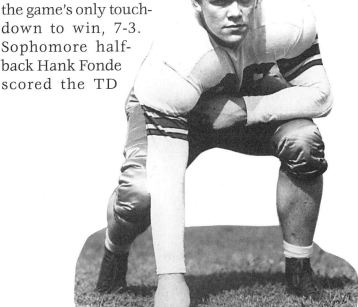

All-American tackle Russ Thomas

with a reverse over OSU's right tackle. The drive's big play was a 25-yard pass from Pete Elliott to Fonde at the OSU 19. Each team had 11 first downs, while Michigan held a very slight edge in total offensive yards, 179-167.

Cline Big Ten MVP

Indiana captured its first conference championship with a league mark of 5-0-1 and an overall record of 9-0-1. The Hoosiers became the final conference school to win a Big Ten title in football. Army (9-0) was voted the national champion, followed by Navy (7-1-1), Alabama (9-0), and Indiana (9-0-1). Michigan (7-3) was sixth in the final poll, and Ohio State (7-2) placed 12th. Warren Amling, Ollie Cline, and Russ Thomas were selected All-Americans, and Cline was chosen the Big Ten's MVP.

Unprecedented Job Exchange

Not all was happy in Buckeyeland. After compiling an outstanding two-year record

---

Hoosier Success

Indiana has won two Big Ten football titles—outright in 1945, and a three-way tie with Minnesota and Purdue in 1967. The Hoosiers and Buckeyes did not meet either of these two seasons.

---

of 16-2, Carroll Widdoes asked to return to his old job as an assistant coach.

Widdoes was a very quiet and religious individual, who did not relish the limelight. He preferred spending his evenings with his wife and three children rather than speaking to alumni groups around the country. Widdoes never aspired to become a head coach—he was much happier as an assistant. Athletic Director Lynn W. St. John agreed. On January 2, 1946, assistant coach Paul Bixler was elevated to Ohio State's head coach, and Carroll Widdoes returned to his former role as an assistant. It was one of the most astonishing switches in college football history, and the Buckeye football program was gaining a reputation as the "graveyard of coaches."

All-American fullback Ollie Cline,
Big Ten MVP

1945

September 29	Missouri	W	47	6
October 6	Iowa	W	42	0
October 13	Wisconsin	W	12	0
October 20	Purdue	L	13	35
October 27	at Minnesota	W	20	7
November 3	Northwestern	W	16	14
November 10	at Pittsburgh	W	14	0
November 17	Illinois (HC)	W	27	2
November 24	at Michigan	L	3	7
Total Points			194	71

Season Record: 7-2
Conference: 3rd Place

Bixler Is Named OSU Coach

Widdoes Returns To Assistant Job At Own Request

Columbus Dispatch, Thursday, January 3, 1946

1946

Paul Bixler, a native of Louisville, Ohio, began his coaching career at Canton Central Junior High School, following his graduation from Mt. Union College in 1929. At Mt. Union, he played both guard and fullback on the football team. Bixler moved to Canton McKinley High School as head basketball coach and assistant football coach in 1932, the same season Paul Brown took over the Massillon Tigers program. It was during his Massillon team's preparation to face McKinley each fall, that Brown became impressed with Bixler.

After three years as McKinley's line coach, Bixler spent a total of six years as head basketball coach and assistant football coach at both Akron University and Colgate University, before accepting Brown's offer to join him at Ohio State in 1941. At Colgate, he was end and wingback coach under noted head coach Andy Kerr. Paul Brown had recently offered Bixler an assistant coach position with his newly formed Cleveland Browns. Bixler was a keen, forth-

right, popular individual, who was well-known for his accurate and comprehensive scouting reports of upcoming opponents. The 39-year-old father of five had never been a head football coach until accepting the position at Ohio State.

Many former players were back on campus after the war to complete their education and return to the college gridiron. A controversy developed when some returning veterans decided to sign professional contracts with Paul Brown's new Cleveland Browns, rather than return to Ohio State. Most no-

Fullback Joe Whisler (36) scoring one of his three touchdowns at Southern California.

How the Ball Moved
Ohio State 21 - Southern California 0

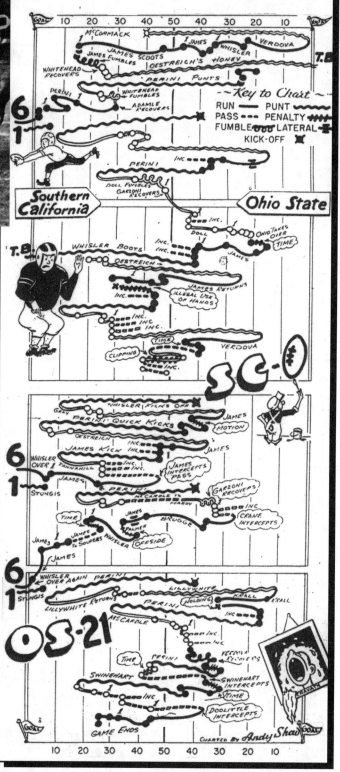

Columbus Citizen, Sunday, October 6, 1946

table among those with remaining college eligibility who signed with Cleveland were end Dante Lavelli, guard Lin Houston, fullback Gene Fekete, guard George Cheroke, and tackle Lou Groza, who had been a freshman at Ohio State in 1942.

Discouraging Start

The heavily favored Buckeyes were tied by Missouri, 13-13, in their September 28 season opener, before an Ohio Stadium crowd of 65,004. Coach Don Faurot's Tigers had opened its season the previous Saturday with a 42-0 loss at Texas. Paul Bixler was disappointed with his team's showing, expressing concern over his team's mistakes. The Buckeyes lost three fumbles, threw one interception, and were guilty of seven penalties.

It looked like an entirely different team the following week, as Ohio State blasted Southern California, 21-0, before a crowd of 80,407 at the Los Angeles Coliseum. Sophomore fullback Joe

Halfback Tommy James (66) swings right for extra yardage against Purdue.

Whisler ran for 73 yards and scored all three of the game's touchdowns on short plunges. Southern California designated the contest as the Howard Harding Jones Memorial Game, in tribute to their very successful coach who died in 1941. Jones had also been Ohio State's head coach in 1910.

The Buckeyes had a rough plane trip to Los Angeles. Ohio State ended up using three DC-3's, after its plan to use one large plane was cancelled by the government shortly before the flight. Using the smaller planes, stops had to be made in St. Louis, Oklahoma City, and Albuquerque. On the flight back, fog forced the team to spend Sunday night in Albuquerque, delaying the return home until late Monday evening.

After a couple of days of practice, the team headed to Madison by train Thursday evening for an October 12 encounter with Wisconsin. Before a Camp Randall Stadium crowd of 45,000, the Badgers came from behind to defeat Bixler's very tired Ohio State squad, 20-7. OSU led 7-0 at halftime but just couldn't sustain the effort needed in the final two quarters of play.

Too Many Missed Opportunities

The Buckeyes and Purdue Boilermakers played to a 14-14 tie the following Saturday, leaving Ohio State with a disappointing record of 1-1-2. The Ohio Stadium crowd of 76,025 watched OSU open up with a 14-0 lead that it could not maintain. Bob DeMoss and Ed Cody provided the fireworks for Purdue, just as they had done in 1945. DeMoss passed 40 yards to Cody to complete a 95-yard drive for Purdue's first touchdown, and Cody raced 78 yards through the entire OSU defense for the other.

Ohio State missed several golden opportunities in the scoreless fourth period. Fullback Pete Perini lost a fumble just inches from the Purdue goal line, another Ohio State drive stalled at the Purdue 22-yard line, and Johnny Stungis missed a field goal attempt from the Purdue 25. Each team finished the afternoon with 339 net yards of offense.

Vast Improvement

The Buckeyes rebounded from the Wisconsin and Purdue games to demolish Minnesota, 39-9, before an October 26 Ohio Stadium attendance of 76,611. After spotting the Golden Gophers an early 6-0 lead, OSU roared back with one of its finest efforts in

the last two seasons. Halfback Bob Brugge, flashing much of his pre-war talent and speed, was the game's leading runner with 102 yards. Brugge scored twice on runs of 31 and 24 yards, and also threw a touchdown pass to Ernie Parks. Dave Bonnie accounted for OSU's final TD with an 18-yard interception return.

Bixler's team made it two in a row, winning a real wild one at Northwestern the following Saturday, 39-27, before a Dyche Stadium crowd of 47,000. The scoring pattern marked the very first game in Ohio State history with both teams scoring in each quarter, as follows:

	1	2	3	4	Final
Ohio State	7	6	12	14	39
Northwestern	7	6	7	7	27

The lead changed hands three times, and the game was tied twice. The Buckeyes were not assured of the victory until Tony Adamle returned an interception 15 yards to the NW 30, setting up Ohio State's sixth and final touchdown with just three minutes and 25 seconds remaining. OSU led in first downs, 19-8, and in total offense, 424 yards to 268. Each team threw three interceptions and lost two fumbles.

Ohio State made it three straight, narrowly defeating the Pitt Panthers on November 9, 20-13. Playing before a home crowd of 74,743, the highly favored Buckeyes were not nearly as effective as they had been at Northwestern the previous week. First-year coach Wes Fesler, former Buckeye great, had his Panther squad primed for an upset. With Pittsburgh's defense stacked to stop OSU's ground game, freshman

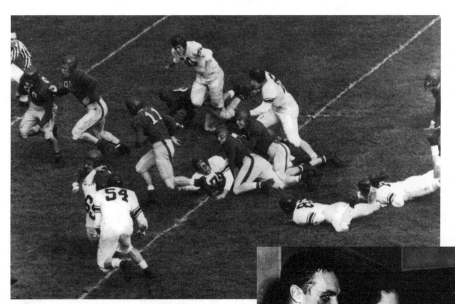

Halfback Bob Brugge (11) follows guard Warren Amling (90) against Northwestern. At bottom of picture is Wildcat center Alex Sarkisian (54).

Jubilant Buckeyes celebrate high-scoring victory at Northwestern. Left to right are quarterback George Spencer, halfback Jerry Krall, halfback Alex Verdova, guard Bob Gaudio, placekicker Johnny Stungis (in background), guard Hal Dean, and head coach Paul Bixler.

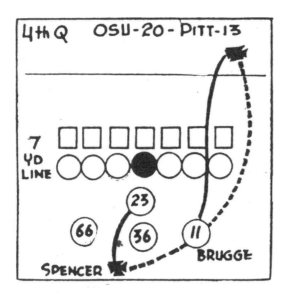

George Spencer passes seven yards to Bob Brugge for Ohio State's third touchdown against Pittsburgh.
Columbus Citizen, Sunday, November 10, 1946

quarterback George Spencer completed nine of 13 passes for 215 yards and all three Buckeye touchdowns. His first scoring toss went to Cy Souders, and the last two were caught by Bob Brugge. Ohio State's overall record was now 4-1-2.

One of the biggest college games of all time was played this same afternoon at Yankee Stadium in New York City. Top-ranked Army and second-ranked Notre Dame battled to a scoreless tie. Notre Dame finished the season as the *AP* national champion with a record of 8-0-1, followed by Army at 9-0-1.

Rose Bowl Still a Possibility

Ohio State still could have earned a trip to the Rose Bowl with victories over Illinois and Michigan in the season's final two games. But those dreams were quickly drowned in a sea of mud at Illinois, where coach Ray Eliot's Fighting Illini upended the Buckeyes, 16-7, breaking OSU's winning streak at three. Playing in the rain most of the afternoon, the Buckeyes advanced deep into Illinois territory midway through the third period, trailing 9-7. With a fourth-and-three at the Illini

four, Spencer tried to pass to Tommy James in the right flat for the first down. Illinois freshman Julius Rykovich stepped in front of James, intercepted at the two, then raced 98 yards for a touchdown which gave his team its nine-point victory.

The November 23 season finale against Michigan was a total disaster. Playing before a homecoming crowd of 78,634, at the time the fourth largest in Ohio Stadium history, the Buckeyes were completely embarrassed by the Wolverines, 58-6. To add insult to injury, and with the score 55-0 late in the final period, Michigan elected to kick a 22-yard field goal to boost its score to 58.

Ohio State avoided a shutout on this cold and cloudy afternoon, when Bill Doolittle and Rodney Swinehard connected with a 63-yard "sleeper" scoring pass with just 59 seconds remaining. The slaughter was OSU's worst conference defeat since joining the Big Ten in 1913. The Wolverines led in first downs, 22-4, and total offensive yards, 509-155. Michigan used 16 different ballcarriers throughout the afternoon.

One of the first to console Paul Bixler after the game was Andy Kerr, who had just retired after 18 seasons as head coach at Colgate, where Bixler served as one of Kerr's assistants in '39 and '40. Kerr was at Ohio Stadium to scout players for the annual East-West Shrine Game in San Francisco on New Year's Day. It was rumored that Kerr was also in Columbus to talk with Bixler about the possibility of Bixler returning to Colgate as Kerr's replacement.

New Year's Tradition

The tradition of matching up the champions of the Big Ten and Pacific Coast (later named Pacific Eight and Pacific Ten) Conferences in the New Year's Day Rose Bowl began with the 1946 season. Illinois defeated UCLA in Pasadena on January 1, 1947, 45-14.

later rejoined Paul Brown in Cleveland with the Browns organization.

All-American end Cy Souders, team MVP

1946				
September 28	Missouri	T	13	13
October 5	at Southern Cal	W	21	0
October 12	at Wisconsin	L	7	20
October 19	Purdue	T	14	14
October 26	Minnesota	W	39	9
November 2	at Northwestern	W	39	27
November 9	Pittsburgh	W	20	13
November 16	at Illinois	L	7	16
November 23	Michigan (HC)	L	6	58
Total Points			166	170

Season Record: 4-3-2
Conference: 6th Place (Tie)

The Buckeyes finished the season with a very disappointing record of 4-3-2, and many fans were wondering if Bixler was the right man for the Ohio State job. Captain Warren Amling was selected an All-American for the second straight season, this time as a tackle (Amling was an All-American guard in 1945). Cy Souders was also tabbed for the All-American teams and was chosen the team MVP.

The average home attendance of 74,203 per game in 1946, marked the first time in the 25-year history of Ohio Stadium that OSU averaged more than 70,000 at home. Since then, the season average per game has never been less than 70,000.

On February 5, 1947, Paul Bixler resigned his Ohio State position to accept the head coaching spot at Colgate, citing the "pressure of the Ohio State job" as a major reason for his change. Most Ohio State followers were stunned, especially after learning that Colgate's stadium on the Hamilton, New York, campus seated approximately 15,000. Ohio State's reputation as the "graveyard of coaches" was steadily getting stronger. Bixler stayed at Colgate five seasons, compiling an overall record of 14-27-2. He

1947

With the Buckeye football program begging for stability, Ohio State selected 39-year-old Wesley Fesler, who had been one of the finest athletes in school history. Other coaches who were rumored to be candidates to become the fifth Ohio State coach in the last eight seasons were Sid Gillman, former Buckeye captain and presently coach at Miami (Ohio); Jack Mollenkopf, highly successful coach at Toledo Waite High School; and Missouri's Don Faurot.

Bring Back Brown

There was also a campaign among some Buckeye fans to bring Paul Brown back to Columbus. The State of Ohio House of Representatives passed a resolution, suggesting that Ohio State find out if Brown would be interested in returning. It is not clear how much attention (if any) Ohio State gave to this resolution. The overall selection process

OHIO STATE GIVES FESLER CONTRACT FOR FIVE YEARS

New Football Coach Assumes Duties at Once

Lyal Clark and Dick Fisher To Be Brought From Pittsburgh

Columbus Dispatch, Saturday, February 15, 1947

was somewhat of a joint effort between Athletic Director Lynn W. St. John and his future successor, Dick Larkins (St. John would retire July 1 at age 70). The selection of Fesler was announced on February 14, 1947. Fesler and Larkins had been teammates at Ohio State and were long-time friends.

Wes Fesler, who grew up in Youngstown, won nine varsity letters at Ohio State—three each in football, basketball, and baseball. He was a three-time All-American end and fullback in 1928-29-30, and was the team captain and Big Ten MVP his senior season.

Fesler was an All-Big Ten guard in basketball, and was so versatile on the baseball diamond that he played first base, second base, and center field. He graduated from Ohio State's College of Commerce in 1932.

Fesler's first coaching position was as an assistant to Sam Willaman at Ohio State in '31 and '32. He moved to Harvard for eight years as an assistant in football and head basketball coach. Fesler moved to Connecticut Wesleyan as head football coach in '41 and '42. When Wesleyan dropped football during the war, he worked for two years in Washington, D.C., with the Office of Strategic Services.

After the war, Fesler was head basketball coach and a football assistant at Princeton for one year, before replacing head coach Clark Shaughnessy at the University of Pittsburgh in 1946. His only Pitt team was 3-6-1, but Ohio State officials were very impressed with the Panthers' efforts during Pitt's 20-13 loss at Ohio State. Fesler became just the second Ohio State graduate to be named the school's head football coach—Sam Willaman, Fesler's coach in '29 and '30, was the first.

Buckeyes Lose James and Adamle

Fesler used the single wing offense to a much greater extent than did Widdoes or Bixler. He learned a lot about the single wing

Captain Bob Jabbusch, Big Ten Scholar-Athlete 1947

OHIO STATE
MISSOURI

The Columbus Citizen

Local Weather—Increasing cloudiness and somewhat warmer today.

VOL. 49—No. 212 ★ ★ ★ COLUMBUS 15, OHIO, SUNDAY, SEPTEMBER 28, 1947

SUNDAY EDITION
10c
DAILY AND SUNDAY,
30c PER WEEK

BUCKS BEAT MISSOURI, 13 TO 7

25c

losing to the Purdue Boilermakers in a real thriller, 24-20. The Buckeyes twice came from behind to take the lead, and almost did it a third time before losing possession on downs at the Purdue 30 with one minute to play. Purdue's new coach this fall was Stu Holcomb, a former Fesler teammate at Ohio State who had been the Buckeyes' captain in 1931.

Buckeyes Suffer First of Four Shutouts

Southern California scored in each quarter to thoroughly trounce Ohio State, 32-0, before 76,559 stunned spectators at Ohio Stadium on October 11. At the time, it was the largest margin of defeat ever dealt an OSU squad by a team from the west coast. The afternoon was

during his year at Princeton, and the Buckeyes ran this formation from an unbalanced line, making extensive use of flankers and the buck-lateral series. Ohio State was weakened when two of its finest players jumped to the professional ranks. Halfback Tommy James, Captain-elect for '47, signed with the NFL's Detroit Lions for one year, then joined the Cleveland Browns of the ACC the following season. Center Tony Adamle became a Cleveland Brown after considering an offer from the NFL's Chicago Bears. On the plus side, Dean Sensenbaugher was back in a Scarlet and Gray uniform after completing his assignment at West Point.

The Buckeyes opened at home September 27 with a relatively unimpressive 13-7 win over Missouri, before an anxious crowd of 59,444. After a scoreless first half, OSU put together scoring drives of 75 and 84 yards to seal the victory. Fullback Joe Whisler, the game's leading rusher with 65 yards, scored both touchdowns on short power plunges.

Wes Fesler suffered his first Ohio State loss the following weekend at West Lafayette,

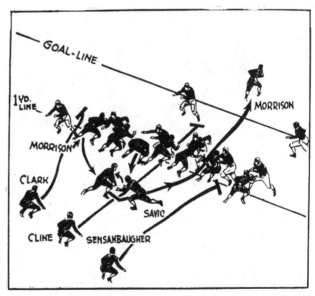

Ohio State used the old-fashioned end around play to tie Iowa, 13-13. With just 52 seconds to play, quarterback Pandel Savic faked a handoff to fullback Ollie Cline, then slipped the ball to Curly Morrison coming around from left end. Morrison sliced off right tackle for the final yard and the touchdown. Emil Moldea's extra point tied the score.
Columbus Citizen, Sunday, October 19, 1947

Dad of Dads

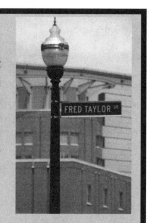

The honored Dad of Dads at the Ohio State Dad's Day game against Iowa was Mr. John F. Taylor of Zanesville, Ohio, whose son Fred was a sophomore in the College of Education. Interestingly, son Fred would excel in both basketball and baseball for the Buckeyes, and would later coach the Ohio State basketball team to its only NCAA title in 1960. Taylor is a member of the Basketball Hall of Fame. The drive on the west side of Ohio State's Schottenstein Center is named in Fred Taylor's honor.

Ohio State's Schottenstein Center on Fred Taylor Drive

Pitt's Only Victory

The underdog Pitt Panthers surprised Ohio State, 12-0, before an appreciative Pitt Stadium homecoming crowd of 55,217 on October 25. By winning their only game of the 1947 season, Pitt snapped a 24-game losing streak to Big Ten Conference opponents. The Panthers finished the year at 1-8, being outscored, 267-26. They managed only four touchdowns all season—two of them were against the Buckeyes. It was a particularly tough afternoon for Wes Fesler, who offered sincere congratulations to Panther head coach Walt Milligan, Fesler's former assistant at Pitt the previous season.

Although their play was much improved the following weekend, the Buckeyes lost a bruising battle to Indiana, 7-0, before a very disappointed Ohio Stadium crowd of 75,882. The Hoosiers' George Taliaferro scored the game's only touchdown with a five-yard

a stark contrast with the Buckeyes' 21-0 triumph over the Trojans at Los Angeles the previous season.

Fesler's squad was much improved at home the following Saturday, coming from behind to tie Iowa, 13-13, after trailing 13-0 with just nine minutes remaining in the final quarter. Fullback Ollie Cline carried five yards over center for OSU's first touchdown to complete an 80-yard drive, and Curly Morrison scored the other TD on a two-yard end around play, finishing off a 72-yard march. The Buckeyes' season record stood at 1-2-1.

Wrong Sideline Two Years Running

Wes Fesler was the losing coach in two consecutive Ohio State—Pittsburgh games, even though he changed jobs between seasons. Ohio State defeated Fesler's Pitt Panthers in 1946, 20-13, and Pitt upset Fesler's Ohio State Buckeyes the next season, 12-0.

smash over his own left tackle, completing an 80-yard first-quarter march. The drive's long gainer was a 63-yard pass from Taliaferro to Melvin Groomes, who was downed at the OSU 12. The triumph was Indiana's first conference win of the season, and left Ohio State as the only Big Ten team without at least one conference victory.

Uncanny Ending Earns Buckeyes Much Needed Win

The November 8 game against Northwestern produced one of the most bizarre and hectic finishes in college football history. With the game knotted at 0-0 after three quarters, NU halfback Frank Aschenbrenner scored from the one-yard line on the second play of the fourth period to put the Wildcats on top, 6-0. Jim Farrar's conversion attempt was wide—it was just his second miss of the season.

Late in the game, the Buckeyes drove from midfield to the Northwestern one-yard line, where they were held on downs with just one minute and 47 seconds remaining. At that point, many of the 70,203 fans headed for the exits, apparently conceding the game to the Wildcats. Northwestern was soon forced to kick after failing to register a first down, and OSU's Bob Demmel returned Tom Worthington's punt to the NU 36-yard line with just 31 seconds remaining.

On first down, quarterback Pandel Savic passed 24 yards to Demmel at the Wildcat 12—there were 13 sec-

onds left. Savic's next pass was intercepted by L. A. Day as time expired, and Northwestern had apparently won, 6-0. The Ohio State marching band started onto the field for its postgame show, and fans were now pouring out of the stadium by the thousands. However, Northwestern had 12 men on the field during the last play, and Ohio State would have one more down.

The Buckeyes tried a deep reverse with Rodney Swinehart carrying, but Swinehart was tackled at the two. But wait—Northwestern had two players lined up offside, and OSU would have yet another play. This time Savic fired a lobbing pass to Jimmy Clark in the back corner of the end zone to tie the score, 6-6.

Emil Moldea's extra point, four plays after time had expired, gives Ohio State a 7-6 victory over Northwestern.

Emil Moldea's conversion attempt was blocked, but AGAIN two Northwestern players were offside. Moldea's second attempt was good, giving Ohio State the win, 7-6. Three Northwestern penalties had enabled the Buckeyes to score all seven of their points on the second and fourth plays after time had expired.

Headlinesman E. C. Curtis, a 25-year veteran Big Ten official, called the three penalties against Northwestern after time had expired. Wildcat coach Bob Voigts might have been more disturbed if field judge Irish Krieger had flagged any of NU's infractions— Irish's son, George, was a reserve guard on Ohio State's squad. The game also marked the first time OSU's Bonnie twins, Dave and Dale, had seen game action together, since their playing days at Columbus North High School. Interestingly, earlier that morning the Ohio State junior varsity had beaten

Halfback Jimmy Clark with coach Wes Fesler.

Northwestern's JV squad, by the same 7-6 score.

In the November 15 home finale, 70,036 shivering and rain-spattered fans watched Illinois score two touchdowns in the fourth period to win over the Buckeyes, 28-7. The Illini led in first downs, 16-9, and total offensive yards, 318-216. At Ann Arbor the following weekend, the Buckeyes played their hearts out before losing to Michigan, 21-0. The Wolverines finished their season at 9-0 under retiring coach Fritz Crisler.

Ohio State completed the year at 2-6-1, finishing last in the Big Ten Conference (1-4-1) for the only time in school history. Fullback Ollie Cline was the team's leading rusher with 332 yards, and quarterback Dick Slager led the team in passing with 236 yards. Guard David Templeton was chosen the team MVP. It had been a tough year for first-year coach Wes Fesler, but better times were just around the corner.

Quarterback
Dick Slager

1947

September 27	Missouri	W	13	7
October 4	at Purdue	L	20	24
October 11	Southern California	L	0	32
October 18	Iowa	T	13	13
October 25	at Pittsburgh	L	0	12
November 1	Indiana	L	0	7
November 8	Northwestern	W	7	6
November 15	Illinois (HC)	L	7	28
November 22	at Michigan	L	0	21
Total Points			**60**	**150**

Season Record: 2-6-1
Conference: 9th Place

1948

Fesler's second year at the helm was much improved. The players were now more accustomed to his system, and the 1947 season had given Fesler and his coaching staff a season to work together and mature. Two of Ohio State's major objectives were to improve the offense (OSU scored only 60 points the previous season) and reduce the number of turnovers. On the downside, two of the Buckeyes' backfield veterans, who were eligible for the professional draft since their classes had graduated, decided to give up their remaining college eligibility—halfbacks Dean Sensenbaugher and Bob Brugge were both drafted by the Cleveland Browns.

The Buckeyes opened September 25 with a convincing 21-7 triumph over coach Don Faurot's Missouri Tigers, before an Ohio Stadium throng of 57,042. Fullback Curly Morrison and halfback Jimmy Clark, both juniors, played major roles. Morrison replaced Joe Whisler after Whisler was injured while scoring the Buckeyes' first touchdown on a 14-yard cut back over right guard. Morrison finished the afternoon with 68

yards and scored the game's last TD on a short plunge in the final period. Clark was the game's leading ground gainer with 70 yards, including a two-yard dash over tackle for Ohio State's second score.

Quarterback Pandel Savic had a solid afternoon, completing all five of his passes for 84 yards. Savic's big toss was a 35-yarder to end Bob Dorsey during OSU's first scoring drive. Ohio State led in first downs, 20-11, and total offensive yards, 349-179.

What a Difference a Year Makes

The Buckeyes astonished even their most ardent supporters the following weekend, soundly defeating Southern California,

Columbus Citizen, Sunday, October 3, 1948

20-0, before another excellent Ohio Stadium crowd of 75,102. The game was a complete contrast to USC's 32-0 victory in 1947. Joe Whisler scored twice on short plunges from inside the one, and Jerry Krall caught a six-yard toss from Pandel Savic for the final touchdown of the afternoon. The game was broadcast nationally by Harry Wismer of ABC and NBC's Bill Stern.

The October 9 conference opener was a much different story. Iowa upset the Buckeyes, 14-7, before a disappointed home crowd of 63,394. OSU suffered from four lost fumbles and a number of mental errors. It was the Hawkeyes' first win in Columbus in 20 seasons.

The Buckeyes looked much better the next weekend, shutting out Indiana, 17-0, before a homecoming crowd of 34,000 at Bloomington. The blocking and tackling had improved over the Iowa game, and the team played with a lot more poise and confidence. Whisler and Clark scored touchdowns in the opening period, and Jimmy Hague added a 24-yard field goal in the final quarter. The Buckeyes had a decided edge in the game's statistics, leading in first downs, 20-6, and total offensive yards, 333-99.

Buckeye Air Attack Sinks Badgers

Ohio State's October 23 encounter with Wisconsin was one of the most exhilarating games between the two schools. The Buckeyes outlasted the Badgers, 34-32, with all of OSU's five touchdowns being scored through the air. The inspired Wisconsin players tried desperately to win this one for their coach,

Harry Stuhldreher, who was under attack from alumni and fans after his team started the season at 1-3. Most of the Ohio Stadium Dad's Day crowd of 77,205 was breathless and limp by the end of the afternoon. Following is the scoring by quarters:

	1	2	3	4	Final
Wisconsin	12	7	13	0	32
Ohio State	0	20	7	7	34

It was definitely a "team victory" in every sense. The lead changed hands four times, and three times the Buckeyes battled back from a 12-point deficit. Three players passed for the five OSU touchdowns—Pandel Savic and Jerry Krall each had two, and the other was thrown by Alex Verdova. Verdova was also on the receiving end of both of Krall's throws and Savic's first TD toss.

Halfback Jimmy Clark (12) skirts right end for some of his game-high 75 yards rushing against Wisconsin.

Savic's other scoring pass went to Joe Cannavino, while Verdova's was caught by Sonny Gandee.

Ohio State's winning score came on Krall's second TD pass to Verdova, a four-yarder early in the fourth quarter. OSU led in first downs, 17-14, and total offense, 421 yards to 317. Jimmy Clark was the game's leading rusher with 75 yards on 14 carries, while Savic connected on eight of 11 passes for 162 yards. This triumph over Wisconsin was Ohio State's 500th football game. The Buckeyes all-time record stood at 313-151-36 (66.2%).

At sunny Evanston the following weekend, Northwestern dashed Ohio State's faint Rose Bowl dreams, 21-7, before a thrilled homecoming crowd of 47,000. The Wildcats' overall team speed was one noticeable difference in the two teams. Sophomore halfback Johnny Miller, who had played a total of only 30 minutes in the season's first five games, led the powerful Northwestern rushing attack with 124 yards and two of his team's three touchdowns. Ohio State was

now 4-2 on the season, 2-2 in conference play.

The Buckeyes had no trouble overpowering Pittsburgh, 41-0, at home on November 6. Fesler used a total of 42 players, including many members of the OSU Junior Varsity team who had played that morning in a game against Pitt's JV squad. OSU's 41 points provided the largest margin of victory in any of the 13 games that had been played in the series. The previous Tuesday, Harry Truman pulled the fall's biggest upset, de-

Varsity "O" at Last

Arthur Huntington, who won a football letter in 1895, finally received his award 53 years later. Renick Dunlap, the 1895 captain, was reviewing a list of Varsity "O" members, and realized Huntington's name was missing. Dunlap notified the Ohio State Athletic Department and Huntington's monogrammed sweater was finally sent to him in 1948.

How the Ball Moved
Ohio State 34 - Illinois 7

Columbus Citizen, Sunday, November 14, 1948

feating Thomas Dewey in the 1948 Presidential election.

The Buckeyes stunned Illinois, 34-7, playing one of their best games of the season before an Illini homecoming crowd of 65,732. The Champaign weather was perfect for football, and Ohio State got stronger as the game wore on, scoring three of its five touchdowns in the fourth period. OSU made up for its lack of great team speed with superb timing on offense and smart anticipation on defense.

One of the afternoon's longest plays was a 39-yard pass from Bucky Wertz to Jimmy Hague at the Illini five, setting up OSU's fourth touchdown. It was a surprising play, since Wertz and Hague both played mostly on defense. The team dedicated the game to retired Athletic Director Lynn W. St. John, whose wife hadpassed away the day before the game.

Superb Showing
Against Wolverines

Ohio State returned home November 20 to face top-ranked Michigan, whose winning streak now stood at 22. The Wolverines' last setback was at home to Illinois, 13-9, over two years earlier on October 26, 1946. OSU at 6-2 was ranked 18th nationally. The homecoming crowd of 82,754 was, at the time, the second largest in Ohio Stadium history. The Buckeyes, who were still in the game with five minutes left, put up a brilliant battle before losing, 13-3. In the end, it was Michigan's superior speed that spelled the difference.

Football Capital of the World. Broad and High Streets in Columbus the morning of an Ohio State-Michigan game. *Columbus Citizen,* Saturday, November 20, 1948

OSU quickly went out in front 3-0 on Jimmy Hague's 30-yard field goal, with 9:29 remaining in the first quarter. Michigan drove 90 yards midway through the second period to grab the lead, 7-3, and a 62-yard Wolverine march in the final quarter finished the scoring. Ohio State had the better of the game statistics, leading in first downs, 14-9, and total offensive yards, 203-170. It was the only game all season in which the Buckeyes were held without at least one touchdown.

The Wolverines won their second consecutive outright Big Ten title but could not return to the Rose Bowl because of the "no repeat" policy in place at that time. This was quite an accomplishment for Bennie Oosterbaan, who was in his first season as UM's head coach. Second-place Northwestern made the New Year's trip to Pasadena, defeating California, 20-14, in one of the most exciting bowl games ever played. Michigan (9-0) captured the national title, Northwestern (8-2) finished seventh, and Minnesota (7-2) placed 16th.

The 1948 season had been very successful for Fesler, whose second OSU squad finished the year at 6-3. Fullback Joe Whisler was chosen the team MVP. The Buckeye foot-

Fullback Joe Whisler, team MVP

1948			
September 25	Missouri	W 21	7
October 2	Southern California	W 20	0
October 9	Iowa	L 7	14
October 16	at Indiana	W 17	0
October 23	Wisconsin	W 34	32
October 30	at Northwestern	L 7	21
November 6	Pittsburgh	W 41	0
November 13	at Illinois	W 34	7
November 20	Michigan (HC)	L 3	13
Total Points		**184**	**94**

Season Record: 6-3
Conference: 4th Place

1949

ball program would continue to improve, and the following season's squad would develop into one of the most determined teams in all of Ohio State football.

Ohio State began fall practice with 27 lettermen back, plus one of the finest sophomore classes in school history. Two years

First Come, First Serve

The 1948 Ohio State-Michigan game at Ohio Stadium attracted media coverage from all over the country. In those years three radio networks, CBS, NBC, and Mutual, each did a "game of the week" national broadcast. Retired OSU Sports Information Director Marv Homan remembers that each network normally followed an unwritten policy of notifying the home school by Monday if that school's game the following Saturday had been selected for broadcast.

CBS, with sportscaster Ted Husing, had selected the Ohio State-Michigan game several weeks in advance. By Monday evening prior to the game, Wilbur Snypp (then SID) had not heard from NBC, so he assumed NBC was going elsewhere. However, Bill Stern, NBC's prominent sportscaster, called Snypp on Wednesday to request a booth for the broadcast of Saturday's Ohio State-Michigan game. Stern was furious when told that all of the Ohio Stadium radio booths had been assigned, and there was no space for NBC to air his broadcast.

With the press box full, Snypp had a temporary open-air platform erected, extending from the stadium's southwest corner and adjacent to C deck. With Stern were two student spotters, Dick Mantanaro for Ohio State and Ray Collins for Michigan. Even though the view of the playing field wasn't the greatest, it was from this small make-shift platform overlooking the south end zone that the famous Bill Stern aired nationally the Ohio State-Michigan game of 1948.

Starting offensive lineup in 1949. Line from left to right: Jimmy Hague, Jack Wilson, Richard O'Hanlon, John Biltz, Jack Lininger, George Toneff, and Sonny Gandee. Backfield from left to right: Ray Hamilton, Curly Morrison, Pandel Savic, and Jimmy Clark. Backs Jerry Krall and Vic Janowicz also saw considerable action this season.

earlier, an organization known as the "Frontliners" was formed to help recruit top talent for the Ohio State football program. Ed Weaver, then field secretary with the Ohio State Alumni Association, and assistant coach Ernie Godfrey organized the group, which was comprised primarily of prominent graduates, top businessmen, and enthusiastic supporters, who would help direct the top high school talent toward Columbus. This season's excellent class of sophomores was partly the result of the Frontliners' fine efforts.

One of these top sophomores was Vic Janowicz, a highly talented youngster from Elyria, Ohio, who had been one of the most recruited prospects in college football history. Janowicz picked Ohio State over more than 60 other schools, partly because of the influence of Mr. John Galbreath, a wealthy Columbus businessman who loved sports. The impact of the multi-talented Janowicz was felt immediately, particularly at defensive safety. Another exceptionally talented sophomore who would play right from the start was halfback Ray Hamilton from McKinley High School in Canton.

Assistant coach Carroll Widdoes left Ohio State to become head coach of the Ohio University Bobcats. His son, Dick Widdoes, was a junior halfback at Ohio State in '49, and played a prominent role in the Buckeyes' defensive backfield.

First TV from Ohio Stadium

Ohio State's 35-34 victory over Missouri in the September 24 season opener was a thriller from start to finish. It also was the

MISSOURI
OHIO STATE

25¢

SEPTEMBER 24, 1949

ing pass with 3:52 remaining in the third period. The touchdown was set up by center Jack Lininger's interception return to the Missouri 30-yard line.

Hague Five For Five

The Tigers scored again early in the fourth period, but John Glorioso's conversion attempt was wide, leaving OSU with a 28-27 lead. The two teams traded touchdowns to

BUCKS EDGE MISSOURI, 35-34

Columbus Citizen, Sunday, September 25, 1949

conclude the scoring at 35-34. Ohio State's final score was another TD toss from Savic to Hamilton, this one covering 24 yards. Jimmy Hague was successful on all five of

very first contest televised from Ohio Stadium (WLW-C TV, now NBC4-TV). Playing before an Ohio Stadium crowd of 66,510, the Buckeyes were fortunate to be tied 14-14 at halftime—Missouri was plagued by three first-half fumbles. Starting left halfback Jimmy Clark suffered a shoulder separation in the second period, and was out for the rest of the afternoon. Following is the scoring by quarters:

	1	2	3	4	Final
Missouri	7	7	7	13	34
Ohio State	0	14	14	7	35

Ohio State's first-half scores came on a two-yard plunge over center by fullback Curly Morrison and an eight-yard cut back inside right end by halfback Jerry Krall. Missouri scored first in the third period to lead 21-14, but Ohio State again tied the score on a 31-yard pass from Krall to end Jimmy Hague. The Buckeyes took their first lead, 28-21, when quarterback Pandel Savic teamed with Ray Hamilton on a 30-yard scor-

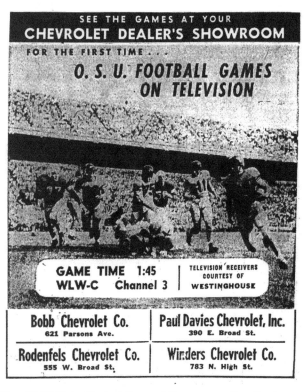

SEE THE GAMES AT YOUR
CHEVROLET DEALER'S SHOWROOM
FOR THE FIRST TIME...
**O. S. U. FOOTBALL GAMES
ON TELEVISION**

GAME TIME 1:45 WLW-C Channel 3	TELEVISION RECEIVERS COURTESY OF WESTINGHOUSE

Bobb Chevrolet Co. 621 Parsons Ave.	**Paul Davies Chevrolet, Inc.** 390 E. Broad St.
Rodenfels Chevrolet Co. 555 W. Broad St.	**Winders Chevrolet Co.** 783 N. High St.

The 1949 Ohio State-Missouri Game was the first to be televised from Ohio Stadium. *Columbus Citizen,* Friday, September 23, 1949

Ohio State's 1949 coaching staff. Left to right, Ernie Godfrey, Harry Strobel, Lyal Clark, head coach Wes Fesler, Dick Fisher, Esco Sarkkinen, and Gene Fekete.

Janowicz and Skip Doyle each scored their first collegiate TDs. OSU led in first downs, 25-4, and total offensive yards, 508-96. Indiana University Athletic Director Paul Harrell had all kinds of bad luck. Harrell missed the game altogether, after his automobile broke down just outside of Indianapolis on Saturday morning, as he was heading for Columbus.

The Buckeyes won the statistical battle, but finished with a 13-13 tie against Southern California in Los Angeles on October 8. Each team missed an extra point attempt. Sophomore Frank Gifford,

his conversion attempts, which was the difference in the single-point victory. Missouri still had a shot with just eight seconds remaining and the ball at the OSU 26, but Glorioso's attempted field goal fell low and just short of the goal post.

Ohio State head coach Wes Fesler was especially pleased with the play of Hamilton, who rushed for 111 yards on five carries and caught five passes for 115 yards and two touchdowns. This game also marked the varsity football debut of senior end Dick Schnittker, a 6'5" All-American basketball player. Schnittker joined the football squad just 10 days earlier after injuries had depleted Fesler's end corps. The loss was a tough one for Missouri coach Don Faurot—his team led in first downs, 25-15; outgained Ohio State, 505 yards to 424; and ran 87 plays to OSU's 62.

The following Saturday's game was much different. Ohio State overwhelmed Indiana, 46-7, before a home crowd of 70,568. Jerry Krall was the game's leading rusher with 128 yards and two touchdowns, while

INDIANA OHIO STATE

OCTOBER 1, 1949   25 CENTS

1949 Big Ten Co-Champions and Rose Bowl Champions

who later would star for the NFL's New York Giants, missed his first attempt of the season following USC's first touchdown. Jimmy Hague's kick after OSU's second touchdown was blocked. The Buckeyes piled up 407 yards to the Trojans' 194, but made too many mistakes to win (seven fumbles and two interceptions). College football's biggest story this weekend came from Ann Arbor, where Army defeated Michigan, 21-7, breaking the Wolverines' winning streak at 25.

Season's Single Setback

Back home the following Saturday, Minnesota's huge Golden Gophers completely shut down Ohio State's offense, 27-0. Coach Bernie Bierman's bone-crushing line paved the way for the Gophers' fourth straight win of the season, holding OSU to just 48 yards on the ground. Two linemen who especially caused problems for the Buckeyes were 255-pound tackle Leo Nomellini and 246-pound center Clayton Tonnemaker, both All-Americans. Halfbacks Dick Gregory and Billy Bye led Minnesota's ground attack with 131 and 83 yards, respectively.

Ohio State's record was now 2-1-1, and few of the 82,111 fans leaving Ohio Stadium that afternoon would have predicted that the

Buckeyes would finish the season in the Rose Bowl. To make matters worse, several thousand bogus souvenir programs were sold outside the stadium, costing the Ohio State Athletic Department several thousands of dollars in lost revenue. The counterfeit programs apparently contained team rosters and records from the previous year.

Minnesota's MVP this season was All-Big Ten end Bud Grant, who later was enshrined in the Professional Football Hall of Fame after coaching the NFL Minnesota Vikings to four Super Bowl appearances. The game's referee was Jay Berwanger, former Chicago All-American and winner of the first Heisman Trophy in 1935.

Back on Track

The Buckeyes bounced back with an impressive 21-0 triumph at Wisconsin on October 22. It was Ohio State's first game against the Badgers' new coach, Ivy Williamson. Curly Morrison and Jimmy Clark scored first-quarter touchdowns on short runs, and Jerry Krall passed ten yards to Pandel Savic for OSU's third six-pointer in the final period.

Ohio State's kicking could hardly have been any stronger. Morrison and Pete Perini averaged 51.6 yards on seven punts. One of Morrison's kicks went 68 yards, rolling dead at the Badger three. Minnesota lost at Michigan, 14-7, putting many teams including Ohio State back in the Big Ten title picture. At 3-1-1, Ohio State moved into the Associated Press weekly top 20, placing 18th.

Back home the following Saturday, the Buckeyes had little trouble defeating Northwestern, 24-7. OSU's smooth-working offense scored in each quarter, while the Buckeye defense kept the Wildcats in their own territory the entire first half. Northwestern was penalized four times for unsportsmanlike conduct, causing several boos from the highly partisan Dad's Day crowd of 81,872.

Ohio State moved into a first-place tie with Iowa in the league standings, after getting some much needed help from Michigan and Purdue. The Wolverines dropped Illinois from the unbeaten ranks, 13-0, and Purdue handed Minnesota its second straight setback, 13-7. The Buckeyes advanced from 18th to 11th in the weekly *AP*.

OSU was fortunate to escape Pittsburgh with a 14-

Quarterback Pandel Savic

10 victory the following Saturday, November 5. The Buckeyes played poorly most of the afternoon, possibly because they were looking ahead to the season's last two conference games. The Ohio State Marching Band made its first out-of-town trip of the season.

The Panthers entered the game at 5-1. Pittsburgh led 7-0 at halftime on a second-quarter, 17-yard touchdown pass from quarterback Carl DePasqua to end Earl Sumpter. The Panthers increased their lead to 10-0 with Nick Bolkovac's 38-yard field goal three minutes into the third quarter, much to the delight of the Pitt Stadium homecoming crowd of 54,789.

Ohio State then took advantage of two big breaks. OSU tackle George Toneff recovered a Panther fumble at the Pitt 12-yard line, leading to Ohio State's first touchdown—a one-yard sneak by quarterback Pandel Savic. Next, halfback Billy Newell intercepted Lou Cecconi's pass at the OSU 30, setting up a 70-yard march for the winning touchdown. Ray Hamilton out-maneuvered four defenders on a 22-yard scamper around left end for the score. The fourth quarter was scoreless, and Fesler's squad gladly settled for the four-point victory. Pitt outgained Ohio State, 287 yards to 198.

"Comeback Kids" Do It Again

The Buckeyes returned home November 12 for a crucial encounter with coach Ray Eliot's Illinois squad (3-2-2). On this beautiful, warm afternoon, before a homecoming crowd of 81,085, Fesler's squad blew three first-half scoring opportunities and trailed 10-0 at halftime. But the second half was a different story. The Buck-

Sophomore halfback sensation Ray Hamilton (10) skirts left end for yardage during homecoming victory over Illinois. Other players pictured are tackle Jack Wilson (79), end Ralph Armstrong (81), and quarterback Pandel Savic (25).

eyes scored 30 points and twice came from behind to win, 30-17. Quarterback Pandel Savic passed 17 yards to end Ralph Armstrong for OSU's first touchdown, then Vic Janowicz scored on a four-yard cut back over right tackle to give his squad its first lead of the afternoon, 14-10. On the ensuing kickoff, halfback Johnny Karras showed why he was one of the finest ever to play for the Fighting Illini, returning the ball 95 yards to put Illinois back in front, 17-14.

But the Buckeyes retaliated with two more touchdowns, first on a 34-yard toss from Savic to Ray Hamilton, followed by a beautiful 36-yard run by Curly Morrison. Late in the game, middle guard Shag Thomas sacked Illini quarterback Don Engels in the end zone, for a safety. Ohio State's season record now stood at 6-1-1 overall, and 4-1 in the conference. OSU moved up four spots to seventh place in the Associated Press poll.

Sweetest Tie in Ohio State Football

The Buckeyes headed for Michigan the

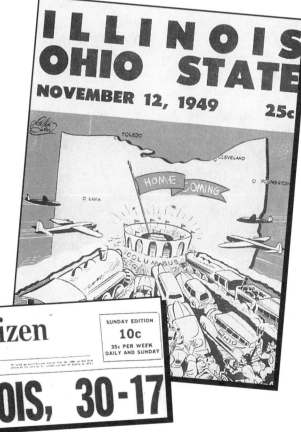

following weekend, knowing that a win or tie would send them to their first Rose Bowl since the Big Ten-Pacific Coast agreement was initiated in 1946. The Wolverines at 4-1 in conference play needed a victory to become the first school in Big Ten history to capture three consecutive undisputed conference titles. Michigan was ranked fifth nationally with an overall record of 6-2.

The Wolverines went out in front, 7-0, on their second possession of the afternoon. Walt Teninga jump-passed 15 yards to Leo Koceski for the touchdown, completing a 44-yard march, and Harry Ellis kicked the extra point. Defensive halfback Billy Newell provided the Buckeyes with two golden scoring opportunities in the first half, intercepting a Chuck Ortmann pass at the UM 35-yard

Quarterback and linebacker
Bucky Wertz

line and recovering fullback Don Dufek's fumble at the UM 25-yard line. But Ohio State could not capitalize on either break, and Michigan led at halftime, 7-0.

The third quarter was scoreless. With ten minutes remaining in the final period, Ohio State took possession at its own 20, still trailing, 7-0. A six-play 80-yard scoring march, highlighted by a 49-yard pass from Savic to Hamilton, brought the Buckeyes within one at 7-6. Fullback Curly Morrison hammered twice for the final four yards and the touchdown. It was now up to placekicker Jimmy Hague for the all-important extra point, since a tie would send the Buckeyes to the Rose Bowl (the two-point conversion option did not become a part of college football until 1958).

Before a Michigan Stadium crowd of 97,239 and the first television audience to ever view an Ohio State-Michigan game, Hague missed the extra point . . . but wait, the Wolverines had lined up offside, and Hague was given a second chance. Ohio State may NEVER have benefitted from a more timely penalty! Jimmy Hague's second attempt was good, the game ended in a 7-7 tie, and the Buckeyes were Pasadena bound.

Tale of the Momsen Brothers

On the playing field this cold November afternoon were the two Momsen brothers from Toledo, who played on opposite sides. Tony Momsen was Michigan's center,

Women At Last

Among the 306 people packed inside the Michigan Stadium press box were eight women who operated the Western Union teleprinter machines. It was the first season women had been permitted in this section of the stadium. The working press box at Michigan, like most other schools, had previously been a "men only" area.

Wake Up Call

The Ohio State marching band spent Friday evening at a Toledo hotel before continuing on to Ann Arbor for the game against Michigan. Band members Jimmy Thompson and Merv Durea recalled that the trumpet section decided to provide the Saturday morning wake up service. Scattered throughout the hotel, all 40 of the trumpeters sounded reveiry promptly at 6:00 a.m. The other members of the band were quickly awakened, as were all of the hotel's other guests.

while younger brother Bob played tackle for Ohio State. Ironically, the Wolverine who lined up offside on Hague's first extra point attempt was center Tony Momsen. Since Tony had been offside, Bob was able to play in the Rose Bowl.

The Buckeyes led in first downs, 14-10, but the Wolverines won the total offensive yardage count, 288 to 231. Ohio State and Michigan tied for the Big Ten crown with identical league records of 4-1-1, but OSU was given the Rose Bowl nod since the Wolverines had played in Pasadena two years earlier. Over 10,000 ecstatic well-wishers, mostly students, greeted the team when its train arrived back at Union Station shortly after midnight. Led by Mayor James Rhodes, the celebration was believed to have been the largest ever to greet an Ohio State team upon its return to Columbus.

Come-From-Behind Wins Become Habit Forming

The California Golden Bears were the Buckeyes' opponent in the January 2, 1950, Rose Bowl. Coach Lynn "Pappy" Waldorf's team entered the game at 10-0, ranked third in the Associated Press standings. The Bears had not been beaten since losing the previous season's Rose Bowl to Northwestern, 21-14. It had been a season of courage and determination for Wes Fesler's senior-dominated squad, that entered the game with an overall record of 6-1-2. The Buckeyes had "come from behind" for three of their six victories.

After a scoreless opening quarter, fullback Curly Morrison appeared to have scored the game's first touchdown with a powerful ten-yard burst

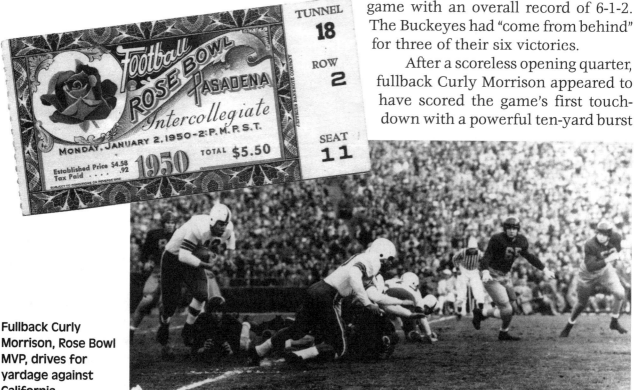

Fullback Curly Morrison, Rose Bowl MVP, drives for yardage against California.

over left guard, but the Buckeyes were penalized back to the California 23-yard line for illegal use of hands. Morrison fumbled on the next down, and the Golden Bears recovered on their own 26-yard line. California then marched 74 yards to take a 7-0 lead, with halfback Jim Monachino scoring from four yards out on a pitch-out around the Buckeyes' right end. Monachino previously played for Cleveland's John Adams High School.

Janowicz Interception Huge Play

The Golden Bears moved the ball freely after receiving the third-quarter kickoff, and threatened to increase their lead to 14-0. But halfback Vic Janowicz ended the drive with a jumping interception of Bob Celeri's pass at the Ohio State 25-yard line, and returned it all the way to the California 31. From there the Buckeyes tied it up, 7-7, with Morrison going over the middle on a fourth-down call from the two. Another key play during the drive was a seven-yard jump pass from Jerry

Krall to Ralph Armstrong on a fourth-and-five from the Golden Bear 14. Years later, when discussing the game, quarterback Pandel Savic recalled, "Vic's interception and return turned things around for us, and it really took the spirit out of California's attack."

California started its next drive from its own 26-yard line. After three plays netted only two yards, Buckeye tackle Bill Trautwein blocked Celeri's punt attempt, and center Jack Lininger carried the pigskin to the six. It again required four downs for Ohio State to score, with Krall taking it over left tackle from inside the two. Jimmy Hague's conversion made the score, 14-7, and the Buckeyes had tallied twice within a span of three minutes and 40 seconds.

The Golden Bears retaliated to tie the game on their next possession. Aided by a

All eyes are glued on Jimmy Hague's successful field goal attempt, which meant a Rose Bowl victory for Ohio State.

key block from fullback Pete Schabarum, Monachino scored his second touchdown, this time on a picture perfect 44-yard run around end with just 31 seconds remaining in a very frenzied third quarter.

With the game still tied 14-14 and just over three minutes remaining, Bob Celeri was forced to punt on fourth down with the ball resting at the California 16-yard line. Celeri momentarily fumbled a low pass from center, then kicked the ball off his wrong foot (left) on the run. It rolled out of bounds at the 13, giving the Buckeyes one of the game's biggest breaks.

Three running plays netted just over eight yards, so Fesler sent Dick Widdoes and Tom Watson in with instructions for Hague to attempt a field goal on fourth down. The team, wanting to go for the first down, signaled them off the field, so Widdoes and Watson returned to the sideline. Fesler, however, sent them back onto the field, but by this time the Buckeyes were penalized five yards for delay of game. With Widdoes spotting the ball at the 18-yard line, Hague responded beautifully under tremendous pressure and booted the ball through the uprights for one of the biggest field goals in Ohio State history. The Buckeyes led, 17-14, with 1:55 remaining.

Coach Wes Fesler is carried from field following Ohio State's Rose Bowl victory over California.

The Golden Bears made a courageous effort in the closing seconds, but Widdoes intercepted "Boots" Erb's pass at the OSU 11-yard line, and the Buckeyes ran out the clock to preserve their first Rose Bowl victory. Erb was the son of Charlie Erb, who quarterbacked California to its victory over Ohio State in the 1921 Rose Bowl, while Widdoes was the son of coach Carroll Widdoes, who guided the Buckeyes to the National Civilian Championship with a record of 9-0 in 1944.

Senior Curly Morrison, who gained 119 yards on 25 carries, had played the finest game of his career and was selected the game's MVP. Fesler, who was carried off the

Robert Hooey Remembered

On behalf of his teammates, Captain Jack Wilson presented the Rose Bowl game ball to Mrs. Robert Hooey, widow of the *Ohio State Journal* Sports Editor who died five weeks earlier from an automobile accident on November 28. Robert Hooey was extremely close to Buckeye football for many years. He died before he could realize his dearest wish—covering an Ohio State victory in the Rose Bowl.

Center and team MVP Jack Lininger

field by his team, claimed, "This is the biggest thrill I've ever had in football. Every boy dreams of playing in the Rose Bowl and winning.....and we coaches do, too. It was a great football game." It was the first Rose Bowl to be decided by a kick.

The Ohio State marching band, with its usual snap and precision, received extremely high praise from the crowd of 100,963, at the time the second largest ever to attend a college football game.

For California's Lynn "Pappy" Waldorf, losing to Ohio State on a late fourth-quarter field goal was nothing new. Waldorf had been Northwestern's coach when Ohio State's Max Schnittker's 32-yard field goal, with just one minute and 28 seconds remaining, lifted the Buckeyes to a 16-14 win over the Wildcats in 1945.

Ohio State finished the season at 7-1-2, good for sixth place in the final *AP* poll. Four times the team came from behind to win, including the Rose Bowl. Senior center Jack Lininger, a standout all season, was chosen as the team's MVP.

But not all was well for coach Wes Fesler. There were strong rumors that Fesler was unhappy with all the pressure associated with being Ohio State's head coach. Sports Editor Lew Byrer of the *Columbus Citizen* wrote in his January 3, 1950, column that, "Fesler is unhappy about the abuse his family has had to take in his experience as Ohio State coach. He doesn't think it is all worth it—even in the moments following a Rose Bowl victory. You can expect his resignation at most any time—as soon as it's cleared by the Athletic Board and by his boss, Athletic Director Dick Larkins."

Mr. Byrer's prediction was not quite correct, at least not yet. Fesler was considering leaving Ohio State and going into the business world, but decided to stay after conferring with Ohio State President Howard Bevis and three members of the Board of Trustees on Saturday, January 7. Fesler was prom-

ised a full professorship in the Department of Physical Education, if and when he decided to leave his coaching position. Wes Fesler's next season would be one of the most interesting and highly unusual in all of Ohio State football.

1949

September 24	Missouri	W	35	34
October 1	Indiana	W	46	7
October 8	at Southern Cal	T	13	13
October 15	Minnesota	L	0	27
October 22	at Wisconsin	W	21	0
October 29	Northwestern	W	24	7
November 5	at Pittsburgh	W	14	10
November 12	Illinois (HC)	W	30	17
November 19	at Michigan	T	7	7
January 2	California*	W	17	14
Total Points			207	136

*Rose Bowl

Season Record: 7-1-2
Big Ten Co-Champion

1950

With the graduation of 21 lettermen from the '49 Rose Bowl championship squad, Wes Fesler and his staff faced a rebuilding effort in 1950. Gone from the line were ends Jimmy Hague, Chuck Gilbert, and Dick Schnittker; tackles Jack Wilson, Jack Jennings, and Richard O'Hanlon; guards George Toneff, George Mattey, and Shag Thomas; and center Jack Lininger. Missing from the backfield were fullbacks Curly Morrison and Pete Perini, halfbacks Jimmy Clark, Jerry Krall, Billy Newell, and Rodney Swinehart; and quarterbacks Pandel Savic and Bucky Wertz.

Even with the departure of a fine senior class, the Buckeyes returned 18 lettermen and a very promising group of sophomores. Ends Tom Watson and Ralph Armstrong were back, along with Sonny Gandee who missed the '49 campaign with a neck injury. Captain Bill Trautwein, Bill Miller, Julius Whitman, and Bob Momsen provided experience at tackle, and John Biltz and Jerry Manz returned at guard. Bob McCullough took over at center, backed up by Bob Heid. Sophomores who would contribute included guard Lou Fischer and end Bob Grimes.

With the Buckeyes using both the T-formation and single-wing attacks, Fesler stationed Janowicz at quarterback to take advantage of his all-around talents. Halfback returnees included Ray Hamilton, Walt Klevay, Skip Doyle, Karl Sturtz, and Dick Widdoes, who was used primarily on defense. Chuck Gandee was the most experienced returnee at fullback. Sophomores who would see action included halfbacks Fred Bruney and Bernie Skvarka, quarterback Tony Curcillo, and fullback John Hlay.

Remembering Fred Benners

Ohio State faced Southern Methodist for the very first time in the September 30 season opener before a crowd of 80,672, at the time the largest opening day attendance in Ohio Stadium history. The weather could hardly have been better—sunshine with temperatures in the mid-70s. SMU had opened the previous Saturday with a 33-13 win over Georgia Tech. The contest featured the play of Ohio State's Vic Janowicz, who this season would win the Heisman Trophy, against SMU's Kyle Rote, who would finish as the runner-up in the Heisman voting. The afternoon also produced one of the most miraculous comebacks in Ohio Stadium history— much to the disappointment of Ohio State fans.

The Buckeyes appeared to have the game well under control, leading 24-7 midway through the third quarter. Down by 17 points, Mustang coach Rusty Russell decided to go with reserve quarterback Fred Benners and instructed Benners to throw from the spread formation on every down. The lanky 6'3" junior from Dallas (who also pitched for the SMU baseball team) responded by passing for 325 yards and four touchdowns in the game's final 20 minutes. Southern Methodist won the game, 32-27.

Interestingly, after the game Fesler told the press, "Believe it or not, but we set our defense to stop a passing attack!" The game lasted two hours and 48 minutes, at the time the longest ever played in Ohio Stadium. The halftime included a silent tribute to former Athletic Director Lynn W. St. John, who had passed away the previous evening at age 73.

Janowicz Six-For-Six—Four TDs

The Buckeyes struck like a bolt of lightning at home against Pittsburgh the next Saturday, scoring three touchdowns in each of the first two quarters to lead at halftime, 41-0. Fesler flooded the field with all available reserves in the second half, or the final score of 41-7 would have

Name Game

Earle Bruce was strongly recruited by his namesake, Penn State assistant coach Earl Bruce, in 1949. A star halfback at Allegany High School in Cumberland, Maryland, Bruce eventually decided to play at Ohio State under coach Wes Fesler.

Halfback Earle Bruce in 1950, 29 seasons before taking the reins as Ohio State's head coach in 1979.

Four experienced Buckeyes returning in 1950 were (left to right) end Tom Watson, defensive back Dick Widdoes, multi-purpose back Vic Janowicz, and tackle Bill Trautwein, team captain.

been much higher. Vic Janowicz was moved from quarterback to left halfback, making way for his former high school teammate, Tony Curcillo, to move into the starting quarterback role.

Janowicz was sensational, completing six of six passes for 151 yards and four of OSU's six touchdowns. He also punted twice for a 55-yard average. Walt Klevay rushed for 103 yards in just three carries, including a 74-yard scoring run. This same afternoon, unranked Purdue upset top-rated Notre Dame at South Bend, 28-14, breaking ND's unbeaten streak at 39.

The competition was a little stronger at Bloomington the following Saturday, where Ohio State defeated Indiana in its Big Ten opener, 26-14. The Memorial Stadium Dad's Day crowd of 29,000 enjoyed a perfect autumn afternoon for college football. The Hoosiers drove 82 yards early in the second period to go out in front, 7-0. Walt Klevay

pittsburgh ohio state

25 cents

october 7, 1950

quickly tied the score, returning the ensuing kickoff 93 yards for OSU's first touchdown. Janowicz passed eight yards to Curcillo for Ohio State's second score, just seven seconds before halftime, to give the Buckeyes their first lead of the afternoon, 13-7.

Fullback Chuck Gandee scored from the three late in the third period, and finished the day as the game's leading rusher with 74 yards in 13 carries. Midway through the final quarter, Skip Doyle pitched a perfect six-yard touchdown toss to Ray Hamilton, who was standing all alone in the end zone. IU led in net yards gained, 313 to 270, but suffered from three interceptions and two lost fumbles.

Armstrong Praises Fesler

Playing before an October 21 Memorial Stadium crowd of 52,115, the Buckeyes routed Minnesota, 48-0. Ohio State gained some revenge for the Golden Gophers' 27-0 victory at Ohio Stadium in '49. The score could have been worse, but Wes Fesler cleared his bench early in the afternoon, using all 40 of his available players. Seven different players scored Ohio State's seven touchdowns—Chuck Gandee, Tom Watson, Dick Widdoes, Ralph Armstrong, Tony Curcillo, Carl Sturtz, and Fred Bruney.

At the time, it was Minnesota's second worst setback in a Big Ten game. It also was Ohio State's largest margin of victory in conference play since defeating Chicago in 1939, 61-0. Minnesota's new Athletic Director, Ike Armstrong, praised Fesler and classified the Buckeyes as "The greatest football team I ever saw." Fesler and Armstrong first met the previous day at a Junior Chamber of Commerce luncheon, held at the Nicolet Hotel in Minneapolis. Ironically, in just two months, Fesler and Armstrong would be spending a lot of time together. Ike Armstrong–remember the name!

A College Football Classic

If Armstrong was impressed with Fesler's team against Minnesota, he should have been in Columbus on October 28, when Ohio State defeated Iowa, 83-21. It was another delightful autumn afternoon for college football, with the temperature in the low-70s and a slight wind blowing out of the southwest. The Dad's Day crowd of 82,174, at the time the third largest in Ohio Stadium history, saw Vic Janowicz play one of the finest games in all of college football. The 3-1 Buckeyes were a three-touchdown favorite over the Hawkeyes, whose season record stood at 2-2.

Janowicz kicked off ten yards beyond the end zone to start the game. Iowa's Jerry Faske fumbled on first down, and Janowicz recovered at the Iowa 23. After the Buckeyes advanced the ball to the Iowa 11-yard line, Janowicz scored the game's first touchdown on a trap play over left guard. Janowicz kicked the extra point, making the score 7-0 at the 13:05 mark.

All-American tackle Bob Momsen

The Columbus Citizen

OFFICIAL FORECAST—Rather cloudy and warm; low of 58, high of 78.

SUNDAY EDITION
10c
35c PER WEEK
DAILY AND SUNDAY

VOL. 52—No. 243 Phone AD. 1111   COLUMBUS 15, OHIO, SUNDAY, OCTOBER 29, 1950 ★ ★ ★

OHIO 83
IOWA 21
DOWN YDS
TIME TO PLAY
MIN SEC

The Scoreboard Tells the Story . . .

OHIO STATE SMOTHERS IOWA

Janowicz again kicked off beyond the end zone. After the Hawkeyes failed to gain ten yards, Glenn Drahn punted on fourth down. Janowicz took the punt on his own 39 near the east sideline, swerved to miss one tackler, dodged another, cut back and outran the others for his second touchdown. Veteran *Columbus Citizen* sportswriter Lew Byrer referred to Janowicz's return as "the finest bit of open field running I've seen since the days of Ohio State's Chic Harley (1919) and Illinois' Red Grange (1925)." Janowicz's second conversion increased the lead to 14 with 11:31 remaining in the first quarter.

Janowicz's kickoff again was far out of the end zone. On second down, fullback Bill

Forty years later, All-American Vic Janowicz recalls Ohio State's convincing 83-21 victory over Iowa in 1950. Janowicz captured the 1950 Heisman Trophy, and was named the Big Ten MVP.

"Jim Zabel, You Still Owe Me One!"—Jack Buck

Jim Zabel, Sports Director at WHO Radio in Des Moines, Iowa, is a legend in his own time. He followed Ronald Reagan as the sports voice at WHO, and has been a part of the broadcast of every Iowa football game since 1950.

Zabel's first trip to Ohio Stadium to broadcast the 1950 Ohio State-Iowa game, developed into a "long afternoon" in more ways than one. Jim signed on the air for his pregame show without taking into consideration the one-hour time difference between Columbus and Des Moines. As the pregame show progressed, Zabel soon realized he had an additional hour of air time to fill.

In the booth next to Zabel was Jack Buck, an Ohio State graduate, who was doing the Buckeyes' play-by-play on WCOL Radio in Columbus. Zabel brought Buck into his booth for an interview. Then, during commercial breaks, Buck quickly arranged for other people in the press box to be Zabel's guests. "It was a really long pregame show," Zabel recalls, "but with Jack Buck's help, we made it."

Jack Buck became a Baseball Hall of Fame announcer as the voice of the St. Louis Cardinals over KMOX Radio. Buck still remembers that afternoon in Ohio Stadium back in 1950. Today, when Buck is trying to fill air time during a baseball rain delay, he has been known to say, "Jim Zabel, where are you when I need you? You still owe me one!"

All-American center Bob McCullough

Reichardt's fumble was recovered by Janowicz at the Iowa 26-yard line. After Ohio State advanced to the 12-yard line, Janowicz fired a jump-pass into the outstretched arms of Tony Curcillo for the Buckeyes' third touchdown. Janowicz kicked his third extra point, just five minutes and 10 seconds into the first quarter. With almost 25 minutes remaining in the first half, Ohio State held a 21-point lead, but Vic Janowicz was just getting warmed-up.

Janowicz finished the afternoon by scoring two touchdowns, completing five of six passes for 133 yards and four touchdowns, kicking ten extra points, punting twice for a total of 84 yards, and playing his usual fine game at defensive safety. The talented junior played very little in the second half, as Fesler emptied his bench for the fourth time in five games. Following is the scoring by quarters:

	1	2	3	4	Final
Iowa	0	14	0	7	21
Ohio State	35	20	7	21	83

Halfback Bob Wilson scored Iowa's first touchdown on a 15-yard pass from Glenn Drahn. Wilson's father, John "Red" Wilson, lettered three seasons at Ohio State in 1922-24. The game lasted three hours; Ohio State kicked-off at 2:00 p.m., and the final gun sounded precisely at 5:00 p.m. The 83 points are the most ever scored by the Buckeyes in a Big Ten conference game. It also is Ohio State's third highest single-game score, exceeded only by OSU's 128-0 win over Oberlin in 1916 and an 85-7 victory over Drake in 1935.

Nine different players scored the Buckeyes' 12 touchdowns. Bob Demmel's 87-yard punt return for a second-quarter touchdown is the longest in Ohio State history. Demmel also returned an interception 37 yards for another score in the final period. OSU led in first downs, 21-13, and total offensive yards, 432-251. The Hawkeyes threw five interceptions and lost seven fumbles. With a record of 4-1, the Buckeyes moved up two places to fourth in the weekly Associated Press poll.

NOT What the Doctor Ordered!

Retired Ohio State greenskeeper Tony Aquilla had been released from University Hospital, where he was treated for a kidney ailment in early October. Aquilla was recovering at the home of his daughter, Mrs. Edith McCoy, who lived just east of the Ohio State campus at 256 Woodruff Ave. On the afternoon of the Iowa game, when Mrs. McCoy wasn't watching, Aquilla slipped out the back door and headed for Ohio Stadium without telling anyone. A *Columbus Citizen* reporter found Aquilla sitting in the west stands at the stadium's open end. "I feel pretty good," Aquilla quipped, "and I just couldn't stay home with the boys playing in the stadium."

Five Straight

The Buckeyes struck quickly and often to hand Northwestern a decisive 32-0 defeat, before a saddened homecoming crowd of 50,000 at Dyche Stadium. Temperatures were near freezing, and snow fell in Evanston on Saturday morning, making the playing field wet and slippery. Halfback Karl Sturtz carted the opening kickoff 94 yards to the Wildcat four—three plunges by fullback Chuck Gandee gave the Buckeyes their first touchdown just one minute and 20 seconds into the game. Northwestern moved the ball well at times, but was unable to dent the Ohio State end zone. OSU's defense again created a number of turnovers; the Wildcats lost five fumbles and threw two interceptions. At 5-1, the Buckeyes advanced to second place in the *AP* standings behind top-ranked Army (6-0).

Huge Win Over Badgers

In one of the season's biggest games, Ohio State edged Wisconsin, 19-14, to strengthen its hold on first place in the Big Ten standings. The 15th-ranked Badgers entered the afternoon with a record of 5-1, having lost at Michigan on October 21, 26-13. At the time, the media coverage was the largest in the history of Ohio Stadium. Unfortunately, the stadium elevator broke down 45 minutes before kick-off, forcing many of the reporters to make a long climb to the press box. The date was November 11, Armistice Day, and the half-frozen crowd of 81,535 applauded proudly when the Ohio State marching band paid tribute to those who died defending our country.

On one of the coldest Saturday afternoons in many seasons, Wisconsin scored the game's first and last touchdowns, and the Buckeyes scored 19 points in between. The Badgers led at halftime, 7-6, using a new spread formation that gave Ohio State some serious problems. Wisconsin quarterback John Coatta was magnificent, connecting on his first 10 passes, and finishing the afternoon with 12 completions for 119 yards and his team's first touchdown.

By halftime, Fesler and his staff had solved the Badgers' spread attack, changing the game's complexion dramatically. In particular, tackle Bob Momsen sacked Coatta repeatedly for sizable losses in the second half.

Halfback Walt Klevay

Fullback Chuck Gandee supplied much of OSU's offensive punch, finishing the day with 145 yards on 37 carries.

Season Crumbles

The Buckeyes at 6-1 headed for Champaign as the nation's No. 1 ranked team, but they didn't stay at the top very long. In the weekend's major upset, Illinois broke Ohio State's six-game winning streak with a 14-7 victory, before a capacity Dad's Day crowd of 71,119 at Memorial Stadium. The difference in the game was simply turnovers. The Fighting Illini did not once turn over the ball, while the Buckeyes lost four fumbles and threw three interceptions.

The scoring all took place in the second quarter. Illinois went up 14-0 with two touchdown passes from left-handed quarterback Fred Major to left halfback Don Stevens (plays covering 52 yards and five yards). Less than three minutes before the half, Janowicz plunged four yards over right tackle for OSU's only touchdown, completing a 10-play, 83-yard drive. Altogether, it was Ohio State's poorest showing of the season.

Even after the loss at Illinois, Ohio State could still capture the outright conference championship with a victory over Michigan. Heading into the last week of play, the Buckeyes were 5-1 in the league, Michigan was 3-1-1, and Illinois was 4-1. To go to Pasadena, the Fighting Illini needed to defeat Northwestern and the Wolverines to beat Ohio State. Michigan could make the California trip with a win over the Buckeyes, providing Northwestern defeated Illinois. Because of the no-repeat policy at that time, Ohio State could not return to the Rose Bowl.

The Buckeyes were rated a six-point favorite, primarily on the basis of their offensive strength. OSU was averaging almost 35 points per game, while Michigan was scoring 17. But the Wolverines, who were now playing excellent football, had improved as the season progressed. The 1950 Ohio State-

Bierman's Replacement at Minnesota?

It was strongly rumored that Minnesota coach Bernie Bierman would retire this fall, after 16 seasons as head coach of the Golden Gophers. The November 19, 1950, *Columbus Citizen* reported the possibility of Paul Brown leaving the Cleveland Browns to replace Bierman. Citing a reliable source, columnist Lew Byrer reported that Minnesota Chancellor J. Louis Morrill was possibly in favor of Brown, and that Brown had indicated he wouldn't turn down the position if sufficient financial inducements were attached. (INTERESTING! Bierman's replacement would be a former Ohio State head coach, but it wouldn't be Paul Brown.)

Michigan game should have been a good one—but how good, we'll never know.

The Unbelievable "Snow Bowl"

The forecast for Saturday, November 25, was for cloudy and cold weather with little or no snow. By Saturday morning, however, a blizzard was sweeping across northern and central Ohio. With the temperature hovering near 10 degrees and winds whirling at 40 miles per hour, Columbus was soon completely paralyzed by one of the worst snowstorms ever to hit central Ohio.

Other games in the area were cancelled, but Athletic Directors Dick Larkins and Fritz Crisler (after considering cancellation) decided that the game would be played. It was rumored that Crisler told Larkins that if they did not play now, the game would not be played, because Michigan would not return at a later date. It was homecoming weekend and more than 80,000 tickets had been sold. Yet, no one was at the stadium gates on Saturday to collect tickets, and fans simply went inside and found a seat.

Amazingly, a reported 50,503 fans were able to make it inside the horseshoe to wit-

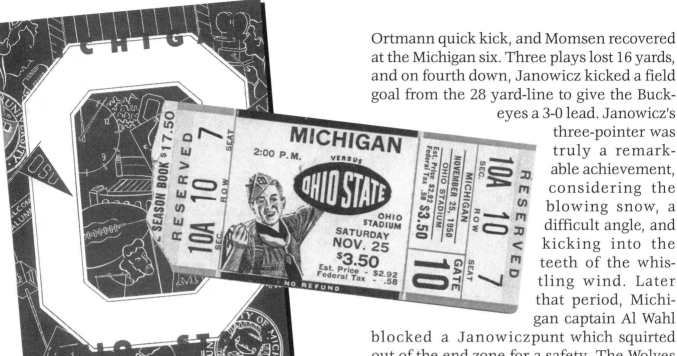

Ortmann quick kick, and Momsen recovered at the Michigan six. Three plays lost 16 yards, and on fourth down, Janowicz kicked a field goal from the 28 yard-line to give the Buckeyes a 3-0 lead. Janowicz's three-pointer was truly a remarkable achievement, considering the blowing snow, a difficult angle, and kicking into the teeth of the whistling wind. Later that period, Michigan captain Al Wahl blocked a Janowicz punt which squirted out of the end zone for a safety. The Wolves had cut the margin to 3-2.

A very controversial play selection was made in the final 47 seconds of the first half—Ohio State had a third-and-six at the Michigan 13-yard line, when Fesler instructed Janowicz to punt. Michigan center Tony Momsen blocked the kick and fell on the ball for the game's only touchdown. Harry Allis' extra point made it 9-3 and that was the ball game. There was no scoring in the second half. Tony Momsen was the older brother of OSU's Bob Momsen, whose earlier recovery set up Janowicz's field goal.

ness one of the most unusual football games ever played. The start of the game was delayed 20 minutes until the frozen tarp could be removed from the playing field. Ohio Stadium chief groundskeeper Ralph Guarasci often said, "I never saw anything like it, and I hope I never have to see anything like it again." Guarasci's crew was faced with the impossible task of keeping the field clear of snow prior to kickoff. Cars were snowbound for days following the game, and many out-of-town fans did not return home until the following Tuesday.

Michigan won the encounter, 9-3, without registering a single first down! With the rushing attacks all but halted by the conditions, both squads frequently punted on first or second down. Michigan's Chuck Ortmann punted 24 times for 723 yards, and Ohio State's Vic Janowicz punted 21 times for 685 yards.

The game's scoring all resulted from blocked punts. In the first period, OSU's Joe Campanella and Bob Momsen blocked an

Better Late Than Never

Paul Schodorf, Jr., was born in Columbus on November 25, 1950, the day of the "Snow Bowl." Paul, Sr., took his wife, Bette, to Mt. Carmel Hospital that morning, but there was just one problem—their doctor had gone to the Ohio State-Michigan football game. After leaving the stadium and fighting the impossible elements, Dr. Robert J. Henry finally reached the hospital at 6:00 p.m., "looking like a snowman." Paul, Jr., was born at 7:00 p.m.

Playing in blizzard conditions, Michigan defeated Ohio State, 9-3, without registering a single first down.

Behind the blocking of tackle Julius Wittman (67) and fullback Chuck Gandee (32), Vic Janowicz (31) plows for yardage in the infamous "Snow Bowl." In the background is quarterback Tony Curcillo (25).

Fans strongly second-guessed Fesler's decision to punt on third down, instead of simply running out the clock with only 47 seconds remaining. "We had two plays left," Fesler said, "but too much time to close out the end of the period. So rather than take a chance of anything happening, I wanted to get the ball out of there."

The game's final offensive statistics probably best describe the deplorable playing conditions. Ohio State rushed for 16 yards, Michigan for 27. The Buckeyes registered three first downs, Michigan had none. Ohio State completed 3 of 18 passes for 25 yards, while Michigan was unable to connect on any of nine throws.

At the 1988 Ohio State-Michigan game, WJR Radio's Warren Pierce reminisces with Tony and Bob Momsen, brothers who played on opposite sides and figured prominently in the scoring of the 1950 "Snow Bowl." Tony (in the middle) played center for Michigan, and Bob (right) played tackle for Ohio State.

Lost Boy Scout

The Ohio Stadium grounds crew had an almost impossible task removing the canvas from the frozen surface, so the "Snow Bowl" between Ohio State and Michigan could get started. Many spectators, including several boy scouts, came down out of the stands to assist with clearing the field. Soon after the game started, a rumor spread that one of the boy scouts had been caught and wrapped up in the canvas as it was being rolled from the field. The scout in question was Roy Case, who had fallen on the icy surface. Fortunately, the story proved to be a false rumor—Case had been able to roll aside after falling to avoid being caught in the rolling tarp. Today, Roy Case is still involved with the Boy Scouts and the Buckeyes. For years he has been supervising scouts who serve as ushers for each home game.

(Illustration by Tom Hayes)

"Snow Bowl" Souvenirs

Mr. John Hummel was in charge of distributing football programs for many seasons at Ohio Stadium. Approximately 4,000 of the 28,000 printed for the "Snow Bowl" were sold. After the heavy snow cleared the following week, Hummel arranged for a truck to haul away the other 24,000. "What a mistake. We later had many requests from people wanting to purchase one of them. Just think of the money the university lost by not having those available as collectors' items," he suggested years later.

Columbus Dispatch, Wednesday, December 6, 1950

Graveyard Of Coaches No Longer

Fourteen days after Ohio State's loss to Michigan, Wes Fesler resigned as Ohio State's head coach. Fesler indicated the pressure of coaching in Columbus was "just too much," and that he was concerned about how the job was affecting his health and his family.

Fesler entered the real estate business in Columbus, but lightning would soon strike again. Just 47 days after resigning from Ohio State, Fesler accepted the head coaching position at Minnesota. The announcement was made by Minnesota Athletic Director, Ike Armstrong, who had so strongly praised Fesler's Ohio State squad, after Ohio State's

Northwestern defeated Illinois, 14-7, sending Michigan to the Rose Bowl to face California (Wolverines won, 14-6). The Buckeyes finished the year at 6-3, good for 14th place in the final *AP* poll. Vic Janowicz, tackle Bob Momsen, and center Bob McCullough were chosen as All-Americans, and Janowicz became the second Ohio State player to receive the Heisman Trophy, an award given annually to the nation's top college football player. Janowicz was also picked the Big Ten MVP.

Snow Bowl Attraction

Marilyn Soliday was one of many Buckeye fans who braved the weather to attend the infamous "Snow Bowl" between Ohio State and Michigan in 1950. She had a ticket for section 18C, but ended up sitting in 18B because of the icy aisles.

During the second half, she noticed one of the portals seemed almost frozen from the cold, and offered to share one of her two blankets with him. His name was Barney Atkinson. When Marilyn had to leave to catch a bus to her home in Bexley, Barney offered her a ride since he drove through Bexley on his way home to Pataskala.

Marilyn recalls that it took about three hours of driving through the heavy snow before he dropped her off at home. The long drive gave them a chance to get to know each other, and the following Tuesday Barney called and asked her to go out. They continued to date, and the following May 11 they were married.

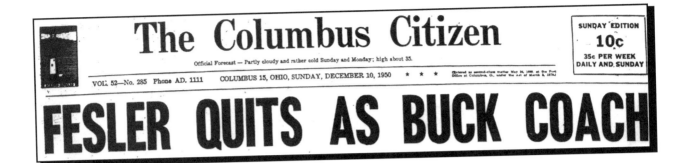

The Columbus Citizen

SUNDAY EDITION
10c
35c PER WEEK
DAILY AND SUNDAY

Official Forecast — Partly cloudy and rather cold Sunday and Monday; high about 35.

VOL. 52—No. 285 Phone AD. 1111   COLUMBUS 15, OHIO, SUNDAY, DECEMBER 10, 1950   ★ ★ ★   (Entered as second-class matter May 24, 1898, at the Post Office at Columbus, O., under the Act of March 3, 1879.)

FESLER QUITS AS BUCK COACH

crushing 48-0 victory over the Golden Gophers the previous fall.

For Fesler, it meant a new job, a new environment, and most of all a new start. Fesler's resignation also created a significant change for Ohio State. He was replaced by a man who, at that time, was relatively unknown in the national coaching circles—this man was Woody Hayes. Ohio State's reputation as the "Graveyard of Coaches" would eventually disappear, and Ohio State football would be changed—forever.

1950				
September 30	Southern Methodist	L	27	32
October 7	Pittsburgh	W	41	7
October 14	at Indiana	W	26	14
October 21	at Minnesota	W	48	0
October 28	Iowa	W	83	21
November 4	at Northwestern	W	32	0
November 11	Wisconsin	W	19	14
November 18	at Illinois	L	7	14
November 25	Michigan (HC)	L	3	9
Total Points			**286**	**111**

Season Record: 6-3
Conference: 2nd Place (Tie)

WOODY TAKES COMMAND

With the resignation of Wes Fesler following the 1950 season, Ohio State began a search for an individual who would become the school's sixth head football coach within the 12-year period of 1940 through 1951. Yes, Ohio State had well earned its dubious distinction as "the graveyard of coaches," but that reputation would soon change dramatically.

Athletic Director Dick Larkins coordinated a six-man search committee that selected and interviewed seven finalists for the position: Paul Brown, head coach and general manager of the Cleveland Browns, who had led the Buckeyes to the 1942 national title; Don Faurot, prominent head coach of the Missouri Tigers; Warren Gaer, head coach at Drake University; Sid Gillman, OSU's 1933 captain and now head coach at Cincinnati; Woody Hayes, head coach at Miami of Ohio; Chuck Mather, accomplished head coach at Massillon High School; and Harry Strobel, freshman coach under Fesler at OSU following an effective stint as head coach at Barberton, Ohio, High School.

Brown had just finished his fifth highly successful season as head coach of the Browns, the team he created in 1946 following World War II. Many fans wondered why he would be interested in returning to the college game. In his book, *PB: The Paul Brown Story*, Brown described his first two seasons at Ohio State as the happiest, most exciting and rewarding period of his life. He was extremely popular with many Buckeye fans, but his candidacy was highly controversial with some members of the Ohio State administration. In 1946, Brown had signed players to his first Cleveland team who still had remaining years of eligibility to play at Ohio State. He met with the Ohio State selection committee on Saturday, January 27, 1951, but it was not clear how interested he was to return as head coach of the Buckeyes.

Be Careful What You Wish For — It Might Come True

Faurot was the committee's top choice. The Missouri coach had nearly been picked for the Ohio State job ten years earlier in

Woody Hayes meets with a portion of the search committee after accepting the head coaching position in 1951. Left to right are Athletic Director Dick Larkins, Ralph Paffenbarger (Engineering Drawing), Hayes, Paul Lehoczky (Industrial Engineering), and Herman Miller (Accounting).

1941, prior to the selection of Paul Brown. Faurot met with the selection committee in Columbus on Saturday, February 10, 1951, and accepted Ohio State's offer to become the Buckeyes' new head coach. It appeared his ambition to lead the Buckeye program had finally become a reality.

The following Monday, Larkins received a very unexpected call from Faurot at about the time the OSU Sports Information Department was planning a press conference to announce Faurot's appointment. Larkins was stunned when Faurot told him he had changed his mind and decided to stay at Missouri, and he really gave no specific reason for his decision. Apparently the Missouri Athletic Board had convinced Faurot to remain in his position.

After Faurot's rejection, the selection committee decided to offer the position to Woody Hayes, who accepted immediately. The date was Sunday, February 18, 1951, and few could have envisioned the impact this decision would have on Ohio State football. Hayes (who was born on Valentine's Day, 1913) had been captain of his football team at Newcomerstown High School, where his father, Wayne Benton Hayes, was Superintendent of Schools. He graduated from Denison University in 1935 with a major in English and history. At Denison, he played tackle on the football team and outfield for the baseball squad.

After college, Hayes was an assistant football coach at Mingo Junction High School for two seasons before moving to New Philadelphia High School in 1937 as an assistant to head coach John Brickles. Brickles introduced Hayes to Miss Anne Gross, an attractive and charming graduate of Ohio Wesleyan University, who would later become Mrs. Woody Hayes. In 1938 when Brickles moved to Huntington, West Virginia, Hayes became New Philadelphia's head coach. After enlisting in the Navy in 1941, he advanced to Lieutenant Commander and commanded two ships in the Pacific during World War II.

Hayes returned to Denison University as head coach in 1946, to rebuild a football program that had been discontinued during the war. There his teams compiled a three-year record of 19-6, even though his first squad won only one game. Hayes moved to Miami of Ohio in 1949, where his first team went 5-4. His 1950 squad lost its opener to Xavier, 7-0, then won nine straight, including a 34-21 Salad Bowl triumph over Arizona State. One of his star players at Miami was tackle Bo Schembechler, who would later play a prominent role both as an assistant coach and as an opposing coach during Hayes' stay at Ohio State.

1951

Hayes' first season could be described as "so-so" at best.

The Buckeyes returned a lot of talent from Wes Fesler's last squad, including All-American Vic Janowicz, the 1950 Heisman Trophy winner. However, Fesler's offense, which showcased Janowicz's many talents, was built around the single wing attack, and the '51 team had a lot of difficulty adjusting to Hayes' T-formation offense. Secondly, many of the players were offended by Hayes' aggressive, demanding style of coaching, and team morale was often very low. To say that the new coach was not the team's favorite person would, at times, be a huge understatement.

Senior center Bob Heid of Fremont captained Hayes' first Ohio State team. OSU opened at home September 29 against Southern Methodist, with the Buckeyes winning,

End Bob Joslin scored the only touchdown during Woody Hayes's first Ohio State game.

Woody Hayes and his first Ohio State staff in 1951. Front row: Gene Fekete, Bo Schembechler, Bill Arnsparger, and Bill Hess. Back row: Doyt Perry, Harry Strobel, Hayes, Esco Sarkkinen, and Ernie Godfrey.

7-0. The attendance of 80,735 was, at the time, the largest opening-day crowd in Ohio Stadium history. Ohio State's new T-formation offense sputtered most of the afternoon, and the game's only touchdown came on a pass—something Hayes earned quite a reputation for shunning in the years ahead. In the third period, quarterback Tony Curcillo connected with end Bob Joslin from 21 yards, and Janowicz added the extra point.

The Famous "Transcontinental Pass"

The following Saturday coach Clarence "Biggie" Munn brought his top-ranked Michigan State Spartans to Columbus to face the seventh-ranked Buckeyes. Michigan State would join the conference two years later in 1953, replacing the University of Chicago (Chicago dropped football following the 1939 season).

It was an extremely hard-fought contest, with OSU holding a 20-17 lead late in the final period. The Buckeyes then lost a fumble on their own 45-yard line. MSU was soon faced with a fourth-and-six at the OSU 28-yard line, as Munn inserted reserve quarter-

Quarterback Tony Curcillo

back Tom Yewsic, a sophomore, at left half-back. Quarterback Al Dorrow lateraled to Yewsic, who ran to his right—stopped sud-denly—then passed back across the field to Dorrow, who eluded two Buckeye defenders before falling into the end zone with the win-ning touchdown. The Spartans had won a real thriller, 24-20.

This miraculous play, known as the "transcontinental pass," had been drawn-up on the sidelines by Munn just seconds be-fore it was executed. It was Yewsic's very first collegiate pass.

Two of Ohio State's touchdowns were scored by end Ray Hamilton on a 19-yard pass from halfback Vic Janowicz and a 25-yard throw from quarterback Tony Curcillo.

Against Wisconsin at Madison the next weekend, the Buckeyes were very fortunate to escape with a 6-6 tie. OSU could muster just 106 yards of total offense, compared with the Badgers' 346 yards. Ohio State scored in the final period with a four-yard pass from Janowicz to end Ralph Armstrong. The Buck-eyes were penalized five yards on the con-version attempt for having only ten men on the field, and a bad pass from center con-tributed to Janowicz's missed extra point.

Things went from bad to worse at home the following Saturday, October 20, when 17-point underdog Indiana stunned Ohio State, 32-10. The Buckeyes committed five turn-overs, which set up three of the Hoosiers' five touchdowns. IU quarterback Lou D'Achille was particularly effective, throw-ing for two first-period scores and directing his team to a 26-3 lead at halftime. This 22-point loss would be the Buckeyes' highest margin of defeat until Iowa defeated Ohio State by 23 points (35-12) in 1960.

Curcillo to the Rescue

Ohio State's record stood at 1-2-1 after four games, and team morale was very low. Many players felt that football was no longer fun under Hayes' style of leadership, and they resented his long and rugged practices.

Live From Michigan Stadium?

Jimmy Crum, former veteran sports anchor at Channel 4 in Columbus, did the broadcast of Ohio State foot-ball on WRFD Radio in the early 1950s. A dilemma developed when WRFD sponsors had been signed to air the 1951 Ohio State - Michigan game, but the station was un-able to obtain a broadcasting booth at Michigan Stadium. So, Crum and broad-casting partner Dave Collins watched the game on a small black-and-white televison in the WRFD studios, and aired the game as if they were inside Michigan Stadium. Years later Crum related that if this story had been known at the time, WRFD might well have lost its broadcasting license.

Fans were also beginning to question his se-lection as head coach. Sensing the anxiety, the new coach held a party for his players before their next game against Iowa.

After scoring a total of only 16 points against Wisconsin and Indiana the two pre-vious weeks, Hayes decided some position changes would be in order. At practice the Monday afternoon prior to facing Iowa, Hayes moved Tony Curcillo from quarter-back to fullback and inserted junior Bill Wilkes as the starting quarterback.

Curcillo worked the entire week at full-back without taking a single snap at the quar-terback position.

But when Wilkes went out with an in-jury in the first quarter against Iowa, Curcillo was quickly returned to quarterback. He re-sponded by passing for 292 yards and four touchdowns, to lead his squad to a 47-21 vic-tory. Curcillo connected with four different receivers for the scores. First, it was 30 yards to halfback Doug Goodsell, then nine yards to end Bob Grimes. His third was a 35-yard strike to end Ralph Armstrong, and his final scoring toss went 18 yards to end Bob Joslin. Curcillo also scored twice himself on short plunges. This was a very welcome victory for the Buckeyes, who had not won since the season-opener four weeks earlier against SMU.

Unfortunately, the Buckeye high-scoring offense was short lived.

Three times OSU's defense held Northwestern on downs inside the 15-yard line the following week, and Vic Janowicz's 26-yard fourth quarter field goal gave Ohio State a weak 3-0 victory over the Wildcats. It was more of the same at Pittsburgh the next Saturday, November 10, where the Pitt Panthers completely dominated their homecoming game before losing, 16-14. Again, it was a Janowicz field goal of 20 yards that provided the margin of victory. The Buckeye defenders held Pitt inside the OSU 10-yard line three times to secure Hayes' first road victory.

Season's Best Showing

Illinois provided the Homecoming opposition the following Saturday, November 17, in the season's last home game. Coach Ray Eliot's Fighting Illini entered the game as heavy favorites with a record of 7-0. The Buckeye players were really up for the game. They staged a private spirited pregame meeting after locking Woody Hayes out of their stadium dressing room, then went out and held the league leaders to a scoreless tie. It was the season's only blemish for Illinois, who finished the year with a record of 9-0-1 after walloping Stanford in the Rose Bowl, 40-7.

Ohio State closed out the season with a disappointing 7-0 loss at Michigan on November 24, before a crowd of 95,000. The nationally televised contest was one of the dullest Ohio State - Michigan games ever staged. The Wolverines marched 49 yards in the second quarter for the game's only touchdown, with halfback Don Peterson scoring on an end sweep from six yards out. OSU committed eight turnovers and never advanced beyond the Michigan 24-yard line.

Hayes's first Buckeye squad finished the year at 4-3-2. The 1951 Buckeye offense had been able to generate only 109 points after

Center Bob Heid was captain of Woody Hayes's first Ohio State squad in 1951.

scoring 286 in 1950. The conversion to Hayes' T-formation offense had been slow and painful, and the new coach had acquired more than his share of critics. Hayes took much of the blame and promised that better days were ahead. The following season would prove to be a step in the right direction.

1951				
September 29	Southern Methodist	W	7	0
October 6	Michigan State	L	20	24
October 13	at Wisconsin	T	6	6
October 20	Indiana	L	10	32
October 27	Iowa	W	47	21
November 3	Northwestern	W	3	0
November 10	at Pittsburgh	W	16	14
November 17	Illinois (HC)	T	0	0
November 24	at Michigan	L	0	7
Total Points			109	104

Season Record: 4-3-2
Conference: 5th place

1952

In his second year at Ohio State, coach Woody Hayes introduced a new offense, the split-T formation, which had the offensive linemen positioned further apart to provide better blocking angles. Hayes selected sophomore John Borton, a fine drop-back-style passer from Alliance, to lead his new attack. Senior Tony Curcillo, the starter at quarterback the past two seasons, was moved to defensive linebacker. Ohio State entered the season with a "wait and see" outlook, since 16 lettermen had been lost to graduation and many untested players would be counted on early in the schedule.

"Hopalong" Arrives

The Buckeyes opened with a bang, knocking off the Indiana Hoosiers, 33-13, in one of the most celebrated openers in all of Ohio State football. The game, played September 27 at Ohio Stadium, atoned for the previous season's 32-10 loss to IU.

Freshman Howard "Hopalong" Cassady, playing in his first collegiate game, scored three touchdowns and thrilled the sun-bathed crowd of 70,208 with his spirited running and pass receiving. The 18-year-old Cassady, who weighed just 168 pounds, was a product of Columbus Central High School, where he had excelled in football, basketball, and baseball.

The Buckeyes led 6-0 early in the first period, when quarterback John Borton connected with fearless Fred Bruney on a 15-yard scoring toss. The Hoosiers then went ahead 7-6 later in the quarter.

Cassady's first touchdown came midway through the second quarter, with a sensational leaping endzone catch of a Bruney-thrown pass. The play covered 27 yards.

Indiana came back to tie it up 13-13 at halftime.

The third period was scoreless as the Hoosiers of first-year coach Bernie Crimmins hung tough. But the heavier Buckeyes really took command with a 20-point fourth quarter. Cassady got his second score on a five-yard sweep around left end to make it 20-13. Indiana came right back and drove to the OSU three, but the Bucks' defense stiffened to hold IU on downs. The key play was tackle George Jacoby's eight-yard sack of Hoosier quarterback Lou D'Achille. The Buckeyes then put it away with two more touchdowns, the first a 27-yard burst over right guard by fullback John Hlay, followed by Cassady's third touchdown of the game from the IU three.

Hayes offered much praise for his team's spirited effort and the play of Cassady, Bruney, and end Bob Joslin. Cassady's performance was just the beginning of one of the most outstanding careers in Buckeye history. In four seasons he would help Ohio State capture a national title, two undisputed

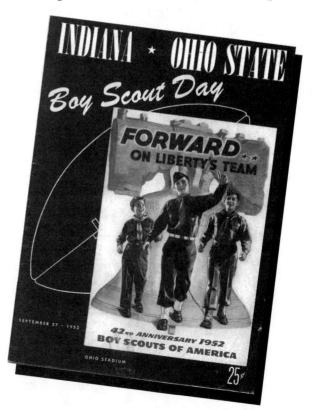

Big Ten championships, and three triumphs over Michigan. In 1955 Cassady would become the third Ohio State player to win the coveted Heisman Trophy.

Turnovers Are Your Worst Enemy! — Woody Hayes

Hayes always detested turnovers, but this strong feeling really intensified after Ohio State lost at home to Purdue, 21-14, in the season's second game. The Boilermakers' three touchdowns resulted from a fumble recovery, a blocked punt, and an interception.

Less than four minutes into the game, the Boilermakers needed just five plays to lead 7-0, after recovering fullback John Hlay's fumble at the Ohio State 26-yard line. In the second period, Purdue end Johnny Kerr blocked Bill Peterson's punt, guard Tom Bettis scooped up the loose ball at the nine and rambled into the end zone for his team's second score.

In the third quarter, Purdue safety Phil Mateja intercepted a John Borton pass and returned it to the Ohio State 30-yard line. Fullback Max Schmeling scored from the three just five plays later, and the Boilermakers had their third touchdown—thanks to three Buckeye turnovers. This was a costly defeat for Ohio State. A victory would have ultimately earned the Buckeyes the 1952 Big Ten title. Hayes' intense efforts to avoid turnovers in the seasons ahead resulted (at least partially) from this setback.

Woody's First "Big Win"

Things improved drastically the following Saturday, October 11. Coach Ivy Williamson's Badgers invaded Ohio Stadium as the nation's No. 1 ranked team, following lop-sided victories over Marquette and Illinois.

Led by the passing of John Borton and the running of Hopalong Cassady and senior Fred Bruney, the Buckeyes scored on drives

Sophomore quarterback John Borton led Ohio State's new split-T attack.

of 88, 64, and 55 yards, to upend the nation's number-one team, 23-14.

Linebacker Tony Curcillo spearheaded the defense that five times held the Badgers' potent offense on downs inside the Ohio State 20-yard line.

Badger fullback Alan Ameche, who led the league in rushing, was held without a touchdown against Ohio State for the second consecutive year. This was the Buckeyes' first significant win under Woody Hayes, and it couldn't have come at a better time.

Washington State came to Columbus the next weekend for its very first encounter with Ohio State. The Cougars had great difficulty getting to the game. After flying to Milwaukee, the team rode to Columbus by train. From Union Station in downtown Columbus, the Cougars boarded a bus and mistakenly traveled to Delaware, Ohio, then returned to stay at the old Deshler-Wallick hotel near Broad and High Streets.

John Borton was really beginning to feel comfortable with Hayes' new split-T offense. He completed 15 of 17 passes for 312 yards and all five touchdowns during a 35-7 triumph. Borton's touchdown tosses covered 12, 54, 15, 70, and 26 yards. Four of Borton's scoring passes were caught by senior end Bob Grimes, who had ten receptions for 187 yards.

Borton's five touchdown passes set an Ohio State single-game record, which was tied by Bobby Hoying against Purdue in 1994 and at Pittsburgh in 1995. Grimes' four touchdown catches also set a school single-game record, which was tied by Terry Glenn in the 1995 Pittsburgh game. Ironically, Washington State was expected to have the better passing attack. In 1951, Cougar quarterback Bob Burkhart established a new Pacific Coast Conference record with 15 touch-

down passes, while end Ed Barker set an NCAA receiving record with 847 yards.

The Buckeyes hit the low point of the season at Iowa the next Saturday. The Hawkeyes of first-year coach Forest Evashevski pulled off a major upset, defeating Ohio State 8-0. It was homecoming at Iowa City. For the three-touchdown underdog Hawkeyes, it was their first conference victory in two seasons, and they had been winless in their last ten games. Iowa led 2-0 at halftime and sealed the decision with a touchdown early in the fourth period. Ohio State simply couldn't get its offense in gear, being held to 215 net offensive yards, including just 42 on the ground.

Fourth-Quarter Heroics

OSU hit the road again the following week with much better success at Northwest-

Woody Hayes and assistant coach Ernie Godfrey watch action in Ohio State's 23-14 win over top-ranked Wisconsin at Ohio Stadium in 1952.

ern, winning 24-21, but the resilient Buckeyes had to rally with 17 fourth-quarter points. The nationally televised thriller was played at Dyche Stadium in Evanston, before a crowd of 35,000. Northwestern had led 21-7 heading into the final 15 minutes of play.

Ohio State took the game's opening kickoff, and moved 66 yards with ease to take an early 7-0 lead. With the ball at the Wildcat seven, Hopalong Cassady took a pitchout around left end, then cut back across the middle to cross the goal line standing-up. After tying the score late in the first period, the Wildcats really took charge of the game in the second quarter, scoring twice on long passes from quarterback Dick Thomas to end Joe Collier to give Northwestern a 21-7 halftime lead.

The third period was scoreless, but the Buckeyes had moved to a fourth-and-one at the Northwestern one as the quarter ended. On the fourth period's first play, Ohio State lost a golden opportunity to score when Northwestern took over on downs after spilling Cassady for a one-yard loss. But the kicking game would be Northwestern's undoing in the game's final 15 minutes.

After the Wildcats were unable to move, an extremely poor punt gave Ohio State possession at the Northwestern 18-yard line. The Buckeyes moved it in, with halfback Fred Bruney packing the pigskin the final yard around right end. Tad Weed's extra point reduced OSU's deficit to seven, at 21-14.

Northwestern was again forced to punt, with Norman Kregseth's 27-yard kick rolling dead at the NW 42-yard line. On first down, Borton passed to Bruney, who caught the ball at the 18 and sprinted into the end zone for his second touchdown of the quarter. Weed's third conversion tied the game at 21 with six minutes remaining.

After Northwestern was again unable to move, Kregseth's punt was blocked by tackle Irv Denker and recovered by linebacker Tony Curcillo at the Wildcat six. Three plays and a penalty moved the ball back to a fourth

All-American guard Mike Takacs

down at the 11. With the ball held at the 17-yard line, Weed booted a field goal from a very difficult angle for the three-point victory. His fine kick was a fitting reward for the many long hours of practice he had spent preparing for just such a moment. Late in the final period, interceptions by the Buckeyes' Marts Beekley and George Rosso ended the last two Wildcat threats and preserved one of the most thrilling Ohio State wins of all time.

Back home the next week, the Buckeyes had more than they could handle against Pittsburgh in the season's seventh game. The Panthers of coach Red Dawson scored in each of the first three quarters to win 21-14. Ohio State's John Borton had another productive day, completing 25 tosses for 282 yards, and both Buckeye touchdowns. But the Panther defense made the difference, holding the Buckeyes to just 51 rushing yards on 35 carries.

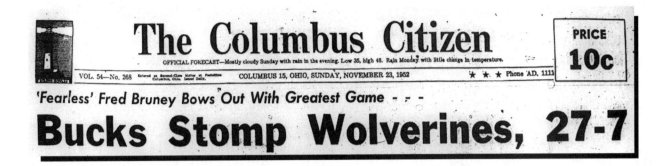

The Columbus Citizen

OFFICIAL FORECAST—Mostly cloudy Sunday with rain in the evening. Low 35, high 48. Rain Monday with little change in temperature.

PRICE
10c

VOL. 54—No. 268 Entered as Second-Class Matter at Postoffice Columbus, Ohio, Issued Daily.   COLUMBUS 15, OHIO, SUNDAY, NOVEMBER 23, 1952   ★ ★ ★ Phone AD. 1111

'Fearless' Fred Bruney Bows Out With Greatest Game - - -

Bucks Stomp Wolverines, 27-7

Leading the Pitt defensive attack that afternoon was the Panther captain, All-American linebacker Joe Schmidt. Years later when recalling this game, Woody Hayes referred to Schmidt's defensive play as one of the finest his teams had ever faced. Schmidt later gained fame as a middle linebacker with the NFL's Detroit Lions.

Record Six Interceptions
Spark Victory at Illinois

Ohio State finished the '52 campaign on the upswing, defeating Illinois at Champaign and Michigan at the Horseshoe by identical scores of 27-7. At Illinois, before a Dad's Day gathering of 60,077, the Buckeyes used a relentless running attack to break a 7-7 halftime tie and secure their fifth win of the season. OSU rushed for 252 yards, as compared with 51 the previous week against Pitt. In his postgame press conference, Hayes said the outstanding play of offensive tackle George Jacoby was one of the major reasons for his squad's improved running attack.

Defensively, Ohio State employed a specially constructed "super-umbrella," which used as many as seven deep defenders against the Illini's fine quarterback, Tommy O'Connell. The senior signal-caller was able to connect on 19 throws for 254 yards, but OSU intercepted six of his passes—at the time, the most ever against Illinois in a single game.

Woody's First of Sixteen

An alert defense and the strong passing of quarterback John Borton keyed the vic-

tory over favored Michigan the following Saturday, before a jam-packed Ohio Stadium crowd of 81,541. It was Ohio State's first win over UM in eight seasons.

The Buckeyes' vicious tackling and well-executed game-plan forced eight Wolverine turnovers. Michigan, averaging 25 points per game, was shut out until late in the final quarter. Fearless Fred Bruney, the senior halfback from Martins Ferry, played brilliantly, setting an OSU single game record with three first-half interceptions. Borton had his finest game as a Buckeye. The sharp-shooting sophomore threw for three touchdowns and

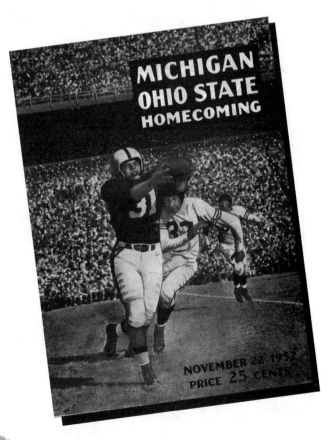

scored another on a four-yard keeper. Borton's first scoring aerials were snagged by junior end Bob Joslin of Middletown, giving the Bucks a 14-0 advantage at halftime. His third went to Joslin's former high school teammate, senior end Bob Grimes.

A Michigan victory would have earned the Wolverines the Big Ten championship and Rose Bowl berth. Instead Purdue and Wisconsin tied for the title, with the Badgers getting the trip to Pasadena.

Prior to 1952, Ohio State had won only 12 of its 48 previous encounters with Michigan, but that trend was about to change. From 1952 through 1975, Woody Hayes-coached-teams would be 16-7-1 against "that team up North," and 13 of those 24 games would have a direct bearing on the Big Ten Conference championship.

Hayes' image had improved considerably from his first season, but Ohio State was still a year away from one of its most successful and memorable autumns.

1953

Expectations were pretty high when Ohio State opened camp in the fall of 1953. John Borton was returning at quarterback after setting a single-season passing mark in '52 with 1,555 yards (a school single-season record which would stand until 1979). Two experienced halfbacks were back in sophomore Hopalong Cassady and junior Bobby Watkins, who complemented each other very effectively.

All major colleges faced a significant change this season when the NCAA rules committee eliminated two-platoon football, meaning that players would be required to play both offense and defense. Hayes was

1952				
September 27	Indiana	W	33	13
October 4	Purdue	L	14	21
October 11	Wisconsin	W	23	14
October 18	Washington State	W	35	7
October 25	at Iowa	L	0	8
November 1	at Northwestern	W	24	21
November 8	Pittsburgh	L	14	21
November 15	at Illinois	W	27	7
November 22	Michigan (HC)	W	27	7
Total Points			197	119

Season Record: 6-3
Conference: 3rd place

definitely not in favor of the change, partly because it forced a vital restructuring of practices since players would be going both ways.

The Buckeyes opened impressively on September 26 by defeating Indiana, 36-12. OSU rolled-up a 23-0 halftime margin before an Ohio Stadium crowd of 75,898, at the time the largest ever to attend an Ohio State-Indiana game. Borton was particularly impressive, completing eight of 13 throws for 122 yards and two touchdowns.

At Berkeley the next weekend, the Buckeyes downed the California Golden Bears, 33-19, after trailing 13-6 at halftime. Watkins had one of his best games as a Buckeye, plunging for 129 yards and equaling a school single-game record with four touchdowns.

He was particularly inspired when a Berkeley newspaper the day before the game compared Watkins with California's right halfback Don Marks, and "gave the edge to California." Ohio State was now an impressive 2-0 on the season, but that would change very abruptly.

Enter J. C. and Mickey

The following Saturday, October 10, Illinois routed the Buckeyes, 41-20. Coach Ray Eliot unveiled two previously unheralded halfbacks in J. C. Caroline and Mickey Bates, who teamed to provide one of the most explosive offensive performances ever witnessed in Ohio Stadium. The two ran the halfback counter play to perfection, as Caroline rushed for 192 yards and two touchdowns and Bates scampered for 147 yards and four six-pointers.

If anything, the setback was even more one-sided than indicated by the final score. Caroline had a long touchdown run called back by an offside penalty, and the Illini blew another scoring opportunity, losing a fumble on the Ohio State one-yard line. It was quite apparent that the Buckeyes had many glaring defensive weaknesses. Additionally, Borton was seriously injured against the Illini

The Victory Bell

Ohio State's victory bell has been sounding after every home win since 1953. A gift from the class of '43, the bell is located in the south east tower of Ohio Stadium. The original plans called for the bell to be located on the oval and sounded after every athletic victory, not just football. After the bell was cast nearly ten years later, it was placed in its present location.

Initial Toss

Howard "Hopalong" Cassady's first collegiate pass was a 25-yard touchdown toss to end Tommy Hague during OSU's 27-13 win over Northwestern on October 31, 1953.

and never regained the passing brilliance he exhibited as a sophomore.

Dave Leggett started at quarterback the next weekend against Pennsylvania at Franklin Field in Philadelphia. The Buckeyes struggled offensively, but still managed to come away with a ragged 12-6 win. OSU broke a 6-6 tie with a 93-yard scoring drive late in the fourth period. It was Ohio State's first game against an Ivy League opponent since losing at Cornell, 21-7, in 1940.

Madison Magic

Leggett's play improved considerably at Madison the following Saturday. The Buckeyes came back from a two-touchdown fourth-quarter deficit to nip Wisconsin by a single point, 20-19, before a then-record crowd of 52,819 at Camp Randall Stadium. The sensational comeback was completed when Ohio State quarterback Dave Leggett connected with halfback Hopalong Cassady on a perfectly thrown 60-yard touchdown pass play, with just two minutes and 31 seconds remaining.

It was Dads' Day, and both teams entered the game with 3-1 records. Coach Ivy Williams' Badgers wanted this one badly—Ohio State had upset them in Columbus the previous year, 23-14, knocking them from their number-one national ranking. Wisconsin was led by junior fullback Alan "The Horse" Ameche, who had led the Big Ten in rushing in both 1951 and 1952.

Ohio State scored first midway through the first quarter, with Cassady powering himself into the end zone from the three. Tommy Hague's all-important conversion made it 7-0. Wisconsin then took charge of the game, scoring in each of the first three quarters to lead, 19-7, heading into the final period. Quarterback Jim Miller scored the first and third touchdowns on end sweeps from the OSU 12 and 10-yard line. He passed four yards to end Norbert Esser for the other. But the Badgers missed their first two conversion attempts, which became very costly in the end.

The Buckeyes nearly scored in the second quarter, but Cassady was run out-of-bounds at the Badger one after catching a fourth-down pass from Leggett. Finally, on the first play of the fourth quarter, OSU's Bobby Watkins bulled into the end zone from the three to cap a 59-yard drive and narrow the Badger lead to 19-14.

Late in the final stanza, Ohio State held Wisconsin on downs at the Wisconsin 40-yard line. With a fourth-and-two, linebacker Mike Takacs nailed Ameche for no gain at the line of scrimmage. On first down Leggett connected with Cassady for the 60-yarder. The fleet halfback never broke stride, after hauling in the perfectly thrown strike on the dead run at the 36-yard line. Woody Hayes' never-say-die warriors had taken the lead, 20-19, with two-and-one-half minutes remaining.

But the Badgers came right back, driving to the OSU 17-yard line. With just 22 seconds left, Bill Miller's 23-yard field goal at-

tempt was wide to the right by inches, and the Buckeyes had won a real thriller. Hayes couldn't have been prouder as he heaped praise upon the efforts of both squads. His team had just captured one of the most thrilling Buckeye-Badger tilts of all-time.

After two weeks on the road, Ohio State treated its October 31 homecoming crowd of 80,562 to a well-executed 27-13 win over Northwestern. The offensive line played its best game of the season, Dave Leggett's passing continued to improve (6 of 10 for 110 yards), and Hopalong Cassady raced 65 yards for one of OSU's four touchdowns.

Ohio State led in first downs, 22-19, and in total offensive yardage, 476-302. Altogether Hayes used ten different ballcarriers, five separate passers, and five different receivers. The Buckeyes were now 5-1 and appeared to be hitting their stride just in time for the season's biggest game against highly talented Michigan State.

Halfback Bobby Watkins led the Buckeyes in scoring in both 1953 and 1954.

Chic Honored

At halftime of the Michigan State game, the legendary Chic Harley, All-American in 1916-17-19, was honored for his induction into the College Football Hall of Fame. A plaque was presented to Harley by his coach, Dr. John W. Wilce.

Flying High

Early arriving fans at the 1953 Michigan State game wondered what was flying from the flagpole at the stadium's open end. Assistant coach Ernie Godfrey, who was the brunt of many practical jokes, found his practice pants had been hoisted to the top of the pole.

Powerful Staff

Among Spartan coach Biggie Munn's 1953 assistant coaches were Bob Devaney, who later built a powerful program at Nebraska; Dan Devine, who went on to success at Missouri, Notre Dame, and with the Green Bay Packers; and Duffy Daugherty, who became head coach following Munn's retirement after the 1953 season.

Bucks Fall Short Despite Season's Best Effort

The defending national champion Spartans, who in '53 became a member of the Big Ten, had won 30 of their last 31 games dating back to the fourth week of the 1950 season. On a cold and windy November 7, Ohio State likely played its best game of the year, but it just wasn't quite enough. The Spartans earned a hard-fought 28-13 victory, increasing their season record to 6-1.

MSU's speedy "pony backfield" of quarterback Tom Yewsic, halfbacks LeRoy Bolden and Billy Wells, and fullback Evan Slonac weighed just 180, 163, 175, and 170 pounds, respectively. The elusive Bolden, with 128 yards in 18 carries, dazzled the Ohio Stadium crowd of 82,328 with touchdown runs of 37, 20 and 3 yards.

The Buckeyes, who trailed only 14-13 after three quarters, lost any hope for an upset after failing to convert on two golden opportunities in the final period. First George Rosso intercepted an Earl Morrall pass and returned it to the OSU 45-yard line. But the Buckeyes soon surrendered the ball on downs at the Spartan 20 after four consecutive rushes gained only nine yards. Next Dave Leggett picked off a Yewsic throw and returned it back to the Michigan State 23-yard line. However, Tad Weed's field goal attempt on fourth down from the MSU 27-yard line was blocked, killing any chances of a Buckeye win.

MSU awarded a game ball to end Bill Quinlan, whose brilliant play was a big factor in the Spartan victory. Michigan State went on to defeat UCLA in the Rose Bowl, 28-20, after sharing the '53 Big Ten crown with Illinois.

Ohio State bounced back to defeat Purdue, 21-6, in the home finale on November 14. Before a Dads Day crowd of 77,465, OSU spotted the Boilermakers a 6-0 first-pe-

1953				
September 26	Indiana	W	36	12
October 3	at California	W	33	19
October 10	Illinois	L	20	41
October 17	at Pennsylvania	W	12	6
October 24	at Wisconsin	W	20	19
October 31	Northwestern (HC)	W	27	13
November 7	Michigan State	L	13	28
November 14	Purdue	W	21	6
November 21	at Michigan	L	0	20
Total Points			182	164

Season Record: 6-3
Conference: 4th place

riod lead, then roared back behind the fine running of Watkins and Cassady for their sixth victory of the campaign. Leggett and Borton split the signal-calling duties, with Leggett completing six passes for 53 yards and Borton connecting on five attempts for 78 yards.

Major Disappointment at Ann Arbor

The next week Ohio State headed north in search of its first victory at Michigan since 1937. Hayes' 6-2 squad was highly favored over the 5-3 Wolverines, but lost badly, 20-0. The Buckeyes could hardly have looked worse, throwing five interceptions, losing a fumble, and gaining a mere 98 yards on the ground. This was the beginning of a long, cold winter for the third-year coach, and many fans began calling for his removal. The following season was obviously going to be a critical period for Woody Hayes.

1954

While addressing the *Columbus Dispatch* Quarterback Club one evening during the 1975 season, Coach Woody Hayes told of an incident that occurred during the summer of 1954. He recalled relaxing on his porch one Saturday evening, while some neighbors were having a small get-together nearby. Apparently the neighbors were talking about the Ohio State football program, and Hayes overheard one neighbor remark, "This is the year we get Woody!"

Hayes' teams had a combined record of 16-9-2 during his three previous seasons, and the neighbor was obviously thinking the coach would be fired after the 1954 season. Hayes said that incident provided additional motivation for him to do his very best that fall.

"I even got up an hour earlier each day, so I could prepare all the more for our sea-

son," he stated. As it turned out, the 1954 season was the turning point in the Woody Hayes era at Ohio State. The team went 10-0 through a very strong Big Ten schedule, to capture the Associated Press national title.

Lyal Clark Great Addition

The '53 Buckeyes had barely outscored their opposition, 182-164. To help strengthen his defense, Woody Hayes brought coach Lyal Clark back to Ohio State from Minnesota. Clark was an excellent defensive line coach, who served under Wes Fesler at Ohio State through 1950, and had moved with Fesler to Minnesota in 1951.

Clark rightfully received a lot of the credit for OSU's improved defense in '54, which surrendered only 75 points during its rugged ten-game schedule.

Bucks Picked Fifth in Preseason

Ohio State's excellent showing in '54 came as a surprise to most sportswriters and analysts. The Buckeyes were selected for fifth place in the conference race, behind Illinois, Michigan State, Wisconsin, and Iowa. The Big Ten was especially strong during the 1950s, and in 1954 the conference went 17-9-1 against non-league competition.

Alan Ameche of Wisconsin captured the 1954 Heisman Trophy. Most players played both ways because of the limited substitution rules in effect at that time.

Seniors Dean Dugger and co-captain Dick Brubaker were the starting ends, and junior Frank Machinsky and seniors Dick

Two of Northeast Ohio's Finest

Alliance (Ohio) High School produced two excellent quarterbacks in the early 1950s—John Borton, who was an Ohio State co-captain in 1954, and Len Dawson, who co-captained Purdue in 1956.

Hilinski and Don Swartz were the tackles. Senior Jim Reichenbach (a four-year starter) returned at guard, and was joined by massive Jim Parker, a talented sophomore who would become one of the finest linemen in school history. Junior Kenny Vargo was the center.

Dave Leggett, a very fine option-style runner, won out over co-captain John Borton at quarterback. Both were seniors. The halfbacks were senior Bobby Watkins, a strong power-type runner, and junior Hopalong Cassady, who was a real game breaker. Sophomore Hubert Bobo, a very effective runner and blocker, was the starting fullback.

Impressive Right From The Opening Whistle

Ohio State opened the season at home September 25 with a 28-0 shutout over Indiana. Watkins and Cassady each scored twice to lead the Buckeye offense, and Hayes was very pleased with his team's defense, which created four IU turnovers.

Cassady scored two more the following week, as the Buckeyes fought hard to defeat California at home, 21-13. With Ohio State leading just 14-13 midway through the final period, Cassady also intercepted a Golden Bear pass to set up the Buckeyes' final touchdown.

Ohio State opened its Big Ten season the next Saturday with a 40-7 triumph at Illinois, avenging the previous season's 41-20 loss to the Illini. On a hot afternoon with the temperature near 80 degrees, OSU scored at least once in each quarter to rout the Illini. The Buckeyes led in first downs, 24-8, and in total offensive yardage, 479-123. Illinois avoided a shutout when J. C. Caroline re-

turned an interception 42 yards late in the final period for his team's only score.

It was a costly win, however, as center Ken Vargo was lost for the remainder of the regular season with a broken arm. Vargo was ably replaced by Bob Thornton, a senior from Willard. Ohio State was now 3-0 and had jumped to fourth place in the weekly Associated Press poll.

Iowa Inflicts Season's Closest Call

The Buckeyes returned home October 16 to face the rugged Iowa Hawkeyes of coach Forest Evashevski. This game was a thriller to the very end. Iowa halfback Earl Smith had quite a day, scoring both Hawkeye touchdowns, the first on a 67-yard interception return and the second on a 75-yard punt return. Ohio State led 20-14 midway through the fourth period on touchdowns by Watkins, Leggett, and Brubaker, but the conversion at-

All-American end Dean Dugger

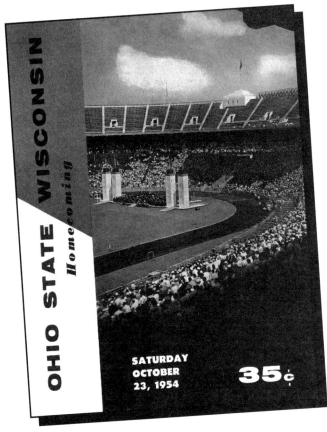

OHIO STATE WISCONSIN Homecoming

SATURDAY
OCTOBER
23, 1954

35¢

tempt was unsuccessful following the third score.

Late in the game, Iowa drove inside the Ohio State five, but was held on downs with under two minutes remaining. The Buckeyes had survived a close one, and were now 4-0. This six-point win would turn out to be the season's smallest margin of victory.

Cassady Interception
An Ohio Stadium Classic

One of the 1954 Buckeyes' major tests came in the homecoming game October 23 against second-ranked Wisconsin. Both teams were 4-0. It was the key game in the nation that weekend.

Woody Hayes' Buckeyes were rated the Big Ten's top offensive team while the Badgers were the league's best defensively. A record 400 press passes were issued to sportswriters and broadcasters from all over the country, who were covering one of the year's top college games.

Wisconsin coach Ivy Williamson, realizing the Badgers had not won in Columbus since 1918, tried to change their luck by having his squad stay Friday evening in Springfield, Ohio, rather than a Columbus hotel. Winning this game was also a personal goal for Williamson, who had compiled a fine 34-12-4 record during his six seasons as the Badger boss. Ohio State was the only Big Ten opponent his teams had not defeated. The Badgers had two veteran quarterbacks in Jim Miller and Jim Haluska, an excellent fullback in Alan Ameche, and two very capable ends in Ron Lockland and Jim Temp.

The Buckeyes had their chances during a very bruising first half, but trailed 7-3 at intermission. Late in the third period, Wisconsin seriously threatened to increase its four-point lead. With second-and-four at the OSU 20-yard line, quarterback Jim Miller took to the air.

Hopalong Cassady intercepted at the twelve, and, behind several key blocks, electrified the crowd with a spectacular 88-yard touchdown return which soundly shifted the game's momentum. It was Miller's first interception of the '54 season, and the first time all year the Badgers had been scored upon in the second half.

Cassady's memorable run completely fractured Wisconsin's poise, and end Dean Dugger staged a one-man campaign against any Badger comeback. Dugger participated in every tackle as OSU held Wisconsin on downs during a crucial series early in the fourth quarter. On fourth down he nailed Badger halfback Billy Lowe for a 12-yard loss, and the Buckeyes took over at the Wisconsin 27-yard line. Ohio State scored three times in the final quarter to win, 31-14—the game was much closer than suggested by the final score.

The Buckeyes limited talented Badger fullback Alan Ameche to just 42 yards in 16 carries. Ameche, who that season would win the Heisman Trophy, had been unable to score against Ohio State for the fourth consecutive year. Cassady finished third to Ameche in the balloting and captured the award the following season. Wisconsin finished the year at 7-2, good for ninth place in the season's final Associated Press poll.

It was quite a weekend for Ohio State, who jumped to the number-one spot in the weekly AP poll. Michigan handed Minnesota its first conference loss, 34-0, leaving the Buckeyes and Wolverines as the only undefeated teams in league play.

Ohio State struggled at Evanston the next weekend, before finally defeating Northwestern, 14-7. Dave Leggett connected with Bobby Watkins on a 24-yard scoring pass in the fourth quarter to break a 7-7 tie. But the big news of the day came from Ann Arbor, where Indiana upset the Michigan Wolverines, 13-9. Ohio State was now 6-0 overall,

and all alone atop the Big Ten with a 4-0 league record.

The Buckeyes had little trouble the next two weeks, defeating Pittsburgh 26-0 at home and besting Purdue 28-6 at West Lafayette.

The stage was now set for what turned out to be one of the greatest struggles between OSU and "that team up north."

Goal-Line Stand One of Buckeyes' All-Time Great Moments

The Big Ten title and Rose Bowl berth were on the line when 12th-ranked Michigan invaded Ohio Stadium on November 20. Ohio State was 6-0 in league play, Michigan was 5-1. Coach Bennie Oosterbaan's Wolverines had lost only to Indiana in conference action, and could force a tie for the Big Ten crown with a victory. The game was nation-

The Buckeyes' fourth-quarter goal-line stand against Michigan is one of the finest moments in all of Ohio State football.

Success Far Beyond the Gridiron

One of the most significant single plays during Woody Hayes' 28 seasons as Buckeye boss was created by a relatively unknown reserve linebacker. Near halftime in the Buckeyes' crucial game against Michigan in 1954, Hubert Bobo re-injured his foot and was replaced at linebacker by Jack Gibbs, a senior with very little game experience. Two plays later (with the Wolverines leading, 7-0), Gibbs intercepted a Michigan pass and returned it to the ten-yard line, setting up OSU's first touchdown, which tied the game at halftime. This interception completely changed the game's momentum, and the Buckeyes went on to win, 21-7.

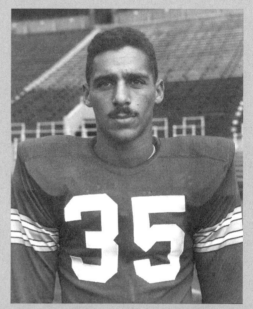

Jack Gibbs' interception in the 1954 Michigan game was one of the most significant plays during Woody Hayes' 28 seasons at Ohio State.

The story of Jack Gibbs is a description of extraordinary success that extends far beyond the college gridiron. Gibbs was told he was too small to play football at Columbus West High School. After graduation he worked two years to help support his family before enrolling at Ohio State, where he received the support of Woody Hayes to give college football a try even without high school experience.

Gibbs progressed steadily and was expected to see considerable action at fullback in 1953 until a broken ankle kept him idle most of that season. More determined than ever, he returned for his senior year and by Michigan week had moved up to the second team. Gibbs worked a 40-hour-week on the night shift at North American Aviation, attended classes during the day, and practiced football in the late afternoon. He graduated summa cum laude in the fall of 1954.

Gibbs joined the Columbus Public Schools where he quickly earned the reputation of being a high achiever. He became Principal at East High School and later served as the first Director of the Fort Hayes Career Center. Lee Williams, a '54 Ohio State teammate who began teaching at East High School in 1961, described Gibbs as "one of the best educators I've ever known." Ruth Ann Gibbs remembered her husband as "a very giving and unselfish person who was always available when students needed help." Son Jack, Jr., recalled how much his father enjoyed helping other people succeed.

Gibbs was a member of the Ohio State Board of Trustees in the late-1960s. He passed away in 1982. The street in front of the Fort Hayes Career Center in Columbus has been renamed in his honor.

Jack Gibbs Boulevard is located in the northeast section of downtown Columbus.

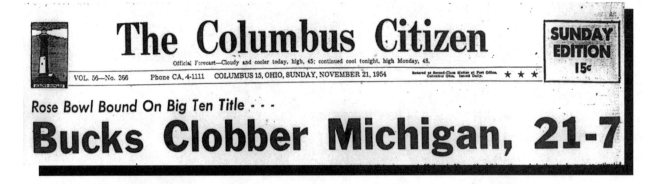

The Columbus Citizen

SUNDAY EDITION 15¢

Official Forecast—Cloudy and cooler today, high, 45; continued cool tonight, high Monday, 48.

VOL. 56—No. 266   Phone CA. 4-1111   COLUMBUS 15, OHIO, SUNDAY, NOVEMBER 21, 1954   ★ ★ ★

Rose Bowl Bound On Big Ten Title · · ·
Bucks Clobber Michigan, 21-7

ally televised, with former Michigan great Tom Harmon and veteran sportscaster Bill Stern handling the announcing. Press passes were issued to over 500 media representatives, at the time the largest ever to cover a Big Ten game.

Michigan immediately took charge, driving 68 yards after receiving the opening kickoff for an early 7-0 lead. The visitors surprised everyone with a new offensive formation, that showed an unbalanced line with just one player—a tackle—on the left side of center. The Wolverines used a perfect blend of power, speed, and deception with their multiple offense, scoring the touchdown on a seven-yard double handoff reverse around left end to halfback Dan Cline. Buckeye fans were already concerned!

The Wolverines dominated the first half but were unable to increase their lead. With a little more then three minutes remaining until halftime, Michigan quarterback Jim Maddock's pass was intercepted at the OSU 43-yard line and returned to the ten by linebacker Jack Gibbs. Gibbs, who had not been considered big enough to play football at Columbus West High School, was a seldom-used player who had just entered the game. From there, end Fred Kriss scored his first collegiate touchdown on a pass from quarterback Dave Leggett, and suddenly it was 7-7.

The third period was scoreless, but the Wolverines opened fourth-quarter play with a first down at the Ohio State four. With their backs to the wall, Ohio State's defense demonstrated great poise and confidence, hold-

ing Michigan on downs just six inches shy of the OSU goal. Particularly effective during this memorable goal-line stand were guards Jim Parker and Jim Reichenbach, tackle Frank Machinsky, and linebacker Hubert Bobo.

Leggett then moved his team just six inches short of 100 yards the other direction for one of OSU's biggest touchdowns of all time. End Dick Brubaker caught Leggett's second TD aerial, Hopalong Cassady scored another during the game's final seconds, and

Ohio State
Michigan
Saturday November 20, 1954
35¢

Tad Weed's third conversion gave Ohio State the 21-7 victory.

Woody Hayes would coach many more big wins during his remaining 24 seasons —but none would be much bigger than this come-from-behind victory over Michigan. For the first time in Woody Hayes' career, the Buckeyes were Pasadena-bound.

Leggett Rose Bowl MVP

Playing in the rain and mud, Ohio State defeated Southern California, 20-7, in the January 1, 1955, Rose Bowl.

Sportsmanship at Its Best

Late in the January 1, 1955, Rose Bowl, Woody Hayes began substituting liberally, allowing each player the opportunity to play at least one down. One player who had seen no action that afternoon was senior co-captain John Borton, who had lost his starting quarterback position that season to Dave Leggett. As Hayes called upon Borton to relieve Leggett, Borton very unselfishly suggested that third-team quarterback Bill Booth be inserted instead. Borton was aware that Booth's father, Dick Booth, had played fullback for the Pitt Panthers against Stanford in the 1928 Rose Bowl.

Hayes proudly shook Borton's hand, then beckoned Booth, who quarterbacked the last three plays of the game. John Borton was Ohio State's only able-bodied player not to see action that afternoon, but his thoughtfulness will always be remembered by Bill Booth as "the greatest act of sportsmanship I have ever seen." Booth's proud father was in attendance that afternoon—they became the first father-son combination to have appeared in a Rose Bowl.

The game was played in an all-day downpour—players were slipping and slithering in a quagmire that extended from end zone to end zone. Over 100,000 tickets had been sold, but only 89,191 drenched fans attended. Ticket scalpers were forced to sell tickets for little more than 50 cents. Serious problems developed in the open press box, when the rain damaged Western Union circuit wires, preventing many writers from filing their pregame stories.

Ohio State entered the game a 13-point favorite. On the eve of the game, a "Good Luck Telegram" was received from Columbus carrying the signatures of approximately 4,200 Buckeye fans—the document measured over 40 yards in length.

Late in the first period, OSU put together an 11-play, 69-yard drive that produced the game's first touchdown. Quarterback Dave Leggett sneaked three yards over right guard on the second play of the second quarter, and Weed converted to make it 7-0. The key play of the series was a 26-yard sweep around left end by halfback Jerry Harkrader.

The Trojans fumbled on their next possession, and Leggett recovered on the USC 35. On second down, Leggett combined with Bobby Watkins on a 21-yard scoring pass for OSU's second touchdown. Watkins' conversion made it 14-0, with almost 13 minutes of the second period remaining. The fine senior halfback from New Bedford, Massachusetts, had just realized a lifetime dream—scoring a touchdown in the Rose Bowl.

Near the half, Southern Cal's Aramis Dandoy fielded Hubert Bobo's punt at his own 14 and started up the east sideline. Picking up two key blocks, Dandoy headed back toward midfield. Ohio State's fleet Jimmy Roseboro was gaining ground in pursuit, but a tenacious block cut him down, allowing Dandoy to score standing up. Dandoy's 86-yard scamper is the longest punt return in Rose Bowl history.

The third quarter was scoreless, but USC really caused some anxious moments. First, the Trojans held OSU on downs at the USC four. Then, on first down, Southern Cal's Jon Arnett circled his own right end and dashed 70 yards to the Ohio State 26-yard line as the

Woody's Favorite Meringue Pie

Dave Diles, former anchor for ABC's college football telecasts, covered sports for the Associated Press, both in Columbus and Detroit, before moving to New York with ABC.

Diles recalls that Woody Hayes agreed to speak at the 1954 high school football banquet in Middleport where Diles went to high school. When Ohio State found itself headed for the Rose Bowl, though, Hayes asked if they could re-schedule the banquet until the following January—the school agreed. "The place was filled to capacity that night," Diles recalls, "and Woody really captivated them."

Hayes met Diles' parents that evening, and a strong friendship developed over the next several years. The coach would call when he was going to be in the area and ask Mrs. Diles to bake one of her lemon meringue pies. When assistant coaches Ernie Godfrey and Esco Sarkkinen spoke at Middleport banquets in later years, Hayes insisted they first stop and have a piece of "Lucille Diles' lemon meringue pie—the world's finest!"

1954 National Champions

A Rose Bowl First

The January 1, 1955, Rose Bowl clash between Ohio State and Southern California was the first Rose Bowl to be covered by a female sportswriter, as Miss Faye Lloyd reported game highlights for the United Press International.

was needed the most. End Dean Dugger and halfback Hopalong Cassady were selected as All-Americans.

Ohio State became the first Big Ten team to win seven conference games in one season since Amos Alonzo Stagg's Chicago team won seven in 1913, the year Woody Hayes was born. The 1954 season was not only one of the finest in Buckeye history, it also was the turning point in Hayes' career.

third period ended. But the Buckeye defense stiffened as USC was able to gain only three yards on its next four tries.

Starting from the OSU 23-yard line, Leggett guided his team 77 yards for the game's clincher. Harkrader scored the TD from the eight on a pitchout around USC's right end, to conclude the scoring at 20-7. By this time, the Buckeyes were mud-soaked to the skin, but it didn't matter—they had concluded a perfect 10-0 season and could hardly have been happier. Leggett was selected the game's MVP, after handling the ball 80 times in the mud and rain without a single fumble.

The Buckeyes had completed the season with a perfect 10-0 record, and were awarded the mythical national title by the Associated Press. Playing one of the toughest schedules in school history, this team was always able to make the right play when it

1954

September 25	Indiana	W	28	0
October 2	California	W	21	13
October 9	at Illinois	W	40	7
October 16	Iowa	W	20	14
October 23	Wisconsin (HC)	W	31	14
October 30	at Northwestern	W	14	7
November 6	Pittsburgh	W	26	0
November 13	at Purdue	W	28	6
November 20	Michigan	W	21	7
January 1	Southern California*	W	20	7
Total Points			**249**	**75**

* Rose Bowl

Season Record: 10-0
Big Ten Champion
National Champion

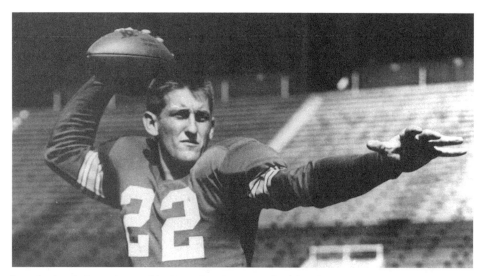

Quarterback Dave Leggett - Rose Bowl Most Valuable Player

Greatest Rose Bowl NEVER Played!

The "Dream Rose Bowl" of January 1, 1955, would have matched undefeated Ohio State (9-0) and undefeated UCLA (9-0). Ohio State was awarded the 1954 Associated Press national title, while UCLA was chosen for the same honor by United Press International. The Bruins of coach Red Sanders featured tailback Primo Villanueva, fullback Bob Davenport, and All-American linemen Jim Salsbury and Jack Ellena.

This was one of UCLA's finest teams, but the "no repeat rule" at that time prevented teams from appearing in consecutive Rose Bowls. The Bruins had played in the previous year's classic, losing to Michigan State, 28-20.

1955

Expectations for 1955 were high, even with the graduation of seven senior starters from the '54 national title team. Hopalong Cassady, an electrifying runner with a quick change of pace, was returning for his fourth season. The fiery redhead from Columbus Central High School was also a keenly alert defender, as demonstrated with his classic 88-yard interception return in the '54 Wisconsin game. The team mourned the loss of tackle Dick Hilinski, who had recently lost his life in an automobile accident.

With both Dave Leggett and John Borton graduated, Woody Hayes moved junior Frank Ellwood to quarterback. Ellwood had played quarterback at Dover High School, but shifted to end his sophomore season at Ohio State. Although not an overly effective passer, Ellwood was very adept at running and handling the ball, which were

vital for Ohio State's ground-pounding attack. He also was an excellent student.

Nebraska Visits Columbus

The Buckeyes opened the season September 24 with an exciting 28-20 victory over the Nebraska Cornhuskers. It was the very first meeting between the two schools, and the Ohio Stadium crowd of 80,171 witnessed a tense, absorbing thriller that wasn't decided until the final minutes. Cassady had a magnificent afternoon, scoring Ohio State's first three touchdowns and setting up the fourth with a 43-yard jaunt to the Nebraska two-yard line.

Woody Hayes' squad twice came from behind for the eight-point victory. Linebacker John Edwards gave Nebraska its first lead early in the second quarter, with an electrifying 87-yard return of a stolen lateral. Edwards' timing was perfect as he intercepted an option pitchout, then darted the opposite direction for the Ohio State end zone. Buckeye halfback Jim Roseboro made a key interception late in the game, grabbing quarterback Don Erway's pass at the Ohio State 10-yard line.

Cornhusker coach Bill Glassford, a native of Lancaster, Ohio, felt his team's four

Buckeyes' Weed Leads All-Stars over Browns

Place kicker Tad Weed, a senior in '54, paced the College All-Stars to a 30-27 upset win over the NFL's defending champion Cleveland Browns. The game was played August 12, 1955, at Soldier Field in Chicago. Weed scored 11 of the All-Star's 30 points with three field goals and two extra points.

The game's MVP was All-Star quarterback Ralph Guglielmi, an All-American from Notre Dame. Weed and Guglielmi had been teammates at Columbus' Grandview Heights High School from '47 through '50.

Hopalong Cassady's three touchdowns in the 1955 Nebraska opener increased his career total to a school record 25, two more than Chic Harley's 23 career touchdowns in 1916-17-19.

held scoreless for only the second time in OSU's last 25 games.

The offense got back in gear at home the next weekend in the conference opener against Illinois. Ohio State won, 27-12, even though the game was somewhat closer than suggested by the final score. Illinois scored the game's first and last six points, and the Buckeyes put 27 consecutive markers on the scoreboard in between. Cassady led all runners with 95 yards while scoring two of OSU's four touchdowns. Altogether, Hayes used ten different ball carriers and five different passers throughout the afternoon. The Illini led in first downs, 17-16, and in total offensive yards, 371-351.

turnovers played a big factor in the game's outcome. Ohio State led in rushing yardage, 321 to 138, with Cassady leading all runners with 170 yards. Nebraska had a decided edge in passing, 189 yards to 17.

Winning Streak
Shattered

In a nationally televised contest the next Saturday at Palo Alto, Stanford took the opening kickoff and drove 72 yards for the game's only score to win, 6-0. The loss broke Ohio State's two-season winning streak at 11 games. The Indians' defensive scheme to stop Cassady worked well, holding him to just 37 yards in 11 carries. Hayes was deeply concerned about his offense, which was

Halfback Jerry Harkrader (44) gains ground against the Nebraska Cornhuskers while massive Jim Parker (62) prepares to block.

Duke surprised a lot of fans around the country the following Saturday, roaring back for a 20-14 triumph over OSU after trailing early, 14-0. The Buckeyes scored on two long plays, a 44-yard end sweep by halfback Jim Roseboro and a 38-yard punt return by Hopalong Cassady. But the Blue Devils changed the game's momentum with their first of three touchdowns, a five-yard pass from halfback Bob Pascal to halfback Bernie Blaney, just one second before halftime.

The visitors tied the score with Pascal's one-yard plunge early in the third period, then staged a 17-play, 82-yard, fourth-quarter drive for the deciding score. Junior quarterback Sonny Jurgenson, who went on to a successful NFL career with the Philadelphia Eagles and Washington Redskins, sneaked across from the one for the winning touchdown. Ohio State committed six turnovers and never crossed the 50-yard line in the second half. The Buckeyes' season was now at the crossroads with a 2-2 record after four games.

Huge Afternoon at Wisconsin

At Madison on October 22, before what was then an all-time Camp Randall Stadium crowd of 53,529, Ohio State came from behind for a very key 26-16 win after spotting favored Wisconsin a 14-0 lead. In typical Woody Hayes fashion, the Buckeyes put together sustained marches of 66, 30, 73, and 80 yards for their four touchdowns. OSU had 304 yards on the ground and only 32 through the air.

Ellwood directed his team almost flawlessly and scored three of Ohio State's four touchdowns on short plunges. Cassady scored the other TD and led all rushers with 100 yards. Jimmy Roseboro, second-team right halfback behind ailing Jerry Harkrader, ran for 96 yards in 15 attempts, including two carries for 53 yards during OSU's third touchdown drive. Hayes called the win one of the most significant during his first five years at Ohio State, and praised assistant coach Esco Sarkkinen for his excellent scouting of Wisconsin.

Back at Ohio Stadium for homecoming the following week, the Buckeyes scored in each quarter to overwhelm the Northwestern Wildcats 49-0 and go 4-2 on the season. The 49-point victory was the most lopsided in the OSU-NW series since Ohio State won 58-0 back in 1913. Honored at halftime before a crowd of 82,214 were the 1905 and 1930 squads, who were holding their 50th and 25th anniversaries.

Six different Buckeyes broke into the scoring column. Cassady ran for 77 yards and scored twice to increase his career touchdown total to 31, before sitting out the entire second half. He tied what was then a Big Ten Conference career TD record set by Red Grange at Illinois in 1923-24-25. Halfbacks

New Attendance Mark

The 1955 season was the first year each game at Ohio Stadium drew more than 80,000 fans.

Joe Cannavino and Jim Roseboro scampered for 137 and 104 yards to pace an Ohio State ground attack that netted 395 yards. Linebacker Jim Parker scored OSU's third touchdown after recovering a Wildcat fumble in mid-air and racing 42 yards.

At home the next Saturday, the Buckeyes had all they could handle before defeating unexpectedly stubborn Indiana, 20-13. Hayes admitted his team did not have its finest afternoon, but offered that championship teams must find a way to win even when they're not playing their best. The big news of the weekend came from Champaign, where Illinois upset previously unbeaten Michigan, 25-6. The Buckeyes were now on top of the conference standings with a league record of 4-0.

Cassady was again the workhorse, racing for 124 yards and scoring OSU's first two touchdowns. Jerry Harkrader scored the third TD with a three-yard smash over left tackle late in the fourth quarter. Indiana led in first downs, 20-16, and in total offensive yards, 301-251. Ohio State attempted only two passes and both were incomplete.

Home Finale for 13 Seniors

The November 12 Iowa game was Dad's Day. The emotion-filled afternoon marked the final appearance in Ohio Stadium for Hopalong Cassady and 12 other seniors, including the team's co-captains—tackle Frank Machinsky and center Ken Vargo. The Hawkeyes were one of the preseason favorites for the league title and would present one of the season's biggest tests, even though they entered the game with a disappointing record of 3-3-1. A Western Union telegram containing the names of nearly 3,000 Hawkeye fans was delivered to the Iowa dressing room right before the game, in an effort to inspire the Hawkeyes.

Hopalong Cassady receives congratulations from Woody Hayes as he leaves the Ohio Stadium playing field for the last time on November 12, 1955. Cassady scored three touchdowns that afternoon to lead OSU past Iowa, 20-10.

The Nation's Finest

The 1955 Iowa game featured the opposing play of the nation's two finest guards, Jim Parker of Ohio State and Calvin Jones of Iowa. Both were from Ohio (Parker-Toledo, Jones-Steubenville), both were consensus All-Americans, both would win the Outland Trophy (Jones-'55, Parker-'56), and both wore jersey No. 62.

Cassady rushed for 169 yards (his best effort of the season) and scored all three touchdowns, to pace Ohio State to a 20-10 victory. His first score came on a 45-yard sprint off right tackle on his first carry of the afternoon. That touchdown boosted his career scoring total to 204 points, three better than the previous school record amassed by Chic Harley. The two teams' statistics were nearly identical. Each had 16 first downs, while OSU barely led in total offensive yards, 273-272. For the second week in a row, Ohio State had zero yards passing.

One of the game's key plays was center Ken Vargo's interception of Iowa quarterback Jerry Reichow's pass at the Iowa 29-yard line with 7:37 left in the game. Cassady was jubilantly carried off the field by his teammates, much to the delight of the 82,701 spectators.

In his postgame conference, Hayes especially praised the play of guard Jim Parker and the blocking of fullback Don Vicic. A game ball was presented to Dr. Howard Bevis, who was retiring as Ohio State's president. The Buckeyes were now 6-2 on the season, and had tied the school's consecutive Big Ten victory record with 12.

Spartans Appreciate Buckeyes' Effort

The Big Ten title was again on the line as Ohio State traveled to Ann Arbor to battle Michigan. Coach Benny Oosterbaan's Wolverines were 5-1 in the conference, while Ohio State was 5-0. Michigan could capture the conference title and Rose Bowl berth with a win over Ohio State, since the Wolverines played seven league games compared with the Buckeyes' six. This battle was Michigan's 600th all-time football game, and the Michigan Stadium crowd of 97,369 was at the time the largest for a college-owned stadium.

Michigan State also had a real interest in the game. The Spartans were 5-1 in the conference, and had completed league play the previous Saturday. An Ohio State win over Michigan would place Michigan State second in the final conference standings and send the Spartans to the Rose Bowl, since Ohio State could not return to Pasadena under the no-repeat rule in effect at that time.

Center Ken Vargo, left, and tackle Frank Machinsky, 1955 co-captains.

Spartans Show Support for Buckeyes

To help support the Buckeyes against Michigan in '55, one of Michigan State's cheerleaders joined Ohio State's cheerleaders at Michigan Stadium, while MSU was defeating the Marquette Warriors 33-0 in a non-conference game that same afternoon at Spartan Stadium. The Buckeyes' 17-0 victory over the Wolverines sent Michigan State to the Rose Bowl.

The Spartans' support may have helped—Ohio State shut out the Wolverines, 17-0, with the Buckeyes' defense allowing Michigan to cross the 50-yard line only once (on a penalty). On the following play, massive Jim Parker spilled the Wolverines for a loss, putting them back into their own territory. In a surprise switch that confused Michigan's defense, Cassady started at right halfback and Don Sutherin (who played the game's entire 60 minutes) moved to Cassady's normal left halfback spot.

Ohio State used every method of scoring except a conversion. End Fred Kriss gave his team a 3-0 halftime lead with a 13-yard second quarter field goal (his first as a collegian). In the second half, Cassady and Vicic each scored TDs on short plunges, and the Buckeye defense recorded a safety. The game got out of control at the end with penalties being assessed on almost every play, and two Michigan players were ejected for unsportsmanlike conduct. Buckeye fans tore down both goal posts immediately following the game, while numerous scuffles among opposing fans developed along the snow-covered sidelines.

Ohio State had captured its first win at Ann Arbor since 1937. The Buckeyes led in first downs, 20-5, and in total offensive yards, 337-109. Hayes had his team throw only three passes, completing one for four yards—it was the Buckeyes' first pass completion in three weeks. This game brought to an end the fabulous collegiate career of Hopalong Cassady, who rushed for 146 yards on the afternoon. Dr. Harlan Hatcher, President of the University of Michigan and former Dean of Ohio

Overnight Guest

Tackle Dick Guy was a very outgoing individual who always liked to have fun at whatever he was doing. Hayes apparently thought Guy should take a little more serious approach to football. In the dressing room following practice the Monday evening prior to the 1955 Ohio State-Michigan game, Hayes told Guy, "You're moving in with me for a few days."

Guy spent the next three nights at the Hayes' home. "Woody drilled me right up until bedtime every night," Guy recalls. Hayes would repeatedly ask, "What do you do on this play?" Then they would start all over again early the next morning. Thursday, Hayes finally allowed Guy to return to his campus room after he was convinced Guy knew all his assignments. "Man, was I glad to get out of there," Guy reflects. Saturday at Ann Arbor Guy played one of his finest games, and Ohio State won, 17-0.

Safety First

Imagine completing a forward pass and having a safety scored against you—all on the same play. It happened in the '55 OSU-UM game. The Wolverines, trailing 9-0 in the fourth quarter, had possession deep in their own territory. Quarterback Jim Maddock faded back into his own end zone, then flipped a short pass out into the flat to halfback Terry Barr. Before Barr could move up field, the Buckeyes' Bill Michael and Aurealius Thomas tackled him behind the Michigan goal line for a safety.

State's English Department, paid a visit to OSU's dressing room to offer congratulations. Ohio State had captured its second consecutive outright conference title, while Michigan State went on to represent the Big Ten Conference with a thrilling 17-14 Rose Bowl win over UCLA.

Cassady and Parker were chosen All-America, and Cassady became the third Ohio State player to capture the coveted Heisman Trophy, following in the footsteps of Les Horvath in 1944 and Vic Janowicz in 1950. He finished with a career total of 2,466 yards and 222 points, both school records at that time. Hayes was now establishing himself as a very capable big-time college coach after a wobbly start his first three seasons, and Ohio State was finally shaking its image as the graveyard of coaches.

1955			
September 24	Nebraska	W	28	20
October 1	at Stanford	L	0	6
October 8	Illinois	W	27	12
October 15	Duke	L	14	20
October 22	at Wisconsin	W	26	16
October 29	Northwestern (HC)	W	49	0
November 5	Indiana	W	20	13
November 12	Iowa	W	20	10
November 19	at Michigan	W	17	0
Total Points			201	97

Season Record: 7-2
Big Ten Champion

1956

In a real strange twist of events, Ohio State entered the 1956 season with a one-year NCAA probation, which would prevent the Buckeyes from participating in the Rose Bowl

should they qualify. During one of his weekly television shows in 1955, Woody Hayes mentioned how difficult it was for some of his players to stay in school because they had very little money. Because their rigorous time commitment to football allowed them little opportunity for any part-time jobs, he indicated he often loaned small amounts of money to players who were in need of financial assistance. These loans came from his own pockets, and the coach later admitted he did not keep an accurate count of the loans and could not completely verify which ones had been repaid.

The story appeared in *Sports Illustrated* and quickly made its way to the Big Ten and NCAA offices. This prompted an immediate investigation, since loans of this nature would be a direct violation of NCAA rules. Hayes stated the aid was merely casual assistance in time of need, and that he was not aware it was in violation of any code. The university agreed that he undoubtedly did not know he was breaking any rules, but acknowledged that his small charitable givings were against NCAA regulations.

Investigation Leads to Probation

The NCAA investigation led to a probe of the Ohio State "jobs program for athletes" that coordinated employment opportunities with outside employers. Many irregularities were discovered, including athletes being paid even though they often did not show up for the work. In April of 1956 Big Ten Commissioner Kenneth "Tug" Wilson announced the one-year probation.

The NCAA probation banned all Ohio State sports teams from participating in NCAA-sanctioned tournaments. Hayes felt the penalty was too severe for the infractions incurred, but agreed to abide by the rulings without appeal. University President Howard Bevis stated that steps would be taken to eliminate any practices which violated the rules.

Despite the Rose Bowl ban, football analysts predicted the Buckeyes would have another very fine season in 1956. Many talented players returned, including All-American guard Jim Parker, quarterback Frank Ellwood, Bill Michael who had shifted to tackle from end, and newcomer Don Clark, a swift and powerful sophomore halfback. Ohio State entered the season with two primary goals: become the first school to capture three consecutive outright Big Ten titles, and break the league record of 15 consecutive conference game victories that was set by Michigan in 1946-47-48.

Powerful Beginning

The Buckeyes opened September 29 with a strong 34-7 pounding of Nebraska, before a sun-baked Ohio Stadium record-opening-day crowd of 82,153. End Leo Brown scored early in the first quarter after blocking a Cornhusker punt and returning the ball 18 yards. In his first college game, Clark had touchdown runs of 35 and 38 yards. Hayes used 10 different ball carriers and three different passers to garner 478 yards of total offense, compared with 253 for Nebraska.

John Brodie Impresses Record Crowd

Next, it was Ohio State's high-powered running attack that outscored Stanford's high-powered passing attack, 32-20, before what was then a record Ohio Stadium crowd of 82,881. Stanford's John Brodie staged one of the greatest passing demonstrations in stadium history, completing 21 throws for 256 yards and two of the Indians' three scores. The senior quarterback would go on to become one

of the NFL's premiere quarterbacks with the San Francisco 49ers.

Don Clark had another outstanding afternoon, rushing for 141 yards and two of the Buckeyes' five touchdowns. The game was tied 20-20 after three quarters. The surprise play of the day, which put the contest out of reach, was a Clark-to-Jim Roseboro 19-yard scoring pass for OSU's final touchdown. Halfback Joe Cannavino made two key defensive plays with an interception and a fumble recovery.

Ohio State ran its season record to 3-0 with a rugged 26-6 win at Illinois on October 13. The Illini's fleet halfbacks—Abe Woodson, Bobby Mitchell, and Harry Jefferson—gave the Buckeyes some anxious moments, including Jefferson's surprise 44-yard sprint for the game's first touchdown on a fourth-and-

Fullback Galen Cisco carries against the Stanford Cardinals.

one. But OSU's smashing offense drove 79 and 85 yards for two TDs, and an alert defense provided an interception and a fumble recovery to set up the other two scores.

Jim Roseboro ran for a game-high 101 yards and junior fullback Galen Cisco added 98. Parker had another excellent afternoon with his jarring tackles all over the field. The Buckeyes now had won 14 consecutive conference games, just one short of the record held by Michigan.

Nittany Lions Pull Surprise

The Buckeyes returned home October 20 as a three-touchdown favorite over non-conference opponent Penn State. It was just the second meeting between the two schools. The Nittany Lions had humbled the Buckeyes 37-0 in a controversial 1912 meeting at old Ohio Field. Head coaches Woody Hayes and Rip Engle were no strangers. Hayes had coached the East squad in the previous season's East-West Shrine Game, with Engle as one of his assistants.

The first quarter belonged to Penn State. The Lions put together two effective drives on their first two possessions, but were unable to score. Buckeye linebacker Tom Dillman intercepted quarterback Milt Plum's pass at the OSU 10-yard line to interrupt a drive that started from the PSU 24. Then, OSU's Don Sutherin picked off another Plum aerial at the OSU 4-yard line after the Lions had marched from their own 29.

Penn State's defense was giving the Bucks all kinds of problems. Ohio State finally secured its initial first down two minutes into the second period. The Scarlet and Gray moved to the enemy 18, where, on a fourth-and-five, Frank Kremblas' field goal attempt fell short. This would be the closest Ohio State would get to the Lion goal in the first two quarters.

After a scoreless first half, Ohio State's offense appeared to be taking charge early in the third period. In machine-like fashion, the Bucks used 17 consecutive running plays

(and nearly 12 minutes of playing time) to move 84 yards from their own 13-yard line to the Penn State three. The big play had been Don Clark's 21-yard sprint around right end for an apparent touchdown, but the Lion's Bruce Gilmore pulled him down from behind at the five.

With third-and-three from the three-yard line, quarterback Frank Ellwood attempted his first pass of the drive—Gilmore seemed to come out of nowhere to intercept in the end zone and return the ball to his own 21. This unexpected third-down call would be debated by Buckeye fans "long into the night." Woody Hayes defended his quarterback's decision, stating, "It was okay for Ellwood to pass. I was going to send Kremblas in for a field goal on fourth down if the pass was incomplete."

Tension really mounted in the fourth quarter. On a fourth and less-than-one at their own 23-yard line, it appeared the Buckeyes would go for the first down. But a late substitution caused a five-yard delay-of-game penalty, forcing a kick. Don Sutherin's 34-yard punt was returned by Billy Kane to the Buckeye 45-yard line, and the Lions were in business. Milt Plum engineered a 13-play scoring drive, with Gilmore plunging over left guard for the touchdown. Plum's conversion made it 7-0 with just 3:35 showing on the clock.

But the Buckeyes came right back, moving 80 yards in five plays for a touchdown.

"Fill-ins" Surprise Buckeyes

Penn State's 7-6 victory in 1956 broke Ohio State's eight-game winning streak. It was OSU's first loss since Duke upset the Buckeyes 20-14 in the fourth game of 1955. Ironically, Duke and Penn State had been recent "fill-ins" on the Ohio State schedule, after Navy canceled a two-game series with the Buckeyes.

Hayes used the "halfback-option pass" for the drive's two long gainers. Jim Roseboro rifled a cross-field pass to end Leo Brown for 23 yards to the Penn State 45-yard line. Next, Clark hooked up with Brown on a 42-yard option which carried to the Lion three. From there Clark exploded over right tackle for the score.

As Kremblas set up for the conversion attempt, Hayes (thinking he had only ten men on the field) sent Leo Brown dashing onto the field. Ohio State was penalized five yards for having 12 men in the game. Kremblas' ensuing placement attempt from the 15-yard line was just a few inches wide to the left, and the score remained 7-6. It was OSU's seventh missed conversion in 15 tries this season.

On their following possession, the Lions ran out the clock to preserve the one-point win. The Buckeyes suffered a very unexpected defeat, while Penn State registered one of the most significant wins in the school's history.

Penn State quarterback Milt Plum was given a lot of credit for leading the Lion of-

Last Laugh

Penn State's 1956 win over the Buckeyes was especially sweet for Nittany Lion captain Sam Valentine, a 5'11", 200-pound senior guard from DuBois, Pennsylvania. Valentine had wanted to play at Ohio State, but had been told by the Buckeye coaches he might be too small. He was selected for All-America honors at Penn State in 1956.

fense, and for his excellent punting. He had a 56-yard punt that rolled dead at the Ohio State two-yard line in the second quarter, and a 72-yard fourth-quarter kick that rolled out of bounds at the Ohio State three. Plum's coach was a young assistant who had played quarterback under Engle at Brown in the late 1940s . . . and his name was Joe Paterno.

This was the first Ohio State loss resulting from a missed conversion attempt since the Buckeyes lost to Southern California 13-12 in 1937. The crowd of 82,584 was (at the time) the largest to ever see Penn State play. Rip Engle told reporters, "This has been our greatest victory. I admire Big Ten football . . . . I think it's tremendous." Little did Engle realize that 37 years later his university would become a member of the conference he so admired.

Back on Track

Things got better the following Saturday, October 27, when Ohio State rolled to a 21-0 homecoming triumph over Wisconsin to tie the Big Ten consecutive conference victory record of 15. Clark had another great day with 151 yards rushing, including a 23-yard dash right through the middle of the Badger defense for OSU's first touchdown. Frank Ellwood scored the other two on one-yard plunges.

Much to the delight of Ohio State fans, Illinois upset top-ranked Michigan State 20-13 at Champaign this same afternoon, to

Penn State Ohio State

Saturday, October 20, 1956 35¢

break the Spartans' 13-game winning streak. This appeared to be an important outcome for the Buckeyes, since Ohio State and Michigan State did not meet in 1956.

Big Ten Consecutive Victory Record Established

The Buckeyes were unimpressive the next weekend, but managed to slip past Northwestern 6-2 and set a new league record with 16 consecutive wins. This four-point triumph was OSU's smallest margin of victory during the 16 games. Ohio State had not lost a Big Ten game since being shutout 20-0 at Michigan on November 21, 1953.

OSU was a 17-point favorite, but new Wildcat coach Ara Parseghian had his squad primed for an upset which nearly developed.

Northwestern led 2-0 after one quarter when Al Viola blocked Frank Ellwood's punt attempt from the Ohio State end zone for a safety. The Buckeyes were unable to gain a single first down during the game's first 15 minutes of play. OSU finally got on the board with a seven-yard scoring toss from Ellwood to end Leo Brown just 16 seconds before the half.

Northwestern turned out to be its own worst enemy after being flagged for 100 yards in penalties compared with just 15 against the Buckeyes. Ohio State was now 5-1 on the season and 3-0 in league play.

School and Conference Rushing Record Set

At home for Dad's Day the ensuing weekend, the Buckeyes used a record-setting ground attack to push their conference winning streak to 17 with a 35-14 win over Indiana. Ohio State netted 465 yards rushing to set (what was then) both school and conference single-game records. The Buckeyes eclipsed the OSU mark of 440 yards against Fort Knox in the 1942 opener, and the Big Ten record of 454 set by Purdue against Indiana in 1948.

Three backs each ran for more than 100 yards—fullback Galen Cisco (160), and halfbacks Jim Roseboro (157) and Don Clark (112). OSU completed only one pass all afternoon, a five-yarder in the first quarter from Frank Ellwood to Leo Brown for the game's first touchdown.

Biggest Win in Iowa History

Ohio State now had a league record of 4-0 and seemed ready to accomplish its second primary goal of becoming the first school to claim three straight outright Big Ten titles. That dream was shattered in a bruising battle at Iowa City the following Saturday, November 17, where coach Forest Evashevski's Hawkeyes posted a 6-0 shutout.

Two-time All-American Jim Parker, one of the finest linemen in college history, was awarded the Outland Trophy in 1956.

Halfback Leads '56 Passing Attack

Woody Hayes had a strong reputation for shunning the forward pass. This was quite evident in 1956, when Ohio State's leading passer was not quarterback Frank Elwood, but rather left halfback Don Clark. Clark completed 3 of 7 "halfback option passes" for 88 yards to lead the team in passing that season. Clark was also the team's leading rusher with 797 yards in 139 carries. Elwood was successful on 7 of 20 passes that year for 86 yards.

After a scoreless first half, Iowa quarterback Kenny Ploen completed an 80-yard drive with a 17-yard third-quarter touchdown toss to end Jim Gibbons for the game's only score. The hard-charging Hawkeyes, led by tackle Alex Karras, held Ohio State's faltering attack to just nine first downs and 147 yards in total offense. This may well have been the biggest win in all of Iowa football. The Hawkeyes were assured of their first-ever postseason bowl and at least a share of the Big Ten title.

With Ohio State's Big Ten victory streak snapped at 17 and the chance to capture a third consecutive outright league crown ruined, the Buckeyes could at least share the 1956 league title with a season-ending win at home over arch-rival Michigan. Unfortunately, matters did not improve for the Scarlet and Gray. Six Buckeye turnovers helped the Wolverines post a 19-0 shutout and gain revenge for their humiliating setback in '55.

Michigan opened strongly with a 13-0 first-quarter lead, and often seemed to be daring the Buckeyes to pass by deploying what was essentially an 11-man defensive line. Ohio State completed just one of five passes for ten yards. The loss left Iowa in sole possession of the conference championship, its first since 1922. The Hawkeyes made their first postseason bowl a good one

with a 35-19 win over Oregon State in the Rose Bowl.

Jim Parker was again selected for All-America honors and became the first Ohio State player to capture the Outland Trophy as the nation's top interior lineman. He became the "benchmark" against which Hayes measured all future offensive linemen. The following spring Parker was a first-round pick of the NFL's Baltimore Colts, where he enjoyed a distinguished career as a perennial all-pro selection.

After some excellent play during most of the fall, the 1956 season really fell apart when OSU failed to score in either of its last two games. But better times were ahead, and the Buckeyes would surprise a lot of people the following season.

1956

September 29	Nebraska	W	34	7
October 6	Stanford	W	32	20
October 13	at Illinois	W	26	6
October 20	Penn State	L	6	7
October 27	Wisconsin (HC)	W	21	0
November 3	at Northwestern	W	6	2
November 10	Indiana	W	35	14
November 17	at Iowa	L	0	6
November 24	Michigan	L	0	19
Total Points			**160**	**81**

Season Record: 6-3
Conference: 4th Place (Tie)

1957

"A football team improves more between the first and second games, than any other time of the season!" That well-known quotation by Woody Hayes applied perfectly to his 1957 squad. After sustaining a discouraging upset in its opening game, Ohio State rebounded with nine consecutive triumphs to capture the United Press International National Championship.

The Buckeyes had made a strong run at a third outright league title in 1956, before losing the final two games to Iowa and Michigan. Going into the 1957 season, Ohio State was picked fifth in the Big Ten, behind Michigan State, Minnesota, Iowa, and Michigan. Only 18 lettermen returned; Hayes's losses from '56 included two-time All-American guard Jim Parker, winner of the Outland Trophy, and starting quarterback Frank Ellwood. Also gone were tackle Dick Guy, end Bill Michael, center Tom Dillman, halfback Jimmy Roseboro, and fullback Don Vicic.

Ohio State's 1957 starting lineup included ends Leo Brown, a 171-pound senior from Portsmouth, Russ Bowermaster, a junior from Hamilton, and sophomore Jim Houston of Massillon. The tackles were manned by senior John Martin of Waverly, junior Dick Schafrath of Wooster, and Jim Marshall, a quick and talented sophomore from Columbus.

The Buckeyes had two excellent guards in seniors Aurealius Thomas of Columbus, an All-American this season, and Bill Jobko of Lansing who was selected the team's Most-Valuable-Player. Playing time at center went to big Danny James, a 258-pounder from Cincinnati, and 189-pound Danny Fronk of Dover.

Hayes picked Frank Kremblas, a junior from Akron, to direct his team's split-T attack. Kremblas was an excellent student, he had good speed and power running the ball, and he was a very adequate passer. The early-season starter at fullback was Galen Cisco, a senior from St. Marys. Bob White, a rugged sophomore from Covington, Kentucky, saw considerable action at fullback as the season progressed.

Returning at halfback was speedster Don Clark of Akron, an excellent runner, who was the team's leading rusher in '56 with 797 net yards. Teaming with Clark was Dick LeBeau, a junior from London, Ohio. Also seeing considerable playing time at halfback were seniors Joe Cannavino and Joe Trivisonno of Cleveland and Don Sutherin of Toronto, Ohio.

Ohio State's offense was primarily ground-oriented in 1956, netting 2,468 yards rushing and only 278 yards passing in nine games. This emphasis on the run would change very little in '57.

First Season-Opening Loss for Hayes

The Buckeyes were two-touchdown favorites over Texas Christian University in the September 28 opener. But the Horned Frogs pulled off an 18-14 upset before an Ohio Stadium crowd of 81,784, largest ever to watch a TCU team in action. It was Woody Hayes' first opening-game loss in seven years at OSU and the Buckeyes' third consecutive defeat over two seasons.

The lead changed hands after each touchdown. Ohio State led 7-6 after the first period, on a two-yard sweep by Dick LeBeau. On the opening play of the second quarter, TCU's Jim Shofner returned a Don Sutherin punt 90 yards down the west sideline to put the visitors back in front 12-7. Shofner's scamper stands yet today as the longest punt return in the 79-year history of Ohio Stadium.

Ohio State put together an 18-play, 68-yard drive with Clark getting the TD to lead 14-12 at intermission. But the Horned Frogs scored another in the third period to go ahead 18-14 and conclude the scoring. At this stage, Ohio State resembled anything but a contender for national honors.

The second week found Ohio State in Seattle to take on the Washington Huskies. After a 7-7 halftime deadlock, Don Sutherin weaved his way upfield with an 81-yard punt return to break the tie and lead the way to a 35-7 victory. The Bucks used 11 different ball carriers to outgain the Huskies 353 yards to 221 in total offense. Years later, Hayes frequently referred to Sutherin's punt return as "the play that turned our '57 season around."

"We just seemed to gel from this point forward," Hayes said.

Impressive Conference Opener

The Buckeyes were back home the following Saturday, October 12, for a 21-7 win over Illinois before a crowd of 82,239 in the conference opener for both schools. Don Clark, who led all rushers with 133 yards in 33 carries, scored the game's first touchdown on a nine-yard plunge in the first quarter. After a scoreless second period, the Illini tied the game with a beautifully executed 59-yard scoring toss from quarterback Tom Haller to end Rich Kreitling to start the second half.

Ohio State then used a 13-play 63-yard march to regain the lead, 14-7. Kremblas scored on a plunge from inside the one, and added the game's final touchdown with a 6-yard toss to Don Sutherin in the fourth quarter. This same afternoon Michigan State blasted Michigan 35-6 at Ann Arbor to be-

Strongest Finish!

The 1957 Buckeye squad is the only team in Ohio State history to win the remainder of its games after losing the opener.

come the odds-on favorite in the Big Ten race.

Woody Hayes used 17 different ball carriers the next Saturday while demolishing undermanned Indiana, 56-0. Nine different players scored in one way or another. The Buckeyes led in first downs, 24-6, and in total offensive yardage, 458-146. The big news of the day, however, came from East Lansing, where winless Purdue upset mighty Michigan State, 20-13. Suddenly Ohio State was tied with Iowa for the league lead at 2-0.

Huge Win at Wisconsin Keeps Bucks Tied for League Lead

OSU traveled to Madison the following Saturday, October 26, to face 3-1 Wisconsin before a Dad's Day crowd of 50,051 at Camp Randall Stadium. The Badgers had been pointing for this one, and quickly jumped off to a 13-0 lead with two first-quarter touchdown sprints by halfback Danny Lewis.

Once again it was Don Clark who got the Buckeye of-

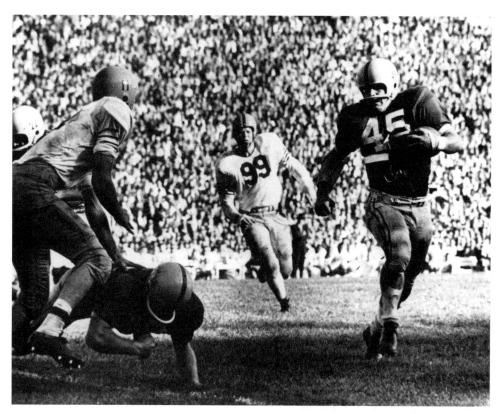

Halfback Don Sutherin
in action against Illinois.

fense going. The Akron speedster put his team on the board with a sensational 71-yard scamper around his own right end. Following his interference to perfection, Clark scored standing up to make it 13-7, Wisconsin. Galen Cisco got OSU's second TD on a three-yard plunge to tie the game at 13 all after one quarter.

After a scoreless second period, Don Sutherin booted a 20-yard field goal early in the third quarter to put the Buckeyes on top, 16-13, and conclude the scoring. Wisconsin moved to the OSU seven late in the final period, but a key fumble recovery by the Bucks' Bob White ended the threat. Ohio State (4-1) had posted a significant win over a fine Wisconsin team, and suddenly the league title and Rose Bowl were realistic possibilities.

The following week's Homecoming game was simply no contest, as OSU overwhelmed Ara Parseghian's Northwestern Wildcats, 46-7. Don Clark had one of his finest games, rushing for 127 yards in 19 carries and scoring four touchdowns. That same afternoon Iowa and Michigan played to a 21-21 tie at Ann Arbor, leaving the Buckeyes alone atop the Big Ten standings. Ohio State had now won five in a row and had moved up to sixth place in the AP and UPI weekly polls.

Buckeyes Hold Off Boilermakers to Maintain League Lead

Tenacious Purdue gave Ohio State all it could handle the next Saturday, November 9, before 79,177 shivering fans at Ohio Stadium. The Buckeyes built up a 20-0 halftime lead with touchdowns by Clark, LeBeau, and Kremblas, and seemed to have the afternoon pretty well under control. OSU drove 73 yards in eight plays for its first touchdown, and used 13 plays to march 91 yards for its second score. Clark was injured late in the first quarter and was lost for the rest of the afternoon.

INDIANA OHIO STATE

SATURDAY, OCTOBER 19 35¢ 1957

But the second half was an entirely different game. The Boilers scored quickly on a 24-yard pass play from Ross Fichtner to Tom Fletcher. Ohio State's fine defense then held the visitors five times inside the OSU 16 to preserve the 20-7 victory.

A relieved Woody Hayes told the press he was happy to win by 13 points. He also said "The team that wins the second half usually wins the game, but that wasn't true today." Iowa defeated Minnesota 44-20 at Iowa City to go 4-0-1 in league play (6-0-1 overall) and set up a showdown at Ohio Stadium the following week.

An Afternoon to Treasure

The Ohio State campus was really jumping the week prior to the November 16 clash between fifth-ranked Iowa and sixth-ranked Ohio State. Buckeye spirits were somewhat dampened when it was learned Clark would not play because of the leg injury he suffered against Purdue. The Hawkeyes were rated six-point favorites in the game that would decide the Big Ten championship.

The crowd of 82,935 was, at the time, the largest in Ohio Stadium history. Ohio

Iowa - Ohio State

Dad's Day   Nov. 16, 1957

35¢

Sophomore fullback Bob White's performance against Iowa is one of the best remembered in all of Ohio State football.

State took an early 3-0 lead with Don Sutherin's field goal from the Iowa 15-yard line. Iowa came back to go ahead 6-3 on an eight-yard pass from quarterback Randy Duncan to end Bob Prescott. The Hawkeyes featured a flashy double-wing attack with multiple laterals and reverses.

OSU drove 80 yards in the second quarter to take a 10-6 halftime lead. Frank Kremblas got the score on a one-yard quarterback sneak, and the drive was highlighted by Kremblas' faking and ball handling and the powerful running of fullback Bob White. Iowa regained the lead in the third quarter, 13-10, with Duncan scoring from the one to conclude a 70-yard march.

Early in the final period Iowa punted to OSU's Joe Cannavino, who was downed at his own 32-yard line at the stadium's north end. With just 7:51 remaining in the game,

the Buckeyes realized this might be their last chance. They were 68 yards away from the Big Ten title and trip to Pasadena.

Fullback Bob White plunged over right tackle for four yards, and then over left guard for nine and a first down at the OSU 45. White next broke over right guard for 29 yards for a first down at the Iowa 26-yard line. By this time the entire crowd was on its feet—the noise level was unbelievable.

Dick LeBeau carried for two, then White took it up the middle for six more. On third-and-two, White gained another ten for a first down at the Iowa eight. The big fullback then hit the middle for three, and followed it with a five-yard burst over left tackle for one of the biggest touchdowns in Ohio State history. White had carried on seven of the eight plays for 66 of the 68 yards.

Sutherin converted to end the scoring at 17-13. With just over three minutes remaining Iowa mounted another drive, but guard Bill Jobko ended the threat when he intercepted Duncan's pass at the Ohio State 32. Iowa coach Forest Evashevski explained, "We knew what was happening, but we were just powerless to stop it. It was fantastic". Most of the then-record crowd of 82,935, which included Vice-President Richard Nixon, stayed long after the game to savor the win.

Ohio State moved up to third in the AP poll and Iowa fell to eighth. Even with the league title secured, the Buckeyes turned their full attention to the November 23 battle at Michigan with the 19th-ranked Wolverines (5-2-1). Injured Don Clark was again unable to play. With White gaining 163 yards in 30 attempts, OSU came back from a 14-10 half-

All-American guard Aurealius Thomas

Precious Record

Guard Bill Jobko, who was a member of Ohio State's 1954 and 1955 teams, is the only player in Big Ten history to play on three undisputed league champions. The Buckeyes were 20-0 in Big Ten play during the '54, '55, and '57 seasons.

time deficit to smash the Wolverines, 31-14, before a chilled crowd of 101,001. The Wolverines put some double-reverse fancywork back into their attack, and dented OSU's defense with 270 yards on the ground and 107 through the air. Michigan's All-American halfback Jimmy Pace was the game's leading rusher with 164 yards in 22 carries.

The Buckeyes' touchdowns were scored by LeBeau (two), Kremblas, and Cannavino. Sutherin added a 30-yard field goal in the second period. Kremblas engineered his team brilliantly while easily playing the finest game of his career.

Hayes was extremely jubilant after his team outscored the Wolverines 21-0 in the second half. Ohio State's 31 points was the Buckeyes' highest output against Michigan since OSU won 38-0 at Ann Arbor in 1935. It also was OSU's second consecutive 17-point win at Michigan Stadium (17-0 in 1955). After losing the opener, the Buckeyes had won eight in a row and were Pasadena-bound.

Buckeyes Win Rose Bowl - Capture UPI National Title

Ohio State was heavily favored over the Oregon Ducks in the January 1, 1958, Rose Bowl, but struggled to win, 10-7. OSU drove 79 yards on its first possession to lead, 7-0. Kremblas scored the touchdown from the one after passing 18 yards to Jim Houston to set up the touchdown. The Ducks drove 80 yards in 10

1957 National Champions

Game Oregon Club Bows to Ohio State, 10 to 7

Columbus Dispatch,
Thursday, January 2, 1958

Dr. Robert Murphy served the Ohio State football program with distinction for 41 years. He began in 1952 as Associate Team Physician and was Head Team Physician from 1970 through 1992. In the early 1950s, college football players were not encouraged to drink water during practices, and occasionally some players suffered from heat strokes. Dr. Murphy, a noted pioneer in changing this long-established philosophy, lectured throughout the country about the need to provide water at all practices.

Woody Hayes guided Ohio State to three outright Big Ten titles and two national championships from 1954 through 1957.

Don Sutherin's 34-yard fourth-quarter field goal was the margin of victory over Oregon in the Rose Bowl.

quarterback Jack Crabtree pitched out to halfback Jim Stanley for the final five yards. Crabtree handled his team so expertly he was a near-unanimous choice as the game's Most Valuable Player.

After a scoreless third period, Don Sutherin booted a 34-yard field goal early in the fourth quarter for the three-point margin of victory. Ironically, Oregon's co-captain Jack Morris had missed on a third-quarter field-goal attempt from the same distance. Ohio State became the first school to post three Rose Bowl victories since the Big Ten and Pacific Coast Conferences agreed to play in the January 1 classic beginning in 1946.

The Buckeyes (9-1) were awarded the UPI National Championship and finished second to Auburn (10-0) in the final AP rankings. Woody Hayes was selected college football's Coach of the Year. Ohio State had allowed only six points in the fourth quarter all season.

After stumbling against TCU in the season opener, the 1957 Buckeyes had rebounded to complete one of the most successful seasons in all of Ohio State Football.

1957				
September 28	Texas Christian	L	14	18
October 5	at Washington	W	35	7
October 12	Illinois	W	21	7
October 19	Indiana	W	56	0
October 26	at Wisconsin	W	16	13
November 2	Northwestern (HC)	W	47	6
November 9	Purdue	W	20	7
November 16	Iowa	W	17	13
November 23	at Michigan	W	31	14
January 1	Oregon*	W	10	7
Total Points			267	92

*Rose Bowl

Season Record: 9-1
National Champion
Big Ten Champion

317

Ohio State was the pre-season choice by both the Associated Press and the United Press International to capture the national championship in 1958. The OSU backfield, which was expected to be one of the most productive in school history, returned three seniors in quarterback Frank Kremblas and halfbacks Don Clark and Dick LeBeau. Junior Bob White would step in at fullback after seeing considerable playing time the last half of the '57 season. Two sophomore halfbacks who would contribute were Jim Herbstreit and Tom Matte.

Returning veterans on the line included senior center Dan Fronk, and three juniors; guard Ernie Spychalski, tackle Jim Marshall, and end Jim Houston. Senior Dick Schafrath moved from tackle to end, and sophomores Oscar Hauer and Jim Tyrer advanced into starting positions at guard and tackle.

A then-record Ohio Stadium crowd of 83,113 watched Ohio State hold on for a thrilling 23-20 triumph over frisky Southern Methodist University in the September 27 season opener. The Mustangs were led by the passing of junior quarterback Don Meredith, who directed scoring marches of 61 and 75 yards. Throwing from the spread formation much of the afternoon, he completed 19 passes for 213 yards. Meredith later gained fame as a quarterback with the NFL's Dallas Cowboys, and as a commentator for ABC's Monday Night Football.

Don Clark, the game's leading runner with 98 yards, scored OSU's first two touchdowns as the Buckeyes hung on to a precarious 15-14 lead at halftime. In the third period, Bob White plunged five yards through the middle for OSU's final score by carrying two defenders across the goal line. This was Ohio State's tenth consecutive win over two years.

Huskies Nearly Pull Upset

Washington made its very first trip to Columbus the next weekend, and the 20-point underdogs nearly pulled off the season's first big upset. Frank Kremblas was unable to play because of a slight shoulder separation sustained late in the SMU opener, but was ably replaced by sophomore Jerry Fields. The Buckeyes took advantage of two Huskie turnovers to squeeze out a 12-7 win.

Washington scored first to lead 7-0 early in the first period. Bob White set up the Buckeyes' first touchdown with an interception at the Huskie 27, and Fields sneaked across from inside the one. The conversion was missed, leaving Washington with a single-point lead.

The Huskies hung on to their 7-6 lead until early in the fourth quarter. When Washington punter Bob Schloredt received a bad pass from center, guard Oscar Hauer blocked the kick and tackle Jim Marshall recovered at the Washington 27-yard line. The Buckeyes moved the distance in seven plays, with halfback Don Clark going the final four yards on a slant over right tackle for the winning score.

Washington came right back, but its drive stalled at the Ohio State 21-yard line with just 2:14 remaining. Turnovers made the difference. Ohio State had no miscues, while

Change in Scoring

The two-point conversion option was added to college football in 1958. Ohio State's first two-pointer came on a pass from quarterback Frank Kremblas to halfback Dick LeBeau following the Buckeyes' first touchdown in the 1958 opener against Southern Methodist.

its early season showing.

Back home the following weekend, Ohio State blasted out-manned Indiana, 49-8. White accounted for 116 of OSU's 236 yards on the ground, and tied (what was then) a school single-game record with four touchdowns. The Hoosiers only entrance into Ohio territory came late in the afternoon against OSU's fourth team. IU scored its only touchdown with just four seconds to play.

The game's most "unusual play" unfolded in the second half with Woody Hayes throwing his sport coat to the ground and darting out to the middle of the playing field. With the game being held up, he protested to the officials about what he considered unnecessary roughness against his squad. The outcome of his tirade—a 15-yard penalty for unsportsmanlike conduct. Indiana coach Phil Dickens strongly defended his players and felt Hayes' outburst was out of line, especially with Ohio State leading 35-0 at the time.

Washington threw three interceptions and lost three fumbles in addition to the blocked punt.

Things didn't get any easier at Illinois the following Saturday. Ohio State scored twice in the third period, then held off the Illini to slip through, 19-13. With just one minute remaining, Illinois quarterback Bob Hickey passed to halfback Dick McDage, who momentarily held the ball before dropping it for an incompletion at the Ohio State three yard line.

Woody Hayes made an important halftime adjustment that helped his third-quarter offense, shifting to an unbalanced line with left tackle Jim Tyrer moving to the right side. Don Clark again was the Buckeye sparkplug, rushing for 105 yards and scoring the winning touchdown on a 42-yard sprint around right end. Bob White played the game's entire 60 minutes, and Clark logged nearly 57. Even with his team now 3-0, Woody Hayes was a little disappointed with

Mr. Hospitality!

Many of the midwest's writers and broadcasters who covered Big Ten football in the '50s and '60s were known as the Big Ten skywriters. As a group each fall they would visit each school to preview the season. When they arrived in Columbus to see Ohio State's team in early September of '58, Woody Hayes was upset with his squad's practice and refused to allow the skywriters to watch the drills. Visibly upset, many of the writers and broadcasters abruptly left and moved on to the next city.

Ohio State's athletic administration was embarrassed by Hayes' actions and issued a letter of apology to the Big Ten Conference. The following season Hayes could not have been more charming, and extended his hospitality by serving the skywriters lemonade and cookies.

Winning Streak Snapped

The fiery Hayes had more than officiating to worry about the next three weeks. First, his second-ranked team was tied by Wisconsin on a rainy homecoming afternoon, 7-7. After a scoreless first half, Badger quarterback Dale Hackbart raced 64 yards on a punt return to put the visitors in front 7-0 in the third period. The Buckeyes then put together their only sustained march of the day, going 66 yards in 20 plays with White bulling across from the one for the tieing score.

Wisconsin nearly pulled it out in the final quarter. The Badgers drove from their 31 to OSU's eight, where Jim Herbstreit made a key interception in the end zone to end the threat. After Ohio State was unable to mount any additional offense, Wisconsin was back at the Ohio State 12-yard line where Jim Tyrer recovered Hackbart's fumble to curtain another Badger effort. The Buckeyes' winning streak had been stopped at 13, but matters would get worse before they improved.

Next came a November 1 trip to Northwestern. Fifth-ranked Ohio State was favored over the improved Wildcats of third-year coach Ara Parseghian, who entered the contest at 4-1 after having lost every game the previous season. After a scoreless first half, Northwestern quarterback Dick Thornton became a one-man show, passing for two touchdowns and scoring a third himself to lead the Wildcats to a 21-0 victory. He also kicked the three extra points.

Thornton's first scoring toss was a perfectly executed 67-yard strike to halfback Ron Burton of Springfield, Ohio. The upset provided an exceptionally happy Homecoming for the Dyche Stadium crowd of 51,102. It was the Buckeyes' first setback in 15 games and destroyed any possibility of finishing the season as the nation's number-one team.

"Lineman's Dream"

Ohio State's offense failed again to score the following Saturday against Purdue for Dad's Day, even though the Buckeyes led 14-0 at intermission. The first half was a "lineman's dream" for tackle Jim Marhshall who scored both of the Buckeyes' touchdowns. In the first period he scooped up a blocked punt and rambled 22 yards for his first score, then returned an interception 25 yards for his second touchdown late in the second quarter. End Jim Houston assisted with both of Marshall's scoring plays, blocking the first-quarter punt and deflecting the second-quarter pass into Marshall's arms.

Ohio State's offense could muster only one first down and 37 yards of offense in the second half. The Boilermakers tallied twice in the final period, and the game ended in a 14-14 tie. The visitors had outgained the Buckeyes, 374 yards to 180, and led in first downs, 22-11.

Purdue coach Jack Mollenkopf, who had an outstanding stint at Toledo Waite High

Woody Hayes openly expresses his view of the officiating during the Indiana game.

School, was miffed when he stated that Hayes made no attempt to shake hands after the game. The Buckeyes were now 4-1-2 on the season and trending downward, having gone 0-1-2 and been outscored 42-21 over their last three games. Injuries had really hurt, but the offense had been so inconsistent that many fans gave the Buckeyes little chance to win either of their last two games.

Another Buckeye-Hawkeye Classic

Ohio State traveled to Iowa City for a November 15 showing against Coach Forest Evashevski's Hawkeyes. The game had been sold out since mid-September, and the crowd of 58,463 was (at the time) the largest in Kinnick Stadium history. Iowa had already secured the outright Big Ten title with a 28-6 win at Minnesota the previous week. The Buckeyes were 14-point underdogs. Interestingly, that week it was being strongly rumored that coach Woody Hayes would be leaving Ohio State after the 1958 season to accept a position with the Ford Foundation.

Ohio State's offense really came together, as the Buckeyes handed Iowa its only loss of the season, 38-28. It was one of the most thrilling and dramatic games ever staged between the two schools. The game's scoring pattern was incredible. Ohio State and Iowa alternated touchdowns until the fourth period, when the Buckeyes finally went ahead to stay. Ohio State took the lead on each of its five touchdowns, yet Iowa responded after the first four to tie the game

at 7-7, 14-14, 21-21 (halftime) and 28-28 (three quarters). OSU secured the win with ten unanswered points in the final period.

The game was fast and furious from the opening whistle. Bob White and Don Clark led Woody Hayes' patented ground attack with 209 and 157 yards, respectively, and scored all five touchdowns. Clark scored both of his touchdowns on sweeps around right end, the first on a 25-yarder and the second from 37 yards out.

White powered 71 yards for his first score on a third-and-inches situation in the second quarter. His others were one-yard plunges in the second and fourth periods. Dave Kilgore's 19-yard field goal put the game out of reach with just two minutes and 12 seconds to play.

Hayes offered special praise

All-American tackle Jim Marshall scored both of Ohio State's touchdowns against Purdue.

Halfback Don Clark's excellent play sparked 38-28 win at Iowa.

for Ohio State quarterback Jerry Fields, who directed the Buckeye attack like a veteran while filling in for Frank Kremblas who was injured. OSU's line play was superb, with Jim Houston, Dick Schafrath, and Ernie Wright playing the entire 60 minutes.

Iowa quarterback Randy Duncan, the Big Ten's MVP in '58, completed 23 passes against the Buckeyes' defense for 249 yards and one touchdown. The Hawkeyes went on to defeat Oregon State 38-12 in the Rose Bowl (with 516 yards of offense) and finish the season with an overall record of 7-1-1. They placed second to Louisiana State in the final Associated Press poll.

Too Close for Comfort

Ohio State returned home November 22 for its traditional season finale against the struggling Michigan Wolverines, who entered

the game with a dismal record of 2-5-1. The Wolverines had already given up 191 points during their first eight games, more than any team in Michigan history. Northwestern had defeated the Wolverines 55-24 earlier in the season—the most points surrendered by UM in one afternoon since losing to Cornell, 58-12, in 1891.

This was the 100th and final game as Michigan's head coach for Bennie Oosterbaan, a three-time All-American end for the Wolverines in 1925-26-27, who had decided to retire at season's end. It also was Oosterbaan's 34th Ohio State-Michigan game —three as a player, 20 as an assistant coach ('28-'47), and 11 as head coach ('48-'58).

Michigan almost pulled off the upset, but the highly favored Buckeyes somehow held on for the victory, 20-14. Trailing 14-12 at the half, Ohio State put together an 80-

yard third-quarter scoring drive for its first lead of the afternoon and the winning touchdown. Michigan led in first downs, 24-12, and in total offensive yards, 376-252. Bob Ptacek, senior quarterback from Cleveland, put on one of the finest passing exhibitions in Ohio Stadium history, completing 24 attempts for 241 yards. Twelve of Ptacek's completions went to halfback Brad Myers.

The Wolverines nearly pulled it out at the end. Facing a fourth-and-one at the Ohio State four with just 40 seconds remaining, Myers fumbled after being hit hard by Dick Schafrath. Jerry Fields recovered for the Buckeyes to preserve the victory. It was a heartbreaking loss for the Wolverines, who had made every effort to send their coach out with a win. Oosterbaan's career record as Michigan's head coach was 63-33-4, including a mark of 5-5-1 against the Buckeyes.

Ohio State finished the '58 season at 6-1-2, good for seventh and eighth places in the final UPI and AP polls. Jim Houston, Jim Marshall, and Bob White were named All-America, and White was chosen for the Academic All-America squad. Woody Hayes now had an abundance of supporters, especially with five victories over Michigan during his first eight seasons.

Ohio State entered the 1959 season "cautiously optimistic." Only 16 returned from 1958, but they included end and team captain Jim Houston, tackle Jim Tyrer, and guards Oscar Hauer and Ernie Wright. Fullback Bob White was back for his senior season as was quarterback Jerry Fields, who had logged considerable playing time as a dependable back-up the previous season.

Substitution rules were relaxed a little this year. The new rules permitted coaches to re-enter one player at a time when the clock was stopped, regardless of how many times this particular player had been in and out of the game. Previously a player could not re-enter the game more than once during each quarter. This new rule enabled teams to make better use of "specialists" such as punters and placekickers.

Matte Becomes a Quarterback at Halftime

On September 26, in one of Ohio State's most thrilling openers, the Buckeyes edged Duke 14-13 before a nervous Ohio Stadium crowd of 82,834. The victory broke Duke's record of never having lost to a Big Ten opponent. Fans were generally pleased with Woody Hayes' new "more wide open" attack, which featured an unbalanced line with split ends and flanked halfbacks.

Ohio State took the opening kickoff and drove 58 yards in eight plays to seize an early 7-0 lead. Sophomore left halfback Bob Ferguson (who would become an All-American fullback the following two seasons) bolted 15 yards through right guard for the touchdown. There was no further first-half scoring, but the Buckeyes suffered a real blow near halftime—starting quarterback

1958				
September 27	Southern Methodist	W	23	20
October 4	Washington	W	12	7
October 11	at Illinois	W	19	13
October 18	Indiana	W	49	8
October 25	Wisconsin (HC)	T	7	7
November 1	at Northwestern	L	0	21
November 8	Purdue	T	14	14
November 15	at Iowa	W	38	28
November 22	Michigan	W	20	14
Total Points			182	132

Season Record: 6-1-2
Conference: 3rd Place

Jerry Fields injured his right arm and was lost for the rest of the afternoon.

With Fields injured, Woody Hayes decided at halftime to try starting right halfback Tom Matte at quarterback. While most of the squad went to the dressing room under the guidance of the assistant coaches, Hayes took Matte, center Jene Watkins, and reserve halfbacks Dave Tingley and Ron Houck to the practice field outside the south end of Ohio Stadium. During this impromptu rehearsal, Matte practiced taking snaps from center and running plays from the quarterback position.

Matte returned to his right halfback position for most of the second half. While sophomore quarterback Jack Wallace was unable to consistently move the Buckeyes, Duke scored twice to take a 13-7 lead. As Ohio State took possession at its own 37-yard line with just over four minutes remaining, Woody Hayes made his move—he shifted Tom Matte to quarterback.

In almost magical style, Matte courageously drove his team 63 yards in nine plays for the winning score. Interestingly, the touchdown came on a fourth-down 22-yard rollout pass from Matte to end Chuck Bryant. Dave Kilgore converted to give Ohio State its single-point come-from-behind victory.

A Weekend to Forget

The next week Ohio State took to the road for a rare Friday evening game, October 2, against Southern California at the Los Angeles Coliseum. This would turn out to be one of the worst weekends during Hayes' Ohio State career. The Buckeyes lost 17-0 to the clearly superior Trojans. Led by the McKeever twins, Mike and Marlin, USC's defense held the Buckeyes to just 84 yards on the ground (1.9 yard average per rush) and 59 yards through the air.

In addition to the humiliating shutout, Ohio State suffered a very sound physical beating. Seventeen players were hurt, and the injuries subsequently limited their play-

SATURDAY, SEPTEMBER 26, 1959 35¢

ing time the remainder of the season. To make matters worse, Los Angeles area sportswriters Al Bine and Dick Shafer accused the coach of hitting them in the team dressing room following the game. Hayes denied he hit them, saying he might have shoved one of them when the two were slow to leave the dressing room so he could meet privatcly with his team following the defeat. Needless to say, this controversy did nothing to enhance Hayes' image with the California press.

Ohio State's offense didn't look much better at home against Illinois the next week in the Big Ten opener. The Illini won, 9-0, after scoring the game's only touchdown in the first period on a 73-yard pass from quarterback Mel Meyers to halfback Johnny Counts. Senior tackle Don Yeazel of Dayton,

Goal Posts Widened

In 1959 college goal posts were widened from 19 feet and two inches to 24 feet apart, to encourage more field goals.

Ohio, booted a 27-yard field goal late in the fourth quarter to seal the victory.

The Buckeyes were able to muster only 160 yards in total offense, compared with 369 yards for the visitors. This was a sweet victory for "Mr. Illini" Ray Eliot, who was retiring at the end of the season after 18 very successful campaigns as head coach at Illinois. The loss to the Illini was OSU's 600th all-time game (383-175-42).

Surprise! Surprise!

Ohio State's October 17 homecoming game with Purdue was a delightful change for Ohio State fans. The Buckeyes intercepted three Purdue passes and scored in almost every possible way to stun the sixth-ranked Boilermakers, 15-0. Purdue finished the '59 season with a league record of 4-2-1. Had the Boilers defeated Ohio State as expected, they would have captured the outright Big Ten title, which instead was won by Wisconsin with a conference mark of 5-2.

Placekicker Dave Kilgore booted field goals of 36 and 35 yards, and kicked the extra point after quarterback Tom Matte scored the game's only touchdown on a 32-yard scamper in the second quarter. Ohio State also recorded a safety when Purdue's Jim Tiller was tackled in the end zone. Tiller fielded a punt at the Purdue 16-yard line and raced backward in an attempt to avoid being tackled.

Before a rain-soaked crowd of 55,440 at Madison the following Saturday, Wisconsin's twelfth-ranked Badgers defeated Ohio State 12-3 for their first victory over the Scarlet and Gray since 1946. The scoring all took place in the first half. Wisconsin first scored a safety as tackle Danny Lanphear blocked a punt which rolled out of the end zone. Next, quarterback Dale Hackbart capped a 54-yard drive with a seven-yard end sweep for the game's only touchdown. Badger placekicker Karl Holzwarth nailed a 27-yard field goal seconds before the half. Dave Kilgore's second-quarter field goal, also from 27 yards, prevented the Buckeyes from suffering their third shutout of the season.

Matte's First Quarterback Start Highly Successful

Back home October 31, the Buckeyes scored in each quarter and played their best game of the year to defeat highly favored Michigan State, 30-24. On this dark and rainy afternoon, Ohio State rose to heroic proportions. Junior Tom Matte, who had switched from halfback, started his first game at quarterback and guided his squad to 420 yards in total offense, its highest total since the prior year's win at Iowa.

Matte fired scoring passes of 57 and 17 yards to end Jim Houston in the first half, and a 13-yard TD toss to halfback Billy Wentz in the third period. It was the first time Ohio State passed for three touchdown passes in one game since John Borton tossed for three against Michigan in 1952. Dave Kilgore added a 26-yard field goal in the first period.

The clincher in this tense struggle between two very spirited offenses was a fine effort by sophomore halfback Bob Ferguson. With the Buckeyes leading 23-17 midway through the fourth period, Ferguson broke a tackle at the line of scrimmage and sprinted 55 yards for OSU's final touchdown.

This was Ohio State's very first win over the Spartans, following losses in 1912, 1951, and 1953. The loss cost Michigan State the Big Ten title—the Spartans finished second with a league record of 4-2 behind Wisconsin at 5-2.

Buckeyes' Last Scoreless Tie

Emotionally drained from their upset over Michigan State, the Buckeyes and underdog Indiana settled for a scoreless tie in one of the most lethargic games ever held in Ohio Stadium. It was hard to imagine this was the same team which had scored 30 points just seven days earlier. OSU managed just 127 yards of offense and seven first downs, while IU gained only 179 yards and 11 first downs.

The Hoosiers came within a whisker of pulling the upset when its 23-play, 85-yard first half march died two inches from the Ohio State end zone. Indiana coach Phil Dickens strongly protested that fullback Vic Jones crossed the goal on the drive's last play, but game officials saw it otherwise. OSU's only scoring threats ended with missed field goals of 48 and 50 yards. The Buckeyes were now 3-3-1 on the season.

Ohio State dropped its November 14 Dad's Day home finale to Iowa, 16-7, in a contest that was not as close as suggested by the final score. The Hawkeyes dominated play but lost four fumbles that nullified several scoring efforts. Fullback Roger Detrick scored from inside the one to cap an eight-play, 31-yard march, and give Ohio State an early 7-0 lead. The drive followed the recovery of an Iowa fumble by tackle Jim Tyrer.

Iowa scored six points in the first quarter and 10 in the final period. The Hawkeyes

Two-time All-American end Jim Houston was Ohio State's 1959 captain. Houston was team MVP in 1958 and 1959.

dominated the statistics, leading in first downs, 17-13, and in total offensive yards, 338-181. Bob White, who was a real nemesis of the Hawks the last two seasons, was injured on OSU's fourth play from scrimmage and lost for the remainder of the season. It was Iowa's first victory in Ohio Stadium since 1948.

First Losing Season Under Hayes

The 1959 Ohio State-Michigan game was played solely for pride. The Buckeyes traveled north for their November 21 clash at Ann Arbor with an overall record of 3-4-1. Michigan entered the contest at 3-5. Before a chilled crowd of 90,093, the lively Wolverines made several "clutch plays" and scored in each quarter to win, 23-14. The victory was UM's first over OSU in three seasons.

Rare Finish

The Ohio State and Michigan football programs have both been extremely successful over the years. Only once during the 97 seasons Ohio State and Michigan have met through 2000, have BOTH teams finished a season with losing records—1959. The Wolverines' record was 4-5 in '59, while the Buckeyes' was 3-5-1.

Senior quarterback Stan Noskin, playing his final game for the Maize and Blue, provided flawless direction of the spirited Michigan wing-T attack. Noskin passed eight yards to fullback Tony Rio for UM's first touchdown, scored the second on a one-yard plunge, and set up his team's third TD with two key third-down passes.

Each squad had 20 first downs, and Ohio State actually had the edge in total offensive yardage, 358-306. But the Buckeyes were their own worst enemy with three pass interceptions and two lost fumbles. Roger Detrick was the game's leading runner with 139 yards in 33 carries. It was the sophomore's first start for the Scarlet and Gray.

Woody Hayes created a lot of attention along the sidelines with several critical blasts at the officials. The fiery coach spent much of the cold overcast afternoon in shirt sleeves after hurling his coat to the surface. He slammed a folding chair against the ground after one call, and several times kicked at the yard markers when he thought the decisions were not correct.

Hayes kept reporters waiting nearly 30 minutes after the game, then held the shortest press conference in his nine seasons at Ohio State—it lasted all of 73 seconds. He simply stated that Michigan played a fine game, that Bump Elliott had done an excellent job coaching the Wolverines, but that he was proud of his players who didn't quit. He then left the conference without taking any questions.

The '59 Buckeyes finished at 3-5-1—the first of only two losing seasons during Hayes' 28 seasons. Injuries sustained in the season's second game at Southern California hindered the team the remainder of the year. Jim Houston was the team captain, and for the second consecutive season was selected an All-American and chosen the team's MVP. Bob White was named to the Big Ten's All-Academic team for the third year.

1959

September 26	Duke	W	14	13
October 2	at Southern Cal.	L	0	17
October 10	Illinois	L	0	9
October 17	Purdue (HC)	W	15	0
October 24	at Wisconsin	L	3	12
October 31	Michigan State	W	30	24
November 7	Indiana	T	0	0
November 14	Iowa	L	7	16
November 21	at Michigan	L	14	23
Total Points			83	114

Season Record: 3-5-1
Conference: 8th Place (Tie)

1960

Woody Hayes began planning for the 1960 season by welcoming another change in substitution rules by the NCAA that virtually allowed a return to two-platoon football. Instead of using a few "iron men" who often would be on the field for practically all 60 minutes of each game, Ohio State now planned to utilize many more players who would specialize in either offense or defense.

Tom Matte was solidly installed as the starting quarterback and Bob Ferguson was moved from left halfback to fullback, which was his more natural position. Matte and Ferguson would handle the bulk of the running attack, with halfbacks Bob Klein, Bill Wentz, and Jim Herbstreit used primarily as blockers. Experienced returning linemen included ends Tom Perdue and Chuck Bryant, tackle Jim Tyrer, guard/linebacker Mike Ingram, and guards Gabe Hartman and Oscar Hauer.

Complete Two-Platoon System

Using 22 separate players as starters on offense and defense, the Buckeyes opened at home September 24 with an impressive 24-0 triumph over Southern Methodist. OSU displayed a more wide open attack than in previous seasons. The Buckeyes built up a 21-0 halftime lead on a 14-yard scoring pass from Matte to Bryant and short plunges by Ferguson and backup fullback Roger Detrick. Sophomore Ben Jones added a 25-yard field goal in the third quarter. Interceptions by Herbstreit led to two of the scores.

Ohio State continued its fast start with a 20-0 blanking of Southern California at Ohio Stadium the following Saturday, and gained some measure of revenge for the 17-0 pasting at Los Angeles in 1959. Ferguson had another great afternoon, scoring all three touchdowns on runs of 74, 2, and 19 yards. OSU held a huge advantage in rushing yards, 274-69, and dominated the game even more than reflected by the final score. The Buckeyes also lost two other scoring opportunities with an interception and a lost fumble inside the USC ten.

Ohio State's defense played a key role, intercepting four Trojan passes and recovering a fumble. This game marked just the second time Southern California had lost five consecutive games since it fielded its first football team in 1888.

#4 Versus #5

The Buckeyes, now ranked fifth nationally, opened the Big Ten season October 8 by overpowering fourth-ranked Illinois 34-7 at Champaign. The stunned homecoming crowd of 71,119 watched Ohio State pound out a 13-0 halftime lead, with Ferguson and Detrick scoring on short plunges. Illinois could advance no further than the Ohio State 40 in the first half.

Halfback Bill Wentz took the second-half kickoff 100 yards to increase the lead to 20-0, and that was pretty much the ball game. Matte and Klein scored on gallops of 57 and 42 yards, before Illini fullback Jim Brown plunged across in the final period to prevent Ohio State from registering its third consecutive shutout.

Hayes Holds 45-Second Press Conference After First Defeat

The season's complexion changed abruptly at West Lafayette the following Saturday, where Purdue played its best game of the season to edge Ohio State 24-21. Senior fullback Willie Jones, who had never before scored a touchdown in college, accounted for all three Purdue six-pointers on runs of two, three, and 26 yards.

Ferguson scored twice on short plunges to run his season touchdown total to seven, and Matte fired a 31-yard scoring toss to end Tom Perdue, but the OSU defense could not contain the Boilermakers. Purdue quarterback Bernie Allen, a senior from East Liverpool, Ohio, passed effectively in clutch situations and booted a 32-yard third-quarter field goal that was the eventual margin of victory.

Woody Hayes showed his strong disappointment by barring reporters from the

History Repeats Itself

Ohio State's 20-0 win over Southern California in 1960 marked the Trojans' first game at Ohio Stadium since 1948, when they lost by the same exact score.

SATURDAY *October* 1 1960

dressing room following the game. Hayes met outside with the press for approximately 45 seconds, and simply stated, "Both teams moved the ball well, but Purdue moved it better." The writers were hardly impressed. The Purdue Athletic Department issued a brief written text that read, "Woody Hayes, noted as possibly the most outspoken coach in the United States, was all but speechless. He made a brief, almost fruitless appearance in the corridor outside the dressing room."

Ohio State returned to the victory trail the following week, with a 34-7 pasting of Wisconsin before a delighted homecoming crowd of 83,246. Playing Hayes' favorite type of possession football, the Buckeyes put together touchdown drives of 89 and 66 yards the first two times they had the ball.

Tom Matte, playing one of his finest games, displayed excellent passing, running, and ball handling to lead the assault on the defending Big Ten champions. Matte passed five yards to Bob Klein and 53 yards to Chuck Bryant for two touchdowns, carried the ball 17 times for 108 yards, and punted five times for a 37-yard average. Ferguson scored twice

on a two-yard plunge and a 52-yard scamper, and Detrick bolted two yards for OSU's final score. Hayes used nine different ball carriers to accumulate an even 300 yards on the ground.

Initial Game at East Lansing

On October 29, Ohio State made its very first trip to Michigan State a memorable one, winning 21-10 before a then-record Spartan Stadium crowd of 76,520. Coach Woody Hayes' eighth-ranked Buckeyes entered the game at 4-1, while Duffy Daugherty's tenth-ranked Spartans were 3-1-1. It was just the fifth meeting between the two schools—the Spartans held a 3-1 edge during the four previous games played in Columbus.

Halfback Bob Klein (a native of Athens, Michigan) scored the game's first touchdown on a 45-yard halfback trap in the second period. It caught MSU completely by surprise, especially since Ohio State's halfbacks had been used primarily as blockers in Hayes' quarterback-fullback-run-oriented offense. The conversion attempt was missed and OSU led 6-0.

Later that period, end Tom Perdue blocked and recovered a Spartan punt to give the Buckeyes possession on the Michigan State 21. Four plays later Bob Ferguson rammed the ball across from the three, and a two-point conversion pass from Tom Matte to Klein extended the lead to 14-0. Michigan State finally got on the scoreboard when Art

Family Affair

Pete Elliott was the new coach at Illinois in 1960. His brother Bump had taken over the Michigan program in 1959. The classic coaching encounter at Ann Arbor on November 5, 1960—brother against brother—was a first in the history of the Big Ten. The Wolverines won, 8-7.

Brandstatter booted a 25-yard field goal right before halftime.

Ohio State increased its lead to 21-3 late in the third quarter, when Matte connected on a 25-yard throw to end Bob Middleton, who evaded two tacklers and continued untouched into the end zone for the Buckeyes' final score. Michigan State recorded its only touchdown in the final period on a 17-yard throw from quarterback Tom Wilson to halfback Herb Adderley.

Hayes was especially proud of his team's defensive effort, and praised the play of tackle Daryl Sanders, end Sam Tidmore, linebacker Mike Ingram, and halfback Jim Herbstreit who all delivered key tackles or pass deflections. Ferguson led all rushers with 112 yards on 18 carries while Klein added 70 on seven attempts. Matte, who had led OSU to a thrilling 30-24 victory over the Spartans in 1959 during his first start at quarterback, added 52 yards on 16 tries.

Back in the friendly confines of Ohio Stadium the next Saturday, Ohio State had no difficulty with Indiana, winning 36-7. Like the 20-0 win over USC earlier in the season, this game was also more one-sided than indicated by the final score. The win, however, did not register in the conference standings or statistics, since the Hoosiers were under probation for recruiting violations.

1960 Co-Captain Jim Herbstreit

The Buckeyes led in first downs, 29-4, and in total offensive yards, 394-60. Hayes used 58 players during the afternoon, including 12 different ball carriers. Matte passed for three touchdowns and Ferguson and Klein each scored on short plunges.

The same afternoon Ohio State was whipping Indiana, top-ranked Iowa played at Minnesota in the nation's key contest. Both entered the game undefeated and untied. Minnesota won 27-10 to take over first place in the weekly AP poll. Missouri was now second, Ohio State moved up to third, and Iowa fell to fifth place.

Hawkeye Sets Record with Longest Run

Ironically, the Buckeyes faced Iowa the following week in a November 12 nationally televised game at Kinnick Stadium. They

Great Recommendation from Mrs. Hayes!

Anne Hayes gave her husband some good advice preceding the 1960 Michigan State game. After reading a *Sports Illustrated* article, she told him how a Texas coach praised Ohio State's use of the "trap play." Woody decided to put it back into his offense, and Bob Klein raced 45-yards on a "halfback trap" for the game's first touchdown.

In his last game for the Scarlet and Gray, quarterback Tom Matte powers for extra yardage during victory over Michigan.

found the Hawkeyes at a fever pitch, primarily because it was the last home game for retiring Forest Evashevski who had led Iowa to its greatest success during his nine seasons as head coach. Also, after losing at Minnesota, the Hawkeyes needed a victory to have any chance for at least a share of the Big Ten crown.

Running from a complex winged-T formation, Iowa unleashed a furious rushing attack and rapped the Buckeyes, 35-12. Two of the Hawkeyes' five touchdowns were scored from long distance—a 49-yard first-quarter burst by fullback Joe Williams for the game's first points, and Larry Ferguson's unbelievable 91-yard sideline dash in the final period. Ferguson's run is the longest ever by an Ohio State opponent. It was the first game all season Ohio State had not scored at least three touchdowns.

Approximately 30 Ohio State players were stricken with dysentery the prior evening and were not at full strength Saturday, but the illnesses probably made little difference. Iowa was just too strong this afternoon, collecting 487 yards in total offense against the confused Buckeye defenders. The Hawkeyes also received some good news from Minneapolis, where Purdue upset top-ranked Minnesota, 23-14, to give Iowa at least a share of the 1960 conference championship.

For the second consecutive season, the Ohio State-Michigan game was "strictly for pride," since the Buckeyes had two losses in league play and the Wolverines had three.

Both teams failed to show the offensive strength each had exhibited earlier in the season, and after three quarters it appeared the rivalry might have its first scoreless tie since the second game of the series in 1900. In the final stanza, Ohio State finally put together a 42-yard scoring drive, with Ferguson churning the last 17 yards for the game's only score.

The Buckeyes won 7-0 to finish the season with a record of 7-2, Michigan finished at 5-4. The Wolverines won the game's statistical battle, leading in first downs 17-9 and in total offensive yards 218-168. Minnesota and Iowa shared the conference title with identical league records of 5-1. The Golden Gophers were granted the Rose Bowl berth and lost to Washington, 17-7.

Ferguson was named All-American and shared the Big Ten individual scoring title with Iowa's Wilburn Hollis (48 points). Matte was selected the team's Most Valuable Player. Woody Hayes had finished his first decade at Ohio State with an overall ten-year record of 64-23-5 (72.3 percent), but the tireless taskmaster was really just getting started. His teams had captured three outright Big Ten titles and two National Championships, and his record against Michigan was 6-4—not bad for a coach who had been the selection committee's "second choice" in 1951.

It's Hard To Get Ahead Of Woody

Before freshmen players became eligible for varsity competition in 1972, they normally sat together for all home games in section 17 directly behind the Ohio State bench. Two of the Buckeyes' most promising freshmen in 1961 were halfbacks Paul Warfield and Matt Snell. As the two reached their seats just prior to kickoff at the November 19, 1960, game against Michigan, both were instructed to meet with Woody Hayes in the Ohio State dressing room right after the game. There was no further explanation—just meet the coach there when the game is over.

Approximately 45 minutes after the Buckeyes had defeated Michigan, 7-0, and with the stadium basically cleared, the coach came back out onto the field with his two prize freshmen halfbacks dressed in sweat suits. Senior quarterback Tom Matte (OSU's MVP in '60) had just played his last collegiate game, and Hayes was already considering a shift of either Warfield or Snell to quarterback. Also, Hayes was not breaking any NCAA rules, since practices could be held through the day of the season's last game.

The two worked out for about one hour, throwing passes and practicing handouts. By the fall of '61, Warfield and Snell had moved into the starting halfback positions, and John Mummey, Bill Mrukowski, and Joe Sparma shared the duties at quarterback.

1960				
September 24	Southern Methodist	W	24	0
October 1	Southern California	W	20	0
October 8	at Illinois	W	34	7
October 15	at Purdue	L	21	24
October 22	Wisconsin (HC)	W	34	7
October 29	at Michigan State	W	21	10
November 5	Indiana	W	36	7
November 12	at Iowa	L	12	35
November 19	Michigan	W	7	0
Total Points			209	90

Season Record: 7-2
Conference: 3rd Place

1961-1970

THE TURBULENT '60s

The 1960s was a decade of immense transformation in the United States. It was a period characterized by extensive industrial development, expansion of computer technology, growth of the civil rights movement, extended campus unrest, and involvement in the Vietnam War.

Ohio State football also experienced extensive change in the 1960s. Some of the Buckeyes' all-time "highest highs" and "lowest lows" would transpire between 1961 and 1970. The Ohio State football program would be dealt one of the greatest disappointments ever experienced by a college football team —it also would win a national title with a squad dominated by sophomores.

1961

The 1961 Ohio State Buckeyes were expected to contend for national recognition,

primarily because 26 lettermen returned from the fine 1960 squad that won seven and lost only two. Woody Hayes' biggest concern was finding a quarterback replacement for the talented Tom Matte, 1960 team MVP, who had graduated and was now playing with the NFL's Baltimore Colts. Also gone were halfbacks Jim Herbstreit, Bill Wentz, and Bill German, tackle Jim Tyrer, and guards Don Young, Oscar Hauer, and Gabe Hartman.

NCAA rules permitted member schools to open their 1961 fall practices on September 1. With Ohio State not playing its season opener until September 30, Hayes waited until September 4 to begin fall workouts, in an effort to minimize some of the boredom often associated with long pre-season practices.

The starting offensive ends were veterans Chuck Bryant of Zanesville, Bob Middleton of Marion, and sophomore Ormonde Ricketts of Springfield. Hayes had two excellent tackles in Bob Vogel of Massillon and Daryl Sanders of Mayfield Heights, both juniors. The two would become

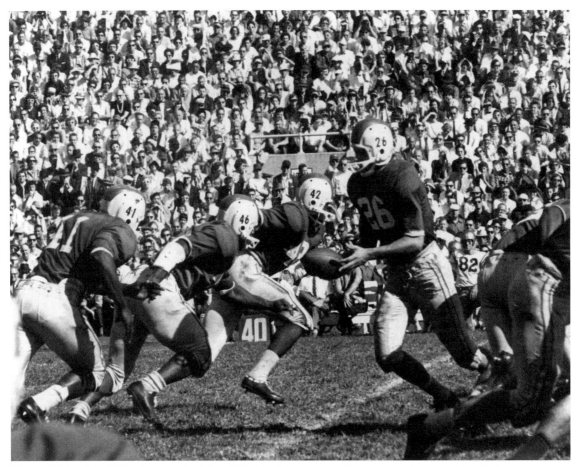

The 1961 backfield featured Matt Snell (41), Bob Ferguson (46), and Paul Warfield (42). Quarterback Bill Mrukowski (26) had the enviable job of handing off to three of Ohio State's finest runners.

first-round selections in the NFL draft following the 1962 season. The guards were co-captain Mike Ingram of Bellaire and Rodney Foster of Cleveland, while Billy Joe Armstrong of Huron manned the center position.

The backfield was built around fullback Bob Ferguson of Troy, a consensus All-American the previous year when he led the Buckeyes with 853 yards rushing and 13 touchdowns. The quarterbacks were juniors Bill Mrukowski of Elyria and John Mummey of Painesville, both fine runners. Mrukowski and Mummey had each been an All-Ohio selection at fullback in high school. In passing situations Hayes often used sophomore Joe Sparma of Massillon, a fine athlete who later became a major league pitcher with the

Detroit Tigers. Mummey would serve as an OSU assistant coach from 1969 through 1976.

The halfback spots went to two highly publicized sophomore speedsters, Paul Warfield of Warren and Matt Snell of Locust Valley, New York. Both were fine runners, and at one time Hayes even considered converting one of them to quarterback in his ground-oriented offense. Bob Klein, a junior from Athens, Michigan, who had scored five touchdowns the previous season, would also play a prominent role in '61.

Ohio State's defensive unit had veterans Sam Tidmore of Cleveland and co-captain Tom Perdue of Wellston at the ends. The tackles were George Tolford of Swanton and Dick Laskoski of Shamokin, Pennsylvania. The middle guard position was manned by Wayne

Betz of Cuyahoga Falls and Larry Stephens of Coshocton. Gary Moeller of Lima, who later served as head coach at Illinois and Michigan, was at linebacker.

The defensive backfield included returning regulars Billy Hess of Springfield and Ron Houck of Troy. They were joined by Ed Ulmer of Brookfield and Howard Lambert of Bellefontaine.

After a rocky start, this team would develop into one of the finest and most well-balanced Ohio State squads of all time. It also would be dealt an almost unbelievable disappointment at the end of the season. The Buckeyes were ranked third in the weekly Associated Press poll the week prior to their opener with Texas Christian. Iowa was ranked first, followed by second-place Mississippi. Michigan State was tenth.

TCU Does It Again!

Texas Christian University was the opponent for Ohio State's September 30 opener at Ohio Stadium. The Horned Frogs had opened their season the previous week with a 17-16 upset of eighth-ranked Kansas.

The Buckeyes marched 56 yards on their first possession to take a 7-0 lead, with the

Ohio State's three quarterbacks were John Mummey (25), Bill Mrukowski (26), and Joe Sparma (24).

335

touchdown coming on a roll-out pass from Mrukowski to Bryant from the TCU two. Sophomore placekicker Dick VanRaaphorst added the conversion. The score remained 7-0 until the final period, when TCU's 6'7" quarterback Guy "Sonny" Gibbs passed 12 yards to end Jim Glasscock for a touchdown. Horned Frog placekicker Jim McAteer made it 7-7 and that's how the game ended.

Ohio State had a chance late in the fourth quarter with a second-and-seven at the TCU 10-yard line, but Gibbs intercepted a Mrukowski pass at the goal line to end the threat. It was a very disappointing start for Ohio State. Coach Woody Hayes took most of the blame for the tie, stating, "That was as bad a game as I've ever coached." He admitted he should never have called for the pass at the TCU ten, which resulted in Gibbs' interception. "We should have chopped away for at least two more plays since we were within field goal range," he said.

Ohio State fell to eighth in the weekly AP rankings. Ironically, TCU had been the "spoiler" in 1957, upsetting Ohio State 18-14

in that season's home opener. The '57 squad became the only Buckeye team ever to win every game after a season-opening loss.

For a while, things didn't look much better the next week against UCLA. Coach Bill Barnes' Bruins, running from their famed single wing attack, led 3-0 after three quarters. Finally, in the fourth period, Ohio State's sophomore halfbacks broke things open. First Warfield scored on a 13-yard dash over tackle. Snell then zipped 33 yards through the same hole for another TD to conclude the scoring at 13-3.

UCLA did a fine job defensing Ferguson, holding him to just 29 yards in 13 carries. The Ohio Stadium attendance of 82,992 was the 20th consecutive crowd in excess of 80,000. The Big Ten dominated the *AP* poll: Iowa (2-0), was second; Michigan State (2-0), fifth; and Michigan (2-0), sixth. The Buckeyes at 1-0-1 had moved up one place to seventh.

Buckeyes Impressive in Conference Opener Against Illinois

Ohio State had little trouble in its October 14 Big Ten opener, downing Illinois 44-0. On a cold and windy afternoon at Ohio Stadium, coach Woody Hayes used 61 players including 10 different ball carriers. Ferguson scored four times, and Warfield thrilled the crowd of 82,974 with a sparkling 35-yard scoring cutback around left end in the second period. This same afternoon Michigan State shut out Michigan 28-0 at Ann Arbor, and advanced to first place in the weekly AP. The Buckeyes remained seventh.

The following Saturday at Dycke Stadium in Evanston, Ohio State had all it could handle before conquering Northwestern, 10-0. Coach Ara Parseghian's Wildcat defense held OSU to just three points in the first three quarters—a 24-yard second-period field goal by VanRaaphorst that was his first as a collegian. In the final quarter Mrukowski went 20 yards on a roll-out inside his own left end for the game's only touchdown.

Woody Unleashes "Double-Fullback" Attack

Wisconsin was sky-high for its October 28 homecoming battle with Ohio State. Badger quarterback Ron Miller played an exceptional game, completing 13 of 23 passes for 219 yards and two touchdowns. Six of Miller's throws went to All-American end Pat Richter (who later became Wisconsin's Director of Athletics) for 104 yards and one TD.

But Woody Hayes' mighty ground attack proved to be superior, as Ohio State ground out a hard-earned 30-21 victory. Fullbacks Bob Ferguson and Dave Katterhenrich (212-pound junior from Bucyrus) led an awesome rushing effort that netted 357 yards. Ferguson ran for 120 yards in 20 attempts, and Katterhenrich added 91 in 17 carries including the game's first touchdown on a 17-yard burst through the center of the Badger defense.

While Ohio State was undoing Wisconsin, Purdue was upsetting fifth-ranked Iowa, 9-0, for the Hawkeyes' first loss of the season. Ohio State, Michigan State, and Minnesota were in a three-way tie for first place in the Big Ten with 3-0 conference records. But the Buckeyes would need plenty of outside help if they were to win the league title. Michigan State and Minnesota each played seven conference games, compared with Ohio State's six, and the Buckeyes would not meet either the Spartans or Golden Gophers this season.

Iowa — Biggest Test-to-Date

Heading into the first weekend of November, Michigan State (5-0) was ranked number one nationally; Ohio State (4-0-1), fifth; Iowa (4-1), ninth; and Minnesota (4-1), eleventh. After two weeks on the road, the Buckeyes returned to Ohio Stadium November 4 for their biggest test of the season—a homecoming clash against Iowa. The Hawkeyes had beaten OSU the two previous seasons, and no team had won three in a row

Hayes Honored

Woody Hayes so greatly influenced co-captain Tom Perdue that Perdue named his son Hayes Perdue in honor of his coach. In addition to playing football, Tom was an All-American in baseball. His single-season batting average of .469 is still an Ohio State record. He also was selected an Academic All-American his senior year.

over Hayes-coached teams at this point in his career.

Before a homecoming crowd of 83,795, at the time the largest in Ohio Stadium history, the Buckeyes pulled off a huge win, 29-13. OSU's defense led the way to a 12-0 halftime lead. End Tom Perdue returned an interception 55 yards for the game's first score. OSU's second touchdown, an 18-yard pass from Sparma to Bryant, followed Dave Tingley's interception return to the Iowa 30.

The Buckeyes' last 17 points came in the fourth quarter. First Sparma again connected with Bryant on a 63-yard scoring pass. VanRaaphorst kicked a 24-yard field goal, and Bob Ferguson scored from the 11-yard line to make it 29-7. Ferguson's TD followed a 53-yard interception by Gary Moeller down the west sideline to the Iowa 21-yard line.

Hayes was extremely proud of his defense and especially the play of ends Perdue and Tidmore. In later years, Hayes frequently referred to Bryant's 63-yard score as "one of the greatest individual efforts I have ever seen." Bryant had eluded seven different tacklers and carried an eighth over the goal line for the touchdown.

While Ohio State was defeating Iowa, Minnesota upset Michigan State, 13-0, to leave the Buckeyes and Golden Gophers alone atop the Big Ten with 4-0 records. OSU

(5-0-1) advanced to third in the *AP* rankings, below Texas (7-0) and Alabama (7-0). Minnesota (5-1) was up to fifth, while Michigan State (5-1) fell from first to sixth.

Mrukowski Shifts to Defense

Hayes was not completely satisfied with his team's offense. He decided to shift Mrukowski to defense and go with Mummey and Sparma at quarterback. His squad did not look overly spectacular the next week, but managed a 16-7 win at Indiana. It was the Buckeyes' first trip to Bloomington since 1950.

Sparma passed for both touchdowns against the Hoosiers—five yards to Warfield in the second period and nine yards on a diagonal pattern to Bryant for the game's only second-half score. Mummey rushed for exactly 100 yards in 17 attempts, while the IU defense held Ferguson to just 49 yards on 14 carries. The Buckeyes were penalized 10 times for 76 yards—in their six previous starts they had been flagged for only 107 yards.

Three Exceed 100-Yard Mark in Woody's 100th Game

The Buckeyes returned home for a 22-12 Dad's Day win over Oregon on November 18. It was Woody Hayes' 100th game at Ohio State, and nothing could have pleased him more than having three backs each rush for more than 100 yards. Bob Klein netted 103, which included a brilliant 72-yard end sweep for OSU's first touchdown on the game's second play from scrimmage. Mummey had 116 and Ferguson 101.

Hayes also bragged about his team's flawless execution, which included no fumbles, no interceptions, and no penalties. OSU was 5-0 in league play and 7-0-1 overall heading into its traditional grudge match at Michigan. Minnesota had won close encounters over Iowa and Purdue in their last two games, to go 6-0 in the conference (7-1 overall) with one game remaining at Wisconsin. Alabama was now number one in the nation,

followed by Ohio State and Minnesota. Hayes' 11-year Ohio State record was now 71-23-6.

All-Time Triumph No. 400

The Buckeyes traveled north to Ann Arbor on November 25, the Saturday following Thanksgiving. The Wolverines under coach Bump Elliott entered the game at 6-2, 3-2 in league play. This contest developed into one of the wildest and most offensive games in the storied Ohio State-Michigan series.

Two-time All-American fullback Bob Ferguson finished second to winner Ernie Davis of Syracuse in the 1961 Heisman Trophy race.

No Stranger to Michigan's Press Box

Calling the Buckeyes' offensive plays during their 50-20 triumph at Michigan was Ohio State assistant coach Bo Schembechler. Who could ever have imagined that, in just eight years, Schembechler would begin leading the Wolverines to some of their most successful seasons.

The Buckeyes erupted for a 50-20 shellacking, even though the score was only 21-12 after three quarters. It was Ohio State's 400th all-time victory (400-180-44). The 50 points is Ohio State's highest point total against Michigan (it was equaled with a 50-14 OSU win in 1968).

This game had everything! Bob Ferguson, playing his last collegiate game, rushed for 152 yards and four touchdowns to become the first Ohio State player to score four TDs in an Ohio State-Michigan game. Joe Sparma and Bob Klein connected on an 80-yard touchdown pass, the longest scoring pass play in an Ohio State-Michigan game. Michigan's Davey Raimey, from Dayton, Ohio, scored on a 90-yard kickoff return—it is the only kickoff to be returned for a touchdown in series history.

But the game's most spectacular play was executed by Paul Warfield. On a counterplay right, the fleet halfback turned the end, cut back upfield, faked Michigan's safety off his feet, and raced 69-yards for the second longest scoring run from scrimmage in an Ohio State-Michigan game.

Altogether Ohio State led in first downs 22-16 and in total offensive yards, 512-271. With the score 48-20, Hayes elected to go for a two-point conversion, which was successful. When later questioned if he was deliberately running up the score, Hayes indicated long-time kicking coach Ernie Godfrey was

celebrating his 70th birthday and would be retiring at the end of the season after 32 years as an assistant coach. (Godfrey continued to work with the kickers for many seasons). He wanted the game's total points to equal 70 in Ernie's honor. As might be expected, Wolverine fans were not so enchanted with the idea.

While Ohio State was taking care of Michigan, Wisconsin upset Minnesota 23-21 at Minneapolis, allowing Ohio State to capture its fourth outright conference title in the last eight seasons. The second-ranked Buckeyes were all set for a January 1 Rose Bowl date with UCLA, a team they had beaten 13-3 in the season's second game. The team was awarded the National Championship by the Football Writers Association of America.

The Bitter Disappointment

An agreement between the Big Ten Conference and Pacific Eight Conference (later the Pacific Ten with the addition of Arizona and Arizona State) had been signed in 1946, allowing the conference champions to meet in the Rose Bowl each January 1. However,

1961 National Champions

in 1959, the Big Ten split five-to-five on renewing the pact, which meant the agreement would expire following the January 2, 1960 Rose Bowl.

Although there was no formal agreement in force the following year, the Rose Bowl invited 1960 Big Ten Champion Minnesota to face Washington in the January 1, 1961, game. Minnesota, even though it had been opposed to the agreement, accepted the bid and made the trip to Pasadena to play in its first Rose Bowl. Ohio State also opposed the agreement, but nevertheless accepted its share of the Rose Bowl gate (the Big Ten splits its Rose Bowl receipts equally among its members, after allowing for the participating team's expenses).

With Ohio State winning the conference championship in 1961, the Rose Bowl invitation was extended to the Buckeyes. For Ohio State fans, Tuesday, November 28, 1961, became one of the darkest days in all of Ohio State football. The Ohio State faculty council, by a reported vote of 28 to 25, voted against playing in the Rose Bowl.

Apparently a majority of the council felt football was getting too big at Ohio State. In the council's words, the university was becoming known as a "football school," which

hurt its academic image. Many of the faculty and administration also thought the Rose Bowl was becoming too commercial. The Tournament of Roses next extended an invitation to second-place Minnesota, who accepted and made its second consecutive trip to Pasadena. The Ohio State faculty council still voted to accept what it considered "its share of the Rose Bowl receipts," even after declining to participate in the game.

Even with the bitterness of the Rose Bowl situation, Ohio State had had an excellent year, finishing at 8-0-1 for second place behind Alabama in both the AP and UPI polls. Bob Ferguson was again a consensus All-American and finished second to Syracuse's Ernie Davis in the '61 Heisman Trophy voting. He led the conference in both rushing and scoring. Tom Perdue was chosen the team's Most Valuable Player. Ferguson and Mike Ingram were named All-Big Ten.

When the team returned to campus for its 25th reunion in 1986, many recalled those great moments of their 8-0-1 season—and they also remembered the overwhelming disappointment of being denied the Rose Bowl after achieving one of the finest records in school history.

1961

September 30	Texas Christian	T	7	7
October 7	UCLA	W	13	3
October 14	Illinois	W	44	0
October 21	at Northwestern	W	10	0
October 28	at Wisconsin	W	30	21
November 4	Iowa (HC)	W	29	13
November 11	at Indiana	W	16	7
November 18	Oregon	W	22	12
November 25	at Michigan	W	50	20
Total Points			221	83

Season Record: 8-0-1
National Champion
Big Ten Champion

1962

The bitterness of being denied the Rose Bowl trip still lingered when the Buckeyes assembled to begin preparation for 1962. Nevertheless, Ohio State was ranked number one in the AP's preseason poll, mainly because of the many talented players returning. The offensive line was built around two gifted senior tackles, Bob Vogel and Daryl Sanders, who would both become first-round picks in the 1963 NFL draft.

Three quarterbacks returned in John Mummey (the runner), Joe Sparma (the passer) and Bill Mrukowski (who also played defense). Three senior fullbacks—Dave Francis, Dave Katterhenrich, Bob Butts—all saw considerable playing time, and Matt Snell was used primarily at defensive end. Halfbacks Paul Warfield and Bob Klein were back, and Warfield was used as a runner, receiver, and defender. Bill Hess returned at defensive back and Gary Moeller at linebacker. Moeller would become even more familiar to Ohio State backers as head coach of the Michigan Wolverines from 1990 through 1994.

Highest Season-Opening Score in 27 Years

The Buckeyes opened September 29 with a convincing 41-7 win over North Carolina before a then-record Ohio Stadium crowd of 84,009. It was OSU's largest opening-game score since defeating Missouri 47-6 on this same date in 1945. Ohio State scored on its first two possessions, then exploded with 27 points in the second half.

Warfield electrified the record crowd with two touchdowns—a 42-yard over-the-shoulder scoring catch from Mummey and a four-yard sweep around right end. Hayes used 72 different players throughout the afternoon, including ten different ball carriers.

The Buckeyes should have kept some of their opening-day touchdowns for the second game. UCLA produced the first major upset of 1962, winning 9-7 at the Los Angeles Coliseum. Sophomore Larry Zeno booted a 24-yard goal with just 1:35 remaining for the Bruins' come-from-behind shocker. Ohio State won everything but the final score, leading in first downs, 18-8, total offensive yards, 276-186, and running 72 plays from scrimmage compared with 38 for UCLA. Three times the inspired Bruins held the Buckeye offense at the one-yard line.

In the third quarter Joe Sparma passed six yards to Matt Snell for OSU's only score. Interestingly, the Bruin's touchdown came on their very first play from their newly in-

League Encounters Top Priority

Woody Hayes developed a powerful reputation for winning consistently in the conference, while not concentrating as strongly on non-conference games. Fans pointed to the 1962 loss at UCLA as another example of Hayes focusing primarily on the Big Ten.

stalled T-formation. After UCLA recovered a fumble at the OSU 45 early in the game, halfback Kermit Alexander dashed through left tackle and went the distance. The Bruins had switched from the single-wing offense to the T, and this was their first game of the season.

Another Impressive Big Ten Opener at Illinois

Ohio State bounced back mightily October 13 to win the conference opener at Illinois, 51-15. Using 11 different ball carriers, the Buckeyes rushed for 517 yards to establish, at the time, a new Big Ten single-game record. This erased the old league mark of 465 yards set by Ohio State against Indiana in 1956. Quarterback John Mummey led the relentless ground attack, netting 114 yards in a dozen carries. The Buckeyes attempted only seven passes, connecting on two for just nine yards.

Most of the Illinois homecoming crowd of 56,107 had vacated Memorial Stadium by the time the Illini posted their second touchdown with just 15 seconds remaining. It came on a 90-yard pass play from quarterback Mike Taliaferro to end Mike Yavorski—the longest pass play ever against Ohio State.

Wildcats on Road to Nation's Top Ranking

After two weeks on the road, the Buckeyes returned home October 20 to battle the highly improved Northwestern Wildcats who entered the game at 3-0. It was homecoming, and halfback Bob Klein electrified the record crowd of 84,376 with a 90-yard return of the opening kickoff for the game's first touchdown. Later that quarter Ohio State marched 71 yards for its second score, a nine-yard run by fullback Dave Francis, to lead 14-0.

But the rest of the sunny afternoon belonged to coach Ara Parseghian's Wildcats. Parseghian, an Akron native, had recruited well within his home state. Twenty-four

Too Little, Too Late

On Tuesday, October 9, 1962, four days before the season's first conference game at Illinois, the Ohio State Faculty Council voted to send the football team to the Rose Bowl if an invitation was received. This decision reversed the council's prior position, when a Rose Bowl invitation was declined after Ohio State had captured the 1961 Big Ten title.

Gary Moeller, linebacker and Co-Captain

members of his '62 squad were from Ohio, including two all-Americans—sophomore quarterback Tom (Gun) Myers of Troy and junior guard Jack Cvercko of Campbell. Northwestern smoothly controlled the last three quarters and tallied three times for a well-deserved 18-14 victory. Myers was outstanding, completing 18 tosses for 177 yards and guiding his squad with the composure of a veteran.

Ohio State had two third-quarter touchdowns nullified by penalties. Halfback Bo Scott's 62-yard interception return was negated by a pass interference penalty, and a short scoring plunge by fullback Bob Butts was nullified by a backfield-in-motion call.

Northwestern defeated Notre Dame, 35-6, the following Saturday and rose to number-one in the weekly Associated Press poll. The Wildcats stayed there until they lost at Wisconsin, 37-6, two weeks later.

Hayes was very critical of the officiating following the loss to Northwestern, and even showed one controversial call three times on his Sunday television show. The outspoken coach found himself in trouble again with Big Ten Commissioner Bill Reed because of his faultfinding remarks, and reluctantly sent the commissioner a letter apologizing for his outbursts.

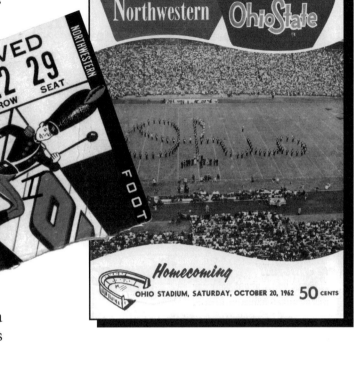

Badgers' Sole Setback

The Buckeyes rebounded from the Northwestern setback with success and authority, to hand talented Wisconsin its only loss of the regular season, 14-7. OSU scored in the first quarter with Joe Sparma passing 21 yards to Paul Warfield, who outmaneuvered three defenders to find his way to the end zone. The Badgers retaliated right before the half on a beautifully executed 47-yard scoring toss from quarterback Ron VanderKelen (later named '62 Big Ten MVP) to halfback Ron Smith. Midway through the fourth period, Hayes alternated his three senior fullbacks—Francis, Katterhenrich, Butts—eight straight times through the middle of the Wisconsin defense to advance the ball 57 yards to the opponent's one. Mummey sneaked across for the deciding score.

All-American end Pat Richter was held to just two catches, thanks primarily to

Bucks Grind It Out In 4th Quarter And Budge Badgers, 14-7

Columbus Dispatch, Sunday, October 28, 1962

the defensive heroics of Paul Warfield. His string of at least one touchdown reception was snapped at eight games. Ironically Richter started his streak by scoring against Ohio State at Wisconsin in the 1961 game. This was a much needed win for the Buckeyes who were now 3-2 on the season.

But the enjoyment didn't last long. On November 3 the "on again-off again" Buckeyes lost any chance of repeating as Big Ten champions with a crushing 28-14 setback at Iowa. The Hawkeyes jumped out to a quick 14-0 first-quarter lead, and were aided throughout the afternoon by four OSU turnovers. This was the Buckeyes' fourth loss in their five most recent trips to Iowa City.

Iowa held Ohio State to just 174 yards on the ground and 20 yards through the air (three completions in 10 attempts). The Bucks were now 3-3 on the season.

Bucks Fortunate to Avoid Huge Upset

At rain-soaked Ohio Stadium the following Saturday, Ohio State was an 18-point Dad's Day favorite over an Indiana team that had lost 17 consecutive Big Ten games over three seasons. Paul Warfield scored on a dazzling 75-yard scamper to give Ohio State a 7-0 halftime lead. But the Buckeye offense had trouble the rest of the afternoon, and Hoosier quarterback Woody Moore tied the game 7-7 with a one-yard sneak in the third period.

After several stalled drives, Ohio State finally moved to the Indiana 11-yard line with just eight seconds remaining. Placekicker Dick VanRaaphorst calmly booted a 27-yard field goal, and the Buckeyes escaped with a 10-7 win. It was a moral victory for the Hoosiers, who nearly pulled off what would have been one of the season's biggest upsets.

After dodging a bullet against Indiana, Ohio State played exceptionally well with a 26-7 non-conference win over Oregon. The

Line coach Bo Schembechler, an Ohio State assistant for five seasons, poses with his 1962 tackles, Daryl Sanders (76) and Co-Captain Bob Vogel (73). Both were NFL first-round draft picks in 1963, Sanders by the Detroit Lions and Vogel by the Baltimore Colts.

flashy Ducks entered Ohio Stadium with a record of 6-1-1. It was a cold overcast afternoon with just 72,828 spectators on hand. Mummey, Klein, VanRaaphorst, and Scott all sat this one out with injuries.

Ohio State scored in each of the four quarters. Bill Mrukowski moved back to quarterback from defense, and had a fine afternoon with two four-yard rollout runs for touchdowns. Woody Hayes again alternated his three senior fullbacks, who combined for 47 carries and 214 of the team's 316 rushing yards. Oregon committed three turnovers and simply could not contain the Buckeyes' power.

Triple Fullback Delight!

Ohio State closed out its '62 season November 24 with an impressive 28-0 drubbing of Michigan. Hayes' love of his patented fullback-dominated ground attack may never have been more evident.

Playing their last game in Ohio Stadium, the senior fullback trio of Francis, Katterenrich, and Butts scored all four touchdowns, and placekicker Chuck Mamula added the four conversions. The Buckeyes, who used 69 different players throughout the afternoon, led in first downs, 19-9, and in total offensive yardage, 337-142. Michigan never moved beyond the Ohio State 21-yard line.

Ohio State finished the inconsistent season with a record of 6-3, good for 13th place in the final AP poll but a far cry from the top spot where it was expected to finish. Warfield and center Billy Joe Armstrong were All-Big Ten picks, and Armstrong was selected the team's MVP.

Katterhenrich made the Academic All-Big Ten team. Francis led the Big Ten in rushing with 418 yards (75 atttempts) in six conference games. The Buckeyes now had three consecutive wins over Michigan, and had averaged in excess of 80,000 fans at each home game for the ninth straight year.

1962				
September 29	North Carolina	W	41	7
October 6	at UCLA	L	7	9
October 13	at Illinois	W	51	15
October 20	Northwestern (HC)	L	14	18
October 27	Wisconsin	W	14	7
November 3	at Iowa	L	14	28
November 10	Indiana	W	10	7
November 17	Oregon	W	26	7
November 24	Michigan	W	28	0
Total Points			205	98

Season Record: 6-3
Conference: 3rd Place (Tie)

Fullback Dave Francis powers his way into the Michigan end zone after taking a hand off from quarterback Bill Mrukowski (26).

1963

Woody Hayes' 13th season at Ohio State would require a major rebuilding effort, particularly on offense where only three starters returned. Paul Warfield was back for his final year and would play a prominent role as a runner, pass receiver, defensive back, and punt and kickoff returner. Senior Matt Snell was moved from defensive end to fullback, and dependable placekicker Dick VanRaaphorst would make a real impact throughout the season. Sophomores would be relied upon to play key roles, especially at quarterback.

First Meeting with Texas Aggies

Ohio State opened at home September 28 with an impressive 17-0 win over Texas A & M, in the first meeting between the two schools. The Aggies, who had opened the previous week with a 14-6 loss to Louisiana State, was held to just one first down in the first three quarters.

The Buckeyes ran 74 plays to the visitors' 49, and led in total offensive yards, 280 to 110. Sophomore Don Unverferth started at quarterback, Warfield led all ground gainers with 85 yards, halfback Tyrone Barnett added another 69, and Snell scored both touchdowns from short range. Dick VanRaaphorst finished the day's scoring with a 37-yard field goal in the final period. The game was one of the shortest in Ohio Stadium history, lasting just under two hours.

It was more of the same the second week at Indiana. The "surprising Buckeyes" shut out the Hoosiers 20-0 before a then-record Memorial Stadium crowd of 42,296. Unverferth (who played with more certainty than in his debut the week before) passed for two touchdowns, a 24 yarder to sophomore end Greg Lashutka and a four yarder to Warfield.

Snell was the game's leading ground gainer with 72 yards. VanRaaphorst's first of two field goals was 48 yards, which set a Big Ten record, breaking the old mark of 47 yards established two seasons earlier by Wisconsin's Jim Baaken. The Buckeyes also tallied a safety in the final period.

Play Selection Debated by Both Sides

The Buckeyes returned to Columbus for an October 12 homecoming matchup against talented Illinois, a preseason favorite for the Big Ten title. The game drew an Ohio Stadium-record crowd of 84,712. In one of the most suspenseful thrillers in the series, the two battled to a 20-20 tie. Fans from both schools would "second guess" certain coaching decisions long into the night.

The first controversial call came 22 seconds before halftime, with Ohio State having possession at the Illini 17-yard line, fourth-and-three. Illinois had a 7-3 lead. Rather than go for a relatively short field goal, Hayes called for a pass that ended up being

September 28, 1963

OHIO STATE

TEXAS A&M

50

batted down in the end zone. The Illini kept the four-point lead at the half.

The Buckeyes scored twice in the third period on short plunges by fullbacks Matt Snell and Will Sander to forge ahead, 17-7. At this point, Ohio State appeared to be headed for its third win of the season. But Illinois scored twice in the final quarter to recapture the lead, 20-17. Trailing 17-13 after the first TD, the Illini tried a two-point conversion in an attempt to pull within two points of the Buckeyes—the attempted pass failed. Had the visitors kicked the extra point, they likely would have won the game, 21-20.

With just 1:53 remaining, VanRaaphorst connected on a 49-yard field goal to tie the game, 20-20, and that's how it ended. The kick broke his own Big Ten record of 48 yards set just one week earlier at Indiana, but it was of little consolation. Coach Pete Elliott's Illinois squad went on to capture the '63 league title, and finish the season with a 17-7 triumph over Washington in the Rose Bowl.

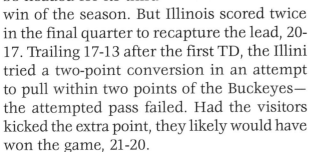

Another Bad Day at the Coliseum

The following weekend Southern California riddled the fourth-ranked Buckeyes 32-3 in Los Angeles. Led by the outstanding running and passing of quarterback Pete Beathard, the Trojans outplayed Ohio State in every phase of the game, and outgained the Buckeyes, 407 yards to 178. Ohio State completed only three of 17 passes and had four intercepted. Woody Hayes was now 0-3 in games played at the Los Angeles Memorial Coliseum.

Are We Going to Let Them Do This to Us?

After the poor showing on the west coast, Ohio State was a huge underdog against undefeated and second-ranked Wisconsin at Madison. While taking a walk near Lake Mendota on the Wisconsin campus around 6:00 a.m. the morning of the game, Woody Hayes spotted a morning newspaper that predicted, "This is the year we finally get Woody!" The Badgers had been able to defeat OSU only once during Hayes' first dozen seasons, and the local publication was obviously forecasting better results this af-

Versatility-Plus

Matt Snell, one of Ohio State's 1963 co-captains, was a starter three consecutive seasons at three different positions. Snell started at right halfback in 1961, defensive end in 1962, and fullback in 1963.

ternoon for the Badgers. Hayes immediately purchased a huge stack of the papers. Back at the hotel he quickly awakened the entire team, showed them the story,and prodded them with, "Are we going to let them do this to us?"

The coach's impromptu pep talk obviously had some effect. Even though his young Buckeyes were clearly outmanned, they played their hearts out that afternoon and upset the Badgers, 13-10. The fiery coach, now 50 years old, could not have been more pleased with his team's effort.

Ohio State outplayed Wisconsin in the early going, and led 6-3 at halftime on VanRaaphorst's field goals of 36 and 45 yards. The fine placekicker from Ligonier, Pennsylvania, now had six for the season, setting a new Big Ten record. Sophomore quarterback Tom Barrington played remarkably well in his first game. Barrington had been idle the first four weeks of the season after sustaining a broken jaw in an industrial accident that summer. The concern at halftime was if Ohio State could sustain its gutty performance for another 30 minutes.

Wisconsin's offense came alive in the second half.

Sticking mostly with their ground attack, the Badgers put together a 12-play, 76-yard touchdown march to take the lead at 10-6. Junior halfback Carl Silvestri scored around end from 12 yards out on a much-used pitchback play.

Ohio State got a big break midway through the final period, when Don Hendrickson's 44-yard field-goal attempt hit the right upright and bounced back onto the playing field. With the Buckeyes then taking over at their own 20-yard line, Hayes switched to Don Unverferth at quarterback, who very impressively directed his squad 80 yards for the game-winning touchdown.

Unverferth kept the winning drive alive with three key third-down completions to end Tom Kiehfuss. Matt Snell plunged across from the two for the clinching touchdown. Snell had been questionable for the afternoon because of injuries, but the big fullback played one of his finest games and finished with 93 yards rushing.

Wisconsin made one last effort to pull it out, but Paul Warfield's interception ended the drive on the game's last play. Ohio State was now 3-1-1 on the season and seemed to be heading in the right direction.

Offense Continues to Struggle

After two weeks out of town, the Buckeyes returned home to shade Iowa, 7-3. This was not one of the most exciting college games ever played. The two teams combined for just 21 first downs and 386 yards of total offense. Ohio State had been able to register just a single first down on its first eight times with the ball.

One bright spot was the play of Tom Barrington, who gained 111 yards from both the quarterback and left halfback positons. He led his squad on its lone scoring drive of 74 yards in the third period. Barrington's performance was quite remarkable, especially when considering he had been hospitalized three days with intestinal flu and had missed

Quarterback Don Unverferth

all of the week's heavy practices. Arnie Chonko's interception late in the fourth quarter helped seal the win.

Penn State upset the 10th-ranked Buckeyes 10-7 on November 2, behind the magical ball handling and passing of quarterback Pete Liske. Many among the home crowd of 83,159 felt this was another example of Woody Hayes lack of preparation for a nonconference opponent. Ohio State put together just one sustained scoring drive to lead 7-0 at the half.

The Nittany Lions scored all ten of their points in the third period with a 13-yard scoring toss from Liske to end Bill Bowes and a 23-yard tie-breaking field goal by Ron Coates. The Buckeyes never advanced into enemy territory in six second-half attempts. Ohio State's offense was obviously continuing to struggle, having scored only three touchdowns in its last four games. Hayes was quite disappointed with his team's offense but gave credit to Liske, whom he described as the best quarterback he had ever seen in Ohio Stadium.

While this loss dropped the Buckeyes from the AP top ten, OSU received some unexpected help in the Big Ten race when Michigan upset Illinois, 14-8, at Champaign. The Illini loss left Ohio State and Michigan State as the only two undefeated teams in league competiton, although each had a tie.

Ara Parseghian's Wildcats Do It Again

In the season's last home game, Northwestern eliminated Ohio State from Big Ten title contention with an impressive 17-8 triumph that was even more convincing than suggested by the final tally. Trailing 17-0, the

Buckeyes avoided their first home shutout in four seasons with a 31-yard TD pass from Don Unverferth to Paul Warfield late in the final period. Ohio State threw 32 passes that afternoon, the most by an OSU team in a single game since passing 44 times in the 1952 Pittsburgh game (which the Buckeyes also lost, 21-14).

Ara Parseghian was now 3-1 in his last four games against Woody Hayes. After restoring respectability to the Northwestern program, Parseghian moved to Notre Dame the following season.

Football Virtually at Standstill as Nation Mourns

The Michigan game, scheduled for Saturday, November 23, was postponed one week following the assassination of President John F. Kennedy on Friday, November 22. The announcement came at approximately 10 a.m. Saturday morning, just as the Ohio

One of many unused tickets for the 1963 Ohio State - Michigan game, which was postponed one week due to the assassination of President Kennedy.

State squad was heading to Michigan Stadium from its hotel in Ypsilanti. College football that weekend, including numerous traditional rivalries, was virtually forgotten.

Illinois was scheduled to play at Michigan State this same afternoon, in a game that would decide the Big Ten title. This battle was moved back to Thanksgiving Day, with the Illini coming out on top, 13-0.

The following Saturday, November 30, a crowd of 36,424, smallest at Michigan Stadium in 20 years, saw the Buckeyes rebound from a 10-0 deficit to win, 14-10. It also was the smallest crowd to attend an Ohio State-Michigan game in Ann Arbor since the opening of Michigan Stadium 36 years earlier in 1927. Since neither team was in contention for the league title and Michigan was experiencing its second consecutive losing season, many fans decided against a return trip to Ann Arbor.

Don Unverferth connected with Paul Warfield on a 35-yard scoring pass for the Buckeyes' first score just 41 seconds before halftime. Midway through the final period, Unverferth (who was known more for his passing than running) rolled out five yards around left end for the other touchdown. It appeared the Wolverines might pull it out until their final drive stalled at the Ohio State six with under two minutes remaining.

Ohio State finished the year at 5-3-1. Warfield was again an All-Big Ten selection and Snell was selected the squad's MVP. VanRaaphorst led the team in scoring with 34 points. The Buckeyes had now defeated Michigan "four in a row," and Woody Hayes' 13-year record against the Wolverines was 9-4.

1964

Ohio State approached its 75th anniversary season with great optimism. Warfield and Snell were now enjoying fine rookie seasons in the professional ranks, but three solid juniors returned in the offensive backfield —quarterback Don Unverferth, halfback Tom Barrington, and fullback Willard Sander. Bo Rein, a talented sophomore from Niles, manned the other halfback spot.

The offensive line was anchored around two fine tackles, Jim Davidson and Doug Van Horn, and the defense was built around two experienced junior linebackers, Ike Kelley and Tom Bugel. Arnie Chonko returned in the defensive backfield. Bob Funk was Ohio State's new placekicker, replacing Dick VanRaaphorst who had been very effective the last three seasons.

Offense and Defense Sparkle in Opener

The Buckeyes opened at home September 26 with an explosive 27-8 win over coach Hayden Fry's Southern Methodist Mustangs. Two of the three touchdowns came on long plays, as OSU scored in each quarter. Behind some crisp blocking, Barrington circled right

1963				
September 28	Texas A & M	W	17	0
October 5	at Indiana	W	21	0
October 12	Illinois (HC)	T	20	20
October 19	At Southern Cal	L	3	32
October 26	at Wisconsin	W	13	10
November 2	Iowa	W	7	3
November 9	Penn State	L	7	10
November 16	Northwestern	L	8	17
November 30	at Michigan	W	14	10
Total Points			110	102

Season Record: 5-3-1
Conference: 2nd Place (Tie)

end and cut back across the middle for a 39-yard touchdown in the first quarter. The scoring drive was set up by Chonko's interception at the OSU 27-yard line. Defensive end and tri-captain Bill Spahr accounted for another score by racing 31 yards with a fumble recovery on the second play after halftime.

Sander pounded 42 yards through a huge hole in the Mustang defense for a fourth quarter TD. Bob Funk added field goals of 39 and 27 yards. Ohio State intercepted three SMU passes and recovered three fumbles. The Mustangs scored the game's last TD late in the final quarter to avoid a shutout.

Chonko Ties Interception Record

Indiana, the second week's opponent, provided a much tougher test in the conference opener. The Buckeyes rode the passing arm of Don Unverferth and the pass defending ability of cornerback Arnie Chonko to hold off the talented Hoosiers, 17-9.

Ohio State led 17-3 after three quarters, but the final period belonged to Indiana. Starting at their own 26-yard line, the Hoosiers moved deep inside Ohio territory before Chonko picked off quarterback Rich Badar's pass at the OSU six-yard line to end the threat. After a short punt gave IU possession at the Buckeyes' 33, Badar quickly engineered a scoring drive to tighten things up at 17-9. The touchdown came on a five-yard pass to Rudolph Keuchenberg. Badar's attempted two-point conversion pass was intercepted by Don Harkins.

Indiana soon again took possession on its own 24-yard line after forcing OSU to punt.

All-American defensive back Arnie Chonko

Badar quickly moved his squad the length of the field, only to be interrupted by Chonko's second interception of the quarter at the goal line. IU again held and soon regained possession at its own 47. Badar directed his team to a first down at the OSU three-yard line—a touchdown and two-point conversion would tie the game. But there again was Arnie Chonko, intercepting a pass thrown into the flat with just 14 seconds remaining.

Very few of the Ohio Stadium crowd of 81,834 left early. They had witnessed one of the wildest finishes ever between Ohio State and Indiana. Chonko, whose three interceptions tied an Ohio State single-game record, was awarded the game ball. Indiana outgained the Buckeyes in first downs, 18-16, and in total offensive yards, 322-289. The Hoosiers ran 42 plays in the second half to only 26 for Ohio State, attesting to the pressure IU applied to the Bucks' defense.

Perfect Performance!

The Buckeyes' first road game October 10 at Illinois was the nation's top attraction that weekend. The fourth-ranked Buckeyes were six-point underdogs to the second-ranked defending Big Ten champions, whose returning starters included linebacker Dick Butkus and fullback Jim Grabowski. With almost perfect coordination between its vibrant offense and conquering defense, Ohio State shut out the Illini, 26-0, before a stunned Homecoming throng of

71,227. At the time, it was the largest crowd to ever see a Big Ten conference game at Memorial Stadium.

Ohio State scored on its very first play from scrimmage, with quarterback Don Unverferth bootlegging 24 yards on an option play around his own left end. The touchdown was set up when defensive back John Fill returned his first collegiate interception 47 yards to the Illini 24-yard line.

In the second period, fullback Will Sander plunged over from the one to cap an 84-yard march. The drive's big gainer was a 49-yard completion from Unverferth to end Bob Stock on first down from the OSU 16. Later in the quarter, Bob Funk connected on a 29-yard field goal to increase the lead to 16-0 at halftime.

In the third period, Sander's four-yard touchdown plunge increased the lead to 23-0. The score was set up when end Bill Spahr intercepted quarterback Fred Custardo's pass at the Illini 35. Funk's second field goal of the game in the fourth quarter concluded the scoring at 26-0.

Seldom has an Ohio State team been as well prepared to play. A devastating pass rush, led by Spahr, tackle Ed Orazen, guard Bill Ridder, and linebacker Ike Kelley, kept Custardo off balance all afternoon. Hayes' diversified offense tied together his custom-

Tackle Ed Orazen, team MVP

Michigan in 1948, labeled the Buckeyes "as good as any Ohio State team I've ever seen." Woody Hayes was now seven-for-seven against the Illini in games played at Champaign.

Bucks Pull Out Stops To Smash Illini, 26-0

Columbus Dispatch, Sunday, October 11, 1964

ary rushing attack with a more varied passing attack. OSU even used two tackle-eligible plays, with Jim Davidson catching two passes for 37 yards.

Illinois never moved beyond the Ohio State 31-yard line. Coach Pete Elliott, who had been an All-American quarterback at

Sweet Revenge!

Back at Ohio Stadium the following week, second-ranked Ohio State blanked Southern California, 17-0, to hand the Trojans their first shutout in 29 games. The win helped alleviate some of the humiliation suffered with USC's 32-3 win in Los Angeles the previous year.

Sander's two-yard scoring plunge off right tackle completed a 16-play 63-yard march in the first period. Right before halftime, Don Unverferth passed ten yards to end Greg Laskutka to go up 14-0 at intermission. Unverferth's toss was set up by end Tom Kiehfuss's recovery of tailback Mike Garrett's fumble at the USC 10-yard line. Bob Funk connected on a 24-yard field goal in the final quarter.

The Buckeyes ran 84 plays from scrimmage compared with 55 for USC. Their swarming defense held Southern Cal's famed "student body" ground attack to a mere 64 yards, while forcing five turnovers. The following Monday Ohio State was elevated to the nation's No. 1 spot.

Homecoming fans the following Saturday enjoyed ideal October weather and another excellent showing by the Buckeyes on both sides of the ball. Before a crowd of 84,365, at the time the third largest ever at Ohio Stadium, OSU defeated Wisconsin, 28-3, and extended its streak of not giving up a touchdown to three games. OSU scored twice in both the first and fourth quarters, led in first downs, 29-10, and outgained the Badgers, 408 yards to 188. The impressive Bucks were 5-0 for the first time since 1954, and Woody Hayes was now 11-1-2 against Wisconsin over his first 14 seasons.

Iowa City Is Never Easy

Next it was off to Iowa City, where Woody Hayes' teams had won only one of five previous games against the Hawkeyes at Kinnick Stadium. The Buckeyes were fortunate to escape with a 21-19 win after being outgained 315 yards to 189. Ohio State's first score came just 41 seconds into the game, when Steve Dreffer intercepted quarterback Gary Snook's first pass of the afternoon and raced 36 yards for the touchdown.

The Buckeyes led 21-13 late in the final period, but the Hawkeyes refused to fold. Taking possession at its own 33 with 3:42 remaining, Iowa

Ted Andrick (61) clears the way for Tom Barrington (25) in Ohio State's Homecoming win over Wisconsin.

put together a 67-yard scoring drive climaxed by halfback Craig Nourse's one-yard scoring plunge with just two seconds remaining. Snook attempted a naked reverse around left end for the potential two-point conversion to tie, but Ike Kelley stopped the quarterback just six inches short of the Ohio State goal line to preserve the win. It had been an extremely physical game, and in the end it was the Buckeye defense which made the difference.

Penn State Does It Again— Only Much Worse This time

Ohio State returned home November 7 for a non-conference encounter with Penn State. That same afternoon Purdue suffered its first loss of the season at Michigan State (21-7), to leave the Buckeyes in sole possession of first place in the Big Ten chase.

Normally that would have been cause for jubilant celebration. But while the Spartans were handling the Boilermakers, the Nittany Lions administered one of the most humiliating losses ever suffered by an Ohio State squad. It's doubtful if a team ever slipped into first place in the Big Ten standings on a lower note.

The No. 2 ranked Buckeyes entered the Dad's Day game at 6-0, while Penn State was 3-4. OSU had given up only 39 points in its first six games. The Nittany Lions scored in each quarter to win, 27-0, handing the confused Buckeyes their first shutout in 45 games. Ohio State obtained its initial first down in the third period on a penalty, and finally crossed the midfield stripe late in the final quarter. At the time it was the widest margin of defeat for a Woody Hayes-coached team in Ohio Stadium. The loss shattered Ohio State's winning streak at seven.

Penn State's rushing attack was led by fullback Tom Urbanik with 79 yards. Urbanik's younger brother, Bill, would later become a fine defensive tackle on Ohio State's national title team of 1968.

Coach Rip Engle said he never had a team play a more perfect game. Hayes described the afternoon as the soundest trouncing ever registered against one of his teams. In the first half, the Buckeyes ran only 16 offensive plays for a minus-14 yards of total offense. Penn State led in first downs, 22 to 5, and in total offensive yards, 349 to 63.

Ohio State rebounded with a 10-0 win at home over Northwestern, its first over the Wildcats in three seasons. Will Sander scored the game's only six-pointer from five yards out in the first quarter. The drive was kept alive with a fourth-down fake punt play at the Northwestern 33-yard line. Steve Dreffer was in punt formation, but the ball was centered to blocker Doug Drenik who rocketed straight ahead for five yards and a first down at the Northwestern 28-yard line. Bob Funk delivered a 37-yard field goal shortly before halftime. The stage was now set for Ohio State and Michigan to settle the league title in the season finale.

All-American tackle Jim Davidson

Frigid Finish

Michigan broke a four-game losing streak to the Buckeyes and claimed its first Big Ten title in 14 seasons, with a 10-0 shut-

There's Always a Way

The late Roger Stanton, publisher of the *Football News*, remembered the 1964 Ohio State-Michigan game as the coldest day of his 40-plus years of covering football games. "The Ohio Stadium press box was so cold that the copying machine wouldn't work," he said, "and the staff had no way of providing game statistics for the sportswriters. Finally a resourceful individual poured some vodka into the machine's gears. The 'lubricant' got it going, and the machine hummed along reasonably well the remainder of the afternoon."

Woody and "That Team Up North"

Michigan won only one Big Ten title —1964—during Woody Hayes' first 18 seasons from 1951 through 1968. The Wolverines' record would change radically after Bo Schembechler's arrival in 1969.

Ohio's "Other Team" Goes West

Michigan shut out Ohio State, 10-0, to emerge as the 1964 outright Big Ten champion and representative to the Rose Bowl. Not surprisingly, all four of Ohio State's offensive backs that afternoon were from Ohio—quarterback Don Unverferth of Dayton, fullback Will Sander of Cincinnati, and halfbacks Bo Rein and Tom Barrington of Niles and Lima.

Ironically, Michigan's entire offensive backfield was also from Ohio. All-American quarterback Bob Timberlake hailed from Franklin and halfback Jim Detwiler, who scored the game's only touchdown on a pass from Timberlake, was from Toledo. Fullback Mel Anthony and halfback Carl Ward were both from Cincinnati.

Ohio's "other team" represented the Big Ten well in the January 1, 1965, Rose Bowl, defeating Oregon State, 34-7.

out at Ohio Stadium. It was a bitterly cold afternoon in Columbus, with severe winds whipping throughout the horseshoe and the temperature hovering near 20 degrees.

The frigid weather definitely affected both offenses. Ohio State could muster just 10 first downs, Michigan only nine. The Buckeyes put together a mere 180 yards in total offense, the Wolverines netted just 160.

Ohio State finished the 1964 season at 5-1 in conference action compared with Michigan's 6-1. The Buckeyes were denied a share of the Big Ten title for the second straight season by playing one less conference game. Michigan and Ohio State both finished in the Associated Press top ten for the first time in 15 years, with the Wolverines fourth and the Buckeyes ninth.

After an impressive start, Ohio State finished the 1964 campaign on the downswing. The Buckeyes outscored their first six opponents, 136-39, but were outscored 37-10 in the season's final three games. Jim Davidson, Ike Kelley, and Arnie Chonko were chosen as All-American, and tackle Ed Orazen was named team MVP. Chonko also was a recipient of a National Football Foundation scholarship, which is based upon combined excellence in both athletics and academics.

Ohio State played seven home games for just the second time since Ohio Stadium was dedicated in 1922 (1942 was the other year). The season's home attendance of 583,740 marked the first year it exceeded the half-million mark.

1964

September 26	Southern Methodist	W	27	8
October 3	Indiana	W	17	9
October 10	at Illinois	W	26	0
October 17	Southern California	W	17	0
October 24	Wisconsin (HC)	W	28	3
October 31	at Iowa	W	21	19
November 7	Penn State	L	0	27
November 14	Northwestern	W	10	0
November 21	Michigan	L	0	10
Total Points			146	76

Season Record: 7-2
Conference: 2nd Place

1965

Ohio State's 1965 season was somewhat opposite of 1964. The Buckeyes started slowly, winning just two of their first four, then finished strongly with five straight victories. The squad of just 56 players was the smallest in number of any Ohio State team since 1945. Returnees included the entire offensive backfield of Unverferth, Barrington, Sander, and Rein, linebackers Kelley and Bugel, and placekicker Bob Funk.

Among the experienced linemen were guard Ted Andrick, tackles Bill Ridder and Dick Anderson, and end Greg Lashutka. Ray Pryor shifted from guard to center, and adaptable Doug Van Horn played guard and tackle on both offense and defense.

Nine Game Schedule Contributes to Opening Loss

Ohio State was the only Big Ten school still playing just a nine game schedule (in '65 all other conference teams began playing 10), and it showed in a 14-3 season opening loss to North Carolina on September 25. The Tar Heels had lost 31-24 to Michigan at Chapel Hill the previous Saturday, but the experience of having already played a game was evident when they entered Ohio Stadium.

The Buckeyes squandered four scoring opportunities and could not figure out how to control UNC's "absorbing defense," which held OSU to just 65 yards on the ground. Unverferth connected on 19 passes for 178 yards, but his squad was simply unable to sustain any scoring efforts. It was OSU's first opening game loss in eight seasons.

The Buckeyes next ventured to Seattle for a nationally televised contest with Washington. The Huskies led early, but the Ohio State offense finally came to life with two scores on short runs by Sander and Barrington to lead 14-13 at halftime. Sophomore Arnie Fontes saw considerable playing time at quarterback. The teams traded touchdowns in the third quarter, but Washington regained the lead 21-20 with a successful two-point conversion pass from quarterback Tod Hullin to end Bruce Kramer.

It appeared that's how the game might end before Ohio State put together one last drive, moving the ball to the Washington 10-yard line with just 59 seconds remaining. Bob Funk came through with a 27-yard field goal, and the Buckeyes had won a real thriller, 23-21.

Fortunately for Ohio State, Washington had just missed a 23-yard field goal attempt prior to the Buckeyes' winning possession. Funk was especially elated with the win, since it first appeared that his missed extra point after OSU's third touchdown might leave his team with a single point loss.

Finally—Two in a Row

The Buckeyes returned home October 9 for a rain-spattered Big Ten opener against Illinois. After the Illini took an early 7-0 lead, OSU exploded for 21 second-quarter points en route to a 28-14 victory which was more convincing than the final score. Running primarily from the fullback position, Barrington had his biggest day as a Buckeye with 179 yards in 32 carries and three of the four touchdowns (on runs of 12, 2, and 1 yards).

Fontes started the game at quarterback, but gave way to Unverferth after being unable to move the team in the first period. This win marked OSU's first back-to-back victories since the fifth and sixth games of 1964 against Wisconsin and Iowa.

A featured halftime attraction was the return to campus of William A. Dougherty, a retired attorney who composed "Across the Field" as an OSU junior in 1915. He used a piano placed at midfield to thrill the crowd with a rousing chorus of his creation. Dougherty's spirited march was first played at the Ohio State-Illinois game 50 years earlier.

Woody Hayes with Ohio State's 1965 Co-Captains, end Greg Lashutka (left) and two-time All-American linebacker Ike Kelley.

Spartans Simply Too Talented

Ohio State was back on the road the next two weeks with games at Michigan State and Wisconsin. Michigan State fielded one of the strongest teams in Big Ten history this season. Coach Duffy Daugherty's Spartans were led by defensive end Bubba Smith, linebacker George Webster, halfback Clint Jones, and receiver Gene Washington.

Michigan State dealt the Buckeyes one of the most one-sided setbacks during Woody Hayes' career, winning 32-7 while holding Ohio State to minus 22 yards rushing. MSU rolled up 538 yards of total offense. Interestingly, the burly Spartans had held Michigan to minus 51 yards on the ground during a 24-7 win at Ann Arbor the previous Saturday.

MSU led 7-0 at halftime on a spectacular 80-yard sprint by right halfback Clinton

Jones on the game's second play from scrimmage. Jones, an ex-Ohio high school hurdles champion from Cleveland, raced to his right, then reversed his field for his scoring gallop around his own left end. In the final quarter, Don Unverferth passed 36 yards to Arnie Fontes for the Buckeyes' lone touchdown. Fontes, normally a quarterback, had been inserted into the offense at split end. He broke behind the MSU secondary and went in untouched for the score.

Michigan State's October 16 win over Ohio State ultimately decided the '65 Big Ten title. This was OSU's only conference loss—the Spartans finished 7-0 in league play and Woody Hayes' team finished alone in second place at 6-1.

Ohio State enjoyed a much more pleasant stay at Madison, where they upended Wisconsin, 20-10, before a homecoming crowd of 65,269. The Buckeyes looked anything but spectacular on this cloudy overcast afternoon, and the Badgers had the better of the statistics—18 to 11 in first downs and 229 to 199

All-American Doug Van Horn played guard and tackle on both offense and defense.

Celebrity Support

Comedian Bob Hope, a native of Cleveland, was on hand to help cheer Ohio State to its 20-10 win over the Badgers. Hope was performing in Madison as part of Wisconsin's homecoming activities.

in total offensive yards. But Ohio State found a way to win. This victory perpetuated one of the Big Ten's most one-sided rivalries. Woody Hayes now had a personal coaching record of 12-1-2 against Wisconsin.

The Badgers scored first on Gary Pinnow's 35-yard first-quarter field goal. It marked the fifth straight week Ohio State had spotted its opponent an early lead. OSU scored 17 of its points in the second quarter with two short plunges by Sander and Funk's 19-yard field goal. Funk also connected on a 44-yarder in the final period. The Badgers became their own worst enemy with five turnovers.

OSU was now 3-2 on the season and 2-1 in conference play. Michigan State remained undefeated, but had to rally from a 10-0 halftime deficit at Purdue to defeat the Boilermakers, 14-10, with two fourth-quarter touchdowns.

First Encounter with Golden Gophers in 15 Seasons

Ohio State and Minnesota were virtually strangers when the two faced each other October 30 before an Ohio Stadium homecoming crowd of 84,359. The two had not met since the Buckeyes won 48-0 at Minneapolis during coach Wes Fesler's last season at Ohio State in 1950. The tension-filled afternoon was highlighted by a "fake kick" and a "real kick."

OSU won a cliff-hanger, 11-10, when Bob Funk booted an 18-yard field goal with only a minute and 17 seconds remaining. Fortunately for Buckeye fans, Minnesota missed a field goal from the OSU 15-yard line in the game's final 17 seconds.

The game's real surprise and eventual margin of victory came in the second quarter, on a play that was very uncharacteristic of Woody Hayes' offense. Ohio State scored its lone touchdown on a 25-yard pass from Don Unverferth to halfback Nelson Adderly. OSU then lined up at the Stadium's north end for Funk to apparently kick the extra point. The ball was centered to holder Len Fontes, but Fontes fooled everyone (except his teammates) by bootlegging the ball around his own right end for a very unexpected two-point conversion.

Halfback Bo Rein missed the entire game with an illness. Ohio State emerged with the only single-point victory in the Ohio State-Minnesota series. The win gave the Buckeyes a record of 4-2 after six games.

The following week's home encounter with Indiana was almost as

OSU Tops Gophers By 11-10

Columbus Dispatch
Sunday, October 31, 1965

Eagle Eye

A prankster apparently sneaked into Ohio Stadium the Friday evening before the Minnesota game and strung fine nylon fishing line between the uprights of the north goal post. Fortunately Stadium Superintendent Ralph Guarasci noticed the mesh glistening in the sun Saturday morning, and had it removed. It was through this goal that Bob Funk's fourth-quarter field goal lifted OSU to an 11-10 victory.

important TD from two yards out on the 12th play of a 64-yard drive.

IU dominated the first half, running 45 plays to a mere 20 for the Buckeyes. On a sad note, senior linebacker Tom Bugel suffered a broken ankle that ended his fine career at Ohio State.

Another of Woody's Boys Makes Good

The 1965 Indiana Hoosiers were guided by first-year coach John Pont, who had been an excellent halfback at Miami of Ohio under Woody Hayes in '49 and '50. Pont was the first athlete in Miami history to have his jersey number (#42) retired. In '67 Pont was selected College Coach of the Year—that season he became the only coach to take Indiana to the Rose bowl.

close. After trailing 10-7 at halftime, Ohio State tied the score on Funk's 26-yard third-quarter field goal, then posted the winning touchdown late in the final period to squeeze out a 17-10 victory. Sander scored the all-

The Dad's Day home finale November 13 was a much different story. The Buckeyes walloped Iowa, 38-0, with their largest offensive output in their last 33 games. It also was the Hawkeyes' most one-sided conference setback since losing to OSU in 1950, 83-21.

Barrington and Sander, who were playing their final game at Ohio Stadium, combined for 198 yards rushing and four of the squad's five touchdowns. Unverferth connected on 12 of 19 passes for 99 yards, including a 22-yard strike to Bo Rein for his squad's other six-pointer. Bob Funk added a 26-yard field goal in the second period.

Ohio State led in first downs, 21-13, and in total offensive yards, 349-220. Defensive coordinator Lou McCullough was very pleased with his unit's performance, and offered special praise for linebackers Ike Kelley and John McCoy, end Jim Baas, tackle Dick Himes, and safety Tom Portsmouth.

Fullback
Will Sander

Funk Comes Through Again

With nothing on the line but pride for either team, Ohio State topped Michigan, 9-7, for its fifth win over the Wolverines in the last six seasons. Before a crowd of 77,733 at Ann Arbor, Michigan came out on top in just about every category except the final score. The Wolverines advanced inside the OSU 20-yard line four times without scoring. Ohio State crossed the 50-yard line only three times all afternoon, yet scored twice for the two-point victory.

The Buckeyes drove 76 yards and scored early in the first quarter on a five-yard toss from Don Unverferth to Bill Anders. Bob Funk missed the conversion and the score remained 6-0. Late in the second period Michigan defender Mike Bass returned an

Sweet Sound of Victory Missing

The sound of the Victory Bell was conspicuously absent following Ohio State's 38-0 triumph over Iowa in the last home game of 1965—the bell's clapper had been stolen. Some students did their best by hitting the bell with a hammer, but the sound was too faint to be heard outside the stadium tower. The following week, the clapper was discovered hanging from a rope around the William Oxley Thompson statue in front of the Main Library.

Cutting It Close

Ohio State's 1965 record was 7-2, but without the talents of placekicker Bob Funk, the record might have been 4-5. Three of Funk's eight field goals that season meant the difference between victory and defeat:

- A 27-yard field goal with just 59 seconds remaining earned Ohio State a 23-21 victory at Washington.
- An 18-yard field goal with 1:17 left gave the Buckeyes an 11-10 homecoming win over Minnesota.
- At Michigan, his 28-yard field goal with 1:15 remaining lifted Ohio State over the Wolverines, 9-7.

1965

September 25	North Carolina	L	3	14
October 2	at Washington	W	23	21
October 9	Illinois	W	28	14
October 16	at Michigan State	L	7	32
October 23	at Wisconsin	W	20	10
October 30	Minnesota (HC)	W	11	10
November 6	Indiana	W	17	10
November 13	Iowa	W	38	0
November 20	at Michigan	W	9	7
Total Points			156	118

Season Record: 7-2
Conference: 2nd Place

1966

interception to the OSU 15-yard line. Four straight carries by fullback Dave Fisher provided UM its only touchdown of the afternoon, and Rick Sygar's extra point made it 7-6.

The Buckeyes' struggling offensive unit finally put together a sustained drive late in the final period. Starting at its own nine with just 7:30 remaining, Ohio State drove to a fourth down at the Michigan 11-yard line. With Arnold Fontes holding from a slight angle to the right, Funk slammed a 28-yard field goal with just 1:15 on the clock to secure the two-point victory. A key play was Will Sander's carry for a first down early in the drive on a fourth-and-two at the OSU 16.

The Buckeyes finished at 7-2 for the second straight season. Ike Kelley and Doug Van Horn were chosen as All-Americans and Van Horn was voted the team's MVP. Middle guard Bill Ridder was selected an Academic All-American, and Woody Hayes had concluded his 15th season in Columbus with an overall record of 97-33-7.

A reasonable number of veterans returned in 1966, but sophomores would have to come through at some key vacated positions if Ohio State was to challenge for the Big Ten title. This was especially true at quarterback where sophomores Bill Long and Gary Ehrsam would see most of the action.

Woody Hayes and his staff made a key strategic change in their recruiting this fall. This decision would have no impact on 1966 but would produce dramatic changes in the years ahead. The bulk of Hayes' recruiting had always been within Ohio, since some of the nation's finest high school football takes place within the Buckeye state.

After the Ohio State Faculty Council voted "no" on the Rose Bowl following the 1961 season, other schools immediately intensified their recruiting efforts within Ohio. Opposing coaches successfully convinced many prospects that Ohio State was de-emphasizing football. With a higher proportion of the Ohio high school talent now leaving

Fullback Paul Hudson powers for yardage in season-opening victory over Texas Christian.

the state, Hayes and his staff began recruiting more heavily in other areas of the country. This major shift would produce noteworthy results in just two seasons.

Less-Than-Spectacular Opener

The Buckeyes opened at home September 24 with an unimpressive 14-7 win over Texas Christian. The victory came despite five lost fumbles that contributed to the tension-packed afternoon. Two bright spots were the play of Paul Hudson and Bill Long. Hudson, a senior, gained 92 yards and scored both Buckeye touchdowns in his first start at fullback. Long began his OSU career completing 12 of 14 passes for 106 yards.

The most spectacular play of the afternoon wound up as the first of OSU's five lost fumbles. Senior halfback Will Thomas ran back the opening kickoff 91 yards, and ap-

peared to be ready to score the season's first touchdown. But the speedster from Lima broke stride inside the TCU 10-yard line, faltered slightly, and was caught from behind. His fumble was recovered by the Horned Frogs at the two.

The Buckeyes were far less fortunate the following weekend. Washington devastated the Buckeye defense with a surprisingly easy 38-22 triumph in Columbus. The Huskies built up a 21-0 lead before Long scored OSU's first points on a fourth-down one-yard keeper in the fading moments of the second period.

Washington's 38 points were the most scored against the Buckeyes since Illinois' 41 in 1953. Led by halfback Don Moore's 221 yards, the Huskies rushed for 413 compared with OSU's 34. Long's 228 yards passing was one bright spot for Ohio State, but it was not enough to counter Washington's impressive showing.

Woody's Only Loss at Champaign

Despite three field goals by placekicker Gary Cairns, Ohio State lost a heartbreaker at Illinois the following week, 10-9. It was the Buckeyes' first single-point loss since bowing to Penn State, 7-6, ten years earlier in '56. Cairns' second field goal of 55 yards was (at the time) a Big Ten record, eclipsing a 50-yarder by Indiana's Tom Nowatzke against Ohio State in 1964.

Late in the final period the Illini put together their only sustained drive of the afternoon, moving 74 yards for the game's only touchdown. Quarterback Bob Naponic sneaked across from the one, and Jim Stotz's all-important extra point was the difference. Particularly frustrating for the Buckeyes was a 41-yard slant pass play from Naponic to receiver Johnny Wright which kept the drive moving—it came on a second-and-30 after Illinois had been penalized on two successive downs. This was Woody Hayes' only loss during the 14 games he would coach at Illinois' Memorial Stadium.

Season's Best Showing

Back at rain-soaked Ohio Stadium October 15, the Buckeyes nearly pulled off the season's biggest upset before bowing to No. 1 ranked Michigan State, 11-8. The wet weather played a major role in causing a total of ten fumbles during the afternoon. Although considerably outmanned, the Buckeyes gave the Spartans their strongest challenge of the season.

Ohio State took a 2-0 lead into the dressing room at halftime, after a snap from center sailed far over Spartan punter Dick Kenney's head and rolled out of the end zone for a safety. Michigan State took its first lead, 3-2, on Kenney's 27-yard field goal midway through

October 15, 1966

the third quarter. The Buckeyes regained the lead, 8-3, on the first play of the fourth quarter, using a perfectly-executed 47-yard pass from Bill Long to end Bill Anders.

But the Spartans pulled it out at the end, driving 84 yards in the game's closing minutes. Fullback Bob Apisa scored MSU's only touchdown on a fourth-down carry from inside the OSU one-yard line. The Buckeyes were now 1-3 on the year, and this defeat marked the only time in Woody Hayes' 28 campaigns that Ohio State would lose three consecutive games in one season.

The Buckeyes finally returned to the victory column with a 24-13 homecoming win over Wisconsin. Trailing 13-10 after three quarters of play, Ohio State engineered impressive touchdown marches of 63 and 81 yards to snap their losing streak at three. It was

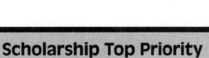

Scholarship Top Priority

For three consecutive years, one of Woody Hayes' former players finished first in the Ohio State College of Medicine's freshman class—Arnie Chonko in '66, Don Unverferth in '67, and John Darbyshire in '68.

a much needed win—OSU had not lost four consecutive games since 1943.

Fullback Paul Hudson tallied all three touchdowns on short plunges, halfback Bo Rein led all runners with 109 yards, and Bill Long completed 14 passes for 154 yards. It was Ohio State's seventh consecutive win over the Badgers.

First Trip to Minneapolis in Sixteen Seasons

Underdog Minnesota, after being humiliated 49-0 at Michigan the previous week, up-ended Ohio State, 17-7. It was the Buckeyes' first trip to Minneapolis since defeating the Golden Gophers 48-0 at Memorial Stadium in 1950. OSU's only touchdown resulted from a 10-yard throw from Long to Rein in the final period.

Ohio State was its own worst enemy when it squandered two golden scoring opportunities with turnovers inside the Minnesota five-yard line. A dejected Woody Hayes spent just 20 seconds with newsmen at his post-game press conference, before retreating back to the team dressing room to contemplate his squad's showing. The defeat pushed the season's record to 2-4.

Woody Hits The Century Mark

Ohio State returned home November 5 for a 7-0 Dad's Day win over Indiana. The offenses were no more exciting than the overcast rainy weather, as the two teams combined for just 475 yards of total offense. This was Woody Hayes' 100th win at Ohio State. His record since coming to Columbus in 1951 now stood at 100-37-7. Simply getting back into the victory column was undoubtedly

more important to Hayes than the personal achievement, since his squad had lost four of its previous five outings.

The Buckeyes drove 59 yards following the second-half kickoff for the game's only touchdown. Interestingly, the drive stalled at the IU 21-yard line and Gary Cairns kicked a 38-yard field goal. But the Hoosiers were called for defensive holding, so OSU elected to take the three points off the board and retain possession at the IU 11-yard line. After Hudson gained three, Long passed

All-American center Ray Pryor

OHIO STATE vs. INDIANA, NOV. 11

WESTERN CONFERENCE CHAMPIONSHIP
1916
NORTHWESTERN
OHIO STATE
NOVEMBER 25

OHIO STATE vs. CINCINNATI
Season 1919

I O
Homecoming Program
Price 25 Cents
NOVEMBER 22, 1919

ILLINOIS vs OHIO STATE
SAT. NOV. 19   2 P.M.

California vs Ohio State
ROSE BOWL
1950
Price Fifty Cents

FOOTBALL CENTENNIAL
55TH ROSE BOWL
OHIO STATE vs. SOUTHERN CAL
PASADENA, JANUARY 1, 1969   OFFICIAL PROGRAM $1
A TRIBUTE TO ONE HUNDRED YEARS OF COLLEGE

OFFICIAL PROGRAM
Rose Bowl
JANUARY 1, 1958
PASADENA, CALIF.
50¢
OHIO STATE UNIVERSITY
vs.
UNIVERSITY OF OREGON

OBERLIN vs OHIO STATE
THE OHIO STADIUM
Main Entrance
Ohio Field, October 8, 1921

SOUVENIR DEDICATION PROGRAM
MICHIGAN versus OHIO STATE

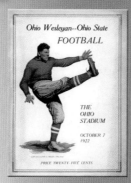

Ohio Wesleyan--Ohio State
FOOTBALL
THE OHIO STADIUM
OCTOBER 7 1922
PRICE TWENTY-FIVE CENTS

MICHIGAN OHIO STATE
OHIO STADIUM
NOVEMBER 15 1924

ILLINOIS OHIO STATE
OHIO STADIUM
NOVEMBER 21 1925
35¢

MICHIGAN OHIO STATE
OHIO STADIUM
NOVEMBER 15-26
HOMECOMING
50¢

CHICAGO OHIO STATE
OCT. 29 1927
25¢

DENISON OHIO STATE

IOWA
OHIO STATE
October 12, 1929 · 25cents

INDIANA
October 4, 1930
OHIO STATE
The Stadium
25¢

1949 Team, 50th Reunion
Rose Bowl Champions

Woody Hayes and the 1978 Buckeyes

Earle Bruce and the 1986 Buckeyes

The Pride of the Buckeyes

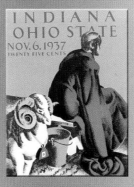

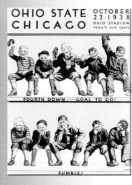

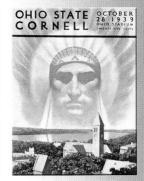

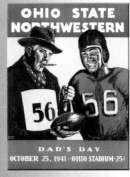

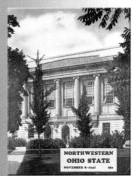

eight yards in the flat to Rein for the six-pointer. Cairns converted with 9:39 remaining in the third period.

At Iowa City the next week, Ohio State evened its season record at 4-4 with a suspenseful 14-10 victory over the Hawkeyes. This was OSU's fourth straight win over Iowa, but it was anything but easy. Two excellent defensive stands allowed the Buckeyes to escape with the four-point victory.

Under the direction of promising sophomore quarterback Ed Podolak, the Hawks drove 61 yards to a first down at the OSU nine with 5:20 remaining. Each of Podolak's first two passes appeared to score what would have been the winning touchdown, but both were dropped in the end zone. His third throw was too high, and sophomore linebacker Mark Stier intercepted his fourth-down toss at the OSU two-yard line to end the suspense with 1:01 on the clock. Earlier the Buckeye defense had held the Hawkeyes on four successive downs inside the Ohio State three.

Strictly for Pride

For the second consecutive year, Ohio State and Michigan squared off strictly for bragging rights. The Buckeyes entered the

game with a record of 4-4, the Wolverines were 5-4. Michigan State had already secured its second straight outright league title, but could not return to Pasadena because of the Big Ten's "no-repeat" policy. Purdue was already assured of second place and its first trip to the Rose Bowl (the Boilermakers defeated Southern California, 14-13, on January 2, 1967).

Michigan dominated early with three drives inside the Ohio State 20-yard line, but came away only with Rick Sygar's 24-yard field goal to lead 3-0 after one quarter. Gary Cairns' 26-yard field goal early in the second period tied the game at 3-3, but that would be as close to the Michigan end zone as the Buckeyes would advance all afternoon.

End Billy Anders

Leading Pass Receiver Did Not Play During High School

Ohio State's leading pass receiver in 1966 and 1967 was end Billy Anders of Sabina. He caught 108 catches for 1,318 yards and six touchdowns during his college career. Since his high school had been too small to field a football team, Anders never had the opportunity to play the game until his days at Ohio State. He and defensive halfback Sam Elliott were the Buckeyes' 1967 co-captains.

The Wolverines scored touchdowns in the second and third periods to win, 17-3. Ohio State was stopped twice on downs inside the Michigan 20 in the final quarter. Halfback Jim Detwiler led the Wolverines rushing attack with 140 yards on 20 carries.

The Buckeyes finished 1966 with an overall record of 4-5. It was the second and final of two losing seasons during Woody Hayes' 28 years at Ohio State (OSU was 3-5-1 in 1959). Center Ray Pryor was selected All-American and was chosen the team's MVP.

Ohio State had not captured a Big Ten title in the last five years, and Woody Hayes' critics were becoming a little more vocal. Some felt it was time for a change. But better times were just ahead, and the following fall would become a "transition period" leading to some of Ohio State's finest seasons.

Lucky Buckeye

Ohio State fans Bill and June Kuhn of Bucyrus carry Buckeyes, gathered from a special tree, to each home game. One evening in 1967, Woody Hayes spoke at the OSU Mansfield Campus where June was a student. She remembers the effectiveness of Hayes' talk, which stressed desire and dedication, and she was thrilled to receive a small Buckeye tree from the coach as a token of friendship and pride.

"That was one of the most significant evenings in my life," she recalls. "Woody Hayes gave us the encouragement and confidence to reach our goals." The Kuhns proudly planted the tree; it's been providing Buckeyes ever since.

1966

September 24	Texas Christian	W	14	7
October 1	Washington	L	22	38
October 8	at Illinois	L	9	10
October 15	Michigan State	L	8	11
October 22	Wisconsin (HC)	W	24	13
October 29	at Minnesota	L	7	17
November 5	Indiana	W	7	0
November 12	at Iowa	W	14	10
November 19	Michigan	L	3	17
Total Points			**108**	**123**

Season Record: 4-5
Conference: 6th Place

1967

The 1967 season was much like 1965 in that the Buckeyes started slowly, but finished on the upswing. They won just two of their first five, then finished strongly with four straight victories. Bill Long returned for his junior year at quarterback and was joined by senior halfback Rudy Hubbard. The other ballcarriers who saw substantial playing time were all sophomores—fullbacks Jim Otis and Paul Huff and halfbacks Dave Brungard and Ray Gillian. Seniors Jim Nein, Sam Elliott, and Tom Portsmouth all returned in the defensive secondary.

The '67 season became known as the "wait-until-next-year" season. Freshmen were not eligible for varsity competition. Word leaked out that the varsity squad was having a tougher struggle during its weekly scrimmages against the '67 freshmen than against most opponents on Saturday afternoon. Fans were already speculating what impact this would have on 1968.

Ohio State opened September 30 with a very embarrassing 14-7 loss to the visiting Arizona Wildcats. It was just the ninth season-opening loss in the first 78 years of Ohio State football.

The Buckeyes scored first to take a 7-0 first-quarter lead. Woody Hayes reached into his files for a play which became legal the previous season, when the rules were changed to allow the quarterback to be an eligible receiver. With the ball at the Arizona 7-yard line, halfback Dave Brungard took a pitchout from quarterback Jerry Ehrsam and headed to his right as if to run an end sweep. Brungard suddenly stopped and passed back to Ehrsam, who had slipped to his left unnoticed and into the end zone for the touchdown after receiving Brungard's pass.

Down 7-0 after one quarter, the Wildcats came back with two touchdowns, a one-yard burst by Wayne Edmonds and a nine-yard sweep by Bruce Lee, to stun the highly favored Buckeyes. There was at least one bright spot for Ohio State. Sophomore defensive back Ted Provost had two interceptions in his first varsity game.

Arizona (now a member of the Pacific Ten Conference) belonged to the Western Athletic Conference in 1967. This was the very first time a member of the Western Athletic Conference had defeated a Big Ten team.

Ohio State rebounded with a vengeance the following week by scoring in each quarter to whip the Oregon Ducks, 30-0. It became a rather unpleasant afternoon for Oregon who was dedicating its new Autzen Stadium. Hayes put a lot more variety into his offense, using reverses, draw plays, and quarterback keepers to supplement his traditional fullback attack. OSU led in first downs, 25-8; rushing yards, 279-106; and passing yards, 103-47.

The Ducks threw four interceptions, with the first two leading to Ohio State's first two touchdowns. Huff scored twice and Otis and Hubbard each entered the end zone once. Gary Cairns booted a 35-yard field goal in the second period.

Thanks, Jack, for Not Making It Worse!

The Buckeyes returned home October 14 for the conference opener against the Rose

---

Woody's Worst

The Buckeye's 35-point loss to Purdue (41-6) was the largest margin of defeat during Woody Hayes' 276 games at Ohio State.

Bowl Champion Purdue Boilermakers. Excitement ran high all week in Ohio as fans felt Ohio State had a reasonable chance to break Purdue's winning streak, which now stretched to eight games over two seasons. How wrong they were.

The Boilermakers romped 41-6, completely overpowering the Buckeyes in every phase of the game. The margin of defeat could have been much worse. After his team built up a 35-0 halftime lead, coach Jack Mollenkopf benched most of his regulars early in the second half. Woody Hayes even thanked him for being so considerate when the two shook hands at midfield following the game.

Purdue grabbed a quick 7-0 lead just 58 seconds into the game. On OSU's third play following the opening kickoff, defender Dennis Cirbes picked off quarterback Jerry Ehrsam's pass in full stride at the OSU 30-yard line and raced down the sideline for the Boilermaker's first of six touchdowns. Sophomore Mike Phipps, who was replacing '66 Big Ten MVP Bob Griese at quarterback, played with the poise of a seasoned professional. Phipps completed 14 of 19 tosses for 210 yards, two touchdowns, and no interceptions, before leaving the game midway through the second half. Purdue led in first downs, 24-16, and in total offensive yards, 470-260.

Fan criticism of Hayes was now becoming much more intense. This was the Buckeyes' second setback in just the season's third game, and their seventh loss in their last 11 over two seasons. Monday morning quarterbacks all over the state were wondering if

the 54-year-old coach, now in his 17th season at Ohio State, had passed his peak—only time would tell!

Ohio State edged Northwestern 6-2 for a much needed win the following Saturday to spoil the Wildcats' homecoming. It seemed to be a game neither team wanted to win, but in the end it was the Buckeyes' defense which made the difference.

After a pretty dull and scoreless first half, OSU made its only sustained drive of the day to score the game's only touchdown. Dave Brungard returned the second-half kickoff to the Wildcat 46-yard line, and nine plays later he scored from the two. Gary Cairns' extra point attempt was blocked, and the Buckeyes led 6-0.

The Wildcats' offense rolled up a lot of yards the rest of the afternoon, but OSU's defense intercepted three second-half passes and twice held Northwestern on downs to protect its slim lead. With his team facing a fourth down at its own 10-yard line with just over a minute to play, Hayes had Ehrsam take a deliberate safety.

Following the game Ohio State received some pleasant news from Minneapolis, where the Minnesota Golden Gophers defeated Michigan State, 21-0. This loss broke the Spartans' conference winning streak at 16, one short of Ohio State's league record of 17 established during the 1954-55-56 seasons.

Fourth Consecutive Loss at Home

Illinois spoiled the Buckeyes' October 28 homecoming, 17-13, after scoring the winning touchdown with less than a minute remaining. It was a bitter setback for OSU whose season record dipped to 2-3. The '67 team now owned the dubious distinction of being the only Ohio State team to have lost its first three home games of the season since Ohio Stadium was dedicated in 1922 (four in a row at home counting the 1966 loss to Michigan).

The Fighting Illini led 10-0 at halftime, but the Buckeyes quickly reduced the lead to 10-6 after receiving the third-quarter kickoff and marching 73 yards for their first score. Halfback Dave Brungard electrified the crowd with a 67-yard scoring dash off right tackle. A two-point conversion pass attempt from Bill Long to Rudy Hubbard was incomplete. A 74-yard drive early in the final period culminated with a 7-yard scoring toss from Long to Bill Anders. Gary Cairns converted and OSU had its first lead of the afternoon, 13-10.

But Illinois saved its best for last. Quarterback Dean Volkman guided his squad 77 yards for the winning TD—a one-yard leap over the line by sophomore Dave Jackson for his second touchdown of the day. It was new Illini coach Jim Valek's first conference victory after losses to Indiana and Minnesota. Ohio State was badly harmed with three lost fumbles and two interceptions.

Hayes's Future in Doubt?

The frustrated 2-3 Buckeyes headed north November 4 for East Lansing to face coach Duffy Daugherty's Michigan State Spartans. The game had no bearing on Big Ten or national rankings, since the Spartans' record was 2-4. Yet, it likely was one of the most significant games during Woody Hayes's career.

touched when his players presented him the game ball.

This desperately-needed victory turned out to be the beginning of the longest winning streak in Ohio State history—22 games. Ironically, this victory was also a significant turning point for Woody Hayes, who would enjoy his greatest success at Ohio State after he turned 55 years old on February 14, 1968. During his last 11 seasons from '68 through '78, Ohio State would capture nine Big Ten titles, two national titles, and tailback Archie Griffin would become the only two-time winner of the coveted Heisman Trophy. Not bad for a coach and staff who midway through the '67 season felt their future was very much in question.

Smallest Gathering in 17 Seasons

The following Saturday, November 11, an Ohio Stadium crowd of just 65,470 sat through a steady rain to see the Buckeyes clip Wisconsin, 17-15. It was the smallest home crowd since the "snow bowl" of November 25, 1950, when the gate was officially announced at 50,503. The game itself was pretty exciting with the lead changing hands four times.

Gary Cairns' 18-yard first-quarter field goal gave OSU its first points. This turned out to be the margin of victory, although the decision was strongly second-guessed at the time. With fourth-and-goal from the Badger

There were rumors Hayes might be replaced after the season. Earle Bruce, then an assistant coach, recalls that Hayes told his staff that he felt all of them would be able to retain their jobs if the Buckeyes could win their final four games and finish the '67 season at 6-3. Otherwise, their coaching future at Ohio State might be somewhat in doubt.

The Buckeyes won, 21-7, before 76,235 surprised homecoming fans at snow-showered Spartan Stadium. Ohio State opened very strongly to lead, 14-0, after one quarter. Bill Long had one of his finest games with nine completions in 11 attempts for 129 yards. Sophomore fullback Paul Huff scored twice and led all runners with 120 yards in 35 carries. The Buckeyes led in first downs, 17-11, and total offensive yards, 337-192. Hayes was very

one, many fans voiced their disapproval of not going for six points.

Bill Long scored OSU's touchdowns on runs of 14 and four yards in the second and fourth periods. The victory bell in the stadium's southeast corner rang for the first time in more than a year (last home victory had been over Indiana, 7-0, on November 5, 1966).

The Buckeyes elevated their victory streak to three with a 21-10 win over Iowa in the November 18 home finale. They used typical Woody Hayes power-and-mistake-free football to score in each period. Jim Otis pulverized the Hawkeye defense with 149 yards in 35 attempts and scored the game's first touchdown.

Bill Long scored from the two shortly before the half, and passed ten yards to Bill Anders for six points on OSU's first possession of the third period. Cairns' 20-yard field goal came just 56 seconds before the final whistle. Iowa gained a lot of yardage in the middle of the field but never advanced beyond the Ohio State 37-yard line in the second half.

Hayes kept reporters waiting almost 45 minutes for his post-game press conference, while he presented the game ball to Lt. General Lewis W. Walt. The two had become close friends during Hayes' recent visits with American troops in Vietnam. Hayes asked Walt to address his team and praised Walt as "a great American hero."

Momentum Building for Next Year

The Buckeyes continued to get stronger each week. They finished the season November 25 with a 24-14 win at Michigan Stadium before a crowd of 64,411. Ohio State scored on its first two possessions, and tallied its third touchdown just seven minutes into the second period. Halfback Rudy Hubbard, playing his final game for the Scarlet and Gray, scored on runs of 22 and 12 yards, and Long accounted for the second-quarter TD with a one-yard sneak. Gary Cairns added a 35-yard

Center John Muhlbach had the distinction of playing at Massillon High School under Earle Bruce and at Ohio State under Woody Hayes. Muhlbach is now a successful insurance executive in Massillon, and also serves as chairman of the Professional Football Hall of Fame's Board of Trustees in Canton.

field goal late in the final period.

Hayes was extremely pleased with the turnover margin—Michigan had four; Ohio State, none. After 17 seasons, his coaching record against Michigan now stood at 11-6, which included wins in six of the last eight meetings.

After losing three of their first five, the '67 Buckeyes won their last four to finish strongly with a record of 6-3. End Bill Anders and tackle Dick Himes were All-Big Ten picks and linebacker Dirk Worden was voted the team's Most Valuable Player.

Ohio State had now gone six seasons without a conference championship, but those close to Woody Hayes sensed that he now was more determined than ever to succeed. Fans were already counting the days until the '68 opener against SMU when the '67 freshmen would finally be eligible for varsity competition—one of the finest periods in the long and glorious history of Ohio State football was just around the corner.

1967

September 30	Arizona	L	7	14
October 7	at Oregon	W	30	0
October 14	Purdue	L	6	41
October 21	at Northwestern	W	6	2
October 28	Illinois (HC)	L	13	17
November 4	at Michigan State	W	21	7
November 11	Wisconsin	W	17	15
November 18	Iowa	W	21	10
November 25	at Michigan	W	24	14
Total Points			**145**	**120**

Season Record: 6-3
Conference: 4th Place

1968

During his early years at Ohio State, Woody Hayes was reluctant to use sophomores in his starting lineups. While addressing the *Columbus Dispatch* Quarterback Club one evening, he stated, "You're bound to lose one game for every sophomore you start, because of their lack of experience." Hayes changed this approach drastically in 1968, when his "super sophomores" led the Buckeyes to an undefeated national title and one of the finest seasons in all of Ohio State football.

OSU's recruiting within its own state was strongly impaired during the early 1960s, after the school's Faculty Council turned down a Rose Bowl invitation in 1961. A lot of the state's good talent was going elsewhere to play, especially with rival recruiters re-

minding them that Ohio State's Faculty Council voted against playing in the Rose Bowl. After working against this competition for three or four years, Hayes and his staff decided to put more emphasis on recruiting out-of-state talent, while still continuing to go after the good Ohio prospects. As a result, their freshman class of 1967 developed into one of the finest and most successful in college football history.

From 1962 through 1967, OSU won 35, lost 18, and tied one. During those six seasons they beat Michigan four of six, but still finished no higher than second in the Big Ten. Ohio State fans were becoming openly dissatisfied—it had been ten years since the Buckeyes had played in the Rose Bowl.

Sophomores Dominate Starting Lineups

Hayes returned some solid upperclassmen in '68, including senior offensive tackles Dave Foley and Rufus Mayes (a converted tight end). Junior Jim Otis, OSU's leading groundgainer in '67, returned at fullback. The center was dependable John Muhlbach, a senior, and the guards were juniors Alan Jack and Tom Backhus. Sophomores Jan White and Bruce Jankowski took over the tight end and wide receiver posts, respectively.

Senior quarterback Bill Long, the starter the past two seasons, joined sophomore Ron "super sub" Maciejowski as backups to sophomore Rex Kern. The halfback spots were manned by sophomores Leo Hayden, Larry Zelina, and John Brockington, with considerable support from juniors Ray Gillian and Dave Brungard.

The defense was anchored around sophomore middle guard Jim Stillwagon, who would soon establish himself as one of the finest linemen in school history. Stillwagon was supported by veteran Vic Stottlemyer. Juniors Paul Schmidlin, Brad Nielsen, and Bill Urbanik returned at tackle, and juniors Dave Whitfield and Mike Radtke were joined at end by sophomore Mark Debevc. The linebackers were seniors Dirk

Worden and Mark Stier, with sophomore Doug Adams stepping in as a superb tackler following Worden's injury in the season's third game.

The defensive backfield was led by sophomore cornerback Jack Tatum, who may very well have been the fiercest tackler in school history. Tatum was joined by sophomores Mike Sensibaugh and Tim Anderson and junior Ted Provost. Their defensive backfield coach was Lou Holtz. All four would become All-Americans during their careers with the Scarlet and Gray.

Hayden's Mustangs Provide Aerial Circus in Opener

Expectations were high when the Buckeyes opened at home September 28 against SMU, before a crowd of 73,855. Last season's outstanding freshman class was finally ready for its first taste of varsity competition. The visitors were coached by Hayden Fry, who was in his seventh year with the Mustangs (and would later guide the Iowa Hawkeyes

SATURDAY, SEPTEMBER 28, 1968

50¢

Southern Methodist

Ohio State

We will only ONCE play this game against SMU!

Defensive end Mike Radtke will never forget his team's win over Southern Methodist on Saturday, September 28, 1968. Friday evening he spent time at Riverside Hospital with his wife, Marty, who was expecting and had just gone into labor.

When Radtke entered the dressing room following Saturday's game, he was presented with a game ball while learning that Marty had given birth to twins, Douglas and Laura, late that afternoon. "It was really a great thrill," he recalls, "and to help me concentrate on football prior to kick-off, Coach Hayes told me that women give birth to babies every day of the year, but we will only ONCE play this game against SMU!"

for 20 seasons). Hayes was beginning his 18th year in Columbus—the Buckeyes had been 13-3-1 in his 17 previous opening games. OSU was aiming for its first Big Ten title since 1961, and its first Rose Bowl appearance since the 1957 season.

SMU had opened its season the previous Saturday with a 37-28 victory at Auburn. Sophomore quarterback Chuck Hixson was impressive as he completed 28 of 40 passes. Ohio State assistant Esco Sarkkinen scouted the Mustangs and warned, "They start passing when they get off the bus." The Buckeyes, who were ranked 15th nationally even though they hadn't yet played, entered the game as an eleven-point favorite.

Southern Methodist moved the ball well on its first two possessions, but was unable to score. Safety Mike Sensibaugh ended the first threat, intercepting a Hixson pass at the OSU nine-yard line. On the second drive, Bicky Lesser's 38-yard field goal attempt was wide-to-the-right.

Ohio State's offense came alive midway through the first period with an 80-yard scoring drive. Rex Kern went the final two yards untouched on an option inside his own right end. The drive's key play was a 44-yard Kern-to-John Brockington completion which moved the ball to the SMU 27-yard line. Dick Merryman's conversion made it 7-0. Merryman was a transfer from Miami (Ohio), who had been with the team just nine days.

Ohio State recovered SMU's fumble of the ensuing kickoff, and quickly moved 28 yards in seven plays to go ahead 14-0. Fullback Jim Otis plunged over left tackle for the final eight yards, carrying a defender with him across the goal.

Hixson directed a 12-play, 70-yard scoring march early in the second quarter, to tighten things up at 14-7. Eleven passes were thrown during the drive, including an eight-yard strike to end Ken Fleming for the TD. The scoring pass was a fine individual effort by Hixson, who was almost trapped before zipping the ball as Fleming was cutting across the end zone.

Next, versatile Dave Brungard exploded for two touchdowns to help give the Buckeyes a 26-7 halftime lead. His first was a 41-yard sideline scamper to complete a 3-play, 51-yard drive, while his second came on an 18-yard pass from Kern with just 35 seconds remaining in the half.

Rex Kern's fine leadership ability became very evident during this last drive. With a fourth and ten at the SMU 41-yard line, he quickly brought his team from the huddle while Woody Hayes was trying to send Mike Sensibaugh in to punt. Kern made 15 yards on an exciting option around right end to keep the drive alive. In his postgame news conference, Hayes admitted it was "one of the game's key plays."

Southern Methodist came back strong after halftime with three sustained drives. OSU's "bend-but-don't break" defense stopped the first two, with Mike Polaski recovering a fumble at the OSU 19-yard line and Mark Stier intercepting Hixson's pass at

the Ohio State two. But the Mustangs finally scored on their third possession, when Hixson threw six yards to Fleming to complete a 51-yard march and make it 26-14.

SMU nearly scored again early in the final period. Hixson drove his squad to the OSU 18-yard line, but the drive stalled on a fourth-and-eight play when Dirk Worden batted down a pass at the Buckeye two. That series turned out to be the Mustang's last threat. Hixson was later tackled by Mark Debevc for a safety to increase OSU's lead to 28-14. Brungard then scored his third touchdown of the afternoon on a 20-yard pass play from Kern, to make it 35-14 and conclude the scoring.

Sophomore quarterback Rex Kern established himself as a genuine leader during his team's season-opening victory over Southern Methodist.

Buckeye fans had witnessed one of the most exciting (and offensive) openers in Ohio State history. With the two teams combining for 93 passes and running a total of 178 plays, the game lasted over three hours—at the time the longest in Ohio Stadium history. SMU threw 76 passes (69 by Hixson and 7 by back-up Gary Carter), completing 40 for 437 yards. It was the most passes ever thrown by one team in an NCAA game until Houston threw 78 (completing 46) against Arizona State on September 23, 1989. But Ohio State intercepted five of Hixson's tosses deep in Buckeye territory (two by Mark Stier), ending drives at the OSU 12, 19, 18, 2, and 20-yard line.

The Buckeyes used 10 different ballcarriers while rushing for 227 yards. Kern ran the offense like an experienced senior rather than a first-game sophomore. His ball handling and play calling were excellent, and he passed for 145 yards. Fry's Mustangs finished their '68 season with a fine 8-3 record, losing other games only to Texas and Arkansas.

At home the next week the Buckeyes overcame six turnovers to outclass Oregon, 21-6. In the first quarter Mike Polaski returned a blocked punt nine yards for the game's first touchdown. After halftime, Jim Otis scored from the Oregon 35 on his patented off-tackle play, and Bruce Jankowski

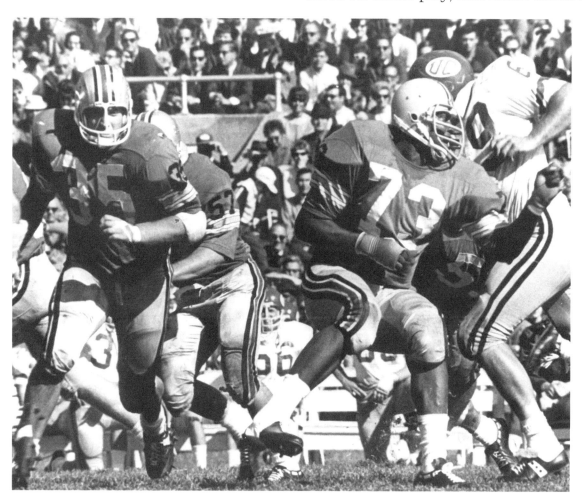

Fullback Jim Otis (35) and All-American tackle Rufus Mayes (73) lead interference against Oregon. Behind Otis is guard Tom Backhus (57).

caught a 55-yard TD strike from Ron Maciejowski. OSU's defense held the Ducks to just six first downs and 140 yards in total offense.

Ohio State's Greatest Victory!

Ohio State opened its conference schedule at home October 12 (Columbus Day) against powerful Purdue, the preseason pick for a second consecutive league title. The Buckeyes, remembering an embarrassing 41-6 loss at home to the Boilermakers the previous season, were more than ready for the nation's number-one ranked team. OSU was rated fourth in the weekly Associated Press poll. Purdue, with highly talented halfback Leroy Keyes and quarterback Mike Phipps, was a solid 13-point favorite.

Although Ohio State dominated from the start, the first half was scoreless. Three times the Buckeyes drove deep into Purdue territory during the first 30 minutes of play, but were unable to score. One drive was stopped at the Boilermaker four. OSU suffered two major injuries in the first half—linebacker Dirk Worden with an injured knee and John Brockington (running from the halfback position) with a sprained ankle. The play of both was affected the rest of the season.

On the fourth play of the second half, with Phipps throwing under heavy pressure, Ted Provost intercepted and scampered 35 yards into the south end zone untouched for Ohio State's first touchdown. Cornerback Jack Tatum had nearly intercepted an outcut pass thrown by Phipps on the previous down. Tatum and Provost switched off on the next play, with Tatum covering deep and Provost protecting the flat. When Phipps saw Tatum go deep, he again threw an outcut into the flat—where Provost was sitting and waiting.

Later that quarter Jim Stillwagon intercepted another Phipps aerial and returned it to the Purdue 25-yard line. Four plays later Kern was shaken up and replaced by senior Bill Long. On his first play, Long faded back

to pass and, finding his main receiver covered, raced 14 yards up the middle for his team's second score. Jim Roman's conver-

What Some Fans Won't Do to Follow the Buckeyes!

Ohio State's great 13-0 victory over Purdue in 1968 was very significant in the life of one of the Buckeyes' most devoted fans—Mr. Ed Linser. Linser grew up in New York City and joined the Navy in 1948 at age 19. While stationed at Great Lakes Training Center, he became good friends with Bill Wade, an enlistee from Chauncey, Ohio, who was an avid Buckeye fan.

After Linser and Wade were discharged from the Navy, they roomed together for a short time in Columbus. Ed became hooked on the Buckeyes, even though he never attended a game. He met his wife, Shirley, and the two moved to New York City in 1951. Finally, after more than 17 years of keeping close tabs on the Buckeyes, the Linsers returned to Columbus to see their very first game in Ohio Stadium—the famous Purdue game of 1968. Ed went insane! He had never been part of anything as fantastic as an Ohio State football game.

The following spring, Linser, deciding that he had to be closer to Ohio Stadium, did something that is almost beyond belief. He quit his job, sold his home, and moved his family to Columbus. Friends told him he was crazy to give up a good job, especially when he had four school-age children to support and no job waiting in Columbus.

The Linsers lived with Shirley's parents until Ed found a job. They purchased a home, but Ohio Stadium became their "second home." Since 1969, Ed has missed only five games in the horseshoe. What some people won't do to support their Buckeyes!

The Cleveland Plain
Dealer
Saturday, October
12, 1968

Quarterback Bill Long scores a memorable touchdown against Purdue.

sion concluded the scoring at 13-0, and the Buckeyes were well on their way to one of the most significant victories in all of Ohio State football.

Ohio State led in first downs, 22-16, and in total offensive yardage, 411-186. Hayes gave tremendous credit to his defensive coaches—Lou McCullough, Lou Holtz, and Bill Mallory. Tatum was magnificent, especially with his guarding of Keyes who was held to a mere 18 yards rushing. Phipps completed just 10 of 28 passes for 106 yards, and he was sacked four times. Otis was the game's leading runner with 144 yards in 29 carries.

Northwestern was Ohio State's homecoming opponent the following Saturday, October 19. Ohio State at 3-0 had climbed to second place in the weekly AP behind Southern California (4-0). The Wildcats led 7-6 after the first period, marking the first time OSU had trailed all season. NU kept it close for three quarters, until the Bucks scored three times in the final stanza to win, 45-21. Kern had an exceptional day, rushing for 120 yards and a touchdown, while throwing for 170 yards and two TDs.

Buckeyes Survive at Illinois—Barely

Ohio State played its first road game October 26 at winless Illinois, before a Memorial Stadium homecoming crowd of 56,174. The Buckeyes dominated the first half, rolling up 17 first downs, 294 yards of offense, and a 24-0 lead. But the second half was an entirely different story. The resurging Illini, operating with a new spread offense, tallied three times and remarkably added three two-point conversions (all on the ground) to tie the game late in the final period, 24-all. OSU's defense was weakened with the loss of Dirk Worden, Mark Debevc, Tim Anderson, and Mike Polaski, all out with injuries.

It was now crunch time, as Ohio State found itself at its own 30-yard line with just over four minutes remaining and Kern out with a head injury. Ron Maciejowski calmly engineered a 70-yard drive for the winning score, a four-yard plunge by Otis. The key play of the drive was a 44-yard completion from Maciejowski to wingback Larry Zelina who carried to the Illini four. Ohio State had won a tough one, 31-24, to up its record to 5-0.

Spartans Render Season's "Closest Call"

Back home the next week, November 2, Duffy Daugherty's Michigan State Spartans gave the Buckeyes as much as they could handle before a Parents' Day crowd of 84,859.

The 16th-ranked Spartans (4-2) had upset Notre Dame, 21-17, the previous week. Ohio State confused MSU from the start, running some plays in sequence without a huddle and having others called by quarterback Rex Kern at the line of scrimmage. Mixing their running and passing very effectively, the Buckeyes took a 7-0 lead with fullback Jim Otis plunging across from the one to complete an 83-yard drive following the opening kickoff.

They increased the lead to 13-0 early in the second period, when Kern fired a 14-yard scoring toss to split end Bruce Jankowski to climax a 64-yard drive. The Spartans tightened things up, 13-7, with quarterback Bill

Ohio State 1968 coaching staff. Front row: Lou Holtz, George Chaump, Rudy Hubbard, and Bill Mallory. Back row: Woody Hayes, Glenn "Tiger" Ellison, Lou McCullough, Earle Bruce, Esco Sarkkinen, Hugh Hindman.

Triplett sneaking over from the one to conclude a 19-play drive.

Kern severely sprained an ankle in the second quarter and was sidelined for the remainder of the afternoon. Maciejowski replaced Kern and immediately guided his team 83 yards in 13 plays to boost OSU's halftime lead to 19-7. Otis notched his second touchdown, this time from the three.

Michigan State's offense took charge in the third period. First Triplett directed a 57-yard scoring drive to bring MSU within five at 19-14. The touchdown was scored by end Frank Foreman on a 14-yard toss from Triplett. The Buckeyes then marched 70 yards, with Maciejowski rolling out around left end for the TD to make it 25-14. Later that quarter MSU's Frank Waters returned Mike Sensibaugh's punt to the Ohio State 31, and the Spartans again were threatening. Halfback Tommy Love dove over the middle for the final yard and the score was now, 25-20.

In the hectic and scoreless final quarter, Ohio State's defense made the difference.

#41 VS. #41

Two former Buckeyes were the leading rushers in the NFL's Super Bowl III, played Sunday, January 12, 1969, at the Orange Bowl in Miami. The New York Jets stunned the favored Baltimore Colts, 16-7. Matt Snell (OSU 61-62-63) was the Jets' leading rusher with 121 yards, and Tom Matte (OSU 58-59-60) led the Colts with 116 yards. Snell and Matte each wore jersey #41 in the pros, the same number they had each worn at Ohio State.

Defensive end Mike Radtke was particularly impressive, first blitzing Triplett into a fumble which OSU end Dave Whitfield recovered at the MSU 31-yard line. On their next possession the Spartans were forced to give up the ball after Radtke spilled Triplett for a 14-yard loss on a key third-and-six at midfield. Finally Radtke helped blind-side Triplett into the game's last fumble with less than two minutes remaining. Whitfield again recovered, this time at the MSU 20-yard line.

Lou Holtz coached Ohio State's defensive backs in 1968. Front row: Suber, Sensibaugh, Tatum, Polaski, Smith, Dale, and Page. Back row: Burton, Trapuzzano, Anderson, Holtz, Wagner, Provost, and Ehrsam.

After the game Hayes praised the efforts of both teams, and complimented defenders Radtke, Bill Urbanik, Jim Stillwagon, and Jack Tatum for their fine efforts. Turnovers helped spell the difference—the Spartans threw three interceptions and lost four fumbles. This five-point win would be the Buckeyes' smallest margin of victory all season.

Things were much easier at Madison the following Saturday, where Hayes' squad scored 33 second-half points to thrash winless Wisconsin, 43-8. With Kern still injured from the Michigan State game, Maciejowski went the distance at quarterback. The "super sub" had a great afternoon, passing for 153 yards and a touchdown and rushing for 124 yards and three scores. Jim Otis contributed 94 yards in 18 carries, along with two touchdowns in the third quarter.

Ohio State ran its record to 8-0 the next week at rain-soaked Iowa City, but it wasn't easy. The Bucks hung on for a 33-27 win over Iowa, after leading 26-6 at the end of the third period. Otis again led the attack with 166 yards and two scores, while Jack Tatum and Mark Stier each ended Hawkeye threats with interceptions. The "Big One" was just one week away, as Ohio State and Michigan were now tied with conference records of 6-0.

#2 Buckeyes Bury #4 Wolverines

Emotions were sky-high as Ohio State and Michigan clashed November 23 to decide the Big Ten title and the representative to the Rose Bowl. The screaming crowd of 85,371 was, at the time, the largest in Ohio Stadium history. For Buckeye fans, it turned out to be one of the most glorious Michigan games of all time. After spotting the Wolverines an early 7-0 advantage, OSU came back to lead 21-14 after two quarters, then out-scored its arch-rival 29-0 in the second half to triumph convincingly, 50-14. It had been many seasons since Ohio State had outplayed an opponent so con-

Fullback Jim Otis scored four touchdowns to lead Buckeyes' 50-14 triumph over Michigan.

Ohio Stadium scoreboard shows final score of Ohio State's victory over Michigan.

vincingly in one half. OSU threw only three passes in the last two quarters.

OSU's 50 points equaled the most points ever scored by a Buckeye 11 against the Wolverines (OSU beat UM 50-20 in 1961). Jim Otis again led the OSU attack with 143 yards and four of the seven touchdowns. The Buckeyes' potent defense, spearheaded by great line play, became stronger as the game progressed. Tatum, Adams, and Art Burton each had interceptions, while end Dave Whitfield had two tackles behind the line of scrimmage. Ohio State led in first downs, 28-17, and in total offensive yards, 467-311.

Students swarmed the field following the monumental victory, ripped down the goal posts, and carried them down High Street to

The Famous Michigan Game Chinstrap

Bob Ferguson and Jim Otis were two of the Buckeyes' finest fullbacks. Ferguson was a two-time All-American in 1960-61, and finished a close second to Ernie Davis in the Heisman Trophy balloting his senior year. Otis was an All-American in 1969, and his career rushing total of 2,542 yards is the highest of any fullback in Ohio State history.

Ferguson was fantastic in his last collegiate game, scoring four touchdowns while leading the Buckeyes to a 50-20 blasting of Michigan at Ann Arbor. Fifty is the most points ever scored by the Buckeyes against the Wolverines. On his way to the dressing room after the game, Ferguson gave his chinstrap to a young Ohio State fan named Scooter who requested it as a souvenir.

Seven years later in 1968, Ohio State was preparing for its game with Michigan, which would determine the outright Big Ten champion. Both teams entered the contest with 6-0 league records. At a huge pep rally on the Ohio State campus the Friday evening prior to the big game, Scooter approached Jim Otis, told Otis the history of the chinstrap, and gave it to him.

Saturday morning Otis taped his new keepsake inside his shoulder pads as a measure of "good luck." In almost magical fashion that afternoon, Otis scored four touchdowns, just like Ferguson, and Ohio State again scored 50 points while defeating the Wolverines, 50-14. Jim Otis still treasures that famous chinstrap— the one that crossed the Michigan goal line eight times.

the State Capitol where fans celebrated long into the night. Around midnight Hayes appeared at the Statehouse with Columbus mayor Jack Sensenbrenner to express their appreciation of the fan support.

The victory earned Ohio State its first Big Ten championship since 1961 and its first Rose Bowl appearance since 1957. With the win, the Buckeyes moved to the top spot in the weekly Associated Press poll, dropping their Rose Bowl opponent Southern California to second.

Ohio State's Last National Title

The Buckeyes have only once played in a game between the nation's two top-ranked teams—the January 1, 1969, Rose Bowl against second-ranked USC. Ohio State entered the game at 9-0, the Trojans were 9-0-1. It was the first Rose Bowl between unbeaten teams, since the Big Ten-Pac Eight contract was initiated in 1947.

After a scoreless first period, USC built its lead to 10-0. Heisman Trophy winner O. J. Simpson took a pitchout to his left, reversed his direction, and raced 80 yards for the game's first touchdown. It was the second-longest scoring run in Rose Bowl history. Down 10-0, the Buckeyes finally got things together to make it 10-10 at halftime. Otis plunged one yard for OSU's first TD, and Jim Roman's 26-yard field goal three seconds before the half tied the score.

Ohio State broke it wide open in the second half. First Roman kicked a 25-yard field goal to make it 13-10 after three quarters. In the final period, Kern threw scoring passes of four and 16 yards, respectively, to halfbacks Leo Hayden and Ray Gillian. The Trojans scored a controversial touchdown with 45 seconds remaining to make the final score, 27-16.

The Buckeye defense was superb, with two interceptions and three fumble recoveries. Ohio State did not commit a turnover. Woody Hayes offered a lot of credit to reserve quarterback Bill Long, who ran the "scout team" in preparation for the game. Kern was named the game's Most Valuable Player. Simpson greatly impressed the Ohio State team when he visited their locker room after the game to offer his congratulations.

Ohio State (10-0) had captured the national title, while completing the fourth undefeated-untied season in school history. Offensive tackles Dave Foley and Rufus Mayes were both named All-American, and Mark Stier was selected as the team's Most Valuable Player. Woody Hayes didn't stay long to savor the win—he left in just two days for one of his many visits with U. S. troops in Vietnam.

Woody Hayes with Ohio State's 1968 Co-Captains, All-American tackle Dave Foley (70) and linebacker Dirk Worden (56).

Halfback Ray Gillian had four receptions in the Rose Bowl, good for 69 yards and a touchdown.

The Buckeyes of 1968 were a great team who gave Ohio State fans many happy and exciting moments and memories. But possibly the finest indication of their greatness came at their 20th reunion in 1988, when they presented their university with a $1.2 million endowment in memory of their beloved coach—a gentleman who meant a lot to them, both on and off the field.

1968				
September 28	Southern Methodist	W	35	14
October 5	Oregon	W	21	6
October 12	Purdue	W	13	0
October 19	Northwestern (HC)	W	45	21
October 26	at Illinois	W	31	24
November 2	Michigan State	W	25	20
November 9	at Wisconsin	W	43	8
November 16	at Iowa	W	33	27
November 23	Michigan	W	50	14
January 1	Southern California*	W	27	16
Total Points			323	150

*Rose Bowl

Season Record: 10-0
National Champion
Big Ten Champion

1969

With most of the Buckeyes' 1968 national championship squad returning, expectations were even higher as Woody Hayes embarked on his 19th season at Ohio State. On offense, Brian Donovan moved from guard to the starting center position vacated by John Muhlbach, and Chuck Hutchison and Dave Chaney replaced All-Americans Dave Foley and Rufus Mayes at tackle. Defensively, Mark Stier's linebacker slot was filled by Phil Strickland who played offensive guard in '68. Tackle Bill Urbanik and halfback Mike Polaski, both senior defensive back-ups, saw additional playing time.

Perfect Opener in All Respects

The September 27 opener could hardly have been more one-sided. The Buckeyes routed Texas Christian, 62-0, before 86,412, at the time the largest crowd in Ohio Stadium history. It was OSU's highest score since defeating Iowa, 83-21, in 1950, and the highest opening game tally since the '33 Bucks walloped Virginia, 75-0. Hayes cleared his entire bench in the second half. It also was the highest margin of defeat ever against TCU.

It would be hard to imagine a more superlative start. After receiving the opening kickoff, quarterback Rex Kern passed 36 yards to split end Bruce Jankowski at the TCU seven, but the play was called back because of a Buckeye lineman illegally downfield. On what then became the season's first official play from scrimmage, Kern and Jankowski connected on a perfectly executed 58-yard touchdown strike, and the rout was on.

Ohio State rolled up a whopping 565 yards in total offense, and set a school single-game record for total offensive plays with 101. Interestingly, the last of nine

Wingback Larry Zelina (16) returns a punt in the season opener against Texas Christian.

touchdowns late in the final period produced one of the game's most spectacular plays— a 62-yard connection from quarterback Kevin Rusnak to halfback Tom Campana, both third-stringers.

The next weekend the Buckeyes gained their 16th consecutive win over three seasons with a 41-14 thumping of the Washington Huskies at Seattle. The game drew a then-record Huskie Stadium crowd of 58,800. Kern started the scoring with a splendid 64-yard option play midway through the first quarter. The Junior signal-caller collected 267 yards in total offense that afternoon, and scored again on a four-yard run midway through the third period.

Fullback Jim Otis added 111 yards on the ground and scored three times from inside the five. Quarterback Ron Maciejowski added the Buckeyes' sixth touchdown on a five-yard end sweep midway through the final quarter.

Ohio State led in first downs, 26-21, and in total offensive yardage, 502 to 328. The Buckeye defense played a big role intercept-

ing two Huskie passes and recovering three fumbles.

This was Washington's third consecutive game against a Big Ten opponent. The Huskies had lost to Michigan State (27-11) and Michigan (45-7) the two previous weekends.

Most Points Ever Against One of Duffy's Teams

Top-ranked Ohio State returned home October 11 to open Big Ten play against No. 19 Michigan State. Another record crowd was on hand, this time it was 86,861. The legendary Chic Harley, OSU's first three-time All-American (1916-17-19), was honored at halftime.

Ohio State's superb defense throttled the Spartans' triple-option veer attack and immediately took control of the game. End Mark Debevc intercepted a Bill Triplett pass, returning it 14 yards for OSU's first touchdown. Triplett had made a hasty toss from his own end zone while being pressured by Buckeye middle guard Jim Stillwagon.

After recovering a Spartan fumble, OSU drove 26 yards for its second score with Kern taking it across from the one. Next, wingback Larry Zelina returned a punt 73 yards for the Bucks' third touchdown and a 20-0 lead after just six minutes of play. After MSU got on the board with a 76-yard Triplett-to-Frank Foreman pass play, Kern scored his second touchdown from the four to make it 27-7 after one quarter.

With MSU's defense geared to halting Woody Hayes' famed ground attack, Kern took to the air, throwing for OSU's next three scores. First he connected on a 24-yarder to tight end Jan White, followed by a 13-yard strike in the end zone to split end Bruce Jankowski. Kern's last toss was a beautifully executed 29-yard connection with sophomore Tom Campana. Quarterback Kevin Rusnak passed five yards to Campana for OSU's final touchdown late in the fourth quarter.

The 54 points were the most ever scored against Michigan State during Duffy Daugherty's 19 seasons as the Spartans' head coach (1954 through 1972). It also was the most points given up by MSU since being shut out 55-0 at Michigan in 1947.

Hayes used 59 players in the game, including 10 different ballcarriers and eight separate receivers. The 1969 season was the 100th anniversary of college football, and the '69 Buckeyes left little doubt they were one of the finest teams the game had ever seen.

No Easy Task at Minneapolis

The following Saturday, Minnesota coach Murray Warmath had his Golden Gophers primed for an upset, and his squad played its heart out before falling to the nation's top-ranked team, 34-7. The game was much closer and more tense than indicated by the final score.

Playing at old Memorial Stadium on the Minnesota campus before a homecoming crowd of 56,016, the inspired Gophers actually outgained Ohio State, 443 yards to 429. But the Buckeye defense interrupted many of Minnesota's scoring threats by recovering five Gopher fumbles. Quarterback Phil Hagen connected on 26 passes for 304 yards (both school records at the time), but couldn't get any of his receivers into the end zone.

Kern and Otis again provided the lion's share of OSU's offense. Kern ran the option and "hidden ball" plays to perfection and was unanimously voted the game ball by his teammates. Otis rambled for 138 yards and scored twice. The Buckeyes' other touchdowns came on short runs by Leo Hayden and Ray Gillian and a 25-yard pass from Kevin Rusnak to Bruce Jankowski. Ohio State's winning streak now stretched to 18, longest in school history.

Perfect Homecoming Afternoon

The Buckeyes' October 25 homecoming game could hardly have been more flawless. On a beautiful sunny fall afternoon before a crowd of 86,576, Ohio State scored in each quarter to whitewash Illinois, 41-0. The Bucks thundered to 31 first downs and 564 total yards, while holding the Illini to eight first downs and a mere 156 yards of total offense.

Linebacker Doug Adams

Illinois crossed the midfield stripe only twice all afternoon, and never advanced further than the OSU 39-yard line.

Once again the offensive tandem of Rex Kern and Jim Otis was outstanding. Kern passed for 193 yards and two touchdowns—both to tight end Jan White. Otis ran for 167 yards to advance his career rushing total to 2,134. He scored the game's first TD from inside the one-yard line. John Brockington scored twice in the final period on short runs of one and two yards.

It was almost as easy the following Saturday, November 1, at Evanston, where the nation's top-ranked team put together 34 first downs and 575 yards of offense to topple Northwestern, 35-6. The Dyche Stadium homecoming crowd of 41,279 was very impressed with the play of Wildcat quarterback Maurie Daigneau, a sophomore, who set then-school records with 22 completions for 294 yards against Ohio State's excellent de-

Coach Woody Hayes (center) with assistant coaches Bill Mallory (left) and Earle Bruce.

"First Lady" Impresses Windy City Club

Mrs. Anne Hayes became the first woman to address the Chicago Quarterback Club, when she dazzled them with her wit and charm at their November 3, 1969, luncheon. Mrs. Hayes provided many "humorous insights" about her husband, and amazed the group with her knowledge of college football.

fense. But the home team committed four turnovers, and most of NU's yardage came between the 20 yard lines.

Hayes substituted liberally, particularly in the second half. The Buckeyes' quarterback trio of Kern-Maciejowski-Rusnak connected 17 times with nine separate receivers for 213 yards. Kern threw 21 yards to Jan White for OSU's second touchdown and Maciejowski teamed with Otis for a 12-yard TD. The big fullback scored two others on short plunges and was the game's leading rusher with 127 yards.

Tailback Leo Hayden thrilled the Scarlet and Gray faithful in attendance, as he broke clear over the middle and outran the Wildcat secondary for a 33-yard touchdown right after halftime. Stan White added all five extra points.

"Mace" Again Dazzles Badgers

Kern reinjured his shoulder late in the Northwestern game, and was unable to see action at home the next week against Wisconsin. But it was difficult to see how he could have played any better against the Badgers than Ron Maciejowski (who also had led OSU to its 43-8 win at Wisconsin in '68). "Super sub" accounted for 247 of the Buckeyes' 595 yards of total offense (including two TD passes) before turning the offense over to Kevin Rusnak early in the second half with OSU leading, 34-0.

Defense Foils Purdue, Phipps For No. 22 in Streak, 41-14

Columbus Dispatch, Sunday, November 16, 1969

PURDUE   OHIO STATE

THE COLLEGE GAME

"HEATING UP THE OLD BOILER"

NOVEMBER 15, 1969 · OFFICIAL PROGRAM · FIFTY CENTS

Ohio State routed Wisconsin that afternoon, 62-7, in one of the most one-sided games during Woody Hayes' 28 years in Columbus. The Buckeyes led in first downs, 33-11, and offensive yards, 595-176. Six different players scored OSU's nine touchdowns, as Hayes rested his first-team players most of the second half. The Badgers scored late in the final period to avoid a shutout.

Victory Streak Reaches 22

With its overwhelming defense and astonishing offense both operating at top speed, Ohio State completely mastered Purdue the following week, 42-14, to tie its own Big Ten record with 17 consecutive conference victories. The victory assured the nation's No. 1 ranked team at least a share of the 1969 league title, and also stretched Ohio State's overall winning streak to 22, longest in school history. Tenth-ranked Purdue entered the game at 7-1, having lost only to Michigan (31-20) five weeks earlier. The 25-degree temperature in snow-covered Ohio Stadium had little effect, as Hayes substituted liberally when the score reached 42-7 after three quarters.

Leo Hayden led the Buckeyes' rushing assault with 130 yards, including a 59-yarder

All-American defensive back Ted Provost, who is fondly remembered by Ohio State fans for his touchdown with an interception return against Purdue in 1968.

for the day's longest gain. One of the game's most spectacular plays was a 57-yard punt return by Larry Zelina for the Buckeyes' final score. Ohio State's defense intercepted five of quarterback Mike Phipps' passes and recovered three Boilermaker fumbles. One bright spot for the visitors was Stan Brown's 98-yard second quarter kickoff return for Purdue's first touchdown.

In his postgame press conference, Hayes rated the Buckeye defense that afternoon as the "best I have ever seen." Later that evening he received a congratulatory telephone call from a good friend—President Richard Nixon—who had watched part of the game on television.

What a Way to Start a War!

Ohio State's November 22 encounter at Michigan would be the Buckeyes' last game of the season, because of the Rose Bowl's "no repeat" policy in effect at that time. The nation's No. 1 ranked team was averaging 46 points and 512 yards per game, and needed one more win to break its own conference record of 17 consecutive victories. A triumph over the arch-rival Wolverines would also assure Ohio State its second straight national title.

The Michigan Stadium crowd totaled 103,588, primarily because Michigan Athletic Director Don Canham and Sports Information Director Will Perry had driven to Columbus the preceding Monday to deliver approximately 25,000 tickets to Ohio State's ticket office. Buckeye fans had purchased all of them by the end of the week.

The Ann Arbor crowd of 103,588 was, at the time, the largest ever to attend a regular-season college football game. Former Woody Hayes assistant Bo Schembechler had taken over the Michigan program that spring, af-

All-American quarterback Rex Kern receives instructions from Woody Hayes.

Two-time All-American middle guard Jim Stillwagon. In 1970, Stillwagon captured the Lombardi Award and was selected Ohio State's MVP.

ter an impressive 40-17-3 six-year record at his alma mater, Miami of Ohio. His twelfth-ranked Wolverines were 7-2, and had outscored their last four opponents, 178-22. Nevertheless, Michigan entered the game a 17-point underdog.

The Wolverines pulled off one of college football's greatest upsets that afternoon, 24-12. The scoring all took place in the first half. In retrospect, this 1969 encounter could be characterized as Michigan's biggest win—EVER, and Ohio State's most shattering loss—EVER! For the Buckeyes, a Big Ten Co-Championship with Michigan was absolutely no consolation.

Ohio State grabbed a 6-0 lead on its second possession. Fullback Jim Otis powered over from the one to cap a short drive after Larry Zelina returned a punt 35 yards to the Michigan 16-yard line. But then Michigan really took charge, scoring the next four times it had the ball. Fullback Garvie Craw's three-yard touchdown burst completed a 45-yard march, and Frank Titas kicked the extra point to give Michigan the lead, 7-6. For the first time all season, the Buckeyes were behind.

Ohio State recaptured the lead, 12-7, going 73 yards in 11 plays with Rex Kern throwing to Jan White for a 22-yard touchdown on the first play of the second quarter. But the Wolverines regained the lead for good on their next possession, driving 58 yards with Craw blasting across for his second touchdown from the one. The drive's big play was a beautiful broken-field run of 28 yards by sophomore Billy Taylor of Barberton, Ohio, Schembechler's hometown.

Next, Barry Pierson returned a punt 60 yards to the Ohio State three, and two plays later, quarterback Don Moorhead sneaked over from the two, and it was 21-12, Michigan. Pierson's punt return was probably the key play of the afternoon. It signaled that the Wolverines were for real, and that the Buckeyes were now in deep trouble. Later that quarter, a

WOLVES UPEND BUCKS TO SHARE BIG10 TITLE

Columbus Dispatch, Sunday, November 23, 1969

Moorhead-to-Jim Mandich touchdown pass was nullified by a motion penalty, and Michigan had to settle for a 25-yard field goal by Tim Killian. The score was 24-12 with 1:15 remaining in the first half, and that's how the game ended.

Ohio State's defense stiffened in the second half, but so did Michigan's. The Buckeyes moved past midfield only once in the final two quarters. The Wolverines virtually shut off the option play, forcing Ohio State to pass. The result was six interceptions, three of them by Pierson.

Those that Stay
Will be Champions! — Bo

The victory was really no big surprise for Schembechler and his staff. He began talking about beating the Buckeyes during practice the previous spring. Schembechler placed a sign in the team's dressing room which read, "What the mind can conceive and believe, the mind can achieve, and those that stay will be Champions!" Not all of the players stayed—some quit. But those that stayed likely learned that, under Schembechler's leadership, they were able to accomplish far more than even they thought was possible. By late Saturday afternoon, November 22, 1969, the pupil had defeated the master, and Schembechler's vision had become a reality.

One of College Football's Greatest!

Even with its season-ending setback, Ohio State's 1969 squad was one of the finest college teams ever assembled. Finishing fourth in the final AP standings with a record of 8-1, the Buckeyes had outscored their opponents, 383-93. Until their season-ending debacle at Michigan, their closest games had been 27-point margins of victory at Washington and at Minnesota. OSU's scoring average of 42.6 points per game (even after registering only 12 at Michigan) is the highest of any season in the 111 years of Ohio State football. Thirteen different players scored a total of 56 touchdowns in just nine games.

Jim Stillwagon, Rex Kern, Ted Provost, Jack Tatum, and Jim Otis were selected All-America. Otis, who was chosen the team's MVP, rushed for 1,027 yards to become the first Ohio State player to total more than 1,000 yards in a single season. His three-year career total of 2,542 is the highest of any fullback in Ohio State history. He had 35 career touchdowns.

Eleven players made the All-Big Ten team—Stillwagon, Provost, Tatum, and Otis were joined by tackle Charles Hutchinson, center Brian Donovan, end Dave Whitfield, end Mark Debevc, tackle Paul Schmidlin, linebacker Doug Adams, and safety Mike Sensibaugh.

Those close to the Ohio State program recall that Hayes, after returning from his team's bitter defeat at Michigan, went directly to his office that Saturday evening and began preparing for next year's game. The stage was being set for the most colossal rematch conceivable—the countdown to November 20, 1970, was well on its way, and the "Ten Year War" between Woody and Bo was just getting started!

1969			
September 27	Texas Christian	W 62	0
October 4	at Washington	W 41	14
October 11	Michigan State	W 54	21
October 18	at Minnesota	W 34	7
October 25	Illinois (HC)	W 41	0
November 1	at Northwestern	W 35	6
November 8	Wisconsin	W 62	7
November 15	Purdue	W 42	14
November 22	at Michigan	L 12	24
Total Points		383	93

Season record: 8-1
Big Ten Co-Champion

1970

The overriding theme surrounding Ohio State's 1970 spring practice was redemption for the previous year's very unexpected and painful loss at Michigan. A large rug bearing last year's 24-12 score was placed at the entrance to the team's dressing room, to serve as a constant reminder of this season's prime objective. The "Super Sophomores of '68" were now preparing for their third and final year. Hayes' teams always spent part of their off-season preparing for the Wolverines, and this spring was certainly no exception.

Rex Kern and Ron Maciejowski continued their 1-2 punch at quarterback, Larry Zelina and Leo Hayden again manned the halfback posts, and John Brockington was now the starting fullback replacing Jim Otis. Ends Jan White and Bruce Jankowski both returned for their third season as starters, and Dave Cheney was joined at tackle by sophomore John Hicks.

Phil Strickland and Dick Kuhn were the starting guards. Strickland moved from linebacker back to the offensive line, where he had played in '68, and Kuhn had been a backup offensive end the last two seasons. Junior Tom DeLeone was the new starting center.

Jim Stillwagon and Mark Debevc were joined on the defensive line by junior end Ken Luttner and tackles Ralph Holloway, a senior, and sophomore George Hasenohrl. Junior Stan White joined Doug Adams at linebacker, and Harry Howard, a junior, moved into the secondary with Jack Tatum, Tim Anderson, and Mike Sensibaugh.

Buckeyes Ambush Aggies

Ohio State scored on its first three possessions and coasted to a 56-13 victory over outmanned Texas A & M, before an Ohio Sta-

dium crowd of 85,657 on September 26. The Aggies were in their 76th season of football, and this was the most points they had ever surrendered in a single game. Even though it was the Buckeyes' season opener, coach Gene Stallings' team was already 2-0 with wins over Wichita State (41-14) and LSU (20-18) the two previous Saturdays.

Woody Hayes substituted frequently, as seven different players scored OSU's eight touchdowns. The Buckeyes led in first downs, 27-19, and total offensive yards, 513-321. They also took advantage of five Aggie turnovers.

Ohio State was a little less impressive the following Saturday, even with a 34-10 win

Coach Woody Hayes examines a rug that reflects Michigan's 24-12 winning score over Ohio State in 1969. All players had to cross the rug when leaving the dressing room for practice. It was a constant reminder of the Buckeyes' goal to defeat Michigan in 1970 (which they did, 20-9).

over Duke. The Blue Devils led 3-0 up until 25 seconds before halftime, when they elected to punt on fourth down from the OSU 44. Ralph Holloway blocked the kick, and Ken Luttner returned it to the end zone for the Buckeyes' first points of the afternoon and a 6-3 lead after two quarters.

Hayes' decision at halftime to pound the visitors with his experienced backs worked well. Three topped the century mark—

All-American safety Mike Sensibaugh

Hayden (155), Brockington (117), and Kern (113)—as OSU scored 21 points in the third period to put the game out of reach.

Solid Ground Attack
Continues in League Opener

OSU rushed for 287 of 338 total offensive yards to whitewash Michigan State, 29-0, at Spartan Stadium on October 10. Ironically, Notre Dame had shut out MSU in East Lansing the previous Saturday by the same exact score. Brockington was again the leading ground gainer with 126 yards, including a 25-yard bolt behind a great block by John Hicks for OSU's final touchdown.

For the second week the Buckeyes started slowly and led just 9-0 at the half. Ohio State's quick defense forced Michigan State to play most of the game in their own territory. Stan White and Jim Stillwagon each had seven solo tackles, and Jack Tatum had five. This victory at East Lansing was OSU's 700th all-time game (456-199-45).

At homecoming the next weekend, the top-ranked Buckeyes reversed their script to defeat Minnesota, 28-8. OSU sprinted away to a 28-0 lead in the game's first 23 minutes,

The distressed Fighting Illini squad threatened to boycott the rest of their season, and did everything possible to give their coach a victory. Illinois led 23-16 early in the third quarter, before a sparse Memorial Stadium crowd of 46,208, but could not maintain the pace for a full 60 minutes. The Buckeyes exploded for five touchdowns on their first five second-half possessions for their fifth win of the year. Illini halfback Darrell Robinson was the game's leading rusher with 187 yards in 43 carries.

Hayes, who was pleased with his team's late game comeback, used his postgame

then coasted to their fourth consecutive win of the season. OSU effectively used the triple-option attack, with Kern and Brockington each scoring twice. Brockington was the game's leading rusher with 187 yards, including a 62-yard effort in the first period for his team's longest run of the year.

On this perfect autumn afternoon, the Buckeye faithful were a little frustrated by their team's inability to score in the second half, and by Minnesota's auspicious passing attack. Golden Gopher quarterback Craig Curry connected 27 times for 298 yards, including a 12-yarder to end Kevin Hamm for the only score by either team in the second half.

Ohio State's record now stood at 4-0. With the return match with Michigan just five weeks away, Buckeye fans were monitoring the Wolverines who were now 5-0 (OSU was still playing just nine games during the regular season, while the other nine Big Ten schools were playing ten).

Inspired Illini Support Their Coach

The Buckeyes returned to the road October 24 to face Illinois. Ohio State survived its worst scare of the season by bouncing back in the game's last 20 minutes for a 48-29 victory. An official announcement from Illinois the morning of the game confirmed a rumor that head coach Jim Valek would be relieved of his coaching duties following the game. The 43-year-old Valek was in his fourth season as head coach with a record of 7-28.

Two-time All-American cornerback Jack Tatum was one of the finest players in Ohio State history.

press conference to blast Illinois officials for removing Valek in the middle of the season. He offered his opinion that such a move might not be legal, and suggested that the

All-American end Jan White

American Football Coaches Association should check this one out very carefully.

Back home on October 31, the Buckeyes again relied on a strong second half to defeat Northwestern, 24-10. OSU trailed the Wildcats, 10-3, at halftime, before what was then an Ohio Stadium record crowd of 86,673. Both squads entered the game 3-0 in conference play.

Woody Hayes went with his traditional fullback offense with great intensity and success. Brockington lugged the pigskin 42 times for 161 yards, as Ohio State outgained Northwestern 336-93 on the ground. The Buckeyes made an unusually high number of mistakes with three interceptions and eight penalties, and also failed on two fourth-down situations.

OSU's record was now 6-0 overall and 4-0 in the Big Ten. Michigan struggled more than expected with a 29-15 win at Wisconsin to run its season record to 7-0.

Two More—Then the Big One!

The Buckeyes hit the road the next two weeks before returning to the friendly confines of Ohio Stadium for the season finale against their friends from the north. OSU

won out over Wisconsin, 24-7, before what was then an all-time Camp Randall Stadium crowd of 72,758 on November 7. Again, Hayes' squad was not overly impressive, and the Badgers trailed just 10-7 at the half.

Wisconsin's inspired defense held OSU's power offense to 161 yards on the ground. But the Buckeyes connected for 158 yards through the air, their best effort of the season, to set up their three touchdowns (scored by Brockington on runs of 11, 4, and 1 yards). Ron Maciejowski connected for 141 of his team's air yards, but he also threw four of OSU's five interceptions, which seriously reduced his team's momentum.

The 7-0 Buckeyes clearly appeared to be "looking ahead" to their showdown with Michigan, and nearly let one get away November 14 at Purdue. Before a chilled crowd of 68,157 in snow covered Ross-Ade Stadium, Ohio State was fortunate to escape West Lafayette with a 10-7 verdict. Fred Schram's 30-yard field goal into a strong wind broke a 7-7 tie with just 2:04 remaining.

Fullback John Brockington's powerful 26-yard scoring burst gave the Buckeyes an early 7-0 first-quarter lead. But Stan Brown returned the ensuing kickoff 96 yards to tie, and there was no further scoring until Schram's winning kick.

The Buckeyes' defense saved the day,

Desire, Dedication, and Determination

Fred Schram never played high school football. His fourth-quarter field goal broke a 7-7 tie to give Ohio State its 10-7 win at Purdue. Schram was selected MVP of the Massillon High School baseball team his senior year, and decided to walk-on as a placekicker at Ohio State in the fall of '68. He credits much of his success to the fine instruction he received from placekicking coach Ernie Godfrey.

holding Purdue to three first downs and 131 yards in total offense. The Boilermakers were in great position to take the lead after recovering a blocked punt at the Ohio State 17-yard line early in the final period, but the effort failed when linebacker Doug Adams stopped Brown in mid-air on a fourth-and-one at the eight. Quarterback Ron Maciejowski's timely fourth-quarter running and passing put the ball in position for Schram's tie-breaker.

While the Buckeyes edged the Boilermakers to up their record to 8-0, Michigan was walloping Iowa, 55-0, at Ann Arbor to run its season record to 9-0. The nationally heralded showdown was just seven days away—it would be the first time BOTH schools entered their season-ending struggle with undefeated-untied records. What fan could have asked for more?

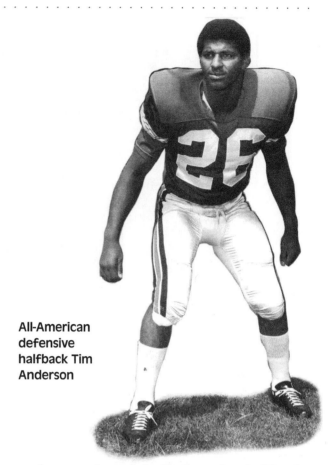

All-American defensive halfback Tim Anderson

This One Is Literally for a Lifetime!

What a difference a year makes! In what might have been the most tense and dramatic struggle in all of Ohio State football, the fifth-ranked Buckeyes captured the outright Big Ten title with a 20-9 triumph over fourth-ranked Michigan on November 21. The highly publicized contest was played before a national television audience and a record (at the time) Ohio Stadium crowd of 87,331. It was the first time since 1905 that two undefeated-untied teams met to settle the Big Ten title—that year Chicago defeated Michigan, 2-0, for the only points scored against the Wolverines that season.

The atmosphere was ecstatic, as Ohio Stadium was virtually filled an hour before kickoff. The Buckeyes took an immediate 3-0 lead on Fred Schram's 28-yard field goal, following the recovery of a Michigan fumble on the opening kickoff. The Wolverines tied it up early in the second period on Dana Coin's 31-yard three-pointer.

Ohio State regained the lead with quarterback Rex Kern connecting with split end Bruce Jankowski on a perfectly thrown 26-yard pass play right before the half. The Buckeyes had gotten a big break when a 72-yard punt by Michigan's Paul Staroba was nullified by a facemask penalty. Staroba's second punt was returned by Tim Anderson to the OSU 47-yard line. From there, Kern drove his team 53 yards in ten plays for the go-ahead touchdown.

Tension really mounted in the third quarter as Wolverine quarterback Don Moorhead guided his team 50 yards to a touchdown, with a pass to Staroba covering the final 13 yards. But Anderson blocked Coin's extra point attempt to leave the score at 10-9.

Schram's 27-yard field goal early in the final period increased the lead to 13-9. On the Wolverines' next series, OSU linebacker Stan White picked off a pass at the Michigan 23-yard line and returned it to the nine. On third down from the four, Kern executed the option to perfection, pitching out to halfback Leo Hayden for the game's final touchdown. Schram's extra point concluded the scoring at 20-9.

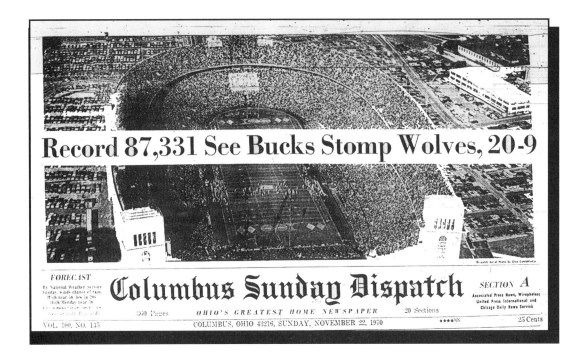

Record 87,331 See Bucks Stomp Wolves, 20-9

Columbus Sunday Dispatch

SECTION A

FORECAST

OHIO'S GREATEST HOME NEWSPAPER

COLUMBUS, OHIO 43216, SUNDAY, NOVEMBER 22, 1970

25 Cents

The Buckeye defense had been superb, yielding just 37 rushing yards to a team that had been averaging 247 yards per game. Hayes had surprised everyone with a two-tight-end offense. Hayden, who consistently gained yardage on a newly installed delay-type play, led all rushers with 117 yards.

In his postgame news conference, Hayes referred to the win as the greatest game in Ohio State history. President Richard Nixon telephoned the jubilant coach within minutes after the victory to offer congratulations. In his pregame pep talk, Hayes had read an excerpt from an anonymous telegram that indicated, "This one is literally for a lifetime." With the win Ohio State advanced to second behind Texas in the weekly AP poll, Michigan fell to eighth.

Learning from the Enemy

Woody Hayes was so impressed with Stanford's passing attack in the Rose Bowl, that he asked Stanford quarterback coach Mike White for some guidance. The following spring, White spent time in Columbus with the Ohio State coaching staff, explaining many aspects of the passing game. White asked Hayes if he would return the favor whenever White was able to land his first head coaching position.

White became head coach of the University of California at Berkeley in 1972, and—true to his word—Hayes spoke at California's coaching clinic that spring, impressing everyone with his knowledge and enthusiasm. White later took over the Illinois program, where in 1983 he led the Fighting Illini to a 17-13 triumph over the Buckeyes. It was Illinois' first victory over Ohio State in 16 seasons.

HOLD YOUR OWN TICKET

MICHIGAN

OHIO STATE

CENTENNIAL

THE OHIO STATE UNIVERSITY
OHIO STADIUM

Plunkett Directs Stanford's Upset

The Rose Bowl against coach John Ralston's Stanford Cardinals was not nearly as pleasant. Heisman Trophy winner Jim Plunkett quarterbacked his squad to an unexpected 27-17 come-from-behind triumph in the January 1, 1971, Pasadena Classic. Stanford scored the first two times it had the ball to grab a quick 10-0 lead, but the Buckeyes came back with two touchdowns to lead at the half, 14-10. John Brockington scored both TDs on short plunges.

After trading third-period field goals, Ohio State drove from its own six to the Stanford 19-yard line, for a "fourth-and-inches" to start the final quarter. Brockington was stacked up for no gain and Stanford took over on downs. This play severely changed the game's momentum. Plunkett drove his squad 81 yards to take the lead at 20-17, then sealed the victory with a 10-yard scoring toss to Randy Vataha for the game's final score.

Woody Hayes described the game as "an afternoon of missed opportunities." He felt Plunkett was a splendid quarterback, but he lamented the fact that Ohio State was able to score only three points in the second half. The Buckeyes held a slight edge in the game's statistics, leading in first downs, 22-21, and in total offensive yards, 439-408. Kern was OSU's leading rusher with 129 yards, followed by Brockington with 101. The setback was Ohio State's 200th all-time loss (462-200-45).

27 and 2

Ohio State finished the season at 9-1, good for fifth place in the final AP rankings. OSU was the National Football Foundation's selection as National Champion. Even with the disappointing finish, the Buckeyes enjoyed another excellent season. Six players were named All-Americans—Stillwagon, Tatum, White, Brockington, Sensibaugh, and Anderson. Stillwagon was chosen the team's MVP. The 1968 through 1970 era produced a three-year record of 27-2, with a winning rate

All-American fullback John Brockington

of 93.1 percent. This percentage is the highest of any three-year period in all of Ohio State football.

1970				
September 26	Texas A & M	W	56	13
October 3	Duke	W	34	10
October 10	at Michigan State	W	29	0
October 17	Minnesota (HC)	W	28	8
October 24	at Illinois	W	48	29
October 31	Northwestern	W	24	10
November 7	at Wisconsin	W	24	7
November 14	at Purdue	W	10	7
November 21	Michigan	W	20	9
January 1	Stanford*	L	17	27
Total Points			290	120

*Rose Bowl

Season Record: 9-1
National Champion
Big Ten Champion

Ohio State Football and Woody Hayes Were Inseparable

ARCHIE ARRIVES

The 1971 season truly symbolized a new era in Ohio State football. The Buckeyes finally scheduled 10 regular-season games, a move other Big Ten schools had made six years earlier in 1965. Interestingly, while OSU was going to 10, the rest of the conference moved to 11 games during the '71 regular season. Ohio State would not add an 11th encounter until 1974.

Lou Fischer Gift in Memory of Joe Campanella

A second major change saw the installation of Astro-turf at Ohio Stadium. The new artificial surface replaced the hallowed grass sod which had supported so many successful seasons during the Buckeyes' first 49 years at the horseshoe. The new carpet was made possible by a generous $380,000 donation from Lou Fischer, a Buckeye guard in 1950 and '51.

Fischer's gift was in memory of his close friend and teammate, tackle Joe Campanella, who played with the NFL's Cleveland Browns and Baltimore Colts after leaving Ohio State.

Fischer and Campanella became business partners with two other Colt players, defensive end Gino Marchetti and fullback Alan Ameche. In 1957, the four of them founded Gino's, a fast food chain, which became very successful. Campanella died unexpectedly of a heart attack in 1968, shortly after being named General Manager of the Colts.

1971

Woody Hayes faced a monumental rebuilding effort with the departure of 17 starters from last year's Big Ten champions. Junior tackle John Hicks would miss the entire fall with a preseason knee operation. Center Tom DeLeone was the only returning starter on offense. Two major concerns were quarterback and fullback. Senior Don Lamka, who had played on the defensive units the past two seasons, replaced Rex

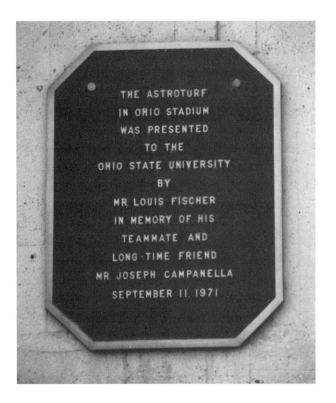

Kern and Ron Maciejowski at quarterback. Junior John Bledsoe moved into John Brockington's fullback slot, even though he had only three minutes of playing time in 1970.

Senior running back Rick Galbos would see considerable action at both halfback and fullback. Junior Merv Teague was moved to offensive tackle from tight end, and senior Tom Campana switched to the defensive backfield after two fine seasons on offense. The defense was also bolstered with the arrival of sophomore Randy Gradishar at linebacker.

Auspicious Start

To the delight of 75,596 rain-soaked fans, the Buckeyes opened at home September 11 with a blistering 52-21 triumph over the Iowa Hawkeyes. It was the first time Ohio State had opened against a member of the Big Ten Conference since defeating Indiana (28-0) in the first game of 1954. OSU roared to a 17-0 advantage in the game's first 10 minutes and was never in any real danger. Lamka was terrific in his first quarterback start, scoring

four touchdowns (21, 19, 6, and 1 yards) while running for an even 100 yards.

Bledsoe ripped huge gains over tackle and up the middle to finish with 157 yards and two TDs. The 52 points was OSU's highest score in its last 10 conference games. It was a very rough initiation for Iowa's new head coach, Frank Lauterbur, who had guided the Toledo Rockets to 23 consecutive wins before moving to Iowa City.

Home Winning Streak Snapped at 19

After an open date the following week, the sixth-ranked Buckeyes played host September 25 to tenth-ranked Colorado in the nation's top intersection clash of the day. The Ohio State marching band unveiled a new script "Woody" formation before the start of the game.

Colorado held on to win, 20-14, to break the Buckeye's home winning streak at 19. OSU's last setback in Columbus was to Illinois, 17-13, on October 28, 1967.

This first meeting between the two schools produced one of Ohio Stadium's most dramatic finishes. Three of the five touchdowns were scored in the game's last five minutes, including Ohio State's only points of the afternoon. The Buffaloes effectively used their triple-option attack and led 13-0 midway through the final period. The lead would have been greater if OSU had not

stopped two other Colorado drives with an end zone interception and a fumble recovery at the one-yard line. The Buffaloes' second six-pointer was a beautifully executed 68-yard punt return by Cliff Branch early in the second period.

Twice during the afternoon Colorado held Ohio State on downs inside the two-yard line. In each instance, Bledsoe was stopped on a fullback plunge up the middle when the Buffaloes were virtually in an 11-man-line defense. Many fans were critical of Hayes' conservative offense and debated the play selection long into the evening, thinking a short pass or option around end would have been much better calls.

Lamka, who was fantastic with 255 passing yards on 22 completions, connected with end Rick Middleton for 14 yards and OSU's second touchdown with just 2:11 remaining to reduce the deficit to six points. Placekicker Fred Schram's ensuing on-side kick was recovered by Ohio State. One official signaled an OSU recovery, but it was eventually ruled that the ball had not traveled the required 10 yards. Hayes blasted the decision in his post-game press briefing, and this controversial call would be pondered by the Buckeye faithful for some time.

Ohio State led in first downs, 24-19, and in total offensive yards, 400-382. End Dick Wakefield finished the afternoon with 11 receptions for 172 yards. Colorado's win over Ohio State was the Big Eight Conference's 20th consecutive victory over the Big Ten.

The Buckeyes started a new Ohio Stadium victory streak the following Saturday, October 2, with a 35-3 victory over the University of California. On a sweltering afternoon with the temperature in the high 80s, OSU rushed to a 14-0 first-quarter lead and finished strongly with 21 points in the final period. Hayes called on nine different ball carriers who netted 317 yards on the ground.

When Lamka was forced to exit the game with a strained right shoulder midway through the first half, sophomore Greg Hare grabbed the controls and engineered the last three scoring drives. Hare looked particularly spectacular on a 40-yard quarterback-keeper for OSU's third touchdown.

Big Eight Superiority

The nation's top three teams in the final 1971 Associated Press poll were also the Big Eight Conference's first three finishers. Nebraska won the national title with a record of 12-0, followed by Oklahoma at 11-1 and Colorado at 10-2. Oklahoma's only setback was to Nebraska, while the Cornhuskers and Sooners handed the Buffaloes their only two defeats.

Ohio State Fortunate at Champaign

The season's first road game was a 24-10 win at Illinois on October 9. On a chilly afternoon before a Memorial Stadium crowd of 53,555, the Illini of first-year coach Bob Blackman finished on top in every category but the final score. The mistake-prone home team (four turnovers) spent most of the afternoon threatening to score before losing its fifth straight game of the season.

OSU's attack was weakened with the loss of John Bledsoe and tight end Fred Pagac, who were out with injuries. Fullback Randy Keith scored twice from short range within a two-minute span in the first quarter, and Hare scored the Bucks' last TD from three yards out to cap a 75-yard drive following the second-half kickoff.

Illinois ran 25 more plays from scrimmage than Ohio State (81 to 56). The Illini led in first downs, 23-15, and offensive yardage, 414-292. Gary Lago was called on to punt seven times, for an average of 39 yards per kick.

Ohio State was weakened at Illinois with three additional injuries. Defensive tackle Shad Williams was lost for the remainder of the season with a serious knee injury, offensive tackle Merv Teague left with a shoulder problem, and middle guard Kevin Fletcher was sidelined with a wounded knee. Hayes referred to the game as "the most expensive victory I can remember."

To bolster its depleted ranks, sophomore Dan Cutillo replaced Williams, and junior tackle Charlie Beecroft was moved from offense to defense to add some much- needed depth. Sophomore linebacker Vic Koegel moved into the starting line up. Defensive coordinator George Hill went to a new alignment

with Koegel as a third linebacker, rather than using another middle guard to replace Fletcher.

At Bloomington the following Saturday, Ohio State relied on its passing game to defeat Indiana, 27-7. The Buckeyes scored in

Tailback Morris Bradshaw scored twice on runs of 88 yards in the homecoming game against Wisconsin. Pictured with Bradshaw are tackle Dan Scott (76) and guard Jim Kregel (63).

Route 88

Morris Bradshaw's two 88-yard scoring runs against Wisconsin in 1971, brought to memory Hopalong Cassady's unforgettable 88-yard interception return, which keyed OSU's win over the Badgers in 1954. Interestingly, these two victories over Wisconsin were both at Ohio Stadium on October 23.

each quarter against the charged-up Hoosiers, whose defense was tightly stacked to stop OSU's ground attack. Lamka and Hare combined for 17 completions and 263 of OSU's 384 total net yards. Tom Campana returned nine punts (76 yards) against IU, an all-time Ohio State single-game high.

Sophomores Bradshaw and Gradishar Shine

The Buckeyes delighted an October 23 rain-soaked homecoming crowd of 86,559, with an impressive 31-6 triumph over the potent Wisconsin Badgers. It was OSU's finest showing of the fall, as the Buckeyes ran from the wishbone-T formation for the first time this season. Ohio State tailback Morris Bradshaw scored twice on 88-yard runs, one from scrimmage in the second period and the other on a kickoff return late in the game.

Sophomore halfback Elmer Lippert gave his team a 7-0 lead early in the second quarter with a 48-yard sprint right up the middle. The Buckeyes had gained possession with linebacker Stan White's recovery of a Badger fumble at the Wisconsin 48-yard line.

OSU's defense, led by Randy Gradishar, recovered three Badger fumbles and intercepted four passes. Gradishar was credited with 11 solo tackles, seven assists, and two of the fumble recoveries. The Buckeyes, 5-1 overall and tenth in the weekly Associated Press poll, were tied with Michigan for the

Big Ten lead with identical conference records of 4-0.

Things were quite different the next Saturday, October 30, at Minneapolis, where Ohio State hung on to edge Minnesota, 14-12. Trailing 6-0 after a miserable first half, the Buckeyes scored in each of the third and fourth quarters to lead, 14-6. In the game's closing minutes, Gopher quarterback Craig Curry (who completed 27 passes for 298 yards at Ohio Stadium the previous season) drove his squad 80 yards to bring Minnesota within two at 14-12. The Gophers' two-point conversion attempt fell just one foot short, when Curry faked a rollout pass and bolted inside his left end for the end zone. Stan White, Harry Howard, and Vic Koegel made the game-saving stop.

On this dark and rainy afternoon, many of the small crowd of 36,281 headed for the exits after Ohio State's second touchdown and missed Minnesota's best drive of the afternoon. Gary Lago played a key role in the win, punting 11 times for a 45-yard average to frequently keep the Gophers deep in their own territory.

Season Changes Drastically

The Buckeyes advanced to ninth in the weekly AP rankings with an overall record of 6-1, as they returned to Ohio Stadium for a November 6 clash with always tough Michigan State. The Spartans were led by tailback Eric "The Flea" Allen, who had rushed for 350 yards during a 43-10 win at Purdue the previous week. Ohio State's defense was magnificent on this bitterly cold afternoon, holding Allen to just 79 yards. But the Buckeye offense sputtered for the second straight

Bucks Edge Gophers, 14-12

The Columbus Dispatch, Sunday, October 31, 1971

403

week, and OSU dropped its first conference game of the season, 17-10.

Hayes took full responsibility for the loss. "It was a case of our defense winning, and our offense losing," he chanted. "I coach the offense, so I'm fully to blame." The Buckeyes threw three interceptions, lost a fumble, completed just two of 15 attempted passes, and finished with a scanty 185 yards of total offense.

Northwestern added to Ohio State's woes with a 14-10 upset November 13 in the Buckeyes' last home game. The setback eliminated any chance OSU might have had of defending its Big Ten title. The Buckeyes scored first with Don Lamka's seven-yard bolt over left tackle late in the first quarter. But the lead didn't last long—NU's Greg Strunk blazed his way 93 yards with the ensuing kickoff to tie the score at 7-7.

Fred Schram connected with a 27-yard field goal late in the second period to put OSU back on top at halftime, 10-7, but it was the Buckeyes' last score of the afternoon. Midway through the final period, coach Alex Agase's squad put together an 18-play 63-yard Ohio State-type possession drive for the winning touchdown. One bright spot was the play of sophomore linebackers Koegel and Gradishar, who led OSU's defense with 21 and 18 tackles, respectively.

Valiant Effort Nearly Enough

Ohio State's trip to Ann Arbor on November 20 was another of those "strictly for pride" contests. The Buckeyes were 6-3 overall (5-2 in the league), while third-ranked Michigan was 10-0 and had outscored its opponents, 399-63. The Michigan Stadium crowd of 104,016 was, at the time, the largest ever to attend a college game.

Since Ohio State was a young team that had suffered numerous injuries throughout the season, not one offensive player who started against the Wolverines in 1970 would be available. In spite of being a decided underdog, the Scarlet and Gray nearly pulled

off the season's biggest upset before losing, 10-7. With the weather frequently changing between snow and sunshine, Hayes' valiant team, riddled by injuries but undaunted in spirit, played one of the most vivacious games in school history.

The Wolverines thoroughly dominated the game's statistics, but somehow Ohio State was repeatedly able to make "the big play" and keep the game close against the Big Ten's most devastating attack. Michigan led in first downs, 20-7, and in total offense, 335 yards to 138 (a season low for OSU). The Wolverines ran 81 plays from scrimmage compared with just 52 by the Buckeyes.

UM led at halftime on a 32-yard second-quarter field goal by Dana Coin. Late in the third period, Tom Campana gathered in a punt at his own 15-yard line, broke up the middle, faked the final defender between himself and the Michigan goal, and scored standing up to put OSU in front, 7-3. Campana's brilliant 85-yard punt return was the first Ohio State had broken for a touchdown all season. He finished the afternoon with five returns for 166 yards.

Midway through the fourth quarter, the Wolverines made their only concerted march of the afternoon, going 72 yards in 11 plays for the winning touchdown. Senior tailback Billy Taylor scored the all-important six-

Schmidt Remembered

At halftime of the Northwestern game, Coach Francis Schmidt was honored posthumously for his induction into the National Football Foundation Hall of Fame. Schmidt guided the Buckeyes from 1934 through 1940. A plaque was presented to the coach's widow, Mrs. Evelyn Schmidt, by former Ohio State assistant coach Ernie Godfrey and Northwestern Athletic Director Tippy Dye. Dye played quarterback for the Buckeyes under Schmidt in 1934-35-36.

pointer from 21 yards out, on an option pitch around end from quarterback Larry Cipa. The clock showed just 2:07 remaining when Taylor crossed the Ohio State goal line.

Woody's Most Explosive Outburst

The Buckeyes began one last drive, but it came to a screeching halt when Michigan's Thom Darden intercepted Don Lamka's pass at the UM 32-yard line. The throw was intended for receiver Dick Wakefield. Darden leaped over Wakefield to spear the ball, but Woody Hayes and his players strongly believed that Darden had interfered with Wakefield. No interference was called.

Hayes thundered to the middle of the field, roaring his disapproval at the referee who had failed to make the call. The official quickly marched off a 15-yard penalty for Hayes' intrusion over the sidelines. The Buckeye general continued to vehemently protest, even appealed to another official, and was eventually escorted to the sidelines by two of his players, Randy Gradishar and Tom Battista.

The fiery coach continued his rampage on the sideline, breaking a down marker over his knee and heaving the pieces onto the field, then ripping a bright orange first down indicator to shreds. Approximately 45 minutes after the game, a team spokesman emerged from the Ohio State locker room and said that, "Woody is not speaking to the press, not at all. That's it. He's talking to no one today." It was the first time in his 21 seasons at Ohio State that Hayes had not met with the media after a game. When asked his reaction to Hayes' conduct, Michigan Athletic Director Don Canham diplomatically stated that Woody's antics and showmanship probably helped draw an additional 30,000 to their games.

Ohio State had now lost three consecutive Big Ten games for the first time since Hayes took over the Buckeye program in

All-American center Tom DeLeone

1951. Michigan finished the regular season at 11-0, and represented the conference in the Rose Bowl. Ironically, the Wolverines lost their bowl game to Stanford, 13-12, the same team that had spoiled Ohio State's perfect season with a 27-17 Rose Bowl victory over the Buckeyes the previous year.

The young Buckeyes finished the campaign with six wins and four losses. Center Tom DeLeone, the team's MVP, was selected as an All-American. For the first time in four seasons Ohio State did not own at least a share of the Big Ten title, but one of the Scarlet and Gray's most successful and enjoyable periods was just ahead.

1971

September 11	Iowa	W	52	21
September 25	Colorado	L	14	20
October 2	California	W	35	3
October 9	at Illinois	W	24	10
October 16	at Indiana	W	27	7
October 23	Wisconsin (HC)	W	31	6
October 30	at Minnesota	W	14	12
November 6	Michigan State	L	10	17
November 13	Northwestern	L	10	14
November 20	at Michigan	L	7	10
Total Points			224	120

Season Record: 6-4
Conference: 3rd Place (Tie)

1972

Woody Hayes was optimistic about the Buckeyes' chances for 1972. Many starters were returning and several sophomores looked very promising during spring practice. In a major NCAA policy change, freshmen became eligible for varsity competition. Ohio State would likely benefit more from this modification in 1972 than any other college team. The Big Ten also abolished its "no repeat" policy for selecting its Rose Bowl representative, meaning essentially that teams could appear in Pasadena every year if they won the league title. In the next four seasons, the Buckeyes would really take advantage of this change.

Veteran offensive players returning included tackles John Hicks and Merv Teague, guards Jim Kregel and Chuck Bonica, tight end Fred Pagac, quarterback Greg Hare, fullback Randy Keith, tailbacks Elmer Lippert, Morris Bradshaw (who would spend most of the season at split end), and Rick Galbos (who shifted to wingback). Sophomores who would either start or add valuable depth included fullback Harold "Champ" Henson,

centers Steve Myers and Steve Luke, guard Dick Mack, tackles Scott Dannelley and Doug France, and ends Mike Bartoszek and Dave Hazel. Junior Blair Conway took over the placekicking duties.

Back on defense were linebackers Randy Gradishar, Vic Koegel, and Rick Middleton (switched from tight end on offense), tackles George Hasenohrl and Shad Williams, end Tom Marendt, safety Rick Seifert, halfback John Hughes, cornerback Lou Mathis, and punter Gary Lago. Sophomores who would contribute defensively included ends Van DeCree and Jim Cope, tackle Pete Cusick, linebacker Arnie Jones, halfbacks Doug Plank and Neal Colzie, and safety Rich Parsons.

The Buckeye freshman class totaled only 15, yet four would make an immediate impact—tailback Archie Griffin, wingback Brian Baschnagel, linebacker Ken Kuhn, and defensive halfback Tim Fox.

This season Ohio State also celebrated the 50th anniversary of Ohio Stadium, which was dedicated in 1922.

Record 114 Players in Uniform

Ohio State opened at home September 16 with a 21-0 win over Iowa. With the new freshman eligibility change, a record 114 players suited up. Basically, the Buckeyes outmuscled the Hawkeyes with three crunching power marches to terminate a three-game losing streak built up at the end of the last season. With the Hawkeye defense stacked to stop OSU's outside game, Hayes' fullbacks got quite a workout between the tackles. Keith and Henson combined for 35 carries and 160 of the Buckeyes' 255 rushing yards—they scored all three touchdowns on short plunges.

Hasenohrl, Marendt, and Gradishar were each credited with eight tackles as Ohio State posted its first shutout in 18 games. Late in the afternoon Hayes inserted many of his reserves, including freshman Archie Griffin, an 18-year-old tailback from Columbus

Eastmoor High School. Griffin was in for only one play. He and reserve quarterback Dave Purdy misconnected on a pitchout, and Purdy recovered the fumble for a five-yard loss. Griffin went to the sideline and wondered how this fumble might affect his career.

An Unforgettable Afternoon

Since OSU played one fewer regular-season game than the rest of the conference, the Buckeyes had two weeks to prepare for their September 30 game against North Carolina. Ohio State started very slowly against the Tar Heels, and gained only 13 yards on its first two possessions. Meanwhile, North

Freshman tailback Archie Griffin scores his first collegiate touchdown while rushing for 239 yards against North Carolina.

Carolina had grabbed an early 7-0 lead after blocking Gary Lego's punt and recovering it in the end zone. Needless to say, Coach Hayes was not very happy!

Griffin was listed as the fifth-team tailback this week, but backfield coach Rudy Hubbard had been telling Hayes all week that the freshman was practicing very well and should be given some playing time. With the offense sputtering early, Hayes decided to follow Hubbard's advice and sent Griffin into the game late in the first quarter. This move by the old master would develop into one of the most momentous decisions in all of Ohio State football.

Griffin, who had hoped "just to get into the game," was so startled he started onto the field without his helmet. Before the afternoon was complete, Griffin produced one of the most spectacular performances in Ohio State history, setting (what was then) a school single-game rushing record with 239 yards. The prior record of 229 yards was es-tablished 27 years earlier by fullback Ollie Cline, during a 14-0 win at Pittsburgh in 1945.

Ohio State defeated North Carolina, 29-14. In his Sunday column, noted *Columbus Dispatch* Sports Editor Paul Hornung stated, "Probably never in the 50-year history of Ohio Stadium has there been so sensational a debut as that of 18-year-old Eastmoor grad Archie Griffin." Griffin ran for 116 first-half yards to lead his team to a 9-7 lead at half-time. OSU's first score came on a 22-yard first-quarter field goal by Blair Conway. Quarterback Greg Hare scored on a 17-yard option play early in the second period.

The Buckeyes scored twice in the third period on touchdowns by fullbacks Randy Keith and Champ Henson. Henson's one-yard plunge was set up by Griffin's longest run of the day, a 55-yard dash down the east sidelines to the North Carolina 14-yard line. Midway through the fourth quarter, Griffin scored his first collegiate touchdown on his final carry of the afternoon, a nine-yard slash outside left tackle.

Ernie Honored

In a special ceremony before the Illinois game, coach-emeritus Ernie Godfrey was honored for his induction into the National Football Foundation Hall of Fame. While the Ohio State marching band spelled out "Ernie," Godfrey was presented his plaque by former Buckeye All-American Bill Willis and John Galbreath, who represented the Hall of Fame.

Godfrey served the Buckeyes as an assistant for 33 seasons from 1929 through 1961 under seven different head coaches, and he is credited with developing many of Ohio State's fine placekickers. Godfrey continued to tutor the kickers for many seasons after his formal retirement. The Columbus Chapter of the National Football Foundation is named in Godfrey's honor.

Ernie Godfrey

Tailback Elmer Lippert also helped the cause, rushing for 116 yards, including a 68-yard sprint for the game's longest run. Hayes strongly complimented the blocking of Keith, Hicks, France, and Bonica. Koegel led the defense with 17 tackles.

Two Middleton Interceptions Spark Comeback

The next Saturday, October 7, the Buckeyes rallied from a 9-3 halftime deficit to defeat the University of California, 35-18, at Berkeley. Interceptions deep in California territory by linebacker Rick Middleton set up two of the Buckeyes' five second-half touchdowns. Champ Henson scored three times, his longest a 25-yard thrust to conclude an explosive four-play 75-yard march early in the third period.

Ohio State used a number of big plays to generate 379 yards of offense, compared with 233 for the Golden Bears. Greg Hare clicked on eight passing attempts for 151 yards, including a nine-yard toss to Mike Bartoszek for OSU's final touchdown.

Back home the following week, Ohio State ran its record to 4-0 with a 26-7 win over Illinois before a crowd of 86,298. The Buckeyes erupted for a 19-7 lead at halftime, with Henson scoring three times from short

range to increase his season touchdown total to nine. The firepower of the attack was supplied by Archie Griffin, who gathered 192 yards in 27 carries.

OSU was not effective in the second half, and was forced to punt on its first seven possessions after failing each time to penetrate beyond the Illinois 40-yard line. Ohio State's last touchdown was a 10-yard strike from reserve quarterback Dave Purdy to tight end Fred Pagac with no time on the clock.

Stadium Golden Anniversary Celebrated

The Buckeye offense was far more impressive the next Saturday, October 21, as Ohio State shellacked Indiana, 44-7. OSU more than met the challenge of their toughest test of the season thus far. Hayes was particularly impressed with his offensive team's execution, and the dedication of the OSU defense, which played most of the game without injured linebackers Vic Koegel and Randy Gradishar. It was IU's first conference setback after victories over Minnesota (27-23) and Wisconsin (33-7).

Ohio State scored at least once in each quarter before an Ohio Stadium Golden Anniversary crowd of 86,365. Henson bulldozed his way to 116 yards and two touchdowns, while Hare also scored twice on well-executed option plays. Reserve quarterback Steve Morrison directed both of his team's last two scoring drives, as Hayes substituted liberally in the fourth quarter.

50 Years Ago Today

The Indiana game was played at Ohio Stadium on October 21, 1972, the exact 50th anniversary of the stadium dedication game against Michigan on October 21, 1922. Honored on the field at halftime were 14 former Buckeyes who had played in the 1922 dedication game.

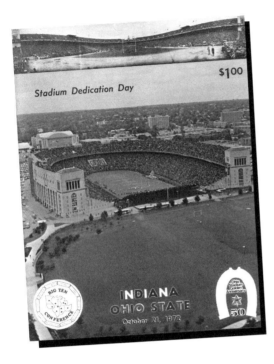

Stadium Dedication Day

$1.00

INDIANA
OHIO STATE
October 21, 1972

Game No. 200

It was far more difficult the following weekend at Madison, where the fired-up Wisconsin Badgers nearly gave a crowd of 78,713 what it had hoped to see—an enormous upset. It was, at the time, the largest crowd ever to see a game at Camp Randall Stadium. The Badgers entered the game at 3-3 overall and 1-2 in the conference. Three-touchdown-favorite Ohio State jumped out to a 28-7 halftime advantage, then held on for a nerve-racking 28-20 victory to increase its season record to 6-0.

This was Woody Hayes' 200th game since taking over the Ohio State program in 1951. His OSU career record now stood at 146-47-7. It also was Ohio State's 13th consecutive win over Wisconsin.

The first half belonged to OSU, the last half to the Badgers. The Buckeyes scored each of the four times they had the ball in the first two quarters, putting together two long marches and using fumble recoveries as springboards to the other two touchdowns.

Rick Galbos scored on a three-yard pass from Greg Hare, Champ Henson notched two TDs on short plunges, and Hare collected the final TD with an eight-yard sweep around right end.

The Badgers got back into the game after recovering two OSU fumbles in the third quarter, one at the Wisconsin 33-yard line and the second at the Wisconsin 20. UW quarterback Rudy Steiner engineered two second-half scores and finished the afternoon with 16 completions for 252 yards and two TDs. The Badgers battled right down to the last play. With the ball at the OSU 34-yard line, Steiner's last-gasp pass into the end zone was batted down by Neal Colzie as time expired, and Buckeye fans could finally breath a little easier.

Punters' Vacation

Interestingly, neither team punted the entire game. Wisconsin held a slight edge in the game's statistics, leading in first downs, 27-24, and total yards of offense, 442-419. The Badgers ran 88 plays from scrimmage, compared with 73 for the Buckeyes. Hayes gave a lot of credit to Wisconsin. He also praised Ohio State's defense unit which "hung in there until the end," despite having to finish the game without six regulars who were sidelined with injuries. Freshman linebacker Ken Kuhn was particularly impressive with 10 solo tackles and nine assists. OSU's season record now stood at 6-0.

The game at home against inspired Minnesota the following Saturday, November 4, was very similar. To the amazement of 86,439 Homecoming fans, the four-touchdown-underdog Golden Gophers (who entered the game with a record of 1-6) jumped ahead 13-7 in the first quarter. Ohio State took a 21-13 halftime lead, after scoring twice in the second period, and went on to finish with a 27-19 win that was anything but easy.

Champ Henson again powered the Buckeye running attack with 131 yards and his team's first two touchdowns. Archie Griffin scored OSU's third six-pointer with an 11-yard blast over the middle, and Greg Hare passed 23 yards to tight end Ted Powell for Ohio State's only points in the second half.

For the second straight week, Ken Kuhn led his team in tackles with 14. His interception of quarterback Bob Morgan's pass near the Ohio State goal line near halftime was one of the game's key plays. Kuhn returned the interception to the OSU 31-yard line, setting up a march of 69 yards for Ohio State's third touchdown. The Buckeyes were now 7-0 and ranked fifth in the weekly AP.

Errors Bring End to Winning Streak

Ohio State committed close to a season's worth of mistakes the following Saturday, November 11, and stumbled at Michigan State, 19-12. Three lost fumbles led to two MSU field goals and a touchdown, and one of two intercepted passes led to another MSU field goal. The underdog Spartans also were still riding the emotion of the announced retirement of coach Duffy Daugherty. The popular veteran was in his 19th season as head coach. Daugherty had told his players on Friday before MSU's 22-12 upset over Purdue the previous week that the 1972 season would be his last.

Twelve of the Spartans' 19 points came from field goals by walk-on soccer-style kicker Dirk Kryt, a transfer student from the Netherlands who was not even listed in the official program. This was his first varsity football game. Since Kryt knew so little about football, Daugherty needed to explain to him that the ball had to be kicked "over the crossbar, not underneath it." Kryt's field goals were from distances of 24, 40, 22, and 23 yards.

The underdog Spartans ran 81 plays to OSU's 57. They led in first downs, 20-12, and in total offense, 356 yards to 176. Woody Hayes' press conference lasted a full 14 seconds. He told the reporters that making all those mistakes was not exactly typical of an Ohio State team. After stating that his squad deserved the whipping it received, Hayes walked away from the reporters without taking any questions.

It's Henson's Day

The Buckeyes moved back into the victory column, November 18, with a 27-14 win at Dyche Stadium over the inspired Northwestern Wildcats. Hayes went back to his old "robust" fullhouse backfield formation for most of the afternoon. Fullback Champ Henson carried the ball 44 times, the most ever by an Ohio State player in a single game. He gained 153 yards and scored all four of his team's touchdowns on short plunges. That ran Henson's season total to 19, which was (at the time) a new Ohio State single-season record. The previous high had been 17 by Jim Otis in 1969 and John Brockington in 1970.

The Buckeyes' season record was now 8-1, 6-1 in the Big Ten. While OSU was defeating Northwestern, the Michigan Wolver-

Two-time All-American tackle John Hicks

ines edged Purdue, 9-6, at Ann Arbor to run their record to 10-0, 7-0 in conference play. Ohio State could gain a share of the Big Ten title and a trip to the Rose Bowl with a victory over Michigan the following week in Columbus. A Wolverine triumph would earn UM the outright league crown. Michigan would then return to Pasadena for the second consecutive season, since the conference had abolished its "no repeat" policy at the beginning of this season.

Defensive Wonder

The Buckeyes and Wolverines squared-off on a cold and rainy November 25 before a crowd of 87,040, at the time the second largest in Ohio Stadium history. UM entered the game ranked third in the country, OSU was ranked ninth. The Wolverines were favored by six points.

The Buckeyes won, 14-11, primarily because of two dramatic goal-line stands. It was one of the most fantastic defensive efforts ever by an Ohio State team. Michigan ran a total of 12 plays from inside the OSU five-yard line, and came away with only one touchdown. The two finished as Big Ten Co-Champions, with the Buckeyes getting the nod to meet Southern California in the Rose Bowl.

Michigan went ahead 3-0 on Mike Lantry's 35-yard field goal on the third play of the second quarter. OSU fought back to take the lead, 7-3, with Champ Henson's one-yard plunge, his 20th touchdown of the season. Near halftime the Wolverines moved to a first down at the Ohio State one-yard line. Tailback Chuck Heater, a sophomore from Tiffin, Ohio, lost one around right end on first down, then regained the yard on sec-

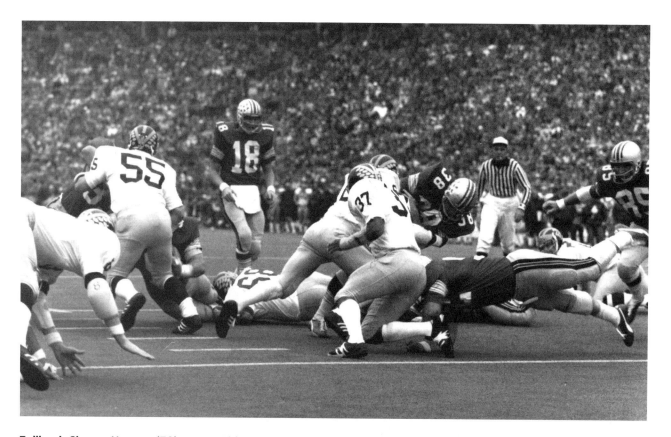

Fullback Champ Henson (38) scores Ohio State's first touchdown against Michigan, after taking handoff from quarterback Greg Hare (18). On ground is tight end Fred Pagac (80), and at right is tight end John Smurda (85).

ond down. Fullback Bob Thornbladh plunged over right tackle to the one-foot line. On fourth down, quarterback Dennis Franklin, a sophomore from Massillon, Ohio, fumbled and the ball was recovered at the two. **GOAL-LINE STAND #1** was in the books, and the Buckeyes went to the dressing room with a 7-3 lead at halftime.

Ohio State returned the second-half kickoff to its own 22-yard line, then used just two minutes and 28 seconds to march 78 yards and build its lead to 14-3. The 78-yard drive was highlighted by two huge plays. Quarterback Greg Hare rolled to his right on an option and, after sliding off a tackle, churned 35 yards down the sidelines to the UM 30-yard line. On the next play, Archie Griffin sped through right tackle, veered to his right, faked out Michigan's safety, and zoomed into the west corner of the south end zone standing up for one of the biggest touchdowns of his career.

The Wolverines quickly retaliated with their only touchdown of the afternoon, but it wasn't easy. After driving the length of the field to the OSU five-yard line, it took four plays before fullback Ed Shuttlesworth, a junior from Cincinnati, Ohio, bolted into the end zone from inside the one. Franklin passed three yards to Clint Haslerig for a two-point conversion, and the Buckeye lead had been narrowed to three at 14-11.

Early in the last period, UM's Randy Logan picked off one of Hare's passes at the OSU 29-yard line. The Wolverines quickly moved to a first down at the five, and once again the Buckeye defense would be severely tested. On first down, tailback Harry Banks, a junior from Cleveland, Ohio, swept right end for one. Banks next bolted over right guard for two, and on third down Banks rammed through right tackle to the one-foot line. The Wolverines protested that Banks had scored, but game officials saw it otherwise and placed the ball just inches short of the Ohio State goal line. Franklin failed to gain with a quarterback sneak on fourth down, and **GOAL-LINE STAND #2** was in the books.

Michigan mounted two last drives, but was not able to make another serious threat. The Wolverines swept nearly all the game statistics except the one that counted most —the final score. UM led in first downs, 21-10, and in total offense, 344 yards to 192.

Michigan ran 83 plays from scrimmage compared with just 44 for Ohio State. Sophomore linebacker Arnie Jones, playing for injured Vic Koegel, led the Buckeyes with 24 tackles. Rick Middleton was next with 17 followed by Randy Gradishar with 15.

The Wolverines could have tied the game (14-14) with a field goal on either of the two possessions when they were stopped on fourth down. A tie would have given them the outright league title and sent them to the Rose Bowl. Bo Schembechler strongly defended his decisions stating, "We should have scored from the one! We had too many opportunities to win this game and didn't. That's not like us." Woody Hayes told the press that OSU's first goal-line stand at the end of the first half was the game's turning point.

Trojans Definitely National Champions

Ohio State faced undefeated and top-ranked Southern California in the January 1, 1973, Rose Bowl before an audience of 106,869, at the time the largest crowd ever to see a football game. The younger Buckeyes fought a valiant first half and went to the dressing room tied 7-7 at halftime. But the Trojans scored touchdowns on their first

Overmatched

Southern California's 42 points in the Rose Bowl were the most scored against the Buckeyes in any of the 276 games coached by Woody Hayes from 1951 through 1978.

five possessions of the second half to win, 42-17. Two interceptions and a lost fumble led to three of USC's scores.

Southern Cal's all-around brilliance and depth had much to do with its 25-point victory. Senior fullback Sam "the Bam" Cunningham set a Rose Bowl record with four touchdowns—all dives into the end zone over goal-line pile-ups. Tailback Anthony Davis was USC's leading ground gainer with 157 yards, Griffin led the Buckeyes with 95.

Southern California (12-0) was a unanimous choice for the national title, receiving all 50 first-place votes. Michigan (10-1) finished sixth and Ohio State (9-2) ended up ninth in the final Associated Press poll. Randy Gradishar and John Hicks became All-Americans, and co-captain George Hasenohrl was chosen the team MVP. The '72 Buckeyes surprised a lot of people, possibly even to the extent that some observers praised the squad as "overachievers." Woody Hayes had completed his 22nd year at Ohio State, but some of his happiest days were just ahead.

1973

What was Ohio State's greatest all-time team? Some Buckeye fans would say 1954 (10-0), Woody Hayes' first national title squad; or 1968 (10-0), the year of the "Super Sophomores;" or 1969 (8-1), a team that averaged 42.6 points per game. Others might pick Coach Paul Brown's 1942 squad (9-1), the first Ohio State team to capture the national title. Earle Bruce's first team in 1979 went 11-1—its only loss was by a single point to USC in the Rose Bowl. The 1996 (11-1) or 1998 (11-1) teams, two of John Cooper's finest, could be logical choices. But the 1973 Buckeyes, at 10-0-1, may well have been the finest Ohio State team ever assembled.

Many successful teams are characterized by either a high-scoring offense or a stingy defense, but the '73 Buckeyes were truly outstanding on both sides of the ball. They outscored their opposition, 413-64, and led the nation in scoring defense, surrendering an average of only 4.3 points per game during the regular season. Except for a 10-10 tie at Michigan, their closest call was a 21-point Rose Bowl triumph over Southern California, 42-21. The Bucks of '73 averaged 37.5 points per game, third highest of any team in school history (42.6 in 1969, 37.9 in 1996).

Ohio State entered the '73 campaign with high expectations, since a large nucleus returned from the '72 squad that went 9-2. Sophomore Archie Griffin was back for his second season at tailback, and another sophomore, fleet footed Cornelius Green, edged out senior co-captain Greg Hare as the starting quarterback. A third sophomore, Brian Baschnagel, returned at wingback, and junior Champ Henson resumed his familiar spot at fullback.

1972

September 16	Iowa	W	21	0
September 30	North Carolina	W	29	14
October 7	at California	W	35	18
October 14	Illinois	W	26	7
October 21	Indiana	W	44	7
October 28	at Wisconsin	W	28	20
November 4	Minnesota (HC)	W	27	19
November 11	at Michigan State	L	12	19
November 18	at Northwestern	W	27	14
November 25	Michigan	W	14	11
January 1	Southern California*	L	17	42
Total Points			280	171

*Rose Bowl

Season Record: 9-2
Big Ten Co-Champion

The offensive line was built around senior tackle John Hicks, whom Woody Hayes once labeled "the greatest interior lineman I have ever coached." Kurt Schumacher handled the other tackle, Jim Kregel and Dick Mack were the guards, and Steve Myers very capably manned the center spot. The offensive ends were Fred Pagac, Dave Hazel, and Mike Bartoszek.

The defense featured three exceptional senior linebackers in co-captain Rick Middleton, Randy Gradishar, and Vic Koegel who was recuperating from knee surgery. Middleton was very versatile and often played himself into a state of near-exhaustion, Gradishar had great speed and excellent lateral pursuit, and Koegel was an extremely hard hitter with a real knack for diagnosing plays.

Arnie Jones, another exceptional linebacker, was shifted to defensive tackle so that he could be part of the starting lineup. Pete Cusick was the other tackle, and Van DeCree and Jim Cope manned the defensive ends. In the backfield, Tim Fox was at cornerback, Neal Colzie and Steve Luke handled the halfback duties, and Rich Parsons was the safety. Senior Blair Conway was the placekicker, and freshman Tom Skladany took over the punting duties.

Opener Indication of Great Season Ahead

Ohio State, picked third in the AP preseason poll, opened the season at home September 15 by scoring at least once in each quarter to overpower Minnesota, 56-7. Griffin and Colzie provided plenty of long-range

Ohio State's stout defense was paced by linebackers Rick Middleton (left), Vic Koegel (center), and two-time All-American Randy Gradishar.

fireworks, with Griffin scoring on a 93-yard kickoff return and Colzie on a 78-yard punt return. Henson, who was the nation's leading scorer in '72, tallied three times from close range. Greene played like a veteran in his first start at quarterback, directing the Buckeyes to touchdowns on four of their first six possessions.

Hayes, now in his 23rd season at Ohio State, said his team's performance was the best of any opening game he could remember. He was lavish in his praise of the offensive line, and was pleased with the way OSU's defense controlled the Golden Gophers and kept them from breaking any long plays. Ohio State led in first downs, 25-13, and had a decided edge in total offense, 457 yards to 199.

OSU's last touchdown accounted for almost all of the team's 74 passing yards—a 55-yard scoring bomb from Greg Hare to wide receiver Bill Ezzo. Frank Mosco, Minnesota's sophomore punter, was impressive averaging 48.2 yards on eight punts

Ohio State was still playing a ten-game regular-season schedule while the other Big Ten members played 11. After being idle a week, OSU had little trouble disposing of TCU on September 29, 37-3. An Ohio Stadium crowd of 87,439 sat through a rare, severe storm, complete with thunder and lightning. But it was a costly victory. Champ Henson suffered a torn knee cartilage and was lost for the remainder of the regular season.

Big running plays again sparked the attack. Griffin scored on a 68-yard scamper on OSU's second play of the game, while Greene later scored on a beautifully executed 72-yard run. The Buckeyes' outstanding linebacking trio of Gradishar, Koegel, and Middleton combined for 33 tackles and almost completely closed off the Horned Frogs' option attack. After the TCU victory, OSU moved to number one in the Associated Press poll, a position it would hold for the next eight weeks.

Elia Returns to Fullback

With Henson out, Hayes moved reserve linebacker Bruce Elia to fullback the following Monday. Elia, a junior, began his sophomore year at fullback, but had shifted to linebacker midway through the season. Elia's return to fullback would prove to be an excellent decision. Just five days after rejoining the offense, he and Griffin each scored

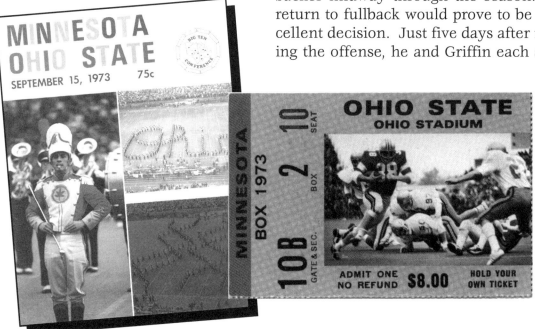

twice to lead the Buckeyes past Washington State, 27-3, at home on October 6.

Ohio State started very slowly, gaining only 23 yards with no first downs in the first period, then burst forth for all 27 points in the second and third quarters. Griffin had 128 yards rushing for his third consecutive game of 100-yards-plus. Gradishar led the defense with a career high 22 tackles, and freshman Tom Skladany averaged 48.3 yards on four punts.

Shutouts Become Habit Forming

The Bucks shut out Wisconsin 24-0 at Madison, October 13, in a game somewhat more difficult than might be implied from the final score. The Badgers hung tough on defense in the early going, allowing OSU to lead only 7-0 at halftime. Elia scored in the first and final quarters from short range, and Greene added another touchdown with a two-yard sneak on his team's first possession of the second half. Blair Conway connected on a 36-yard field goal in the fourth quarter.

The Buckeye defense was again marvelous. The Badgers moved into Ohio State territory only four times and never advanced beyond the 34-yard line. Gradishar and tackle Pete Cusick each had a dozen tackles. Wisconsin tailback Billy Marek, who was averaging 120 yards in his first four games, was held to 49. Griffin led Ohio State's attack with 169 yards, Greene added 81, and Elia had 74.

The Buckeyes were on the road again the next week, October 20, crushing Indiana at Bloomington, 37-7. The crowd of 53,183 was, at the time, the second largest ever to see a game at IU's Memorial Stadium. The nation's No. 1 ranked team, scoring in each quarter, lived up to its rating with 419 yards of total offense.

Elia scored twice and rushed for a personal-high 123 yards, while Griffin led all rushers with 130 yards. Greene scored two touchdowns on short runs, and Neal Colzie thrilled the crowd with a 55-yard interception return for a touchdown early in the third

Two-time All-American end Van DeCree.

quarter. Coach Lee Corso's Hoosiers scored the game's last points with a 51-yard toss off a reverse from flanker Mike Flanagan to end Trent Smock. Flanagan's father, Dick Flanagan, had been a starting halfback on Ohio State's undefeated National Civilian Championship squad in 1944.

Seven Players Score Touchdowns

After two weeks on the road, the Buckeyes were back at Ohio Stadium October 27 for their annual homecoming game against Northwestern. Ohio State erupted for a 60-0 victory, its most one-sided triumph of the season. Seven different Buckeyes scored eight touchdowns, including cornerback Tim Fox on a 12-yard blocked kick return and

Guard Dick Mack and quarterback Cornelius Greene head for the sideline following Greene's touchdown against Northwestern.

Colzie with a 19-yard pass interception. The Wildcats played well in the early going, holding OSU scoreless in the first 15 minutes of play. But NU couldn't sustain the effort—the Buckeyes scored 27 points in the second period and 26 in the third.

Bruce Elia injured his back after only three carries and did not return to action. Wingback Brian Baschnagel moved over to fullback for much of the afternoon, and 232-pound Pete Johnson saw his first significant action as a Buckeye. The powerful freshman churned for 37 yards on six attempts, including a 19-yarder on which he blasted over two defenders before finally being brought down.

Fighting Illini First Major Test

Heading into November, three teams were tied at the top of the Big Ten with conference records of 4-0—Ohio State, Illinois, and Michigan. The Buckeyes traveled to Champaign November 3 for their toughest challenge of the season to date, a head-to-head meeting with Illinois. The Fighting Illini were noticeably inspired with a pregame pep talk by former coach Ray Eliot, who very successfully led their program from 1942 through 1959. A dinner honoring Eliot was held Friday evening, with several of his former players returning to campus to recognize him.

Illinois played magnificently on defense in the early going, and Ohio State was forced to settle for a precarious 3-0 halftime lead on a 25-yard field goal by Blair Conway. The Buckeyes lost a fumble and had two touchdowns called back because of penalties. It was the only game all season that OSU did not score at least one touchdown in the first half. Ohio State's defense took charge in the second half, setting up four touchdown drives which covered only 41, 16, 31, and 31 yards. The Buckeyes won, 30-0.

Griffin scored from the one to boost the lead to 10-0 after three quarters, Greene added two more in the fourth, and Pete Johnson finished the scoring with his first career touchdown. Illinois was able to gain only 74 yards in total offense all afternoon.

While Ohio State was handling Illinois, Michigan crushed Indiana, 49-13. The Buckeyes and Wolverines were now tied for the conference lead at 5-0, and fans were already looking ahead three weeks to their November 24 clash at Ann Arbor.

Colzie Establishes Punt Return Mark

Back home the following Saturday, November 10, the Buckeyes swept aside Michigan State, 35-0, using a magnificent defense, a relentless ground attack, and Neal Colzie's spectacular punt returning. It was the season's fourth shutout, as OSU held the Spartans to four first downs and a sparse 94 yards of total offense. Van DeCree had a grand afternoon, collecting four tackles behind the line of scrimmage. The Spartans did

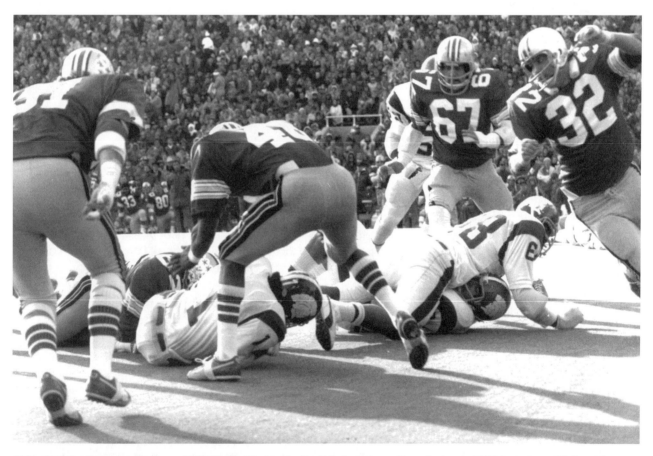

Ohio State's defense shuts out Michigan State for its third consecutive shutout of the season. Pictured are end Jim Cope (91), halfback Steve Luke (46), tackle Dan Cutillo (67), and linebacker Rick Middleton (32).

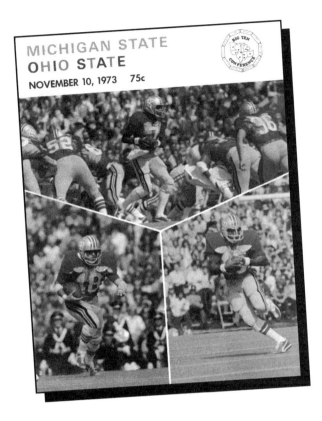

MICHIGAN STATE
OHIO STATE
NOVEMBER 10, 1973   75¢

breaking his old record of 239 set against North Carolina the previous season.

Elia netted just 11 yards in nine attempts, but four of his carries were for touchdowns from inside the three. The junior fullback now had 13 for the year, even though he hadn't joined the offense until the season's third game. With the score 48-0, the Hawkeyes dented the Buckeye reserves for two fourth-quarter scores. Ohio State had gone 15 consecutive quarters without surrendering a touchdown. Michigan defeated Purdue, 34-9, setting up a "showdown" against OSU in the regular season finale.

not cross the 50-yard line until midway in the final period, when they moved to the OSU 32 before turning over the ball on downs.

Colzie set an Ohio State single-game punt-return record, returning eight kicks for 170 yards and one touchdown, a 43-yarder in the second quarter. Archie Griffin smashed MSU for 131 yards to top the century mark in rushing for the eighth consecutive week. Griffin ran his season rushing total to 1,019 yards, to become just the third Ohio State back to rush for more than 1,000 yards in a single season. Elia scored three times and Johnson once, all from short range. The Buckeyes had outscored their first eight opponents, 306-20.

The Bucks closed out their home season November 17 with a 55-13 shellacking of winless Iowa. Thirty seniors made their last appearance in Ohio Stadium. Griffin established (what was then) a new school single-game rushing mark of 246 yards,

Enterprising Young Gate Crasher

Fans unable to obtain tickets to Ohio State games sometimes resort to devious methods of entry. Some have tried slipping through the north gates with the marching band, others have tried the emergency exits inside the Stadium Scholarship Dormitories, and a brazen few have scaled the gates.

Frank Buffington, Superintendent of Gates, remembers a clever incident back in the early 1970s. A young boy, about 11, approached Gate 10 carrying a bag of ice on each shoulder. He explained that a concession manager had sent him out to obtain the ice. The ticket takers were somewhat suspicious of the boy's story, but finally decided to let him through. Buffington recalls one of the gatemen saying, "Now let's see what he does."

After walking approximately 60 feet inside the stadium, the youngster suddenly dropped both sacks of ice and took off running at full speed. Buffington laughingly remarks, "What an ENTERPRISING young gate crasher! Just think, this youngster engineered his way inside Ohio Stadium for the cost of two 25-cent bags of ice!"

Two Team Conference

With Ohio State and Michigan dominating conference play, the Big Ten of the 1970s was commonly called the "Big Two and Little Eight." This was never more evident than in '73, when each team brought a 7-0 league record into their November 24 encounter before a Michigan Stadium crowd of 105,223. The Buckeyes had not played Purdue (4-4); Michigan did not meet Northwestern (4-4).

OSU, at 9-0 overall, had outscored its nine opponents, 361-33, while 10-0 UM had been outscoring its ten foes, 220-58. Ohio State entered the game ranked first in the nation, Michigan was fourth. The winner would be Rose Bowl bound, since the controversial "no-repeat" rule had been abolished prior to the '72 season.

The game began as a titanic defensive struggle, with neither team able to sustain a drive in the first quarter. The Buckeyes then opened up a 10-0 lead at halftime on Blair Conway's 21-yard field goal and Pete Johnson's five-yard touchdown plunge. The big fullback's score was set up by Archie Griffin, who carried five consecutive times for 41 yards on a drive starting at the UM 46.

The third quarter was scoreless, but Michigan took control late in the period after stopping Cornelius Greene on a fourth-and-two at the UM 42-yard line. This play would turn out to be a turning point of the game. The Wolverines marched to the OSU 13-yard line, where placekicker Mike Lantry put Michigan on the scoreboard with a 30-yard field goal.

After the Buckeyes were unable to sustain a drive, the Wolverines took advantage of a short punt and gained possession at their own 49-yard line. Quarterback Dennis Franklin quickly hit tight end Paul Seal with a 31-yard strike to the OSU 20-yard line. Three plays later it was fourth-and-inches at the 10. After faking a handout to fullback Ed Shuttlesworth, Franklin shot in-side OSU's left end and into the end zone. With the game tied 10-10, the Michigan faithful were delirious.

On the Wolverines' next possession, Franklin fell on his right shoulder after releasing a pass and broke his collarbone—this injury eventually damaged Michigan's Rose Bowl chances in more ways than one. When backup Larry Cipa was unable to sustain the drive, Lantry missed a field goal attempt of 57 yards.

Woody Hayes replaced Greene with Greg Hare, who was the better passer of the two. On first down, Wolverine defender Tom Drake intercepted Hare's throw at the OSU 33, and the Wolverines seemed to have everything going their way. When the clock moved down to 24 seconds, Lantry missed another field goal try, this time from 44 yards. Ohio State and Michigan had played to a tie for the first time since 1949. Who would go to the Rose Bowl? The Buckeyes dropped to third in the weekly AP poll, behind undefeated Alabama and once-tied Oklahoma, and Michigan remained fourth.

The Big Ten's Big Controversy

With Ohio State and Michigan tying for the Big Ten title with identical 7-0-1 league records, the conference athletic directors met Sunday in Chicago to select the Rose Bowl representative. This may well have been the most famous vote in conference history. To the surprise of many, Ohio State was selected. The league office would not release the vote count, but the *Detroit Free Press* reported it to be six to four. The story stated that Ohio State received votes from Illinois, Michigan State, Wisconsin, Purdue, and

Big 10 Vote Delights Hayes, Football Squad

The Columbus Dispatch—Monday, November 26, 1973

Northwestern, while Michigan got the support of Indiana, Iowa, and Minnesota.

Michigan coach Bo Schembechler was extremely bitter, stating that his team deserved the trip because he felt his team had outplayed Ohio State. Schembechler cited his team's lead in first downs, 16-9, and in total offensive yards, 333 to 204. He also protested that Ohio State had been to Pasadena the previous season. Ironically, Michigan Athletic Director Don Canham had been one of the strong backers to abolish the "no repeat" policy.

The condition of Wolverine quarterback Dennis Franklin probably influenced some of the votes. Franklin would not have been able to play because of the broken collarbone suffered late in the game. Schembechler was furious and insisted that Larry Cipa was an excellent replacement, but apparently the athletic directors thought otherwise.

Ohio State Deserving Representative

The Buckeyes really made the most of the Rose Bowl opportunity, defeating Southern California, 42-21. Trailing 21-14 early in the third quarter, Ohio State scored the game's last 28 points to give the Big Ten its first Rose Bowl triumph in five years.

The Ohio State offense accounted for 449 yards, 320 of them on the ground. Archie Griffin led all rushers with 149 yards in 22 carries, including a beautiful 47-yard run for the game's final touchdown. Big Pete Johnson scored three on power plunges of 1, 1, and 4 yards, while Bruce Elia and Cornelius Greene scored on runs of 1 and 2 yards, respectively. Greene's TD followed a spectacular 56-yard punt return by Neal Colzie.

Greene was named the game's MVP because of his slick ball handling and pinpoint passing. His throwing was decisive on several drives, and he completed six of eight tosses for 129 yards. Tight end Fred Pagac, later OSU's Assistant Head Coach, was Greene's prime receiver with four catches for 89 yards.

Rose Bowl Remembrances

Ohio State All-American tackle John Hicks became the first college player to appear in three Rose Bowls (1971, 1973, 1974). Two-time Heisman Winner Archie Griffin is the only player in college history to have started four Rose Bowls (1973 through 1976).

Postseason Honors Galore

Four Buckeyes were selected as All-Americans; seniors Randy Gradishar and John Hicks repeated the honor, and were joined by junior end Van DeCree and sophomore tailback Archie Griffin. Griffin led the conference in both rushing and total offense and became the only sophomore to be chosen the Big Ten's Most Valuable Player. Hicks captured both the Outland Trophy and

Tight end Fred Pagac.

Lombardi Award, and finished second to Penn State's John Cappelletti in the race for the Heisman Trophy. Gradishar was awarded a graduate scholarship from the National Football Foundation, based upon his excellence in both athletics and academics.

Bruce Elia tied with Wisconsin's Billy Marek for the conference scoring title with 66 points. The '73 Buckeyes finished second behind undefeated Notre Dame in the final Associated Press poll. Yes, this team may well have been the finest Ohio State team ever assembled.

Bruce Elia was the team's leading scorer as a fullback in 1973 with 84 points. As a linebacker in 1974, Elia was the team's leading tackler with 144 tackles.

1974

Woody Hayes' future was the Ohio State football program's biggest concern as the 1974 season approached. Hayes suffered a heart attack on Thursday, June 6, and an uncertainty about his role was inevitable. It was exactly 100 days until Saturday, September 14, when the Buckeyes would open their 1974 campaign at Minnesota. The 61-year-old veteran spent most of the summer recuperating. Rumors persisted that Hayes would decide to retire, but nothing could have been further from the truth. By fall Hayes had shed about 25 pounds, appeared "more relaxed," and was cleared for his normal autumn duties.

That summer Defensive Coordinator George Hill represented Ohio State at the annual Big Ten luncheon and media gathering in Chicago. When introduced to the group as Woody Hayes's "replacement," Hill reminded everyone that, "NO ONE replaces Woody Hayes—today I'm simply substituting for Coach Hayes while he is at home continuing his recovery."

High Expectations

Ohio State anticipated making another strong run at the national title, especially with the return of 16 starters from the excellent '73 squad. The explosive backfield of Cornelius Greene, Archie Griffin, Brian Baschnagel, Champ Henson, and Pete Johnson was intact, as was the entire defensive backfield of Neal Colzie, Tim Fox, Steve Luke, and Rich Parsons. Senior Doug Plank and sophomore Bruce Ruhl would see considerable playing time as the season progressed.

One big assignment was replacing the outstanding linebacking trio of Gradishar,

1973				
September 15	Minnesota	W	56	7
September 29	Texas Christian	W	37	3
October 6	Washington State	W	27	3
October 13	at Wisconsin	W	24	0
October 20	at Indiana	W	37	7
October 27	Northwestern (HC)	W	60	0
November 3	at Illinois	W	30	0
November 10	Michigan State	W	35	0
November 17	Iowa	W	55	13
November 24	at Michigan	T	10	10
January 1	Southern California*	W	42	21
Total Points			413	64

*Rose Bowl

Season Record: 10-0-1
Big Ten Co-Champion

Koegel, and Middleton. Bruce Elia returned to defense from fullback to fill one spot and Arnie Jones was used effectively at both tackle and linebacker. Senior Brian Bowers, sophomore Ed Thompson, and junior Ken Kuhn all saw extensive playing time. On offense, junior Scott Dannelley took over John Hicks' tackle slot, junior Ted Smith converted from linebacker to replace guard Jim Kregel, and 6'6" senior Doug France moved from tackle to fill Fred Pagac's tight end position.

Rushing Record Shattered

The Buckeyes opened the season September 14 with a wild victory, 34-19, at Minnesota before a crowd of 45,511. The contest marked the golden anniversary of the Golden Gophers' Memorial Stadium, which was dedicated 50 years earlier in 1924. Archie Griffin was the game's leading ground gainer with 133 yards, increasing his career rushing total to 2,577, a new school record. The junior tailback moved into the top spot ahead of Jim Otis (2,542 yards) and Hopalong Cassady (2,466 yards).

Ohio State jumped off to a 21-3 lead at halftime and increased its advantage to 28-3 after three quarters. Champ Henson scored OSU's third touchdown from 36 yards out on his very first carry of the year, after missing most of the last season with a knee injury. But the Gophers rode the passing of quarterback Tony Dungy and the running of tailback Rick Upchurch, to score two fourth-quarter

touchdowns and two two-point conversions and tighten the score at 28-19.

After Minnesota's second touchdown, the Buckeyes brought the ensuing kickoff out only to the OSU 14-yard line, and Gopher fans sensed that an upset was still possible. After Ohio State moved the ball out to its own 43, Cornelius Greene (on a third-and-five) completely fooled the defense with a 57-yard scamper around end for the game's last score.

Woody Hayes was moderately happy with the win, but was quick to point out that his team would have to eliminate many of its mistakes in the weeks ahead. This was the first game after his summer heart attack; the coach said that he felt tired, but no more than usual after a game. The pollsters were apparently impressed with the Buckeyes' first game. Ohio State advanced from fourth to second in the weekly AP poll behind Notre Dame.

Eleven at Last

In 1974, Ohio State followed in the footsteps of the other Big Ten schools when it

All-American tackle Kurt Schumacher

Unusual Start

Ohio State's 34-19 season-opening victory at Minnesota marked the first time the Buckeyes had opened away from home in 62 seasons. Their last road opener had been a 55-0 win at Otterbein College in Westerville, Ohio, on October 5, 1912.

extended its regular-season schedule from 10 games to 11. Oregon State traveled to Columbus September 21 for a contest that had been added to the schedule within the last year. The Buckeyes clobbered the Beavers, 51-10, despite losing four fumbles. After Woody Hayes cleared his bench in the second half, Oregon State managed to score its only touchdown midway through the final period.

With Ohio State holding a 23-3 halftime lead, junior college transfer Lenny Willis grabbed the second-half kickoff and sprinted 97 yards down the east sideline for the first touchdown of the third quarter. Archie Griffin sped for 134 yards to increase his streak of 100-yard-plus games to 13. Freshman tailback Ray Griffin, Archie's younger brother, scored his first two collegiate touchdowns late in the game on runs of nine and 12 yards.

Southern Methodist invaded Columbus the next Saturday, September 28, to battle a Buckeye squad that had advanced to the top spot in the weekly AP following its 41-point victory over Oregon State. Ohio State scored once in each quarter to put away the Mustangs, 28-9, but the game was somewhat more tough than predicted.

The OSU offense sputtered at times while gaining 403 net yards, and the defense yielded 337 yards including 281 on the ground. SMU ran 83 plays from scrimmage, OSU ran 61.

Wingback Brian Baschnagel ran two reverse plays to perfection, scoring on a 44-yard run in the second quarter and repeating the same play for 64 yards in the fourth period to set up his team's final touchdown. When asked about the reverse, Hayes said he borrowed it from Army's Red Blaik who had developed the play in the mid-1940s for the Cadets' Heisman Trophy winner Glenn Davis. Baschnagel finished the afternoon with 140 yards on just seven carries, Griffin was the game's leading rusher with 156 yards on 24 attempts.

Hey, Buddy, I Think You're Sitting in My Seat!

The Buckeyes blew out Oregon State, 51-10, in their home opener on September 21. But some of the REAL action that afternoon came, not from the playing field, but up in the stands. As fans began arriving, Portal Chief Kenny Tinkler suddenly realized he had a big problem—all seats for section 9B had been double-printed and double-sold. In essence, two different fans each held identical tickets for every seat. Tinkler estimates about 700 seats were duplicated. Obviously, most of the spectators were anything but overjoyed with the predicament.

Some fans were seated on top of the press box, others on temporary folding chairs placed on the running track, while others simply sat in the aisles. Portal Superintendent Dick Weber has remarked, "Those displaced fans probably can't recall the opponent, the final score, or even the season—but they'll always remember the confusion associated with the double-printing of the game tickets for section 9B."

Ohio State defeated Washington State, 42-7, in the third and final non-conference game of the regular season. The encounter was held October 5 at Huskie Stadium on the University of Washington campus, rather than the Washington State campus in Pullman. WSU moved the game to Seattle in anticipation of drawing a larger crowd. The attendance was estimated at 50,000.

The Buckeyes put everything together to play their finest game of the young 1974 season. After building up a 35-7 lead at halftime, Hayes used his second units most of the third and fourth quarters. For the fourth straight week Ohio State scored on its first possession. Archie Griffin was the game's top runner with 196 yards, including a spectacular 75-yard touchdown sprint—the longest run of his college career. Fullback Champ Henson got his first start of the season and scored twice. Woody Hayes was most pleased that his team had committed no turnovers.

Buckeyes Destroy Badgers

The top-ranked Buckeyes returned home October 12 to entertain ambitious Wisconsin. Coach John Jardine's 13th-ranked Badgers were 3-1 after impressive wins over Purdue, Nebraska, and Missouri, and a three-point loss to Colorado. Wisconsin opened impressively by taking the opening kickoff and moving 80 yards in just six plays to grab an early 7-0 lead. But from there it was all Ohio State. The Badger offense never advanced farther than the OSU 29-yard line the rest of the afternoon.

OSU quickly retaliated with a field goal and seven touchdowns to rout the visitors, 52-7. Five interceptions by the defense aided OSU's scoring assault. Safety Bruce Ruhl, who started in place of Rich Parsons (after Parsons suffered a broken arm the previous week) made three of the interceptions to tie a school single-game record. It was the Badgers' most one-sided setback since losing at Ohio State, 62-7, on November 8, 1969.

With the Badger defense obviously set to neutralize Griffin, OSU countered the strategy with the play of Cornelius Greene. The junior quarterback finished the afternoon with his top offensive game as a Buckeye— 146 yards rushing, 81 passing yards (5 of 7), and two touchdowns. Griffin still managed 112 yards, his 16th consecutive 100-yard-plus game.

Ohio State continued its excellent play at home the following week with a convincing 49-9 rout of coach Lee Corso's Indiana Hoosiers. The Buckeyes

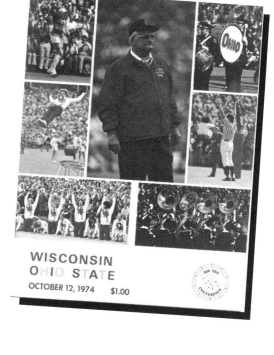

WISCONSIN
OHIO STATE
OCTOBER 12, 1974 $1.00

stormed through IU for a staggering 568 yards, while holding the opposition to 266. OSU had 377 yards by halftime to lead, 35-3. Hayes cleared his bench in the second half, and had used 16 different ball carriers by the time the final whistle blew. Linebacker Bruce Elia led the defensive charge with 14 tackles.

The Ohio Stadium crowd of 87,671 included members of Ohio State's 1954 national champions who were back on campus for their 20-year reunion.

Archie Griffin ran for 146 yards and became, what was then, the Big Ten's all-time career rushing leader. The junior tailback's career total of 3,321 yards eclipsed the previous high of 3,315 held by Otis Armstrong of Purdue (1970-71-72). The Buckeyes surprised Indiana (and everyone else) with their aggressive passing attack. Greene topped his prior week's game against Wisconsin with

330 yards of total offense—235 yards passing (9 of 11) and 95 on the ground.

It was more of the same October 26 in Evanston where Ohio State routed Northwestern, 55-7. OSU scored eight of the 10 times it had the ball. It also was the seventh straight game the Buckeyes scored the first time they had the ball. Hayes used 13 different ball carriers, and seven different players scored the team's eight touchdowns. Tom Klaban successfully converted after the first six touchdowns and increased his consecutive streak to 36. The soccer-style kicker's next attempt, however, veered left of the upright, leaving him three short of the then Ohio State record of 39.

At 7-0 overall and 4-0 in the conference, the Buckeyes strengthened their hold on the top spot in the weekly Associated Press poll. Oklahoma was second, followed by the Michigan Wolverines, whose record was identical to Ohio State's. Analysts were already looking ahead four weeks to what seemed to be an annual clash between the Buckeyes and Wolverines that would settle the Big Ten title, Rose Bowl representative, and possibly the national championship.

No. 200 and #18

Saturday, November 2, 1974, was heroic. Woody Hayes joined a select circle of American coaches with his 200th career victory, and Archie Griffin became the first player in major college football history to rush for 100 or more yards in 18 consecutive regular season games. Ohio State destroyed Illinois that after-

noon, 49-7, before a homecoming crowd of 87,813, at the time the largest in Ohio Stadium history.

Griffin finished the afternoon with 144 yards. The carry which took him over the century mark was a 22-yard touchdown sprint with 3:21 remaining in the third quarter. Griffin's string was actually 19 if the previous season's Rose Bowl is included, but bowl games are not considered with this particular NCAA record. Ray Griffin replaced his brother late in the game and picked up 86 yards in eight carries. Greene finished the afternoon with 127 yards rushing and 127 yards passing. The Buckeyes pounded the Illini for 644 yards of total offense, a modern day single-game record that stood until the 1986 squad amassed 715 yards against Utah.

Hayes' all-time college record was now 200-60-8, including totals of 167-49-8 at Ohio State. He had a three-year mark of 19-6 at Denison and a two-season total of 14-5 at

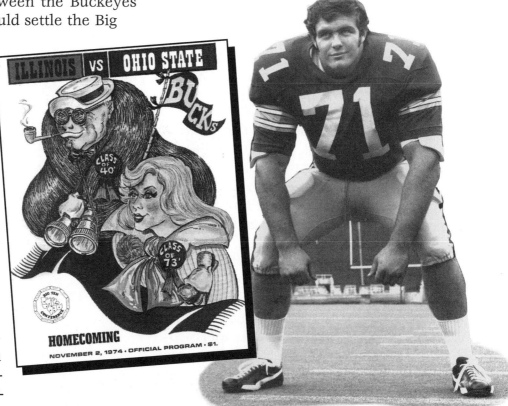

All-American tackle Pete Cusick

Miami (Ohio) before arriving at Ohio State in 1951. While Ohio State routed Illinois, Michigan kept pace with a solid 21-7 victory at Indiana.

Who Won?

Ohio State's unbeaten record and its number-one national ranking came crashing down November 9 at the hands of inspired underdog Michigan State, 16-13. The game, played before a Spartan Stadium crowd of 78,533, ended in a controversy that will be sadly remembered for as long as the Buckeyes play football. Ohio State entered the game at 8-0, having outscored its opponents, 360-75. The Buckeyes had given up no more than one touchdown in each of their last seven games. Michigan State was 4-3-1 on the season, with wins over Northwestern (41-7), Syracuse (19-0), Purdue (31-7), and Wisconsin (28-21); losses to UCLA (14-56), Notre Dame (14-19), and Michigan (7-21); and a 21-21 tie with Illinois.

The game was tied 3-3 at halftime, after two lost fumbles and an interception curtailed Ohio State's first-half offensive efforts. The Buckeyes opened the second half with a march from their own 18 to a first down at the MSU 9-yard line. The drive stalled, and Tom Klaban booted his second field goal to put OSU on top, 6-3.

Early in the final period, Steve Luke recovered quarterback Charlie Baggett's fumble at the MSU 44-yard line. Champ Henson and Archie Griffin combined forces behind great blocking, especially by Steve Myers and Ted Smith, to increase Ohio State's lead to 13-3. Henson charged one yard over right tackle for the touchdown with 9:03 left in the game. On the ensuing possession, Baggett connected with end Mike Jones on a 44-yard scoring pass to tighten the score at 13-9 (a two-point conversion attempt failed).

Ohio State was unable to sustain a drive on its next possession, but punter Tom Skladany came through with a 55-yard punt to put the Spartans deep at their own 12-yard line. On first down, fullback Levi Jackson

broke through a hole over right tackle, eluded three tacklers, and scored standing up with 3:17 remaining to put Michigan State on top for the first time all afternoon, 16-13. Jackson's 88-yard sideline sprint is the second longest in history by an Ohio State opponent.

The Buckeyes quickly marched from their own 29-yard line to the Spartan five, where fullback Champ Henson plunged to within inches of the goal line. There were 29 seconds remaining and Ohio State had used all its timeouts. MSU's defenders were very slow to get up following Henson's plunge, and Ohio State had difficulty getting off an additional play. When the ball was finally snapped, it squirted between the legs of quarterback Cornelius Greene and was picked up and carried into the end zone by wingback Brian Baschnagel. Headlinesman Ed Scheck signaled touchdown, but field

All-American Center Steve Myers

With Brian Baschnagel holding, Tom Klaban kicks one of his four field goals against Michigan.

judge Robert Dagenhardt indicated time had run out before this last play.

To say that confusion followed is a strong understatement. Approximately 40,000 of the 78,533 fans were still in the stadium when, 46 minutes later, commissioner Wayne Duke announced Michigan State had won the game, 16-13. Referee Gene Calhoun informed Duke time had run out before OSU's last play. Calhoun also stated the Buckeyes would have been penalized (if time had not run out), because they did not come to a required one-second set before the ball was snapped.

The Buckeyes' lofty number-one ranking was a thing of the past. Michigan won at Illinois, 14-6, to move into sole possession of first place in the conference, and the complexion of the Big Ten race had changed radically.

After the ambush at East Lansing, Ohio State moved back into the victory column by defeating Iowa, 35-10, before a chilled Kinnick Stadium crowd of 48,700. The Hawkeyes were led by first-year coach Bob Commings, who played at Iowa in the mid-1950s and more recently enjoyed a very successful stint as head coach of the Massillon High School Tigers. The Buckeyes were not especially sharp and were fortunate to win by 25 points. Iowa, who trailed just 14-10 at the half, ripped OSU's defense for 339 yards and seriously threatened to score three times in the final period.

Henson scored three times on short plunges, Griffin added another on a 19-yard burst through the middle, and Pete Johnson powered his way 12 yards for the game's final score. Griffin finished with 175 yards to extend his consecutive 100-or-more yard games to 21. Michigan blasted Purdue at Ann Arbor, 51-0, and the stage was now set for the season's biggest game.

Kickers Take Center Stage

In what had become an almost annual event, Ohio State and Michigan squared off the last weekend of the regular season to decide the Big Ten title and representation to the Rose Bowl. Excitement in Columbus and around Ohio intensified so much during the week, that by Saturday afternoon, November 23, Ohio Stadium was at an almost unparalleled fever pitch. The demand for tickets was one of the fiercest in many seasons, and the attendance of 88,243 was (at the time) the largest to ever pack the horseshoe.

Ohio State was the Big Ten's top offensive team, Michigan was ranked number one in defense. The Wolverines (10-0, 7-0) could capture the outright title with a victory, while an Ohio State (9-1, 6-1) triumph would force a co-championship that would require a Sunday vote of the conference's athletic directors to decide the Rose Bowl delegate. Michigan entered the epic battle ranked third in the national rankings (behind Oklahoma and Alabama), Ohio State was fourth.

The Wolverines opened convincingly, scoring on their fourth play of the afternoon with a 42-yard TD toss from quarterback Dennis Franklin to wingback Gil Chapman. On the ensuing possession, OSU lost a fumble at the UM 26-yard line. Franklin directed his team downfield until the march stalled at the OSU 20-yard line. Mike Lantry calmly booted a 38-yard field goal, and the Maize and Blue were in solid command, 10-0, with 4:57 of the first period still remaining.

The second quarter belonged to Ohio State. Driving into the closed end of Ohio Stadium with the wind at their backs, the Buckeyes called upon Tom Klaban for three second-quarter field goals of 47, 25, and 43 yards, to tighten the score at 10-9 after two periods. Klaban, a junior from Cincinnati who learned to play soccer in Europe, had never played football until Hayes granted him a tryout. He had settled in the U.S. just 10 years earlier, after he and his family escaped to Canada from Czechoslovakia and later settled in Cincinnati.

Early in the third period, Klaban booted his fourth three-pointer, a 45-yarder (also at the stadium's north end), to put Ohio State on top, 12-10. Much of the credit is also due Klaban's holder, wingback Brian Baschnagel. Two of the four snaps from center were extremely low, but Baschnagel was able to accurately make the placements, thus enabling Klaban's masterful feat.

There would be no further scoring after Klaban's fourth connection, even with 25 minutes and nine seconds remaining to be played. But the tension generated the rest of the afternoon is nearly impossible to describe. Late in the third period Michigan ap-

Streak Broken

Ohio State's 12-10 triumph over Michigan marked the first time in 81 games the Buckeyes had been held without a touchdown. The last was November 19, 1966, when Michigan defeated Ohio State, 17-3.

peared to have positioned itself to regain the lead, holding the Buckeyes deep and forcing them to punt from their own end zone. But Tom Skladany's booming 63-yard kick and Ray Griffin's excellent coverage forced the Wolverines to take possession at their own 30, and the threat of giving Michigan an easy field-goal attempt was eliminated. Skladany came through with one of his finest punts when it was needed the most.

With 16 seconds remaining in the game, Michigan had one final chance with the ball

The Dispatch
SUNDAY, NOV. 24, 1974 FXX E-1

SPORTS SECTION

*Outdoor Features,
Jim Murray Column,
Race Results*

Bucks' Toe Beats Bo, 12-10

Klaban's Four Field Goals Victory Margin, Ohio, Michigan Share Title; Bowl Pick ???

on the Ohio State 16-yard line. Kicking into the stadium's closed end with a strong wind at his back, Mike Lantry attempted a 33-yard field goal that would mean not only the difference between winning or losing the game, but also the league title and possible Rose Bowl trip. The left-footer's kick was wide to the left by a mere 18 inches, and the Buckeyes had really "dodged a bullet." Final score: Ohio State 12, Michigan 10.

Schembechler Correct

Michigan coach Bo Schembechler had predicted earlier in the week that the outcome would be decided by the "kicking game." How right he was! Woody Hayes could not say enough about his team's defense, which made the "big play" numerous times to hold Michigan scoreless the last three quarters. He especially praised the play of tackles Pete Cusick and Nick Buonamici, end Van DeCree, linebackers Ken Kuhn and Bruce Elia, and cornerback Neal Colzie.

Elia was credited with a season-high 19 tackles, and his second-quarter interception led to Klaban's second field goal. Colzie (who was questionable for the game after being hospitalized most of the week with the flu) had a huge second-half play, intercepting one of Franklin's passes after Michigan had advanced to the OSU 39-yard line.

Ohio State and Michigan finished the regular season as the conference's co-champions (both were 10-1, 7-1). The Wolverines won the battle of the statistics, leading in first downs, 18-14, and total offensive yards, 291-253. Archie Griffin was the afternoon's leading ground gainer with 111 yards, his 21st consecutive game of exceeding the 100-yard mark. Skladany was outstanding, averaging 45.2 yards on five punts. Hayes gave Tom Klaban the game ball and immediately awarded him a full scholarship for the rest of his stay at Ohio State.

In their Sunday "bowl ballot," the conference athletic directors selected Ohio State as the Big Ten's representative to face Southern California in the Rose Bowl. Hayes' team was the AD's choice, at least partly because it had defeated Michigan in head-to-head competition. For the third consecutive year it would be the Buckeyes and Trojans in Pasadena on New Year's Day.

All But Three

Michigan's excellent three-year record from 1972 through 1974 was 30-2-1. The only three games the Wolverines failed to win were their three against Ohio State. The Buckeyes won in 1972 (14-11) and 1974 (12-10), and the two battled to a 10-10 tie in 1973.

431

Ohio State celebrated a very special award as it prepared to meet USC. On December 3, Archie Griffin was selected the winner of the coveted Heisman Trophy, which is presented annually to the nation's top college player. Griffin became just the fifth junior to capture the prize, which was first awarded to Jay Berwanger of the University of Chicago in 1935.

Father-Son Act Aids USC in Rubber Match

The Rose Bowl was promoted as a dual between the nation's two top tailbacks, since USC's Anthony Davis finished second to Griffin in the Heisman Trophy voting. It also was billed as a "rubber match," since the two schools had split the last two Rose Bowls—OSU over USC (42-21) the previous year, and USC over OSU (42-17) two years before. Southern California won the "tie-breaker," 18-17, in one of the wildest, "anything-can-happen" match-ups in Rose Bowl history.

The game developed into a battle of the quarterbacks rather than tailbacks. Davis suffered a chest injury in the first half and never returned to action, although Allan Carter played well as Davis' replacement. Davis finished with 67 yards, Carter with 75. Griffin also completed the afternoon with 75, marking the first time in the last 23 games (including bowls) that the Buckeyes' star tailback had been held under 100 yards.

Both teams squandered numerous scoring opportunities during the first three periods, which ended with Ohio State on top, 7-3. Champ Henson had scored with a powerful two-yard blast with 4:42 remaining before the half. In the third period the Buckeyes twice had the ball inside the USC 10-yard line but failed to score.

After USC marched 72 yards for a touchdown and a 10-7 lead early in the fourth quarter, Ohio State scored on its first two possessions of the final period to go back on top, 17-10. Cornelius Greene engineered an 82-yard march, scoring the touchdown himself

untouched with a rollout around end after Pete Johnson made a great fake into the line. Two plays later OSU got a big break when Van DeCree recovered a Trojan fumble at the USC 30-yard line. But the offense was unable to go the distance, and Klaban's 32-yard field goal built the lead to seven. There was 6:38 remaining in the game.

After bringing the kickoff out to its own 17-yard line, Southern Cal calmly used nine plays to drive 83 yards and bring the Trojans within one at 17-16. The touchdown was a 38-yard pass from quarterback Pat Haden to end J. K. McKay, son of USC head coach John McKay and Haden's teammate and good friend since high school. With just 2:03 showing on the clock, Haden rifled a pass to Shelton Diggs, who made a diving catch in the end zone for a two-point conversion which spelled a single-point victory over Ohio State.

All-American defensive back Neal Colzie

The Buckeyes made one last attempt, moving to the USC 48-yard line with 21 seconds to play. Tom Skladany's desperation attempt for a 62-yard field goal was on line but fell just short in the end zone. Coach John McKay maybe best described the afternoon's play when he told the press, "It was a great game between two great teams. When the game ended we had 18 points and they had 17." An obviously disappointed Woody Hayes was very cordial while spending about 20 minutes with reporters, and admitted his team simply did not play quite well enough to win. Haden and J. K. McKay shared the game's MVP award.

Ohio State's Finest 10-2 Team

The Buckeyes finished fourth in the final 1974 Associated Press poll. Oklahoma (11-0) captured the national title, followed by Southern California (10-1-1) and Michigan (10-1). It was a great season with two near misses—the controversial ending at Michigan State and the single-point setback in the Rose Bowl. It's doubtful if there ever was a better Ohio State team to finish with two losses. The Buckeyes outscored their 12 opponents, 437-129, while scoring 59 touchdowns and amassing 5,252 yards of total offense.

1974				
September 14	at Minnesota	W	34	19
September 21	Oregon State	W	51	10
September 28	Southern Methodist	W	28	9
October 5	at Washington State	W	42	7
October 12	Wisconsin	W	52	7
October 19	Indiana	W	49	9
October 26	at Northwestern	W	55	7
November 2	Illinois (HC)	W	49	7
November 9	at Michigan State	L	13	16
November 16	at Iowa	W	35	10
November 23	Michigan	W	12	10
January 1	Southern California*	L	17	18
Total Points			437	129
*Rose Bowl				

Season Record: 10-2
Big Ten Co-Champion

Griffin and DeCree repeated as All-Americans and were joined on the select team by Neal Colzie, Pete Cusick, Kurt Schumacher, and Tom Skladany. Archie Griffin, who rushed for 1,695 yards over the season's 12 games, was chosen the Big Ten's MVP for the second consecutive season.

1975

Ohio State entered the 1975 season with great optimism, even though Hayes and his staff faced a major rebuilding effort. Only nine starters from the '74 season were back —six on offense and three on defense. Gone from the offensive unit were tight end Doug France, All-American tackle Kurt Schumacher, All-American center Steve Myers, guard Dick Mack, and split end Dave Hazel. Fullback Champ Henson elected not to return in '75, even though he was granted an additional year of eligibility because of a leg injury that sidelined him for most of 1973.

Ohio State had to rebuild almost its entire defense. Missing from '74 were ends Van DeCree and Jim Cope, tackle Pete Cusick, linebackers Bruce Elia and Arnie Jones, and defensive backs Neal Colzie, Steve Luke, Rich Parsons, and Doug Plank. DeCree, Cusick, and Colzie had been All-Americans.

Backfield Intact

The Buckeyes returned one of the finest and most explosive backfields in school history. Archie Griffin was again at tailback, after rushing for 4,139 yards his first three seasons. Versatile Brian Baschnagel, an excellent blocker and pass receiver, returned at wingback. Cornelius Greene, a nimble and exciting speedster, continued at quarterback, and big Pete Johnson was set at fullback. Griffin, Baschnagel, and Greene were se-

Ohio State's splendid backfield of wingback Brian Baschnagel, quarterback Cornelius Greene, fullback Pete Johnson, and tailback Archie Griffin.

niors, Johnson a junior. Heading into 1975, Griffin had rushed for more than 100 yards in 21 consecutive regular season games.

Senior Lenny Willis, the squad's fastest player (:09.5 in the 100 yard dash), took over at split end. The tackles were senior veteran Scott Dannelley and sophomore Chris Ward. Returning senior Ted Smith was joined at guard by junior Bill Lukens. Junior Rick Applegate, a reserve tackle in '74, shifted to center. Placekicker Tom Klaban, who will always be remembered for his four field goals against Michigan in '74, returned for his senior season.

Defensively, senior Pat Curto and junior Bob Brudzinski took over at the ends. Returning junior Nick Buonamici was joined at tackle by sophomore Eddie Beamon. The linebackers were senior Ken Kuhn, junior Ed Thompson, and sophomore Aaron Brown. Senior Tim Fox and junior Bruce Ruhl re-

turned in the secondary, and were joined by senior Craig Cassady and sophomore Ray Griffin, who shifted to defense after playing tailback his freshman season. All-American punter Tom Skladany had led the Big Ten in '74 with an average of 46.1 yards per punt.

Michigan was the Big Ten's preseason favorite, with Ohio State a close second. In the national polls Oklahoma was everyone's choice to repeat as national champion. Michigan was picked second and the Buckeyes third.

Gigantic Big Ten Opener

Ironically, Ohio State launched the 1975 season September 13 against eleventh-ranked Michigan State at East Lansing, before a record crowd of 80,383. With memories of the '74 debacle still very vivid, OSU shut out the Spartans, 21-0, in one of the most highly publicized openers in Big Ten football.

The team was pleased to settle the year-old score, and 62-year-old Woody Hayes was especially thrilled with the play of his young defense.

Ohio State held the explosive Spartans to just 11 first downs and 173 yards in total offense. Senior defensive halfback Craig Cassady (son of Hopalong Cassady, '55 Heisman winner) tied a school single-game record with three interceptions. It was his first start as a Buckeye.

Ohio State began slowly and had horrible field position the first quarter. But the booming punts of Tom Skladany kept Michigan State at bay until the offense could get rolling. Skladany averaged a superb 45 yards on four punts. OSU finally put together a 57-yard scoring march late in the second period to lead 7-0 at halftime. The touchdown came on a six-yard burst over left tackle by fullback Pete Johnson.

The Buckeyes made it 14-0 on their first possession after intermission, with Cornelius Greene hooking up with Lenny Willis on a 64-yard pass play. Willis juggled the ball at the MSU 25-yard line, eluded defender Joe Runt, and raced into the end zone untouched. In the final period, Johnson scored his second six-pointer from the nine, and Tom Klaban added his third conversion to complete the scoring. The Buckeyes led in first downs, 15-11, and total offense, 313 yards to 173. Brown, Kuhn, and Buonamici each had 11 tackles, and Ray Griffin played well in his first game at safety. Archie Griffin led all rushers with 108 yards.

First Victory over Nittany Lions

The following week Ohio State defeated Penn State, 17-9, in its September 20 home opener before a crowd of 88,093. It was OSU's very first win over the Nittany Lions after

Ohio State's defense shuts out Michigan State in the season opener. Pictured are Jim Savoca (57) and Bob Brudzinski (84).

losses in 1912, 1956, 1963, and 1964. It also was the initial meeting between coaches Woody Hayes and Joe Paterno. The Buckeyes were ranked third in the weekly AP poll, the Nittany Lions seventh. The Ohio State Marching Band saluted Hayes on his 25th season as head coach with a "WOODY" formation in its pre-game show.

Ohio State opened the afternoon with an 80-yard drive to lead 7-0. The key play of the series was a surprise 49-yard reverse by wingback Brian Baschnagel. Fullback Pete Johnson scored the touchdown from the three, behind a key block by Archie Griffin.

PSU came right back with a 55-yard field goal by Chris Bahr to make the score 7-3. At the time, Bahr's field goal was the longest in the history of Ohio Stadium (it is now the second longest). OSU's Tom Klaban followed with his first field goal of the season, a 45-yarder, to put the Bucks on top after one quarter, 10-3.

The Lions' defense stiffened to hold the Bucks scoreless the next 30 minutes. Meanwhile, Bahr connected on a 31-yard second-quarter field goal, and a 25-yarder after halftime, to really tighten things up at 10-9 heading into the final period.

The Buckeye offense finally got rolling again, with Johnson scoring his second touchdown on a powerful burst from the Nittany Lion 11-yard line. Klaban's conversion concluded the game's scoring at 17-9. The drive was kept alive when Archie Griffin made a breathtaking one-handed grab of a Cornelius Greene pass, on a third and 11 from the OSU 32-yard line.

Griffin led all rushers with 128 yards— it was his 23rd consecutive regular-season game of rushing for more than 100 yards. Tom Skladany averaged 47.6 yards on five punts. Hayes was especially proud of his young defense, which had not given up a touchdown in its first two games. It was the

Penn State's Joe Paterno and Ohio State's Woody Hayes faced each other for the first time in 1975.

first time Penn State had been held without a touchdown in its last 27 outings.

Archie and Pete Set New Records

The following Saturday, September 27, the Buckeyes defeated North Carolina at home, 32-7. After a scoreless first quarter, OSU had little trouble the rest of the afternoon. Pete Johnson scored all five touchdowns to set an OSU single-game scoring record with 30 points (the record was equaled by Keith Byars against Illinois in 1984). Eddie Beamon was the game's leading tackler with 15, and Tom Skladany averaged 46 yards on four punts.

Ohio State led in total offensive yardage, 535 to 193. Archie Griffin scorched the Tar Heel defense for 157 yards on 22 carries, making him the school's new career total offense leader with 4,532 yards. Griffin moved past Rex Kern who had 4,518 career yards.

While Ohio State's record now stood at 3-0, Michigan played its second consecutive tie to start its season at 1-0-2. After opening with a 23-6 win over Wisconsin at Madison, the Wolverines were tied at home by Stanford (19-19) and Baylor (14-14).

Next, it was UCLA in an October 4 night game at the Los Angeles Coliseum, before a crowd of 55,482. Hayes' team scored at least once in each quarter to win a real wild one, 41-20, after leading 38-7 midway through the third period. Griffin was the game's leading rusher with 160 yards in 21 carries.

Greene had an excellent evening, rushing for 120 yards and two touchdowns, and completing six of nine passes for 98 yards. He was chosen the top offensive player of the game, and tackle Eddie Beamon was chosen the game's top defender. The Buckeyes were now 4-0 and advanced to first place in the Associated Press poll, a position they would hold for the next nine weeks. Michigan at 2-0-2 was ninth.

Perfect Performances

Ohio State returned to Big Ten play against Iowa, October 11, before a very appreciative Ohio Stadium crowd of 87,826. In almost faultless fashion, the Buckeyes scored the first seven times they had the ball and won convincingly, 49-0. Griffin led all rushers with 120 yards, stretching his regular season streak of 100 yards or more to 26. Greene clicked on all eight of his passes for 117 yards —one of his tosses was a nine-yarder to tight end Larry Kain for OSU's third touchdown.

We'll Meet Again — Woody

After the Buckeyes' 41-20 win over UCLA in Los Angeles, Woody Hayes told his players that they would likely see the Bruins again that season in the Rose Bowl. How right he was!

All-American guard Ted Smith

The only bright spot for Iowa was winning the coin toss to start the game. Pete Johnson scored three times on short plunges from inside the five, to boost his season touchdown total to 14, while Tom Skladany was not called upon to punt all afternoon. Freshman quarterback Rod Gerald entered the game in the fourth quarter and scored on runs of 45 and 14 yards—they were his only two carries of the afternoon.

In an almost repeat production the following week, Ohio State scored at least once in each quarter to completely overwhelm Wisconsin, 56-0. Using a balanced powerful attack, with emphasis on both offense and defense, the Buckeyes enjoyed their second straight shutout. Seven different players scored OSU's eight touchdowns. Defender Tim Fox thrilled the homecoming crowd of 87,820 by turning a complete flip in the end zone after returning a Badger punt 75 yards for OSU's third score. Wisconsin severely hurt itself with five lost fumbles and an inter-

ception, while Ohio State had no turnovers for the second consecutive week.

After outscoring their six opponents, 216 to 36, the Buckeyes' record now stood at 6-0. Ohio State's first four victims—Michigan State, Penn State, North Carolina, and UCLA—were all playing well. The combined record of these four teams was now 16-3-1, excluding their losses to Ohio State, and their three setbacks had been by a total of only 18 points.

Archie Sets the Record

On October 25, Archie Griffin became major college football's all-time rushing leader, as the Buckeyes triumphed 35-6 over Purdue. The talented tailback rushed for 130 yards that afternoon to increase his career total to 4,730 yards, 15 higher than the previous NCAA mark held by Cornell's Ed Marinaro. The record-breaking play was a 23-yard burst inside tackle midway through the fourth quarter. The game was played at West Lafayette before a crowd of 69,405, at the time the third largest in Ross-Ade Stadium history.

It was Ohio State's first meeting with Purdue since 1970, and their first experience playing on Ross-Ade Stadium's Prescription Athletic Turf (PAT). The surface is a system that utilizes natural grass planted over a layer of sand and topsoil on top of a plastic liner.

Coach Alex Agase's hard-luck Boilermakers entered the contest with a record of 1-5.

After Purdue could not move on its first possession, Ohio State took over at its own 40-yard line. Pete Johnson got the Buckeyes on the scoreboard in a hurry, going 60 yards up the middle for his 17th touchdown of the season on OSU's very first play from scrimmage.

The big hole was opened when tackle Scott Dannelley neutralized Purdue's tackle, center Rick Applegate took out the middle guard, and guard Ted Smith blocked the inside linebacker. Purdue's safety went for a fake pitch to Griffin, and Johnson was on his way. Tom Klaban's conversion made it 7-0 just one minute and 37 seconds into the game. Interestingly, Griffin had kidded Johnson the previous evening about scoring on his very first carry of the afternoon.

The Boilermakers came back with a 22-yard field goal by Steve Schmidt to make the score 7-3. These were the first points against Ohio State by a Big Ten opponent this season.

Griffin returned the ensuing kickoff 53 yards to the Purdue 37. Seven plays later, Johnson scored his second touchdown of the quarter on a plunge from the three, to make it 14-3. The drive's biggest gainer was a 16-yard toss from quarterback Corny Greene to split end Lenny Willis. Schmidt kicked his second field goal, a 27-yarder, midway through the second quarter to cut the Buckeye margin to eight at 14-6.

OSU created some breathing room on its next possession, driving 80 yards in 12 plays to expand its lead to 21-6 at the half. The touchdown came on a perfectly thrown ball from Cornelius Greene to wingback Brian Baschnagel, who waltzed untouched into the right corner of the end zone. At this point, it appeared that Griffin might not break Marinaro's record until the following Saturday at home against Indiana. At halftime he had only 36 of the needed 116 yards.

The Buckeyes received the second-half

Archie Griffin in action during his record-breaking afternoon at Purdue.

kickoff and quickly increased their lead to 28-6. Greene passed for his second touchdown of the game, this one a 41-yarder to Lenny Willis, to complete an 80-yard, 10-play drive.

Later in the third period the Buckeyes put together one of Woody Hayes' patented ball-control marches, going 90 yards in 11 plays for their fifth and final touchdown of the afternoon. On the first play of the fourth quarter, Greene scampered 28 yards around end for six points. Klaban's placement finalized the scoring at 35-6, but the best was yet to happen.

After an exchange of punts, Ohio State's defense held Purdue on downs at the Boilermaker 38, and the Buckeye offense returned to the field with just 8:26 remaining to be played. Griffin had run for 107 yards, needing just nine more for the record. On first down he carried for 23 yards to become major college football's most prolific ground gainer. The play was an off-tackle slant behind Scott Dannelley, that Griffin cut inside for the record. The gifted tailback received a standing ovation from the entire crowd, as OSU's starting offensive unit was replaced by the second team. It also was his 28th consecutive regular-season game of rushing for more than 100 yards.

Griffin gave much of the credit to his offensive line. "Yards were tough to get today," he said, "but our offensive line was grinding it out all the way. I've always played with great lines ever since I've been at Ohio State." Woody Hayes was especially elated over Archie's latest milestone, because the squad regarded it as a team accomplishment.

The game's statistics were somewhat peculiar—Purdue led in first downs, 22 to 21, and in total offensive plays, 81 to 60. The Boilermakers had possession of the ball for more than 33 minutes. Johnson led all rushers with 131 yards, Griffin had 130. The Buckeyes led in total offensive yardage, 458 to 358.

Corso's Very Imposing Hoosiers

In Columbus the following Saturday, November 1, Indiana gave the nation's number-one team a very unexpected scare. Ohio State led 17-0 at halftime, but the hepped-up Hoosiers roared back with two third-quarter touchdowns to make matters very tense at 17-14. Few if any of the 87,835 partisan fans left early. The Buckeyes finally put another touchdown on the board in the final period to win, 24-14.

After Tom Klaban's 43-yard field goal had paced OSU to a 3-0 first-quarter advantage, the Buckeyes twice crossed the Hoosier goal line in the second period—a five-yard pass from Cornelius Greene to freshman tight end Jimmy Moore and a four-yard scamper by Greene.

Fullback Rick Enis, an impressive sophomore from Union City, Indiana (on the Ohio-

No More Mr. Nice Guy

The Buckeyes were 7-0 as they prepared for the season's eighth game against Indiana. The Hoosiers had won only two of their first seven starts, and had lost at Michigan the previous Saturday, 55-7. Woody Hayes did something that week that, for him, was a first—he gave his players "Monday off without practice." After seven games, Hayes thought the rest would be good for his squad, especially since Indiana appeared to be an easy test.

Saturday afternoon's game was much more tougher than anticipated. Ohio State had all it could handle before winning, 24-14, and the game was even closer than the final score suggests. Woody Hayes was NEVER again known to cancel a Monday practice.

Indiana border), led the Hoosiers' second-half charge. Enis scored both IU touchdowns and finished the afternoon with 148 yards in 29 carries. The talented Hoosier was no stranger to Woody Hayes, who had tried to recruit Enis for his own team.

Bruce Ruhl created a big break for the Buckeyes early in the final period with an over-the-head interception at the Indiana 33-yard line. From there the offense drove the distance to ease the plight. Pete Johnson crashed over from the one to register his 19th touchdown of the season, and the Buckeye faithful were breathing a little easier.

After the game Hayes told the press, "Maybe we should feel fortunate we didn't get knocked off." Hayes offered a special salute to cornerback Max Midlam, who replaced Tim Fox after Fox left the game with an injury in the second quarter. IU coach Lee Corso was visibly proud of his young team, which included 20 sophomores and 19 freshmen on its traveling squad of 48 players.

Archie Griffin was the game's leading runner with 150 yards in 28 attempts. Corso was very familiar with Ohio State's three Griffins. One of their older brothers, Larry, had played under Corso at the University of Louisville.

Three Weeks and Counting

Ohio State (8-0 overall) and Michigan (6-0-2 overall) were tied for the league lead with conference records of 5-0. The Buckeyes continued their stronghold on first place in the weekly Associated Press poll, while the Wolverines had gradually moved up to sixth. It now seemed almost certain that the Big Ten's "Big Two" would each be 7-0 in conference play when they collided November 22 in Ann Arbor.

Ohio State had little trouble defeating Illinois, 40-3, before a crowd of 67,571 at Champaign on November 8. After spotting the Fighting Illini a 3-0 first-quarter lead on Dan Beaver's 36-yard field goal, the Buckeyes scored 10 points in the second and third periods, then finished strongly with 20 points in the final 15 minutes of play. Tom Skladany set a school record with a 59-yard field goal. Pete Johnson established what was then a Big Ten record with his 20th and 21st touchdowns of the season, breaking the conference record of 20 set by OSU's Champ Henson in 1972.

Tim Fox turned his second end zone flip of the season, after returning an interception 20 yards for Ohio State's second touchdown. Archie Griffin sprinted 30 yards for his team's first touchdown, and finished the afternoon with 127 yards, giving him 30 consecutive games of rushing for more than 100 yards. Michigan blanked Purdue, 28-0, and advanced to fourth place in the weekly AP.

In the home finale the following Saturday, Ohio State clobbered Minnesota, 38-6, before a vocal Ohio Stadium crowd of 87,817. It was very fitting that each member of the Buckeyes' talented starting backfield scored at least once to pilot the attack. Griffin scored on a 19-yard scamper, Greene ran for a pair of touchdowns from 14 and 31 yards out, Johnson (the backfield's only junior) notched his 22nd TD of the season with an eight-yard ramble, and Baschnagel scored the game's final touchdown with a 21-yard reverse to the left midway through the final period. Senior Tom Klaban scored the game's first points with a 29-yard field goal.

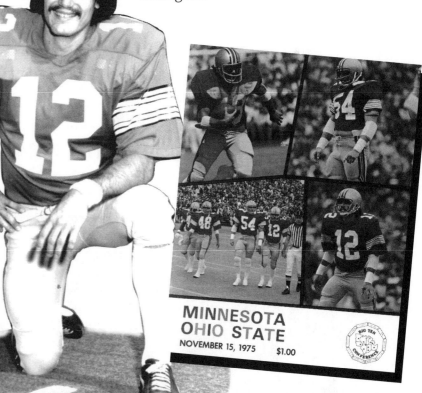

MINNESOTA
OHIO STATE
NOVEMBER 15, 1975 $1.00

All-American defensive back Tim Fox

In his last appearance at Ohio Stadium, Griffin gained 124 yards before leaving to a thunderous ovation with 3:57 left in the game. Ohio State led in first downs, 30-16, and total offense, 491 yards to 232. The Buckeyes' home winning streak now totaled 24, dating back to the 1972 opener against Iowa. While OSU was handling the Golden Gophers, Michigan struggled to win at Illinois, 21-15. The biggest test of the season was just seven days away—a November 22 visit up north to confront coach Bo Schembechler's fourth-ranked Michigan Wolverines.

Ray Griffin's Interception
"Play of the Season"

For the seventh time in the last eight seasons, the Ohio State—Michigan game would decide the Big Ten title and representative to the Rose Bowl. The 1975 season was also the first year conference teams were permitted to play in bowls other than the Rose Bowl. The Big Ten had arranged for the loser of the OSU-UM game to meet Oklahoma in

Thank You, Mrs. Griffin

A popular bumper sticker in 1975 read, "Thank You, Mrs. Griffin." It acknowledged the contributions that three of Mrs. James Griffin's sons were making on the football field that fall. Archie won his second Heisman Trophy that season, Ray was the starting defensive safety, and Duncan, then a freshman, was a member of the Buckeyes' specialty teams.

the Orange Bowl. The Michigan Stadium crowd of 105,543 was, at the time, the largest to ever attend an NCAA regular-season game. The Wolverines had not lost in their last 41 home contests.

Ohio State grabbed an early 7-0 lead, driving 63 yards in 15 plays on its first possession with Pete Johnson scoring on a seven-yard pass from Cornelius Greene. Tom Klaban, the hero of the '74 game, kicked the extra point. The next 15 minutes of play

1975 Big Ten Champions

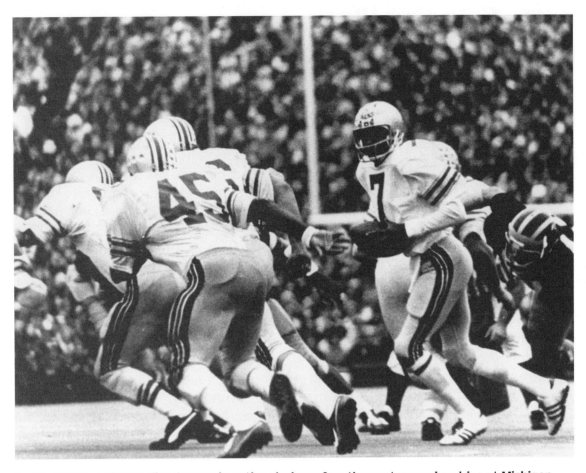

Archie Griffin and Cornelius Greene in action during a fourth-quarter scoring drive at Michigan.

were marred by a raft of turnovers. The Buckeyes threw two interceptions and lost a fumble, while the Wolverines had two passes picked off and lost one fumble. OSU was really floundering—the offense made a first down with 13:11 remaining in the second quarter, but would not gain another first down until midway through the fourth period.

UM put together a fine scoring drive right before the half, moving 80 yards to tie the game 7-7 at intermission. Tailback Gordon Bell connected with wingback Jimmy Smith on an 11-yard option pass for the touchdown, and Bob Wood booted the conversion. The Wolverines had little success in the third quarter, with their only serious threat, a 43-yard field-goal attempt, falling short.

The game changed radically in the final period. After forcing the Buckeyes to punt

from their end zone, Michigan took possession at the OSU 43-yard line and went the distance with freshman quarterback Rick Leach getting the touchdown from the one. The UM drive was kept alive when OSU's defense was offside on a third-down play, which otherwise was an incomplete pass. Michigan was now in front 14-7 with 7:11 left in the game, and Ohio State (averaging 35 points per game) had still not registered a first down since early in the second period.

But the Buckeyes soon made up for lost time and began to play like the nation's No. 1 team. Starting from the OSU 20-yard line, Greene (after escaping near disaster while passing on first and second downs) engineered one of the season's finest drives to tie the score, 14-14. Johnson got his second touchdown of the afternoon on a fourth-down plunge from the one with just 3:18 re-

most significant plays in the history of the Ohio State—Michigan series. He was outstanding on defense that afternoon with 14 tackles, including ten solos. Two were safety blitzes that resulted in losses totaling nine yards. Archie rushed for 46 yards, snapping his string of rushing for more than 100 yards at 31 games. Tom Skladany was a big factor, punting eight times for a 45-yard average.

Michigan won the statistical battle by a wide margin, leading in first downs, 19-12, and total offensive yards, 361-208. The Wolverines ran 77 offensive plays, the Buckeyes ran 61. But Ohio State won the struggle of the scoreboard, thereby claiming both the outright Big Ten crown and a postseason date in Pasadena for the fourth consecutive year.

Second Time Around Much Different

Ohio State was a solid 15-point favorite over UCLA in the January 1, 1976, Rose Bowl, especially after having defeated coach Dick Vermeil's Bruins by 21 points at the Los Angeles Coliseum in the season's fourth game. UCLA finished the regular season at 8-2-1 and shared the Pacific Eight Conference title with California. The West Coast writers gave the home team little chance of upsetting the nation's No. 1 team, although most conceded UCLA had improved considerably as the season progressed.

The Buckeyes took the opening kickoff and marched to the Bruin 25-yard line, where Tom Klaban booted a 42-yard field goal with 12:11 remaining in the first quarter to put his team on top, 3-0. That was the extent of the scoring in the first half. Ohio State held

maining. One of the drive's key plays was a 17-yard completion from Greene to Baschnagel on third down from the OSU 20-yard line.

The pressure was suddenly on Michigan, since a tie would send Ohio State to Pasadena. The Wolverines took over at their own 20-yard line and came out throwing. On first down Leach was spilled by middle guard Aaron Brown for a nine-yard loss, and his second-down throw was incomplete. On third down, Ray Griffin intercepted Leach's pass at the UM 32-yard line and streaked 29 yards to the three. It's hard to imagine an Ohio State team ever benefiting from a more timely interception. On first down Johnson bolted over for his third touchdown, and suddenly the Buckeyes were back on top, 21-14, with 2:19 remaining. What a change! A team that had gone more than 30 minutes of play without a first down, had now scored two touchdowns within a span of 59 seconds.

Michigan desperately tried for another touchdown, but Craig Cassady intercepted Leach on a fourth-down-and-eight pass with just 1:15 remaining. It was his second interception of the afternoon. Johnson carried four times for 19 yards, Greene fell on the ball with eight seconds remaining, and Ohio State had attained one of its most cherished victories. Woody Hayes, who now was 16-8-1 against "that team up north," told the press, "It was our greatest comeback, and the greatest game I've ever coached."

Ray Griffin's interception was one of the

Michigan Stadium Is Bo's House

Ohio State's 21-14 victory at Ann Arbor was the first conference loss at Michigan Stadium for coach Bo Schembechler, who was in his seventh season as the Wolverines' head coach after taking over the program in 1969.

UCLA without a first down until late in the second quarter, but squandered several scoring opportunities after generating 11 first downs and gaining 174 yards by halftime.

Vermeil and his staff made the proper halftime adjustments, and the third period really damaged Ohio State's hopes. The Buckeyes opened the game with man-for-man pass coverage and an almost eight-man defensive front. Vermeil decided to exploit OSU's man-to-man protection in the second half, by using short passes instead of trying to beat them with the bomb. UCLA's change in strategy was very successful.

After Bruin place-kicker Brett White tied the game at 3-3 with a 33-yard field goal, quarterback John Sciarra (who finished seventh in the Heisman Trophy voting) threw two damaging touchdown strikes to flanker Wally Henry. The first score went for 16 yards, and Henry simply outran the Buckeye secondary to go 67 yards for the second. UCLA led at the end of three quarters, 16-3, and time was starting to weigh heavily against the Scarlet and Gray.

Ohio State retaliated with a 12-play 65-yard march to tighten things up at 16-10 with 11:46 remaining to be played. Johnson powered across from the one for the touchdown. White had missed the extra-point attempt after UCLA's first touchdown, and for a while it appeared this single point might be significant. The OSU defense stiffened on the ensuing series, and Craig Cassady picked off Sciarra's pass and brought the pigskin back to midfield. A personal foul against UCLA as Cassady was tackled moved the ball to the Bruin 35-yard line, and the Buckeyes' fortune seemed to be changing—another touchdown and extra point would give them a one-point lead.

On first down, Greene checked off at the line of scrimmage and underthrew Lenny Willis who was open around the Bruin 10. UCLA's Barney Person intercepted the throw at the 13-yard line and brought it back to the UCLA 43. Ohio State's defense forced UCLA

History Repeats Itself

UCLA's 23-10 upset of top-ranked Ohio State in the January 1, 1976, Rose Bowl came exactly ten years after the Bruins upset previously undefeated and number-one rated Michigan State, 14-12, in the same bowl on January 1, 1966.

Ironically, UCLA had lost to each of these bowl opponents earlier in the regular seasons. The Buckeyes won over the Bruins, 41-20, on October 4, 1975, while the Spartans defeated UCLA, 13-3, at East Lansing on September 18, 1965.

to punt, giving OSU the ball at its own 29-yard line with 5:29 remaining. But again a Greene pass intended for Willis was picked off—this time by Pat Schmidt—and the Bruins were in possession at their own 39-yard line. Eddie Ayers rambled for seven yards on first down, then Wendell Tyler streaked 54 yards up the middle for another touchdown to make the score 23-10, and that's how the game ended.

Woody Hayes, visibly frustrated and disappointed beyond description, met very briefly with the press following the game. "We got outcoached and just got beat," he explained. "Our defense played magnificently for the first half, but this UCLA staff just outcoached us."

The 39-year-old Vermeil was very gracious with his compliments towards Hayes and the OSU squad. "I think we probably were a little underestimated by a lot of people," he said. "We've been improving continually throughout the season and it all came to a head today." Vermeil also volunteered that he felt his team had a big edge in preparation from a mental standpoint, since Ohio State had defeated his squad so handily during the regular season.

In the second half, UCLA registered 366 of its 414 total yards and 17 of its 19 first downs. Ohio State finished with 20 first downs and 298 yards. Archie Griffin fractured his hand on the third play of the game, but still managed to continue, finishing with 93 yards in 17 carries. Tyler netted 172 yards in 21 tries, while Sciarra connected on 13 of 19 tosses for 212 yards including the two TD strikes to Henry.

The setback, one of the most devastating in Ohio State history, deprived the Buckeyes of what would have been a sure national title. In the final Associated Press poll, Ohio State (11-1) finished fourth behind Oklahoma (11-1), Arizona State (12-0), and Alabama (11-1). UCLA (9-2-1) placed fifth, and Michigan (8-2-2) came in eighth after losing to Oklahoma, 14-6, in the Orange Bowl.

The End of a Golden Era

Archie Griffin concluded his outstanding career by winning almost every national award, including his second Heisman Trophy. He finished with 5,589 career yards and 26 touchdowns. Griffin and Skladany repeated as All-Americans and were joined by Ted Smith and Tim Fox. Pete Johnson led the nation in scoring with 150 points on 25 touchdowns, and Cornelius Greene was selected the Big Ten's MVP. Craig Cassady's nine interceptions tied a school single-year record.

The 1975 season concluded a remarkable four-year period that saw Ohio State go 40-5-1 (88.0%). The Buckeyes won outright or shared four Big Ten titles and made four appearances in the Rose Bowl. They were 3-0-1 against Michigan, and finished these seasons ranked ninth, second, fourth, and fourth, respectively, in the final Associated Press polls.

1975				
September 13	at Michigan State	W	21	0
September 20	Penn State	W	17	9
September 27	North Carolina	W	32	7
October 4	at UCLA	W	41	20
October 11	Iowa	W	49	0
October 18	Wisconsin (HC)	W	56	0
October 25	at Purdue	W	35	6
November 1	Indiana	W	24	14
November 8	at Illinois	W	40	3
November 15	Minnesota	W	38	6
November 22	at Michigan	W	21	14
January 1	UCLA*	L	10	23
Total Points			384	102

*Rose Bowl

Season record: 11-1
Big Ten Champion

1976

The Buckeyes faced a major rebuilding effort in 1976, particularly on offense with only three returning starters: fullback Pete Johnson, tackle Chris Ward, and guard Bill Lukens. Seven defensive regulars were back; linemen Eddie Beamon, Bob Brudzinski, Aaron Brown, and Nick Buonamici, linebacker Ed Thompson, cornerback Bruce Ruhl, and safety Ray Griffin. Michigan was favored to capture the Big Ten title, with OSU predicted to be a close second.

Enormous Start

Ohio State wasted no time igniting the post-Archie Griffin era, shattering Michigan State in the September 11 season opener, 49-21, before a very appreciative Ohio Stadium crowd of 86,509. The Buckeyes built up a 35-0 halftime lead, using a ground attack which was too much for the Spartan defense. Junior tailback Jeff Logan scored three times, including a 75-yard sprint on the second play

of the third quarter and a 68-yard punt return in the final period. Logan had a fourth scoring jaunt of 60 yards called back because of a penalty.

Sophomore quarterback Rod Gerald scored twice while running the option play very effectively in his first start. Veteran Pete Johnson accounted for the other two touchdowns, his second a 58-yard power run over OSU's left side early in the second quarter. Michigan State had little success with its ground attack in the early going, but was able to score three times through the air in the second half.

Woody Hayes elected to skip his regular postgame interview, sending assistant coaches Ralph Staub and George Hill to meet with the media. The Michigan State student newspaper had run a series of late-summer articles accusing Hayes of improper recruiting activities, and an East Lansing daily newspaper had recently joined the attack on the veteran coach. Hayes had steadfastly branded the charges as ridiculous falsehoods unworthy of his time. But since scribes from both publications were in Columbus to cover the game, Hayes apparently felt it best to avoid any potential confrontation with his accusers.

While OSU was humbling the Spartans, Michigan defeated Wisconsin at Ann Arbor, 40-27. The Wolverines moved to the top spot in the weekly AP, and Ohio State advanced

to second. Fans were already looking ahead 10 weeks to the "Big Two's" head-to-head collision at Ohio Stadium.

First Encounter at Happy Valley

The following weekend the Buckeyes traveled to Penn State for a non-conference match up between coaching legends Woody Hayes and Joe Paterno. It was Ohio State's very first trip to the State College campus, after home games against the Nittany Lions in '12, '56, '63, '64, and '75. Penn State was still 17 seasons away from becoming a member of the Big Ten Conference.

Led by Gerald's clever ball handling and Logan's excellent running, OSU won a very close one, 12-7. Gerald gave Ohio State a 6-0 halftime lead with an eight-yard option-keeper around left end in the second period. A bad pass from center prevented Tom

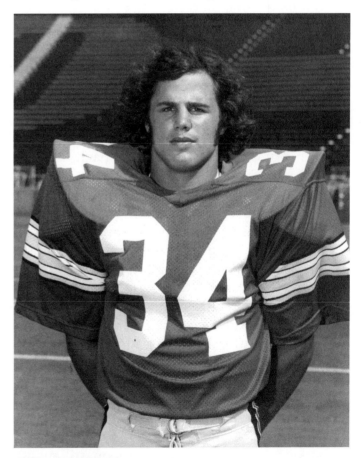

Tailback Jeff Logan

Skladany from attempting the conversion.

The third quarter was scoreless, but the Buckeyes dominated play by controlling the ball 12:43 of the 15-minute period. The game-clinching touchdown was scored by halfback Bobby Hyatt on a surprise option sweep around left end from the Penn State eight-yard line. It came on a fourth-and-two early in the final period, with Penn State expecting Pete Johnson to carry up the middle for the first down. This was Hyatt's first and only Ohio State touchdown, and his only carry of the 1976 season.

Ohio State's defense shut off two Nittany Lion marches inside the five-yard line. Safety Ray Griffin intercepted a pass deep in his own end zone to stop one drive, while end Bob Brudzinski recovered a Penn State fumble at the Ohio State four-yard line to end the other. The Nittany Lions avoided a shut-out by driving 87 yards late in the game for their only score, a one-yard dive over the middle by freshman fullback Matt Suhey.

OSU led in rushing yardage, 280 to 150, while PSU out-passed the Buckeyes, 178 yards to 10. Logan was the game's leading runner with 160 yards. The setback was just the sixth at Beaver Stadium for Joe Paterno in his first 11 seasons as head coach.

Home Winning Streak Stopped at 25

Missouri's undaunted Tigers posted a dramatic 22-21 upset the following Saturday, September 25, in front of a stunned crowd of 87,936. The setback broke a 25-game home winning string for Ohio State, who had not lost at Ohio Stadium since falling to Northwestern, 14-10, on November 13, 1971. It also was Missouri's first ever victory over the Buckeyes after 10 previous tries.

Ohio State took a 21-7 halftime lead on three touchdowns by fullback Pete Johnson and appeared to have the game well under control. The big fullback, hobbled by an ankle injury most of the afternoon, still managed to rush for 119 yards in 23 carries. But a Missouri touchdown in the third period re-

The Sergeant and the Professor

Pat Harmon, former Historian/Curator at the College Football Hall of Fame, tells a story about Woody Hayes driving all night to get home from Philadelphia after the evening's last flight was cancelled. Hayes was not too happy, and as he was making arrangements for a rental car, a young Air Force Sergeant named David Buller overheard Hayes and asked if he could ride with him. Hayes readily agreed as Buller explained his need to get to Dayton to make a connection to his home in Ogden, Utah.

The two drove all night, and as they reached the outskirts of Columbus about 3:00 a.m., Hayes called John Mummey, one of his assistant coaches, and asked Mummey to drive Buller on to Dayton. As Mummey started for the Dayton airport, Buller told Mummey how impressed he was with Mr. Hayes' knowledge of history and how enlightening it was to talk with him.

With that, Mummey asked, "Do you know who you were riding with?" "He said his name was Hayes," Buller replied, "and he sure sounded like a history professor." Mummey asked, "Are you aware this Mr. Hayes is coach Woody Hayes of Ohio State?" "You're kidding, THE Woody Hayes? He never once even mentioned football," the open-mouthed sergeant answered. "I can't believe it. Just wait until I tell my parents!"

Mummey took Buller on to Dayton, then headed straight back to Columbus for an 8:00 a.m. coaches' meeting—and there was Woody, eager to get started after a very short night's sleep.

ally tightened things up at 21-14, heading into the fourth quarter.

Late in the final period, and still trailing by seven points, the Tigers marched 80 yards for their third touchdown, to come within one point of the Buckeyes, 21-20, with just 12 seconds remaining. Missouri's first attempt at a two-point conversion failed, but

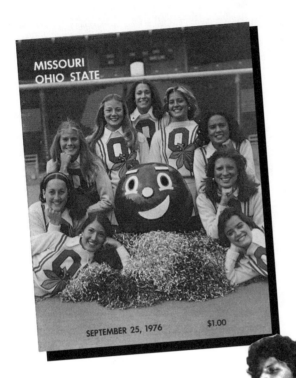

MISSOURI
OHIO STATE

SEPTEMBER 25, 1976 $1.00

Matters were not much better at the horseshoe the next week, where Ohio State and UCLA battled to a 10-10 tie. The game, played in mid-summer temperatures before a crowd of 87,969, was billed as the "rubber match," since the Buckeyes and Bruins had faced each other twice in '75. Terry Donahue, 32, had taken charge of the Bruin program, replacing Dick Vermeil who left to coach the NFL's Philadelphia Eagles. UCLA at 3-0 entered the game ranked fourth in the nation.

Defenses dominated the afternoon's action. Ray Griffin set up the Buckeyes' lone touchdown with a 17-yard punt return to the UCLA 46-yard line with 11:41 remaining in the second quarter. Seven plays later Johnson bolted four yards over left tackle for a touchdown, and Skladany converted to give Ohio State a 7-0 lead at halftime. The Bruins could penetrate no farther than the OSU 44-yard line during the first 30 minutes of play.

UCLA finally got on the board with Frank Corral's 47-yard field goal at the 9:35 mark of the third period. The Bruins took the lead, 10-7, driving 83 yards for the touchdown after recovering a Buckeye bobble at the Bruin 17. The drive was kept alive when Theotis Brown carried 25 yards to the OSU 49-yard line with a fake punt run on fourth-and-one, completely fooling the Buckeye punt return team.

On OSU's following possession, Tom Skladany booted a tying 25-yard field goal on a fourth-and-three from the Bruin eight. Buckeye fans were somewhat perplexed when Woody Hayes elected to have his team punt on fourth down from the UCLA 48-yard line in the game's final minute of play. Hayes singled out safety Ray Griffin for his excellent

Ohio State was penalized for holding, giving the Tigers another chance. On his second attempt, Tiger quarterback Pete Woods moved to his left and dove into the end zone for the two points, giving Missouri a miraculous 22-21 win.

Woods was a sophomore filling in for regular quarterback Steve Pisarkiewicz who was injured. The game's first downs were exactly the same as the final score; Missouri had 22, Ohio State had 21. The Tigers also had a slight edge in total offensive yards, 324 to 305. Coach Al Onofrio called it the biggest win in Missouri history—and it probably was, much to the dismay of Buckeye fans who had not witnessed a loss in Ohio Stadium for nearly five years.

Three-time All-American punter Tom Skladany.

game, and also praised freshman cornerback Mike Guess for his play while replacing Bruce Ruhl who was injured. Ohio State's record was now 2-1-1.

Back on Track with Two Road Wins

The Buckeyes returned to the victory column October 9 with a 34-14 win over the Iowa Hawkeyes at Kinnick Stadium. Ohio State marched to touchdowns on its first three possessions, but showed signs of inconsistency throughout the final three quarters. Hayes told reporters after the game he was happy with the win but hinted his offense will need to eliminate a lot of errors in the weeks ahead. OSU threw two interceptions and lost a fumble in the second period.

Pete Johnson scored three times on short blasts to set, what was then, a Big Ten record with 48 career touchdowns. Tom Skladany was noticeably effective in each department, kicking off into (or over) the end zone on all but one attempt, going two-for-two on field goals, punting twice for a 41-yard average, and kicking all four extra points.

At Madison, October 16, the Buckeyes outscored Wisconsin, 30-20, before what was then a record Camp Randall Stadium crowd of 79,579. Ohio State ran from the I-formation most of the afternoon, after using pro-set and veer offenses in its first five games. Badger coach John Jardine admitted he was surprised by the tactical switch, which caused problems for his team with its defensive adjustments.

Injuries forced OSU to use a lot of new faces, especially on offense. Freshman Paul Campbell split time at fullback with Johnson, whose ailing ankles were reinjured, and junior college transfer Ron Springs looked good at tailback in place of Logan who went out after getting kicked in the calf. Quick-footed Rod Gerald continued to play well at quarterback, netting 81 yards in 13 carries and using his acceleration to score OSU's last

touchdown with a 29-yard scamper on a broken play which was to have been a handout to Logan.

Pacenta to the Rescue

After a very slow start and a narrow 3-0 lead after two quarters, the Buckeyes played their best second half of the season to defeat Purdue, 24-3, before a rain-soaked homecoming crowd of 87,890. But the victory was very costly. Rod Gerald injured his back at the 4:14 mark of the first quarter, and was lost for the remainder of the regular season with a hairline fracture of the lumbar vertebrae.

Jim Pacenta, who had played a total of 19 minutes in the season's six previous games, came off the bench and directed his squad to its sixth victory of the season. The senior from Akron excelled as a drop-back-style passer, as compared with Gerald whose best strength was executing the option. Jeff Logan had one of his finest games as a Buckeye, picking up 175 yards on 27 carries and scoring his team's first two touchdowns.

Johnson scored the other TD, the 51st of his career. Linebacker Tom Cousineau caused problems for the Boilermakers all afternoon, and finished as the game's leading

Two-time All-American tackle Chris Ward

tackler with 18. Tackle Eddie Beamon had four tackles behind the line of scrimmage for a total loss of 18 yards.

The Buckeyes continued their drive toward a fifth consecutive Big Ten title, with a 47-7 triumph at Indiana on October 30. The weather was rainy and cold for the second straight week, which partly explains why only 39,633 showed up at Memorial Stadium to watch the game. OSU led just 12-7 at the half, following what Woody Hayes described as, "About as bad a first half as we've ever played." In the first 30 minutes of play, his team lost two fumbles, had two costly clipping penalties, and fumbled the snap on the extra point try following its first touchdown.

OSU scored five times in the second half, partly because the defense continually provided the offense with good field position. In his first start at quarterback, Pacenta got stronger as the game progressed and finished with five completions in seven attempts for 90 yards—including a 59-yard perfect pitch play to Jim Harrell for the Scarlet and Gray's fourth touchdown. Ron Springs fashioned one of the game's most impressive moments with a 62-yard sprint through left tackle for the game's final score.

The improving Buckeyes headed into November ranked eighth in the weekly *AP* with an overall record of 6-1-1. The Wolverines of Michigan at 8-0 were the nation's No. 1 team ahead of the Pitt Panthers who also were 8-0. With the Ohio State–Michigan clash just three weeks away, the two were tied at the top of the Big Ten with identical conference marks of 5-0.

Hail Purdue!

As expected, Ohio State crushed Illinois 42-10 at home on November 6, but the real story of the afternoon came from West Lafayette where unheralded Purdue (3-5) shocked top-ranked Michigan, 16-14, to hand the Wolverines their first setback of the year. Boilermaker Rock Supan kicked a 23-yard field goal late in the game's fourth quarter to

Joint Effort

Tackle Nick Buonamici and safety Ray Griffin combined on a 95-yard interception return for Ohio State's first touchdown at Indiana. Buonamici picked off Scott Arnett's pass at the OSU five-yard line, rambled 30 yards down the sideline, then lateraled to Griffin who raced the remaining 65 yards for the score.

highlight the biggest surprise of the college season to date.

Back at Ohio Stadium, quarterback Jim Pacenta effectively led the assault on the Fighting Illini, and Pete Johnson scored four of the Buckeyes' six touchdowns on short runs from inside the five-yard line. Johnson's four scores ran his career total to 57, including 53 during regular-season games. The NCAA does not recognize statistics from postseason competition, and four of Johnson's touchdowns were scored in Rose Bowl competition.

Ohio State's triumph was as consistent as it was easy, even when Hayes substituted

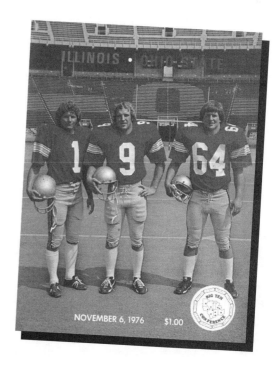

NOVEMBER 6, 1976 $1.00

liberally throughout the second half. OSU's defense kept Illinois under control with only a field goal until the game's last three seconds, when the visitors scored their only touchdown on a 17-yard pass from quarterback Mike McCray to tight end Marty Friel.

The defense also scored Ohio State's other two touchdowns. Ed Thompson returned an interception 81 yards down the east sideline for the game's first points, and Dave Adkins brought one back 19 yards for OSU's final score of the afternoon with just two minutes remaining.

The Buckeyes (7-1-1, 6-0) were now in sole possession of first place in the Big Ten and remained eighth in the weekly AP. Michigan (8-1, 5-1) fell to fourth place in the national ranking behind Pittsburgh (8-0), UCLA (8-0-1), and Southern California (7-1).

Record Fifth Consecutive League Title Guaranteed

It wasn't pretty, but Ohio State assured itself of at least a share of a record fifth consecutive Big Ten championship with a 9-3 win at Minnesota on November 13. It also was OSU's 17th straight Big Ten victory, which tied another record. While the Buckeyes were edging the Golden Gophers, Michigan blasted Illinois, 38-7, to set up the fol-

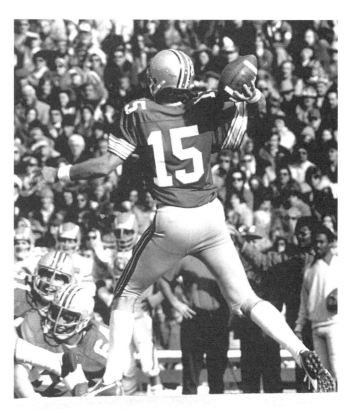

Quarterback Jim Pacenta directed Ohio State to four consecutive victories after Rod Gerald was injured in the Purdue game.

lowing week's title showdown in Columbus.

The game's scoring all took place in the first half. The Buckeyes combined their single sustained scoring drive with Tom Skladany's 39-yard first period field goal to extend their season record to 8-1-1. OSU's defense was superb, especially against the rush. Minnesota could gain only 46 yards in 35 running plays, while quarterback Tony Dungy connected 16 times with his receivers for 201 yards but no touchdowns. Middle guard Aaron Brown played brilliantly and was credited with four tackles of Dungy behind the line of scrimmage for a total loss of 42 yards.

Ohio State's second-quarter touchdown drive covered 73 yards in 14 plays, with Jim Pacenta getting into the end zone from the four-yard line for his first career touchdown. Jeff Logan ran for 116 yards in 30 carries, increasing his season total to 1,106 and becoming the fifth player in Buckeye history

Are You Kidding?

While Ohio State was winning at Minnesota, ABC television was reporting that Woody Hayes would be announcing his retirement the following Friday to spark his squad in its game the following afternoon against Michigan. ABC indicated the report was circulating among reporters in the Notre Dame press box during its televised game between Alabama and the Fighting Irish. Hayes emphatically denied the rumor, stating, "The report is ridiculous without one word of truth."

to amass more than 1,000 yards in a single season.

The stage was now set. With a victory over Michigan, Ohio State would claim its second straight outright conference crown, while Michigan could secure a share of the championship with a triumph over the Buckeyes. With a victory, the Buckeyes would also establish a new Big Ten record with 18 consecutive league wins.

Wolverines Just Too Good

Ohio State had its opportunities in a scoreless first half, but Michigan used its overall strength to roll up a 22-0 verdict before a mostly disappointed audience of 88,250. At the time, it was the largest crowd ever to attend a game at Ohio Stadium. The Wolverines so dominated play that the Buckeyes had possession of the ball only four times in the second half.

OSU mounted its only serious scoring effort in the final four minutes of the second quarter. Starting from their own 26-yard line, the Buckeyes benefited from the fine running of Logan and Pacenta and quickly moved to the UM 10. On second down, Pacenta fought off several would-be tacklers and lofted a pass intended for tight end Greg Storer, but Wolverine defender Jim Pickens intercepted in the end zone, and the Ohio State threat was dead. The Buckeyes were held to 173 net yards of offense, their lowest total of the season.

Led by the punishing running of tailback Rob Lytle and fullback Russell Davis, Michigan produced three impressive scoring drives and the outcome was never in doubt. All 366 of the Wolverines' total offensive yards came on the ground, led by Lytle with 165 and Davis with 83. Tom Skladany helped keep UM off the scoreboard in the first half, averaging 52.2 yards with eight kicks.

In his postgame comments, Hayes took the blame for calling the pass that

Unpleasant Memories

Michigan's 22-0 victory was the first shutout inflicted against Ohio State since the Wolverines defeated the Buckeyes, 10-0, at Ohio Stadium 12 years earlier on November 21, 1964. Ohio State had scored in each of its last 122 games.

was intercepted late in the second quarter. "I just called a bad play. Without the interception we could have gone in at the half with at least a three-point lead," he offered. Hayes told reporters that Michigan was obviously a better team that day. He praised Bo Schembechler for coming back from open heart surgery in the spring, and stressed that Schembechler would definitely get his vote for coach of the year.

Bo Schembechler and Woody Hayes exchange pleasantries before the Big Game.

"Quick Backfield" Leads Orange Bowl Victory

Ohio State played in a postseason bowl other than the Rose Bowl for the very first time, meeting Big Eight co-champion Colorado in the January 1, 1977, Orange Bowl. The Buckeyes won convincingly, 27-10—the Buffaloes scored the game's first 10 points, the Buckeyes scored the last 27. Colorado was coached by Bill Mallory, who had been a Woody Hayes assistant from 1966 through 1968.

When Ohio State found it difficult to move against the Buffaloes in the early going, Hayes went to a "quick backfield set" instead of his regular power attack. Rod Gerald, now recovered from the back injury suffered October 23 against Purdue, entered the game at the 3:54 mark of the first quarter and immediately sparked his squad with a 17-yard scamper on his first carry. With

All-American end Bob Brudzinski

Ron Springs positioned at tailback and Jeff Logan shifting to fullback, the speedy trio completely revitalized OSU's attack. Growing stronger as the game progressed, Ohio State rolled up a total of 330 yards including 271 on the ground.

As the offense picked up momentum, the Buckeye defense shut off the Buffaloes in the final three periods. Tom Cousineau and Nick Buonamici were particularly outstanding. Colorado rushed for 97 yards in the first half but could add only 37 more in the final two quarters. The Big Eight co-champ gained 137 yards through the air, including an 11-yard toss from quarterback Jeff Knapple to wingback Emory Moorehead for its only touchdown.

Logan, Johnson, and Gerald scored Ohio State's touchdowns. Tom Skladany effectively handled the punting and kickoffs, and was the game's leading scorer with two field goals and three extra points.

OSU finished the season at 9-2-1, good for sixth place in the final Associated Press ranking. The Pitt Panthers (12-0) with Heisman Trophy winner Tony Dorsett won the national title, Michigan (10-2) placed third after losing the Rose Bowl to Southern California, 14-6.

Skladany was chosen as an All-American for the third consecutive season, and was joined on the honor team by defensive end Bob Brudzinski and offensive tackle Chris

Ward. Brudzinski was selected the team's MVP. Pete Johnson finished his outstanding four-year career as the school's all-time leading scorer with 348 points on 58 touchdowns.

1976

September 11	Michigan State	W	49	21
September 18	at Penn State	W	12	7
September 25	Missouri	L	21	22
October 2	UCLA	T	10	10
October 9	at Iowa	W	34	14
October 16	at Wisconsin	W	30	20
October 23	Purdue (HC)	W	24	3
October 30	at Indiana	W	47	7
November 6	Illinois	W	42	10
November 13	at Minnesota	W	9	3
November 20	Michigan	L	0	22
January 1	Colorado*	W	27	10
Total Points			305	149
*Orange Bowl				

Season Record: 9-2-1
Big Ten Co-Champion

1977

After winning outright or sharing the Big Ten title the last five seasons, expectations were again very high as Woody Hayes began his 27th season at Ohio State. Eight offensive starters from '76 were back; tight end Greg Storer, tackle Chris Ward, guard Jim Savoca, center Mark Lang, and the entire backfield of quarterback Rod Gerald, tailback Ron Springs, wingback Jimmy Harrell, and fullback Jeff Logan.

The defense was also in good shape with seven regulars returning; linebacker Tom Cousineau, end Kelton Dansler, middle guard Aaron Brown, tackle Eddie Beamon, safety Ray Griffin, and halfbacks Joe Allegro and Mike Guess. With the graduation of three-time All-American Tom Skladany, David McKee took over the punting duties and Vlade Janakievski assumed the place-kicking responsibilities.

Unimpressive Beginning

Ohio State struggled while grinding out a 10-0 win over coach Lou Saban's Miami of Florida Hurricanes in the September 10 season opener. The Ohio Stadium crowd of 86,287 expected a lot more scoring from the OSU offense, which put all of its 10 points on the board in the second quarter. After OSU's first sustained march stalled at the Miami 14-yard line, Vlade Janakievski staked his squad to a 3-0 lead with a 31-yard field goal. Jeff Logan suffered a severely sprained ankle and was lost for the rest of the afternoon.

Sophomore tailback Ricky Johnson came off the bench to spark a seven-play 93-yard march which delivered the game's only touchdown. Johnson zig-zagged his way wide for 32 yards on his first carry of the afternoon, and Ron Springs took a lateral from Rod Gerald on an option play and scampered 21 yards to the outside for the six

points. A sprained knee and thigh bruise forced Johnson to the sideline in the third quarter.

While Hurricane quarterback E. J. Baker harried OSU's defensive secondary with short sideline and over-the-middle completions totaling 210 yards, the Buckeyes completely eliminated Miami's running game, holding the visitors to minus-13 yards on the ground. The Hurricanes were aided by the outstanding punting of Robert Rajsich who averaged nearly 45 yards on nine punts. Springs was the game's leading rusher with 114 yards on 27 attempts.

The next Saturday a far more effective offense led Ohio State to a 38-7 trouncing of Minnesota, before a sunbaked Ohio Stadium crowd of 86,287. The Buckeyes, who were nearly as hot as the 85-degree afternoon temperature, scored in each quarter and led in total offense, 518 yards to 138. Five different players scored Ohio State's five touchdowns, and Janakievski booted his second field goal of the season.

With Logan and Johnson both unable to play because of injuries suffered in the Miami opener, senior Ray Griffin returned to the offensive backfield for the first time since his freshman season and delivered 58 yards in 14 carries. The lone bright spot for the Golden Gophers was Bobby Weber's 100-yard kickoff return late in the third period for his team's only score. Springs again led the offense with 27 carries for 147 yards, and Woody Hayes was especially proud of the Buckeye defense which had held its first two opponents scoreless.

All-American safety Ray Griffin

An Afternoon Never to be Forgotten

Few events in all of Ohio State athletics created the anticipation and excitement as the Buckeyes' September 24 collision with the Oklahoma Sooners. If anything, the very first meeting between these two powers even exceeded all expectations, although a different outcome would definitely have been preferred by those with allegiance to the Scarlet and Gray. Both teams were 2-0. In the weekly AP poll, Oklahoma was third and Ohio State fourth behind Michigan and Southern California.

Before a packed and nervous Ohio Stadium crowd of 88,119, Oklahoma won, 29-28, in one of the most dramatic games ever staged. On this overcast 78-degree afternoon, a strong 15-mile-per-hour wind streamed out of the south. The two offenses scored 54 of the game's 57 points at the stadium's north end with the wind to their backs. This struggle was composed of three chapters—Oklahoma opened by tallying the game's first 20 points, Ohio State retaliated with the next 28, and Oklahoma finished the tense afternoon by scoring the final nine. It also developed into one of the most physical battles experienced by either team in many seasons.

Running from the wishbone formation, the Sooners relied primarily on their great speed to score the first four times they had the ball. Elvis Peacock rocketed 33 yards for a touchdown, Billy Sims darted 15 yards for another, and Uwe von Schamann (remember the name) booted field goals of 23 and

33 yards. His 33-yarder was the game's only score at the stadium's south end.

Ohio State was yet to register a single first down by the time the score was 20-0, defensive ace Tom Cousineau had suffered a shoulder separation and was done for the afternoon, and a rout seemed entirely possible. OSU twice rejected fourth-down field goal attempts in the second quarter, one at the Oklahoma 12 and another at the Sooner 25—the Buckeyes came up empty both times.

ABC-TV was carrying the game regionally, and decided (at this point) to shift some of its affiliated stations to the Maryland-Penn State game because of the one-sidedness of the Buckeye-Sooner tilt. But there was an abrupt reversal in the tone of the game in Columbus. In a complete turnabout, the Buckeyes scored 28 consecutive points during the second and third quarters. First Ron Springs scored from 30 yards out on a pitchout to finish off an 80-yard march. On the second play of Oklahoma's ensuing possession, linebacker Dave Adkins recovered a Sooner fumble at the Ohio State 19, setting up a first-down scoring dash by Rod Gerald. Suddenly the halftime score was 20-14.

On the Buckeyes' second possession of the third period, freshman fullback Joel Payton plunged across from the one to complete a 52-yard drive. The crowd went totally bananas as Vlade Janakievski's extra point put Ohio State ahead for the first time all afternoon, 21-20.

Sooner option-style quarterback Thomas Lott had been injured and was replaced by

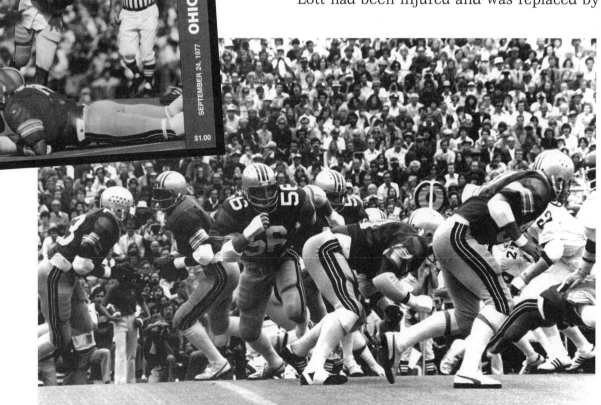

Quarterback Rod Gerald hands off to tailback Ron Springs as guard Ken Fritz pulls to lead interference against Oklahoma.

Dean Blevins who was a better passer. Two minutes later OSU's Kelton Dansler intercepted one of Blevin's passes at the Oklahoma 33-yard line. Three plays later Gerald suffered a head bump and was replaced at quarterback by Greg Castignola, who immediately fired a 16-yard touchdown pass to tight end Jimmy Moore. Suddenly Ohio State led, 28-20, and ABC-TV had its affiliated stations tuned back to Ohio Stadium for the remainder of the game.

Oklahoma then got a big break with the recovery of an Ohio State fumble at its own 43 with 6:24 remaining in the game. Peacock's one-yard touchdown dive at 1:29 finished off a 13-play 57-yard drive, which really tightened the score at 28-26. The march was sustained when Ohio State was off-side on a down when the Sooners failed to convert a fourth-and-four situation at the 12. Oklahoma went to Peacock on an option pitch for an attempted two-point conversion, but Paul Ross, Mike Guess, and Tom Blinco dropped him short of the goal line, and Ohio State's lead of 28-26 appeared to be safe.

von Schamann Delivers

The Sooners did the obvious—an onside kick—which they recovered at the 50-yard line with 1:21 remaining. Four plays moved the ball to the OSU 23. The game's outcome now centered on the foot of von Schamann, a German-born soccer-style kicker who moved with his family to Fort Worth, Texas, from West Berlin when he was 14 years old. Woody Hayes called time out to let him think about his challenge, but it didn't matter. With just three seconds on the clock, von Schamann calmly sliced a 41-yarder through the uprights for the game-winning field goal.

Many of Ohio State's disheartened defenders dropped to the turf, too shocked to move. After coming back from a 20-point deficit, the defeat was doubly difficult to digest. Many fans remained in their seats long after the final gun sounded, too emotionally

Hayes In A Hurry

While opening up his Lane Avenue barber shop one summer morning in the late 1970s, Howard Warner spotted Woody Hayes headed for his campus office with his briefcase riding on top of his car. Apparently the coach had forgotten he had placed it there as he was leaving his home.

Howard immediately telephoned Mrs. Hayes, told her what he had just seen, and jokingly expressed his concern that Woody's plans for the Michigan game might be inside. She called and relayed the message to the coach, who went outside and found his briefcase still sitting on top of his car—plans for the Michigan game were safe!

drained to leave. Oklahoma coach Barry Switzer told newsmen, "I am sure glad football games are 60 minutes. This game had more drama, more tension than any game I have been associated with."

A visibly disappointed Woody Hayes gave Oklahoma much credit and told the press, "We had our chances to win and we did not cash in on them. It was just like that. Our defense played enormously well after the poor start." He lamented the loss of Cousineau, but praised Tom Blinco for playing well as Cousineau's replacement.

The Sooners led in first downs, 18-14, and in net offensive yards, 294-202. Turnovers were a big factor; Oklahoma lost four of seven fumbles and threw two interceptions, while Ohio State lost two of three fumbles with no interceptions. The Sooners moved to the top spot in the weekly *AP*, and the Buckeyes fell to sixth.

Seven Interceptions in Dallas

Rod Gerald dazzled a Cotton Bowl crowd of 51,970 as he guided Ohio State to a 35-7 victory over Southern Methodist on Saturday evening, October 1. It was a grand homecoming for the junior quarterback, who connected on three long passes in the Buckeyes' first scoring drive, and jaunted 33 yards for a TD on a broken play to lift OSU to a 21-0 first-period lead. Gerald had attended South Oak Cliff High School in Dallas, where his father was a Baptist minister.

The Buckeye defense intercepted seven Mustang passes, just one short of the school record of eight set during a 42-7 victory over Chicago on October 22, 1938. Mike Guess tied a school single-game record with three of the seven thefts. On the downside, Jeff Logan re-injured his left ankle, and defensive back Leonard Mills suffered a concussion.

SMU, trailing 35-0, avoided a shutout with its only touchdown late in the fourth period. Hayes was openly proud of his team's pass defense, but confessed his concern over having both a punt and a field goal attempt blocked.

The Buckeyes were exceptional in almost every aspect with a 46-0 romp over Purdue the next Saturday in Columbus. Hayes described the afternoon as, "About as perfect a game as we could play against a team as good as Purdue." Ohio State jumped out to a 29-0 lead after intercepting Boilermaker quarterback Mark Herrmann twice in the first quarter, built the lead to 39-0 at halftime, then substituted liberally throughout the second half. Joel Payton's 26 points increased his season total to 50, making him the nation's leading scorer.

Defense Continues Domination

At Iowa City, October 15, the Buckeyes' ground-oriented offense chewed up both time and yardage in defeating the Hawkeyes, 27-6. But for the third straight weekend,

Hayes preferred to praise the Ohio State defense, which consistently gave the offense good field position. OSU outgained Iowa, 464 yards to 220, but the veteran coach was most bothered by his team's four lost fumbles and three interceptions, which kept the margin of victory from being much more one-sided.

Jeff Logan returned to the playing field and contributed 64 yards in 10 carries. Gerald connected on nine tosses for 91 yards and also was the game's leading runner with exactly 100 yards on 13 trys. Ohio State's record was now 5-1 overall and 3-0 in conference play at the halfway point of the season. The Michigan Wolverines at 6-0 had been elevated to the nation's number-one ranking, the Buckeyes moved up to fourth, and another "two-team race" for the Big Ten title was well underway.

OSU's 35-15 victory the next weekend at Northwestern was anything but pretty. Playing before a Dyche Stadium crowd of just 29,563 on a very raw and rainy afternoon, the Buckeyes were intercepted twice and lost four of eight fumbles. While the offense made more than a season's worth of errors, the defense was riddled for 321 yards by

Payton Points

Freshman fullback Joel Payton scored 26 of Ohio State's 46 points against Purdue, at the time the most ever scored against the Boilermakers by one player in a single game. The record stood 16 seasons until Minnesota's Omar Douglas dented Purdue for 30 points during the Golden Gopher's 59-56 win on October 9, 1993.

an opponent that now had a season record of 0-7.

Big plays were the primary reason OSU was able to score 35 points. In the first quarter, Ron Springs ripped off a 72-yarder to set up Joel Payton's first of two short scoring plunges. In the final period, Jeff Logan's 63-yard jaunt enabled Paul Campbell to score OSU's final touchdown from the Northwestern one.

While Ohio State was struggling at Evanston, the big story of the day came from Minneapolis where unheralded Minnesota stifled top-ranked Michigan, 16-0, to hand the Wolverines their first setback of the year. The Buckeyes were now in sole possession of the Big Ten lead.

Bucks Bury Badgers

Third-ranked Ohio State looked considerably better at home the next Saturday, October 29, smashing Wisconsin 42-0 before a homecoming crowd of 87,837. The Buckeyes wasted no time as Rod Gerald and wingback Jimmy Harrell connected on a 79-yard touchdown pass on the second offensive play of the afternoon. While watching the Badgers on film during their week of preparation, the Ohio State coaches noticed that Wisconsin's safety tended to play very shallow. They felt Harrell could get behind him early in the game, and the play worked exactly as planned.

A strong defense, which created four interceptions (total of 21 for the year), was

Buckeyes Smother Illini 35-0

The Columbus Dispatch, Sunday, November 6, 1977

again one of the keys to the Buckeyes' seventh win of the year. Six different players scored their team's six touchdowns, and back-up quarterback Mike Strahine moved the squad effectively in the final period. It was Ohio State's 18th consecutive win over Wisconsin, since losing 12-3 at Madison in 1959. Michigan got back on track with a 23-6 win over Iowa to maintain its close second place in the league standings.

It was more of the same at Champaign, where the Buckeyes posted their fourth shutout of the season and dampened Illinois' homecoming activities, 35-0. The Ohio State cheerleaders arrived late at Memorial Stadium, so Woody Hayes led the Buckeye fans in some pregame yells. Hayes wanted to make sure the partisans understood how much he and the players appreciated their support, especially on the road.

The OSU offense very systematically amassed 28 first downs and 402 yards on the ground, with most of the gains of the six-to-eight-yard variety. Eleven different Ohio State backs carried at least once against the Fighting Illini, with five of them scoring the game's five touchdowns. Linebacker Tom Cousineau had another excellent afternoon with 17 tackles.

All-American middle guard Aaron Brown

Record Sixth Consecutive Big Ten Championship

Indiana scored first to take a 7-0 lead in the Buckeyes last home game on November 12. Hoosier coach Lee Corso immediately had a portion of his squad photographed with the scoreboard in the background. "I wanted our players to seize this rare opportunity, since we may never again be leading Ohio State," he explained. Corso was right! The Buckeyes won, 35-7, to clinch at least a share of their record sixth consecutive Big Ten title or co-title.

The game was tied at the half, 7-7, with OSU seemingly playing with little emotion. This changed radically with four second-half touchdowns, three in the third period. Jeff Logan showed his ankle was now okay, running for a game-high 148 yards on 20 carries. The Buckeyes again used a lot of players, with five different backs scoring touchdowns. Ron Springs became just the sixth Ohio State back to ever rush for more than 1,000 yards in a single year—his 72 yards pushed his season total to 1,003. Vlade Janakievski's five conversions gave him what was then a school record of 44 in a row without a miss.

All efforts now focused on the November 19 game at Michigan, which once again would decide just about everything. Ohio State was 7-0 in conference competition, the second-place Wolverines were 6-1. Michigan needed a win to earn at least a piece of the top prize. Both teams were 9-1 overall, with OSU fourth in the Associated Press ratings and UM fifth.

Simply Too Many Errors

"This is by far the best game we ever played and lost," a downcast Woody Hayes told the press after his team fell to their archrival Wolverines, 14-6. Seldom has an Ohio State team so dominated a game and not won. A Michigan Stadium crowd of 106,024 (then the largest ever to see a regular-season college football game) saw Ohio State

lead in first downs, 23-10, and total offensive yards, 352-196, yet lose the contest by eight points.

Two lost fumbles were very damaging. Michigan scored its second touchdown after Wolverine linebacker Ron Simpkins recovered Ron Springs' fumble at the UM 20 on OSU's first offensive play of the second half. Late in the final period, with Michigan leading 14-6, the Buckeyes were at the Wolverine eight, first-and-goal. A touchdown and two-point conversion would tie the game, earning Ohio State both the Rose Bowl bid and an undisputed league championship. On first down Gerald optioned to his right but fumbled when hit hard by linebacker John Anderson. Michigan's Derek Howard recovered, and the Buckeyes' chances had all but evaporated.

As the OSU offense came off the field following their last turnover, Hayes vented his frustration by ripping off his headset and throwing it to the ground. As Hayes turned and discovered a television camera focusing on his reactions from very close range, he

Finally

Michigan's victory over Ohio State in 1977 marked the first time the Wolverines had been able to defeat the Buckeyes two-in-a-row during Woody Hayes' first 27 seasons at Ohio State.

lunged at ABC-TV cameraman Mike Freeman—before a national television audience. Hayes' actions drew a reprimand and one-year probation from Big Ten Commissioner Wayne Duke, although Duke conceded the cameraman had broken NCAA guidelines by being just a couple of yards from the coach instead of the regulation 10 yards.

A bubbling Bo Schembechler told reporters, "I've been down there (Columbus) when we got all the statistics and they got the points. Now this one time, we got the points. We got two touchdowns and they got two field goals. That's what the game is all about. It was a great, great victory for us, and I can describe it best by saying our team was extremely tenacious." In their nine games against each other from '69 through '77, Hayes and Schembechler were all even at 4-4-1.

Woody and Bear

With Michigan headed to Pasadena because of its head-to-head win over Ohio State, the Buckeyes accepted an invitation to meet Alabama in the January 2, 1978, Sugar Bowl. The game was advertised as "the classic confrontation" between college football's two winningest active coaches—Woody Hayes and Alabama's Paul "Bear" Bryant. Unfortunately, the game itself was anything but a masterpiece. The Crimson Tide manhandled the Buckeyes, 35-6, before a crowd of 76,811 in the Louisiana Superdome.

The outcome was pretty well decided by the time Rod Gerald threw a 38-yard scoring toss to Jimmy Harrell in the final period for OSU's only points. The team had been in New Orleans for two weeks, fearing that late-December weather in Ohio would hinder practices. Some of the players felt the stay was too long and dulled their competitive edge, especially since Alabama practiced at home until just four days before the game.

After playing exceedingly well most of the season and outscoring its first ten oppo-

nents, 331-71, Ohio State scored only 12 points in its last two games to finish the year at 9-3 and place eleventh in the final national rankings. Dave Adkins was elected the team's MVP. Chris Ward repeated as an All-American, and Aaron Brown, Tom Cousineau, and Ray Griffin were also selected to the honor team.

1977

September 10	Miami (Florida)	W	10	0
September 17	Minnesota	W	38	7
September 24	Oklahoma	L	28	29
October 1	at Southern Methodist	W	35	7
October 8	Purdue	W	46	0
October 15	at Iowa	W	27	6
October 22	Northwestern	W	35	15
October 29	Wisconsin (HC)	W	42	0
November 5	at Illinois	W	35	0
November 12	Indiana	W	35	7
November 19	at Michigan	L	6	14
January 1	Alabama*	L	6	35
Total Points			**343**	**120**

*Sugar Bowl

Season Record: 9-3
Big Ten Co-Champion

1978

The 1978 Ohio State football season was anything but normal. Most discussions among fans centered around who would start at quarterback. Would it be incumbent Rod Gerald, the fleet-footed master of the option who was returning for his senior season, or would it be freshman Art Schlichter from Miami-Trace High School, one of the state's most heralded high school stars since Vic

Janowicz was recruited out of Elyria in 1948? Everyone had an opinion, and Woody Hayes was staying rather quiet, only saying that he felt Ohio State would have another fine team this year.

Gerald practiced at both quarterback and split end in fall drills, partly because he felt his chances of having a successful professional career might be better as a receiver than as a quarterback. After several ups-and-downs throughout the fall, the '78 season would also end much differently than anyone could have imagined.

Unusual Beginning

The September 16 opener against Joe Paterno's Penn State Nittany Lions was hardly routine. It was Ohio State's first game, while Penn State had already played twice, defeating Temple (10-7) and Rutgers (26-10) the two previous weekends. For the first time in anyone's memory, OSU drum major Dwight Hudson failed to catch his baton after throwing it over the goal post in the band's pregame show. It is supposed to mean bad luck for the Buckeyes if the drum major fails to catch the baton.

In OSU's final week of fall practice, broadcasters and reporters had not been able to find out who would be Ohio State's starting quarterback, even on the morning of the opener. When Penn State kicked off into the end zone to start the game, Hayes stood along the sideline with both Schlichter and Gerald at his side. As the ball was being placed at the 20-yard-line, he directed both of them onto the field—Schlichter going to quarterback and Gerald at split end. The roar from Ohio State fans was deafening.

The 18-year-old freshman completed his first pass for six yards to flanker Doug Donley, and his next toss for 13 yards to Gerald. But it would eventually turn out to be a long afternoon for the Ohio Stadium crowd of 88,203. Penn State won, 19-0, on four field goals by place-kicker Matt Bahr and

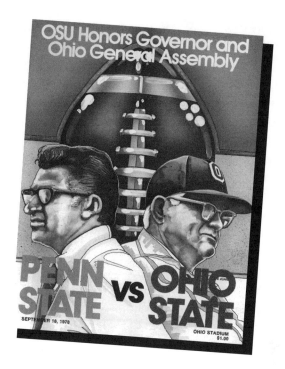

a 13-play 80-yard drive in the third quarter for the game's only touchdown. Bahr was the younger brother of PSU placekicker Chris Bahr, who booted three field goals in Ohio Stadium for PSU's only points during the

---

Looking for Clues at 1711 Cardiff Road

Dale Keitz, a defensive lineman at the University of Michigan from 1976 through 1979, played high school football at Upper Arlington in Columbus. During the summers, Keitz worked on one of the Upper Arlington Sanitation Department trucks, picking up garbage.

One of his "customers" was the Woody Hayes family at 1711 Cardiff Road. Dale took a lot of good-natured kidding about sorting through Woody's trash, looking for clues to Ohio State's game plan for the Michigan game.

Dale likely also talked with his father, Dick, to gain an insight into Hayes' game planning techniques. The elder Keitz played football under Hayes at Denison University in 1947-48.

Buckeyes' 17-9 victory over Penn State in 1975.

Hayes had his quarterbacks throw 34 passes, the most by an Ohio State team since Don Lamka and Greg Hare combined for 39 throws during a 27-7 victory at Indiana on October 16, 1971. Schlichter completed 12 of 26 throws for 182 yards, but suffered five interceptions. Greg Castignola was four of eight for 65 yards. The Buckeyes lost three fumbles for a total of eight turnovers.

Ohio State's problems intensified as the game progressed. The Buckeye offensive line was not able to handle the ferocious pass rush of PSU's defensive tackles Bruce Clark and Matt Millen, and OSU's pass receivers needed more experience working with a new quarterback. Joe Paterno told the press after the game that Hayes' decision to start Schlichter caught Penn State completely by surprise, but that the Nittany Lion's defense was prepared for whatever might come their way.

The same afternoon Ohio State lost to Penn State, Purdue defeated Michigan State, 21-14, at West Lafayette in the season opener for both teams. Although little attention was given to the outcome at that time, this game would become a major factor in deciding the Big Ten title.

Change in Strategy

It looked like an entirely different Ohio State team that defeated Minnesota, 27-10, the following Saturday in Minneapolis. Most of the Memorial Stadium crowd of 55,200 likely expected to see the first Golden Gopher victory in the series since 1966—what they saw was the Buckeyes' domination of the game by effectively returning to their patented ground at-

Two-time All-American linebacker Tom Cousineau

tack. OSU started quickly and led 21-3 at the half. Ohio State rushed 73 times for an even 300 yards, while completing just three of eight tosses for 57 yards. Schlichter improved a lot over his first game and seemed to be more comfortable running the offense.

Hayes Achieves Ohio State Victory No. 200

The Buckeyes defeated Baylor on September 30, 34-28, in the first of two consecutive home games against opponents from the Southwest Conference. The win was the 200th for Woody Hayes since he took command of the OSU program in 1951 (200-58-9).

Ohio State went away from its passing plans after Schlichter threw two interceptions in the first period. Baylor turned both of its thefts into touchdowns to lead 14-7 after the first quarter. Bear quarterback Steve Smith tormented the Buckeye defense with 17 completions for 249 yards and three touchdowns. But in the end it was Woody's famous ground attack that made the difference—a whopping 373 net yards on 81 carries.

The next week Ohio State and Southern Methodist played to a 35-35 tie, leaving both teams disappointed with the outcome. Down 21-14 at halftime, the Buckeyes outscored SMU 21-0 in the third period and seemed to have the game under control. But Mustang quarterback Mike Ford twice plunged across from the one in the game's final 15 minutes to force the tie.

SMU gave Ohio State a real workout, running 107 plays from scrimmage for a total of 501 yards. Woody Hayes blamed himself for the

tie, telling the media he substituted a little too liberally when his team took a 14-point lead into the final quarter. He blamed injuries and a lack of depth in the OSU secondary as the major elements of their defensive problems, but promised his team would get better in the weeks ahead.

Clancy's Annual Ritual

A familiar happening for many seasons was the return of Clancy Issac at homecoming to lead his annual cheer, "Yea Ohio, Yea Ohio, Let's Go, Let's Fight, Let's Win!"

Issac was an Ohio State cheerleader in the late 30s. He was the originator of the Block "O" card section in 1938. He got the idea after seeing a similar activity at the University of Southern California when the Buckeyes played there in '37.

Clancy returned for his familiar homecoming cheer for 40 consecutive years from 1939 through 1978. His final appearance at the '78 Iowa game was an emotional moment, as the marching band spelled out CLANCY as a tribute to his many years of loyalty and enthusiasum.

In 1970 Clancy Issac was honored by his alma mater as "one of 100 distinguished alumni selected during The Ohio State University's first 100 years."

Unusual Day—Ohio State and Michigan Both Upset

Ohio State's chances of capturing a seventh consecutive Big Ten title were weakened with an unexpected 27-16 loss at Purdue on October 14. The game was much different than the Buckeyes' 46-0 win in 1997. OSU outgained the Boilermakers, 507 yards to 328, but lost four fumbles during the afternoon and was flagged for nine penalties totaling 116 yards. OSU's record was now 2-2-1.

Purdue quarterback Mark Herrmann was very effective with his short passes, finishing with 22 completions for 210 yards and a touchdown. It was Purdue's first win over Ohio State since 1967, and it gave the Boilermakers a 2-0 league record and sole possession of first place in the conference standings. This same afternoon Michigan State stunned a Michigan Stadium crowd of 105,132 with a 24-15 upset over the previously undefeated Wolverines. It was the Spartans' first win in this bitter rivalry in nine seasons.

Bob Hope Highlights Homecoming

Ohio State returned to the victory column for the first time in three weeks with a 31-7 pasting of Iowa at homecoming. The second and third teams saw considerable action after the Buckeyes did all their scoring in the first half. Big plays gave OSU two of its touchdowns–Ron Springs's 39-yard touchdown gallop and a 78-yard bomb from Art Schlichter to flanker Doug Donley. Freshman Bob Atha added a 27-yard field goal, fullback Paul Campbell powered into the end zone from five yards out, and middle guard Mark Sullivan grabbed a ball tipped by end Paul Ross and scored his first career touchdown with a 13-yard interception return.

The halftime show was highlighted with comedian Bob Hope dotting the "i" in the band's traditional Script Ohio. Woody Hayes introduced his squad to Hope as they returned to the field for the second half, explaining to his players the wonderful work

Bob Hope is greeted by Woody Hayes shortly after Hope dotted the "i" in Script Ohio at homecoming on October 21.

Hope had done for people all over the world. Hayes and Hope were close friends. The Cleveland native had visited the coach at University Hospital four years before when Hayes was recovering from his heart attack.

The Buckeyes routed overmatched Northwestern, 63-20, at home on October 28. Hayes used almost his entire squad throughout the afternoon, as seven different players

Highest High

The 63 points registered against Northwestern were the most scored by Ohio State in one game during Woody Hayes' 28 seasons as head coach from 1951 through 1978.

scored OSU's nine touchdowns. Ohio State tied a school single-game record with 33 first downs, and ground out 511 rushing yards — just six shy of another OSU single-game mark.

Woody Hayes used his postgame press conference to throw a slight "zinger" at the Ohio State Athletic Council. Apparently the group had recently met and reported that Ohio State would be interested in playing in only one of the four major postseason bowls. When a writer asked about this report, Hayes told him, "We have four tough games ahead. We don't talk about bowl games at this time if other people haven't first. But I am TOO NEW here to be consulted!" Hayes then quickly left the interview room.

Not Your Typical Buckeye Victory

After a game-opening 77-yard touchdown drive, the Buckeyes relied heavily on their defense and special teams to romp over Wisconsin, 49-14, on November 4. A Camp Randall Stadium crowd of 79,940 watched in disbelief as their Badgers threw four interceptions and lost two fumbles, paving the way for Ohio State to score in almost every way conceivable. OSU added two more touchdowns in the second period, first on a blocked punt by Todd Bell which Otha Watson recovered in the end zone, followed by Tyrone Hicks' 96-yard kickoff return.

In the second half, the Buckeye offense put three more TDs on the board, after Vince Skillings scored with a 61-yard interception return just 99 seconds after halftime. The game statistics were somewhat bizarre. Wisconsin led in first downs, 22-19, and total offensive yards, 327-316, yet lost the game by five touchdowns.

Ohio State was now 5-2-1 overall and 4-1 in the Big Ten. Purdue continued to lead the league at 5-0 (7-1 overall), while Michigan and Michigan State were both tied with the Buckeyes at 4-1 in conference play. The

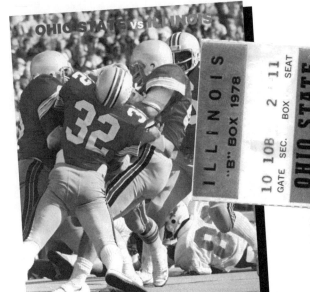

(September 16 at Purdue), but an NCAA probation would prohibit the Spartans from playing in a postseason bowl. If Michigan could defeat Purdue and Ohio State could win at Indiana the next week, the Buckeyes and Wolverines would again be meeting in two weeks to battle for at least a share of the Big Ten title (regardless of how the Spartans fared in their last two games against Northwestern and Iowa).

Purdue-Michigan clash at Ann Arbor in two weeks would play a major role in the Buckeyes' quest of their seventh consecutive league title.

After a slow start, Ohio State had little trouble defeating Illinois, 45-7, at home the following Saturday. All six of OSU's touchdowns were scored on short runs from inside the Illini 10-yard line, as 313 of the Buckeyes' 429 net offensive yards came on the ground. Possibly thinking ahead to the Michigan game in two weeks, Hayes used Rod Gerald at quarterback a couple of times throughout the afternoon. Gerald was very effective, especially with a seven-yard roll option to the right for OSU's sixth TD. Many felt Hayes was sending Bo Schembechler a message that Michigan might want to be ready for the offensive style of either Schlichter or Gerald in two weeks.

The big story of the afternoon came from Madison, where Wisconsin scored a touchdown and a two-point conversion in the game's final 25 seconds to tie Purdue, 24-24. Michigan State was still very much in the title picture with just one conference setback

Woody's Last Victory

The Buckeyes' game at Indiana was one of the most exciting and evenly played ever between the two schools. Coach Lee Corso's Hoosiers were a better team than suggested by their 4-5 record. He had practiced his squad behind closed doors all week, in an attempt to register IU's first victory over the Buckeyes since 1951—the Hoosiers were 0-21-1 in their last 22 meetings with Ohio State. A Memorial Stadium crowd of 47,450, including approximately 11,000 OSU fans, saw Ohio State come from behind to nip the home team, 21-18.

The Buckeyes took an early 7-0 lead, driving 83 yards in 13 plays on their very first possession with fullback Paul Campbell

Last Win at the Horseshoe

Ohio State's 45-7 win over Illinois on November 11, 1978, was Woody Hayes' last victory in Ohio Stadium. Ironically, the Illini were coached by Gary Moeller, one of Hayes' 1962 co-captains, who later was head coach at Michigan from 1990 through 1994.

going over from the four. Ohio State gambled and failed on its next possession, trying for a first down on a fourth-and-one at the OSU 32-yard line. Indiana immediately marched 32 yards in seven plays to tie the score, with Hoosier tailback Mike Harkrader plunging into the end zone from the one. Harkrader's father, Jerry, had been a fine halfback under Woody Hayes, and had scored the final touchdown during OSU's 20-7 win over Southern Cal in the January 1, 1955, Rose Bowl.

The Buckeyes had great difficulty moving the ball the remainder of the first half, and IU's David Freud kicked a 30-yard field goal in the second period to give the Hoosiers a 10-7 lead at intermission. With Paul Campbell and Ron Springs both injured, Ricky Johnson and Ric Volley took over at running back after halftime. On their second possession of the third quarter, the Buckeyes used one of Woody Hayes' patented ball-control drives to go 98 yards in 20 plays and take the lead, 14-10. Quarterback Art Schlichter scored the touchdown from the three.

Early in the final period, Johnson raced 46 yards for a touchdown to increase OSU's lead to 21-10. Schlichter had caught the Hoosier defense in a nine-man front, and Johnson had clear sailing behind key blocks from wide receiver Rod Gerald and guard Ken Fritz.

But IU came right back with sophomore quarterback Tim Clifford guiding his team 72 yards in 14 plays. Tailback Darrick Burnett bolted across for the score after a pass-interference penalty against Ohio State advanced the ball to the one. Clifford passed to split end Mike Friede in the corner of the end zone for a two-point conversion, reducing OSU's lead to three points at 21-18.

After forcing Ohio State to punt, the Hoosiers had one last opportunity for the upset. Pulling out all the stops, Corso called for a pass off of an end-around-reverse, with Friede throwing deep into Ohio State terri-

Mike Guess' interception ended Indiana's final threat.

tory. But Mike Guess wasn't fooled—he intercepted at the OSU 27-yard line to end IU's last threat with just 1:37 remaining.

A disappointed Corso was nevertheless extremely proud of his team's play. "We used everything we had," he said, "because we thought we had a shot at winning. We were going for the win all the way. Our game plan worked real well, but we just didn't have it at the end. We played the best we could and lost." The Hoosiers had used a lot of reverses, and even quick-kicked three times for 52, 66, and 76 yards.

Corso Reflects

Lee Corso has fond memories of that afternoon in 1978 and his association with Woody Hayes. Corso's good friend, Al Carpenter, an avid Hoosier fan, attended all the games and most of IU's practices. Carpenter, who had cerebral palsy, watched most of the games from the IU bench. As Ohio State's squad warmed up that day, Carpenter asked

Corso if it might be possible for Carpenter to meet Woody Hayes. When the two head coaches met at midfield, Corso told Hayes about Carpenter and recalls how Hayes gladly went out of his way to talk with him. "It was heartwarming," Corso remembers. "He autographed Al's program and took such a sincere interest in speaking with him. Al Carpenter couldn't have felt greater."

After Hayes finished, Carpenter graciously thanked Corso, who in turn kidded Carpenter by saying, "Al, I've known you for several years, and you've never asked me for MY autograph." "That's right, coach," a joyous Carpenter replied, "but then, you're not Woody Hayes!"

Corso remembers that when long-time Indiana assistant coach Howard Brown passed away in 1974, Woody Hayes was the only other Big Ten coach to attend his funeral. Brown, a guard, had been selected the Hoosier's MVP in '45 and '47. A plaque recognizing Brown's dedication to Indiana football is proudly displayed in IU's Memorial Stadium.

Corso also recalls the day in 1982 when he was relieved of his job, following his 10th season with the Hoosiers. "Mrs. Anne Hayes was the very first person to call Betsy, my wife. Mrs. Hayes offered a lot of warmth and encouragement, and wanted us to know it wasn't the end of the world. In our book, Woody and Anne Hayes were two very special people."

As the teams left the Indiana playing field late that afternoon of November 18, 1978, no one could have realized that Woody Hayes had just coached his very last victory. Ohio State would play two more games, but soon Hayes's outstanding career as head coach would end abruptly.

The Ten-Year War's Final Chapter

While the Buckeyes were winning at Indiana, Michigan handed Purdue its first conference setback of the year, 24-6, and Michigan State easily defeated Northwestern, 52-

3. The Buckeyes, Wolverines, and Spartans shared the Big Ten lead with identical conference records of 6-1. Purdue was next at 5-1-1. The winner of the November 25 Ohio State-Michigan game would earn at least a share of the league title and a berth in the Rose Bowl (Michigan State was on probation).

The Buckeyes and Wolverines were meeting for the 75th time. It was the first game since 1972 that both teams were not ranked in the nation's top ten. Michigan (9-1, 6-1) was ranked sixth nationally, but Ohio State (7-2-1, 6-1) was listed sixteenth. A then-record Ohio Stadium crowd of 88,358 watched as the Wolverines defeated the Buckeyes, 14-3. Ohio State had now lost three straight to the Wolverines for the first time since losing four consecutive games from 1945 through 1948.

Senior quarterback Rick Leach made a big difference in the game. After Bob Atha's

Tailback Ron Springs

29-yard field goal gave Ohio State an early 3-0 lead, Leach very effectively moved the Wolverines while passing for both of their touchdowns. Michigan led in first downs, 21-11, and in net offensive yards, 364-216. UM ran 80 offensive plays to just 61 for OSU. The Wolverine defense grew stronger as the game progressed, holding Ohio State to just a single first down in the second half.

Michigan State had no trouble handling Iowa, 42-7, to share the Big Ten title with the Wolverines at 7-1. Purdue defeated Indiana, 20-7, to finish in the third spot at 6-1-1, while the Buckeyes dropped to fourth with a record of 6-2. The Spartans' success meant that for the first time in 11 seasons, a team other than Ohio State or Michigan had claimed at least a portion of the conference championship. Indiana, Purdue, and Minnesota tied for the league crown in 1967. Ohio State completed the regular season with an overall record of 7-3-1, its worst since going 6-4 in 1971.

Fateful Night in Jacksonville

It had been arranged that the loser of the Ohio State-Michigan game would play in the Gator Bowl against seventh-ranked Clemson (10-1), champion of the Athletic Coast Conference, on December 29. The Tigers were directed by Danny Ford, who had been elevated to the top job just three weeks earlier after Charlie Pell left for the head coaching position at Florida. The 30-year-old Ford was working as a head coach for the first time at any level.

Ohio State's squad had practiced well in Jacksonville, and Hayes was happy with the attitude and condition of his squad as game night approached. Rain and gale-like winds prevented either team from practicing as planned under the Gator Bowl lights the night before the contest. Ford cancelled his Tigers' final drill, but Hayes, wanting to follow his team's normal pregame routine, put the Buckeyes through their planned practice in the rain and mud at nearby Sandalwood

High School. Interestingly, Clemson entered the game as a two-point favorite.

The Gator Bowl drew a crowd of 72,011 for the Friday evening contest. Clemson drove 80 yards for the game's first touchdown midway through the second quarter to put the Tigers on top, 7-3, after Bob Atha's 27-yard field goal had staked Ohio State to an early 3-0 lead late in the first period. Five minutes before halftime, Schlichter took his team 78 yards for its first touchdown, which he scored from four yards out. Janakievski's extra-point attempt was blocked, but OSU had regained the lead, 9-7. There was just enough time remaining for Obed Arari to boot a 47-yard field goal and put the Tigers back on top, 10-9, after 30 minutes of play.

Ohio State missed scoring on two grand first-half opportunities, either of which might have changed the game's final outcome. On a fourth-and-two, fullback Ric Volley was stopped for no gain on a wide pitchout at the

The Rest of the Story

Keith Jackson did ABC-TV's play-by-play of the 1978 Gator Bowl. One evening in early January, 1979, Jackson was a guest on John Gordon's nightly Sportstalk call-in show on WBNS Radio (1460 AM) in Columbus, giving his view on Woody Hayes' last game.

On the fateful down when Art Schlichter's pass was intercepted by Clemson's Charlie Bauman, Jackson explained that ABC had one of its isolated cameras focused on OSU flanker Doug Donley. Watching the replay in his television booth, Jackson discovered that Donley had been wide open on this play. Jackson told the WBNS audience that, "Had Schlichter noticed Donley he likely would have thrown to Donley for an easy touchdown, Ohio State would have won the game, and Bauman's interception would never have occurred."

Clemson two-yard line. On another possession, fullback Paul Campbell missed a first down by inches on a fourth-and-one at the Clemson 21.

The third quarter belonged to the Tigers, who used a 19-play 84-yard touchdown march to increase their lead to 17-9. Schlichter scored his second touchdown of the evening on a two-yard run in the final period, climaxing an 88-yard drive. Ohio State now trailed 17-15 with 8:11 left in the game. A two-point conversion attempt failed when the freshman quarterback was stopped on an option keeper.

Buckeye middle guard Tim Sawicki gave his team new life when he recovered a Clemson fumble at the OSU 24-yard line with 4:22 remaining. Schlichter quickly moved his team downfield, knowing that a field goal would give Ohio State the victory. On a third-and-five at the Clemson 24-yard line, Schlichter fired a short pass across the middle intended for tailback Ron Springs. Tiger middle guard Charlie Bauman, who had dropped back out of the line of scrimmage, intercepted Schlichter's pass and was run out of bounds in front of the Ohio State bench with 1:59 left to play.

In an obvious fit of frustration, Woody Hayes struck Bauman and had to be physically restrained by some of his players and assistant coaches—the rest is history. Ironically, one of Hayes' good friends, retired

Clemson coach Frank Howard, sent Hayes a pair of boxing gloves as a gag gift. The gloves had been presented to Hayes at the Gator Bowl luncheon the day before the game.

Art Schlichter had played the finest game of his young career, completing 16 of 20 passes for 205 yards and running for another 70 on 18 carries. He came within one vote of being a unanimous choice as Ohio State's MVP of the game.

Hayes talked briefly with his squad following the game, then asked defensive coordinator George Hill to represent him at the postgame press conference. Hill, who had been seen trying to restrain Hayes on the sideline, was pressed by an army of writers for exactly what happened following Bauman's crucial interception. "I have no idea what happened," Hill said. "I was with the defense, getting them ready to go back in." Hayes, whose spirits likely were never lower, remained in the dressing room for more than an hour after the game before boarding the team bus to return to the hotel.

Ohio State Athletic Director Hugh Hindman and President Harold Enarson met late into the night, and it was decided that the 65-year-old coach would be relieved of his duties. Saturday morning Hindman met with Hayes in Hayes' hotel room and, in a very tense session, apparently told the coach he could "resign or be relieved."

For the previous several years Hayes

had stated publicly that when he decided to retire, his close friend Paul Hornung, Sports Editor of *The Columbus Dispatch,* would be the first to know. Around 8:00 a.m. that morning, Hayes called Hornung and announced, "I have resigned as of now."

At a hastily called 9:00 a.m. press conference in Jacksonville, Hindman stated that Hayes had been relieved of his duties, and that the decision had the full support of President Enarson. As the Ohio State team's chartered plane approached the Columbus airport later that morning, Hayes used the plane's public address system to tell his team, "I will not be your coach next year." He wished all his players the best of success and encouraged them to continue to do well in the classroom.

Hayes' punching situation was described by many as "the last straw," in spite of his enormous success both on and off the playing field. The fiery competitor had been involved in a number of recent incidents, many somewhat magnified because they were captured on national television.

Ohio State finished its 1978 season with an overall record of 7-4-1. Linebacker Tom Cousineau was a repeat All-American and was chosen the team's MVP.

The 1978 season brought to a close one of the most colorful and successful coaching careers in college football history. Woody Hayes' 28-season Ohio State record was an outstanding 205-61-10, and his 33-year lifetime coaching record was 238-72-10. Hayes' teams captured 13 Big Ten titles, and 56 of his Ohio State players were named first-team All-Americans.

Hayes was an associate professor who took great pride in teaching classes at Ohio State during the off-season. He had a passion for military history. After football, Hayes continued to be a very active goodwill ambassador for The Ohio State University. He passed away on March 12, 1987, at the age of 74, but Hayes' positive influence will continue for many future generations.

Woody Hayes delivered Ohio State's commencement address on March 22, 1986, an honor he considered the greatest day of his life.

1978

September 16	Penn State	L	0	19
September 23	at Minnesota	W	27	10
September 30	Baylor	W	34	28
October 7	Southern Methodist	T	35	35
October 14	at Purdue	L	16	27
October 21	Iowa (HC)	W	31	7
October 28	Northwestern	W	63	20
November 4	at Wisconsin	W	49	14
November 11	Illinois	W	45	7
November 18	at Indiana	W	21	18
November 25	Michigan	L	3	14
December 29	Clemson*	L	15	17

Total Points			339	216

*Gator Bowl

Season Record: 7-4-1
Conference: 4th Place

THE EARLE BRUCE ERA

"Who will replace Woody Hayes?" That emotionally debated subject was a frequent topic of conversation among Buckeye fans during the 1970s. The question was answered on January 12, 1979, when 47-year-old Earle Bruce, a 1953 Ohio State graduate and former Woody Hayes assistant, became the Buckeyes' 20th head coach. The selection was announced by Athletic Director Hugh Hindman, who had served four seasons with Bruce as a Hayes assistant from 1966 through 1969. Hindman described Bruce as " . . . an individual with all the credentials to be a great coach at Ohio State. He has coached at every level and always has been successful."

Earle Bruce was born in Pittsburgh, Pennsylvania, and at age 10 moved with his family to Cumberland, Maryland, where he became a star halfback and sprinter at Allegeny High School. Ohio State Coach Wes Fesler recruited Bruce in the fall of 1949. A knee injury his freshman year, followed by a reinjury of the knee prior to the 1951 sea-

son, cut short his playing career. Discouraged and tempted to drop out of school, Bruce was persuaded by first-year coach Woody Hayes to stay, earn his degree, and serve as a student assistant coach.

Hayes's encouragement and Bruce's efforts paid off. After graduation, Bruce launched his coaching career as an assistant at Mansfield Senior High School in the fall of 1953. Three years later he became head coach at Salem High School, where his teams compiled a four-season record of 28-9. At Sandusky High School, Bruce's four squads were 34-3-3 from 1960 through 1963, and he finished his high school stint with a 20-0 record at nationally known Massillon High School in '64 and '65. Bruce completed his high school coaching with a 42-game winning streak. He was honored three times as the Ohio High School Coach of the Year in '60, '64, and '65.

Bruce returned to Ohio State as an assistant in 1966, coaching the defensive secondary for two seasons and tutoring the of-

Bruce Succeeds Woody At OSU *Complete Details In Sports Section*

WEATHER
Snow, freezing rain tonight,
Saturday. Low mid-30s tonight.
High Saturday in mid-30s.
Low of 7:33 a.m., sets at 5:33 p.m.
(Map, Data on Page B-5)

The Columbus Dispatch

HOME
FINAL
Associated Press, United Press
International and
Copley News Services

60 Pages   OHIO'S GREATEST HOME NEWSPAPER   4 Sections

VOL. 108, NO. 196   COLUMBUS, OHIO 43216, FRIDAY, JANUARY 12, 1979   •   15 Cents

fensive line the next four. The University of Tampa offered him his first head coaching opportunity at the college level in 1972. Bruce guided Tampa to a record of 10-2, which included a 21-18 Tangerine Bowl (now Florida Citrus Bowl) victory over Kent State, champion of the Mid-American Conference. The Golden Flashes were coached by Don James, who later was highly successful at the University of Washington.

The following fall Bruce was chosen head coach at Iowa State of the powerful Big Eight Conference, replacing Johnny Majors who had moved to the University of Pittsburgh. It wasn't easy competing in a league dominated by Nebraska, Oklahoma, and Colorado, and his first three teams were moderately successful at 4-7. But Bruce's efforts began to show when his next three Cyclone squads posted regular-season records of 8-3, and Bruce was twice selected Big Eight Coach of the Year. It was the first time in 54 years that Iowa State had enjoyed three consecutive winning seasons.

The well-traveled Bruce described his return to Ohio State as a dream come true. "I consider Ohio State the top coaching job in the country, and I will do all I can to ensure that it stays that way. It's a challenge to follow Woody Hayes, but I guess I'm a guy who goes for great challenges. All my efforts will be to keep Ohio State football at its current level of excellence."

1979

Earle Bruce began by retaining Bill Myles and Glen Mason from Woody Hayes' 1978 staff and adding six new assistant coaches; Pete Carroll, Dennis Fryzel, Bob Tucker, Steve Szabo, Fred Zeckman, and Wayne Stanley. Carroll, Tucker, Szabo, and Stanley came with Bruce from Iowa State, and Fryzel had replaced Bruce at Tampa in 1973. Tucker also played under Bruce at Sandusky High School.

There were 11 starters among 45 returning lettermen, including sophomore quarterback Art Schlichter who started all 12 games as a freshman. Gone from the '78 offensive lineup were tight end Jimmy Moore, tackle Joe Robinson, guard Jim Savoca, center Tim Vogler, tailback Ron Springs, and quarterback/receiver Rod Gerald. The defensive losses included tackle Byron Cato, middle guard Mark Sullivan, safety Vince Skillings, and linebackers Tom Cousineau, Kelton Dansler, and Paul Ross. Cousineau had set a school single-season record with 211 tackles his senior season.

Spring practice was very spirited, and the squad was very enthusiastic heading into the autumn schedule. A lot of attention was given to strengthening the defense, which in 1978 had surrendered 216 points (18.0 points per game). It had been the highest defensive scoring average since 1953, when OSU gave up an average of 18.2 points per game.

The 1979 starting offensive line had Tim Waugh at center, Ernie Andria and Ken Fritz at guards, and Tim Burke, Joe Lukens, and Bill Jaco at the tackles. Lukens, just a freshman, was the younger brother of 1976 co-captain Bill Lukens. Ron Barwig and Brad

Dwelle, another freshman, manned the tight end position. Doug Donley returned at flanker, while freshman Gary Williams became the starter at split end. Depth at wide receiver was provided by Chuck Hunter and Tyrone Hicks.

Joining Schlichter in the backfield were fullback Paul Campbell and tailback Calvin Murray. Campbell had been OSU's leading rusher in '78 with 591 yards. Also being counted on for considerable playing time were fullback Ric Volley and freshman tailbacks Tim Spencer and Jimmy Gayle.

The defensive tackles were Luther Henson, Gary Dulin and Jerome Foster. Tim Sawicki and Mark Sullivan were the middle

Leading the Buckeyes onto the field for their opener against Syracuse are Tyrone Hicks (37), Norm Burrows (4), Tim Spencer (46), and Steve Simpson (70).

THE PLAIN DEALER
SUNDAY, SEPTEMBER 9, 1979

Sports

☐ Scores ☐ Races ☐ Opinion ☐ Features

SECTION
3

New-look Buckeyes wallop Syracuse, 31-8

guards. Keith Ferguson, a 1978 starter at offensive tackle, joined Jim Laughlin at outside linebacker. Alvin Washington and freshman Marcus Marek handled the inside linebacking duties. In the defensive backfield were cornerbacks Mike Guess and Ray Ellis, roverback Todd Bell, and safety Vince Skillings.

The September 8 opener with Syracuse marked the first Ohio State game in 29 seasons without Woody Hayes on the sidelines. The Buckeyes looked impressive building up a 21-0 halftime lead, and finishing with a convincing 31-8 triumph over the Orangemen. Greeting an over-crowded room of newsman after the game, Bruce related that he was a little relieved that the first game was a victory. It was also OSU's 800th game (534-218-48).

The first Buckeye to score for a Bruce-coached team was 6'8" tight end Ron Barwig, on an 11-yard pass from Art Schlichter. Cornerback Mike Guess earned Big Ten Defensive Player of the Week honors with 11 tackles and a fumble recovery. OSU led 28-13 in first downs and 464-239 in total net yards. The attendance of 86,205 was the 64th consecutive sellout crowd at Ohio Stadium.

Very Fortunate at Minneapolis

The next week at Minnesota the Golden Gophers won everything but the final score. Using a surprise double-winged T offense, first-year coach Joe Salem's team led in first downs, 26 to 12, and in total offensive yard-

age, 505 to 295. But the injury-plagued Buckeyes somehow managed to win, 21-17, much to the disappointment of the Memorial Stadium crowd of 43,926. Art Schlichter executed brilliantly on key downs and accounted for 238 of his squad's 295 yards.

Minnesota scored on its first two possessions to take a 14-0 lead before OSU could get its offense moving. Schlichter then connected with Tyrone Hicks on a 38-yard scoring pass to make the score 14-7. The Gophers scored a second-quarter field goal and led 17-7 at halftime.

Calvin Murray scored from the one in the third quarter to cut the Gophers' lead to 17-13. In the final period, Schlichter hit end Chuck Hunter for 29 yards, then scrambled the final 32 himself for the game's final touchdown. Schlichter passed to Bill Jaco (playing tight end instead of tackle because of injuries) for a two-point conversion, and Ohio State had its 11th consecutive win over Minnesota.

Fullback Garry White, who scored both Gopher touchdowns, was the game's leading rusher with 221 yards on 34 carries. Quarterback Mark Carlson was successful on 20 of 32 passes for 227 yards with no interceptions. Minnesota ran 80 plays from scrimmage compared with the Buckeyes' 49.

Longest Ohio State Pass

Back at Ohio Stadium on a chilly and overcast September 22, Ohio State outscored Washington State, 45-29. The game featured the longest pass in all of Ohio State football —a short toss over the middle by Art Schlichter to tailback Calvin Murray, who raced the distance for an 86-yard touchdown late in the third quarter.

Murray scored three times, while Schlichter had another big afternoon, completing eight of 13 attempts for 233 yards. Flanker Doug Donley caught five of his tosses, including a 29-yard touchdown pass late in the final quarter to clinch OSU's third win of the season. Linebacker Jim Laughlin recovered a fumble and blocked a Cougar punt, which Tyrone Hicks recovered in the end zone for the Buckeyes' third touchdown. Thirty of the game's 74 points were scored in the fourth period.

Win at UCLA Signals Special Season

Ohio State staged a thrilling 17-13 come-from-behind triumph over UCLA, before a September 29 crowd of 47,228 at the Los Angeles Coliseum. With the Bruins leading, 13-10, Ohio State took possession at its own 20-yard line with just 2:21 remaining to be played. Art Schlichter was near-perfect as he directed the winning drive, connecting on all six passes for 62 of the needed 80 yards and the winning score.

Paul Campbell, normally the starting fullback, had been pressed into service at tight end because of an abundance of injuries at that position. Campbell caught a two-yard toss for the touchdown with just 46 seconds remaining. Calvin Murray was the game's leading rusher with 117 yards, including a 34-yard gallop to the outside in the second period for OSU's first touchdown. Vlade Janakievski booted a 24-yard field goal in the third quarter. The victory was a tremendous confidence builder for the 4-0 Buckeyes, who had now moved up to eighth place in the weekly Associated Press poll.

Following their big win at UCLA, the Buckeyes were sluggish at home the following week, but struggled to a 16-7 victory over stubborn Northwestern. The offense was sty-

We'll be Back

Following the Buckeyes' victory at UCLA, the team plane flew over the Rose Bowl in Pasadena as it began its trip back to Columbus. Seeing the huge stadium from the air, the Ohio State team set a goal of returning there on January 1.

mied by two lost fumbles, an interception, and nine penalties. Schlichter teamed with Brad Dwelle on a four-yard scoring pass for Ohio State's only touchdown. Bob Atha's 50-yard field goal in the fourth quarter secured the win.

While the Buckeyes were defeating Northwestern, Minnesota handled Purdue at Minneapolis, 31-14, for the Boilermakers' only conference loss of the season. This game proved to be extremely significant, since Purdue was the only Big Ten team Ohio State did not face in 1979.

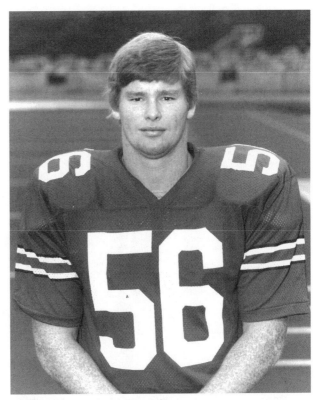

All-American guard Ken Fritz

Moving Into High Gear

Playing at Ohio Stadium the next three Saturdays, the Buckeyes outscored their opponents, 147-6. After routing Indiana 47-6, they whitewashed Wisconsin and Michigan State by scores of 59-0 and 42-0. Ohio State was now 8-0 overall, 5-0 in the conference, and had advanced to fifth in the AP poll. Michigan, also 5-0 in the Big Ten and 7-1 overall, was ranked tenth.

Earle Bruce's team continued to win big the following week at Champaign, with a 44-7 thrashing of Illinois on November 3. The Buckeyes converted two pass interceptions, a fumble recovery, and a blocked punt into scores.

Back at home on November 10, OSU built up a 27-0 halftime lead and coasted to an easier-than-expected 34-7 win over Iowa. The Buckeye defense again dominated, recovering five Hawkeye fumbles and intercepting five passes. Five of the Hawk's 10 turnovers were inside the Iowa 25-yard line.

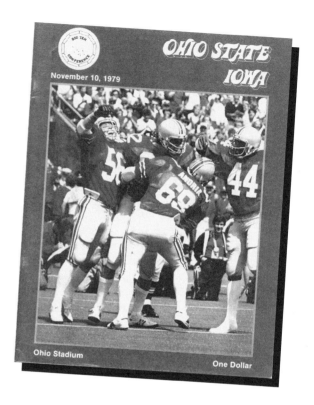

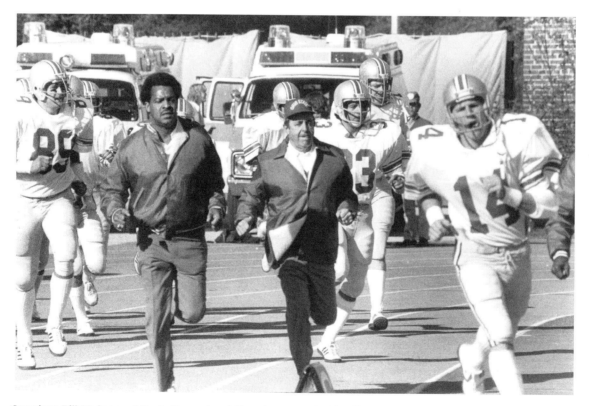

Coaches Bill Myles and Earle Bruce lead the charge onto the field at Illinois' Memorial Stadium. Left to right are Chuck Hunter (89), John Epitropoulos (33), and Brian Schwartz (14).

But the big news of the day came from West Lafayette, where Purdue defeated Michigan, 24-21. Ohio State was now alone atop the Big Ten at 7-0, and Michigan and Purdue were tied for second with league records of 6-1. The Buckeyes could take it all with a win at Ann Arbor the following week.

Jim Laughlin's "Block Party"

Going into their November 17 showdown, the Buckeyes (10-0 overall) had moved into second place in the weekly AP behind Alabama. Michigan, at 8-2, was ranked thirteenth. Tickets were at a premium, as Ohio State was shooting for its first undefeated regular season since 1975. The Michigan Stadium attendance of 106,255 was, at the time, the largest regular-season crowd in college football history.

After a scoreless first quarter, Vlade Janakievski put Ohio State on top, 3-0, with a 23-yard field goal. Michigan grabbed the lead, 7-3, when quarterback John Wangler teamed with Anthony Carter on a scoring pass of 59 yards. Janakievski connected on a 25-yarder with just eight seconds remaining in the second period to bring OSU within one at 7-6. Ohio State had been able to score only two field goals after being inside the UM 40-yard line five times in the first half.

The Wolverines missed a golden opportunity in the second quarter to increase their lead when they failed to convert a fourth-and-inches situation inside the OSU two-yard line. Al Washington and Marcus Marek smothered Michigan's Rick Hewlett (a surprise starter at quarterback) at the OSU four-yard line before the play could develop.

In the third period, Schlichter hit end Chuck Hunter with an 18-yard scoring strike to put Ohio State ahead 12-7. The ball was tipped by Michigan's Mike Jolly

Distance Is NO Problem

Airplane banner towing over Ohio Stadium on a football Saturday is a popular means of commercial advertising and of conveying personal messages. Pilot Bill Watts, who began towing stadium banners in 1969, recalls messages of "Joe Loves Sue," "Happy 50th Birthday, Harry," and "Judy, Will You Marry Me?"

One remarkable tow took place in 1979. Enthusiasm was running high as the undefeated Buckeyes headed north to tangle with Michigan. Three Columbus businesses hired Watts to fly all the way to Ann Arbor that Saturday and tow a "Go Bucks Go" banner over Michigan Stadium. Watt's banner must have helped.....Ohio State won, 18-15.

before Hunter made a leaping catch in the corner of the end zone. A two-point conversion attempt failed. Hunter's catch was the first Ohio State touchdown scored against Michigan since Pete Johnson scored three at Ann Arbor four years earlier in 1975. The Wolverines retaliated with Roosevelt Smith's one-yard TD plunge and a two-point conversion to go back in front, 15-12, after three quarters.

With just over four minutes remaining in the game and Ohio State's 10-game winning streak in jeopardy, the Buckeyes forced Michigan to punt deep in their own territory. Linebacker Jim Laughlin came through with one of the biggest plays in the history of the

Sports SECTION B

THE PLAIN DEALER, SUNDAY, NOVEMBER 18, 1979

OSU defeats U-M, 18-15

A blocked punt comes up Roses

All-American quarterback Art Schlichter started 48 consecutive games from 1978 through 1981.

Ohio State-Michigan series when he blocked Brian Virgil's punt. Todd Bell scooped up the loose pigskin and scrambled 18 yards into the Michigan end zone for one of the season's biggest touchdowns. The Buckeyes rushed ten men on the play, and Laughlin went through untouched for the block. Janakievski's extra-point attempt was no good, leaving the score at 18-15, and that's how the game ended.

With Purdue defeating Indiana that afternoon, 37-21, Ohio State's trip to the Rose Bowl was assured regardless of the outcome at Ann Arbor. But for most Ohio State players and fans, the win over Bo Schembechler's Wolverines was a higher priority than spending January 1 in Pasadena.

#1 Versus #3

Ohio State had advanced to the top of the weekly AP following the close of the regular season. Rose Bowl opponent Southern California, at 10-0-1, was third behind second-place Alabama (11-0). A win over the Trojans would earn Ohio State the national championship in Earle Bruce's first season. Bruce received quite a scare right after the regular season, when he was hospitalized with chest pains. The condition was eventually diagnosed as a severe cold, and the coach was soon able to resume preparation for the Rose Bowl.

Southern Cal scored first to lead 10-0 early in the second period. But the Buckeyes came back to tie the game at halftime with Janakievski's 35-yard field goal and a 67-yard scoring pass from Art Schlichter to Gary Williams. Janakievski scored twice again from 37-yards and 24-yards in the third and fourth periods, to put his team on top, 16-10, with less than ten minutes to play.

But Southern Cal, even after surrendering 16 consecutive points, wasn't finished. With Heisman Trophy winner Charles White leading the charge, the Trojans used eight plays to drive 83 yards and win the game.

Small Town, U.S.A.

Don Hoaglin of Battle Creek, Michigan, enjoys showing Ohio State fans a copy of the state of Michigan's 1979 official transportation road map. The layout engineer became very creative when he inserted two "new" cities just south of the Michigan-Ohio line. One labeled "beatosu" is placed on Route 66 between Archbold and the Ohio Turnpike. The other, "goblu," is located on Route 2, just east of Toledo.

White got the touchdown from the one, and Eric Hipp's conversion made the final score 17-16 in favor of Southern Cal. Ohio State, now 11-1, had come within one point of a national title.

Coach of the Year

The Buckeyes placed fourth in the final AP poll. Alabama (12-0) won the national championship, followed by Southern Cal at (11-0-1) and Oklahoma (11-1). It was a tremendous accomplishment for an Ohio State team that had received no consideration for national honors before the season started.

Schlichter and guard Ken Fritz were chosen as All-Americans and Jim Laughlin was selected the team's MVP. In just his first season at the helm, Earle Bruce was named college football's Coach of the Year. With an 11-1 record in 1979, the Buckeyes had completed the 1970s with a ten-year mark of 91-20-3. Their opponents had been outscored 3,405 points to 1,317. An overall winning rate of 81.1 percent made the 1970s the winningest decade in the first 111 years of Ohio State football.

The wait-and-see attitude that surrounded the 1979 season was gone when Earle Bruce entered his second year at Ohio State. With 15 key starters and 41 lettermen returning from the '79 team, which finished at 11-1, the Buckeyes were the top pick in the Associated Press preseason poll.

The biggest challenge was replacing center Tom Waugh, guards Ken Fritz and Ernie Andria, and tackle Tim Burke on the offensive line. Seniors Jim DeLeone and Scott Burris moved into the starting lineup at center and guard, and sophomore Joe Lukens shifted from starting tackle to the other starting guard spot. Senior Luther Henson switched from defensive tackle to offensive tackle and 6'8" senior Ron Barwig moved from tight end to the other tackle slot. Sophomore Tim Spencer shifted from tailback to replace Paul Campbell and Ric Volley at fullback.

Syracuse Opener Much Different

Syracuse was the opening-game opponent for the second consecutive season, but very little else resembled the previous year's opener. Before a September 13 Ohio Stadium crowd of 86,463, the Orangemen used a variety of formations with a lot of motion, and stormed to a 21-9 lead at halftime. The listless Buckeyes scored just nine first-half points on three field goals by Vlade Janakievski. After the game, Bruce presented Janakievski with a game ball for his outstanding kicking, which kept his team in the game until it could get its offense on track. It was the first time Bruce had presented a game ball since becoming Ohio State's head coach.

The tempo changed considerably when the Buckeyes took the second-half kickoff

1979				
September 8	Syracuse	W	31	8
September 15	at Minnesota	W	21	17
September 22	Washington State	W	45	29
September 29	at UCLA	W	17	13
October 6	Northwestern	W	16	7
October 13	Indiana	W	47	6
October 20	Wisconsin	W	59	0
October 27	Michigan State (HC)	W	42	0
November 3	at Illinois	W	44	7
November 10	Iowa	W	34	7
November 17	at Michigan	W	18	15
January 1	Southern California*	L	16	17
Total Points			390	126
*Rose Bowl				
	Season Record: 11-1			
	Big Ten Champion			

Earle Bruce awarded Vlade Janakievski a game ball for his three first-half field goals in the season-opening win over Syracuse. Janakievski is Ohio State's fourth all-time scoring leader with 295 points from 1977 through 1980.

Janakievski's four field goals of 27, 22, 27, and 27 yards (all in the first half) tied a school single-game record set by Tom Klaban (Klaban's four field goals enabled Ohio State to defeat Michigan 12-10 in 1974).

Golden Gopher freshman quarterback Tim Salem (son of Minnesota coach Joe Salem) connected on his first nine passes and finished with 12 completions for 100 yards with two interceptions, but was unable to move his squad into the end zone. Tim Salem was later Ohio State's quarterback coach under John Cooper. The Buckeyes' five touchdowns all came on runs by Tim Spencer, Jimmy Gayle, Bob Atha, and two by Art Schlichter.

Ohio State's defense was well prepared and motivated to stop the Gophers' run-and-shoot attack, especially after Minnesota's fine offensive showing at Minneapolis in '79. Linebacker Glenn Cobb was out with an injury and was replaced by John Epitropoulos, who made the first start of his college career. The senior linebacker from Warren, Ohio, had an incredible afternoon with an interception, a fumble recovery, and a team-leading 17 tackles.

and drove 80 yards in six plays for their first touchdown. Quarterback Art Schlichter connected with flanker Doug Donley on a perfectly executed 47-yard play-action toss for the score.

OSU scored two more on runs of four and ten yards by tailback Ricky Johnson and Schlichter to win, 31-21. Bruce told the press he was happy anytime his team could win by ten after trailing by 18 (down 21-3 at the end of the first quarter), but admitted he was concerned throughout most of the afternoon.

The conference opener at home the following Saturday was much different. Practices that week had been more intense than prior to the Syracuse opener. Ohio State exploded to a 33-0 first-half lead and coasted to a 47-0 win over error-prone Minnesota.

OHIO STATE MINNESOTA

September 20, 1980

Ohio Stadium $1.50

It was an offensive festival at home against Arizona State on September 27, as the two teams combined for 51 first downs and 1,031 yards of total offense on 160 plays from scrimmage. ASU was led by former Michigan State coach Daryl Rogers. The Buckeyes really "aired it out" for a 38-21 victory in their very first meeting with the Sun Devils.

Schlichter tossed three touchdown passes for the first time in his college career, connecting with Doug Donley in the second and third periods (23 and 10 yards) and Gary Williams in the fourth quarter (13 yards). OSU took advantage of ASU's over-commitment to stopping the Buckeyes' running game. Schlichter finished with 14 completions in 19 attempts for 271 yards.

Line Deficiencies Revealed

Ohio State's fourth consecutive home game October 4 was far less pleasant than the first three. Eleventh-ranked UCLA completely dominated the line of scrimmage on both sides of the ball to shut out the second-ranked Buckeyes, 17-0. It was the first time OSU had been held scoreless in its last 27 games.

After leading 3-0 at the half, UCLA scored touchdowns on its first two possessions of the third quarter. Schlichter, who had passed so brilliantly against Arizona State the previous week, was sacked five times and kept off balance all afternoon by the Bruins' strong rush. He completed only 11 of 27 attempts for 128 yards and had two passes intercepted.

This was the Bruins' third victory over a Big Ten opponent in as many weeks, all on the road. UCLA defeated Wisconsin (35-0) at Madison on September 27, and Purdue (23-14) at West Lafayette September 20.

At Evanston, October 11, the Buckeyes got back on track with a 63-0 shellacking of outmanned Northwestern. Obviously the caliber of opposition had changed, but this game was a welcome switch from the UCLA

First Lady of Football

Dan Heinlen, President of the Ohio State Alumni Association, and his wife have had their Ohio Stadium seats in 16B for many years, and have gotten to know the portal workers in this section. One Saturday around 1980 they were greeted by a new portal worker, dressed in the standard red cap and coat, and having a good time helping people find their seats—Mrs. Anne Hayes. Dan recalls the fun and excitement she was creating, and how people came into the section specifically to talk with her.

encounter. It was Ohio State's highest away-game score since winning 76-0 at Western Reserve on November 3, 1934. It also was the most points ever scored by one team in Dyche Stadium, where the Wildcats had been playing since 1926.

Earle Bruce used his entire 60-man traveling squad. Tailback Calvin Murray led all runners with 120 yards on nine carries. The Buckeyes led in first downs, 30-12, and in total offensive yards, 575-222. They averaged 7.2 yards on each of their 80 plays from scrimmage.

Happy Birthday Calvin Murray

Ohio State returned home October 18 to face Indiana. Each team entered the game with an overall record of 4-1, best in the Big Ten conference after five weeks of play. Hoosier coach Lee Corso returned 39 lettermen from his 1979 squad, which went 8-4 for Indiana's first winning season since 1968. His offense was led by senior quarterback Tim Clifford, the Big Ten's MVP in '79, and two quality tailbacks in seniors Mike Harkrader and Lonnie Johnson. Harkrader was the son of former Ohio State halfback Jerry Harkrader, who had scored a touchdown during OSU's 20-7 triumph over Southern California in the January 1, 1955, Rose Bowl.

Earle Bruce's smoothly coordinated offense and defense combined for a 27-17 victory, before a crowd of 87,957. Calvin Murray celebrated his 22nd birthday that afternoon by rushing for 224 yards and two touchdowns to lead the Scarlet-and-Gray attack.

The Buckeyes built-up a 17-10 halftime lead on a three-yard touchdown bolt by Murray, Vlade Janakievski's 20-yard field goal, and a 20-yard TD burst by tailback Jimmy Gayle. Safety Rod Gorley's two timely interceptions led directly to OSU's two second-half scores. Janakievski's second field goal, a 27-yarder, came in the third quarter, while Murray's second touchdown came on a superbly executed 37-yard sprint down the sideline in the final period.

Following the action, Bruce told reporters, "This was a big game for us. Indiana really came to play.....they put a lot of emphasis on this game. One big factor was our offensive line's ability to control the line of scrimmage." Ohio State led in first downs, 26 to 14, and in total offensive yards, 499 to

251. It was Ohio State's 17th consecutive win over the Hoosiers following a scoreless tie in 1959. Indiana finished the 1980 season at 6-5.

At Madison the following week, Ohio State defeated Wisconsin 21-0 before a shivering crowd of 79,253. With the temperature in the mid-30s and intermittent snow flurries in the air, the Buckeye defense forced four turnovers and secured good field position for the offense most of the afternoon. Wisconsin's furthest penetration was to the OSU 34-yard line midway through the first quarter. After that the Badgers never crossed the midfield stripe.

The scoring all took place in the first half, and Earle Bruce was disturbed by writers' postgame questions which suggested Ohio State should have won by a larger margin. Art Schlichter accounted for the Buckeyes' first two scores on short runs, and Tim Spencer broke loose for 50 yards up the middle midway through the second period for the third touchdown.

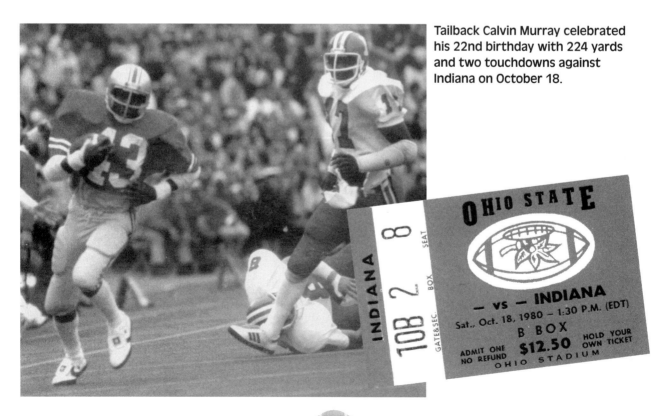

Tailback Calvin Murray celebrated his 22nd birthday with 224 yards and two touchdowns against Indiana on October 18.

After a 48-16 win at Michigan State November 1, Bruce was very pleased with the way the offense and defense fit together, and with the offensive balance that netted 603 yards from scrimmage—381 rushing and 222 passing. He felt his team's 88-yard 10-play scoring drive in the final 1:20 before halftime was one of the keys to his team's success. Schlichter passed 19 yards to Gary Williams for the touchdown with just seven seconds on the clock. This gave the Buckeyes a 24-10 advantage at intermission and provided needed momentum for the second half.

Schlichter passed for 212 yards to increase his career total to 4,085. He became just the seventh player in Big Ten history to pass for more than 4,000 career yards. Murray was the game's leading runner with 115 yards on 16 carries. Quarterback Bob Atha made the game's most exciting play, running wide and sprinting 63 yards for a touchdown early in the final period.

Illinois quarterback Dave Wilson completed an amazing 43 passes for 621 yards and six touchdowns in a losing effort. Pressuring Wilson are Keith Ferguson (65) and Tony Megaro (90).

Buckeyes Withstand Aerial Assault—Barely

Ohio State returned home November 8 to outscore Illinois, 49-42, in one of the wildest games ever staged in the horseshoe. It was the most points scored by an opponent in Ohio Stadium since Michigan defeated the Buckeyes 58-6 on November 23, 1946. Ohio State jumped out to a 28-0 advantage midway through the second quarter, then nearly let it slip away as Illini quarterback Dave Wilson completed 43 of 69 passes for 621 yards and all six touchdowns.

Five of Wilson's TD tosses and 344 of his passing yards came in the second half. He was able to establish (or tie) five NCAA records. Wilson's statistics tended to overshadow one of Art Schlichter's finest games. The junior quarterback connected on his first

11 passing attempts and finished with 17 completions in 21 throws for 284 yards and four touchdowns. It was the only time during his 48 games at OSU from 1978 through 1981 that Schlichter passed for four touchdowns in one game.

Ohio State moved out to what seemed like a safe 49-35 lead when Tim Spencer scored from two yards out to complete a 72-yard drive at the 10:55 mark of the final period. But "old rubber arm" Wilson just kept

coming back. On the Illini's next series a pass to flanker Mike Martin covered 62 yards, but Martin fumbled when finally hit by Buckeye cornerback Vince Skillings, and Ray Ellis recovered for Ohio State at its own eight. Illinois' next possession ended when Skillings intercepted Wilson's pass in the end zone with 3:06 on the clock. His final scoring pass to halfback Greg Foster came with 11 seconds left in the game. Bruce stated afterwards that Skillings' interception probably saved the victory.

The game lasted three and one-half hours. Illinois led in first downs, 36-17, and in total offensive yardage, 659-398. But the Illini committed seven turnovers (three interceptions, four lost fumbles) while Ohio State lost just one fumble. Ironically, the Buckeyes entered the game with the conference's top-ranked pass defense, allowing just 525 passing yards and three touchdowns during their first five conference games.

The succeeding week's game at Iowa City was far less nerve-wracking, even though it was plagued by errors on both sides. Ohio State overcame three lost fumbles and an interception to outclass Iowa, 41-7. The Hawkeyes lost two fumbles and threw four interceptions. Calvin Murray rushed for 183 yards to increase his season total to 1,154 and become the seventh Ohio State player to run for more than 1,000 yards in a single season.

Buckeyes and Wolverines Again Decide League Title

For the ninth consecutive season, Ohio State and Michigan were squaring off to decide the Big Ten title and Rose Bowl representative. The loser would end up with a Fiesta Bowl date against Penn State.

The fifth-ranked Buckeyes and tenth-ranked Wolverines were both 7-0 in league competition. Ohio State had suffered its non-conference setback to UCLA, while Michigan had lost twice outside the league in September to Notre Dame (29-27) and South

Two Team Race

The Big Ten Conference was nick-named the "Big Two and Little Eight" from 1968 through 1980. Ohio State and Michigan were each 6-6-1 against each other, with each team scoring exactly 176 points over these 13 games. In addition, the Buckeyes and Wolverines were each 83-5 those 13 seasons against the "Little Eight." No question about it — the Big Ten title chase those seasons was simply a two-team race.

Carolina (17-14). However, the Wolverines dramatically improved as the season progressed. They had shut out their last three opponents by a combined score of 85-0.

Before what was then the largest crowd in Ohio Stadium history (88,827), Michigan's defense totally controlled the game and led the Wolverines to a 9-3 triumph. It was Earle

Doug Donley was Ohio State's leading receiver in 1978-79-80.

Bruce's first conference loss since taking control of OSU's program the previous year.

Coach Bo Schembechler's strategy was to control the ball and keep Ohio State's offense off the field, and his game plan worked to perfection. Michigan maintained possession for more than 37 of the game's 60 minutes. The Maize and Blue ran 84 plays from scrimmage compared with Ohio State's 58. The frustrated Buckeyes successfully converted only four of 15 third-down calls.

Early in the second quarter Vlade Janakievski's 33-yard field goal gave OSU its only lead of the afternoon. Michigan's Ali Haji-Sheikh tied the game with a 41-yard field goal six minutes before halftime. Ohio State fumbled the ball away at the Michigan 44 on its initial possession of the third quarter. The Wolverines then drove 56 yards in 14 plays for the game's only touchdown—a 13-yard pass on a slant pattern from quarterback John Wangler to wide receiver Anthony Carter.

Haji-Sheikh's extra-point attempt hit the left upright and bounced back, leaving the score at 9-3. This missed conversion loomed large as the game wore on, but Ohio State simply could not reach the Michigan end zone.

Season Ends on Downturn

Penn State dealt the Buckeyes a solid 31-19 defeat before a crowd of 66,738 in the December 26 Fiesta Bowl. There could hardly have been a bigger contrast between the two halves. After tailback Curt Warner sprinted 64 yards on PSU's first play from scrimmage to give the Nittany Lions an early 7-0 lead, Schlichter let loose with two touchdown passes to Doug Donley and a third to Gary Williams to lift OSU to a 19-10 advantage at halftime.

The Nittany Lions played with a lot of emotion in the second half, keeping the Buckeye offense off balance with their timely blitzes and stunts. With the temperature in the 70s, their superior depth also

helped them outscore OSU 21-0 in the third and fourth quarters. Schlichter passed for 244 yards in the first half, but managed only 58 in the last two quarters, mainly because of PSU's defensive changes. In the third period Ohio State gained zero net yards and never advanced beyond its own 36. It was OSU's fourth consecutive bowl defeat.

Ohio State did not have an All-American for the first season since 1967, although nine players were selected All-Big Ten. Calvin Murray was chosen the team MVP, and Art Schlichter finished sixth to George Rogers of South Carolina in the Heisman Trophy race. The '80 season would turn out to be the first of six consecutive years with records of 9-3.

1980

Date	Opponent			
September 13	Syracuse	W	31	21
September 20	Minnesota	W	47	0
September 27	Arizona State	W	38	21
October 4	UCLA	L	0	17
October 11	at Northwestern	W	63	0
October 18	Indiana	W	27	17
October 25	at Wisconsin	W	21	0
November 1	at Michigan State	W	48	16
November 8	Illinois (HC)	W	49	42
November 15	at Iowa	W	41	7
November 22	Michigan	L	3	9
December 26	Penn State*	L	19	31
Total Points			387	181

*Fiesta Bowl

Season Record: 9-3
Conference: 2nd Place (Tie)

1981

Defensive improvement was one of Ohio State's top priorities heading into the '81 season. Four juniors returning were linebackers Marcus Marek and Glen Cobb and tackles Jerome Foster and Chris Riehm, but experience was lacking at the other positions, especially the defensive backfield.

The offense was in better shape. Both Art Schlichter and Bob Atha were back for their senior seasons at quarterback, and junior Tim Spencer shifted back to tailback from fullback to replace Calvin Murray who had graduated. Linemen Jim DeLeone, Joe Smith, and Joe Lukens returned, along with senior wide receiver Gary Williams.

Most Important Conference Game Never Played

The 1981 Big Ten season will always be remembered for the single league game that was not played. Eight of the conference teams played each of the other nine members of the conference, while Ohio State and Iowa played only eight. The Buckeyes and

Tailback Tim Spencer takes off on an 82-yard touchdown run against Duke.

Hawkeyes were the only conference teams not to face each other this season. Ohio State and Iowa tied for the '81 conference title with identical league marks of 6-2. Had they played each other they would have been battling for the outright conference championship. Ironically, what would have been the season's most important league game was the only one not played.

Off and Running

Tailback Tim Spencer raced 82 yards on a draw play off right tackle for a touchdown on the season's very first play from scrimmage. Spencer finished the afternoon with 172 yards on 19 carries to lead Ohio State to a 34-13 win over Duke in the September 12

Woody Returns

Woody Hayes watched the 1981 season opening win over Duke from the Ohio Stadium press box. It was the first game he and Mrs. Hayes had attended since his departure as head coach following the 1978 Gator Bowl. Hayes had steadfastly refused to attend games the previous two seasons, feeling that his presence might detract from Earle Bruce and interest in the games.

Rapid Start!

Tailback Tim Spencer's 82-yard touchdown on the 1981 season's very FIRST play from scrimmage is the fourth longest run in all of Ohio State football. Spencer, who became the Buckeyes' backfield coach in 1994, finished his playing career in 1982 with a four-year total of 3,553 yards. He currently is third in school career rushing behind Archie Griffin (5,589) and Eddie George (3,668).

Williams and a one-yard plunge by Tim Spencer. Earle Bruce was disappointed with the defense's lackluster showing in the second half, but overall was happy to be 2-0 on the season.

Schlichter Versus Elway

The Buckeyes earned a "big victory" September 26 with a 24-19 win over the Stanford Cardinal in front of a Stanford Stadium crowd of 76,102. The game was billed as a battle between the nation's two finest college quarterbacks, Art Schlichter and John Elway, and each played extremely well. Schlichter connected on 16 of 32 passes for 240 yards, no interceptions, and two touchdowns. Elway completed 28 of 42 tosses for 248 yards, no interceptions, and two touchdowns.

The game went right down to the final minute of play. Ohio State led 24-6 after three periods, but Elway fired his two scoring passes in the final quarter to bring his team within five points of the Buckeyes. For a short time it looked as if the junior quarterback might lead his squad to a third fourth-quarter touchdown. With the ball at midfield, Elway fired a pass to running back Vincent White in the left flat. Vincent fumbled when hit hard, and linebacker Marcus Marek recovered to secure the win with just 44 seconds remaining.

Passing and Receiving Records Go for Naught

Schlichter was even more impressive at home the following week, passing for 458 yards to establish a school single-game high. The senior quarterback, who was starting his 40th consecutive Ohio State game, connected on 31 of 52 tosses with no interceptions and two touchdowns. Gary Williams caught 13 of Schlichter's passes (for 220 yards), setting

opener. After leading only 14-13 at halftime, the Buckeyes used their overall physical strength to wear down the Blue Devils in the final 30 minutes of play.

The following Saturday's 27-13 victory over Michigan State was somewhat the opposite. Ohio State surged to a 17-0 halftime lead before what was then a record Ohio Stadium crowd of 87,084, but was not able to put the game out of reach. MSU came to life in the second half, and the Buckeyes were not assured of their second win until quarterback Bob Atha sneaked 27 yards straight ahead for the game's final touchdown with exactly one minute remaining in the game. The play was an audible at the line of scrimmage, and center Jim DeLeone put a solid block on the middle linebacker to send Atha on his way.

Atha scored 15 of OSU's 27 points with two field goals, three extra points, and the touchdown. Ohio State's first-half TDs came on a 46-yard toss from Art Schlichter to Gary

an OSU single-game record which stood until David Boston made 14 receptions at Penn State in 1997.

Unfortunately, the heroics of Schlichter and Williams were not enough. Florida State took advantage of an inexperienced defensive secondary and pounded the young Buckeyes, 36-27. Interestingly, each team finished the afternoon with 496 yards in total offense.

The Seminoles, who had been idle the previous Saturday, were still smarting from a 34-14 trouncing two weeks earlier at Nebraska, and they effectively used the 14 days to prepare their defense for Ohio State's rushing attack. The Buckeyes were able to generate only 38 yards on the ground in 31 attempts. It was the third lowest single-game rushing total in modern OSU history.

Coach Bobby Bowden's squad led 23-21 at halftime and outscored the Buckeyes 13-0 in the third quarter. Even with 63 points being scored during the afternoon, it was FSU's goal-line stand late in the third period that really did the damage. Trailing 30-21, the Buckeyes lined up with a first-and-goal at the Florida State two-yard line. But three line plunges and an incomplete pass netted only one yard, and Florida State gained possession.

Winning Streak Snapped at 21

The Buckeyes lost 24-21 at Wisconsin on October 10, breaking a string of 21 consecutive victories over the Badgers that began in 1960. It was Wisconsin's fifth consecutive home game, played before a sellout crowd of 78,973. Ohio State led 7-0 when Bob Atha lined up to the right as a wide receiver, then took a lateral from Art Schlichter and passed 34 yards to Gary Williams who had slipped behind the Wisconsin secondary.

The Buckeyes became their own worst enemy, giving up 11 points in the final 24 seconds of the first half. Leading 14-6, Ohio State held the Badgers on downs and forced a punt. But OSU's Jeff Cisco fumbled a fair

On the Air and Out the Window

Rick Rizzs, former Sports Director at WBNS Radio in Columbus and later the play-by-play voice of the Seattle Mariners and Detroit Tigers, was broadcasting the Ohio State-Wisconsin game from Madison in 1981. Rizzs' color commentator that season was former Buckeye great, Jim Stillwagon.

"Jim was really great to work with," recalls Rizzs. "He was a very enthusiastic broadcaster with a tremendous knowledge of the game. That afternoon, while vigorously protesting an official's call, Jim pounded so hard on a table in front of us, his microphone flew out of our radio booth's open window—while we were on the air." Rizzs continued to talk while Stillwagon used the cord to pull his microphone back into the booth.

Wisconsin's 24-21 victory that afternoon was the Badgers' first win over Ohio State in 22 seasons.

catch attempt, and Wisconsin recovered at the Ohio State 29-yard line. After a penalty moved the ball to the 24-yard line, quarterback Jess Cole passed to receiver Marvin Neal for a touchdown, and John Williams' two-point conversion carry made it 14-14 with 18 seconds remaining.

Ohio State returned the ensuing kickoff to the Wisconsin 31-yard line. On first down Schlichter ran an option to his right, but a pitch-out to Tim Spencer was fumbled, and Wisconsin recovered at the OSU 33-yard line with eight seconds on the clock. Wendell Gladem connected with a 50-yard field goal, and the Badgers led at halftime, 17-14. Buckeye fans strongly questioned the wisdom of the option play call.

The two teams traded touchdowns in the second half. Ohio State led in first downs, 19-12, and in total offensive yardage, 314-197. But OSU's five turnovers were too much to overcome, and the Buckeyes had lost two straight regular-season games for the first time in ten seasons.

Disguised Defenses Bring Three Interceptions

Ohio State returned home October 17 for a well-earned and much-needed triumph over Illinois, 34-27, in one of the most nerve-racking contests ever between the two schools. The Buckeyes scored touchdowns the first three times they had the ball, and led 21-10 after the first quarter. The touchdowns came on tailback Tim Spencer's two-yard sprint (after Doug Hill's interception had given OSU possession at the Illini 19), a 28-yard Art Schlichter toss to Gary Williams, and an eight-yard run by Jimmy Gayle. After Bob Atha's 35-yard field goal boosted the Buckeyes' lead to 24-10 at the 13:30 mark of the second period, Illinois scored the quarter's last 10 points to come within four of OSU at halftime, 24-20.

After recovering a Schlichter fumble at the OSU 22-yard line on the second play of the third quarter, Illinois needed six plays to take their first (and only) lead of the afternoon, 27-24. On a fourth-and-three from the OSU four-yard line, quarterback Tony Eason rolled right and dove into the end zone for the touchdown after finding all of his receivers covered. After an exchange of punts, the Buckeyes used 14 plays to march 73 yards to regain the lead, 31-27. Spencer scored his second six-pointer of the afternoon, this time from eight yards out, and Atha added his fourth conversion.

Early in the final period, the Buckeyes' Orlando Lowery recovered an Illinois fumble at the OSU 37-yard line, setting up Atha's 26-yard field goal to increase Ohio State's lead to 34-27— and that's how the game ended. Anthony Griggs stopped the last Illini threat with an interception near midfield with just 2:05 remaining.

In one of the finest passing exhibitions ever in Ohio Stadium, Illini quarterback Tony

Eason completed 27 of 47 attempts for 368 yards and two of his team's three touchdowns. But OSU was able to disguise its defenses effectively enough to intercept Eason three times, which likely meant the difference in the game. Ohio State gained 273 of its 394 yards on the ground and held possession of the ball for 34 minutes and 34 seconds, almost 10 minutes longer than the Illini. Coach Mike White said, "We had opportunities, but we did not take advantage of them. Our running game was nonexistent." Illinois netted only 18 yards on 20 rushing attempts.

Ohio State made it two in a row on October 24 with a 29-10 homecoming win over coach Lee Corso's Indiana Hoosiers. This victory, coupled with Minnesota's unexpected 12-10 win at Iowa the same afternoon, allowed OSU to move into a tie with the Hawkeyes for the Big Ten lead. Earle Bruce was generally pleased with his team's showing, but was disturbed over penalties that

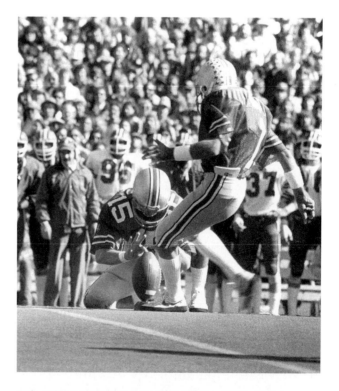

Bob Atha established an Ohio State single-game record with five field goals against Indiana. Holding for Atha is Mike Tomczak.

negated two first-half touchdowns. The Buckeyes led only 12-10 at intermission.

Placekicker Bob Atha set a school single-game record (and tied a Big Ten mark) with five field goals. Atha connected from 25, 23, 41, 46, and 20 yards, and was awarded the game ball. After Tim Spencer went out with a first-quarter ankle sprain, Jimmy Gayle played most of the way at tailback and finished the day with 186 yards in 29 carries. Tight end John Frank scored his first collegiate touchdown with a five-yard reception from Schlichter in the third period.

Wild Afternoon at West Lafayette

Can you imagine a team losing a game by 12 points after its quarterback connected on 31 of 52 passes for 516 yards and three touchdowns? Ohio State outscored Purdue, 45-33, in spite of that phenomenal performance by Boilermaker quarterback Scott Campbell.

It was just Purdue's second loss at Ross-Ade Stadium in its last 23 games. With Illinois upsetting the Iowa Hawkeyes, 24-7, OSU's victory left the Buckeyes alone at the top of the conference standings.

Art Schlichter enjoyed one of the best games of his career. The senior quarterback connected on 19 of 33 tosses for 336 yards and three touchdowns, and was particularly effective calling audibles at the line of scrimmage. Earle Bruce called it "one of the great victories since I've been at Ohio State." The teams combined for 48 first downs, 1,007 yards in total offense, ten touchdowns, and three field goals. Thirty-four of the game's 78 points were scored in the final quarter.

The Buckeyes' porous pass defense continued to get riddled the next week at Minnesota. Ohio State fell to the Golden Gophers, 35-31, primarily because quarterback Mike Hohensee had a field day, completing 37 of 67 attempts for 444 yards and all five Minnesota touchdowns. With exactly 100 passes thrown by both sides, the game lasted over three and one-half hours. The loss

Last Game on Minnesota Campus

Ohio State's 35-31 loss before a crowd of 42,793 marked the Buckeyes' final appearance at the Golden Gophers' old Memorial Stadium. Minnesota began playing its home games at the Metrodome in downtown Minneapolis in 1982.

knocked the Buckeyes into a third-place tie with Iowa in the Big Ten behind Michigan and Wisconsin.

Ohio State jumped off to a 14-0 first-quarter lead, led 21-7 at halftime, and even led 31-21 early in the fourth period. But Hohensee was able to fire two more scoring tosses in the game's final seven minutes to give his team the four-point win. Tight end Jay Carroll caught three of Hohensee's TD tosses, including the last two. The Buckeyes were hurt by three turnovers and a poor kicking game that continually gave the Golden Gophers favorable field position.

OSU returned home November 14 to drub winless Northwestern 70-6 in its final home game of the season. The Buckeyes gained 639 total yards against the overmatched Wildcats who suffered their 30th consecutive loss over three seasons. Tim Spencer rushed for 108 yards to push his season total to 1,011 and become the eighth player in Ohio State history to rush for more than 1,000 yards in a single season.

Maligned Defense Comes Through at Right Time

The Big Ten crown was again on the line when Ohio State and Michigan collided November 21 at Ann Arbor. The Wolverines could capture the outright title with a win over the Buckeyes, while an Ohio State win would earn the Buckeyes at least a portion of the championship. OSU would have to share the title with Iowa if the Hawkeyes won their home meeting against Michigan State the same afternoon. For the Buckeyes to be outright champions, Michigan State would need to defeat Iowa while OSU was beating Michigan.

Ohio State's defense (which had surrendered a total of 68 points to Purdue and Minnesota) really jelled at the right time, holding Michigan to three field goals by Ali Haji-Sheikh to spearhead a 14-9 triumph over the frustrated Wolverines. The Maize and Blue appeared to be in control most of the game, leading in first downs, 20-15, and in total offensive yards, 367-257. The Wolverines entered Ohio State territory eight times during the game but could not cross the goal line.

Ohio State had only two sustained drives all afternoon, but each went 80 yards for a touchdown, and that's all it took. The first scoring drive ended with Schlichter sneaking across from the one to provide a 7-3 halftime lead. Late in the fourth quarter, he scored his second touchdown from the six behind a very key block from sophomore fullback Vaughn Broadnax. The play was a pass-run option to the right, with Schlichter fak-

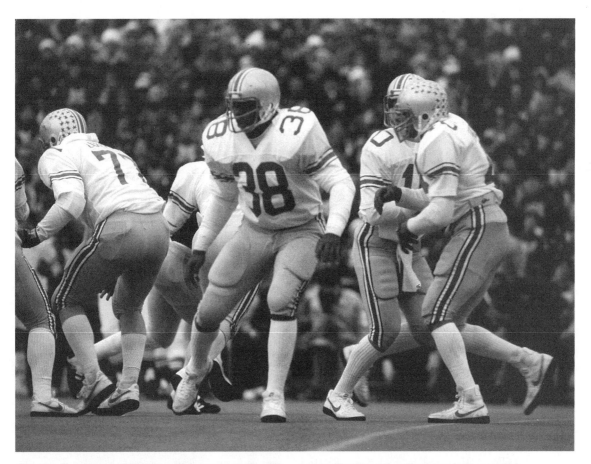

Jim Carson (77) and Vaughn Broadnax (38) offer protection for Tim Spencer (46) and Art Schlichter (10) against Michigan. Broadnax's mammoth block, which cleared the way for Schlichter to score the winning touchdown, is one of the best remembered efforts in the Ohio State-Michigan series.

Ohio State edges Michigan, 14–9;

THE PLAIN DEALER, SUNDAY, NOVEMBER 22, 1981

SECTION B

ing inside, then cutting outside and into the corner of the end zone behind Broadnax's shielding of two defenders.

Enjoying the game from the Michigan Stadium press box was Woody Hayes, who made the trip at the insistence of Earle Bruce. It was his first road trip with the Buckeyes since relinquishing his head coaching position three years earlier.

While Ohio State was winning at Ann Arbor, Iowa was defeating Michigan State 36-7 to share the Big Ten title. The Hawkeyes received the Rose Bowl nod (lost to Washington 28-0 to finish '81 season at 8-4), since they had not been to Pasadena since the 1958 season, and the Buckeyes were there just two years earlier. Ohio State accepted an invitation to meet Navy in the December 30 Liberty Bowl. Michigan defeated UCLA 33-14 in the Bluebonnet Bowl on December 31 to complete its year with an overall record of 9-3.

Bowl Losing Streak Snapped at Four

The Buckeyes won the Liberty Bowl over Navy, 31-28, to finish the year at 9-3 and break a four-year losing streak in postseason bowls. The game was filled with errors on both sides, and the 14-point underdog Midshipmen actually led 20-17 at one point in the third period. Navy mistakes and turnovers led to three touchdowns and a field goal for the Buckeyes. Interestingly, each team scored at least once in each of the four quarters.

This was the last game at the Naval Academy for coach George Welsh, who had announced he would be moving to Virginia at the end of the season. Navy tailback Eddie Myers was voted the game's most valuable player after rushing for 117 yards, the most by a single player against Ohio State this season. Art Schlichter passed for two OSU scores, 50 yards to Gary Williams and nine yards to Cedric Anderson. Jimmy Gayle scored twice on short runs, and Bob Atha delivered a 35-yard field goal in the first quarter that turned out to be the eventual margin of victory.

Even though the '81 Buckeyes finished the season at 9-3 and earned a share of the Big Ten title, the team had the dubious distinction of surrendering 253 points, at the time the most ever scored against Ohio State in a single season. The opposition's average of 21.1 points per game was the highest since Ohio State's first season in 1890, when four opponents averaged 27.5 points per game. OSU's defense had given up an average of only 95 yards per game on the ground, but had surrendered 273 yards per game through the air.

This was Art Schlichter's final season at Ohio State. The excellent quarterback started 48 consecutive games over the four seasons (36-11-1), and was selected the '81 team MVP. He finished fifth in the Heisman Trophy balloting, marking the third consecutive season he had finished in the award's "top ten." Schlichter holds Ohio State career records with 7,547 passing yards and 8,850 yards in total offense.

1981				
September 12	Duke	W	34	13
September 19	Michigan State	W	27	13
September 26	at Stanford	W	24	19
October 3	Florida State	L	27	36
October 10	at Wisconsin	L	21	24
October 17	Illinois	W	34	27
October 24	Indiana (HC)	W	29	10
October 31	at Purdue	W	45	33
November 7	at Minnesota	L	31	35
November 14	Northwestern	W	70	6
November 21	at Michigan	W	14	9
December 30	Navy*	W	31	28
Total Points			387	253
*Liberty Bowl				

Season Record: 9-3
Big Ten Co-Champion

One of Earle Bruce's top priorities entering 1982 was to improve his team's defense, and particularly its ability to protect against the forward pass. He began by making three coaching changes, hiring Randy Hart and Dom Capers and promoting Fred Pagac from graduate assistant to full-time assistant. They replaced Dennis Fryzel, Steve Szabo, and Nick Saban, who were released at the end of the '81 season. The defense would be built around tackles Jerome Foster and Chris Riehm and inside linebackers Marcus Marek and Glen Cobb, all experienced seniors.

Offensively both Tim Spencer and Jimmy Gayle returned at tailback, Vaughn Broadnax at fullback, Gary Williams at wide receiver, and John Frank at tight end. Experienced linemen included tackles William Roberts and Joe Smith, and guards Joe Lukens and Scott Zalenski. The biggest task was replacing quarterbacks Art Schlichter and backup Bob Atha. Sophomore Mike Tomczak earned the starting spot, especially after an excellent showing in the spring intra-squad game.

Unusual Pattern of Wins and Losses

The '82 season is remembered for its high points and low points. After opening with two victories, the Buckeyes lost three consecutive games in Ohio Stadium, then rebounded to finish the year with seven straight wins. The team improved dramatically during its last seven games, and it was felt that Ohio State could have played with anybody in the country by the end of the season.

The Buckeyes opened at home September 11 with a very physical 21-14 win over the Baylor Bears. OSU moved the ball well on the ground with Spencer gaining 147 yards and Broadnax 101, and Bruce was reasonably satisfied with Tomczak's debut at quarterback. Tomczak's one-yard sneak for Ohio State's final touchdown midway through the fourth period concluded a 37-yard drive and broke a 14-14 tie to earn the Buckeyes their seven-point victory. All six officials were from the Big Ten, and after the game Baylor coach Grant Teaff was very quick to voice his displeasure over several of their calls, including a 30-yard third-quarter missed field goal attempt that Teaff thought was good.

Defense Impressive at Michigan State

The Buckeye defense, which struggled most of '81, was the deciding factor the following week at East Lansing. Ohio State emerged with a 31-10 win after being tied 10-10 at the end of the third quarter. OSU's defense applied solid pressure throughout most of the afternoon, and the Spartans netted only two yards on 11 plays from scrimmage in the final 15 minutes of play. MSU quarterback John Leister was sacked three times, twice by Jerome Foster. Linebacker Glenn Cobb finished the day with 18 tackles and an interception.

Broadnax, Spencer, and tailback Kelvin Lindsey scored the fourth quarter TDs on short runs from inside the six. Rich Spangler's 26-yard field goal and a nine-yard scoring toss from Mike Tomczak to Gary Williams provided the Buckeyes their first-half points.

Elway Leads Deciding Drive After Questionable Call

Before what was then a record Ohio Stadium crowd of 89,436, Ohio State appeared to have its third triumph of the season. Leading Stanford, 20-16, the Buckeyes had the ball at the Cardinal's 27, second and 12, with 1:50

Earle Bruce explains the game's finer points.

remaining in the game. Surprisingly, Tomczak attempted a pass intended for Gary Williams. Stanford's Kevin Baird tipped the ball and Charles Hutchings intercepted. It was Tomczak's fourth interception of the afternoon. Earle Bruce took the blame, stating after the game that it was his decision to pass (play-pass 27). With a four-point lead, fans could not understand why Ohio State would not simply keep the ball on the ground and attempt to run out the clock.

With just 1:38 left and the ball at the Stanford 20, quarterback John Elway needed just seven plays and 69 seconds to drive his team 80 yards for the decisive six-pointer and a 23-20 victory. During the afternoon, Elway completed 35 of 63 passes for 407 yards, three interceptions, and two touchdowns. Ohio State led 13-0 at halftime, marking the first time since 1979 the Cardinals had been held scoreless in the first half.

The Buckeyes lost their second straight at home October 2, falling to coach Bobby Bowden's Florida State Seminoles, 34-17. With OSU trailing 21-10 midway through the second quarter, Bruce replaced starting quarterback Mike Tomczak with junior Brent Offenbecher. Ohio State gained some much needed momentum when Offenbecher threw a 31-yard scoring toss to Tim Spencer to complete a 55-yard march and tighten the halftime score at 21-17.

Offenbecher threw interceptions, however, on each of OSU's first two possessions of the second half, and the Buckeyes never recovered. He finished the afternoon completing 11 of 24 for 204 yards, but also had another pass picked off late in the game. Ohio State was now 2-2 on the season, and its offense was really struggling.

Bowden felt the afternoon's 80-degree heat and high humidity worked to FSU's advantage, since his players were accustomed to playing in this type of weather. Bruce disagreed, stating that his offense simply was not executing.

Who Would Have Believed
Three Straight at Home?

Things got worse before they got better! For just the second time since 1922 (the first season at Ohio Stadium), Ohio State lost three in a row at home. Wisconsin upset the favored Buckeyes, 6-0, marching 80 yards for a touchdown on its very first possession of the game. Offenbecher played the entire

Eventful Week for Offenbecher

It had been a busy week for quarterback Brent Offenbecher, who came off the bench to direct Ohio State's offense the last two and one-half quarters against Florida State. Two days earlier wife Jacquie gave birth to daughter Amy at University Hospital. Offenbecher was an All-Ohio quarterback from Massillon who began his college career at Wake Forest before transferring to Ohio State.

game at quarterback. The Buckeyes had only three drives of 10 or more plays the entire afternoon, and had not scored in their last six quarters.

Ohio State made its deepest penetration of the game on its first possession, reaching the Badger eight where freshman Rich Spangler missed a 26-yard field goal attempt on fourth down. Fifth-year senior Jimmy

Badger First

Wisconsin's 6-0 triumph on October 9, 1982, was the school's first ever win at Ohio Stadium after 18 losses and three ties. The Badgers' last victory in Columbus was 14-3 at old Ohio Field on November 23, 1918, four seasons before the Buckeyes moved to the horseshoe.

Gayle started his first game at tailback, while regular tailback Tim Spencer moved back to fullback in place of Vaughn Broadnax who was injured. The Buckeyes drove to the Wisconsin 22 midway through the final period with high hopes of squeezing out a 7-6 victory, but Spencer's lost fumble ended the threat, and Wisconsin had its second straight win over Ohio State.

The attendance was 88,344, breaking an Ohio Stadium sellout streak at 86 games. A total of 1,069 tickets went unsold, partly because of an all-day rain that hampered walk-up sales the morning of the game. Ohio State's last home game with a less-than-capacity crowd was a 21-6 win over Oregon before 70,191 fans on October 5, 1968.

It's Friendlier on the Road

After three consecutive home losses, the Buckeyes were "happy to travel" to Champaign the following Saturday, October 16, to face Illinois. Bruce asked former coach Woody Hayes to speak to the team early in the week to encourage them to remain confident about their season. The Illini homecoming crowd of 73,488 was, at the time, the second largest in Memorial Stadium history, exceeded only by the September 28, 1946, Illinois-Notre Dame crowd of 75,119.

The offense came to life with Mike Tomczak's return at quarterback, as he directed his squad to a 21-7 lead after three quarters. OSU's first score was a 74-yard connection from Tomczak to flanker Cedric Anderson. But Illinois came back to tie the game 21-21 with two fourth-period touchdowns.

Tomczak then drove the Buckeyes from their own 21 to the Illinois 10, where Rich Spangler kicked a 27-yard field goal to break the tie. Ohio State added a safety on the game's last play to make the final score 26-21. Tomczak passed for 247 yards on the afternoon, and was selected the Big Ten "player of the week." Tailback Tim Spencer rushed for 151 yards as the Buckeyes rolled up 490

yards in total offense. It was a much-needed win for the Buckeyes, whose season record now stood at 3-3.

The Ohio State pass defense was tested mightily at Indiana on October 23, when Hoosier quarterback Babe Laufenberg threw for 334 yards, four touchdowns, and no interceptions. But the balanced Buckeyes won, 49-25, before a Memorial Stadium crowd of 52,040. Tomczak passed only nine times, completing seven for 145 yards and a pair of first-half scores to Gary Williams and Cedric Anderson. The sophomore quarterback was maturing and playing with much greater confidence. His toss to Anderson covered 72 yards, which (at the time) was a Memorial Stadium record for an IU opponent.

Earle Bruce was particularly pleased with the offensive line that paved the way for 327 yards on the ground. Tim Spencer carried for 187 of those yards, the most by a

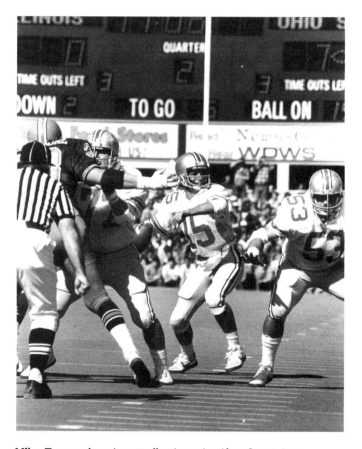

Mike Tomczak gets excellent protection from Joe Lukens (72) and Craig Pack (53) at Illinois.

THE EARLE BRUCE ERA (1979-1987)

Buckeye since Calvin Murray netted 224 yards against the Hoosiers in 1980. One of the afternoon's most spectacular plays was Garcia Lane's 68-yard punt return early in the fourth quarter for OSU's sixth touchdown.

Back Home to "Friendlier Confines"

After two wins on the road, the Buckeyes found Ohio Stadium to be much more hospitable than three weeks earlier after three consecutive setbacks at home. They delighted the October 30 homecoming crowd of 89,341 with a sound 38-6 victory over Purdue. Tomczak connected on two first-period touchdowns, passing 12 yards to tight end John Frank and 33 yards to flanker Cedric Anderson. Rich Spangler's 47-yard field goal with 11:34 remaining in the second quarter boosted OSU's halftime lead to 17-6.

After Ohio State scored touchdowns on each of its first three possessions of the second half, Earle Bruce began flooding the field with substitutes. Tim Spencer and Jimmy Gayle gained 168 and 80 yards, respectively, as OSU's ground game totaled 335 yards—a season high and the second straight game over 300. Nine different Buckeyes carried the ball that afternoon, including freshman tailback Keith Byers who had one attempt for five yards.

Bruce's boys upped their season record to 6-3 at home the next weekend with a rela-

tively easy 35-10 win over Minnesota. Spencer again was OSU's top offensive weapon, totaling 133 yards to increase his season total to 1,057. It was his fourth consecutive game with more than 100 yards, and he became just the second player in Ohio State history to have back-to-back 1,000-yard seasons. The other was Archie Griffin in 1973-74-75.

The Buckeye defense held Golden Gopher quarterback Mike Hohensee in check with just 12 completions in 30 throws for 99 yards (he had riddled the Bucks for 444 yards and five TDs a year earlier at Minneapolis). Ohio State used a lot of five-man coverage, forcing Minnesota to run more than planned—they gained 180 yards on 39 rushing attempts. Linebacker Glenn Cobb was OSU's leading defender with 16 tackles.

At Northwestern on November 13, heavily favored Ohio State jumped out to a 28-14 halftime advantage. But after intermis-

499

sion, the Buckeyes turned the ball over on an interception and two lost fumbles the first three times they had possession, and suddenly what appeared to be an easy win had turned into a real battle. OSU finally emerged with a 40-28 triumph, after giving up 393 passing yards and three touchdowns through the air to freshman quarterback Sandy Schwab.

The 28 points are the most the scrappy Wildcats have ever scored against Ohio State. This '82 Northwestern squad was much improved over the one which lost to OSU 70-6 in '81. NU had defeated Northern Illinois, 31-6, earlier in the season to break a 34-game losing streak that stretched back more than three seasons.

Tailback Tim Spencer once again led the attack with 190 yards, the highest of his career, as the Buckeyes rolled up 605 yards of total offense. Mike Tomczak completed 22 passes for 222 yards, and his first throw was caught by Gary Williams who established what was then an NCAA record by catching at least one pass in 46 consecutive games.

All-American linebacker Marcus Marek is Ohio State's career tackle leader with 572 tackles from 1979 through 1982.

48 in a Row

Wide Receiver Gary Williams established an NCAA record with one or more receptions in each of Ohio State's 48 games from 1979 through 1982. His four-year career statistics include 154 receptions for 2,792 yards and 16 touchdowns.

The Buckeyes had won five in a row and were headed into Michigan week with an overall record of 7-3.

Buckeyes Deal Wolverines Their Only League Setback

Just like '81, eight of the Big Ten teams played a complete round-robin nine-game conference schedule while Ohio State and Iowa played only eight league games. The Buckeyes and Hawkeyes did not meet for the second consecutive year. This scheduling oddity again worked against the Buckeyes.

Michigan entered Ohio Stadium with a conference record of 8-0, Ohio State was 6-1. A then-record crowd of 90,252 watched Earle Bruce's team score ten unanswered fourth-quarter points to defeat the Wolverines 24-14. Unfortunately, Michigan had already wrapped up the Rose Bowl bid and outright league title by playing one additional league game. This season marked the first time the loser of the annual Ohio State-Michigan game would play in Pasadena.

Ohio State's defense helped create six Wolverine turnovers which aided immensely. Linebacker Marcus Marek, playing his last game in the horseshoe, had 19 tackles and a fourth-quarter interception which set up a 33-yard field goal by Rich Spangler to

Defensive tackle Jerome Foster

clinch the victory. As usual, Tim Spencer (also making his last home appearance) was the game's leading runner with 124 yards.

Strong Finish Continues

Ohio State faced Brigham Young in the December 17 Holiday Bowl at Jack Murphy Stadium in San Diego. It was the first meeting between the Buckeyes and Cougars, and Ohio State dominated throughout the evening, scoring in each quarter to win, 47-17. The offense was led by the tailback tandem of Spencer and Gayle, who each scored two of the Buckeyes' seven touchdowns. Spencer rushed for 167 yards, including a 61-yard touchdown sprint in the second quarter, Gayle ran for 80.

The Cougars were led by quarterback Steve Young, who passed for 341 yards and both BYU touchdowns (Young threw for 3,100

yards during the regular season). But the Ohio State defense, led by linebackers Marcus Marek and Glen Cobb, held the Cougars to just 19 net yards rushing. Ohio State's 47 points are the most ever scored by the Buckeyes in a postseason game.

For the third straight year, OSU finished at 9-3. Marcus Marek was selected All-American, and Tom Spencer was chosen the team's MVP. After four seasons in Columbus, Earle Bruce was now 38-10 and owned a 3-1 record against Bo Schembechler's Michigan Wolverines.

1982			
September 11	Baylor	W	21 14
September 18	at Michigan State	W	31 10
September 25	Stanford	L	20 23
October 2	Florida State	L	17 34
October 9	Wisconsin	L	0 6
October 16	at Illinois	W	26 21
October 23	at Indiana	W	49 25
October 30	Purdue (HC)	W	38 6
November 6	Minnesota	W	35 10
November 13	at Northwestern	W	40 28
November 20	Michigan	W	24 14
December 17	Brigham Young *	W	47 17
Total Points			348 208
*Holiday Bowl			
	Season Record: 9-3		
	Conference: 2nd Place		

1983

Expectations were high for 1983. Fourteen starters were back (seven on each side of the ball) from the '82 team that won its last seven games. Offensive linemen William Roberts, Scott Zalenski, Jim Carson, and John Frank returned along with flanker Cedric Anderson and fullback Vaughn

Broadnax. Junior Mike Tomczak was back at quarterback, and Kelvin Lindsey and Keith Byars would step in at tailback to replace Tim Spencer and Jimmy Gayle. Thad Jemison moved in at split end in place of Gary Williams.

Defensively, the entire backfield of Doug Hill, Garcia Lane, Shaun Gayle, and Kelvin Bell was back. Big holes to be filled were those vacated by tackles Jerome Foster and Chris Riehm and linebackers Marcus Marek and Glenn Cobb. Punter Karl Edwards and placekicker Rich Spangler also returned.

Nine Conference Games

For the first time in school history, the Buckeyes would play a complete round-robin nine-game conference schedule, which included away games at Iowa, Illinois, and Michigan. The schedule also featured a highly anticipated trip to Oklahoma in the season's second weekend.

The Buckeyes opened at home September 10 with a very fine 31-6 win over Oregon before a crowd of 88,524. Mike Tomczak could hardly have been more impressive, completing 21 of 25 tosses for 273 yards and all four touchdowns. Broadnax was the game's leading runner with 76 yards, and the Buckeye defense intercepted three passes and recovered two fumbles.

Earle Bruce was concerned over his team's first-half mistakes, but was very pleased with the pass protection provided for Tomczak. The junior quarterback hit on 13 of 14 second-half throws for 182 yards before leaving the game midway through the final period.

Buckeyes Shut Down
No. 2 Ranked Sooners

Ohio State's 24-14 victory over Oklahoma on September 17 at Owen Field in Norman was one of OSU's most impressive non-conference showings during the 1980s. On an afternoon when the field temperature was reported to have reached 135 degrees,

New Tradition

The 1983 opener against Oregon featured the first annual Alumni Cheerleader Reunion. Sixty former cheerleaders were on the sidelines, from as far back as the 1947 squad.

the sixth-ranked Buckeyes scored in each quarter to upend the second-ranked Sooners before a heavily partisan crowd of 75,008.

The triumph was especially pleasing to Earle Bruce, who had lost every year to Oklahoma during his six seasons as head coach at Iowa State from '73 through '78.

Touchdown passes from Mike Tomczak to tight end John Frank of 16 yards in the first period and 15 yards early in the second quarter built Ohio State's lead to 14-0. Frank entered the game following a two-day fast because of the Jewish holiday Yom Kippur. The Sooners retaliated with a four-play 80-yard drive capped by fullback Spencer Tillman's 37-yard touchdown run to make the score 14-7, but failed to capitalize after intercepting a Tomczak pass on OSU's next series.

The two teams traded TDs in the third period, and Rich Spangler's 22-yard field goal at the 9:15 mark of the final quarter completed the game's scoring. Ohio State led in first downs, 24-14, and in total offensive yardage, 412-347. Tailback Kelvin Lindsey and Keith Byars each rushed for 57 yards, while Tomczak hit on 15 of 25 tosses for 234 yards, one interception, and the two TD throws to Frank.

Buckeyes Whip Sooners 24-14

Cleveland Plain Dealer, Sunday, September 18, 1983

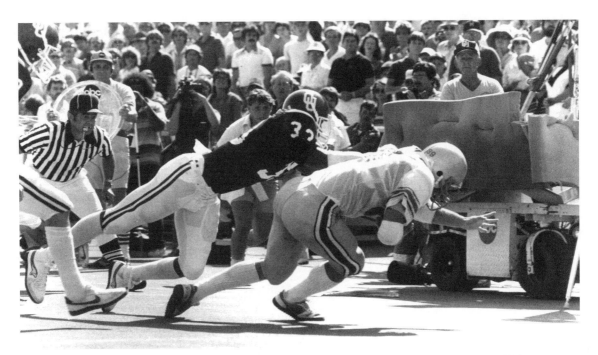

Tight end John Frank's outstanding play was a key factor in Ohio State's victory at Oklahoma.

Winning Streak Snapped at Iowa

The luster of the Oklahoma victory didn't last long. Underdog Iowa upset the Buckeyes, 20-14, the following week to terminate Ohio State's winning streak at nine. Before a then-record crowd of 66,175 at Kinnick Stadium, the Hawkeyes broke a 16-game losing streak to OSU which began in 1963. After the game Iowa players told the media that "all the Ohio State talk the past two seasons of the Buckeyes not being able to go to the Rose Bowl because they didn't play Iowa" really helped inspire the Hawkeyes to play their best.

The Buckeyes led 7-3 at halftime but were outscored 17-7 in the final two periods. Ohio State's attack was hurt when tailback Keith Byars (who had already rushed for 98 yards) strained ligaments in his left knee late in the second quarter and was lost for the afternoon. Iowa quarterback Chuck Long shredded the Buckeye defense for 276 yards and both Hawkeye touchdowns, including a 73-yard scoring bomb to Dave Moritz in the final quarter.

Back home after two weeks on the road, Ohio State demolished inept Minnesota, 69-

18. It was the Golden Gophers' worst Big Ten loss ever with respect to points surrendered and margin of defeat. This was a very physical game with the Buckeyes scoring 31 points in the second quarter and another 24 in the third period. Minnesota committed seven turnovers with four lost fumbles and three interceptions. This same afternoon Ohio State hopefuls were also pleased to learn that Illinois had dealt Iowa its first setback of the season (33-0 at Champaign).

Garcia Lane Rescues the Offense

At home on October 8, Ohio State led Purdue only 12-7 at halftime after penalties and an interception stopped three scoring attempts. Garcia Lane came to the aid of the frustrated offense with two third-quarter touchdowns on punt returns of 63 and 71 yards. Lane is the only player in Ohio State history to score twice on punt returns in one game.

The Buckeyes won, 33-22, but Earle Bruce promised that the offensive line would receive extra work in practice the next week. OSU's defense surrendered 15 points in the

Garcia Lane scored twice on punt returns against Purdue.

terback Jack Trudeau immediately directed an 83-yard five-play touchdown drive, which used only 37 seconds and earned his squad the four-point win. The Buckeyes were now 4-2 on the season and 2-2 in conference play.

Karsatos' First Start Impressive

Back home October 22 in rain-soaked Ohio Stadium, OSU defeated Michigan State 21-11 behind Karsatos' continued fine play. Mike Tomczak was still feeling the effects of the concussion suffered the previous week at Illinois. With the Spartan defense stacked to halt Ohio State's running attack, Karsatos was very effective in completing eight of 11 first-half passes for 163 yards and a 14-3 lead at intermission. The Buckeye defense was very impressive throughout the afternoon. Michigan State's only touchdown resulted from recovering a blocked punt in the end zone in the game's last minute of play.

The following week's 45-27 homecoming victory over Wisconsin was much more explosive. The opposing head coaches that afternoon were old friends who were facing each other for the fifth consecutive season. Earle Bruce and Dave McClain had both been Woody Hayes assistants during the Buckeyes' championship seasons of '69 and '70.

The Ohio State offense scored in each quarter and accounted for 525 yards of total offense. Tailback Keith Byars rushed for 174 yards, and quarterback Mike Tomczak hit on 12 of 14 passes for 162 yards. At one point, Tomczak tied a school record with 11 consecutive completions.

Badger quarterback Randy Wright connected on 23 passes for 319 yards and three touchdowns, but the Buckeyes intercepted

game's final four minutes. Ohio State was now 4-1 on the season.

Illinois all but eliminated the Buckeyes' Rose Bowl hopes the following week, with a 17-13 come-from-behind win at Champaign before a Memorial Stadium crowd of 74,414. The Illini had lost 15 in a row to Ohio State from 1968 through 1982. Redshirt freshman quarterback Jim Karsatos saw the first serious action of his career, taking charge of the offense late in the first half with his team trailing 10-0. Bruce went to the freshman after Tomczak was forced to the sideline with a concussion and senior backup Brent Offenbecher lost a fumble and threw an interception.

Karsatos rallied his team to a 13-10 lead, and the Buckeyes appeared to have the game under control. Late in the final period Ohio State gave up possession on downs at the Illinois 17 with just 1:43 remaining. Illini quar-

four of Wright's throws to help limit Wisconsin's scoring. Kelvin Bell picked off two of Wright's tosses, and Rowland Tatum and Shaun Gayle each made one interception.

The Buckeyes had little trouble the next two Saturdays, winning 56-17 at Indiana on November 5, and humiliating Northwestern 55-7 the following Saturday in the season's last home game. Ohio State scored 14 points in each quarter against the Hoosiers, while the OSU defense had three more interceptions to run their season total to 18.

After mounting a 41-0 halftime lead over Northwestern, Bruce rested many of his regulars for the entire second half. Keith Byars ran his season rushing total to 1,011 yards to become the first Big Ten sophomore to rush for more than 1,000 yards in a single season since Archie Griffin in 1973.

Turnovers Costly at Michigan

The November 19 Ohio State-Michigan game was played primarily for pride. Head-ing into this final weekend of play, Illinois was all alone at the top of the big Ten with a league record of 8-0 while Michigan was 7-1 in conference competition. The Buckeyes were 6-2 in the conference and completely out of the title chase. Michigan could share the league crown with Illinois if the Wolverines defeated Ohio State and Illinois lost at Northwestern. The Wolverines beat the Buckeyes, 24-21, before 106,115 fans at Michigan Stadium, while the Illini overwhelmed the Wildcats, 56-24, to capture their first outright Big Ten championship since 1963.

Turnovers were the big difference at Ann Arbor. Ohio State threw two interceptions and lost two fumbles, while Michigan was turnover free. After the Wolverines took a 10-0 first-quarter lead, Keith Byars scored in each of the second and third periods to put the Buckeyes ahead 14-10 heading into the final 15 minutes of play. Michigan regained the lead, 17-14, early in the fourth quarter.

Ohio State began its next drive on its own 20 and quickly moved to a first down at

Linebacker Rowland Tatum intercepts a Wisconsin pass. Linebacker Clark Backus is #17.

Woody Hayes receives one of Ohio Stadium's strongest ovations while dotting the "i" in Script Ohio at homecoming.

Memorable Script

Tom Hamilton, former sportscaster with WBNS Radio (AM 1460) in Columbus and now the play-by-play voice of the Cleveland Indians, was the color commentator with the University of Wisconsin Football Radio Network in 1983. Tom's first game in Ohio Stadium was the Buckeyes' homecoming game that season against the Wisconsin Badgers.

"I was doing a halftime interview," remembers Hamilton, "when suddenly the crowd's applause became so deafening, I simply couldn't continue with the interview. We all looked out of the radio booth to see what was happening down on the field—Woody Hayes had just dotted the "i" in Script Ohio."

the UM 38-yard line in just three plays. After an incompletion on first down, Bruce called "Lachey Right"—a seldom-used play that had worked well in practice all week.

Center Joe Dooley was instructed to snap the ball to Mike Tomczak, then take the ball right back from Tomczak and place it on the ground. Tomczak whirls as if to pitch out to tailback Keith Byars who is heading left. In the meantime, left guard Jim Lachey is to pick up the loose football and head for the end zone. Somehow the ball got kicked before Lachey could pick it up, and Michigan tackle Mike Hammerstein recovered at the UM 40-yard line.

Each team scored another touchdown, and the Wolverines had broken a two-year losing streak to the Buckeyes. OSU led in first downs, 22-20, and in total offensive yards, 448-414. But the four turnovers were just too much for Ohio State to overcome. Michigan finished its season at 9-3 with a 9-7 Sugar Bowl loss to Auburn. OSU accepted a Fiesta Bowl invitation to meet the Pitt Panthers.

39 Yards and 39 Seconds

The 14th-ranked Buckeyes pondered their "what could have been" season. Their three losses (by a total of 13 points) were all games that could have been victories. OSU considered itself the nation's best 8-3 team as it began preparing for 15th-ranked Pittsburgh (8-2-1).

The January 2, 1984, Fiesta Bowl turned out to be one of the most explosive and exciting bowl games in Ohio State history. Trailing 23-21 late in the fourth quarter, the Buckeyes drove 89 yards for the winning touchdown, which came on a 39-yard pass from Mike Tomczak to split end Thad Jemison, with just 39 seconds remaining. The play (louie pass zone left) was intended to go about 10 yards the other direction to Cedric Anderson. But when Anderson was covered, Tomczak went the distance to Jemison. Ohio State won, 28-23.

Better Late Than Never

Fred and John Zimmerman, whose firm was involved with publishing the Ohio State football programs for many seasons, had a few anxious moments prior to one of the 1983 home games. The Zimmermans guaranteed the programs would be at the stadium on time—otherwise they would have to pay for the programs (at $2.00 apiece).

The programs were printed in Dayton, and the schedule called for them to be delivered at the stadium by noon on Friday. One particular Friday morning, Fred received a call from the printer telling him he should be concerned about the condition of the truck that just left for Columbus with the programs. Soon Fred received another call from the driver, explaining that his truck was stuck with a broken axle on Interstate 70, about one-half hour east of Dayton. When Fred reached the scene, he discovered the truck driver was unloading the programs onto the ground, even though there was a strong threat of rain.

Another truck was acquired and loaded, and the programs finally reached Ohio Stadium around 7:00 p.m. By this time, the stadium maintenance crew that normally unloads the truck had gone home, and the stadium was locked. The only opening was a ticket window near gate 28, just wide enough for one box to be handed through. So, one by one, all 500 boxes (weighing 20 pounds each) were passed through this window. Tired, sore, and hungry, Fred and his crew finished about 11:00 p.m.

Buckeyes bomb Pitt in Fiesta

Cleveland Plain Dealer,
Tuesday, January 3, 1984

The Buckeyes and Panthers combined for 897 yards in total offense. Thirty of the game's 51 points were scored in the fourth quarter, including a touchdown by Keith Byars on a 99-yard kickoff return.

Jemison was named the game's most valuable player, after establishing a then-Fiesta Bowl record with eight receptions for 131 yards. The Buckeye defense was led by linebacker Rowland Tatum with 13 tackles. Pitt quarterback John Congemi riddled OSU's defense with 31 completions for 341 yards and two of the Panther's three TDs.

For the fourth straight season, Ohio State finished at 9-3, and the Buckeyes had won 16 of their last 19 games over two seasons. Keith Byars led the Big Ten in both rushing and scoring. John Frank was selected the team MVP and was chosen an Academic All-American for the second straight year.

1983

September 10	Oregon	W	31	6
September 17	at Oklahoma	W	24	14
September 24	at Iowa	L	14	20
October 1	Minnesota	W	69	18
October 8	Purdue	W	33	22
October 15	at Illinois	L	13	17
October 22	Michigan State	W	21	11
October 29	Wisconsin (HC)	W	45	27
November 5	at Indiana	W	56	17
November 12	Northwestern	W	55	7
November 19	at Michigan	L	21	24
January 2	Pittsburgh*	W	28	23
Total Points			410	206

*Fiesta Bowl

Season Record: 9-3
Conference: 4th Place

1984

Graduation had taken a heavy toll on the Buckeyes as Earle Bruce began preparation for his sixth Ohio State season. Only five regulars returned on offense and three on defense. The offensive line was in the best shape with guards Jim Lachey and Scott Zalenski, center Kirk Lowdermilk, and tackle Mark Krerowicz all back for their senior season. Lowdermilk had been a second team All-Big Ten guard in '83. Mike Tomczak and Keith Byars returned in the backfield.

Defensively, tackles Dave Crecelius and Dave Morrill and safety Kelvin Bell were the only returning starters. Some outstanding incoming freshmen would be counted on to add strength on both sides of the ball. Spring practice went very well until Tomczak broke his leg in the second quarter of the annual spring intra-squad game. It was very uncertain how quickly he would be able to recover and how effective he would be in the fall. Sophomore Jim Karsatos was the only other quarterback with game experience.

Scary Opener

The heavily favored sixth-ranked Buckeyes opened September 8 with a somewhat disappointing 22-14 win over Oregon State, before an Ohio Stadium crowd of 88,072. Karsatos started and went the distance at quarterback. Ohio State had trouble early on with the Beavers' changing defenses and blitzing outside linebackers, Ron Heller and Ellis Dozier, and trailed 14-3 at halftime.

After making some necessary adjustments, the Buckeyes scored TDs on three consecutive second-half possessions for the victory. A key play was Sonny Gordon's 25-yard interception return to the Oregon State 42, which set up the first touchdown. Byars

led the second-half resurgence and finished the afternoon with 182 yards on 34 carries. Five freshmen who played meaningful roles in this opener were linebacker Chris Spielman, wide receiver Cris Carter, punter Tom Tupa, and defensive backs William White and Terry White.

Tomczak Returns to Standing Ovation

Things were entirely different the following Saturday, as OSU completely overwhelmed Washington State, 44-0, before an Ohio Stadium crowd of 89,297. Karsatos again started and led his team to an early 10-0 lead. On the Buckeyes' fourth possession, Mike Tomczak entered the game to one of Ohio Stadium's loudest and longest standing ovations in many seasons. The senior quarterback was seeing his first game action since breaking his leg in the spring.

It was very comforting to Earle Bruce and his staff when Tomczak directed the Buckeyes to touchdowns on each of their next three possessions.

The defense held Cougar quarterback Mark Rypien to just 14 completions in 31 attempts for 123 yards and three interceptions. Byars again carried the load for OSU, netting 145 yards in 26 carries.

Sweet Revenge

For the second consecutive season, each Big Ten team would play a complete round-robin nine-game conference schedule. Ohio State opened league competition at home September 22 by scoring in each quarter to conquer Iowa, 45-26. Mike Tomczak went all the way at quarterback, completing 14 passes for 150 yards. He called the game the biggest win of his career. Iowa entered the game with what was considered the Big Ten's top defense.

Tomczak's counterpart, Hawkeye quarterback Chuck Long, connected on 22 attempts for 275 yards and two touchdowns, but Long also threw two interceptions and lost a fumble that led directly to three Ohio State scores. It was a pleasant retaliation for the Buckeyes, who lost to the Hawkeyes at Iowa City in '83, 20-14. Keith Byars was brilliant as he rushed for 120 yards, scored two touchdowns on the ground and another on a 14-yard pass from Tomczak. Byars also threw a 35-yard scoring toss down the left sideline to flanker Mike Lanese.

Midway through the second period, linebacker Larry Kolic made a one-handed interception off a tipped pass from Long and returned it 25 yards to put Ohio State ahead 24-10. This was a key play from which the Hawkeyes never recovered. Kolic finished the afternoon with 10 tackles, seven of them solos. Interestingly, Kolic had walked out of the program for per-

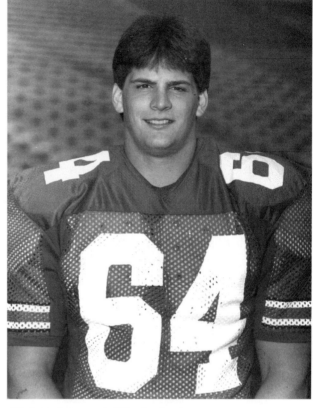

All-American guard Jim Lachey

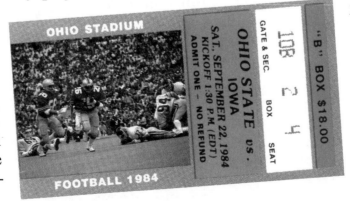

sonal reasons following the Oregon State opener and did not rejoin his teammates until the Monday after the Washington State game.

The Buckeyes next defeated Minnesota, 35-22, in a rare Saturday night game before a crowd of 47,543 at the Minneapolis Metrodome. Golden Gopher fans were showing a renewed interest in their football program with the addition of Lou Holtz as head coach. Ohio State went up 21-0, but Minnesota came back to make a game of it at 21-14 with 8:01 remaining in the third quarter. Byars and Tomczak again had excellent games—Byars rushed for 164 yards and scored two touchdowns and Tomczak hit on 13 of 19 passes for 181 yards with two scoring tosses to Cris Carter.

Boilermakers Deal Buckeyes First Loss of Season

Purdue defeated Ohio State, 28-23, before a crowd of 66,261 at Ross-Ade Stadium on October 6. Earle Bruce was very disappointed his team didn't score more points after leading in first downs, 30-16, and offensive yards, 570-376. He was also visibly upset with OSU's pass defense, which allowed Boilermaker quarterback Jim Everett to throw for 257 yards and three touchdowns. The Buckeyes led 17-7 early in the third period before giving up 21 straight points to trail 28-17.

Byars Leads "Greatest Comeback"

Earle Bruce called it "the greatest comeback after the worst start I've ever been associated with." Down 24-0 early in the second period before an Ohio Stadium homecoming crowd of 89,937, the Buckeyes rallied to conquer Illinois 45-38 in one of the most exciting games in the series. Keith Byars led the resurgence, setting a school single-game rushing record with 274 yards in 39 carries. He scored five touchdowns to tie a school record established by fullback Pete Johnson during OSU's 32-7 win over North Carolina in 1975.

The two rivals were fighting for survival in the Big Ten title chase. The Illini entered with an overall record of 4-2 and 3-1 in the conference, while 8th-ranked Ohio State was 4-1 and 2-1, after losing at Purdue the previous Saturday. The Buckeyes were still smarting from their devastating 17-13 loss at Champaign in 1983.

Midway through the first quarter, Illinois took a 7-0 lead on a three-yard pass from quarterback Jack Trudeau to wide receiver Randy Grant. The Illini had driven 80 yards in 11 plays, with the big gainer being a 38-yard gallop to the OSU five by fullback Thomas Rooks. On their next possession, Chris White booted a 26-yard field goal to increase the lead to ten.

Following the ensuing kickoff, quarterback Mike Tomczak took to the air on first down—the Illini's Mike Heaven intercepted and returned the pigskin to the OSU 21-yard line. From there it took Trudeau just four plays to hit split end David Williams with a nine-yard scoring aerial to increase the visitors' lead to 17-0. Williams had entered the game as the nation's leading receiver with 53 catches for 793 yards.

For Ohio State, it only got worse before it got better. Byars fumbled on first down, and safety Craig Swoope recovered for Illinois at the OSU 21-yard line. Six plays later Trudeau connected with tight end Cap Boso for an eight-yard touchdown, and the Illini held a 24-0 lead just 13 seconds into the second quarter. Sportswriters were quickly reviewing their press guides to determine if Ohio State's "most one-sided loss in Ohio Stadium" might be in the making.

Ohio State finally began to move on its next possession, but the drive stalled at the Illini 13-yard line when a fourth-down pass fell incomplete. After forcing Illinois to punt, the Bucks took possession at their own nine and drove 91 yards in six plays for their first score with 4:13 remaining prior to half-

Golden Anniversary

October 13 was the date of Ohio State's gigantic 45-38 triumph over Illinois in 1984. Exactly 50 years earlier on October 13, 1934, Illinois defeated Ohio State at Champaign, 14-13. It was the only loss that season for the Buckeyes of first-year coach Francis Schmidt, and it prevented Ohio State from sharing the 1934 Big Ten title with Minnesota.

All-American tailback Keith Byars lost his left shoe while racing 67 yards for his fourth of five touchdowns against Illinois.

time. Byars scored the touchdown from the sixteen. The drive's longest gainer was a 36-yard toss from Tomczak to Cris Carter.

The Illini's Craig Swoop was ejected from the game following a flagrant dead-ball personal foul on the touchdown. Many observers felt this was the game's turning point —with the 15-yard penalty assessed on the ensuing kickoff, Ohio State tried an onside kick from the Illini 45-yard line, and linebacker Joe Jenkins recovered for the Buckeyes at the Illini 31. On second down, Tomczak connected with Carter for a 30-yard touchdown, and Ohio State had scored twice within a span of 50 seconds. Rich Spangler's second conversion made it 24-14, and the Buckeyes were back in the ballgame.

Roverback Sonny Gordon set up Ohio State's next touchdown with a diving intercep-tion of a Trudeau pass at the OSU 38-yard line. Ten plays later, Byars dove four yards into the end zone to cut the Illinois lead to 24-21, with just 23 seconds left before halftime.

The Illini's Ray Wilson fumbled the second-half kickoff after being hit hard by Steve Hill—William White recovered, and the Buckeyes were back in business at the Illini 26. Byars carried on four consecutive plays for his third touchdown, and Ohio State took its first lead of the afternoon, 28-24. The Illini came right back with a 46-yard Chris White field goal to cut OSU's advantage to one.

Byars Scores Again After Losing Left Shoe

But the Buckeyes kept right on charging. Byars scored his fourth touchdown on a 67-yard jaunt down the east sideline into the stadium's closed end, to widen the lead to 35-27. The big tailback never broke stride, even after losing his left shoe around the Illini 40-yard line.

Illinois retaliated with a 63-yard scoring march, capped by a nine-yard TD toss from Trudeau to Ray Wilson. Trudeau then rolled right for a two-point conversion to tie the game at 35 with 1:09 remaining in the third quarter.

The two weary opponents traded field goals in the final period. First Rich Spangler hit from 47 yards at the 10:21 mark. Chris White booted a 16-yarder on a fourth-and-goal from the OSU one with just 3:18 remaining.

For the Buckeyes it was now or never. After nearly 57 minutes of play and almost 1,000 yards in combined offense, the score was tied at 38. Ohio State met the challenge, going 80 yards in 11 plays with Byars scoring the clincher from the three with just 36 seconds remaining. Spangler's fifth extra point made it 45-38, and fans had witnessed one of the most explosive and exciting games in all of Big Ten football. Trudeau completed 32 of 52 passes for 313 yards and all four Illini touchdowns. Illinois led in first downs, 27-

23, and Ohio State led in total offensive yardage, 564-509.

OSU Dodges Bullet at East Lansing

The Buckeyes were fortunate to win at Michigan State, 23-20, before a Spartan Stadium crowd of 75,133 on October 20. With just six seconds remaining, MSU placekicker Ralf Mojsiejenko's 43-yard field-goal attempt was low and to the right, and Ohio State avoided a tie. It was Mojsiejenko's first miss of the season after five successful kicks.

This was a very physical game. The Buckeyes dominated early and led 16-0 midway through the third period. But the Spartans put themselves back into the game with two huge scoring plays—a 75-yard pass from quarterback Dave Yarema to flanker Mark Ingram and Larry Jackson's 93-yard kickoff return.

Ohio State completely dominated the game's statistics, leading in first downs, 20-8; offensive yards, 410-223; and time of possession, 37:49 to 22:11. Tomczak had another fine game with 16 completions for 256 yards, and Byars (who now had scored one or more touchdowns in 17 consecutive games) was the afternoon's leading runner with 121 yards.

1984 Big Ten Champions

Badgers Do It Again

Ohio State was now 4-1 in league play, with the offense carrying the bulk of the load. In five conference games, the Buckeyes were averaging 34.2 points per game, while the opposition was scoring at the rate of 26.8 points. With this in mind, Wisconsin coach Dave McClain successfully went to a ball-control offense and defeated the Buckeyes, 16-14, at rainy Madison on October 27. The game was much more one-sided than indicated by the final score.

McClain's plan was to take advantage of Ohio State's defensive weaknesses and keep the ball away from the potent Buckeye offense, and it worked. The Badgers led in first downs, 25-14; offensive yards, 461-320; and ran 84 plays from scrimmage compared with OSU's 64. The Buckeyes suffered a serious blow when center Kirk Lowdermilk went out with a broken leg on the third play of the game.

Wisconsin led 10-0 at halftime and 16-7 late in the final period. Ohio State drove 70 yards to score its second TD with 3:04 remaining, but it was too little too late. Ironically, the Badger attack was led by Marck Harrison from Columbus Eastmoor High School, who started his first game of the season at tailback in place of injured Larry Emery and gained a career-high 203 yards on 31 carries. The Buckeyes had dropped to 4-2 in league play, and this loss appeared to be a serious blow to their Rose Bowl chances.

Ohio State had little trouble the next two weeks, routing Indiana 50-7 in Columbus and Northwestern 52-3 at Evanston. The Buckeyes received some much needed help the afternoon of the Northwestern win, with Michigan State upsetting league-leading Iowa, 17-16, and Wisconsin besting Purdue, 30-13. Suddenly Ohio State was alone atop the league standings and could capture its first outright title in five years with a win over Michigan.

Brutus's Return

Former reporter and news anchor Tom Burris considers the following story one of his favorites among the many Ohio State activities he covered for WSYX-TV6 in Columbus. The date was Friday, November 16, 1984, the day before the Michigan game at Ohio Stadium.

Eric Mayers, that season's Brutus Buckeye, was doing traffic reports that week at WSNY-Sunny 95 Radio as part of Michigan week activities. Early Friday morning as Mayers was leaving for the station, he discovered the Brutus head had been stolen from his car sometime during the night. Eric had a real problem—there was no other head available, and the next day's big game was his last home appearance as Brutus Buckeye.

As part of Mayers' traffic reports that morning, WSNY announced a $500 reward for the return of Brutus' head. Mayers also joined Burris for Burris' noon news telecast from the Ohio Union, and described his predicament. An official from GTE joined them and announced GTE would add $1,000 to the reward fund. WSNY and WSYX-TV received a lot of calls early that afternoon, but none led to anything meaningful.

Finally around 3:30 p.m. a gentleman named Eli telephoned to report he had the missing head. After finding it in a trash dumpster near campus, he took it home to his children thinking it was a doll. Fortunately his wife, who had heard Burris and Mayers on the noon news, recognized the item as the missing Brutus head. Eli returned it, collected his $1,500 reward, and described his find with Burris and Mayers live from Ohio Stadium on the 6:00 p.m. news.

Mayers couldn't have been more grateful. His Brutus head had been returned in time for the 7:00 p.m. Friday evening pep rally, and of course for the Michigan game Saturday——which Ohio State won, 21-6.

Double Trouble

The Michigan football team stayed at the same hotel near the Ohio State campus on the Friday evenings prior to their games in 1982 and 1984. A water main outside the hotel burst during the night in '82, and the entire hotel was without water Saturday morning. It's hard to believe, but the same thing happened in '84 — a water main broke Friday night, and the hotel was again without water Saturday morning.

Steve Held, the hotel's maintenance manager, recalls that the Michigan players absolutely believed they had been sabotaged the second time. As might be expected, Coach Bo Schembechler selected a different hotel when his team returned to Columbus in 1986.

Pasadena Bound

The Buckeyes made the most of their opportunity and defeated Michigan, 21-6, before a November 17 crowd of 90,286, at the time the largest to see a game in Ohio Stadium. The Buckeyes drove 61 yards midway through the first quarter to grab an early 7-0 lead, but Michigan's defense stiffened to hold Ohio State scoreless in the second and third quarters. Meanwhile, the Wolverines' Bob Bergeron booted a 37-yard field goal on the last play of the second period to make the score 7-3 at halftime.

Michigan controlled the ball for more than 12 minutes in the third quarter, but could score only three points on Bergeron's second field goal, a 45-yarder, to bring the Wolverines within one point of the Buckeyes at 7-6. The Ohio State offense came back to life in the final period with Byars scoring two more touchdowns to make the final score 21-6, and send OSU to the Rose Bowl to face Southern California.

The Ohio State defense limited Michigan to just 100 yards on the ground and 164 through the air. Bruce singled out defenders Chris Spielman, Pepper Johnson, Sonny Gordon, Larry Kolic, Byron Lee, Anthony Giuliani, and Dave Morrill for special praise. Gordon's second-quarter end zone interception ended the Wolverines' only serious touchdown threat of the afternoon.

Trojans Better Opportunists

Ohio State won the statistical battle, but Southern California took better advantage of its scoring opportunities and defeated the Buckeyes in the January 1, 1985, Rose Bowl, 20-17. OSU led in first downs, 19-16, and to-

Earle Bruce welcomes Woody Hayes to
Senior Tackle.

tal offensive yards, 403-261, but was forced
to settle for field goals by Rich Spangler in
each of the first three quarters.

The Buckeyes trailed 20-9 heading into
the final 15 minutes of play. Midway through
the fourth period, Ohio State marched 88
yards for its only touchdown of the afternoon
on an 18-yard pass from Mike Tomczak to
Cris Carter. Tomczak added a two-point conversion on a keeper to reduce the margin to
20-17. The Buckeyes could advance no farther than the USC 38-yard line on their final
possession.

Tomczak connected on 24 passes for 290
yards but had three interceptions. It was
Ohio State's fourth consecutive loss in the
Rose Bowl and the Big Ten's 10th setback in
the last 11 seasons. For the fifth straight year
the Buckeyes finished with a record of 9-3.

Guard Jim Lachey and tailback Keith
Byars were selected as All-Americans, and
Byars was selected as the team MVP. Byars

Rose Bowl's Longest

Placekicker Rich Spangler's 52-yard
field goal during Ohio State's 20-17
loss to the Southern California Trojans on January 1, 1985, is the longest in
Rose Bowl history.

also led the nation in rushing (1,764 yards)
and scoring (144 points) and finished second
to Boston College's Doug Flutie in the
Heisman Trophy voting.

1984

September 8	Oregon State	W	22	14
September 15	Washington State	W	44	0
September 22	Iowa	W	45	26
September 29	at Minnesota	W	35	22
October 6	at Purdue	L	23	28
October 13	Illinois (HC)	W	45	38
October 20	at Michigan State	W	23	20
October 27	at Wisconsin	L	14	16
November 3	Indiana	W	50	7
November 10	at Northwestern	W	52	3
November 17	Michigan	W	21	6
January 1	Southern California*	L	17	20
Total Points			**391**	**200**

*Rose Bowl

Season Record: 9-3
Big Ten Champion

1985

Ohio State wanted to accomplish what
no conference team had been able to achieve
in the last 19 seasons—capture consecutive
outright Big Ten titles. Michigan State last
mastered the feat in 1965 and '66, and the
Buckeyes had won back-to-back undisputed

league championships in 1954-55 and 1916-17. The biggest challenge was rebuilding the offensive and defensive lines, which had both been hit hard by graduation.

The offense would be built around senior tailback Keith Byars and three fine receivers in Cris Carter, Mike Lanese, and tight end Ed Taggart. Byars was a preseason favorite to become Ohio State's fifth Heisman Trophy winner. Quarterback Mike Tomczak had graduated, but the coaches had total confidence in junior Jim Karsatos, who had played well the past two seasons when Tomczak was injured.

The entire starting defensive backfield of Sonny Gordon, William White, Greg Rogan, and Terry White was intact, along with linebackers Pepper Johnson, Larry Kolic, Byron Lee, and Chris Spielman. Placekicker Rich Spangler was back for his senior season, and sophomore Tom Tupa returned to handle the punting.

Severe Setback

Monday, September 2, just 12 days prior to the September 14 opener against the Pitt Panthers, the Buckeyes were dealt a devastating blow when Byars broke a bone in his foot while running a play around left end in a non-contact practice drill. The early prognosis was that he would be sidelined at least six weeks and possibly for the entire season. Junior John Wooldridge, the team's second-leading ground gainer in '84 with 633 yards, was suddenly thrust into the starting role at tailback.

The Buckeyes opened with a come-from-behind 10-7 win over Pitt in the first true home night game in Ohio State history. The inexperience in the offense showed as the Buckeyes rushed for just 48 yards against a veteran Panther defense. Karsatos passed for 246 yards, including a one-yard strike to Cris Carter for the winning touchdown with just 4:19 remaining. Bruce credited

his veteran defense with keeping the game close. William White made a key interception at the OSU 44-yard line to stop the Panthers' final drive at the 1:43 mark of the fourth period.

Offense Begins to Jell

There was a noticeable improvement in the offense that helped the seventh-ranked Buckeyes defeat Colorado, 36-13, before 47,022 at Folsom Field in Boulder on September 21. The Buckeyes led in first downs, 23-16, and total offensive yards, 343-251. Karsatos had another solid game with 18 completions for 181 yards and three touchdowns, and Wooldridge rushed for 119 yards.

Colorado scored first and last while the Buckeyes scored 36 consecutive points in between. The defense had its second fine outing, forcing coach Bill McCartney's wishbone offense into four turnovers that led directly to four OSU scores. Outside linebacker Eric Kumerow was his team's leading tackler with 10, including five solos and two for losses totaling six yards.

The offenses took center stage at Ohio Stadium the next weekend as Ohio State outscored Washington State, 48-32. Both teams scored in each of the four quarters. The Buckeyes (who scored four TDs in the second period) really opened it up, amassing 497 yards in total offense while the Cougars totaled 481 yards. Ohio State's offensive line continued to show improvement,

and Karsatos had his third fine game of the season, hitting on 18 of 24 attempts for 228 yards and two touchdowns with no interceptions. At one stretch OSU scored three TDs in a span of two minutes and 58 seconds.

Conference Opener Bitter Disappointment

On October 5, explosive Illinois handed Ohio State its first loss of the season, 31-28, before an enthusiastic crowd of 76,343 at Memorial Stadium. With the wind blowing strongly, Earle Bruce decided to take the wind at his team's back after winning the coin toss. The Illini proceeded to score twice into the wind to lead 14-0 after one quarter. OSU retaliated with four consecutive touchdowns to take what appeared to be a commanding 28-14 advantage near the end of the third period. But after playing the last 32 minutes without scoring, Illinois quickly scored twice to tie the game, 28-28.

After Ohio State was unable to sustain a drive, the Illini took possession on their own 42 following a Buckeye shanked punt that went just 28 yards. Illinois quarterback Jack Trudeau made perfect use of the clock and moved his team into possession for placekicker Chris White (son of head coach Mike White) to boot a 38-yard game-winning field goal with no time remaining.

It was a tough loss for the Buckeyes who fought back to take a 14-point lead after trailing by 14 early in the second period. Trudeau was hard on OSU's defense with 28 completions for 294 yards. Freshman tailback Vince Workman rushed for exactly 100 yards including a 35-yard TD sprint on his first carry of the afternoon. Workman replaced John Wooldridge, who went out with a concussion in the second period. Linebackers Pepper Johnson and Chris Spielman were the game's leading tacklers with 18 each.

At home the following week, Ohio State rebounded with a 48-7 win over under-

Karsatos grabs spotlight in Buckeyes' 48-32 win

Columbus Dispatch, Sunday, September 29, 1985

manned Indiana. Bruce used 11 different ball carriers and 10 separate receivers to account for 507 yards of total offense. For the second time this season, OSU scored four touchdowns in the second period.

Byars's Return to Action Impressive

The Buckeyes enjoyed an emotional 41-27 triumph over Purdue before 89,888 delirious homecoming fans on October 19. Keith Byars received a standing ovation as he made his first appearance of the season midway through the first period. Ohio State jumped out to a 17-0 lead, only to have the Boilermakers surge back and tie the score 27-27 at the 8:35 mark of the final period. Purdue quarterback Jim Everett riddled OSU's defense for 497 yards and two touchdowns, but five Boilermaker turnovers played a big role in the game's outcome.

Byars rushed for 106 yards on the afternoon and scored two fourth-period touchdowns that became the margin of victory. His second score was set up with linebacker Byron Lee's first collegiate interception at the Purdue 48 with 4:12 remaining. Lee's theft broke Everett's string of 153 consecutive passes without an interception. Lee played an excellent game with eight tackles, including two sacks totaling 20 yards. Jim Karsatos had another fine afternoon, passing for 174 yards and OSU's first three touchdowns.

Gallant Comeback Against Holtz's Golden Gophers

Ohio State needed another valiant effort the following week at Minnesota to bring home a 23-19 come-from-behind win. Second-year Golden Gopher coach Lou Holtz had been pointing for the Buckeyes all fall.

The ninth-ranked Buckeyes and twentieth-ranked Gophers each entered the nationally televised contest with records of 5-1. The tremendous noise created by the record homecoming crowd of 64,455 at the Metrodome frequently disrupted Karsatos' signal-calling.

Two Chip Lohmiller field goals of 36 and 50 yards gave the Gophers an early 6-0 advantage. Ohio State then took the lead, 7-6, driving 80 yards with tailback Keith Byars getting the score on a two-yard option pitch around right end. Rich Spangler's 38-yard field goal increased the lead to 10-6.

But the momentum really shifted when Golden Gopher quarterback Rickey Foggie, master of the triple-option attack, scored from the two just nine seconds before halftime to put Minnesota back on top, 12-10. Early in the third period, Foggie completed an 89-yard drive with a one-yard plunge, increasing the lead to 19-10, and Minnesota could smell the upset.

Buckeyes Battle Back

With their backs to the wall, Earle Bruce's squad marched 90 yards to narrow the deficit to 19-17 early in the final period. Karsatos, who kept the drive moving with a

Preparing to stop the Purdue Boilermakers are "Pepper" Johnson (98), Darryl Lee (95), Eric Kumerow (14), Chris Spielman (36), Larry Kolic (33), Fred Ridder (90), and Byron Lee (82).

28-yard strike to Doug Smith, connected with tight end Ed Taggart on a one-yard toss for the touchdown.

Next, cornerback William White helped quiet the crowd by picking off a Foggie pass (Foggie's first interception of the year) at the OSU 47-yard line. With Byars and John Wooldridge both injured, freshman Vince Workman entered the game at tailback. After Karsatos moved his team to the Gopher 16-yard line, Workman swept around left end for the winning touchdown behind key blocks by guard Jim Gilmore and tackle Larry Kotterman.

But Holtz's squad was far from finished. Starting from their own nine, the Gophers moved to a fourth-and-inches at the Ohio State 12-yard line with just 48 seconds remaining. Unfortunately for Minnesota, Foggie had been injured on the third-down carry and was replaced on fourth down by reserve Alan Holt. Holt handed the ball to halfback Valdez Baylor on a straight-ahead dive play, but linebacker "Pepper" Johnson was there to meet him for no gain, and the Buckeyes could finally breath a little easier.

With the lead changing hands four times, Bruce was extremely pleased with the poise exhibited by his team. Linebacker Chris Spielman played one of his finest games, leading the defense with 13 solo tackles.

Ohio Stadium Classic

Eighth-ranked Ohio State returned home November 2 to face top-ranked Iowa. Before a national television audience and a rain-soaked Ohio Stadium record crowd of 90,467, the Buckeyes defeated the Hawkeyes 22-13 for one of the school's all-time "great" victories.

Iowa, with a record of 7-0, entered the battle as a 1-and-½ point favorite. It was the first time Ohio State had been an underdog in its own stadium since the 1977 Oklahoma game, which the Sooners won 29-28. Ohio State owned the nation's longest

home winning streak at 19. The Hawkeyes were the first No. 1 ranked opponent to appear in Ohio Stadium in 17 years, dating back to October 12, 1968, when the Purdue Boilermakers were a 13-0 victim.

Iowa had lost its last 11 games in Ohio Stadium, extending back to 1961. Coach Hayden Fry's team was led by three All-Americans; quarterback Chuck Long, tailback Ronnie Harmon, and linebacker Larry Station. Long entered the game as the nation's top passer, having thrown for 1,984 yards and 21 touchdowns while giving up only eight interceptions. Harmon was fifth nationally in all-purpose running, averaging 170.4 yards per game.

Ohio State quarterback Jim Karsatos was the nation's fifth-ranked passer, with 1,247 yards, 14 touchdowns, and only four interceptions. The Buckeyes were leading the Big Ten in scoring, averaging 35 points per game, but were ranked seventh in total defense and ninth in pass defense.

The Buckeyes played without tailback Keith Byars, who had re-injured his right foot the previous week at Minnesota. But the senior co-captain, who had one of the biggest games of his career against Iowa the previous year, delivered an inspirational pregame speech which really ignited his teammates. Byars became so excited he swiped a food tray from a table, broke a water glass, and kicked a chair while giving his pep talk.

Additional motivation was provided by a very uncomplimentary article in the Saturday morning *Columbus Citizen-Journal*, which belittled the defensive secondary's chances against the nation's top passer—the Buckeyes were not impressed! With Byars out, freshman Vince Workman got his first start at tailback. Rich Spangler's 28-yard field goal and a blocked punt by roverback Sonny Gordon (that went out of the end zone for a safety) gave Ohio State a 5-0 first-period lead —it was the first time all season Iowa had been scored upon in the first quarter.

Excellent Defensive Game Plan

Meanwhile, the Buckeye defenders were confusing Long with their beautifully disguised pass defenses. Early in the second quarter, tailback John Wooldridge (who did not start because of bruised ribs) sped 57 yards on his very first carry of the game to put Ohio State ahead 12-0. The touchdown was set up when William White intercepted a Long pass, and returned it eight yards to the OSU 38-yard line. Later that quarter, Greg Rogan's theft of a Long pass set up Spangler's second field goal, a 26-yarder, to increase the Ohio State lead to 15.

The Hawkeyes finally got their offense on track, driving 88 yards for their first touchdown with just 28 seconds remaining before halftime. Harmon scored from the three on the drive's 14th play. The effort had been kept alive when Long connected with David Hudson for 21 yards on a third-and-eight from the Hawkeye 25-yard line.

Sonny Gordon blocks an Iowa punt for a safety.

The third period was scoreless, but the Hawkeyes had a golden opportunity when safety Jay Norvell intercepted Karsatos, and returned the ball seven yards to the Ohio State 19-yard line. After two carries by Harmon moved the pigskin to the eleven, he again tried the middle—but linebacker Pepper Johnson slipped a block and nailed him at the ten. With Coach Hayden Fry passing up a 27-yard field-goal try, the Hawks again went to Harmon on fourth-and-one. But this time it was linebacker Chris Spielman who nailed him to the wet turf for no gain, and the Buckeyes had met the challenge.

The two teams traded touchdowns in the final period, with the Buckeyes scoring first on Workman's four-yarder over left tackle and Iowa's coming on a two-yard burst by Harmon. Johnson and Spielman (with 19 tackles each) had led a vicious defense that forced Iowa to start its first seven possessions at its own 19, 17, 20, 21, 26, 12, and 20-yard lines. Long (averaging 324 yards-per-game) had been held to 169 yards in 17 completions and was intercepted four times, two by Spielman. Seventeen of the Buckeyes' 22 points resulted from turnovers.

An elated Earle Bruce had just coached one of the finest games of his career. His team simply dominated Iowa. Also jubilant was Woody Hayes, who was especially impressed with Ohio State's defensive efforts. Hayes watched the game at his home where he was recovering from a heart attack. Karsatos completed 10 of

Highest High from Lowest Low

Ohio State's outstanding 22-13 triumph over top-ranked Iowa was played at Ohio Stadium on November 2, 1985, the exact 50th anniversary of one of the most agonizing losses in Ohio State history—an 18-13 setback to the Fighting Irish at the horseshoe in the famous Ohio State-Notre Dame game of November 2, 1935.

17 passes for 157 yards with two interceptions, while fullback George Cooper rushed for 104 yards to become the first Buckeye fullback to rush for 100 or more yards since Vaughn Broadnax in 1982.

Ohio State had little trouble the following Saturday at rainy Northwestern, winning 35-17. OSU led 35-0 before Bruce began

THE PLAIN DEALER
SPORTS
THOM GREER/FORUM, PAGE 2
NBA/MISL/NHL, PAGE 11
IN BRIEF/PEOPLE, PAGE 12
C
SUNDAY, NOVEMBER 3, 1985

Buckeyes down No. 1 Hawkeyes
OSU defense sparkles

John Wooldridge's 57-yard touchdown sprint through the Iowa defense came on his first carry of the afternoon.

THE OFFICIAL OHIO STATE FOOTBALL ENCYCLOPEDIA

multiple second-half substitutions. The Buckeyes lost two fumbles in the inclement weather, their first lost bobbles of the season. Their second touchdown was a 75-yard scoring pass from Jim Karsatos to Mike Lanese.

Who Would Have Believed

The Buckeyes were 5-1 in league play as they prepared for their last home game November 16 against Wisconsin. The Badgers were 1-5 in conference competition and tied for last place with Northwestern and Indiana. Most fans were looking ahead to the following week's game at Michigan, where a victory would send Ohio State to the Rose Bowl for the second consecutive season—assuming the heavily favored Buckeyes had defeated lowly Wisconsin. Bad assumption! The Badgers embarrassed Ohio State, 12-7. It was one of OSU's most unexpected and devastating losses in many seasons.

The Buckeyes lost three fumbles, one more than they had given up in their first eight games. One lost fumble at the Ohio State 22 set up the Badgers winning touchdown late in the third quarter. Another bobble at the Badger three in the final period prevented what could have been the winning touchdown. All three fumbles were recovered by Wisconsin's Michael Reid.

After the Wisconsin loss, Iowa moved to the top of the Big Ten standings. For the Buckeyes to make the Rose Bowl they would have to defeat Michigan, and Iowa would have to lose to Minnesota. Neither happened. The Wolverines topped Ohio State, 27-17, while the Hawkeyes captured the outright league championship with a 31-9 win over the Golden Gophers at Iowa City.

Ohio State and Michigan were tied 10-10 at halftime, but the Wolverines moved to a 20-10 advantage after the Buckeyes were able to run only six plays from scrimmage in the third period. Early in the final quarter a 36-yard TD strike from Jim Karsatos

to Cris Carter cut Michigan's lead to 20-17. But on a second-and-seven from the UM 23-yard line following the ensuing kickoff, Wolverine quarterback Jim Harbaugh and freshman flanker John Kolesar connected on a 77-yard scoring pass to put the game out of reach.

The Buckeye defense simply couldn't contain Harbaugh, who completed 16 of 19 tosses for 230 yards and all three Wolverine touchdowns. Coach Bo Schembechler really opened up his team's attack in the second half. Michigan led in first downs, 19-14, and in total offensive yards, 424-269. The Buckeyes were now 8-3 and had slipped to a fourth-place tie with Michigan State in the final league rankings behind Iowa, Michigan, and Illinois.

Defense Dominates BYU

Ohio State faced Brigham Young in the December 28, 1985, Citrus Bowl in Orlando, Florida. Surprisingly, it was the defenses, and not the offenses, that dominated as the

All-American linebacker Thomas "Pepper" Johnson

Buckeyes won a close one, 10-7. Defensive coordinator Gary Blackney developed a new unorthodox defense with several new looks, including linebackers dropping back to successfully confuse BYU's pass patterns.

BYU quarterback Robbie Bosco completed 26 passes for 261 yards, but four interceptions by the Buckeye defense prevented BYU from scoring in the second half. Ohio State's only touchdown came on a 14-yard interception return by linebacker Larry Kolic on the third play of the third quarter. Kolic was named the game's most valuable player. Altogether the Cougars committed six turnovers. Rich Spangler had booted a 47-yard field goal early in the second quarter to give OSU a temporary 3-0 lead.

Tailback John Wooldridge led the Ohio State rushing attack with 92 yards, and quarterback Jim Karsatos completed 19 passes for 196 yards. Keith Byars was forced to leave the game with an aggravation to his right foot during the Buckeyes' second offensive series.

For the sixth consecutive year Ohio State won nine and lost three. This season finished on the downside with two losses in the last three games. The Buckeye offense averaged 32.3 points-per-game over the first nine games, but only 11.3 during the last three. Linebacker Pepper Johnson became an All-American, and Jim Karsatos was chosen the team's MVP.

Byars was able to play in only four games, gaining 213 yards on 555 carries. He finished his excellent four-year career with exactly 3,200 yards rushing and 50 touchdowns. Flanker Mike Lanese was selected an Academic All-American for the second consecutive season, and became the first Ohio State football player to be awarded a Rhodes Scholarship.

1985				
September 14	Pittsburgh (N)	W	10	7
September 21	at Colorado	W	36	13
September 28	Washington State	W	48	32
October 5	at Illinois	L	28	31
October 12	Indiana	W	48	7
October 19	Purdue (HC)	W	41	27
October 26	at Minnesota	W	23	19
November 2	Iowa	W	22	13
November 9	at Northwestern	W	35	17
November 16	Wisconsin	L	7	12
November 23	at Michigan	L	17	27
December 28	Brigham Young*	W	10	7
Total Points			325	212

*Citrus Bowl

Season Record: 9-3
Conference: 4th Place (Tie)

1986

In June of 1986, Earle Bruce became the first modern-era Ohio State football coach to be granted a multi-year contract, when he signed a three-year pact for the 1986-87-88 seasons. His Buckeyes entered the '86 season with their usual high expectations. Quarterback Jim Karsatos, who passed for 2,311 yards and 19 touchdowns in '85, was back along with split end Cris Carter and tight end Ed Taggart, both excellent receivers. Bob Maggs, Jeff Uhlenhake, and Larry Kotterman returned to bolster the offensive line, Vince Workman and John Wooldridge were back at tailback, and George Cooper returned as the starting fullback.

The defense was built around linemen Eric Kumerow, Fred Ridder, and Darryl Lee, linebacker Chris Spielman, cornerbacks Greg Rogan and William White, and rover Sonny Gordon. Punter Tom Tupa (who averaged

44.3 yards per kick over his first two seasons) was back for his junior year. An inordinate number of injuries in spring practice made it impossible for Earle Bruce and his staff to determine their complete starting lineups, and many positions were still undecided when practice opened in the fall.

The '86 schedule was demanding with seven opponents having played in bowl games the previous year. Ohio State added to its season by playing Alabama in the Wednesday evening, August 27, Kickoff Classic at Giants Stadium in East Rutherford, New Jersey. Except for the Buckeyes' very first game played May 3, 1890, this was the earliest opener in school history.

Worst Start in 102 Seasons

Ohio State opened its season with two straight losses for the first time since losing to Akron (12-6) and Wittenberg (6-0) in 1894. Alabama scored 10 unanswered points in the fourth quarter and won the Kickoff Classic, 16-10. The game was relatively ragged on both sides, but it went down to the evening's final play when a 17-yard Karsatos to Carter pass fell incomplete in the end zone.

Three turnovers, six penalties, and a very ineffective kicking game really hindered Ohio State. Two redshirt freshmen started for the Buckeyes—Joe Staysniak at offensive tackle and David Brown at safety. Ohio State had not opened on the road since defeating Michigan State, 21-0, at East Lansing in 1975.

Matters grew worse before they got better. The Buckeyes were totally humiliated at Washington, 40-7. It was OSU's most one-sided setback in 19 seasons since losing to Purdue in 1967, 41-6. September 13 was a rainy day in Seattle, but Earle Bruce told the media, "I don't think the rain had anything to do with it, this was just bad ball handling by us." This game was quite a blow to Bruce's defensive unit, which was expected to be one of the strongest during his eight years at Ohio State.

After a scoreless first quarter, Washington scored 24 points in the second period to lead 24-0 at halftime. The Huskies led in first downs, 24-11, total offensive yardage, 408-186, and they held the ball for 37:50 minutes of the 60 minute game. The Buckeyes lost three fumbles, all of which led directly to Washington scores. Counting the last three games of 1985, Ohio State had scored just five touchdowns in its last five games.

A Win Is a Win Is a Win

The two losses brought much fan criticism, but Bruce defended his coaching methods and predicted the team would still have a successful season. The Buckeyes finally played their first home game September 20 against coach Bill McCartney's Colorado Buffaloes. It wasn't pretty, and the offense still struggled, but the Buckeyes managed their first win of the season, 13-10. Freshman placekicker Pat O'Morrow's 19-yard field goal with just 25 seconds remaining broke a 10-10 deadlock and provided the three-point margin of victory.

The Ohio State offense did a complete reversal the following week, gaining a Big Ten record 715 yards while shellacking outmanned Utah, 64-6. This broke the mark of 713 yards set by Iowa during a 61-21 win over Northwestern on October 8, 1983. The Buckeyes rushed for 394 yards and passed for 321, to become the first Ohio State team to both rush and pass for more than 300 yards in a single game.

Bruce told the press that his staff and players had been stimulated by the steady fan criticism the past two weeks. The 64 points exactly matched the team's total points scored during its last six games over two seasons. It was Ohio State's largest margin of victory since defeating Northwestern 70-6 on November 14, 1981. It was also OSU's 600th all-time win (600-239-48).

Freshman Jaymes Bryant started at tailback and gained 145 yards, while sopho-

THE OHIO STATE UNIVERSITY

BUCKEYES

50Ohio
THE 50th ANNIVERSARY
OF SCRIPT OHIO
1936-1986

COLORADO

BRUTUS

OHIO STATE
VS.
COLORA

OHIO STADI

SAT. SEPT. 20, 1986

TIME SUBJECT TO CHANGE WITH

SEC. 10B

ROW/BX 2

B-BOX GAME 1

Mike Lanese Honored

At halftime of the home opener against Colorado, graduated flanker Mike Lanese received a standing ovation when he received an award from Athletic Director Rick Bay in honor of becoming the first Ohio State football player to earn a Rhodes Scholarship. Lanese was one of 32 American college seniors to be chosen to study at Oxford University in England. The native of Mayfield, Ohio, was an honor student with a dual major in English and political science.

more Vince Workman rushed for 168 yards and three touchdowns. It was the first game since the season-opening win over Baylor on September 11, 1982, that two OSU backs each gained more than 100 yards (Tim Spencer had 147 and Vaughn Broadnax had 101 in the '82 game). Fullback George Cooper scored four touchdowns on short plunges, and Tom Tupa was called upon to punt only once all afternoon.

Three in a Row and Improving

The Buckeyes began Big Ten competition October 4 with a 14-0 triumph over Illinois. Recent games against the Fighting Illini had been high-scoring shoot-outs, and most of the 90,030 in Ohio Stadium that afternoon had been expecting the same. It was OSU's first shutout since whitewashing Washington State, 44-0, on September 15, 1984. It also was just the second of only two shutouts suffered by Illinois during Mike White's eight seasons as head coach from 1980 through 1987.

While the Ohio State defense dominated the afternoon (holding Illinois to 32 rushing yards), the offense was inconsistent and came away without scoring four times after moving inside the Illini 35-yard line. Jim Karsatos scored the first touchdown standing up on a 10-yard option around left end on the first play of the second quarter. Tailback Vince Workman executed perfectly and passed ten yards to wide receiver Nate Harris on a run-pass option for the second TD right before halftime. After their distressed 0-2 start, the Buckeyes were now 3-2 on the season and gaining respectability.

Hoosier State Two Weeks in a Row

Ohio State ran its record to 5-2 with victories at Indiana and at Purdue the following two Saturdays. The Buckeyes had all they could handle before defeating IU, 24-22, in front of an October 11 homecoming crowd of 51,641 at Memorial Stadium. Coach Bill Mallory was in his third season as head coach of the Hoosiers, who entered the game with a record of 4-0.

OSU scored touchdowns in each of the first three quarters on a one-yard plunge by

Ed Taggart (80), Larry Kotterman (72), George Cooper (44), Jaymes Bryant (41), and Nate Harris (26) return to the sideline after scoring against Utah.

Jim Karsatos, a nine-yard run by George Cooper, and a 21-yard toss from Karsatos to Cris Carter. The eventual two-point margin of victory was a key 43-yard field goal by placekicker Matt Frantz at the 9:31 mark of the third quarter. It was his first collegiate field-goal attempt. Frantz, a walk-on who was not chosen for the trip to Bloomington until two days before the game, was not even listed on the team's traveling roster.

The following week's encounter at Purdue was a rare Saturday night game, which Ohio State won handily, 39-11. It was the first night game in Ross-Ade Stadium history. Frantz connected on four field goals of 21, 22, 22, and 21 yards. Safety David Brown put the game out of reach with an electrifying Big Ten record 100-yard interception return early in the third quarter, putting Ohio State on top, 29-3. Karsatos threw scoring passes to Cris Carter (3 yards) and Nate Harris (37 yards), and backup Tom Tupa passed 23 yards to Jamie Holland for the game's final touchdown.

Back home October 25 before 89,936 rain-soaked homecoming fans, the Buckeyes pounded Minnesota 33-0 to put a huge dent in the Golden Gophers' Big Ten hopes. The visitors entered the game tied for the league lead with Ohio State and Michigan at 3-0 in conference play. The Buckeyes scored in

Spielman True to His Word

Will McClure, a 15-year-old freshman at Upper Arlington High School in 1986, was seriously injured while playing football. All-American linebacker Chris Spielman visited McClure at the hospital while he was recuperating and promised him an interception in Ohio State's next game against Illinois. The following Saturday Spielman made an interception during the Buckeyes' 14-0 victory over the Illini. He returned to the hospital and presented McClure with the ball, as promised.

each quarter and outgained Minnesota, 439 yards to 189. Ironically, the Golden Gophers entered the game with the leading rushing offense in the conference.

Tailback Jaymes Bryant rushed for two touchdowns, Jim Karsatos threw two scoring passes to Cris Carter, and Matt Frantz kicked two field goals. Minnesota never advanced beyond the Ohio State 22. Linebackers Chris Spielman and Scott Leach (who made his first start of the season) led a very aggressive defense with 17 and 13 tackles, respectively. It was the first season since 1980 that the Buckeyes had shut out two conference opponents.

Massive Victory at Iowa City

Ohio State was now 6-2 on the season and 4-0 in conference play, as Earle Bruce's team prepared for its biggest test of the season to-date—a November 1 showdown against Iowa who was leading the Big Ten in scoring and total offense. The 17th ranked

Buckeyes traveled to Iowa City as a three-and-one-half point underdog to the 11th-ranked Hawkeyes. Even the most optimistic fan would hardly have predicted Ohio State's 31-10 triumph. After the Hawkeyes went up 7-0 in the first period, the Buckeyes exploded for 21 points within a span of six minutes and 16 seconds in the second quarter to break the game wide open.

It began with Karsatos and Carter connecting on a 72-yard touchdown pass. Karsatos avoided a heavy blitz that left the Hawkeyes trying to cover Carter man-to-man, and OSU had its longest play from scrimmage of the season. The Buckeyes quickly got the ball back and needed just four plays to move 48 yards for their second touchdown. George Cooper carried the last nine over left guard. On Iowa's next possession, cornerback Greg Rogan recovered a fumble in mid-air and raced 31 yards untouched to put OSU on top, 21-7.

Vince Workman (42) takes handoff from Jim Karsatos (16) with George Cooper (44) and Jay Shaffer (69) leading the way against Illinois.

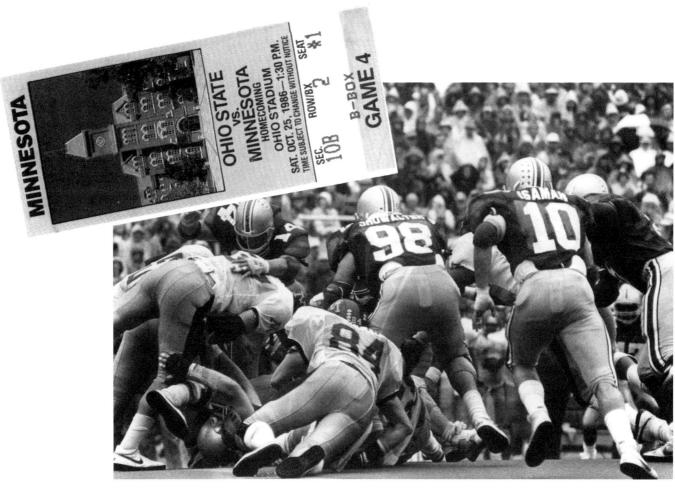

Eric Kumerow (14), Mike Showalter (98), and Derek Isaman (10) pressure the Minnesota Golden Gophers.

In the second half, Karsatos threw a 38-yard scoring strike to Everett Ross, and Matt Frantz connected on a 37-yard field goal. The Buckeyes' "swarm-to-the-ball" defense held Iowa to 192 yards of offense, including just 79 yards on the ground. Chris Spielman was again the leading tackler with 18, and outside linebacker Eric Kumerow had another impressive afternoon with eight solo tackles, a deflected pass, and one sack.

The Buckeyes defeated much-improved Northwestern at home the next week, 30-9, for their eighth straight win. The scrappy Wildcats were limited to a field goal in each of the three final quarters, although they outgained OSU 497 yards to 450. Three interceptions and two lost fumbles kept NU from making the final score much closer.

Minnesota Helps the Cause

Ohio State conquered recent nemesis Wisconsin, 30-17, at Camp Randall Stadium on November 15. Having lost to the Badgers four of the past five years, OSU did not take this game lightly, even though Wisconsin was only 3-7 on the season. Earle Bruce's squad quickly put together a 17-0 first-quarter advantage and never looked back. Cris Carter caught his ninth scoring pass of the year, breaking his own school single-season record of eight set in both '84 and '85.

But the big news of the afternoon came from Ann Arbor, where Minnesota upset Michigan, 20-17, to hand the Wolverines their first loss of the season. This left Ohio State alone at the top of the Big Ten with a

Winning Streak Ends at Nine

On November 22 Michigan derailed the Buckeyes' Rose Bowl express with a heart-stopping 26-24 triumph, before what was then a record Ohio Stadium crowd of 90,674. It earned the Wolverines a tie with Ohio State for the Big Ten title, and a January 1 Rose Bowl trip to meet coach John Cooper's Arizona State Sun Devils. The 50 points was the highest combined score in the series since the Buckeyes defeated the Wolverines 50-14 in 1968.

Ohio State started strongly and led 14-3 after one quarter and 14-6 at halftime. Jamie Holland returned the opening kickoff 47 yards to the Michigan 45-yard line; from there OSU used 10 plays to score their first touchdown on a four-yard throw from Karsatos to Carter. Later that quarter Vince Workman received key blocks from Carter and tight end Ed Taggart and scored on an option pitch from 46 yards out.

Linebacker Michael Kee intercepted Wolverine quarterback Jim Harbaugh at the goal line with 41 seconds left in the second quarter to preserve the eight-point halftime lead. Earlier in the week, Harbaugh publicly guaranteed that Michigan would win this game.

The second half was a different story. Coach Bo Schembechler decided to go with a "two tight end slug it out on the ground" approach and it worked. The Wolverines had touchdown drives of 83, 76, and 86 yards in the final two quarters. At one point they outscored Ohio State, 23-3. The Buckeyes still had a shot late in the game, but Matt Frantz's 45-yard field-goal attempt with just 1:01 remaining hooked just a couple of feet left of the upright.

Both offenses played well. Michigan led in first downs, 27-19, and in total of-fensive yards, 529 to 358. Wolverine tailback Jamie Morris rushed for 210 yards and Harbaugh passed for 261. Workman led the Buckeyes with 126 yards, and Karsatos passed for 188 yards and two touchdowns. Chris Spielman had a career-high 29 tackles.

With this win, Schembechler became the winningest coach in Michigan football with 166 victories, breaking the old school mark of 165 set by legendary Fielding Yost during the first quarter of the century.

Defense Dominates

The Buckeyes became the first Big Ten team to play in the Cotton Bowl when they defeated eighth-ranked Texas A & M, 28-12, before a sellout crowd of 74,188 on January 1, 1987. Ohio State completely confused the Aggies with an entirely new defensive scheme comprised of five linebackers, just two tackles, and four in the secondary. As a result, the 11th-ranked Buckeyes set a Cotton Bowl record with five interceptions, two

All-American split end Cris Carter

Defense Carries Buckeyes to Cotton Bowl Victory

*Columbus Dispatch,
Friday, January 2, 1987*

by Chris Spielman. Scott Leach manned the new "wildcard" position, which could be described as a linebacker-strong safety combination.

Earle Bruce looked very dapper along the sidelines in a new charcoal suit, black patent-leather shoes, a white diagonally striped tie, and a new black fedora with a scarlet feather. The coach surprised everyone with a quick change from his normal coaching gear following his team's pre-game warm-ups. Bruce's players also added a new look to their standard gray pants and white jerseys—red shoes.

The Cotton Bowl was a game of big plays with few sustained drives. Two of the Buckeyes' second-half interceptions went for touchdowns, Spielman taking one 24 yards early in the third period, and Michael Kee going 49 yards in the fourth quarter for the game's final score. Kee's return broke the Cotton Bowl interception record of 47 yards set by Colorado's Bryon "Whizzer" White against Rice in 1947. Jim Karsatos and Vince Workman each scored on short runs, and Sonny Gordon and Eric Kumerow accounted for the other two interceptions.

Spielman, who had 11 tackles and was selected the defensive player of the game, laughingly told the press he thought this was his first interception for a touchdown since a "peewee game" when he was nine years old. OSU outgained the Aggies only 303-296 in total yards, and 18-16 in first downs. A & M's Roger Vick was the offensive player

of the game after a 113-yard rushing performance, and Karsatos was the game's leading passer with 195 yards on 10 completions.

Ohio State finished the season at 10-3 overall, good for a seventh-place ranking in the final Associated Press poll. Michigan (11-2) finished one spot behind the Buckeyes at eighth, after losing the Rose Bowl to coach John Cooper's Arizona State Sun Devils, 22-15. Cris Carter and Chris Spielman made the All-American teams, and Carter was selected Ohio State's MVP.

1986				
August 27	Alabama#	L	10	16
September 13	at Washington	L	7	40
September 20	Colorado	W	13	10
September 27	Utah	W	64	6
October 4	Illinois	W	14	0
October 11	at Indiana	W	24	22
October 18	at Purdue	W	39	11
October 25	Minnesota (HC)	W	33	0
November 1	at Iowa	W	31	10
November 8	Northwestern	W	30	9
November 15	at Wisconsin	W	30	17
November 22	Michigan	L	24	26
January 1	Texas A & M*	W	28	12
Total Points			347	179

#Kickoff Classic
*Cotton Bowl

Season Record: 10-3
Big Ten Co-Champion

1987

The 1987 season was one of the most unusual in the long and glorious history of Ohio State football. Earle Bruce had compiled an eight-year record of 75-22 at his alma mater, as he began preparation for his ninth season. His record included four Big Ten titles or co-titles, victories in five of eight bowl games, and a 4-4 record against the Michigan Wolverines.

Bruce Strongly Considers University of Arizona Offer

In late December of 1986, University of Arizona Athletic Director Cedric Dempsey received permission from Ohio State to contact Bruce about the head coaching position at Arizona. Larry Smith had just announced he was leaving the Tucson school to become head coach at the University of Southern California.

Bruce initially showed no interest in the Arizona job, but Dempsey later persuaded Bruce to stop in Tucson on his way to an NCAA convention in San Diego in early January. At this meeting in Tucson, the Arizona officials apparently convinced Bruce of their commitment to their football program and offered him a five-year contract with a salary higher than he was receiving at Ohio State. The unexpected offer was very tempting, especially since Bruce (now 56) had often thought about living in either Arizona or Florida when he retired.

Ohio State Athletic Director Rick Bay immediately flew to San Diego to persuade Bruce to remain at Ohio State. The two met long into the night, and Bruce finally decided to turn down the Arizona offer, primarily because of his loyalty to his assistant coaches and players and his love for his alma mater. Bay was very relieved to say the least.

Loss of a Legend

The entire football world was saddened March 12 with the passing of Woody Hayes. The renowned coach likely symbolized Ohio State football more than any person ever involved with the program. Hayes became even more dedicated to charitable causes after his final season as head coach in 1978.

In addition to numerous national honors and awards, Hayes received the Medallion of Honor, the Ohio State University's highest award. He delivered the keynote address at Ohio State's 1986 winter quarter commencement, an honor he considered "the greatest day of my life." The street north of Ohio Stadium was named in his honor.

High Expectations

The Ohio State coaching staff was very optimistic as it began preparations for the 1987 season. The defense was expected to be especially strong with eight starters returning from the '86 unit, which allowed just 123 points during the season's last 11 games. The veteran players included All-American Chris Spielman and Fred Ridder at inside linebacker, outside linebackers Eric Kumerow and Derek Isaman, tackle Mike Showalter, and defensive backs William White, Greg Rogan, and David Brown.

Six offensive starters were back. Senior Tom Tupa was ready to step in at quarterback after being an impressive backup to Jim Karsatos. Tupa would also handle the punting chores for the fourth season. Offensive linemen Joe Staysniak and Greg Zackeroff were back, and Jeff Uhlenhake was moved from guard to center to replace Bob Maggs. Veterans Vince Workman and George Cooper returned in the backfield.

A bombshell was dropped on the program in July when the Ohio State Athletic Department revealed that record-setting wide receiver Cris Carter was made ineligible for any further athletic competition. Carter admitted to department officials that he had accepted money from two agents. The subject came to light when Carter was subpoenaed to appear before a grand jury in Chicago as part of an FBI investigation.

Mountaineers Return to Schedule After 84-Year Absence

The fifth-ranked Buckeyes opened their season at home September 12 with a 24-3 victory over neighboring West Virginia. The game (played before a sellout crowd of 88,272) was just the fifth between the two schools, and the first since 1903. The Mountaineers had opened their season at Morgantown the previous Saturday with a 23-3 triumph over Ohio University.

Coach Earle Bruce arrived for the opening kickoff in a stylish gray suit, scarlet tie with gray Os, and a light gray fedora, similar to the black suit and fedora he donned at the Cotton Bowl the previous January 1. A pregame moment of silence honored the memory of Woody Hayes.

This game was over almost before it started. West Virginia committed three turnovers on its first three plays to help Ohio State jump out to a quick 17-0 first-quarter lead. Placekicker Matt Frantz opened the scoring with a 47-yard field goal, at the time the longest of his career. Next, tailback Jaymes Bryant sped seven yards over right guard to cap a three-play, 21-yard drive. Later in the period, quarterback Tom Tupa drove the Bucks 65 yards, with the touchdown coming on a 23-yard pass to flanker Everett Ross.

The Buckeyes' offense was dormant the next two periods. West Virginia made it 17-3 after three quarters, with a 27-yard field goal by Charlie Baumann. In the final period, William White scored on a 29-yard interception return with just over three minutes remaining in the game. It was White's third interception of the afternoon, tying an OSU single-game record. Frantz's third conversion concluded the scoring at 24-3.

The Ohio State defense came up with six interceptions, just two short of the school single-game record of eight against Chicago in 1938. Linebacker Chris Spielman was as intense as ever with 19 tackles and two interceptions. Tupa, starting his first game at quarterback, had four punts of 60 or more yards.

OSU posted a relatively unimpressive 24-14 win over Oregon at home the following week. After leading just 3-0 at halftime,

the Buckeyes scored 14 points within a 74-second span of the third period to lead 17-0. Freshman tight end Jay Koch's first collegiate catch was a four-yard TD pass from Tom Tupa to cap an 88-yard, 14-play drive. After the Ducks were unable to move on the ensuing series, David Brown blocked Jan Cespedes' punt attempt, and Sean Bell recovered at the Oregon 19-yard line. On first down, fullback George Cooper caught a Tupa pass in the right flat and raced the distance for OSU's second touchdown.

Oregon posted its 14 points in the final period to spoil the possible shutout. Vince Workman scored OSU's final touchdown late in the game to complete an eight-play 80-yard march.

Two-time All-American linebacker Chris Spielman receives instructions from coaches Gary Blackney and Earle Bruce.

Major Intersectional Clash in the Bayou

Ohio State, now ranked seventh nationally, traveled to Baton Rouge September 26 to face fourth-ranked Louisiana State before a boisterous Tiger Stadium crowd of 79,263. This first-ever meeting with LSU was one of OSU's most highly anticipated non-conference games since meeting Oklahoma ten years earlier in 1977. The opening kickoff of this nationally televised game was delayed a few minutes—neither team wanted to be the first to leave its dressing room and return to the playing field, following last-minute instructions from the coaching staffs.

The Buckeyes had trouble adjusting to LSU's speedy offense and trailed 10-3 at half-time. Matt Frantz's second field goal of the afternoon cut the Tigers' lead to 10-6 after three quarters. On the third play of the final period, OSU linebacker Mike McCray intercepted Mickey Guidry's pass to give his team possession at the LSU 36-yard line. From there the Buckeyes drove to their first lead of the game, 13-10, when Tupa connected with Jay Koch on an 8-yard scoring toss at the 11:07 mark of the final period.

Louisiana State came right back to tie the game 13-13 on David Browndyke's second field goal of the day, this one a 40-yarder. The remainder of the game was unbelievable! Greg Rogan ended two additional Tiger scoring threats with interceptions in the game's final two minutes and three seconds. The Buckeyes had one last chance to break the tie, but Frantz's 47-yard field goal try on the game's last play was partially blocked.

Defense Preserves Victory in Big Ten Opener

Ohio State started strongly with a 10-0 halftime lead, then hung on for a 10-6 win over Illinois, in the October 3 conference opener at Champaign. The Buckeyes grabbed the opening kickoff and used 17 plays to

move 80 yards for the game's only touchdown, a five-yard option by quarterback Tom Tupa. The drive consumed seven minutes and 16 seconds and appeared to be a carry-over from the Woody Hayes days of ground-control offenses. Late in the quarter, Eric Kumerow recovered an Illini fumble at the Illinois 22 to set up Matt Frantz's 32-yard field goal.

After only five first downs and 68 yards of offense in the first half, Illinois accounted for 16 first downs and 286 yards in the last two quarters. The Illini finally got on the board with an 11-yard touchdown pass from quarterback Scott Mohr to tight end Anthony Williams midway through the fourth period.

The Orange and Blue had one last shot at victory as they advanced to the OSU 20-yard line with 35 seconds remaining. But after throwing three incomplete passes, Mohr was sacked by OSU middle guard Mike Sullivan on fourth down, and Ohio State ran

Fit to be Tied

OSU's 13-13 deadlock at Louisiana State was Earle Bruce's 100th game as head coach at Ohio State. It was also his first tie game as a head coach at the college level. Bruce was 10-2 during his single season at Tampa, and 36-32 over a six-year period at Iowa State. He entered this game against Louisiana State with an Ohio State record of 77-22.

out the clock. For the second consecutive week, the OSU offense could score only one touchdown, and the Buckeyes were fortunate to escape Memorial Stadium with the four-point victory.

Earle's "Darkest Day"

Ohio State's offensive problems continued October 10 at home, where Indiana belted the Buckeyes convincingly, 31-10. The Hoosiers scored in each period and broke a 10-10 halftime tie with three touchdowns in the last two quarters. For the second consecutive week OSU did not score in the second half. IU led in first downs, 21-13, and total offensive yards, 405-264.

Indiana had not defeated Ohio State in its last 31 tries. The Hoosiers most recent victory in the series had been a 32-10 win at Ohio Stadium in 1951, Woody Hayes' first season at OSU. Earle Bruce told the media,

Tom Tupa, quarterback and All-American punter. Tupa's career punting average of 44.7 yards (214 punts) is the highest in OSU history.

"Since I became a freshman at Ohio State in 1949, it's gotta be the darkest day I've seen in Ohio State football." His postgame press conference lasted just two minutes and 22 seconds.

The Buckeyes' second-half woes almost prevented them from posting a much-needed 20-17 win at Purdue's windy Ross-Aide Stadium the next week. Ohio State saw a 17-0 halftime advantage evaporate when the Boilermakers scored on their first three possessions of the second half to tie the game at 17-all. Matt Frantz booted a 50-yard field goal with just 3:10 remaining to break the deadlock. It was an important kick for Frantz, who had missed attempts from 43 and 46 yards in the third period.

In an effort to give his offense the deep receiving threat it had been lacking this season, Earle Bruce moved fleet Vince Workman to the flanker position against the Boilermakers. Workman, who had never before played the position in high school or college, had a fine afternoon with four catches for 88 yards, including a 36-yard scoring toss from Tom Tupa for the game's first touchdown.

Season's Highest Score

Ohio State's 42-9 homecoming victory over Minnesota the following Saturday was one of the team's best efforts of the year. The Golden Gophers entered the game with a record of 5-1, having lost to Indiana the previous week, 18-17, after winning their first five games of the season. Led by freshman Carlos Snow's four touchdowns and 85 yards rushing, the Buckeyes exploded for 28 second-half points to break the game wide open. Snow's overall play ignited the offense, which gained 422 yards, 126 more than its season's average.

Led by linebackers Chris Spielman, Eric Kumerow, and Mike McCray, the defense held the league's most prolific offense to just 269 yards. The Golden Gophers traveled to Columbus averaging 421 yards and 28 points per game.

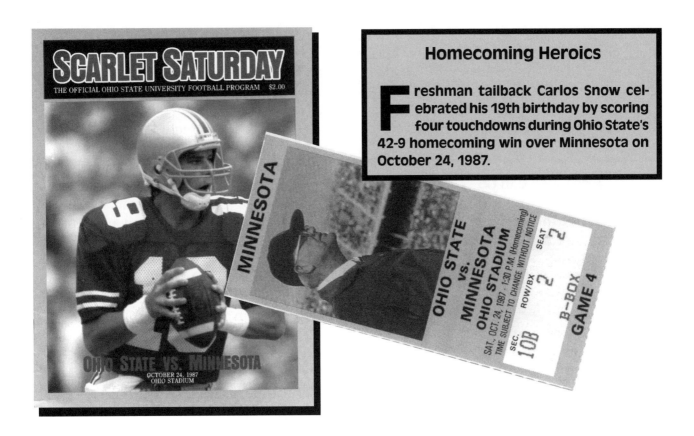

Offense at a Standstill

Fifteen seconds into their October 31 clash with Michigan State, the Buckeyes were celebrating a 7-0 lead, following a well-executed 79-yard scoring pass from quarterback Tom Tupa to split end Everett Ross. The rest of the sunny afternoon belonged to the Spartans, who won more decisively than suggested by the game's 13-7 final score. A puzzled Ohio Stadium crowd of 89,915 watched Ohio State run just 49 plays from scrimmage, make just six first downs, and be held to a meager two yards rushing—the lowest team total since a minus-22 at Michigan State in 1965.

The scoring all took place in the first half. In the first quarter, MSU free safety Todd Krumm returned a punt 27 yards and intercepted a Tupa pass at the OSU 36 to set up the Spartans' lone touchdown and first of two field goals. The Michigan State defense recorded nine sacks, five by nose guard Travis Davis, a sophomore from Harding High School in Warren, Ohio, who was not strongly recruited by OSU even though he had always wanted to play for the Buckeyes. After the 79-yard scoring pass to Ross, the Buckeyes generated only 68 additional yards of offense the rest of the afternoon.

Six Second-Half Turnovers

The following week's outcome at Wisconsin was even more embarrassing. Ohio State committed seven turnovers, six in the second half, and lost to the 18-point underdog Badgers, 26-24, after leading 24-13 at the half. Wisconsin had been winless in five previous Big Ten games. A missed 22-yard field-goal attempt in the fourth quarter would have provided Ohio State with a one-point victory, but the score should not have been so close that a single play could have determined the outcome. OSU was scoreless in the third and fourth quarters for the second straight week.

After recording just six first downs and 147 yards against Michigan State, Ohio State was good for 27 first downs and 512 yards against the Badgers. But few teams will win after committing seven turnovers. Chris Spielman told the media, "We're in a state of shock. It's hard to face, it's kind of embarrassing. It's the lowest point of my OSU career." Ohio State was now 5-3-1 overall and 3-3 in the conference.

What Else Can Go Wrong?

The Buckeyes met Iowa the following week in the season's final home game. It was a gorgeous Saturday afternoon for college football, and Ohio State appeared to have everything going its way with a 14-3 lead early in the second quarter. Tom Tupa had teamed with Everett Ross for two touchdowns, a 24-yarder in the first quarter and a 60-yard bomb midway through the second period. But the Hawkeyes retaliated with Ronnie Harmon's 50-yard touchdown run and two Rob Houghtlin field goals to snatch the lead at halftime, 15-14.

Freshman tight end Jeff Ellis scored his first collegiate touchdown on a 20-yard toss

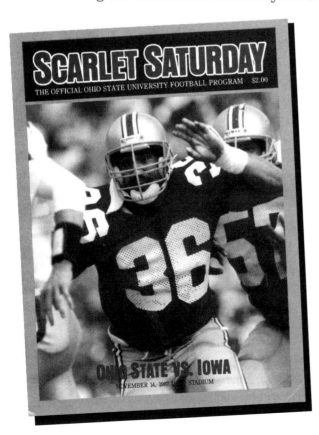

from Tupa to put OSU back on top, 21-15, midway through the third quarter. But the Hawkeyes regained the lead, 22-21, with David Hudson's one-yard dive at the 9:11 mark of the final period. On Ohio State's next possession, Tupa directed an excellent 75-yard scoring drive to regain the lead, 27-22. The Buckeyes converted two third-down plays and another on fourth down to keep the drive alive. Carlos Snow darted the final 14 yards off right tackle, and most of the 90,090 fans were delirious. There was 2:45 remaining in the game.

Using the clock effectively, Iowa moved to a first down at the Ohio State 15-yard line in the stadium's north end. On first down, Eric Kumerow sacked Hawkeye quarterback Chuck Hartleib for an eight-yard loss. Kumerow tripped Hartleib five yards behind the line of scrimmage on second down, and it was now third-and-23. Roverback Ray Jackson blitzed on third down, causing Hartleib to throw wildly, and suddenly the Hawkeyes' last hope rested on a fourth-and-23 from the Ohio State 28-yard line.

Iowa did the impossible! Tight end Marv Cook veered to the right sideline, caught Hartleib's throw at the 10-yard line, then cut to the inside and powered his way into the end zone. There were six seconds remaining. Three different defenders had shots at the big receiver, but simply were unable to stop him. Iowa won, 29-27.

It was the third consecutive loss for the Buckeyes, whose record fell to 5-4-1, 3-4 in the conference. Earle Bruce told reporters, "I just don't quite understand how we can lose like we lose, but we keep doing it." Not since 1966 had Ohio State lost as many as four Big Ten games. Iowa coach Hayden Fry told the press, "I've been associated with a lot of football games in the last 36 years and I don't think I've had a more meaningful victory."

It was rumored in the press box that Athletic Director Rick Bay was on the telephone with Holiday Bowl officials late in the fourth

Athletic Director Rick Bay offers encouragement to Mark Pelini (48), Zack Dumas (21), Mike Giesler (6) and William White (37) during warm-ups before the Iowa game on November 14. Bay resigned two days later in protest of Earle Bruce's dismissal.

quarter, ready to accept a bowl bid immediately after the game. But when Cook scored for Iowa with six seconds remaining, the Holiday Bowl withdrew its intended invitation. The Buckeyes were now 5-4-1, and would need a win at Michigan the following Saturday to salvage a winning season.

Not Your Normal "Beat Michigan" Week

The emotions stirred by Saturday's loss to Iowa were mild compared with the aftershock of the following Monday afternoon's bombshell. President Edward Jennings informed Athletic Director Rick Bay that Earle Bruce's contract was being terminated, and that an announcement would need to be made sometime after Saturday's game at Michigan. Bay, who in January had helped persuade Bruce to turn down Arizona's offer, immediately resigned in protest of Bruce's release.

Rumors had circulated all weekend, particularly on radio talkshows, that Bruce's fu-

ture was in doubt. In addition to disagreeing with Bruce's removal, Bay doubted that the decision could be kept quiet for the remainder of the week. Contrary to Jennings' directions, Bay immediately called a press conference, and by 4:00 p.m. on Monday, November 16, 1987, the entire world knew that Saturday's game at Michigan would be Earle Bruce's last at Ohio State.

Bay told reporters he was disappointed with the decision because he felt Bruce's football program exhibited both excellence and integrity. "It's a shame—it's a dark day for

November 14

Iowa's dramatic 29-27 victory at Ohio Stadium came on November 14. The Hawkeyes had not won at Ohio Stadium since defeating the Buckeyes, 16-7, exactly 28 years earlier on November 14, 1959.

Jennings and Bay Halftime Guests

Ohio State President Edward Jennings and Athletic Director Rick Bay were both interviewed at halftime by veteran Iowa broadcaster Jim Zabel over radio station WHO in Des Moines. Both guests talked about the excitement generated by the first half of play, and how well everything was functioning within OSU's Athletic Department. Just two days later the two would become central figures in the surprise announcement of Earle Bruce's departure.

Ohio State," he said. Jennings did not attend the conference, but instead had a statement read announcing the decision. The statement gave no reason for the dismissal. The next day Jennings explained that reasons for the action could not be disclosed because "it was a personnel issue and we cannot discuss personnel."

Many Ohio State fans, even those who were not solid Earle Bruce supporters, felt the manner in which the 56-year old coach was released left much to be desired. With the president's statement providing no reason for Bruce's removal, a *Columbus Dispatch* columnist predicted that the president would not soon show up in "Profiles in Courage."

First Things First

While most of the radio, television, and newspaper coverage the week of the "big game" centered around the coach's dismissal, including speculation on his successor, Bruce and his players and staff did their best to focus on the Michigan Wolverines. Neither team was in contention for the league championship. The Wolverines entered the game at 7-3 overall, 5-2 in conference play, while OSU, at 5-4-1, was 3-4 in the league. Michigan State was already assured of the outright Big Ten title.

The Ohio State players were very confused early in the week, but by Thursday were able to better concentrate on the game. They entered Michigan Stadium on Saturday wearing white headbands with the inscription "Earle" in support of their coach. The Wolverines built up a 13-0 lead midway through the second quarter, and it could have been worse. With just under six minutes remaining until halftime, OSU defensive tackle Ray Holliman forced fullback Jerrod Bunch to fumble and outside linebacker Mike McCray recovered at the OSU 39.

Tom Tupa led his team 61 yards to its first score of the afternoon, a four-yard toss to Everett Ross, and the Buckeyes had narrowed the gap to 13-7 after the first 30 minutes of play. At this point, Michigan had outgained Ohio State, 283 yards to 91.

Defense Keys Comeback

The Wolverines received the second-half kickoff, but were soon forced to punt after Chris Spielman sacked quarterback Demetrius Brown for a nine-yard loss on a third-and-eight at the OSU 49-yard line. On first down at the UM 30, Tupa tossed a short pass in the left flat to Carlos Snow, who cut behind Ross' block and sped 70 yards down the east sideline for the touchdown. Matt Frantz's extra point gave the Buckeyes their first lead of the afternoon, 14-13.

Two possessions later OSU's David Brown intercepted Demetrius Brown's pass near midfield and returned the ball all the way to the Michigan 19-yard line. Three plays later, Tupa sneaked into the end zone from the one, and the Buckeyes led, 20-13. Frantz missed the conversion attempt, breaking his string of successful kicks at 52. On its next possession, OSU lost a fumble at its own 46, setting up a Michigan scoring drive that tied the game, 20-20, with 1:14 to play in the third period.

The Wolverines appeared to get a huge break on the ensuing kickoff, when UM's

Buckeye players show support for their coach prior to the Ohio State-Michigan game.

Sean LaFountaine recovered an unintentional onside kick at the OSU 45-yard line. But tackle Mike Showalter sacked Brown for a nine-yard loss on a third-and-nine, forcing Michigan to give up possession of the football.

Midway through the final quarter, the Buckeyes marched 77 yards, setting up a 26-yard field goal by Frantz to win the game, 23-20. One of the drive's biggest plays was a 19-yard completion from freshman quarterback Greg Frey to Vince Workman, on a third-and-nine at the Michigan 37. Tupa had been forced to the sideline after being shaken up on the previous down. It was Frey's only play of the afternoon. On UM's ensuing possession, Eric Kumerow recovered Leroy Hoard's fumble at the OSU 47-yard line. Ohio State drove to the UM two before giving up possession with just nine seconds to play. The Buckeye defense had held the Wolverines to 88 yards in the second half.

THE PLAIN DEALER

SPORTS

NBA,MISL,NHL/12
For the record/14
On the outdoors/16

D

SUNDAY, NOVEMBER 22, 1987

Bruce triumphs in his OSU finale

It was an extremely gratifying victory for Earle Bruce, who concluded his stay in Columbus with a record of 81-26-1, best in the Big Ten during his nine Ohio State seasons. Bruce was 5-4 against Michigan and 5-3 in postseason bowls. After the game he told the press, "I had a knot in my stomach all week. But I'm a professional. I'll get a job, I have confidence in that. I'm a good football coach. We teach our players that when they get knocked down, they have to get up and go again . . . . I guess this was the ultimate test for me." Enough said.

Ohio State finished the season at 6-4-1. An invitation to play in the Sun Bowl was declined. Tom Tupa punted 63 times for a 47-yard average and was chosen an All-American. Chris Spielman repeated as an All-American and won the Lombardi Award as the nation's most outstanding lineman.

Placekicker Matt Frantz.

Matt Frantz is hoisted by Joe Staysniak (79) after kicking the winning field goal at Michigan in Earle Bruce's final Ohio State game. Joining the celebration are Greg Zackeroff (51), Scott Powell (13), and Tim Moxley (74). The field goal had not yet been posted to the scoreboard.

1987			
September 12	West Virginia	W	24	3
September 19	Oregon	W	24	14
September 26	at Louisiana State	T	13	13
October 3	at Illinois	W	10	6
October 10	Indiana	L	10	31
October 17	at Purdue	W	20	17
October 24	Minnesota (HC)	W	42	9
October 31	Michigan State	L	7	13
November 7	at Wisconsin	L	24	26
November 14	Iowa	L	27	29
November 21	at Michigan	W	23	20
Total Points			224	181

Season Record: 6-4-1
Conference: 5th Place

COOPER TAKES CONTROL

The 1988 season brought a new chapter to Ohio State football—the John Cooper era. Cooper was one of seven finalists interviewed for the position. The other six were Jack Bicknell of Boston College, George Chaump of Marshall, Willie Jeffries of Howard, Glen Mason of Kent State, Don Nehlen of West Virginia, and former Cleveland Browns coach Sam Rutigliano. Chaump and Mason had also been assistant coaches at Ohio State.

The 50-year-old Cooper, a native of Clinton, Tennessee, played college football at Iowa State, where his senior season he was both the team captain and its most valuable player. After 15 seasons as an assistant coach at Iowa State, Oregon State, UCLA, Kansas, and Kentucky, Cooper began an eight-year reign as head coach at Tulsa from 1977 through 1984. Tulsa won the Missouri Valley Conference league championship each of his last five seasons.

Cooper moved to Arizona State in 1985 where he became an immediate success by compiling a three-year record of 25-9-2. His finest hour was taking the 1986 Sun Devils to their first Rose Bowl, a 22-15 victory over the Michigan Wolverines on January 1, 1987. That season Cooper was a near unanimous choice as college football's Coach of the Year.

John Cooper's 1987 squad completed its 7-4-1 season with a 33-28 Freedom Bowl triumph over Air Force on Wednesday evening, December 30, in Anaheim, California. Cooper immediately flew to Columbus that night to be presented at a December 31 news conference as Ohio State's 21st head coach.

1988

Cooper inherited 13 starters and 45 lettermen from a team that finished 6-4-1 the prior year. The squad possessed one of the finest collections of running backs at Ohio State in many seasons, including tailbacks Vince Workman and Carlos Snow. Defense

John and Helen Cooper meet with reporters when John is introduced as Ohio State's new head coach on December 31, 1987.

was a different story—only five starters were back, and there was a severe lack of depth at many positions. The kicking game was another major concern. Tom Tupa, the nation's leading punter in '87 with a 47.0 average, and placekicker Matt Frantz, the team's top scorer with 56 points, both had to be replaced.

Near-Perfect Opener

The '88 Buckeyes opened September 10 with an exciting nationally televised 26-9 victory over Syracuse. The attendance of 89,768 was, at the time, the largest opening day crowd in Ohio Stadium history. The Orangemen entered the game with the nation's longest undefeated streak at 14. The Buckeyes did not have a penalty or commit a turnover for the first time in 27 seasons.

Sophomore Greg Frey was impressive in his first start at quarterback, completing 12 of 17 passes for 141 yards with no interceptions. After spotting Syracuse a 3-0 first-quarter advantage, Ohio State came back to lead 17-6 at the half and 23-6 after three quarters. Pat O'Morrow's 27-yard field goal, a 14-yard touchdown sprint by tailback Carlos Snow, and a two-yard touchdown toss from Frey to tight end Jeff Ellis accounted for the 17 second-quarter points.

O'Morrow added three more field goals of 33, 41, and 30 yards in the second half. His total of four three-pointers was just one short of the school single-game record of five set by Bob Atha against Indiana in 1981. Fullback Bill Matlock was Ohio State's leading rusher with 67 yards in 13 carries.

The following Saturday's night game at Pittsburgh was a complete contrast with the opener. Before an overflow Pitt Stadium crowd of 56,500, the Panthers humiliated the 18th-ranked Buckeyes, 42-10. If anything, the game was even more one-sided than suggested by the final score. Pittsburgh led 42-3 before Carlos Snow returned a kickoff 100 yards for Ohio State's only touchdown.

Panther quarterback Darnell Dickerson and tailback Adam Walker put on quite a show at the expense of the Buckeye defense. Pitt led in first downs, 29-11; total offensive yards, 504-233; and time of possession, 38:31-21:29. OSU lost two fumbles, suffered one interception, and was penalized seven times for 75 yards.

OSU's versatility beats Syracuse

Cleveland Plain Dealer, Sunday, September 11, 1988

Additionally, senior tailback Vince Workman was released from the team the following Wednesday after admitting he had accepted money from an agent.

The Cooper era begins as John Cooper talks with a television reporter while his squad takes the field for the season opener against Syracuse. Leading the charge are Gary Lickovitch (86), Srecko Zizakovic (96), Tim Moxley (74), Greg Frey (15), Bill Matlock (11), and Greg Zackeroff (51).

Ohio State's dramatic rally beats LSU

Cleveland Plain Dealer, Sunday, September 25, 1988

One of Ohio Stadium's Most Dramatic Finishes

The '88 season was quickly becoming one of the most inconsistent in school history. After a near-perfect season opener and a huge loss the second week, Ohio State returned home September 24 to face Louisiana State. It was the first appearance in Ohio Stadium by a Southeast Conference team since the Buckeyes defeated Kentucky 19-6 on October 5, 1935.

LSU scored its last touchdown at the 4:24 mark of the fourth quarter, and held what appeared to be an insurmountable lead of 33-20. Many of the rain-soaked crowd of 90,584 began heading for the exits. But the Buckeyes amazed even their most optimistic supporters with two touchdowns and a

safety in a span of just one minute and 18 seconds to upset the Tigers, 36-33.

Carlos Snow scored from five yards out to bring OSU within six at 33-27 with 1:56 left in the game. With two time-outs remaining, Cooper decided to kick off deep rather than attempt an on-side kick. The strategy really worked. On LSU's next series, the Buckeyes called a time-out to stop the clock immediately after the Tigers ran the ball on their first two downs. On third down, LSU threw a long pass that fell incomplete and again the clock stopped. Punter Rene Bourgeois intentionally took a safety by running out of the end zone, and the gap was narrowed to 33-29 with 1:34 remaining. LSU's possession had consumed only 22 seconds.

Bourgeois' free kick was taken by Bobby Olive at the OSU 32-yard line and returned 30 yards to the LSU 38. With Workman's departure from the team, Olive was returning punts for the first time in his career. Four plays later   Olive scored the winning touchdown with a diving catch of a 20-yard pass from Greg Frey, and (with 38 seconds remaining) OSU had accomplished what seemed to be the impossible.

The scoring play (called "confirm 63 Y bench") was a simple post pattern toward the center of the field. Greg Frey played extremely well, completing 24 passes (to seven different receivers) for 281 yards, and Snow was the game's leading rusher with 90 yards. Louisiana State began the afternoon having been victorious in its last 14 road games.

Poorest Conference Start in 45 Seasons

The up-and-down Buckeyes were soundly beaten in their October 1 conference opener against Illinois, 31-12. Ironically,

Beating Michigan a Family Tradition

Quarterback Jeff VanRaaphorst passed for two touchdowns to lead John Cooper's Arizona State Sun Devils to its 22-15 win over Michigan in the January 1, 1987, Rose Bowl. Jeff's father, Dick VanRaaphorst, was Ohio State's excellent placekicker from 1961-63. The Buckeyes defeated the Wolverines each of those three years.

Ohio State entered the game as a 14-point favorite. In spite of two fumbles, an interception, seven penalties, and several mental mistakes, OSU trailed only 10-6 entering the fourth quarter. Illini quarterback Jeff George was hard on the Buckeye defense with 18 connections for 224 yards.

John Cooper was anything but happy with his team's showing before an Ohio Stadium crowd of 90,724, and pointed to the inability to control the line of scrimmage as a major factor in the outcome. Illinois coach John Mackovic was in a much better mood as he celebrated his 45th birthday that afternoon. Tailbacks Carlos Snow and Marc Hicks and defensive tackle Mike Showalter all missed the game with injuries. It was Illinois' most one-sided win over Ohio State since defeating the Buckeyes 41-20 in 1953.

Matters got worse at Indiana the next week, where the poised and confident Hoosiers pounded the Buckeyes, 41-7. IU tailback Anthony Thompson splintered the Scarlet and Gray defense with 192 yards and the game's first four touchdowns. Coach Bill Mallory was in his fifth season with the Hoosiers, and at one point his team led 35-0 after scoring on its first five possessions of the afternoon.

The Buckeyes had been outplayed at the line of scrimmage on both sides of the ball. They had given up 147 points in their last four outings, the most ever surrendered by

Ohio State in four consecutive games. It was OSU's first setback at Indiana since losing 8-0 in 1904. It also was Ohio State's largest margin of defeat since falling to Purdue 41-6 in 1967.

At the October 15 homecoming game against Purdue, the Buckeyes appeared to have gotten back on track after taking a 20-7 lead early in the third period. But the then-largest crowd in Ohio Stadium history (90,970) watched in disappointment as the Boilermakers scored 24 points in the game's final 22 minutes to win, 31-26. It was Purdue's first victory in Columbus since 1967.

Boilermaker quarterback Brian Fox, a 17-year-old freshman, engineered the upset with 19 completions for 223 yards and three touchdowns. Fox was particularly effective connecting with fullback Ernie Schramayr, who was repeatedly open slipping out of the backfield. Fox and Schramayr were playing because first-teamers Shawn McCarthy and Scott Nelson were out with injuries.

One bright spot for OSU was the play of a healthy Carlos Snow, who ran for 128 yards including a 58-yard scoring sprint for the game's first touchdown. Ohio State was now 2-4 on the season, and had lost its first three conference games for the first time since 1943.

'68 National Champs Honor Their Coach at 20th Reunion

Sixty members of Ohio State's 1968 national champions were honored during halftime of the homecoming game against Purdue. During the ceremony they presented their university with a $1.2 million endowment for athletic scholarships, which they had raised as a tribute to their coach, Woody Hayes. It is believed to be the largest amount ever gathered by a single college football team.

Victory at Last

John Cooper enjoyed his first conference victory when his Buckeyes held off Minnesota, 13-6, in a Saturday night meeting at the Metrodome in Minneapolis. Ironically, it was the Ohio State defense (which had surrendered 178 points in its last five games) that made the difference. With his team trailing, 13-6, Golden Gopher quarterback Scott Schaffner scrambled 14 yards for a first down at the OSU one-yard line with just 2:28 remaining.

On first and second downs, Minnesota's fine tailback Darrell Thompson was halted for no gain by Buckeye linebacker Orlando Craig. Safety David Brown blitzed on third down and spilled Schaffner for a ten-yard loss. On fourth-and-eleven Schaffner threw a pass incomplete into the end zone, and the Ohio State defense had risen to the occasion. Pat O'Morrow booted field goals of 25 and 20 yards, and Carlos Snow scored from 27 yards out on the first play of the second quarter to account for OSU's only touchdown.

At East Lansing October 29, the Buckeyes let one slip away in a 20-10 loss to Michigan State. With the game tied 10-10 at halftime, Ohio State self-destructed by turning the ball over to the Spartans on their first three possessions of the second half. First, Spartan linebacker Kurt Larson intercepted Greg Frey's intended option pitch to tailback Marc Hicks at the MSU eight to stop what otherwise could have been the Buckeyes' first lead of the game. The next two turnovers, both fumbles, led directly to Michigan State's ten third-quarter points.

A Win Is a Win

At home the following weekend, the weather was rainy, windy, and dreary, but it didn't prevent Ohio State from scoring in each quarter to register a much-needed victory over Wisconsin, 34-12. Quarterback Greg Frey helped account for three second-quarter touchdowns with a one-yard carry, and scoring tosses of 21-yards to Marc Hicks and 13-yards to Jeff Graham. The Buckeyes' season record now stood at 4-5 with two games remaining.

Playing in cold and rainy weather for the second consecutive Saturday, Ohio State and Iowa settled for a 24-24 tie at Iowa City on November 12. For the Hawkeyes, who managed only three points in the game's final 41 minutes after leading 21-7 early in the second period, it was their third tie of the season.

The Buckeyes fought back and finally took their first lead of the afternoon, 24-21, on Pat O'Morrow's 39-yard field goal with 8:21 remaining in the fourth quarter. Late in the game the Buckeyes elected to punt on a fourth-and-two-inches situation at the OSU

40-yard line. Iowa took possession at its own 39 and quickly moved to the OSU 23-yard line, where (with 16 seconds remaining) placekicker Jeff Skillett booted a 40-yard field goal on fourth down to tie the game. Hawkeye fans loudly voiced their disapproval of the play, pleading instead for their team to go for the win. Skillett had missed three previous attempts from 32, 31, and 46 yards.

Ohio State's record now stood at 4-5-1 with only the Michigan game remaining. The Buckeyes were now unable to avoid their first non-winning season since going 4-5 in 1966.

Second-Half Effort
Extremely Impressive

The Michigan Wolverines were assured of at least a share of the Big Ten title and the Rose Bowl trip, when they entered Ohio Stadium on November 19. If Ohio State defeated Michigan and Michigan State defeated Wisconsin, the Wolverines would be forced to share the crown with the Spartans. But Michigan would still be headed to Pasadena, having defeated the Spartans 17-3 on October 8.

In one of the most exciting finishes in the history of the series, the Wolverines grabbed sole possession of the title after holding off Ohio State, 34-31. The two halves were completely different games. Michigan immediately took charge and led 20-0 at half-time—even the most ardent Buckeye fans gave their team little chance of coming back. Heavily favored Michigan had 313 yards of total offense in the first two quarters compared with just 116 for OSU.

In one of the most amazing turnarounds possible, Ohio State scored on its first five second-half possessions, and twice took the lead before losing by three points. OSU drove 70 yards for its first touchdown (4-yard dash by Carlos Snow) and 66 yards for its second (9-yard run over right guard by fullback Bill Matlock). Next, the Buckeyes drove 90 yards with Greg Frey passing 14 yards to Bobby Olive for a third score. Pat O'Morrow's third

Quarterback Greg Frey directs the Buckeye offense against the Wisconsin Badgers.

conversion gave Ohio State its first lead of the afternoon, 21-20.

Critical Missed Opportunity

The Buckeye offense was ripping through Michigan's defense as no team had done all season. On the Wolverines' next possession, OSU nose guard Pat Thomas forced tailback Tony Boles to fumble and linebacker Mike Sullivan recovered at the UM 22-yard line. The Buckeyes ran five plays before settling for a 21-yard field goal by O'Morrow to up their lead to 24-20. In the end this was a crucial series. Ohio State had a first down at the three-yard line but was unable to put the ball in the end zone.

Michigan retaliated with a 76-yard scoring drive to regain the lead at 27-24, but the

Highest Combined
Score in 27 Seasons

Michigan's 34-31 victory in 1988 produced the highest combined score in the Ohio State-Michigan series since 1961, when Ohio State defeated the Wolverines 50-20.

determined Buckeyes marched 92 yards to go back on top, 31-27, with 2:02 left in the game. Bill Matlock, who was unstoppable in the second half, scored his second touchdown of the day right up the middle from 16 yards out.

For the resilient Wolverines, it was now or never. Wide receiver John Kolesar, a senior from Westlake, Ohio, gave his team excellent field position with a 59-yard kickoff

return to the OSU 41-yard line. Two plays later, Kolesar hauled in a 41-yard scoring pass from quarterback Demetrious Brown for the winning score. It was unbelievable.

Starting at their own 29-yard line with 1:36 remaining Ohio State began its sixth drive of the second half, but Michigan intercepted at the UM 39 with just 29 seconds on the clock and the game was over. The two rivals combined for 968 yards of total offense—Michigan had 499, Ohio State 469. Each team had 24 first downs. Michigan's 34 points were the most the Wolverines had scored against OSU since defeating the Buckeyes in 1946, 58-6.

Ohio State finished the year at 4-6-1 and did not participate in a postseason bowl for the second consecutive year. The Buckeyes scored 229 points (20.8 per game average) but the opposition scored 283 for an average of 25.7 points per game—the highest opponent scoring average in modern Ohio State history. John Cooper had suffered through just his second losing season as a head coach. His first Tulsa squad went 3-8 in 1977. Center Jeff Uhlenhake was selected as an All-American and was also chosen the team MVP.

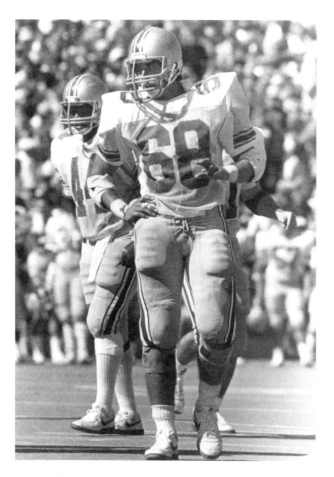

All-American center Jeff Uhlenhake.

1988

Date	Opponent			
September 10	Syracuse	W	26	9
September 17	at Pittsburgh	L	10	42
September 24	Louisiana State	W	36	33
October 1	Illinois	L	12	31
October 8	at Indiana	L	7	41
October 15	Purdue (HC)	L	26	31
October 22	at Minnesota	W	13	6
October 29	at Michigan State	L	10	20
November 5	Wisconsin	W	34	12
November 12	at Iowa	T	24	24
November 19	Michigan	L	31	34
Total Points			229	283

Season Record: 4-6-1
Conference: 7th Place

1989

Ohio State's highest priority as John Cooper prepared for his second season was to improve its defense. Cooper stated, "We have to be more aggressive and start forcing the issue. And we have to develop some depth." The second-year coach and his staff were also aware that the Buckeyes had not had consecutive losing seasons since 1923 and 1924. Eight starters returned on offense, seven were back on defense, and both kickers returned. Greater consistency was needed after a full season under Cooper's new system.

The 1989 season was Ohio State's 100th year of football. The Buckeyes fielded their first team in 1890, and several activites were scheduled for 1989 to commemorate this milestone.

Frey Highly Impressive in Opener
Ohio State opened September 16 with a convincing 37-13 victory over Oklahoma State in front of an Ohio Stadium crowd of 88,760. The Cowboys had lost their season-opener the previous Saturday at Tulsa. The Buckeyes outgained Oklahoma State 437 yards to 259, as quarterback Greg Frey completed 16 of 21 tosses for two touchdowns

and 285 yards, the highest of his career at that time. The defense got stronger as the game progressed and held the visitors to just 90 yards in the second half.

Ohio State led only 16-13 at halftime, then outscored the Cowboys 21-0 in the second half. Carlos Snow scored twice with runs of 20 and two yards. Frey connected with eight different receivers, which included TD passes of 33 and 27 yards to Bernard Edwards and Bobby Olive, respectively. Pat Thomas, Steve Tovar, and Srecko Zizakovic each had nine tackles.

Deja Vu?
The Buckeyes opened their '88 season with an impressive 26-9 victory over Syracuse, then were outclassed the second week at Pittsburgh 42-10. The same pattern was developing in '89. Ohio State was shellacked 42-3 by Southern California at the Los Angeles Coliseum on September 23. After jumping out to a 3-0 first-quarter lead, OSU found it impossible to stop the Trojan stampede. It was Ohio State's most one-sided setback in

43 years, since falling to Michigan 58-6 in 1946.

USC red-shirt freshman quarterback Todd Marinovich threw for four touchdowns, including a school-record 87-yard strike to John Jackson on a third-and-two situation in the second quarter. USC surprised Ohio State by running the option from the I-formation with a three-receiver set, and the Buckeyes had great difficulty adjusting. The Trojans led in first downs, 23-14, and in total offensive yards, 491-223.

Both offenses dominated the next Saturday as Ohio State held off Boston College, 34-29, at Ohio Stadium. It was the first meeting between the two schools, and they combined for 1,107 yards of total offense—602 by OSU and 505 by BC. In the end it was the Buckeye defense that spelled the difference. With just 45 seconds remaining, linebacker Derek Isaman and tackle Mike Showalter stopped fullback Ed Toner in his tracks on a fourth-and-inches at the OSU four, and the Buckeyes could breath a little easier.

After advancing to an impressive 31-7 lead at intermission, the Bucks were outscored in the second half, 22-3. Greg Frey and Jeff Graham combined on an 80-yard touchdown pass on OSU's very first play from scrimmage. The pass was just six yards short of the school record 86-yard TD pass from Art Schlichter to Calvin Murray against Washington State on September 22, 1979.

For the first time since a 64-6 win over Utah on September 27, 1986, Ohio State had two backs each run for more than 100 yards. Fullback

Scottie Graham rambled for 151, including a 70-yard scoring dash down the left sideline right before the half. Tailback Carlos Snow added 147 yards—he scored twice with runs of 24 and 16 yards.

Turnovers and Defensive Deficiencies Mar Big Ten Opener

Illinois scored the game's last 17 points and upended Ohio State, 34-14, before a Memorial Stadium crowd of 69,088. Jeff Graham scored the Buckeyes' last points of the afternoon with a 66-yard punt return late in the third period. The TD brought OSU within three points of the Illini at 17-14 and appeared to provide the spark the Buckeyes needed. But four turnovers, seven penalties, and several defensive breakdowns (especially in the last quarter) were too much to overcome.

The game was played on new turf that had been quickly installed after vandals burned 50 yards of the old turf just 12 days before the start of the season. The Illini led in first downs, 28-10, and in total offensive yardage, 450-288.

Ground Attack Returns

At home on October 14, Ohio State relied primarily on its ground attack to outscore Indiana, 35-31, and break a two-

Tailback Carlos Snow powers into the end zone for one of his two touchdowns against Purdue.

game losing streak to the Hoosiers. IU held a wide margin in the statistical battle, leading in first downs, 28-17, and total offensive yards, 444-290. The Hoosiers did not punt all afternoon.

Greg Frey passed only six times, completing five for 37 yards, but two of his completions were short TD tosses to Jim Palmer (two yards and four yards). The offensive line continued to show improvement as Scottie Graham (124 yards) and Carlos Snow (136 yards) each topped the century mark. Hoosier tailback Anthony Thompson rushed for 177 yards and three of IU's four touchdowns, running his career scoring total to 352 points—a new Big Ten record. The previous conference record of 348 points was established by Ohio State's Pete Johnson from 1973 through 1976.

Late in the final period and deep in their own territory, the Buckeyes decided to take an intentional safety (to make the score 35-31), then free kick the ball to Indiana. Jeff Bohlman's punt from his own 20-yard line hit at the IU 30 near the sideline and rolled to the 16, where OSU's Vinnie Clark grabbed the ball and ran out of bounds with 1:33 remaining. The Hoosiers, apparently not realizing the free kick can be recovered by either team, had let the ball roll. Ohio State had evened its conference record at 1-1 and upped its overall record to 3-2.

The Buckeyes stuck with their ground attack to defeat Purdue, 21-3, in blustery Ohio Stadium, before an October 21 homecoming crowd of 89,091. In what resembled one of Woody Hayes' run-oriented game plans, Ohio State rolled up 371 yards on the ground while completing just four passes for 57 yards. Purdue had also been OSU's homecoming opponent the previous season, when the Boilermakers won 31-26 to hand Ohio State its first homecoming defeat since losing to Illinois, 17-13, in 1967.

OSU jumped out to a 14-0 first-quarter lead, and would have increased the lead to 28-0 at halftime had it not been for losing two fumbles near the Purdue end zone. Carlos Snow had another big afternoon with 149 yards and two TDs, followed by Scottie Graham with 94 yards and freshman tailback Dante Lee with 93.

Record rally
Buckeyes erase 31-0 deficit to win, 41-37

Cleveland Plain Dealer, Sunday, October 29, 1989

Minneapolis Madness

Ohio State's October 28 game at Minnesota became one of the greatest comebacks in all of college football. It also was a pivotal afternoon for John Cooper, whose Ohio State record was 8-8-1 entering the game. Before a crowd of just 33,945 (including many OSU fans) at the Minneapolis Metrodome, the Buckeyes rallied for an unbelievable 41-37 victory after trailing 31-0. Tailback Carlos Snow finally crossed the Golden Gopher goal line for OSU's first score just 10 seconds before halftime.

It's doubtful if Ohio State ever played a game with greater contrast between the first and second halves. While it might have been difficult to play any more poorly than the Buckeyes played in the first half, they scored on six of their last eight possessions and

Turnaround Record

Ohio State's 41-37 triumph at Minnesota, after trailing 31-0, tied what was then an NCAA record for the largest turnaround in a major college game. Maryland had rallied from a 31-0 deficit to defeat Miami (Fla.), 42-40, in 1984. The Buckeyes' previous high had been a 45-38 win over Illinois in 1984 after being behind 24-0.

outscored Minnesota, 41-6, in the game's final 30 minutes and 10 seconds.

Quarterback Greg Frey led the second-half comeback, passing for 362 yards and three touchdowns. His winning toss was a 15-yarder to flanker Jeff Graham with just 51 seconds remaining. It concluded a five-play 73-yard march that included a clutch 34-yard reception by tight end Jim Palmer on a second-and-23.

Ohio State tallied twice on fourth-down situations and made three two-point conversions. Carlos Snow accounted for 278 all-purpose yards and scored OSU's first three touchdowns.

Three Hit Century Mark

The Buckeyes continued to accentuate their ground attack while blasting winless Northwestern, 52-27, at windswept Dyche Stadium on November 4. For the first time since a 34-10 win over Duke on October 3, 1970, Ohio State had three backs each rush for 100 or more yards. Freshman tailback Dante Lee saw his first extended action and responded with 157 yards and three touchdowns, Scottie Graham plunged for 102 yards and a touchdown, and Carlos Snow added 100 yards and one TD.

Ohio State scored on eight of its nine possessions. Senior tailback Jaymes Bryant tallied twice on spectacular plays in the second period—first with a 63-yard sprint, followed by the reception of a 46-yard pass from Greg Frey. Unfortunately, Bryant broke his collarbone on the scoring reception and was lost for the remainder of the season.

First Shutout in 36 Games

In what was the Buckeyes' most impressive showing since John Cooper joined the Ohio State football program in 1988, OSU shut out Iowa 28-0 before a thrilled crowd of 89,536 at Ohio Stadium on November 11. It was the Buckeyes' first shutout in 36 games—their last was a 33-0 win over Minnesota on October 25, 1986. The shutout was very unexpected, since OSU's pass defense was rated last in the conference, and the Hawkeyes' passing offense was ranked first.

Ohio State effectively used a ball-control offense to score once in each quarter on drives of 40, 80, 87, and 79 yards. Freshman outside linebacker Alonzo Spellman had two tackles for losses, and he forced a Hawkeye fumble which set up OSU's first touchdown. Iowa coach Hayden Fry referred to the game as the most frustrating day in his 38 years of college coaching.

OSU defense stands out in shutout

Columbus Dispatch, Sunday, November 12, 1989

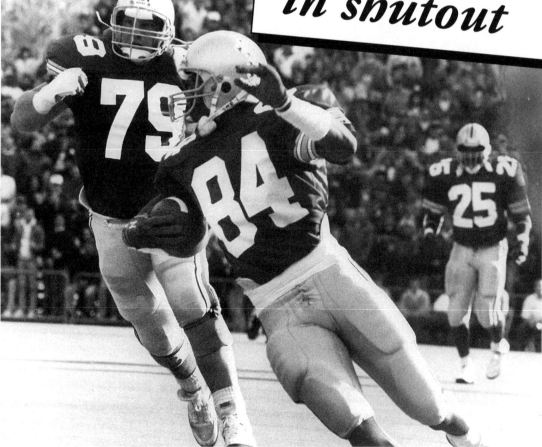

Split end Jeff Graham caught an eight-yard pass from Greg Frey for Ohio State's second touchdown against Iowa. Pictured with Graham are tackle Joe Staysniak (79) and tailback Carlos Snow (25).

Six in a Row

The Buckeyes, now ranked 22nd, ran their winning streak to six with a 42-22 victory over Wisconsin in frigid Ohio Stadium. The offense and defense both continued to improve, and the win gave OSU its first undefeated home season since 1984. With 458 yards of total offense, Ohio State topped the 400-yard mark for the fifth consecutive game. The Badgers managed 257 yards rushing but zero yards through the air. It was the first game in 13 seasons that an Ohio State opponent had failed to gain any yards passing.

Scottie Graham, running from both the fullback and tailback positions, had his best day as a Buckeye with 152 yards and OSU's last two touchdowns. Cornerback David Brown, one of 16 seniors playing their final home game, gave his team a 28-13 halftime lead by returning an interception 43 yards for a touchdown late in the second period. The Buckeyes were now 8-2 on the season and 6-1 in conference play, as they began thinking about the following week's clash at Michigan.

Big Ten Title Possible

What a contrast between entering the Michigan game this season compared with last year. Ohio State had no chance for a winning season in 1988, even with a win over the Wolverines, while this year the Buckeyes held a slim chance of playing in the Rose Bowl. Ohio State and Illinois were both 6-1 in the league standings behind Michigan at 7-0. An OSU win over the Wolverines would force a three-way tie for the league title, assuming Illinois defeated Northwestern the same afternoon the Buckeyes would have to defeat Michigan. If Ohio State beat Michigan, Northwestern (who had lost every game this season) would have to defeat the Fighting Illini for OSU to play in Pasadena.

After a slow start that saw Michigan take a 14-0 lead, Ohio State came to life to seriously challenge the Wolverines before los-

ing, 28-18. Like many other contests in this classic series, this one came right down to the end before a winner was assured. The Buckeyes drew close at 21-18 on Scottie Graham's three-yard touchdown run with 7:04 remaining in the game. Graham's TD concluded an impressive 11-play 80-yard march that consumed five minutes and 18 seconds.

Ohio State's defense held the Wolverines on their following possession, giving the ball back to the Buckeyes on their own 34 with 3:42 to go. On a second-and-twelve, Greg Frey's pass intended for Greg Beatty was intercepted by Wolverine defensive back Todd Plate at the UM 41-yard line. From there, Michigan drove for the game's final touchdown. Plate, a former walk-on who himself was a substitute, made a big difference for Michigan. He had one other interception, and he also broke up a would-be touchdown throw from Frey to Jeff Graham in the left corner of the end zone right before halftime.

The Buckeyes led in first downs, 25-22, and total offensive yardage, 420-410. The at-

U. S. Boxing Team

After winning three letters in 1985-86-87, linebacker Derek Isaman missed the 1988 season to try out for the U. S. Olympic Boxing Team. Isaman returned in 1989 and was selected the team's MVP.

tendance of 106,137 was, at the time, the fourth largest in Michigan Stadium history.

Ohio State returned to bowl competition with a January 1, 1990, matchup against heavily favored Auburn in the Hall of Fame Bowl. The Buckeyes dominated the first half and led 14-3 late in the second quarter, with a one-yard TD plunge by Carlos Snow and Greg Frey's scoring toss of nine yards to Brian Stablein. The Tigers changed the game's momentum with their first touchdown just 11 seconds before halftime to trail 14-10. Auburn dominated the second half, outscoring OSU 21-0 to finish with a 31-14 victory.

Ohio State made significant progress in 1989, and finished with an overall record of 8-4. John Cooper and his staff had turned an up-and-down program into a January 1 bowl participant in just two seasons. Tackle Joe Staysniak was selected an Academic All-American and linebacker Derek Isaman was chosen the team's most valuable player.

One Hundred and Counting

The 1989 season brought to a close the first 100 seasons of football at Ohio State. Over this first century, Ohio State won 626

games, lost 254, and tied 50, for a winning rate of 70.1 percent. The Buckeyes endured only 12 losing seasons, and four of those were between 1890 and 1898. Since joining the Big Ten in 1913, Ohio State won outright, or shared, 25 conference championships.

Ohio State was expected to make a serious run at the Big Ten Conference title, as John Cooper approached his third season in Columbus. The 37 returning lettermen included 11 starters, and a number of promising freshmen were expected to contribute. The offense was built around senior quarterback Greg Frey and junior fullback-tailback Scottie Graham. Frey had passed for more than 2,000 yards each of the last two seasons. The biggest concern was the interior offensive line, where the only returning starter was center Dan Beatty.

Tailback Carlos Snow, the Buckeyes' leading rusher the past two seasons, missed the entire 1990 season after having a benign tumor removed from his right hip in April. Snow's recovery was successful, and he came back for his senior season in 1991.

Improving the defense was still a major priority. Ohio State had surrendered 297 points over 12 games in '89, and 283 points over 11 games in '88. The '90 unit would be built around linebackers Steve Tovar and Judah Herman, linemen Alonzo Spellman and Rich Frimel, and backs Vinnie Clark, Mark Pelini, and Jimmy Peel.

Unimpressive Opener

The Buckeyes opened September 8 with a 17-10 victory over the Texas Tech Red Raiders, before 88,707 unmoved fans at Ohio Sta-

1989				
September 16	Oklahoma State	W	37	13
September 23	at Southern Cal	L	3	42
September 30	Boston College	W	34	29
October 7	at Illinois	L	14	34
October 14	Indiana	W	35	31
October 21	Purdue (HC)	W	21	3
October 28	at Minnesota	W	41	37
November 4	at Northwestern	W	52	27
November 11	Iowa	W	28	0
November 18	Wisconsin	W	42	22
November 25	at Michigan	L	18	28
January 1	Auburn*	L	14	31
Total Points			339	297

* Hall of Fame Bowl

Season Record: 8-4
Conference: 3rd Place (Tie)

Linebacker Judah Herman makes Ohio State's first interception of the season in the opener against Texas Tech. Other members of the defensive unit with Herman are Jim Peel (46), Steve Tovar (58), and Vinnie Clark (7).

dium. Cooper was grateful for the come-from-behind win, but was very disappointed with his team's five turnovers and overall sloppy play. Ohio State trailed 3-0 at halftime and 10-3 late in the third period.

One bright spot was the play of freshman tailback Robert Smith, who came off the bench to put some much needed spark into the attack. Smith accounted for 188 all-purpose yards, and tied the game at 10-10 late in the third period, scoring on a two-yard option pitch to the right corner of the end zone. Jeff Graham brought the fans to life early in the final quarter, when he fielded a punt and raced 50 yards untouched down the left sideline for the winning touchdown.

The Buckeye defense, led by linebacker Steve Tovar's 13 tackles, held the Red Raider offense to 230 yards including just 61 yards on the ground. After starting the game impressively with two quarterback sacks, outside linebacker John Kacherski incurred a season-ending knee injury in the second quarter. This was a major disappointment for Kacherski, who had been forced to sit out the entire '89 season with reconstructive knee surgery.

First Trip to New England

In the season's second game September 15, Ohio State defeated Boston College, 31-10, before an Alumni Stadium crowd of 32,432 in the Boston suburb of Chestnut Hill. This contest marked the Buckeyes' first ever appearance in New England. It also was the first time under Cooper that the Buckeyes started a season at 2-0.

OSU's bullish defense played a big part in the victory, holding BC to 244 yards including just 65 on the ground. The Eagles' lone touchdown resulted from Jay Clark's 24-yard interception return on the first play of the final quarter, which cut OSU's lead to 17-10.

Redshirt freshman Raymont Harris scored the Buckeyes' last two touchdowns, the first at the tailback position from nine yards out and the second from the fullback spot for 35 yards. Harris finished the day with 96 yards in 12 carries, and Robert Smith had another fine game, rushing for 102 yards in 17 attempts. Scottie Graham was forced to leave the game with a sprained ankle in the first half. Tim Williams' 52-yard field goal on the last play of the first half matched the fourth longest in school history.

Greg Fry's quarterback play was inconsistent, so the coaches went to junior Kent Graham in the second quarter. When Graham heaved his second interception of the day, the coaches went back to Fry. Bobby Olive scored OSU's other two touchdowns, the first on a 10-yard throw from Fry in the second period followed by a 21-yard pass from Graham early in the third quarter.

Ohio State was idle the following Saturday, September 22. It was the first time the Buckeyes had had an off-week in 17 seasons —they were idle September 22, 1973, after opening September 15 with a 56-7 win over Minnesota.

First Suspended Game

Southern California's visit to Ohio Stadium September 29 became the first game in modern OSU or USC history to end prior to the regulation 60 minutes of play. Because of a massive storm accompanied by lightning and thunder, the game was called with 2:36 still on the clock. The Trojans were ahead, 35-26, and that's how the game ended.

USC's patented ground attack (student-body left and right) was too much for the Buckeyes to handle. After holding its first

OSU makes it two in a row with 31-10 win

Columbus Dispatch, Sunday, September 16, 1990

two opponents to a combined 126 yards rushing, OSU gave up 331 yards on the ground and another 119 through the air. Trojan tailback Ricky Ervins did the bulk of the damage with 199 yards, including 164 in the first 30 minutes of play. An ankle sprain limited Ervins to just nine carries in the second half.

Down 14-0 after one quarter and 21-10 at halftime, the Buckeyes came back to outscore USC, 16-14, in the second half. Greg Fry completed 19 aerials for 262 yards and two touchdowns, but OSU could muster only 79 yards on the ground.

At the 2:38 mark of the final quarter, Raymont Harris plunged across from the one to complete a 10-play, 50-yard march to bring OSU within nine at 35-26. With fan and player safety on his mind, referee Ron Winter had already conferred with coaches John Cooper and Larry Smith about stopping the game. Cooper told Winter Ohio State would be attempting an onside kick on the ensuing kickoff, and it was agreed that if OSU did not recover the ball the game would be over. Trojan safety Bruce Luizzi smothered the onside kick, and the Buckeyes had suffered their first loss of the 1990 season.

Controversial Lateral Aids Fighting Illini

After outgaining Illinois in total yards, 487-407, Ohio State was unable to maintain a 17-10 halftime lead and lost its conference opener, 31-20. The Fighting Illini's final touchdown resulted from one of the most controversial plays in Ohio Stadium history.

John Cooper and son John, Jr., study game day action. The younger Cooper played football under his father at the University of Tulsa.

With Ohio State down 24-20 early in the final period, Tim Williams was attempting a 51-yard field goal. Linebacker Mel Agee blocked the kick, and defensive tackle Mike Poloskey scooped up the loose ball and headed for the Ohio State end zone. As Poloskey was falling down around the OSU 42-yard line, he tossed the ball to safety Quintin Parker, who raced the distance for a touchdown to put Illinois up, 31-20. Ohio State had only ten men on the field on the play, resulting in a penalty for not having seven players on the line of scrimmage—obviously, Illinois declined the penalty.

Poloskey's toss to Parker was clearly a forward lateral. Most of the Ohio Stadium crowd of 89,404 saw it that way including nearly everyone in the press box. But ref-eree John Nealon saw the play differ-ently and, after conferring with other officials near midfield, signaled "touch-down." Dave Perry, Big Ten supervi-sor of football officials, happened to be watching the game from the press box. When asked about the non-call, Perry stated, "It's just a judgment call, and there's no appeal on a judgment call." The touchdown stood.

In the end, the Buckeyes became their own worst enemy. Greg Frey was able to pass for 244 yards, but tossed three of his four interceptions in the game's final eight minutes. Ohio State also lost two fumbles. Tailback Raymont Harris ran for 118 yards, his first game going over the century mark.

Illini sophomore quarterback Ja-son Verduzco found OSU's zone de-fenses to his liking, passing for 258 yards and two touchdowns. Split end Shawn Wax caught eight of his tosses to account for 159 yards. For the third straight season, Ohio State had lost its conference opener to the Fighting Illini and was 2-2 after four games. Illinois had not beaten the Buckeyes three straight since 1927-28-29.

Matters were not much better the fol-lowing Saturday, October 13, at Bloomington, where Ohio State and Indiana played to a 27-27 tie. No one was happy with the out-come, and both teams lamented lost oppor-tunities that would have given their school the win. IU led 17-14 at halftime, but OSU took the lead for the first time with a beauti-fully executed 65-yard scoring pass from Greg Frey to Jeff Graham on the third play of the third quarter. Two field goals by Tim Will-iams of 29 and 27 yards later in the period upped the score to 27-17.

Indiana scored ten points in the final quarter for the tie, and would have won the contest if a three-yard touchdown plunge by

Cooper's "Razzle-Dazzle" Works to Perfection

John Cooper developed a play for flanker Jeff Graham to pass to quarterback Greg Frey off a reverse, which resulted in a 60-yard touchdown play at Purdue. Cooper got the idea after watching Graham catch punts in practice and pass the ball back to the punter. Graham had been a quarterback at Kettering Alter High School. For the two OSU seniors, it was Graham's first touchdown pass and Frey's first scoring reception of their college careers.

Vaughn Dunbar had not been nullified by a holding penalty. Dunbar finished the afternoon with 188 yards.

Ohio State ran just nine plays and gained only 13 yards in the fourth period. The Buckeyes were hurt when tight end Jeff Ellis suffered a sprained ankle early in the game. OSU was now 1-2-1 against coach Bill Mallory's Hoosiers the last four seasons.

Five in a Row

Ohio State was now 2-4-1 in its last seven games over two seasons, and Buckeye faithfuls were becoming noticeably impatient. Just when it was needed the most, OSU put together a five-game winning streak, outscoring those five opponents, 204-68. First was a 42-2 win at Purdue's homecoming on a gorgeous autumn afternoon in West Lafayette. The Boilermakers were at the bottom of the league standings, but this victory was nevertheless a good confidence builder for the Buckeyes. It was OSU's widest margin of victory since a 64-6 win over Utah on September 27, 1986.

Big scoring plays were the order of the day. Robert Smith tallied first on a 69-yard run. Jeff Graham and Greg Frey reversed their normal roles, with Graham lofting a scoring pass to Frey off a reverse—the play covered 60 yards. Graham also caught TD passes of 48 and 58 yards from Frey. The Buckeyes held Purdue to just four yards rushing and intercepted five Boilermaker passes.

Ohio State's 52-23 homecoming win over Minnesota the following weekend upped the Buckeyes' season record to 4-2-1. OSU scored on six of its first seven possessions and totaled 551 yards in total offense, highest of the season. The offense had 379 yards by halftime. The Buckeye coaches continued to be concerned, however, about the team's porous pass defense which allowed Minnesota quarterbacks Scott Schaffner and Marquel Fleetwood to combine for 307 yards.

Greg Frey effectively mixed up the play selection, and the offensive execution was

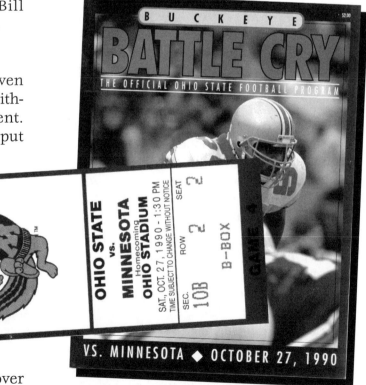

The Columbus Dispatch
Sunday
NOVEMBER 11, 1990 ■■■□

SECTION **E**

Sports

OSU upends Iowa with last–second TD

by far the best of the season. Frey had one of his finest games, completing 16 passes for 257 yards and three touchdowns, and scoring another on a quarterback sneak. John Cooper coached the game from the press box. Cooper was recovering from back surgery the previous Sunday for two ruptured disks.

The Buckeyes had no trouble at home November 3, defeating outmanned Northwestern, 48-7. Ohio State scored on eight of its ten possessions, using 11 different ball carriers and seven separate receivers. Five different players scored six touchdowns and Tim Williams contributed field goals of 26 and 35 yards. OSU led in first downs, 27-10; total offensive yards, 462-174; and time of possession, 37:11-22:49. The Wildcats' 174 yards were the fewest by a Buckeye opponent since 1984.

Thriller at Iowa Is No. 100 for Coop

Ohio State's 27-26 victory at Iowa on November 10 was one of the most thrilling in the Buckeye-Hawkeye series. It also was career victory No. 100 for coach John Cooper, and his 18th at Ohio State. Iowa entered the game ranked 6th in the country with a conference mark of 5-0, which included a 24-23 triumph three weeks earlier at Michigan to spoil the Wolverines' homecoming. The Hawkeyes were leading the Big Ten in both offense and defense.

Iowa took charge early and led 7-0 after one quarter, 17-14 at halftime, and 26-14 with just 11 minutes left in the final period. Quarterback Greg Frey then hit split end Bobby

Olive with a 21-yard touchdown strike and suddenly the score was 26-21.

Trailing by five points and with no time-outs remaining, Ohio State took possession at the Iowa 48-yard line with just 59 seconds to go. Greg Frey used the clock beautifully, passing his squad the 48 needed yards for the winning touchdown, which came on a three-yard scoring toss to Olive with just one second on the clock. It was Frey's third scoring pass of the afternoon.

Linebacker Steve Tovar had a career-high 14 tackles, and outside linebacker Jason Simmons added eight, including three for losses totaling 26 yards. Ohio State had now won four straight and had improved its season record to 6-2-1. The win over Iowa moved the Buckeyes into sole possession of second place in the Big Ten.

Things were a little easier the next week before a Camp Randall Stadium crowd of just 41,403, as OSU outscored Wisconsin 21-0 in the fourth quarter to defeat the Badgers, 35-10. Four Buckeye turnovers in the first half kept the score from being much more one-

Remembering Mom

Bobby Olive was presented the game ball after catching the winning touchdown pass at Iowa with just one second remaining. The game was played on November 10, 1991. Olive said he would give the ball to his mother, Patsy, since it was her birthday.

sided. Jeff Graham's 81-yard punt return for OSU's final touchdown tied for the third longest in school history.

The big story of the afternoon was freshman tailback Robert Smith, whose 171 rushing yards made him just the 26th freshman in NCAA history, and the 15th Ohio State player, to gain 1,000 or more yards in a single season. Smith now had 1,021 yards through ten games, breaking the Ohio State freshman record of 867 set by Archie Griffin in 1972.

Close But Not Close Enough

The Buckeyes were now 5-1-1 in conference play as they began preparation for their November 24 season-ending clash with the Michigan Wolverines. It was the first Ohio State-Michigan game since 1950 in which neither Woody Hayes nor Bo Schembechler was involved. Iowa was still on top of the conference at 6-1. Ohio State would earn a trip to the Rose Bowl if the Buckeyes beat Michigan and Iowa lost at Minnesota (the Golden Gophers were 4-3 in league play and 5-5 overall).

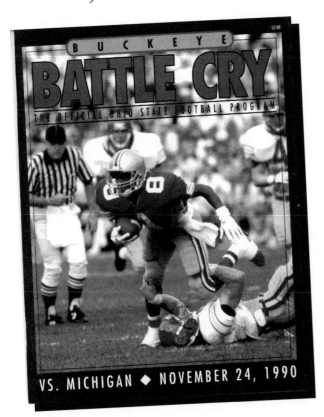

VS. MICHIGAN ◆ NOVEMBER 24, 1990

Minnesota did its part, upsetting the Hawkeyes, 31-24. But Ohio State was unable to hold a 13-6 lead over the Wolverines and lost, 16-13, when J. D. Carlson's 37-yard field goal with no time on the clock broke a 13-13 tie. Iowa, Michigan, Illinois, and Michigan State all tied for the league crown with 6-2 records. Ohio State finished next at 5-2-1. The Hawkeyes received the Rose Bowl nod, having defeated each of the other three co-champions during the season. Iowa lost the Rose Bowl to Washington, 46-34.

Michigan's possession, which led to its winning field goal, resulted from a play selection that would be debated by Ohio State fans long into the winter. With the game tied 13-13 late in the final quarter, Greg Frey passed 15 yards to Bobby Olive for an apparent first down at the UM 44-yard line—the Buckeyes seemed to be moving to at least a winning field-goal attempt. But OSU was called for clipping on the pass completion, and the ball was returned to the OSU 29-yard line for a third-and-one.

A plunge by Raymont Harris gained just a half-yard, and the Buckeyes used their last timeout at the 1:47 mark to decide what to do on fourth down. "Four base" was called, which is an option that was expected to work against any defensive front. Frey was to fake to fullback Scottie Graham up the middle, then peel down the line and either cut up field for the first down or pitch to tailback Butler By'not'e. Unfortunately, Michigan defenders Chris Hutchinson and T. J. Osman tackled Frey before he could do either, and

Even Steven

During the 60 Ohio State–Michigan games from 1931 through 1990, the Buckeyes and Wolverines each scored a total of 883 points. Michigan had a very slight edge in these 60 games, 29-28-3.

the Wolverines took over at the OSU 29. The rest is history!

This was a game the Buckeyes could have won, but three interceptions and eight penalties were simply too much to overcome. Ohio State had lost three straight to the Wolverines for the first time since Woody Hayes' last three seasons of 1976-77-78.

Cold Night in Memphis

After the close call against Michigan, the Buckeyes accepted a December 27 Liberty Bowl invitation to face the Air Force Academy. With players and fans both seeming to show little enthusiasm for the game, the Memphis Chamber of Commerce sent representatives to Columbus in December in an attempt to arouse more interest in the Liberty Bowl festivities.

The 24th-ranked Buckeyes were 17-point favorites over the Falcons, who entered the game at 6-5 and had given up 48 or more points three times during the season. It was a cold and rainy night in Memphis, and the actual crowd was probably closer to 25,000 than the announced 39,262. The Buckeyes were embarrassed by the Air Force, 23-11.

Offensive coordinator Jim Colletto had departed Columbus in December to become head coach at Purdue, and running backs coach Bobby Turner went with him. This may have had some effect on the Ohio State offense, which generated only 214 yards including only 80 on the ground. Greg Frey's third interception of the evening was returned 40 yards for a TD by Air Force cornerback Carlton McDonald to put the game out of reach. The Falcon's effective defense was led by linebacker Brian Hill, son of Ohio State trainer Billy Hill.

After generating a five-game winning streak and playing a very respectable game against Michigan, the Buckeyes finished 1990 on the downslide at 7-4-1. For the second straight season Ohio State did not have an All-American. Greg Frey passed for 2,062 yards to become the only player in school

history to pass for more than 2,000 yards three consecutive seasons. Flanker Jeff Graham was chosen the team MVP.

1990				
September 8	Texas Tech	W	17	10
September 15	at Boston College	W	31	10
September 29	Southern California	L	26	35
October 6	Illinois	L	20	31
October 13	at Indiana	T	27	27
October 20	at Purdue	W	42	2
October 27	Minnesota (HC)	W	52	23
November 3	Northwestern	W	48	7
November 10	at Iowa	W	27	26
November 17	at Wisconsin	W	35	10
November 24	Michigan	L	13	16
December 27	Air Force*	L	11	23
Total Points			349	220

* Liberty Bowl

Season Record: 7-4-1
Conference: 5th Place

1991

John Cooper's first three Ohio State teams had been much stronger offensively than defensively. Over the 35 games played from 1988 through 1990, the Buckeyes scored 917 points for a 26.2 per game average. But the defense surrendered exactly 800 points against those 35 opponents, for an average of 22.9 points per game. This was expected to change in 1991, since the bulk of the Buckeyes' returning strength was on the defensive side of the ball.

Tackles Alan Kline, Mick Shoaf, and Jason Winrow provided experience on the offensive line. Len Hartman, Rod Smith, and Dave Monnot (switched from defense) were the guards, and Paul Long took over at center. Brian Stablein and Bernard Edwards became starters at the wide receiver positions, and Cedric Saunders and Jeff Ellis split time at tight end.

In the backfield, fifth-year senior Kent Graham got the nod to replace three-year starter Greg Frey at quarterback, Scottie Graham returned as a three-year starter at fullback, and Carlos Snow and Butler By'not'e divided the tailback spot. Robert Smith, the previous season's winner of the Big Ten Freshman of the Year award at tailback, left the team two weeks prior to the season opener and did not play in 1991.

Greg Smith, Rich Frimel, and Alonzo Spellman all returned along the defensive front. John Kacherski, Mark Williams, Jason Simmons, and Andy Gurd handled the outside linebacker spots, and Steve Tovar and Judah Herman started at the inside positions. Foster Paulk, the only returner in the defensive secondary, was joined by Bryan Cook, Chico Nelson, and Roger Harper. Tim Williams handled both the punting and placekicking. With the addition of 5,000 new bleacher seats, several new Ohio Stadium single-game attendance records were established this season.

Off and Running

Ohio State opened at home September 7 with an impressive 38-14 triumph over the Arizona Wildcats. Kent Graham did well in his first start at quarterback, but it was the running of two sophomores—tailback Butler By'not'e and fullback Jeff Cothran—that sparked the offensive attack. By'not'e was the game's leading rusher with 189 yards, followed by Cothran with 105. By'not'e's total was the highest for an OSU running back since Keith Byars gained 274 against Illinois in 1984. OSU gained 325 of its total 449 yards on the ground.

The Buckeyes scored at least once in each quarter. By'not'e got the season's first touchdown with an 18-yard run, Cothran tallied on a 39-yard burst, Graham plunged over from the two, fullback Wil-

liam Houston scored twice from short range, and Tim Williams added a 26-yard field goal. Ohio State had possession of the football for nearly 39 of the game's 60 minutes.

The opener could also be described as a game of "big plays," with 279 of the Buckeyes' 449 total yards coming on just 11 separate downs, each of which was 15 yards or longer. The longest was a 57-yard sprint by By'not'e late in the first quarter, which set up William's field goal. Another key play was a 26-yard pass from Graham to Brian Stablein on a 3rd-and-17 in the third quarter, which set up Houston's first touchdown.

Ohio State's first-ever meeting with Louisville the following weekend was a different story. The Buckeyes were penalized 15 times for 118 yards, yet managed to emerge with a 23-15 victory. The Cardinals climbed back for a 16-0 deficit and, with the score 23-15, were in position to tie the game with just 54 seconds left to play. But the Louisville drive died at the OSU 12-yard line when a fourth down pass fell incomplete.

After Butler By'not'e's second touchdown of the afternoon put OSU on top early in the final period, 16-0, Cardinal tackle Leonard Ray blocked Tim Williams' extra point attempt, and safety Ray Buchanan returned the ball 80 yards for the visitors' first two points of the afternoon. Cardinal quarterback Eric Watts, a fifth-year senior making his first start, connected on 22 of 43 passes for 303 yards and both of his team's touchdowns.

Herbstreit Impressive in First Start

The Buckeyes looked much better as they patiently defeated Washington State, 33-19, at Ohio Stadium on September 21. Kirk Herbstreit was very effective running the offense in his first start at quarterback. Kent Graham sat out the game while still feeling the effects from a concussion and slightly separated left shoulder suffered the previous week against Louisville. Herbstreit was eight-of-14 for 158 yards, including a 39-yard option pass completion to Bernard Edwards for OSU's first touchdown less than four minutes into the game.

Ohio State was now 3-0 for the first time in six seasons. Carlos Snow, Butler By'not'e, and Scottie Graham collaborated for 270 of OSU's 321 yards rushing. WSU's aerial assault was directed by sophomore quarterback Drew Bledsoe, who connected 26 times for 287 yards and one touchdown. But Bledsoe was sacked nine times, six by outside linebacker Jason Simmons. Bledsoe's only interception of the afternoon was brought back 42 yards by safety Roger Harper for Ohio State's second touchdown.

Defense Comes Together

After a week off, John Cooper's 14th-ranked Buckeyes opened their conference schedule October 5 with a 31-16 win over Wisconsin, before what was then a record Ohio Stadium crowd of 94,221. The Buckeyes' strengths were running the football and preventing the Badgers from doing the same. OSU gained 221 yards on the ground and gave up just 28. Wisconsin scored its two touchdowns in the last three minutes of the game, gaining 133 of its total 228 yards on those two scoring drives against Ohio State's second and third teams.

Kent Graham played most of the way at quarterback, hitting on nine of 12 tosses for 119 yards, one interception, and a TD to Bernard Edwards (22 yards). Kirk Herbstreit made one of the afternoon's most spectacular plays. Adjusting to the Badgers' blitz on

Herbstreit passes muster at QB in 33-19 victory over Washington State

Columbus Dispatch, Sunday, September 22, 1991

a fourth-and-seven, Herbstreit rolled left to pass, avoided two tacklers, then took off for the other side of the field and eventually hurdled a defender at the goal line for a touchdown. His 32-yard effort put OSU on top, 24-2, with 3:20 remaining in the final period.

Ohio State was dealt its first setback of the season the next weekend at Illinois, 10-7. Kicking into the wind with just 36 ticks left on the clock, placekicker Chris Richardson booted a 41-yard field goal to

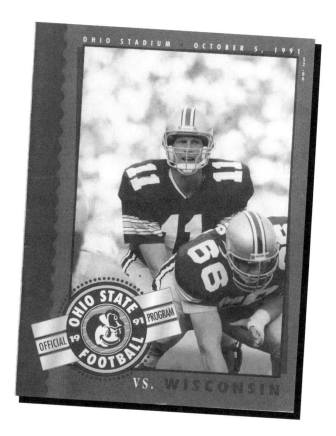

Buckeyes Visit Cleveland

A crowd of 73,830 was on hand at Municipal Stadium for Ohio State's first appearance in Cleveland, since Les Horvath led the Buckeyes over Illinois, 26-12, in this same stadium on November 18, 1944.

The
OHIO STATE
University

VS

NORTHWESTERN
University

$26.00 | **CLEVELAND STADIUM** | SAT. OCTOBER 19, 1991 Game Time T.B.A.

break a 7-7 tie for the three-point victory. Richardson's kick barely cleared the crossbar, but it was enough to earn the Fighting Illini their fourth consecutive win over the Buckeyes.

A game that many predicted would be high scoring turned into a defensive struggle. Coach John Mackovic's team went up 7-0 in the first period with a methodical 13-play, 88-yard drive, capped by Darren Boyer's seven-yard touchdown run up the middle. Following Judah Herman's recovery of an Illini fumble at the OSU 36-yard line, Ohio State finally tied the score late in the final period, going 64 yards in just two plays—Kent Graham's 20-yard toss to Bernard Edwards followed by a 44-yard scoring bomb to Joey Galloway.

The Buckeyes lost a golden opportunity earlier in the fourth quarter when, on second down at the Illini three, Herbstreit's pitchout bounced off By'not'e's shoulder pads and linebacker Julyon Brown recovered for the Illini. Roger Harper helped keep the game close with two interceptions. Harper also stripped the ball from running back Kameno Bell, causing the fumble which Herman recovered to set up OSU's touchdown. Tailback Raymont Harris led the Buckeyes' rushing attack with 73 yards, followed by By'not'e with 71.

Wildcat "Home Game"

Fullback Scottie Graham scored three times to lead a 34-3 rout of Northwestern, October 19, at cold and rainy Municipal Stadium in Cleveland. John Cooper substituted liberally, especially in the second half, using nine different ball carriers to rush for 289 yards. It was Ohio State's 16th consecutive victory over NU. This was a Northwestern "home game," which the Wildcats moved to the Ohio city to attract more fans than would be expected at Dyche Stadium in Evanston.

OSU improved its record to 6-1 overall, 3-1 in the conference, with a fiercely fought homecoming triumph over rugged Michigan State, 27-17. Both teams scored in each of the four quarters. Carlos Snow was the game's star, shredding the Spartan defense for 169 yards on 29 carries. It was a real thrill for the fifth-year senior tailback, who missed

Snow, Buckeyes storm past Spartans

Columbus Dispatch, Sunday, October 27, 1991

the entire 1990 season because of surgery to remove a benign tumor from his right hip.

The Buckeyes' second-half strategy became clear early in the third quarter—don't throw, give the ball to Snow. He gained 112 of his yards on 17 second-half attempts. Ohio State threw just four of its 20 passes in the last two quarters. The Buckeyes led in first downs, 22-16, and total offense, 397 yards to 307.

Hawkeyes Ruin Title Hopes

Eleventh-ranked Iowa shattered 13th-ranked Ohio State's Rose Bowl aspirations, with a 16-9 victory in front of 95,357 at Ohio Stadium on November 2. As the temperature rapidly plummeted during this overcast afternoon, coach Hayden Fry's Hawkeyes were solidly in control, rolling up an advantage of 443 to 221 in total offensive yards.

Iowa's very effective pass rush was led by end Leroy Smith, who sacked Kent Graham four times. The Hawks had possession of the football for slightly more than 36 minutes of the 60-minute game. Ohio State had now scored just one touchdown in each of its two Big Ten setbacks.

Iowa broke a 7-7 tie right before the half with an unusual 61-yard scoring toss from quarterback Matt Rogers to tight end Alan Cross. With a third-and-two at the Iowa 39-yard line, Cross began the play by blocking OSU's tight end while watching the strong safety out of the corner of his eye. When Cross saw OSU's safety blitz the quarterback, he immediately released his block and peeled off to the right sideline. Without a defender in sight, Cross took Rogers' throw and cruised untouched into the stadium's north end for the touchdown. Ohio State scored two points with Jason Simmons' 85-yard return, following Greg Smith's block of the Hawkeyes' extra-point attempt.

It was an emotional weekend for the entire Iowa City community. On Friday afternoon, an Iowa graduate student shot and killed five people in a campus building before taking his own life. There was even thought of postponing Saturday's game because of the tragedy.

Ohio State returned to the victory column with a 35-6 win at Minnesota on November 9. The attendance of 30,145 was the smallest home crowd since the Golden Gophers began playing at the Minneapolis Metrodome in 1982. After a slow start, the Buckeyes scored all 35 of their points in the second and third periods. Five different backs scored OSU's five touchdowns.

Carlos Snow provided the offense with a much-needed spark when he entered the game in the second quarter. Kirk Herbstreit broke loose for the game's final touchdown on a 72-yard option keeper around right end, after breaking a tackle at the OSU 43-yard line where three Minnesota defenders appeared to have him wrapped up. Herbstreit's

Steve Tovar, two-time All-American linebacker

scurry was Ohio State's longest run from scrimmage in 1991.

Hoosiers Provide Major Test

The Buckeyes' 20-16 victory over Indiana in the season's final home game was one of the most thrilling between the two schools. Ohio State scored in each quarter and was fortunate to emerge with the four-point victory after trailing at halftime, 13-10. Coach Bill Mallory's Hoosiers led in first downs, 20-10, and in total offensive yards, 356-225. The IU attack was paced by quarterback Trent Green, who passed for 256 yards and both Indiana touchdowns, and by tailback Vaughn Dunbar, who rushed for 125 yards.

But the Buckeyes moved the ball when it counted. Carlos Snow ran for 124 yards and scored both Buckeye touchdowns. Tim Williams kicked two field goals, a 35-yarder in the first quarter, and a 38-yarder for the only points scored by either team in the final period.

Ohio State was now 8-2 overall, 5-2 in the conference. But the Buckeyes were out of the running for the Big Ten title, since Michigan was undefeated in league play at 7-0.

The November 23 trip to Ann Arbor was not nearly as pleasant (or as close) as the IU game. Michigan walloped OSU, 31-3, to capture the outright conference championship, exploding for 17 points in the second period to put the game out of reach. Desmond Howard, a graduate of Cleveland St. Joseph, impersonated the famed Heisman Trophy pose after bolting 93 yards for UM's fourth touchdown right before halftime. Howard received the coveted award at the end of the season.

The Buckeyes put together two sustained third-quarter marches, but the first ended when OSU was unable to convert a fourth-down at the UM 20-yard line, and a lost fumble just two yards short of the end zone stopped the second drive. Tim Williams' 50-yard field goal early in the second period provided his team's only points of the afternoon.

Big Plays Lead Orange Attack

Ohio State finished the season with a 24-17 loss to Syracuse in the January 1, 1992, Hall of Fame Bowl. Quarterback Marvin Graves shredded the Buckeyes for 309 yards on 18 completions, including two TD tosses of 50 and 60 yards. After trailing 14-3 at the half, OSU battled back to tie the game, 17-17, when linebacker Steve Tovar blocked a punt that was recovered in the end zone by Tito Paul with eight minutes remaining. But Graves threw his second scoring pass less than a minute later, and Ohio State could not mount a serious threat on either of its two last possessions.

The Buckeyes finished the season with eight victories and four losses. Steve Tovar made All-American, and Carlos Snow was selected the team's most valuable player.

1991

September 7	Arizona	W	38	14
September 14	Louisville	W	23	15
September 21	Washington State	W	33	19
October 5	Wisconsin	W	31	16
October 12	at Illinois	L	7	10
October 19	Northwestern#	W	34	3
October 26	Michigan State (HC)	W	27	17
November 2	Iowa	L	9	16
November 9	at Minnesota	W	35	6
November 16	Indiana	W	20	16
November 23	at Michigan	L	3	31
January 1	Syracuse*	L	17	24

Total Points   **277 187**
at Cleveland
* Hall of Fame Bowl

Season Record: 8-4
Conference: 3rd Place (Tie)

1992

Ohio State expected to have a fine season in 1992. John Cooper began his fifth Ohio State season with the return of 36 letterwinners, including 14 starters. The entire interior offensive line from '91 was intact, with tackles Jason Winrow and Alan Kline, guards Dave Monnot and Len Hartman, and center Paul Long. Freshman Korey Stringer started six games at tackle. Cedric Saunders returned at tight end, Brian Stablein at split end, and Chris Sanders replaced Bernard Edwards at flanker.

Fifth-year senior Kirk Herbstreit picked up the reins at quarterback and Jeff Cothran took over at fullback. The Buckeyes had abundant tailback talent with veterans Raymont Harris and Butler By'not'e and the return of Robert Smith, who sat out the '91 season. A freshman who impressed the coaches with his excellent work ethic was Eddie George, who saw action in 11 of the

season's 12 games. Placekicker Tim Williams was back after also handling the punting chores in '91.

The starting defensive backfield of Bryan Cook, Foster Paulk, Roger Harper, and Chico Nelson was in place for another season. Returning linebackers Steve Tovar and Mark Williams were joined by Brent Johnson. Ends Jason Simmons and Derrick Foster and tackle Dan Wilkinson earned starting spots on the defensive line, where middle guard Greg Smith was the only returning regular. Fifth-year senior Joel Kessel took over the punting duties.

No. 400 at the Horseshoe

Ohio State survived 17-point underdog Louisville, 20-19, in the September 5 season opener. With just 33 seconds remaining, Cardinal quarterback Jeff Brohm and halfback Ralph Dawkins were unable to connect on a two-point conversion pass attempt that would have earned Louisville the victory. The Ohio Stadium crowd of 89,653 was only

College Football
OSU smashes Syracuse, 35-12

Cincinnati Enquirer, Sunday, September 20, 1992

the second non-sellout in OSU's last 59 home games. It also was Ohio State's 400th game at Ohio Stadium, which was dedicated in 1922.

The Buckeyes won despite throwing two interceptions, committing six penalties for 44 yards, and losing a fumble in the fourth quarter. Flanker Joey Galloway sprinted 50 yards down the middle of the field on a reverse for OSU's first touchdown, after taking a pitchout from Kirk Herbstreit and picking up a key block from Paul Long.

Steve Tovar made one of the game's biggest plays when he blocked the extra-point attempt following Louisville's first touchdown in the second quarter. Had the Cardinals' kick been successful, the game would have been tied 20-20 at the end—Louisville would then have attempted kicking the extra point after its final touchdown rather than being forced to try for two.

First Ohio Opponent in 58 Seasons

Ohio State defeated Bowling Green at home the following Saturday, 17-6, in the first-ever meeting between the two schools. The Falcons were the defending Mid-American Conference champions, after posting a 1991 record of 11-1 which included a win over Fresno State in the California Raisin Bowl. Bowling Green was coached by Gary Blackney who had been an Ohio State assistant from 1984 through 1990.

It was the Buckeyes' first game against an Ohio opponent since romping over Western Reserve, 76-0, in Cleveland on November 3, 1934. The Buckeye defense took center stage with four interceptions (two by

Marlon Kerner) and two fumble recoveries. The OSU offense continued to struggle and netted just 237 yards compared with the Falcons' 277.

On the first play of the second quarter, BG grabbed a 6-0 lead on Eric White's nine-yard quarterback draw. The short touchdown drive was set up when the Falcons intercepted Ohio State quarterback Bob Hoying at the OSU 22-yard line. Sparked by the running of Raymont Harris, the Buckeyes drove 60 yards on their ensuing possession to take the lead, 7-6. The touchdown was scored from the one by Eddie George, the first of his college career.

Ohio State put ten points on the board in the third period with Tim Williams' 47-yard field goal and Harris' seven-yard touchdown run, which finished off a nine-play 53-yard march. Harris was the game's leading runner with 94 yards. Cooper told reporters he was happy to begin the season with two wins, but emphasized that the offense would have to be more effective in the weeks ahead.

Buckeyes Crush Orangemen

Ohio State's offense was anything but lethargic the following Saturday evening, September 19, at the Syracuse Carrier Dome. Led by Eddie George's three touchdowns and a stingy defense, the 21st-ranked Buckeyes defeated eighth-ranked Syracuse, 35-12. OSU had been pegged a 10-point underdog. It likely was OSU's biggest win during John Cooper's first five seasons in Columbus.

After the game opened with an exchange of punts, the unpredictable Buckeyes scored on their next three possessions to jump out in front, 21-0. Kirk Herbstreit unloaded a 46-yard bomb to Brian Stablein, who beat two defenders for the ball as he dived across the goal line. The offense quickly returned to the field after Tim Walton intercepted quarterback Marvin Graves at the Syracuse 48. Ten plays later, George ripped through the right side of the Orange defense for the final yard, and OSU was on top, 14-0. A key play during the 52-yard march was Stablein's end around 10-yard carry on a third-and-two at the Syracuse 14.

After Syracuse got on the board with John Biskup's 24-yard field goal, Herbstreit flawlessly directed his team 80 yards for its third touchdown at the 10:04 point of the second quarter. George scored from a yard out on a pitchout to the right. Biskup added a 32-yard field goal to make the halftime count, 21-6.

Graves scored his team's only touchdown with a one-yard run in the third quarter. Ohio State put the game out of reach with two fourth-period touchdowns, a 16-yard sprint by Robert Smith and George's two-yard burst with just 13 seconds remaining. The Buckeye defense was magnificent, sacking Graves four times and intercepting four of his 25 passes. The victory was especially gratifying since Ohio State had lost to the Orangemen, 24-17, just nine months earlier in the January 1, 1992, Hall of Fame Bowl.

The Buckeyes welcomed the next weekend without a game before starting conference play at Wisconsin on October 3. Herbstreit and Harris were both nursing ankle injuries, and Robert Smith was still suffering from a cracked rib. Alan Kline was kept out of the Syracuse game with a severe ankle sprain.

Detrimental Conference Start

Ohio State was virtually out of the Big Ten title race after beginning conference play with losses at Wisconsin and at home against Illinois. The Badgers whacked the 12th-

Cooper Leads Coaches

Coach John Cooper served as president of the American Football Coaches Association in 1992. He assumed the presidency in January of that year at the association's annual convention in Dallas.

ranked Buckeyes, 20-16, after putting together two sustained scoring marches to start the second half. Coach Barry Alvarez's emotionally charged defense kept the Buckeye offense off balance most of the afternoon. Wisconsin led in first downs, 20-15, and in total offense, 321 yards to 261. Herbstreit connected on 20 of 33 passes for 216 yards, but OSU could muster only 45 yards on the ground. The Badgers also led in time of possession, 35:14 to 25:46.

Matters went from bad to worse at home October 10 against Illinois. The Buckeyes lost their fifth straight to the Fighting Illini, 18-16, in one of the strangest and most unusual games ever staged between the two schools. The lead changed hands five times, and the Illinois defense scored its team's first nine points. OSU took the opening kickoff and gallantly marched to the Illinois one-yard line. On third-and-goal, Eddie George fumbled the football into the hands of defensive safety Jeff Arneson, who raced 96 yards the opposite direction for the Illini's first touchdown.

OSU retaliated to take the lead, 10-7, with Tim Williams' 50-yard field goal and George's four-yard touchdown blast over the right side of the line. Illinois was unable to sustain its next drive, but really put Ohio State in the hole when Ken Blackman downed Brett Larsen's 37-yard punt inside the OSU one-yard line. After George gained a yard on first down, Blackman bulleted through a gap on the right side to nail Robert Smith in the end zone for a safety. The Buckeyes now led by a single point, 10-9, with 11:24 remaining in the second quarter.

The Illini drove 54 yards to regain the lead with a three-yard keeper by Jeff Kinney, who was making his first start at quarterback. Illinois' Chris Richardson booted the conversion, but coach Lou Tepper elected to take the point off the scoreboard and try for two when OSU was offside on the kick. Kinney's two-point keeper attempt was stopped by Derrick Foster, leaving the score at 15-10 in favor of the Illini.

Right before halftime, Tim Walton intercepted one of Kinney's passes and returned it 59 yards to the Illinois eight-yard line with just five seconds on the clock. Tim Williams connected on a 25-yard field goal on the final play of the first half, and the Buckeyes had cut their deficit to two at 15-13.

Ohio State went back on top, 16-15, on Williams' third three-pointer of the afternoon, a 29-yarder at the 6:47 mark of the third period. On the second play of the final quarter, the Buckeyes created a huge break for themselves when Walter Taylor and Tom Lease blocked an Illinois punt and handed the ball to the offense at the Illini 25-yard line. After a two-yard pick up on the ground, Herbstreit passed 21 yards to Jeff Cothran at the one-yard line. On first down, George took a handoff to the left and cut forward before being thrashed by defenders Dana Howard and Tyrone Washington. The ball popped loose, and Illini strong safety Derrick Rucker recovered at the 10-yard line.

Illinois took advantage of the turnover, using 15 plays to move 86 yards to the OSU four, where Richardson connected on a 21-yard field goal with 4:56 remaining to put the visitors back in front, 18-16. Ohio State still had a shot with 48 seconds to go. Tim Williams' 44-yard field goal attempt into the swirling wind at Ohio Stadium's closed end had the distance but was wide to the left. It was an extremely painful setback for the Buckeyes, who led in first downs, 21-14, and in total offense, 342 yards to 270. OSU had been defeated in its first two conference games by a total of six points.

Season Turns Around

Ohio State rebounded with a much-needed homecoming victory over Northwestern, 31-7, on October 17. Tim Williams started the scoring with a 19-yard field goal, and tailback Raymont Harris scored OSU's first three touchdowns on short plunges. Kirk Herbstreit left the game midway through the second quarter with an aggravation of a sprained ankle, but was effectively replaced by redshirt freshman Bob Hoying.

Midway through the final period, Eddie George broke through right tackle and thundered 60 yards down the sideline to the Wildcat two. On first down Hoying passed to tight end Joe Metzger for the game's last touchdown. It was Hoying's first collegiate

Harris' 3 TDs lift OSU past Northwestern 31-7

Columbus Dispatch, Sunday, October 18, 1992

touchdown pass, and Metzger's very first catch as a Buckeye.

The Buckeyes continued to improve with a 27-17 victory at Michigan State, after trailing 14-3 midway through the second quarter. Ohio State's rally started with a 12-yard scoring pass from Herbstreit to fifth-year senior split end Greg Beatty (his first career TD), followed by a thrilling 15-yard touchdown run by Butler By'not'e. The talented tailback took a handoff to the left and scored untouched, after cutting inside and out behind blocks by Cedric Saunders and Jeff Cothran.

In the third period, Robert Smith rocketed 20 yards through a huge opening at right tackle for the game's final touchdown. Tim Williams added two field goals, a 47-yarder to open the game's scoring and another from 35 yards in the final quarter. It was an im-pressive afternoon for John Cooper's squad, who led in first downs, 21-14, and offensive yards, 412-280. Linebacker Steve Tovar was a terror on defense with 13 solo tackles.

Offense Continues to Jell

Even in the rain and cold of Iowa's Kinnick Stadium, the Buckeyes continued to shine with a 38-15 win over coach Hayden Fry's Hawkeyes. OSU scored touchdowns on its first three possessions and led 28-7 at half-time. Robert Smith carried for 129 of his team's 259 rushing yards, to become the first Buckeye back to exceed the century mark since Carlos Snow's 106 yards against Indiana in 1991.

Ohio State now owned a three-game winning streak and had stretched its overall record to 6-2 (3-2 in the conference).

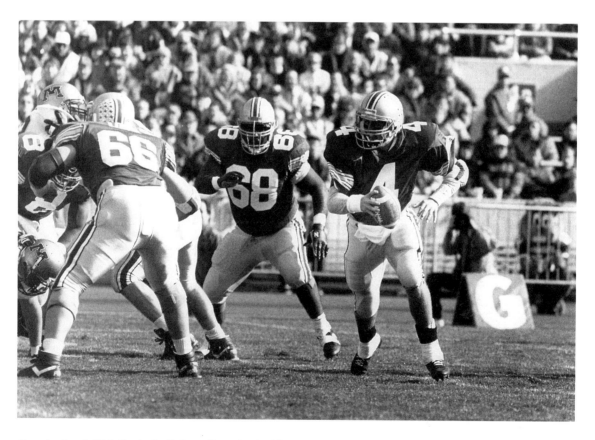

Quarterback Kirk Herbstreit is well protected by center Paul Long (66) and tackle Jason Winrow (68) against Minnesota.

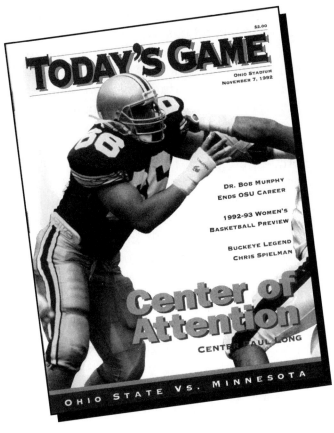

First Shutout Since 1989

After two consecutive weeks on the road, the 22nd-ranked Buckeyes whipped Minnesota at home on November 7, 17-0. It was Ohio State's first shutout since blanking Iowa 28-0 on November 11, 1989. Robert Smith turned in his second straight 100-yard game, running for 119 yards and both touchdowns. Tim Williams added a 22-yard field goal, and Kirk Herbstreit connected on 15 of 23 passes for a career-high 217 yards.

OSU's defense was outstanding, holding Golden Gopher quarterback Marquel Fleetwood to 118 yards through the air. Fleetwood entered the game as the conference's passing leader. Steve Tovar was again the team's busiest tackler with 13. After the game, John Cooper told the media in no uncertain terms how

upset he was with false reports which aired the day before on at least two Columbus radio stations. Rumors were broadcast Friday morning indicating that Cooper would be resigning later that day. Obviously he didn't. Cooper blasted the reporters for airing the reports without verifying them.

The 19th-ranked Buckeyes used a strong second half to defeat Indiana, 27-10, at frigid and snowy Memorial Stadium in Bloomington on November 14. After a slow start and a 3-0 halftime lead, Robert Smith ignited the offense with a 64-yard scoring sprint off right tackle and down the sideline early in the third period. Smith finished the afternoon with a career-high 175 yards on the ground, to become the first Ohio State player with three consecutive 100-yard games since Vince Workman in 1986.

While OSU was defeating the Hoosiers, 28-point underdog Illinois tied third-ranked Michigan, 22-22, at Ann Arbor. However, the tie was enough to guarantee the Wolverines (now 6-0-1 in the conference) the outright Big Ten title, and assure them a January 1 date in Pasadena. The Florida Citrus Bowl announced it would issue Ohio State an invitation to face the runner-up from the Southeast Conference.

Buckeyes-Wolverines Tie

Ohio State tied with Michigan, 13-13, before an Ohio Stadium crowd of 95,330 in

the regular-season finale, breaking the Buckeyes' victory streak at five. OSU led 3-0 after one quarter on a 39-yard field goal by dependable Tim Williams. The Wolverines dominated the next 30 minutes of play, scoring touchdowns in the second and third periods to go out in front, 13-3. Peter Elezovic's missed extra-point attempt following the first touchdown would become very significant as the game progressed. Backup quarterback Todd Collins played almost the entire last three quarters after starter Elvis Grbac suffered bruised ribs while scoring UM's first touchdown.

Williams' second field goal of the afternoon, this one from 30 yards, narrowed the deficit to seven points with 12:16 left in the game. After the Wolverines were forced to punt on their next possession, Kirk Herbstreit took his team 54 yards in 14 plays to tie the game. On a fourth-and-goal from the Michigan five, Herbstreit hit Greg Beatty with a quick slant pass to the right for the touchdown, and Williams' extra point tied the score with 4:24 to play. The Buckeyes got the ball back one last time at their own 45 with 3:19 on the clock, but were unable to sustain a drive.

OSU won the battle of the statistics, leading in first downs, 24-16, and total offensive yards, 362-271. Herbstreit finished the afternoon with 28 completions for a career-high 271 yards, and Chico Nelson led the defense with 11 tackles. Ohio State President Gordon Gee created some good-natured confusion with Buckeye fans by labeling the tie, "one of our greatest wins ever."

The January 1, 1993, Citrus Bowl was correctly billed as a duel between Robert Smith and Georgia's Garrison Hearst. Smith rushed for 112 yards, Hearst had 163, and each scored two touchdowns. Unfortunately, Georgia came out on top on the scoreboard, 21-14, to hand OSU its fourth straight bowl setback.

With the score knotted at 14-14, Ohio State was in good position to go ahead midway through the final quarter. But on a third-and-11 at the Georgia 16-yard line, Herbstreit and fullback Jeff Cothran collided while trying to execute a trap play. The ball popped loose and was recovered by the Bulldog's Travis Jones at the 20. From there Georgia marched 80 yards for the winning touchdown.

The Buckeyes finished the year with a record of 8-3-1, their best since Cooper took the reins as head coach in 1988. Tovar repeated as an All-American, and Herbstreit was chosen the team's MVP. Tackle Korey Stringer was the Big Ten Freshman of the

1992			
September 5	Louisville	W 20	19
September 12	Bowling Green	W 17	6
September 19	at Syracuse	W 35	12
October 3	at Wisconsin	L 16	20
October 10	Illinois	L 16	18
October 17	Northwestern (HC)	W 31	7
October 24	at Michigan State	W 27	17
October 31	at Iowa	W 38	15
November 7	Minnesota	W 17	0
November 14	at Indiana	W 27	10
November 21	Michigan	T 13	13
January 1	Georgia*	L 14	21
Total Points		271	158

* Florida Citrus Bowl

Season Record: 8-3-1
Conference: 2nd Place

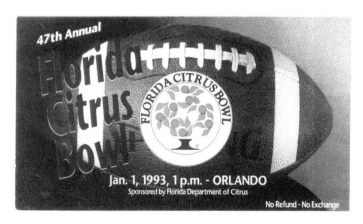

47th Annual
Florida Citrus Bowl
Jan. 1, 1993, 1 p.m. - ORLANDO
Sponsored by Florida Department of Citrus
No Refund - No Exchange

PRICE GATE STAND SEC. ROW SEAT
$35 D SOUTH 227 N 2

year, and Greg Smith and Len Hartman were Academic All-Americans. The Ohio State football program was showing steady improvement, and better seasons were just around the corner.

1993

The Buckeyes were poised for an excellent season as John Cooper began his sixth year in Columbus. A dozen returning starters, evenly divided between offense and defense, formed the nucleus of the '93 squad, plus veteran placekicker Tim Williams was back for his fourth season. Three departed players who played key roles in '92 were quarterback Kirk Herbstreit, linebacker Steve Tovar, and Brian Stablein, the squad's leading receiver.

Four experienced starters on the offensive line were tackles Alan Kline and Korey Stringer and guards Dave Monnot and Jason Winrow (who shifted from tackle to guard). Senior Jack Thrush, who had played all five interior line positions at one time or another, took over at center. Senior Cedric Saunders was back at tight end. The starting wide receivers were flanker Chris Sanders and split end Joey Galloway.

Redshirt sophomore Bobby Hoying moved into the starting role at quarterback with strong support from senior Bret Powers, a transfer two years earlier from Arizona State. Raymont Harris became the starter at tailback, and Jeff Cothran resumed his role at fullback.

The defensive front line was built around returning starters Jason Simmons at end and tackle "Big Daddy" Dan Wilkinson. Randall Brown, who played extensively in

all of the previous season's 12 games, took over at the other end, and redshirt freshman Luke Fickell replaced Greg Smith at nose guard. Outside linebackers Mark Williams and Craig Powell were joined in the middle by Lorenzo Styles. This trio was highly talented with exceptional speed.

The defensive backfield saw returning starter Chico Nelson switch from free safety to strong safety, with Walter Taylor assuming the free safety position. Regular Tim Walton was joined at cornerback by Marlon Kerner, who had started four games in 1992. Junior Scott Terna took over the punting responsibilities. In commemoration of the 25th anniversary of OSU's last national title, the 1993 squad wore 1968-type jerseys with small black playing numbers on the sleeves.

Convincing Beginning

Ohio State had little trouble with Rice in the September 4 opener, 34-7. The Owls had been 6-5 in '92 for their first winning season in 30 years. This was the first game between Ohio State and Rice, and it marked the Owls' first national television appearance in nearly 33 seasons. The Ohio Stadium crowd of 89,040 was, at the time, the largest ever to see the Owls play. The 27-point victory was the Buckeyes' most one-sided opening day win since whipping Michigan State, 49-21, in 1976.

Bobby Hoying was impressive in his first start at quarterback, completing 13 of 22 passes for 144 yards, including a nine-yard touchdown toss to freshman Dimitrious

25th Reunion

The season-opener against Rice featured the 25th reunion of the Ohio State Alumni Band. More than 600 alumni members of TBDBITL (The Best Damn Band in the Land) were back to march down the field "one more time."

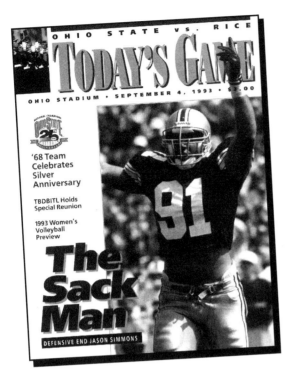

OHIO STATE vs. RICE

Today's Game

OHIO STADIUM · SEPTEMBER 4, 1993 · $3.00

'68 Team Celebrates Silver Anniversary

TBDBITL Holds Special Reunion

1993 Women's Volleyball Preview

The Sack Man

DEFENSIVE END JASON SIMMONS

Stanley. Bret Powers also looked very good in his first appearance as a Buckeye, connecting on five of eight for 102 yards. Powers' 48-yard scoring pass to Joey Galloway was the game's longest play from scrimmage.

Tailback Raymont Harris scored the first touchdown and led the Ohio State ground attack with 76 yards. Rice avoided a shutout when quarterback Josh LaRocca threw a 43-yard scoring pass to split end Herschel Crowe with just 24 seconds remaining.

The atmosphere was quite different the following Saturday when the 16th-rated Buckeyes defeated 12th-ranked Washington, 21-12. It was just the second night game in Ohio Stadium history, and one of the most thrilling and significant wins during John Cooper's first six Ohio State seasons. Jim Lambright had taken over as the Huskies' head coach just four weeks earlier, succeeding Don James who resigned in protest of penalties leveled against his program by the Pacific Ten Conference.

The Buckeyes, who were very unpredictable with their play selection, led 14-9 at halftime on a two-yard touchdown sweep by Raymont Harris and a 35-yard scoring toss from Hoying to Galloway. The mood grew

tense at the 12:46 mark of the fourth period, when Travis Hanson kicked his second field goal of the evening to bring Washington within two points at 14-12. But tailback Butler By'not'e put the game out of reach just 70 seconds later, exploding through a huge hole up the middle and racing 49 yards to put Ohio State ahead, 21-12. By'not'e's 49-yard sprint was OSU's longest rush from scrimmage in 1993.

Highest Score in Seven Seasons

Ohio State had no trouble at Pittsburgh the next weekend, winning 63-28 over coach Johnny Majors's Panthers, after building up a 35-0 lead at halftime. The onslaught began with By'not'e returning the game-opening kickoff 89 yards for OSU's first of four touchdowns in the first period. Fans clad in Scarlet and Gray (who seemed to make up at least half of the Pitt Stadium crowd of 41,511) enjoyed watching the Buckeyes score on their first five possessions.

In the second half, Pitt sophomore quarterback John Ryan passed for all four Panther touchdowns to take a slight edge off the OSU victory. The Buckeye defense surrendered 291 yards through the air, but only 48 on the ground. OSU used 11 different ball carriers and seven separate receivers to rack up 502 yards of total offense. It was Ohio State's highest single-game score since defeating Utah, 64-6, in 1986.

After an idle weekend, the Buckeyes opened Big Ten play with a 52-3 thrashing of Northwestern on October 2. It was one of the few games from Ohio Stadium during the 1990s that was not televised. Ohio State's defense was the dominating factor, intercepting five Wildcat passes (Lorenzo Styles, Chico Nelson, Tim Patillo, and two by Walter Taylor) and holding NU's vaunted passing attack to 76 yards. Northwestern entered the game at 2-1 with a passing average of 212 yards-per-game.

Four of OSU's touchdowns resulted from short drives, after interceptions had turned

Buckeyes collar Huskies

Cleveland Plain Dealer, Sunday, September 12, 1993

Tailback Butler By'not'e races 49 yards for the game-clinching touchdown against Washington.

the ball over to the offense at the NU seven, 20, 31, and 25 yard lines. Hoying was replaced by Bret Powers midway through the third quarter after an inconsistent afternoon. Powers led the offense for four series that resulted in three touchdowns and a field goal. But after the game, offensive coordinator Joe Hollis assured the press that there was no quarterback controversy. "Hoying is our starter, but we're going to need both. It's a luxury to have that second quarterback," he stated.

Victory Over Illinois!

The sixth-ranked Buckeyes conquered Illinois, 20-12, before a crowd of 61,209 at wind-swept Memorial Stadium on October 9. The cherished triumph broke a five-year losing streak to the Fighting Illini, and moved OSU to a 5-0 season start for the first time since 1979. Ohio State's defense again played a key role in the outcome, holding the opposition without a touchdown for the second consecutive week.

OSU benefited from two fumble recoveries to lead 17-3 at halftime. Bobby Hoying needed just three plays to engineer a short 14-yard scoring march, after Jason Simmons recovered quarterback Johnny Johnson's fumble at the Illini 14-yard line on the game's very first play from scrimmage. Hoying passed 11 yards to Joey Galloway for the TD. Late in the second period, Terry Glenn pounced on a fumble by Illinois punter Brett Larsen for his first career touchdown. Larsen was rushed hard from the left by OSU's Tito Paul, forcing the ball to slip through Larsen's hands as he was attempting to punt.

Illinois had its chances in the second half but simply could not cross the Ohio State goal line. With the Buckeyes moving against a 30-mph wind into the stadium's north end, Illinois began four successive possessions at the Illini 47, the OSU 41, the OSU 37, and the OSU 16-yard line. But three field goals by Chris Richardson is all the Buckeye defense would surrender.

Illinois had two good opportunities in the final period but did not score. An apparent 33-yard TD throw from Johnson to tight end Ken Dilger was nullified because of an offensive lineman being beyond the line of scrimmage. OSU's Tim Walton finally sealed the victory when he intercepted Johnson's 36-yard throw in the end zone with just 40 seconds remaining.

Tim Williams added two field goals for the Buckeyes, a 52-yarder in the first quarter and a 36-yarder with just 1:41 remaining in the game. Williams had been perfect through the season's first five games, going six-for-six on field goals and 19-for-19 on PATs.

Fourth-Quarter Drive
Keeps Buckeyes Undefeated

Fifth-ranked Ohio State returned home October 16 for a thrilling 28-21 win over 25th-rated Michigan State. The spirited Spartans were flying high at 3-1 after handing Michigan its first conference loss of the season, 17-7. The festive and rainy homecoming

weekend was highlighted by the 25th reunion of OSU's 1968 national title squad.

The Buckeyes ran their season record to 6-0, in spite of committing five turnovers. Ohio State jumped to a 21-10 halftime lead on the strength of three touchdown catches by Joey Galloway. Two were tossed by Bobby Hoying for distances of 22 and 14 yards, and the other came from backup quarterback Bret Powers. The Powers-to-Galloway play covered 64 yards, which was OSU's longest play from scrimmage in 1993. Powers perfectly executed a play-action fake and side-stepped a rush, then threw long down the right seam to Galloway, who caught the ball in stride at the 26-yard line and was never touched.

Spartan quarterback Jim Miller tormented the Buckeye defense all afternoon

Linebackers Mark Williams (51), Craig Powell (84), and Lorenzo Styles (90) apply pressure during the homecoming victory over Michigan State.

with 31 completions for 360 yards, including a 38-yard TD toss to fullback Scott Greene at the 5:37 mark of the final period. Following the touchdown, Miller tied the game at 21-21 with a two-point conversion throw to flanker Mill Coleman, who leaped high over Marlon Kerner for the ball in the back right corner of the end zone.

With the game on the line, the Ohio State coaches went back to Powers, who used 15 plays to engineer a picture-perfect 80-yard scoring drive for the victory. Tailback Raymont Harris scored the touchdown behind fullback Jeff Cothran's block, on second down from the seven with just 1:06 remaining. One of the march's key downs was Powers' 17-yard bullet to Galloway on a third-and-ten from the MSU 38-yard line. Galloway grabbed the ball at the MSU 21-yard line, and was able to drag both feet in bounds before crossing the sideline.

Michigan State led in first downs, 28-24, and in total offense, 473 yards to 428. But coach George Perles' squad hurt itself with four missed field goal attempts of 34, 33, 20, and 39 yards. Lorenzo Styles spearheaded OSU's defense with 18 tackles, and Harris was the game's leading runner with 103 yards.

The Buckeyes, who had moved up to third in the national rankings, continued to roll with a 45-25 romp at Purdue the following weekend. It was Ohio State's first game against the Boilermakers in three seasons, and OSU relied heavily on its running game for its seventh victory of the season. Harris rushed for 118 yards, George added 96, and By'not'e ran for 95. Bobby Hoying threw only 12 passes, but was very effective with 10 completions for 105 yards.

Ohio State also received some excellent news that same afternoon from Minneapolis and State College. Minnesota dealt Wisconsin its first setback of the season, 28-21, and Michigan handed Penn State its first loss, 21-13, leaving the Buckeyes in sole possession of first place in the league standings.

Tailback Raymont Harris carried for 1,344 yards and scored 12 touchdowns to lead the 1993 Ohio State offense.

Big Ten Now Eleven

Penn State, under the leadership of legendary coach Joe Paterno, began Big Ten play in 1993. It was the first change in conference membership since Michigan State joined in 1953, replacing Chicago who had departed at the end of the 1939 season. Ohio State entertained the 12th-ranked Nittany Lions at cold and snowy Ohio Stadium on October 30. The Buckeyes had faced Penn State eight times in non-conference games between 1912 and 1980, winning only two and losing six.

Ohio State thumped the visitors, 24-6, holding them without a touchdown for the first time all season. The victory was anything but fancy. Playing in a "sea of mud," the Buckeye offense churned its way for 380

OSU snows under Penn State

Columbus Dispatch, Sunday, October 31, 1993

yards, compared with PSU's 271, while the OSU defense pulled off four interceptions and forced a fumble on Penn State's only serious touchdown threat. "Quiet Storm" Raymont Harris topped the 100-yard mark for the third straight weekend, running for what was then a career-high 151.

Cooper told the press that this was probably the biggest win for him so far at Ohio State. He thought the key to the game was OSU's first possession after PSU had taken a 3-0 lead on Craig Fayak's 29-yard field goal early in the first quarter. It was the first time the Buckeyes had been behind all season. Ohio State retaliated with an eight-play 65-yard scoring march to grab the lead at 7-3.

Cold Afternoon at Camp Randall

For the second straight year, the Buckeyes faced Wisconsin at Madison. The 14th-ranked Badgers (7-1, 4-1) were still flying high after defeating Michigan at home the previous Saturday, 13-10. In a rush to celebrate their first victory over the Wolverines since 1981, Wisconsin students knocked down a retaining fence at the base of the stadium and rushed the field, injuring approximately 70 people in the process. In an effort to better control the crowd for its game against the Buckeyes, Wisconsin officials increased its security, and eliminated 200 seats from the student section that overlooks the visiting team's tunnel to the playing field.

With temperatures in the mid-20s, third-ranked Ohio State saw its eight-game winning streak come to an end after battling the Badgers to a 14-14 tie. The Buckeye offense lacked consistency after the first quarter, and suffered from bad field position most of the afternoon. OSU led 7-0 after the first period,

even though it was the first time all season the Buckeyes did not score on their first possession of the game. Wisconsin retaliated with touchdowns in each of the next two quarters to lead, 14-7, heading into the final quarter.

With their backs to the wall after the Badgers had downed a punt at the OSU one with just 4:34 remaining, the coaches turned to Bret Powers, much like they had done three weeks earlier against Michigan State. The senior backup, who had little success moving the offense in the second period, was near perfect with four straight completions for 99 yards and the tying touchdown. Powers hit Joey Galloway on a square-in pattern for 15 yards, then went right back to Galloway for a 47-yard gainer down the left sideline. After Powers threw 11 yards to Cedric Saunders on an outcut pattern, he connected with Galloway for 26 yards down the middle for the touchdown. One of the season's most critical drives had taken just 46 seconds.

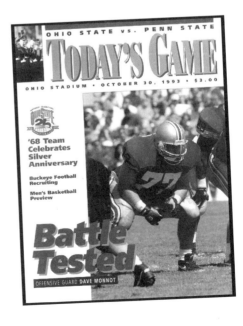

But the Badgers came right back and quickly moved to the OSU 15-yard line with seven seconds remaining. Coach Barry Alvarez turned to his freshman kicker, left-footed Rick Schnetzky, whose first two collegiate field goals a week earlier had meant the difference in Wisconsin's 13-10 win over Michigan. As Schnetzky attempted what could be a game-winning field goal, Marlon Kerner swept in from Schnetzky's right side, got both hands on the ball, and blocked the kick.

Linebacker Lorenzo Styles had another outstanding game, leading his team with 17 tackles. Neither team was happy with the tie, but Ohio State (8-0-1, 5-0-1) was still alone at the top of the Big Ten, and controlled its own destiny with two regular-season games remaining.

Share of Conference Title Assured

The Buckeyes claimed at least a share of their first Big Ten title since 1986, with a hard-earned 23-17 verdict over Indiana in the November 13 home finale. OSU had slipped from third to fifth in the weekly Associated Press poll following its tie at Wisconsin. Coach Bill Mallory's 19th-ranked Hoosiers entered the game at 7-2 overall, their best start in 24 seasons.

Tailback Raymont Harris was a huge factor in the game, rushing for 162 yards to push his season total to 1,044. Both Ohio State touchdowns resulted from short passes, a four-yard toss from Hoying to Galloway on the second play of the second period, and a five-yard throw from Powers to Buster Tillman less than four minutes before halftime. Tim Williams connected on field goals of 36, 23, and 22 yards. A victory the following week at Michigan Stadium would bring Ohio State its first outright league crown and Rose Bowl trip since 1984.

Some Days Nothing Goes Right

The Buckeyes suffered through one of their longest afternoons in many seasons, losing to Michigan, 28-0. The Wolverines so dominated on both sides of the ball, that they looked like anything but the same team that earlier that season had been defeated by Notre Dame, Michigan State, Illinois, and Wisconsin. Using an ideal blend of running and passing, Michigan outgained OSU 421 to 212 in total yards, including an advantage of 256 to 134 in the first half when UM built up a 21-0 lead. After ten weeks of making the big plays at crucial times, Ohio State simply looked like a different team.

The Buckeyes and the rest of the league were forced to wait two weeks for the Rose Bowl representative to be determined. Wisconsin and Michigan State had decided to play their game (originally scheduled for November 20, the same afternoon as the OSU-UM game) in Tokyo, Japan, two weeks later on Saturday, December 4.

For many seasons the Wisconsin-Michigan State contest had no effect on the Big Ten title. But this year it meant everything. Wisconsin (league record of 5-1-1) could gain a tie with Ohio State for the conference championship if it defeated MSU. Unfortunately for OSU, that is precisely what happened. Wisconsin won, 41-20, and was also awarded the Rose Bowl trip, since the Buckeyes had played in Pasadena on New Year's Day more recently than the Badgers.

Harris Leads Triumph Over BYU

Ohio State faced Brigham Young in the Holiday Bowl, played Thursday evening,

December 30, 1993, at Jack Murphy Stadium in San Diego. The Buckeyes won a thriller, 28-21, although the outcome wasn't assured until the game's final 13 seconds. OSU dominated the first period and led, 21-7, when Raymont Harris scored on a two-yard quick trap on the first play of the second quarter. But the Cougars, riding the passing arm of quarterback John Walsh, took charge in the second period and tied the score at halftime, 21-21.

Harris bulled across from one yard out to put the Buckeyes back on top, 28-21, at the 4:11 mark of the third period. BYU drove deep into Ohio State territory three times in the final quarter, but each effort ended with an incomplete pass on fourth down. The last march stalled at the OSU 11-yard line, with just 13 seconds remaining, when Walsh's pass sailed wide of Eric Drage in the left corner of the end zone.

Harris was voted the game's MVP after scoring three TDs and setting a Holiday Bowl rushing record with 235 yards on 39 carries. Tim Patillo accounted for OSU's first TD with a four-yard return of a punt he blocked early in the first period. Walsh put on quite a show, connecting on 25 of 44 attempts for 389 yards and all three Cougar touchdowns. Lorenzo Styles was voted the game's top defensive player. Cornerback Marlon Kerner, who normally wore jersey #46, instead wore #49, the number worn all season by close friend Jayson Gwinn. Gwinn was killed in an automobile accident on December 11.

John Cooper, who had guaranteed OSU fans a bowl victory, was obviously happy with the outcome. The Big Ten co-champions finished the season at 10-1-1, good for 11th place in the final AP poll. It was Ohio State's first 10-win season since 1986.

Tackles Korey Stringer and Dan Wilkinson were each selected All-America, and Raymont Harris was voted the team's MVP. Cooper had completed his sixth campaign with the Buckeyes. After his first team

went 4-6-1 in 1988, his last five squads had posted a very respectable record of 41-16-3. The Ohio State football program was continuing to gain strength each year, and some of the school's finest seasons were just ahead.

1993				
September 4	Rice	W	34	7
September 11	Washington	W	21	12
September 18	at Pittsburgh	W	63	28
October 2	Northwestern	W	51	3
October 9	at Illinois	W	20	12
October 16	Michigan State (HC)	W	28	21
October 23	at Purdue	W	45	24
October 30	Penn State	W	24	6
November 6	at Wisconsin	T	14	14
November 13	Indiana	W	23	17
November 20	at Michigan	L	0	28
December 30	Brigham Young *	W	28	21
Total Points			351	193

* Holiday Bowl

Season Record: 10-1-1
Big Ten Co-Champion

All-American tackles Dan "Big Daddy" Wilkinson (left) and Korey Stringer .

CHAPTER FOURTEEN

1994-2000

COOPER AT THE HELM

John Cooper began the 1994 season as just the fifth coach in Ohio State history to hold the position for seven or more seasons.

Dr. John Wilce was the first to provide the football program with coaching stability, serving 16 seasons from 1913 through 1928. Francis Schmidt, who like Cooper was head coach at Tulsa before coming to Columbus, held the job seven years from 1934 through 1940. Woody Hayes is number one in terms of longevity with 28 campaigns from 1951 through 1978, and Earle Bruce was head coach for the nine seasons following Hayes.

1994

Ohio State posted an outstanding 10-1-1 record in 1993, sharing the Big Ten with Wisconsin. But the Rose Bowl appearance never materialized because of the Big Ten's tie-breaking formula, which sent the Badgers west for New Year's Day. With four returnees on offense and five defensive holdovers, Cooper and his staff had quite a few holes to fill.

One of the biggest concerns was rebuilding the offensive line, where tackle Korey Stringer was the only returning starter. Juan Porter moved from guard to the starting center position, while LeShun Daniels and junior college transfer Jamie Sumner became the starters at guard. Pure freshman Orlando Pace earned the other tackle spot in fall practice. D. J. Jones became the starting tight end, and veterans Chris Sanders and Joey Galloway returned at wide receiver.

Bobby Hoying was back for his second year as the starting quarterback. Junior Eddie George replaced Raymont Harris at tailback, and Jeff Cothran's fullback spot was assumed by Nicky Sualua and Matt Calhoun. Josh Jackson took over the placekicking slot vacated by four-year veteran Tim Williams.

On the defensive line, the biggest gaps were those caused by the losses of end Jason Simmons and tackle Dan Wilkinson.

Those spots were filled with the move of starter Randall Brown from end to tackle and reserve nose guard Matt Finkes to end. Matt Bonhaus also logged considerable playing time at tackle. Mike Vrabel assumed the other end spot, and sophomore Luke Fickell was back at nose guard after starting every game as a redshirt freshman.

The linebacking core was well stocked with the return of Lorenzo Styles and Craig Powell. Sophomore Greg Bellisari picked up the other starting spot, replacing Mark Williams. In the secondary, returner Marlon Kerner was joined by Tito Paul, Tim Patillo, and Shawn Springs. Senior Scott Terna was back to do the punting.

Early Start

Ohio State opened the season with a 34-10 victory over Fresno State in the Disneyland Pigskin Classic at Anaheim, California. The game was played Monday evening, August 29, before a national television audience and an announced stadium attendance of 28,513. The Buckeyes started strong, scoring in each quarter, for their eighth consecutive season-opening win.

Eddie George, who made his first start at tailback, and Joey Galloway each scored twice; Josh Jackson added second-half field goals of 24 and 34 yards. OSU opened the game with an impressive 11-play, 79-yard march, that ended with George plunging into the end zone from the one. The drive's longest gainer was a 28-yard pass from Bobby Hoying to split end Buster Tillman who carried to the FSU 36-yard line.

Later in the first period, Tim Patillo intercepted Fresno State quarterback Adrian Claiborne at the OSU 33-yard line. On first down, Hoying and Galloway connected on a scoring play of 67 yards to boost OSU's lead to 14-0. After faking a reverse to Chris Sanders, Hoying threw long down the right sideline to Galloway, who snagged the ball near the 16-yard line, eluded a tackle attempt, and sped across the goal line. The Bucks in-

College Football Turns 125

The 1994 college season marked the 125th anniversary of the first college game between Princeton and Rutgers, played in 1869. The American Football Coaches Association, National Association of Collegiate Directors of Athletics, and the NCAA joined forces to honor the campaign as a "Season of Celebration." To promote the anniversary, teams were asked to display a 125-year patch on their jerseys. A copy of this patch which Ohio State wore in 1994 is shown below.

creased their lead to 21-0 early in the second quarter, when George's one-yard TD bolt finished off a 58-yard drive.

On OSU's second possession after half-time, with a second-and-goal at the Fresno State eight, Galloway came in motion to his left after splitting out to the right side. The wide receiver took a toss from Hoying, reversed his direction back to the right, and sprinted into the corner of the end zone behind a key block by Hoying. Galloway's TD made the score 31-10, and pretty well put the game out of reach.

Three newcomers who made an impact were Orlando Pace, Rickey Dudley, and

Shawn Springs. Pace and Springs (redshirt freshman) played well in their first college game. Dudley, a 6' 7" tight end who had played three seasons with the OSU basketball squad, saw his first football action since his high school days in Henderson, Texas.

The roles were reversed when Ohio State traveled to Seattle on September 10 to face Washington. The Huskies stunned the Buckeyes with 19 points in the first quarter and a 22-0 lead at halftime. OSU was simply unable to contain Washington tailback Napoleon Kaufman, who shredded the Scarlet and Gray defense for 211 yards on 32 carries. Kaufman used his exceptional speed to score the game's first touchdown, cutting through a gap at right guard and streaking 38 yards untouched down the middle of the field. He was the first back to total more than 200 yards against the Buckeyes since Michigan's Jamie Morris had 210 in 1986.

OSU was a different team after halftime, outscoring the Huskies in the third and final quarters, 16-3. George scored around left end from 24 yards out, and Hoying connected with Tillman on a 13-yard crossing pattern. Hoying passed for a two-point conversion after each touchdown (to Chris Sanders and DeWayne Carter). The offense missed Joey Galloway, who was suspended for two games by the NCAA for accepting a very small amount of money from a financial adviser.

Home at Last!

After two games on the west coast, the Buckeyes were finally able to play in front of the home crowd, defeating the Pitt Panthers 27-3 on September 17. The OSU offense totaled 512 yards and methodically scored in each quarter, in spite of four lost fumbles, an interception, and 96 yards in penalties. Ohio State's third-down efficiency was exceptional, as the offense managed 10 first downs in 13 third-down attempts. Chris Sanders scored his first collegiate touchdown on a 43-yard toss from Bobby Hoying midway through the third period.

The defense looked much improved over the Washington game, holding the Pitt offense to 242 yards. Particularly impressive were sophomore ends Mike Vrable and Matt Finkes, who combined for eight solo tackles and six assists. The Ohio Stadium attendance of 93,454 was, at the time, the largest ever for a Buckeye home opener.

Ohio State had no trouble at home the following weekend, routing Houston, 52-0, in the first-ever meeting between the two schools. OSU scored early and often, building up leads of 23-0 after the first quarter and 36-0 at halftime (it required nearly an hour to complete the first 15 minutes of play). Cooper virtually cleared his bench in the second half. Freshman tailback Jermon Jackson rushed for 54 yards and scored the game's last three touchdowns.

Sign of the Future

The Buckeyes had to rally from a 9-0 halftime deficit to nip Northwestern, 17-15, in the October 1 league opener for both teams. It essentially was a game of two different halves. The Wildcats surprised even their staunchest supporters in the first two quarters, controlling the ball for more than 23 minutes while outgaining the 20th-ranked Buckeyes, 175 yards to 66. NW placekicker Sam Valenzisi accounted for all of the first-half scoring with field goals of 40, 33, and 52 yards. Ohio State fans, who seemed to comprise at least half of the Dyche Stadium crowd of 34,753, were totally shocked.

OSU completely dominated the second half with a decided edge in net offensive yards, 249 to a mere 30. Behind the running of Eddie George, who finished the afternoon with 206 yards, the Buckeyes scored all 17 of their points in the third quarter to lead, 17-9.

Midway through the final period, Ohio State was on its way to putting the game out of reach. But the Wildcats reversed the momentum after recovering George's fumble at the NW 45-yard line, driving 55 yards for a touchdown to pull within two at 17-15 with 5:01 remaining. It was the first touchdown OSU had given up in the second half all season. Matt Finkes submarined and was able to spill Northwestern tailback Dennis Lundy short of the goal line on a two-point conversion attempt, otherwise the score would have been tied, 17-17.

While it may have appeared that the heavily favored Buckeyes should have taken the Wildcats more seriously, coach Gary Barnett was making tremendous progress with the Northwestern program. This improvement would become very evident the next two seasons.

Illinois did it again. The 17th-ranked Buckeyes were defeated at home by the Fighting Illini, 24-10. This was Illinois' sixth win over Ohio State in the last seven seasons, and in some ways it was just the reverse of the previous week's game at Northwestern. The Buckeyes won the first half, 10-7, but the Illini were in control after halftime, outscoring OSU 17-0 in the final 30 minutes of play.

After Illinois went on top, 7-0, scoring on the first play of the second quarter, Ohio State came back with a 67-yard scoring drive (George got the TD from the one) and 35-yard field goal by Josh Jackson to go ahead by three at halftime. Illini quarterback John Johnson inflicted most of the damage in the second half, passing for both of his team's touchdowns to finish the afternoon with 16 completions for 224 yards.

Korey Stringer, two-time All-American tackle

George Ignites Second-Half Assault

Ohio State rallied for a much-needed victory at Michigan State, 23-7. Again, it was a game of two different halves. Down 7-3 at intermission, the Buckeyes outscored the Spartans 20-0 in the third and fourth periods. Eddie George started the turnaround with a 76-yard touchdown burst on OSU's third play from scrimmage in the second half. On a third-and-three at the OSU 24-yard line, George headed to the right sideline with an option pitch from Bobby Hoying, then sped the distance after picking up a key block from Juan Porter near midfield. It gave the

George's TD energizes 23-7 win over Spartans

Columbus Dispatch, Sunday, October 16, 1994

Scarlet and Gray its first lead of the day, and paved the way for the Buckeyes' 16-point victory. This 76-yard run was Ohio State's longest play from scrimmage in 1994.

OSU scored two touchdowns in the final period, first on Hoying's 10-yard run, then on a 35-yard interception return by linebacker Greg Bellisari. Cornerback Marlon Kerner and linebacker Lorenzo Styles led the defense with 10 tackles each, and Scott Turna punted six times for a 42-yard average. The Buckeyes led in first downs, 18-16, and in total offensive yards, 377 to 274.

George finished this beautiful autumn afternoon with 219 yards, to become the only player in Ohio State history to rush for more than 200 yards twice in the same season (206 yards at Northwestern). It also was George's sixth consecutive 100-yard game. John Cooper was thrilled with his teams' second-half play, especially on defense, and he told reporters that the enthusiasm generated by Buckeye fans and the Ohio State marching band was a key factor.

Hoying Ties TD Record

The Buckeyes demolished Purdue, 48-14, in front of an enthusiastic homecoming crowd of 92,865 on October 22. Bobby Hoying delivered one of the finest performances, ever, by an Ohio State quarterback, completing 20 of 24 passes for 304 yards and five touchdowns, before departing early in the third quarter. Three of Hoying's scoring tosses went to split end Joey Galloway, and the other two were snagged by flanker Chris Sanders. Eight different receivers made at least one reception. Hoying's five touchdown tosses tied an Ohio State single-game record, which was set by quarterback John Borton, 32 seasons earlier, against Washington State in 1952.

Pepe Pearson notched Ohio State's other touchdown on a three-yard run through the left side early in the second quarter. Josh Jackson added field goals of 29 and 38 yards. After his team built up a 41-0 halftime lead,

---

Spielman Inspires

Chris Spielman, Detroit Lion linebacker and former Buckeye great, gave the team a pep talk at their East Lansing hotel Friday evening, and encouraged the squad all Saturday afternoon from the Spartan Stadium sidelines. Spielman told the players to control the line of scrimmage, and they would win. Ohio State did both!

Ironically, Greg Bellisari's 35-yard interception return for the game's last touchdown was the first by an OSU linebacker since Spielman returned one 24 yards for a TD in the 1987 Cotton Bowl victory over Texas A & M.

John Cooper used mostly second and third teamers the last two quarters. OSU's 48 points are the most ever scored by the Buckeyes against Purdue in a single game.

The Buckeyes led in first downs, 23-17, and in total offense, 500 yards to 331. Cooper praised his team's "attacking defense"

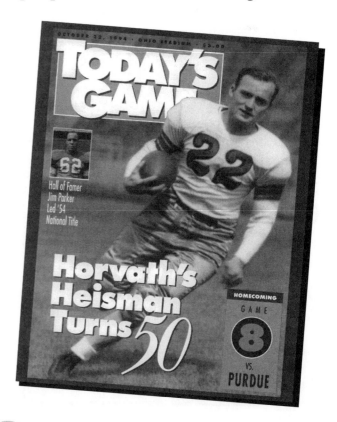

which effectively pressured Boilermaker quarterback Rick Trefzger all afternoon. Purdue came to Columbus averaging 36.5 points per game.

Unhappy Valley

The following week's trip to State College was a complete contrast with the homecoming triumph over Purdue. No. 1 ranked Penn State embarrassed 21st-rated Ohio State, 63-14, in front of a homecoming assemblage of 97,079, at the time the largest in Beaver Stadium history. The 49-point margin of defeat was the highest suffered by an Ohio State team since 1946, when the Buckeyes lost by 52 points to Michigan (58-6). Only twice had OSU yielded more than 63 points in one afternoon. Michigan shut out Ohio State in 1902, 86-0, and in 1890 Wooster defeated the Buckeyes, 64-0.

Penn State both rushed and passed for 286 yards, to amass 572 yards in total offense compared with 214 for Ohio State. Nittany Lion tailback Ki-Jana Carter, who grew up just 10 miles from the Ohio State campus in Westerville, scored four of Penn State's nine touchdowns, and led all runners with 137

Heisman Halftime

Ohio State's four Heisman Trophy winners—Les Horvath, Vic Janowicz, Howard "Hopalong" Cassady, and Archie Griffin—were introduced during the halftime homecoming ceremonies, along with Outland Trophy winner Jim Parker, arguably the school's finest lineman. The Downtown Athletic Club of New York presented Horvath with a ring commemorating the 50th anniversary of his winning the coveted award in 1944.

Also introduced were members of Ohio State's championship teams of 1944, 1949, and 1954. Receiving the crowd's loudest ovation was Mrs. Anne Hayes, who was introduced with Woody Hayes's first national championship squad of '54.

yards. PSU quarterback Kerry Collins tormented the Buckeye defense for 265 yards and two touchdowns.

Buckeyes Bounce Back

Is this the same team? Following the Penn State trouncing, Ohio State put together what may have been its finest all-around effort of the season, throttling Wisconsin 24-3 before an Ohio Stadium crowd of 93,340. The Buckeyes scored in each quarter, while holding the Badgers without a touchdown for the first time in 25 games. It was Ohio State's first victory over Wisconsin in three seasons.

The Buckeyes totaled 411 yards in total offense, while holding the Badgers to 203, including just 49 yards on the ground (lowest in their last 35 games). Ohio State also intercepted four Wisconsin passes. The Buckeyes' excellent execution on both sides of the ball surprised the Badgers, who had won at Michigan the previous Saturday, 31-19.

Quarterback Bobby Hoying passed for 207 yards, including touchdown strikes of 78 and 15 yards to flanker Chris Sanders. Their 78-yarder is the seventh-longest pass play in Ohio State history.

Tailback Eddie George scored the Buckeyes' other touchdown on a one-yard plunge early in the fourth quarter, and was the game's leading runner with 104 yards. It was his seventh game of the year over 100 yards, as he increased his season total to 1,164.

Ohio State picked up its eighth win of the season, defeating Indiana 32-17 in a very physical match-up at Bloomington on November 12. The game was more evenly played than implied by the final score, with IU trailing just 19-17 entering the fourth period. It saddled coach Bill Mallory's Hoosiers with their first four-game losing streak since 1985.

Joey Galloway ran back a kickoff 93 yards for OSU's first touchdown, thrilling the many Scarlet and Gray fans who were among the Memorial Stadium crowd of 44,672. Eddie George scored the Buckeyes' other two

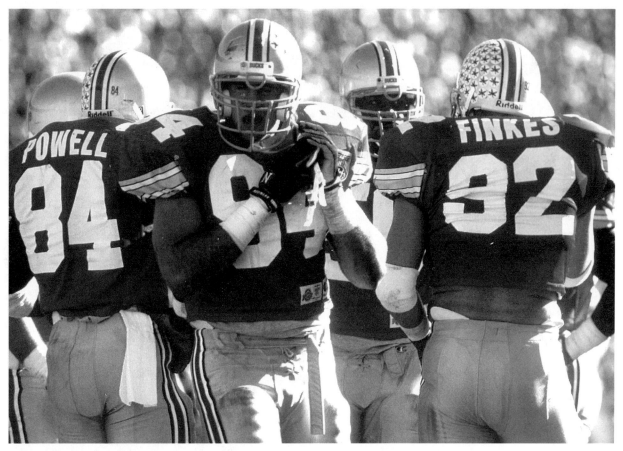

The Buckeye defense gets ready for Wisconsin. Pictured are linebacker Craig Powell (84), end Mike Vrabel (94), and end Matt Finkes (92).

first-half TDs on short runs of one and three yards.

Midway through the third period, the Buckeyes finally started to pull away, using a very methodical 19-play, 86-yard scoring march that consumed more than seven minutes. The drive, which was kept alive with six third-down conversions, culminated with Hoying's two-yard scoring toss to Rickey Dudley at the 14:41 mark of the final period. Hoying also passed 20 yards to Chris Sanders for the final score later that quarter.

Victory at Last!

Ohio State rolled to a cherished 22-6 triumph over Michigan on November 19. The Ohio Stadium crowd of 93,869 included more than 300 former Buckeye players, who formed a spirited human tunnel for the players to run through as they left the dressing room to start the game. Each team was 5-2 in the Big Ten standings. The arch-rivals were playing for the league's second place and a birth in the Florida Citrus Bowl, since undefeated Penn State was already assured of its first Rose Bowl appearance.

The Buckeyes were up 12-0 before the Wolverines got on the board with field goals of 26 and 22 yards by Remy Hamilton in the second and third quarters. Late in the first period, OSU was given a safety when UM quarterback Todd Collins tripped and fell in the end zone, following Scott Terna's 53-yard punt, which was downed by Tito Paul at the Michigan one. In the second quarter, Bobby Hoying scored on a four-yard bootleg to the

Columbus Dispatch, Sunday, November 20, 1994

left side, and Josh Jackson added a 26-yard field goal.

With OSU leading early in the final period, 12-6, Marlon Kerner made one of the game's biggest plays, blocking Hamilton's field-goal attempt at the OSU 23-yard line. Mike Vrabel recovered at the UM 47-yard line, and the Scarlet and Gray moved into position for Jackson's second field goal, a 36-yarder that increased OSU's lead to nine points. With 8:35 remaining, Eddie George scored the Buckeyes' last points with a two-yard TD over right guard, and the rest is history.

UM coach Gary Moeller blamed his offense for the loss. Hamilton's two field goals were all the Wolverines could generate, after being inside the OSU 25 yard-line four times. It was the first time Michigan had been held without a touchdown in 112 games, dat-

ing back nine seasons to a 3-3 tie at Illinois on November 2, 1985 (the same afternoon Ohio State upset top-ranked Iowa, 22-13).

OSU finished its season with a 24-17 loss to Alabama in the Monday, January 2, 1995, Florida Citrus Bowl. The game was tied at halftime, 14-14, after each team tallied twice in the second quarter. The Buckeyes' TDs came from Hoying-to-Galloway passes of 69 and 11 yards. In the final period, Josh Jackson's 36-yard field goal put OSU in the lead, 17-14, but the Crimson Tide retaliated with Michael Proctor's 44-yarder, and the game was again tied, 17-17.

After Ohio State was unable to sustain its next drive, Alabama took over at its own 37. On a second down at midfield, quarterback Jay Barker flipped a short pass across the middle to tailback Sherman Lewis, who caught the ball in full stride and streaked up the middle for the game-winning touchdown. There were 42 seconds remaining when Sherman crossed the OSU goal line.

The Buckeyes completed the 1994 season with an overall mark of 9-4, good for 14th-place in the final Associated Press poll. Tackle Korey Stringer repeated as an All-American, and was also voted the team's most valuable player. John Cooper had led OSU to a very respectable record of 54-26-4 over his first seven campaigns, and some of the finest seasons in all of Ohio State football were right around the corner.

1995

There was great excitement at the 1995 football camp, as Ohio State prepared for one of the strongest schedules in school history. A four-game nonconference schedule included a much-anticipated home date with Notre Dame, and the Buckeyes would begin Big Ten play with back-to-back trips to Penn State and to Wisconsin. OSU had compiled the best record in the conference over the past three seasons at 17-5-2. Coach John Cooper and his staff spent part of spring practice implementing a new "short passing game," designed to provide an additional dimension to an already productive offense.

A total of 32 lettermen returned from 1994, including seven starters on offense and six defensive regulars. The biggest holes to be filled were at wide receiver, linebacker, and the defensive secondary. The offensive line was in good shape with center Juan Porter, guards LeShun Daniels and Jamie Sumner, and tackle Orlando Pace back in the fold. Eric Gohlstin shifted from center to fill the other tackle spot vacated by Korey Stringer. Rickey Dudley moved into the starting role at tight end.

Both wide receivers were gone. Chris Sanders and Joey Galloway were replaced by Terry Glenn and Buster Tillman. There was excellent experience in the backfield with quarterback Bobby Hoying and tailback Eddie George, both seniors. Nicky Sualua, a fine blocker who started the last eight games in '94, was the starter at fullback. Josh Jackson was back to handle the placekicking. All four starters returned on the defensive line—tackle Matt Bonhaus, nose guard Luke Fickell, and ends Mike Vrabel and Matt Finkes. Holdover Greg Bellisari was joined at linebacker by Ryan Miller and Kevin

1994				
August 29	Fresno State#	W	34	10
September 10	at Washington	L	16	25
September 17	Pittsburgh	W	27	3
September 24	Houston	W	52	0
October 1	at Northwestern	W	17	15
October 8	Illinois	L	10	24
October 15	at Michigan State	W	23	7
October 22	Purdue (HC)	W	48	14
October 29	at Penn State	L	14	63
November 5	Wisconsin	W	24	3
November 12	at Indiana	W	32	17
November 19	Michigan	W	22	6
January 2	Alabama*	L	17	24
Total Points			336	211

Disneyland Pigskin Classic
* Florida Citrus Bowl

Season Record: 9-4
Conference: 2nd Place

Johnson. Shawn Springs was the returning starter in the defensive secondary. Tim Patillo, Tito Paul, and Marlon Kerner were replaced by Ty Howard, Anthony Gwinn, and Rob Kelly. Freshman Brent Bartholomew took over the punting duties.

Another Early Start

For the second consecutive season, Ohio State added a preseason game to its schedule. The Buckeyes opened on Sunday, August 27, with a 38-6 win over Boston College in the Kickoff Classic at East Rutherford, New Jersey. It was OSU's ninth straight season-opening triumph and its largest margin of victory in an opener since routing Minnesota, 56-7, in 1973. The Ohio State offense scored each of the five times it moved inside the BC 20-yard line, while the defense intercepted three passes and limited the Eagles to just 91 yards in the second half. OSU led in first downs, 25-14, and total offense, 437 yards to 276.

Shawn Springs returned a kickoff 97 yards to put OSU on top, 14-3, early in the second period. Eddie George scored twice on runs of 12 and nine yards, and Bobby Hoying threw his first scoring pass of the season—a 12-yarder to tight end Rickey Dudley. Ohio State's last touchdown was scored by flanker Dimitrious Stanley on a 12-yard toss from reserve quarterback Tom Hoying, Bobby's younger brother. It was believed to be the first time in OSU history that brothers have thrown touchdown passes in the same game.

20 Days and Counting

Tenth-rated Ohio State had to wait 20 days for its second game, facing 18th-ranked Washington in the September 16 home opener. Before an Ohio Stadium crowd of 94,104, the Buckeyes handled the Huskies, 30-20, in a contest that was not as close as might be suggested by the ten-point margin of victory. OSU entered the fourth quarter

with a 23-point lead, 30-7, but committed two turnovers inside their own 35-yard line, setting up Washington's final 14 points.

Eddie George led the charge with 212 yards and two touchdowns in 36 carries, to become the first Ohio State player to rush for 200 or more yards three times during his career. Washington coach Jim Lambright described George's efforts as "awesome." The Buckeye offense scored five of the six times it was inside the Husky 20-yard line and was successful on 11 of 16 third-down attempts. OSU had a decided edge in time of possession, 37:30 to 22:30. The Scarlet and Gray defense was led by Greg Bellisari with 10 tackles, followed by Ryan Miller who had nine stops and an interception, which set up his team's first touchdown.

Premiere Passing at Pitt

Ohio State routed the Pitt Panthers, 54-14, with one of the finest passing performances in school history. Three Buckeye quarterbacks passed for all seven touchdowns, an OSU record. Bobby Hoying equaled his own school single-game record (and that of John Borton in 1952) with five scoring tosses, while back-ups Stanley Jackson and Tom Hoying each threw for a touchdown in the final period. OSU rolled up 636 yards in total offense, their highest single-game amount since totaling 715 against Utah in 1986. The Buckeye defense forced five turnovers, including four interceptions.

Flanker Terry Glenn was exceptional, grabbing nine passes for 253 yards and four touchdowns. His 253 yards eclipsed the Ohio State single-game record of 220 set by Gary Williams in 1981, and his four touchdown receptions in one game tied a school mark set by Bob Grimes against Washington State in 1952.

Tailback Eddie George added 122 yards on the ground, and the Buckeye offense was successful with 10 of 13 third-down conversion attempts. The Pitt Stadium attendance

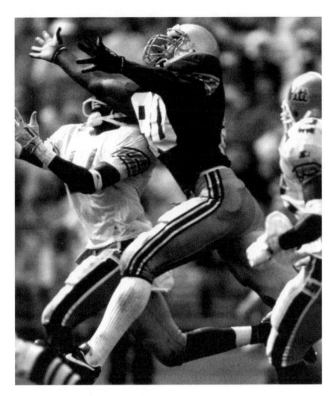

Tight end Rickey Dudley in action against the Pitt Panthers.

it." Cooper had recently experienced his third back operation.

After a slow start, the Buckeyes overcame a 10-0 deficit to win convincingly, 45-26. Ohio State, relying on its superior speed, grew stronger as the afternoon progressed. OSU outscored its opposition 31-9 in the second half after trailing 17-14 at halftime. Midway through the second period, Bobby Hoying threw 10 yards to Terry Glenn on a quick slant pattern for the Buckeyes' first touchdown. Dimitrious Stanley caught Hoying's second TD pass, with an artistic 17-yard over-the-shoulder reception, just 44 seconds before halftime.

Big plays continued to characterize Ohio State's efforts after halftime. ND received the second-half kickoff and impressively drove to a third-and-goal at the OSU two-yard line. End Mike Vrable popped fullback Marc Edwards, causing Edwards to fumble for a two-yard loss, and forcing the Irish to settle for Kevin Kopka's 22-yard field goal.

of 54,917, which included approximately 20,000 Ohio State fans, was Pittsburgh's largest home crowd in five seasons.

Hoying-George-Glenn
Pilot High-Power Offense

The Buckeyes returned home September 30 to face Notre Dame before a crowd of 95,537, at the time the largest to ever jam Ohio Stadium. It had been 60 years since the Fighting Irish made their only other appearance in the horseshoe—a noted 18-13 win over OSU in the "game of the century" on November 2, 1935. Eighteen members of Ohio State's 1935 squad were recognized in the pregame ceremonies.

Notre Dame coach Lou Holtz unexpectedly directed his team from the sideline. Holtz was still recovering from a September 12 back operation, and had planned to view the action from the press box. In their pregame meeting at midfield, John Cooper advised Holtz to make sure he didn't "overdo

After an exchange of possessions, Ohio State broke the game wide open by converting three Notre Dame turnovers into touchdowns within a span of five minutes and eight seconds. Tight end Rickey Dudley took Hoying's short toss and pulled three defenders into the end zone to complete a 15-yard scoring play and put Ohio State on top for the first time, 21-20.

Hoying went back to Glenn for his third touchdown pass of the afternoon, this one covering 82 yards, the second-longest scoring pass in OSU history. Glenn caught the ball at the OSU 29-yard line on a hook pattern, then outran defenders Allen Rossum and LaRon Moore down the middle of the field and into the end zone. Eddie George scored on a five-yard sweep to the left just five seconds into the fourth quarter, and Ohio State had built its lead to 35-20.

After ND pushed across its final touchdown, George scored again with a three-yard smash over left tackle, and Josh Jackson added a 35-yard field goal for the game's final points. Hoying finished the afternoon completing 14 of 22 passing attempts for 272 yards, George rushed for 207 yards on 32 carries, and Glenn's four receptions totaled 128 yards. Greg Bellisari led the Buckeye defense with 12 tackles, followed by Ryan Miller and Luke Fickell with 10 each. The 45 points were the most ever scored against a Notre Dame team coached by Lou Holtz.

Happier Trip to Happy Valley

With a record of 4-0, the Buckeyes advanced to fifth place in the national rankings as they prepared to open Big Ten play at Penn State on October 7. Wisconsin had beaten coach Joe Paterno's squad at State College the previous Saturday, 17-9, snapping Penn State's winning streak at 20 games. Ohio State was still smarting from its 63-14 humiliation at Beaver Stadium in 1994.

In a game filled with magnificent play by both teams, the Buckeyes emerged with a cherished three-point victory, 28-25. The lead changed hands four times. Quarterback Bobby Hoying had another magnificent afternoon, passing for 354 yards and three touchdowns, two to Terry Glenn and a real big one to Rickey Dudley to give the Buckeyes their first lead of the afternoon, 14-10, midway through the second quarter.

Trailing Penn State, 25-21, with just over three minutes remaining, it was "now or never" as the Buckeyes took possession at their own 42-yard line. Hoying was never better as he connected with Buster Tillman on a critical third-down pass, then promptly hit Dudley on the next play for a 32-yard gain to the Penn State 13-yard line. From there, Eddie George needed just two carries to score one of the biggest touchdowns of his career. George finished the afternoon with 105 yards on 24 carries, and Glenn had nine receptions for 175 yards.

Ohio State had a slight edge in game statistics, leading in first downs, 23-21, and total offensive yards, 443-382. Kevin Johnson was the Buckeyes' top tackler with 11, followed by Ryan Miller with 10. Ohio State held the Nittany Lions scoreless on their last three possessions. It was just the fourth time Penn State had lost two straight at home in Joe Paterno's 30 seasons as head coach. While the Buckeyes were beating the Nittany Lions, Northwestern handed sixth-ranked Michigan its first setback of the season, 17-15, at Ann Arbor.

Century Celebration

The Big Ten Conference celebrated its 100th anniversary in 1995. Ohio State joined in 1913 when the league was in its 18th year of activity.

OSU clears a big hurdle

Late drive lifts Buckeyes over Penn State 28-25

Columbus Dispatch, Sunday, October 8, 1995

Quarterback Bobby Hoying led a brilliant fourth-quarter winning drive at Penn State. Pictured with Hoying is left guard Jamie Sumner (72).

Beating the Camp Randall Hex

After five straight wins and a move up to the fourth place in the national rankings, John Cooper's troops traveled to Madison on October 14 to tangle with the always-tough Wisconsin Badgers, who were 2-1-1. OSU was 2-4-1 in its last seven games at Camp Randall Stadium since 1981. Coach Barry Alvarez's squad had two weeks to prepare for the Buckeyes, after registering a 17-9 victory at Penn State on September 30.

Ohio State started slowly and trailed 9-7 at the half. The Buckeyes lost a fumble on their second play from scrimmage, and suffered an interception in the end zone on their third possession. Tailback Eddie George scored Ohio State's lone first-half touchdown, capping an eight-play, 56-yard march, with a one-yard plunge midway through the second quarter.

Right after halftime, Ryan Miller returned an interception to the Wisconsin five, setting up a two-yard scoring toss from Hoying to Glenn to put OSU back in the lead, 13-9. The Badgers retaliated, sending tailback Carl McCullough on a 14-yard draw through some very poor tackling, and regained the lead, 20-16.

But the final quarter belonged to the Buckeyes. Eddie George tallied his second and third touchdowns of the day, the last one

a beautiful 51-yard run after George found a huge hole created by pulling guard LeShun Daniels and fullback Nicky Sualua. Ohio State came out on top, 27-16, with the lead changing hands six times. This was an enormous win for the 6-0 Buckeyes, who were eager to get back to Ohio Stadium after playing four of their first six games away from home.

After impressive road victories at Penn State and Wisconsin, Ohio State celebrated homecoming in the rain with a 28-0 victory over Purdue. While the Buckeyes' high-powered offense had been leading the charge all season, the defense took center stage with its first shutout in conference play since

All-American flanker Terry Glenn

OHIO STATE
VS
PURDUE
FOOTBALL

Homecoming
OHIO STADIUM
SAT., OCT. 21, 1995
1:30 PM
Sec. Row Seat
10B 2 1
B-BOX
GAME 3

the first Ohio State quarterback to pass for 200 or more yards six times in one season.

Terry Glenn caught two of Hoying's scoring tosses, setting an OSU single-season record with 12 TD receptions. The other went to tight end Rickey Dudley. Tailback Eddie George picked up 104 yards and powered across behind Juan Porter from one yard out for the game's first touchdown. Ohio State led in total offensive yards, 435 to 259.

besting Minnesota in 1992, 17-0. With cornerback Shawn Springs injured, freshman cornerback Antoine Winfield was outstanding in his first start, leading the defense with 11 tackles (nine of them solos).

The Ohio State punt return team set the tone early, blocking two Purdue punts, and tackling punter Rob Deignan for a 15-yard loss on another series. Bobby Hoying completed 20 passes for 276 yards and three of the Buckeyes' four touchdowns, becoming

First 56 and Last 35

Ohio State defeated Iowa, 56-35, at Ohio Stadium on October 28, in a game much more one-sided than suggested by the final tally. The scoring pattern was radically unusual—Ohio State scored the first 56 points, Iowa scored the last 35.

The Buckeyes found the end zone on their first six possessions, erupting for 28 points in each of the first two quarters. Tailback Eddie George scored four of the team's eight touchdowns on short runs from inside the 10-yard line, while quarterback Bobby Hoying scored on a 15-yard scamper and threw two scoring tosses to flanker Terry Glenn. Shawn Springs returned an interception 60 yards for the other six points. The Buckeye defense held Iowa to minus-yardage on its first three possessions, intercepted two Hawkeye passes in the first half, and finished the afternoon with 12 tackles for losses.

Who Would Have Believed!

While Ohio State was winning at Minnesota, the big sports story of the weekend was developing in Cleveland, where it was announced that the NFL's Cleveland Browns would be moving to Baltimore after 50 seasons in the lakefront city.

Iowa's 35 points came mostly against OSU's second and third units. The Buckeyes had 396 yards of offense in the first half, but just 42 yards in the final two periods. The 56 points was Ohio State's highest single-game score this season, while Iowa's 35 was the most by an Ohio State opponent.

Fourth-ranked OSU ran its record to 9-0, defeating Minnesota 49-21 on Saturday evening, November 4, at the Minneapolis Metrodome. This victory over the Golden Gophers was Ohio State's 1,000th all-time game (677-270-53). The Buckeyes trailed 14-7 after the first quarter, then exploded for four touchdowns in the second period to lead 35-14 at halftime.

Quarterback Bobby Hoying became the Buckeyes' all-time touchdown pass leader, with the 50th and 51st scoring tosses of his career. Tailback Eddie George scored three times, including an 87-yard gallop early in the third quarter for Ohio State's longest play from scrimmage in 1995. This 87-yard play is also the third longest rush from scrimmage in Ohio State history.

The Ohio State defense, facing Minnesota's unique run-and-shoot attack for the first time, gave up 191 yards in the first quarter, than allowed just 179 yards over the final three periods. The Buckeyes put on a memorable goal-line stand in the first period, stopping the Golden Gophers six times inside the two-yard line. Defensive end Mike Vrable finished with a pair of sacks and his first career interception. The Northwestern Wildcats

continued their winning ways, defeating Penn State 21-10 to remain undefeated in the league standings.

Eddie Tops 300-Mark

It was an afternoon no Buckeye fan will ever forget. Eddie George established a new OSU single-game rushing record with 314 yards on 36 carries, as Ohio State overwhelmed Illinois, 41-3. On an extremely cold and windy November 11 at Ohio Stadium, George started strong, running for 128 yards in the first quarter and totaling 180 yards by halftime. The Illini defense had been allowing just 109 yards on the ground per game.

The superb senior tailback set the tone for the second half, ripping off a 64-yard run on the Buckeyes' very first play from scrimmage in the third quarter. George also caught four passes during the afternoon, including the first of his career for a touchdown—a 13-yarder from quarterback Bobby Hoying late in the third period. After the game, John Cooper told reporters, "I think that was the finest individual effort I've ever seen by a running back." Illini coach Lou Tepper said, "I don't think I've ever had anybody do that against a team of mine." Ohio State led in

The Columbus Dispatch
Sunday
NOVEMBER 12, 1995 ▪▪

Sports

SECTION **E**

George shatters record, Illinois

first downs, 25-9, and total offense, 527 yards to 160.

The Buckeyes' dominance continued the following Saturday with a 42-3 shellacking of Indiana in the season's final home game. Bobby Hoying started the action with two first-quarter scoring passes to Terry Glenn. His 202 passing yards that afternoon built his total to 2,737 for the year, breaking Art Schlichter's single-season record of 2,551 in 1981. Hoying left the game with a mild concussion in the third quarter, giving way to back-up Stanley Jackson, who directed the offense on three consecutive scoring drives of 77, 50, and 49 yards. The 42 points increased Ohio State's season total to 438, breaking the old single-season school record of 437, set in 12 games in 1974.

Unhappy Ending

After 11 straight victories, Ohio State had outscored its opponents, 438-169, and was ranked second in the nation. The Buckeyes still had their traditional regular-season finale at Michigan on November 25. Coach Gary Barnett's surprising Northwestern Wildcats had finished their season November 18 with a 23-8 win at Purdue. NU was 8-0 in league competition and had earned at least a share of the 1995 Big Ten title, its first since 1936. Ohio State and Northwestern did not meet in 1995. If OSU defeated Michigan, the Buckeyes and Wildcats would be league co-champions, but Ohio State would qualify for the Rose Bowl, since the Wildcats had lost a nonconference contest to Miami (Ohio), on September 16, 30-28.

Heisman Trophy winner Eddie George

The 18th-ranked Wolverines (who had lost to Northwestern, Michigan State, and Penn State) dealt the Buckeyes one of their most devastating setbacks in many seasons, 31-23, before a Michigan Stadium crowd of 106,288. UM tailback Tim Biakabutuka played one of the finest games ever witnessed on a college gridiron, shredding the

50th Anniversary

The January 1, 1996, Rose Bowl marked the 50th consecutive season the champions of the Big Ten and Pacific Ten (originally the Pacific Eight) Conferences faced off in the Pasadena Classic.

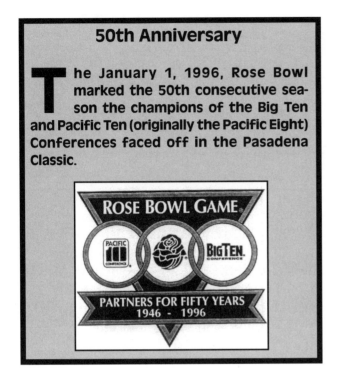

Buckeyes for 313 yards, the most ever against OSU by an opposing player in a single game.

Ohio State had its opportunities in the first half, but had to settle for field goals after twice marching inside the Michigan five. John Cooper told reporters, "If you can't stop the running game in this league, and you can't run the football yourself, you're going to get beaten. That's what happened to us today. They beat us up front unmercifully." Eddie George finished the afternoon with 104 yards on 21 attempts, while Bobby Hoying connected on 22 of 45 passes for 286 yards. Linebackers Ryan Miller and Kevin Johnson each had 11 tackles.

Playing in what resembled a monsoon, Tennessee dealt the Buckeyes their second setback of the season, 20-14, in the January 1, 1996, Florida Citrus Bowl. It was a disappointing finish for Ohio State's high-flying offense, which scored only 43 points in the season's last two games. OSU led 7-0 after one quarter, and was in control most of the first half. The Volunteers created a real momentum booster, sending Jay Graham 69 yards through a huge hole off left tackle just 23 seconds before halftime. Graham's run was a deep draw play on first down.

Tennessee went on top early in the third period with a 47-yard scoring toss from quarterback Payton Manning to Joey Kent, but OSU tied the game at 14-14 when Bobby Hoying passed 32 yards to Rickey Dudley just 12 seconds into the fourth quarter. UT's Jeff Hall provided field goals of 29 and 25 yards for the six-point margin of victory. The Buckeyes had a slight edge in first downs, 17-15, and total offensive yards, 335-327, but OSU's four turnovers were too much to overcome.

Honors Abundant

Ohio State completed the season at 11-2, outscoring its 13 opponents, 475-220, and finishing sixth in the final Associated Press poll. Eddie George became the fifth Ohio State player to win the coveted Heisman Trophy, awarded each season to college football's top player. Terry Glenn captured the Biletnikoff Award as the nation's top receiver, and Orlando Pace seized the Lombardi Award as the outstanding college lineman.

Bobby Hoying received the National Football Foundation's Vincent dePaul Drabby Award, presented annually to the nation's top senior scholar-athlete. George, Glenn, Pace, and Mike Vrabel landed on the All-America teams, and George was chosen the Big Ten's most valuable player.

1995				
August 27	Boston College#	W	38	6
September 16	Washington	W	30	20
September 23	at Pittsburgh	W	54	14
September 30	Notre Dame	W	45	26
October 7	at Penn State	W	28	25
October 14	at Wisconsin	W	27	16
October 21	Purdue (HC)	W	28	0
October 28	Iowa	W	56	35
November 4	at Minnesota	W	49	21
November 11	Illinois	W	41	3
November 18	Indiana	W	42	3
November 25	at Michigan	L	23	31
January 1	Tennessee*	L	14	20
Total Points			**475**	**220**

\# Kickoff Classic
* Florida Citrus Bowl

Season Record: 11-2
Conference: 2nd Place

1996

Ohio State entered 1996 expecting to have another very good football season with a squad dominated by seniors. The team's strengths were its veteran defense and an experienced offensive line, while its major concerns were replacing tailback Eddie George, quarterback Bobby Hoying, flanker Terry Glenn, and six other regulars.

Junior Pepe Pearson moved up to the starting role at tailback, senior Matt Calhoun moved in at fullback, and redshirt freshman Rob Murphy became a starter at guard. D. J. Jones, a starter in 1994, returned at tight end. Jones sat out the 1995 campaign recovering from open-heart surgery. Dimitrious Stanley and freshman David Boston joined Buster Tillman at the wide receiver positions. Stanley Jackson and Joe Germaine split playing time at quarterback, with Jackson starting all but one game.

Junior tackle Winfield Garnett filled the only opening on the defensive line, sophomore Damon Moore moved in at strong safety, and pure freshman Andy Katzenmoyer took charge at middle linebacker. John Cooper began his ninth season at Ohio State and his 20th as a head coach at the college level. The 1996 season was OSU's 75th at Ohio Stadium, which was dedicated in 1922.

What a Start!

The ninth-ranked Buckeyes overwhelmed Rice, 70-7, before an Ohio Stadium opening-day crowd of 93,479 on September 7. OSU scored on 10 of its first 11 possessions, and rolled up 632 yards in total offense. It was Ohio State's highest score since defeating Northwestern on November 14, 1981, 70-6.

Seven different players scored, including two pure freshmen wide receivers, Michael Wiley and David Boston. Quarterbacks Stanley Jackson and Joe Germaine combined for 315 passing yards and five touchdowns, while Pepe Pearson led the ground troops with 119 yards and three TDs. Tight end John Lumpkin's first collegiate catch was a two-yard scoring reception from Jackson on an option pass early in the first quarter.

The OSU defense, using a 4-4 formation most of the afternoon with the strong safety aligned with the linebackers, held the Owls' run-oriented, triple-option attack, to just 218 yards of total offense. Andy Katzenmoyer recorded a team-high eight tackles, including three for losses and a pair of sacks. Katzenmoyer was the first true freshman linebacker to start an Ohio State opening game. Rice head coach Ken Hatfield apparently thought OSU had unnecessarily run up the score, even though John Cooper used 73 different players, including 10 true freshmen and 10 walk-ons.

After an off week, the season's second game on September 21 was nearly a replay of the first. Overmatched Pittsburgh was thrashed, 72-0, after trailing 52-0 at halftime. The Buckeyes scored the first 10 times they had the ball and never punted all afternoon.

Three for Three

In the season-opening victory over Rice, freshman wide receiver Michael Wiley scored touchdowns all three times he touched the ball.

His first was a 49-yard reverse, and the other two came on post pattern catches of 51 and 60 yards from quarterback Joe Germaine. Wiley's afternoon was reminiscent of Howard "Hopalong" Cassady's freshman debut. Cassady scored three touchdowns in OSU's 33-13 season-opening victory over Indiana in 1952.

Only once in 111 seasons of competition has Ohio State defeated back-to-back opponents with a higher combined margin of victory. Coach Jack Ryder's 1892 squad ran over Akron, 62-0, and Marietta, 80-0, on October 22 and 29.

OSU had a decided edge in first downs, 29-4, and in total offensive yards, 602 yards to 120. The Panthers gained only 43 yards in the first half. Pepe Pearson and David Boston each tallied three touchdowns, and Joe Germaine was 8 for 8 in the passing department for 139 yards. Tailback Joe Montgomery scored his first touchdown as a Buckeye with a one-yard run midway through the third period.

Cooper Notches No. 150 at South Bend

In the second of a two-game series between two of college football's most prominent programs, fourth-ranked Ohio State overpowered fifth-rated Notre Dame, 29-16, on September 28. Playing before a Notre Dame Stadium crowd of 59,075, the Buck-

eyes made it two straight over the Fighting Irish and evened the all-time series at 2-2. The Ohio State team awarded the game ball to John Cooper in honor of his 150th career coaching victory. While he proudly cradled the ball, Cooper told reporters, "Obviously, this ball belongs to our team—not John Cooper."

Dimitrious Stanley set the tone of the game, returning the opening kickoff 85 yards to the ND 13-yard line. Four plays later, Pepe Pearson ran it across from the three, the extra point was blocked following a high snap from center, and OSU led, 6-0, just one minute and 45 seconds into the game. The Fighting Irish led briefly later in the quarter, 7-6, when an interception return to the OSU 15-yard line set up a short four-play touchdown drive.

The Buckeyes took command for good, scoring on three of their next five possessions to lead at halftime, 22-7. Matt Calhoun's two-yard touchdown reception from Stanley Jackson finished off an impressive 80-yard drive,

Ann and Brian Timm celebrate Ohio State's victory at Notre Dame. Brian is Senior Account Manager for The Ohio State Football Radio Network.

Josh Jackson came through with a 24-yard field goal, and Pearson's second TD of the afternoon from the one concluded an 84-yard march just 54 seconds before the half. The Buckeyes' blitzing defense, which at times included safeties Rob Kelly and Damon Moore, kept Notre Dame off balance most of the afternoon.

The Irish added a field goal to start the third quarter. OSU countered with a 13-yard scoring strike from Jackson to D. J. Jones, increasing the lead to 29-10. ND's final touchdown was the only score in the final period. Ohio State's superior speed was one of the big differences in the two teams. Pearson finished the afternoon with 173 yards on 29 carries, and Jackson hit on nine of 15 for 154 yards.

Greg Bellisari spearheaded the defense with 14 tackles. Mike Vrable added nine, Kelly had seven, and Moore contributed six. Lou Holtz confessed to reporters, "This is as good a team as we've played for a while. This was an excellent Ohio State team, particularly when they do a lot of things you aren't prepared for."

Complete Dominance

The Buckeyes, now third in the nation at 3-0, opened conference play at home October 5 against the fourth-ranked Penn State Nittany Lions, who were 5-0. In one of its strongest showings in several seasons, Ohio State overpowered Penn State, 38-7. OSU's offense failed to score on its first possession for the first time all season, then tallied the next four times it had the ball to lead at halftime, 24-0. Meanwhile, the Buckeyes' aggressive defense kept the Nittany Lions from crossing midfield until the third period.

Quarterbacks Stanley Jackson and Joe Germaine each passed for two touchdowns.

Ohio State led in total offense, 565 yards to 211, and in first downs, 31-13. Tailbacks Pepe Pearson had 141 yards on 28 carries, Joe Montgomery added 84 on nine carries, and Jermon Jackson contributed 54 yards on nine attempts. Penn State scored the game's last touchdown to avoid what otherwise would have been its first shutout in nine seasons. The Nittany Lions were held to just 68 yards on the ground.

Coupled with the Buckeyes' win over Notre Dame the previous week, this was the first time since 1980 that any college team recorded back-to-back victories over opponents who were ranked in the nation's top five. Penn State was the highest-ranked team Ohio State had defeated since knocking off top-ranked Iowa at Ohio Stadium in 1985, 22-13. It was PSU's most one-sided setback since losing 44-7 at Notre Dame in 1984. North-

Buckeyes overpower Penn State 38-7

Columbus Dispatch, Sunday, October 6, 1996

western remained undefeated in conference action by handing Michigan its first setback of the season, 17-16, at Evanston.

Too Close for Comfort

After four decisive victories, the second-ranked Buckeyes were fortunate to scrape past Wisconsin, 17-14, before an Ohio Stadium homecoming crowd of 94,215. The 3-1 Badgers had two weeks to prepare after losing at home to Penn State, 23-20, on September 28.

Using an eight-man front, they effectively held Ohio State's running attack to 78 yards. Wisconsin took advantage of its size (offensive line averaged 308 pounds) to control the ball more than 18 minutes in the first half. The Buckeyes gave up two fumbles, one interception, and had a field-goal attempt blocked. To OSU's credit, it was an afternoon when a fine team found a way to win when faced with adversity.

Wisconsin led at halftime, 7-3, and regained the lead, 14-10, when free safety

Place Kicker Josh Jackson

Kevin Hartley returned a fumble 36 yards for a touchdown with 13:09 remaining in the fourth quarter. Ohio State's winning possession began with freshman David Boston's 35-yard punt return to the OSU 42-yard line. Joe Ger-maine, making his first and only appearance of the afternoon in relief of Stanley Jackson, needed just four downs to put the Buckeyes back in front to stay.

Two runs by Pepe Pearson netted exactly 10 yards and a first down at the Badger 48. Germaine nearly connected with Boston on a deep sideline route. On second down, he passed eight yards in the left flat to Dimitrious Stanley, who cut upfield and raced untouched into the end zone behind a great block by D. J. Jones. Josh Jackson's extra point made the score 17-14, and the Scarlet and Gray faithful were breathing a wee bit easier. Antoine Winfield and Damon Moore ended Wisconsin's next two possessions with interceptions.

On an afternoon when Ohio State's rushing attack was clearly contained, Jackson completed 18 of 25 tosses for 265 yards, and Germaine added 48 with his scoring connection to Stanley (who hauled in 10 passes for 199 yards). Damon Moore had 19 tackles, and Rob Kelly added 14.

Mike Vrabel, two-time All-American end

Big Plays Spark Sixth Victory

Ohio State rallied from a 14-0 deficit to defeat Purdue, 42-14, at West Lafayette on October 19. This was not the normal Ohio State victory. Knowing it would be difficult to run against the Buckeye defense, the Boilermakers struck early with two long scoring passes to lead 14-0 less than six minutes into the game. On Purdue's third play from scrimmage, quarterback John Reeves passed over the middle to Isaac Jones, who slipped through a seam and raced 86 yards for the game's first touchdown. On their next series, the Boilermakers scored on a 55-yard connection from Reeves to Brian Alford, who had gone in motion out of the backfield.

The 20,000 or more Buckeye fans among the Ross-Ade Stadium crowd of 60,172 were stunned, to say the least. Ohio State retaliated with a touchdown in each of the first two quarters to tie the score, 14-14, while the OSU defense recovered to hold Purdue to 42

yards the rest of the half. Stanley Jackson threw 11 yards to Dimitrious Stanley on a fade route in the corner of the end zone for the first TD, and tailback Pepe Pearson scored the second, cutting back for 26 yards off a sweep to the right side.

Ohio State created a big break on the second-half kickoff, when Kevin Griffin knocked the ball loose from Purdue's kickoff returner, Joe Hagins, and OSU's Mike Burden recovered to the Boilermaker 24-yard line. Five plays later, Jackson scrambled nine yards into the end zone, and OSU had its first lead of the afternoon, 21-14. Later in the period, fullback Matt Keller took a screen pass to the right from Jackson, and raced 63 yards for a score, breaking two tackles along the way.

The Buckeyes continued using the "big play" to put two more TDs on the scoreboard in the final period. Pearson sprinted 64 yards on a sweep to tally his second touchdown of the afternoon, and Rob Kelly returned a fumble 79 yards to close out the scoring. Freshman linebacker Andy Katzenmoyer was outstanding with eight solo tackles (three for losses), two sacks, a forced fumble, and his first collegiate interception. Iowa surprised Penn State, 21-20, at Beaver Stadium,

Airball

For the first time in Ohio State history, two quarterbacks each passed for more than 1,000 yards in the same season. Stanley Jackson threw for 1,298, and Joe Germaine connected for 1,193.

Nifty Fifty

Nose guard Luke Fickell started a school-record 50 straight games from 1993 through 1996.

in 15 attempts, including runs for 50 and 23 yards.

First Since 1979

The Buckeye machine moved into overdrive with convincing shutouts over Minnesota and Illinois, 45-0 and 48-0. It was OSU's first back-to-back whitewashes since blasting Wisconsin (59-0) and Michigan State (42-0) on consecutive weekends in 1979. At home November 2 against the Golden Gophers, Ohio State was hampered with turnovers at the start and led 10-0 at halftime, before erupting for 35 points in the final two quarters.

On this cold and blustery afternoon with temperatures in the mid-30s, the Buckeye defense could hardly have been better. Minnesota only once moved into Ohio State territory. The Golden Gophers, who entered the game as the Big Ten's top passing team averaging 240 yards per outing, were held to 11 completions for a meager 57 yards. The OSU defense picked off four passes and tied a school single-game record with 14 tackles for losses.

The big news of the afternoon came from State College, where Penn State handed Northwestern its first conference setback in two seasons, 34-9. The second-ranked Buckeyes were now alone at the top of the Big Ten standings, followed by Northwestern, Iowa, and Michigan, who had each lost once in league play. For the second consecutive season, Ohio State and Northwestern were not scheduled to meet.

The Buckeyes' 48-0 triumph at Champaign the following Saturday was similar to their win over Minnesota. It was a cold, windy afternoon, and the team began slowly

handing the Nittany Lions their second conference setback and virtually eliminating them from the league title chase.

The second-ranked Buckeyes improved their record to 7-0 with a 38-26 win over 20th-rated Iowa at Kinnick Stadium on October 26. It was the Hawkeyes' first conference setback of the season. Ohio State moved out to a 38-6 lead early in the third period before Iowa scored the game's last three touchdowns.

Safeties Rob Kelly and Damon Moore gave great efforts. Kelly blocked an Iowa punt that Kevin Griffin recovered in the end zone for OSU's first touchdown. Moore had nine tackles, broke up three passes, and tied a school single-game record with three interceptions (all in the first half). Andy Katzenmoyer and Greg Bellisari also had nine tackles, followed by Ryan Miller with eight and Matt Finkes with seven. Sophomore tailback Joe Montgomery came off the bench to contribute a career-high 160 yards

without scoring in the first period. Starting in the second quarter, Joe Germaine directed the offense to touchdowns on seven straight possessions.

Pepe Pearson carried the ball 21 times for 165 yards, increasing his season total to 1,126 to become just the 12th player in OSU history to rush for more than 1,000 yards in a single season. Freshman Michael Wiley saw his first action at tailback, carrying for 88 yards in 12 attempts. Ohio State led in first downs, 24-8, and total offensive yards, 549-130.

Iowa and Michigan suffered their second conference losses, virtually eliminating themselves from the league title chase. The Hawkeyes lost at home to Northwestern, 40-13, while Purdue (with a record of 2-8) shocked Michigan, 9-3, at West Lafayette.

Rose Bowl Clinched at Bloomington

It wasn't easy, but Ohio State was able to seize at least a share of the Big Ten title and its first junket to Pasadena since 1984, with a 27-17 come-from-behind victory at Indiana. Only once before had the Buckeyes been able to grab the Rose Bowl trip the week prior to the Michigan game (in 1957). The Hoosiers were at an emotional high, partly because this was the last home game for Indiana head coach Bill Mallory, who had been informed at mid-season that he would not be returning as head coach in 1997.

With just over six minutes to play and the score knotted at 10-10, linebacker Andy Katzenmoyer stripped the football from IU quarterback Jay Rodgers. End Matt Finkes grabbed the loose pigskin and rambled 45 yards for the go-ahead touchdown, much to the delight of Ohio State fans who seemed to make up more than half the Memorial Stadium crowd of 49,271. Josh Jackson added a 31-yard field goal, and Damon Moore scored on a 28-yard interception return to seal the team's 10th victory of the season.

Joe Germaine had another very impressive game, completing 15 of 27 passes for 167 yards, including a scoring toss to David Boston for the OSU offense's only touchdown (Boston finished with 13 catches for 153 yards). Finkes led the defense with 12 tackles, followed by Greg Bellisari with eight and Mike Vrable with seven. The Hoosiers, who gave it everything they had, looked like anything but a team that had just suffered its 15th consecutive Big Ten loss.

No, Not Again!

History repeats itself. Much like they did in 1995, the Michigan Wolverines spoiled Ohio State's undefeated season, this time with a 13-9 victory at Ohio Stadium on November 23. Coach Lloyd Carr's team entered

All-American cornerback Shawn Springs

Rare Finish

The outcome of the Ohio State-Michigan game has frequently decided which Big Ten team will play in the Rose Bowl. The 1996 season has been the only year the Buckeyes were able to participate in the Pasadena Classic after losing the final game of the regular season to the Wolverines.

the game with three losses in Big Ten play, including setbacks to Purdue and Penn State in its last two games. It was the first time since 1958 that the Wolverines entered "The Game" with a two-game losing streak.

It was essentially an afternoon of two different halves. Joe Germaine started at quarterback for the first time all season. The Buckeyes completely dominated the first 30 minutes of play, yet led only 9-0 at halftime. OSU had put together 220 yards of offense, while holding UM to just 62, but was forced to settle for three field goals instead of putting the ball in the end zone (Josh Jackson from 21, 36, and 21 yards). The second three-pointer was the most disappointing, since OSU began with a first-down at the Michigan two-yard line, but simply couldn't score the touchdown.

The second half was an entirely different story. On the second play from scrimmage, quarterback Brian Griese threw to wide receiver Tai Streets on a quick slant pattern that went for 69 yards and the game's only touchdown. Cornerback Shawn Springs slipped on the play, and Streets had clear sailing into the end zone. Ohio State still led, 9-7, but the game's momentum suddenly had swung toward Michigan, and OSU never recovered. Remy Hamilton added field goals of 43 and 39 yards, and that's all the Wolverines needed to hand the Buckeyes their only loss of the season.

UM controlled the second half, leading in offensive yards, 242-79. Pepe Pearson was the game's leading runner with 117 yards, only 10 of which came after halftime. Michigan's Chris Howard ran for 105 yards to become the first back all season to exceed the century mark against the Buckeye defense. OSU had a slight edge in the game's statistics, leading in first downs, 16-14, and total offense, 304 yards to 299. The loss forced the Buckeyes to share the Big Ten title with Northwestern.

Exceptional Effort!

Ohio State came back convincingly from its devastating setback to Michigan, with a 20-17 Rose Bowl triumph over Arizona State. With the lead changing hands five times, the fourth-ranked Buckeyes outlasted the second-rated Sun Devils in one of the most exciting and nerve-racking finishes possible. The huge throng of Scarlet and Gray loyalists among the crowd of 100,635 were flabbergasted, as they cheered their team to its first Rose Bowl victory in 23 seasons.

Ohio State drew first blood, with Stanley Jackson throwing a nine-yard touchdown

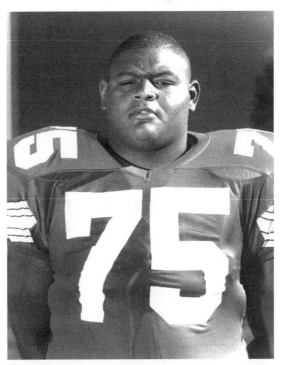

Orlando Pace, two-time All-American tackle, two-time Lombardi Award winner, Outland Trophy winner.

pass to David Boston (remember the name) to finish-off an 83-yard, 11-play march late in the first quarter. The Pac-Ten champions countered with a second period, 13-play, 80-yard drive, to tie the game at halftime. Quarterback Jake "The Snake" Plummer threw 25 yards to Ricky Boyer for the six points.

Arizona State took its first lead on Robert Nycz's 37-yard field goal at the 9:12 mark of the third quarter. The Buckeyes quickly retaliated with the longest pass play in Ohio State bowl history, a 72-yarder from Germaine to Dimitrious Stanley to regain the lead, 14-10. Next it was ASU's turn. Plummer put his squad back on top, 17-14, with a nifty 11-yard scramble on a third-and-goal with just 1:40 remaining in the game. The drive was kept alive when Plummer passed 29 yards to Keith Poole on a fourth-and-three at the OSU 37-yard line.

While the Arizona State team celebrated on the sideline as if the game were over, the Buckeyes knew it was "now or never" as they took possession at their own 35-yard line. Three connections from Germaine to Stanley of 11, 13, and 12 yards moved the ball to the ASU 29-yard line, and Ohio State was on the

Who Is This Guy Named Joe?

Quarterback Joe Germaine was named the Rose Bowl's MVP after directing the winning drive in the game's closing seconds. Ironically, Germaine grew up in Mesa, Arizona, as an Arizona State fan, but elected not to play for the Sun Devils since coach Bruce Snyder was interested in him only as a defensive back.

Exceptional Accomplishment

John Cooper became the first and only coach to guide teams from both the Big Ten and Pacific Ten Conferences to victories in the Rose Bowl. Cooper's Arizona State squad defeated Michigan, 22-15, in Pasadena on January 1, 1987.

move. Two pass interference calls against the Sun Devils advanced the ball to the five. On first-and-goal, with 24 seconds remaining, Stanley drew double coverage running a slant pattern to the back of the end zone. Germaine looked off Stanley, then flipped a short toss on the right side to David Boston, who backpedaled and stepped into the end zone for one of the season's biggest touchdowns. There were 19 seconds on the clock, as Ohio State had staged one of the most dramatic and significant drives in school history.

In the heavy California mist that had beset the giant Rose Bowl stadium, Arizona State was dealt its first loss of the season. The OSU defense was superb, limiting the Sun Devils to 276 yards, including just 75 on the ground. ASU entered the Rose Bowl with

Ohio State Buckeyes
Rose Bowl
CHAMPIONS

FANTASTIC FINISH
OSU 20 ARIZONA ST. 17

Columbus Dispatch, Thursday, January 2, 1997

the nation's fourth-ranked offense, averaging 492 yards and 42 points per game. Damon Moore was the team's leading tackler with nine, followed by Greg Bellisari, Andy Katzenmoyer, and Ty Howard with eight each.

Pearson was the game's leading runner with 111 yards, Germaine had nine completions for 131 yards, and Stanley was the afternoon's top receiver with five catches for 124 yards. Plummer's 19 completions netted the Sun Devils 201 yards. John Cooper was nearly brought to tears as he described the comeback, "The greatest moment in my 35 years of coaching."

Ohio State finished the season as the nation's second-ranked team behind Florida. Florida State was third, Arizona State fourth, and Penn State seventh. The Buckeyes outscored their 12 opponents, 455-131, averaging 37.9 points-per-game while surrendering an average of only 10.9. Orlando Pace became the first two-time winner of the Lombardi Award. He also captured the Outland Trophy as the nation's top interior lineman, and finished fourth in the Heisman Trophy balloting. Pace, Mike Vrabel, and Shawn Springs were named to the All-America team, and Pace was chosen the Big Ten's most valuable player.

1997

John Cooper faced a major rebuilding effort as he began his tenth season at Ohio State. Gone were 14 starters from his excellent '96 squad, including eight on defense. The departees included defensive linemen Mike Vrabel, Matt Finkes, and Luke Fickell, linebackers Greg Bellisari and Ryan Miller, and defensive backs Rob Kelly, Ty Howard, and Shawn Springs. Gone from the offensive unit were interior linemen Orlando Pace, Juan Porter, and LeShun Daniels, tight end D. J. Jones, flanker Dimitrious Stanley, and fullback Matt Calhoun.

The 1997 offensive line was built around returnees Eric Gohlstin, who started at both center and right tackle, and left guard Rob Murphy. Ben Gilbert took over at right guard, Brooks Burris started seven games at right tackle, Tyson Walter moved in at left tackle, and Kurt Murphy started the last six games at center. John Lumpkin took over the tight end responsibilites, and Dee Miller became a starter at flanker. Stanley Jackson and Joe Germaine continued their dual roles at quarterback, Pepe Pearson returned at tailback, and Matt Keller won the starting fullback role.

With tackle Winfield Garnett the only returning starter on the defensive line, the Buckeyes used several players at the other positions in 1997. Matt LaVrar started all but two games at one end, Clinton Wayne, Tony Eisenhard, and Rodney Bailey split time at the other end, and Jim Bell and Joe Brown saw most of the action at nose guard. Middle linebacker Andy Katzenmoyer was joined on the outside by Jerry Rudzinski and Kevin Johnson. Antoine Winfield, Gary Berry, and Ahmed Plummer were united with returnee Damon Moore in the defensive secondary.

1996

September 7	Rice	W	70	7
September 21	Pittsburgh	W	72	0
September 28	at Notre Dame	W	29	16
October 5	Penn State	W	38	7
October 12	Wisconsin (HC)	W	17	14
October 19	at Purdue	W	42	14
October 26	at Iowa	W	38	26
November 2	Minnesota	W	45	0
November 9	at Illinois	W	48	0
November 16	at Indiana	W	27	17
November 23	Michigan	L	9	13
January 1	Arizona State*	W	20	17
Total Points			**455**	**131**
* Rose Bowl				

Season Record: 11-1
Big Ten Co-Champion

Thursday Night Kickoff

Ohio State opened against Wyoming in the inaugural Eddie Robinson Football Classic on Thursday evening, August 28, at Ohio Stadium. The proceeds from this preseason game went to the Black Coaches Association to assist various inner-city youth programs and fund ethnic minority scholarships. The attendance of 89,122 marked the first non-sellout at the horseshoe since the Arizona game on September 7, 1991, breaking a string of 35 straight sellouts.

The Buckeyes came out on top, 24-10, in their first-ever meeting with the surprisingly strong Cowboys. Leading just 10-3 at halftime, OSU struck quickly on its second and third possessions of the third quarter to increase its lead to 24-3. Tailback Michael Wiley came off the bench to spark the offense, rushing for a game-high 121 yards, including a 32-yard touchdown sprint early in the third period. Quarterback Stanley Jackson scampered 41 yards on a keeper for the

season's first touchdown, and connected with a 45-yard sprintout pass to Dee Miller for OSU's last six-pointer of the evening. Dan Stultz added a 40-yard field goal. Antoine Winfield was OSU's leading tackler with 11, followed by Jerry Rudzinski with 10 and Kevin Johnson with 9.

The Buckeyes waited 16 days for their second game, a 44-13 verdict over visiting Bowling Green on September 13. It was the first Ohio State game not to be televised since the 1994 season. John Cooper told reporters he was happy OSU was 2-0, but was particularly bothered with his squad's four lost fumbles in the first half. Michael Wiley had his second fine game, rushing for 72 yards on 10 carries, plus returning a kickoff 100 yards for Ohio State's first touchdown late in the first quarter.

Running Game Stalls

The Buckeyes ran their record to 3-0 with a 28-20 victory over visiting Arizona, but the game's scoring pattern left many of the Scarlet and Gray faithful wondering. Ohio State nearly let the game get away, being outscored 20-0 in the final period after leading 28-0 through three quarters of play. OSU was outgained 380-292 in total yards, committed four turnovers, and was held to 70 yards rushing, its lowest total since gaining just 58 yards on the ground at Michigan in 1993. The team had just four first downs rushing during the afternoon, as the inexperience in the offensive line began to show.

It's Been a Decade

John Cooper joined John Wilce and Woody Hayes as the only head coaches to guide the Ohio State football program for ten or more seasons. Wilce was at the helm 16 years from '13 through '28, while Hayes manned the position 28 seasons from '51 through '78.

On the brighter side, Katzenmoyer returned an interception 20 yards for Ohio State's second touchdown, and Jackson and Germaine combined with 14 completions for 222 yards. The victory was John Cooper's 79th at Ohio State, moving him into third place in school career wins behind Earle Bruce (81) and Woody Hayes (205). Split end David Boston also saw action on defense when Ohio State shifted to a five-man "nickel" defensive backfield in the second half.

Katzenmoyer Changes Game's Momentum

Trailing 10-7 after a sluggish start, the seventh-ranked Buckeyes scored the game's last 24 points to control Missouri, 31-10. It was the first time all season the Buckeyes had trailed an opponent. This was the 11th game between the two schools, and the first to be played at Columbia. The Faurot Field attendance of 58,882 was the largest home crowd to see the Tigers play in 12 seasons. Joe Germaine came off the bench to spark OSU's struggling offense with touchdown passes to David Boston in the second and third quarters.

Holding a lead of 10-7, the upset-minded Tigers were looking at a third-and-ten at their own 15-yard line. Quarterback Corby Jones, who had already very effectively carried 10 times for 69 yards, headed upfield with the ball. Andy Katzenmoyer stopped Jones dead in his tracks with a bone-jarring tackle, one yard short of the first down. The game's momentum shifted on that play, and Missouri never got it back. For the second straight week, OSU had difficulty with its rushing game, finishing with 98 yards on the ground and 269

through the air. Antoine Winfield was all over the field, finishing as the game's leading tackler with 13. Cornerback Rolland Steele and Safety Percy King each made their first career interceptions.

Impressive Conference Opener

The seventh-ranked Buckeyes played their best game of the young season, defeating 11th-rated Iowa, 23-7, in warm and sunny Ohio Stadium. OSU eliminated many of the mistakes and turnovers which characterized its first four games. Ohio State's defense stymied Tavian Banks, holding the talented Hawkeye tailback to 82 yards in 22 attempts. Banks began the afternoon as the nation's top runner, averaging 209 yards-per-game.

The Buckeyes built up a 16-0 lead before Iowa scored its only touchdown of the afternoon midway through the third quarter. Pepe Pearson rushed for a game-high 109 yards, while Michael Wiley added 85 and scored twice from distances of one and 10 yards. Stanley Jackson tossed six yards to David Boston for OSU's other touchdown.

Andy Katzenmoyer again spearheaded the defense, this time with 11 tackles. Katzenmoyer also made his first appearance at fullback, throwing

Buckeye-Badger Streak Snapped

Ohio State and Wisconsin did not meet in 1997, breaking the Buckeyes' third longest continuous series. The two schools had played for 49 consecutive seasons from 1948 through 1996.

an impressive block on Iowa's Eric Thigpen and clearing the way for Wiley's first touchdown.

Late Nittany Lion Rally Too Much

Ohio State suffered its first setback of the season, losing a 31-27 thriller to second-ranked Penn State, before what was then a record Beaver Stadium crowd of 97,282. The afternoon was essentially made up of three different games. The Nittany Lions took command early with a 10-0 lead, Ohio State retaliated by scoring 27 of the game's next 34 points, and Penn State reversed the momentum with a strong running game to account for the contest's final two touchdowns. The loss snapped Ohio State's winning streak at six.

Joe Germaine was brilliant, connecting on 29 of 43 passes for 378 yards and two of OSU's three TDs. But in the end it was PSU's solid ground attack that spelled the differ-

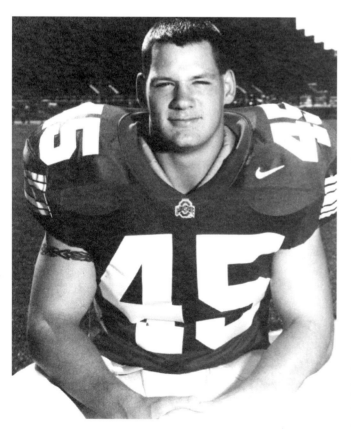

Andy Katzenmoyer, All-American linebacker

ence. With the Buckeyes leading, 27-17, fullback Aaron Harris took a handoff through the left side, bounced back to the right through three attempted tackles, and sprinted 51 yards for a touchdown. There were 20 seconds remaining in the third period. Ohio State still had the lead, 27-24, but the Nittany Lions had given themselves new life.

Penn State went ahead for good with an eight-play, 86-yard scoring drive early in the fourth quarter. Tailback Curtis Enis rocketed the last 26, cutting upfield after starting with a sweep to his right. Enis punished the Buckeye defense for 211 yards on 23 attempts, becoming the first back to break the 100-yard barrier against OSU in 17 games. The Nittany Lions effectively neutralized the pursuit of middle linebacker Andy Katzenmoyer by running straight upfield most of the afternoon.

The loss was a major disappointment for the Ohio State players, especially after racking up 565 total yards of offense. It was career victory 294 for coach Joe Paterno, who told reporters this was a great win for his squad over a very improved Ohio State team. David Boston established a school single-game record with 14 receptions (good for 153 yards and a TD). OSU's ability to stop PSU's running attack was hampered when linebacker Kevin Johnson suffered a sprained ankle late in the first quarter, and saw action only briefly the remainder of the afternoon.

Five Straight

Ohio State, now 5-1 overall and 1-1 in conference play, rebounded strongly from its loss at Penn State to outscore its next five opponents, 189-28. The Buckeyes' closest call during the five-game stretch was a 24-point victory at Michigan State. They returned home October 18 to blast Indiana, 31-0, for their lone shutout of the season. The victory was a real crowd pleaser for the Ohio Stadium attendance of 92,368. Stanley Jack-

son was very solid running the offense, connecting on 13 of 15 passes for 189 yards.

Dan Stultz's 55-yard field goal was the longest ever by an Ohio State player in Ohio Stadium, Clinton Wayne recorded his first career touchdown with a 38-yard interception return, Michael Wiley threw his first collegiate TD pass (eight yards to Steve Wisniewski), and Gary Barry intercepted two IU passes.

The victory was John Cooper's 82nd at Ohio State, moving him into second place on the school's all-time victory list behind Woody Hayes with 205. While the Buckeyes had no trouble with the Hoosiers, Penn State and Michigan were both fortunate to stay undefeated. The Nittany Lions rallied for a 16-15 victory over Minnesota at Beaver Stadium, while the Wolverines came from behind to win at home over Iowa, 28-24. Purdue, the surprise team of the Big Ten under first-year coach Joe Tiller, remained

undefeated in conference play, handing Wisconsin its first league setback, 45-20.

The following weekend, Ohio State treated its homecoming crowd of 92,445 to a 49-6 thrashing of Northwestern, back on the OSU schedule after a two-year absence. The game's statistics were nearly as one-sided as the score. The Buckeyes led in first downs, 32-9, and total offense, 563 yards to 164. Joe Germaine passed for three touchdowns, including a 29-yarder to tight end Tommy Hoying for Hoying's first career reception. OSU's defense had now gone eight straight quarters without surrendering a touchdown.

Berry Sparks Rain-Soaked Victory at MSU

Sophomore cornerback Gary Berry scored two touchdowns within a span of 2:07 late in the first quarter, to spark the ninth-ranked Buckeyes to a 37-13 triumph over 20th-rated Michigan State. Berry picked off Todd Schultz's pass in the flat and raced 45 yards for the afternoon's first touchdown (Schultz had been intercepted five times the week before by Michigan). After OSU forced the Spartans to punt on a three-and-out on their next possession, linebacker Marcel Willis blocked Paul Edinger's punt, and Berry scooped up the loose ball at the one and scored.

Playing in a driving rain storm before a November 1 crowd of 74,903 at Spartan Stadium, OSU had an almost perfect balance on offense with 203 yards passing and 202 yards on the ground. Dan Stultz booted field goals

OSU overcomes early trick play to thump Wildcats

Columbus Dispatch, Sunday, October 26, 1997

Rob Murphy, two-time All-American guard

For the fourth consecutive weekend, the opponent's starting quarterback had fewer than 10 completions against OSU's aggressive "Silver Bullets" defense. In one of the season's biggest games, undefeated Michigan overwhelmed Penn State at Beaver Stadium, 34-8, handing Joe Paterno's Nittany Lions their first setback of the season.

Victory No. 700

Ohio State closed out its home schedule with a 41-6 rout of winless Illinois on November 15. On an extremely cold and snowy afternoon, with temperatures dipping into the 20s, it's doubtful if half of the Ohio Stadium crowd of 92,008 was still on hand when Illinois cornerback Trevor Starghill ran 38 yards with a recovered fumble for his team's only points. It was the last play of the game, and it accounted for the only touchdown the Fighting Illini were able to score against the Buckeyes over the past three seasons.

The victory was the 700th for the Buckeyes, who fielded their first team in 1890. Ohio State's all-time record now stood at 700-274-53. While OSU was running its conference record to 6-1, Purdue and Wisconsin each suffered their second league setbacks of the season at the hands of Penn State (42-17) and Michigan (26-16), respectively.

Second-Half Rally Falls Short

Michigan captured the outright Big Ten title and a birth in the Rose Bowl with a 20-14 victory over Ohio State in the traditional

of 25, 43, and 38 yards, and Joe Germaine connected on 13 aerials for 134 yards (including an 11-yard TD toss to David Boston). Antoine Winfield continued his fine play, leading the defense with 11 tackles. Purdue lost its first conference game of the year, falling to the Iowa Hawkeyes at Kinnick Stadium, 35-17.

The Buckeyes completely dominated Minnesota the following Saturday, winning at the Minneapolis Metrodome, 31-3. It was Ohio State's 14th consecutive victory over the Golden Gophers. Joe Germaine was again especially sharp, completing 17 of 21 tosses for 211 yards and three touchdowns.

The Ohio State defense continued its strong recent play, holding the Golden Gophers to 157 yards of total offense. Quarterback Cory Sauter was sacked five times, Gary Berry and Kevin Johnson each made interceptions, and Andy Katzenmoyer had eight unassisted tackles.

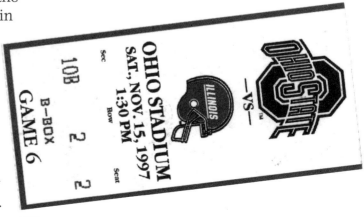

regular-season finale for both schools. The November 22 crowd of 106,982 was, at the time, the largest in Michigan Stadium history.

The Wolverines dominated the first half and led 20-0 early in the third quarter. Michigan scored with a seven-play, 62-yard drive, a 78-yard punt return, and a 43-yard return of an intercepted pass. Ohio State rallied with the game's final two touchdowns—a 56-yard pass from Joe Germaine to David Boston, and a two-yard run by Pepe Pearson after linebacker Jerry Rudzinski returned a Michigan fumble to the two. But the UM defense stopped the Buckeyes three times in the game's last six minutes to secure the victory.

Ohio State completed the season, losing to powerful Florida State in the January 1, 1998, Sugar Bowl, 31-14. The Seminoles took control of the game with two quick touchdowns in the final four minutes of the second quarter to lead at halftime, 21-3. Stanley Jackson and Joe Germaine were pressured all evening by FSU's ferocious pass rush, and were never able to develop any offensive consistency. Seminole quarterback Thad Busby was the game's offensive star, connecting on 22 of 33 tosses for 334 yards.

The Buckeyes finished the season at 10-3, outscoring their 13 opponents, 394-170, and finishing 12th in the final Associated Press poll. Michigan defeated Washington State in the Rose Bowl, 21-16, to complete the year at 12-0, earning a share of a split national title with the Nebraska Cornhuskers. David Boston established a new school single-season receiving record with 73 catches (970 yards, 14 TDs). The previous record of 69 receptions (1,127 yards, 11 TDs) was set by Cris Carter in 1986. Andy Katzenmoyer, Rob Murphy, and Antoine Winfield made the All-America teams. Katzenmoyer became the only sophomore ever to win the Butkus Award as the nation's outstanding linebacker, and Winfield was voted Ohio State's most valuable player.

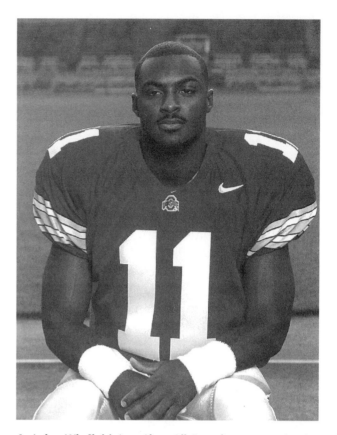

Antoine Winfield, two-time All-American cornerback

1997

August 28	Wyoming#	W	24	10
September 13	Bowling Green	W	44	13
September 20	Arizona	W	28	20
September 27	at Missouri	W	31	10
October 4	Iowa	W	23	7
October 11	at Penn State	L	27	31
October 18	Indiana	W	31	0
October 25	Northwestern (HC)	W	49	6
November 1	at Michigan State	W	37	13
November 8	at Minnesota	W	31	3
November 15	Illinois	W	41	6
November 22	at Michigan	L	14	20
January 1	Florida State*	L	14	31

Total Points		394	170

 # Eddie Robinson Football Classic at Ohio Stadium
* Sugar Bowl

Season Record: 10-3
Conference: 2nd Place (Tie)

1998

Expectations were very high as John Cooper prepared for his eleventh season at Ohio State. A large nucleus was back from the '97 squad, which had gone 10-3 and had outscored its opposition, 394-170. Center Kurt Murphy, guards Rob Murphy and Ben Gilbert, and tackle Tyson Walter were all returning starters, and Brooks Burris replaced Eric Gohlstin at the other tackle spot. Joe Germaine now had the quarterbacking duties all to himself, and an excellent trio of receivers was in place with split end David Boston, flanker Dee Miller, and tight end John Lumpkin. Matt Keller was back at fullback and Michael Wiley replaced Pepe Pearson as the starting tailback.

Great things were expected from the defensive side of the ball. Ohio State may never have had a more effective secondary than the experienced quartet of cornerbacks Antoine Winfield and Ahmed Plummer and

safeties Damon Moore and Gary Berry. The line was deep and talented. Rodney Bailey, Ryan Pickett, Joe Brown, and Brent Johnson started the majority of the season, with fine play also coming from Clinton Wayne, Matt LaVrar, Mike Collins, and James Cotton.

Jerry Rudzinski and Andy Katzenmoyer were joined at the starting linebacker spots by Na'il Diggs who replaced Kevin Johnson. The kicking game was in great shape with the return of Dan Stultz and Brent Bartholomew. Stultz led the Big Ten in kick scoring in '97 with an average of 7.1 points per game, while Bartholomew ranked tenth nationally with an average of 45.2 yards per punt.

Divine Opener

For the first time since 1980, Ohio State was ranked as the nation's top team. The Buckeyes opened Saturday evening, September 5, with an impressive 34-17 triumph at neighboring West Virginia, in one of the most eagerly anticipated openers in school history. Tickets for the contest against the eleventh-ranked Mountaineers were at such a premium, some OSU fans purchased West Vir-

1998 Ohio State coaching staff

ginia season tickets just to be able to see this opener. Not counting three seasons when OSU played in pre-season classics, it was the first time Ohio State had opened outside of Ohio Stadium since defeating Michigan State, 21-0, at East Lansing in 1975.

The rowdy crowd of 68,409, third largest ever at Mountaineer Field, rapidly calmed down after Ohio State sprang to a 17-3 lead early in the second period. After trading first-quarter field goals, the Buckeyes struck twice with drives of 55 and 80 yards. Michael Wiley raced 18 yards around left end for the first touchdown, and Joe Germaine connected from 14 yards out with Dee Miller for the second.

After Dan Stultz increased his team's lead with a 36-yard field goal late in the second period, the Mountaineers put together their most impressive effort of the evening—an 81-yard six-play scoring drive to make it 20-10. Shawn Foreman scored with a six-yard reception from quarterback Marc Bulger just 20 seconds before halftime.

Ohio State dominated the second half with drives of 96 and 74 yards, to increase its lead to 34-10 and break the game wide open. David Boston, who had earlier been shaken up with a hard hit on the artificial turf at the end of a 20-yard punt return, scored his first TD of the season with a perfectly executed 39-yard post pattern from Germaine. Freshman tailback Jonathan Wells finished OSU's

WEST VIRGINIA MOUNTAINEERS VS. OHIO STATE

SAT., SEPTEMBER 5, 1998
MOUNTAINEER FIELD, MORGANTOWN, W.VA

GAME ONE

PHOTO/ VIDEO

244 SUBJECT TO CONDITIONS ON BACK

- ADMISSION STUB -

1 WEST VIRGINIA VS. OHIO STATE SAT., SEPTEMBER 5, 1998

Infrequent Rivals

The season opener at West Virginia marked only the sixth meeting between the neighboring schools, and just the second since 1903. It also was Ohio State's first trip to Morgantown. After losing to the Mountaineers in 1897 (24-0) in a game played at Parkersburg, West Virginia, the Buckeyes won four times in Columbus in 1900 (27-0), 1902 (30-0), 1903 (34-6), and 1987 (24-3).

---

scoring on a seven-yard scamper midway through the final quarter. West Virginia notched its second touchdown, just 13 seconds before the final gun sounded, with a three-yard toss from Bulger to Foreman.

Cooper praised his team's defense and their halftime adjustments which took away WVU's cutback runs. Amos Zereoue was held to minus-three yards in the second half after the fine Mountaineer tailback had gained 80 yards in the first two quarters.

Wiley was the game's leading rusher with 140 yards, and Germaine completed 18 tosses for 301 yards. Antoine Winfield had eight solo tackles. The Mountaineers were successful on only two of 14 third-down conversion attempts. The Buckeyes led in first downs, 26-12, and total offensive yards, 549-310.

Yea!—We All Get to Play!

The following Saturday's home opener against the University of Toledo was never in doubt. The Rockets were the defending champions of the Mid-American Conference's West Division. It was the first-ever meeting between the two schools. Before a crowd of 93,149, the Buckeyes routed the overmatched visitors, 49-0, after vaulting to a 42-0 lead at halftime.

OSU needed only four minutes and 25 seconds to run 11 offensive plays and jump out to a lead of 21-0. Michael Wiley scored his team's first touchdown with a 76-yard run, tying a record for the sixth longest run in school history. The Buckeye defense limited the Rocket offense to 32 yards and one first down in the first half.

Cooper substituted liberally, beginning late in the second period. Ohio State used 11 different ballcarriers and nine separate receivers to accumulate 512 yards, compared with 194 for Toledo. Five different Buckeye defenders made interceptions. Split end Reggie Germany scored his first two collegiate TDs—a five-yard toss from Joe Germaine and a 47-yard bomb from backup quarterback Mark Garcia.

The scoring pattern of Ohio State's third non-conference game September 19 was a stark contrast. The visiting Missouri Tigers (ranked 11th nationally) took advantage of two Ohio State fumbles to lead at halftime, 14-13, even though OSU held a decided advantage in total first-half yards, 306-145. It would turn out to be the only time all season Ohio State would trail at the half.

Matters changed significantly after intermission. The Buckeye offensive line really showed its dominance in the last two quarters, leading Ohio State to its third straight win, 35-14. The Buckeyes very systematically scored on drives of 70, 75, and 70 yards for its three second-half TDs. Germaine and Wiley again had excellent afternoons, passing and running for 211 and 209 yards, respectively. Quarterback Corby Jones was successful running the Tiger's option attack, especially in the early going. Jones finished the day rushing for 91 yards on 20 carries.

John Cooper and Missouri coach Larry Smith, a 1962 Bowling Green grad, were no strangers. Smith guided Southern California

to victories over Ohio State in '89 and '90. He also was head coach at Arizona two of the three seasons Cooper was at Arizona State in the 1980s.

While the Buckeyes were idle the following week, Michigan State visited Michigan in the conference's key encounter. The Wolverines won, 29-17, to even their record at 2-2, after starting the season with losses to Notre Dame and Syracuse. The Spartans' record dipped to 1-3. Penn State was also idle this weekend, giving both the Buckeyes and

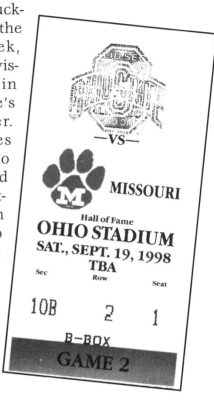

Nittany Lions two weeks to prepare for their October 3 encounter in Columbus.

Defense Dominates

Paced by one of its finest defensive efforts in many games, Ohio State defeated seventh-ranked Penn State, 28-9, before a cold and rain-drenched crowd of 93,479. For the third consecutive season, both teams entered this game unbeaten and ranked in the nation's top ten. After neither squad was able to generate much offense in the early going, Penn State's Travis Forney booted a 42-yard field goal midway through the second period to give his team a 3-0 lead.

OSU stifles Penn State on a day for defense

Cleveland Plain Dealer, Sunday, October 4, 1998

It Finally Happened

Joe Germaine threw a total of 97 passes this season, before finally tossing his first interception. Penn State's David Macklin made the pick-off on the second play of the third quarter.

SPECIAL PULL-OUT COLLECTOR POSTER NO. 3 · ROB MURPHY

Senior Quarterback
Joe Germaine

Ohio State vs. Penn State
OHIO STADIUM · OCTOBER 3, 1998 · $3.00

With four minutes remaining until half-time and the Nittany Lions in possession at their own 13, linebacker Jerry Rudzinski blitzed quarterback Kevin Thompson from the left, forcing him to retreat near his own end zone. Thompson lost control of the ball as he hurriedly attempted to dump it off, and Rudzinski pounced on it for the Buckeyes' first touchdown. Ohio State added to its lead just 23 seconds before the half, when Germaine hit Wiley across the middle with a 20-yard TD pass.

The excellent play of the Buckeyes' defense and special teams continued in the second half. Percy King zipped through and blocked Pat Pedgeon's punt attempt at the goal line—and Joe Cooper fell on the pigskin in the end zone to increase Ohio State's lead to 21-3, early in the third period. Late in the game, after Penn State had scored its only TD, Ahmed Plummer picked off Thompson's pass at the OSU 39, setting up a four-play 61-yard drive for the final score of the afternoon. Tailback Joe Montgomery scored the touchdown from the one.

The Nittany Lions, who could generate only nine first downs and 181 yards of offense, were held for either a "loss" or "no-gain" on 34 of their 59 plays from scrimmage. Ohio State ran 75 plays to collect 17 first downs and 326 yards. The number-one ranked Buckeyes were now 4-0 on the season, and had passed their first big test of the conference schedule.

At Champaign the following Saturday, October 10, Ohio State pounded out its fifth win of the season, 41-0, over heavy under-dog Illinois. On this calm and clear autumn afternoon, Joe Germaine had another excellent game, hitting on 17 attempts for 307 yards and three touchdowns. The Fighting Illini's only serious threat came late in the game, but they lost the ball on downs at the OSU 17.

John Cooper was not completely over-joyed with the victory—his Buckeyes had committed 11 penalties for a total of 104 yards. The Memorial Stadium crowd of 46,390 (with close to half wearing Scarlet and Gray) was the smallest crowd to see Ohio State play this season.

Germaine Superlative

Back home October 17 in the friendly confines of Ohio Stadium, the Buckeyes used an all-out offensive attack to thrash Minnesota, 45-15, before a sun-drenched homecoming crowd of 93,183. Joe Germaine enjoyed one of his finest afternoons, connecting on 29 of 37 tosses for 338 yards and two touchdowns. In doing so, Germaine became the

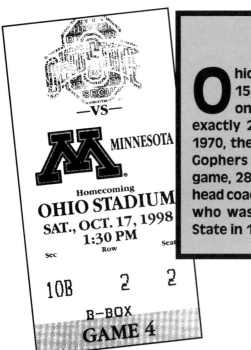

Mason Returns

Ohio State defeated Minnesota, 45-15, in its annual homecoming game on October 17, 1998. Interestingly, exactly 28 years earlier on October 17, 1970, the Buckeyes defeated the Golden Gophers in that season's homecoming game, 28-8. Glen Mason was Minnesota's head coach in 1998—the same Glen Mason who was a reserve linebacker at Ohio State in 1970.

The Buckeyes won their seventh straight at Northwestern the following weekend, 36-10. Joe Germaine was again the difference, particularly in the second half. In his very quiet and effective manner, Germaine completed 19 passes for 342 yards and three touchdowns. Two scoring tosses went to David Boston, who established a new OSU career record with 28. Joe Montgomery ran for exactly 100 yards, including a powerful 19-yard touchdown blast late in the first period.

Clinton Wayne, Brent Johnson, and Steve Bellisari each had interceptions, and Na'il Diggs led the defense's all-out assault

first Ohio State player to pass for more than 300 yards in consecutive games. He also became the first Buckeye to throw for more than 300 yards three times in one season and four times in a career.

It was evident right from the opening whistle that Ohio State was intending to pass. The Buckeyes opened with a four-wideout set, using David Boston, Dee Miller, Reggie Germany, and Ken-Yon Rambo. Boston caught 10 of Germaine's aerials for (what was then) a career-high 191 yards and both scoring tosses. The Golden Gophers also took to the airways frequently against OSU's "Silver Bullets," but with not quite the same degree of success. Quarterback Andy Persby attempted 42, completing 19 for 213 yards and one score.

The Buckeyes led in first downs, 26-16, and total offense, 586 yards to 271. Plummer and Diggs each had eight solo tackles to lead the defense. Although generally satisfied with his team's success, Cooper lamented seven OSU penalties and was most disappointed that one of Brent Bartholomew's punts had been blocked (which resulted in a safety).

Quarterback Joe Germaine, Big Ten MVP

1998 Big Ten Champions

with nine solo tackles and two assists. On the downside, Gary Berry fumbled two punt return attempts, and the squad continued to be frequently penalized (10 infractions for 82 yards).

Passing Game Continues to Flourish

The Buckeye machine continued to roll at Indiana the next Saturday, 38-7. With an abundance of Ohio State fans in the stands this warm Halloween afternoon, the Memorial Stadium crowd of 52,049 was, by far, the Hoosier's highest home attendance of the season. Behind Joe Germaine's 351-yard three-touchdown passing extravaganza, the nation's No. 1 ranked team rolled out 551 yards of offense to run its season record to 8-0. The score would likely have been more one-sided had the Buckeyes not been flagged 12 times for 124 yards.

David Boston started the onslaught with a 70-yard punt return down the right sideline for the game's first score. He and Dee Miller combined to catch 20 of Germaine's 31 completions, good for 269 yards. Boston scored two more on short throws from Germaine, and tight end John Lumpkin gathered in the other scoring toss from six yards out. Michael Wiley, who scored his squad's other TD with a two-yard jaunt, was the game's top runner with 80 yards.

Spartans Supreme Spoilers

In one of the college season's biggest surprises, Michigan State upset the Buckeyes, 28-24, and levied a serious blow to Ohio State's national title hopes. Before a perplexed crowd of 93,595, the underdog Spartans pulled off one of the most stunning come-from-behind wins in the 77-year history of Ohio Stadium. Ohio State led 17-3 after one quarter, but the Buckeyes (who had been averaging more than 38 points-per-game) were held to seven points the rest of this long afternoon. OSU went up 24-9 on Damon Moore's 73-yard interception return for a touchdown early in the second half, but it wasn't enough.

Using the passing arm of quarterback Bill Burke and a relentless blitzing defense, the Spartans scored the game's last 19 points on four consecutive possessions. The composed left-hander from Warren, Ohio, finished the afternoon with 18 completions for 323 yards and a touchdown.

One of the game's key plays came midway through the third period after the Spartans were forced to punt on fourth-down from their own 15-yard line. Craig Jarrett's 34-yard line-drive boot hit an Ohio State player in the back, and MSU's Scott Erneberger recovered at his own 49-yard line. Five plays later

All-American strong safety Damon Moore

Burke hurled a 23-yard TD strike to Lavaile Richardson as the Spartans pulled to within nine at 24-15.

Michigan State's Paul Edinger booted a career-long 49-yard field goal after MSU recovered an Ohio State fumble, and it was 24-18. On their next possession, the Spartans drove 92 yards in eight plays for their first lead of the afternoon at 25-24. Edinger added another field goal to make it 28-24, and that's

Deja Vu

Michigan State's 28-24 upset over top-ranked and undefeated Ohio State on November 7 was practically a carbon copy of 1974 — almost to the day. The underdog Spartans scored two late fourth-quarter touchdowns to win, 16-13, at East Lansing on November 9, 1974, and knock Woody Hayes's previously undefeated squad from its number-one position.

how the game ended. His five field goals tied a school single-game record. The Buckeyes had two more fourth-quarter possessions, but each fell short of the end zone.

The 1998 season was a year of ups and downs for Michigan State. The same team that surprised Ohio State lost to Oregon early in the year by 32 points, and to Penn State by 23 points in the season's last game. Coach Nick Saban was feeling the heat from Spartan fans after his team finished the season at 6-6 (4-4 in the conference). His four-year record at Michigan State now stood at 25-22-1. But on that first Saturday in November of 1998, Saban's team played with the skill and composure of a national champion to deal Ohio State one of its most painful losses in many seasons.

After sitting on top of the national rankings all season, the Buckeyes fell to seventh place. Wisconsin and Michigan, both undefeated in conference play, moved to the top of the Big Ten standings. The same afternoon Michigan State upset Ohio State, Michigan shellacked Penn State, 27-0, to hand the Nittany Lions their first shutout in 11 seasons.

Back on Track

The Buckeyes bounced back at Iowa City the following week, with a 45-14 whipping of coach Hayden Fry's Iowa Hawkeyes. After a slow start, the OSU offense racked up 627 yards, the most by an Ohio State team since gaining 639 against the Northwestern Wildcats in 1981. The Buckeye defense held Iowa to just 180 yards, while recording a school-record 11 sacks.

Joe Montgomery started the onslaught with an 80-yard scoring run on an inside counter play. Joe Germaine passed for 319 yards and three touchdowns, to move past Art Schlichter into first place in career touchdown passes with 52. Two of Germaine's scoring tosses went to David Boston, the other to fullback Matt Keller. Tackle Mike Collins scored his first collegiate touchdown with a

22-yard interception return. Fullback Jamar Martin also notched his first Ohio State touchdown with a 10-yard run in the fourth period.

While the Buckeyes were beating the Hawkeyes, Michigan defeated Wisconsin, 27-10, at Ann Arbor to move into sole possession of first place in the Big Ten. Ohio State could earn a share of the Big Ten title with a win over the Wolverines the following week. OSU's chances of playing in the January 4, 1999, national title game at the Fiesta Bowl were very slim after losing to Michigan State. And even with a win over Michigan, the Buckeyes would qualify for the Rose Bowl only if Penn State defeated Wisconsin.

Aggressive Play Fuels
Season's Biggest Win

Ohio State pounded Michigan, 31-16, with one of its most intense efforts in many seasons. Before a November 21 Ohio Stadium crowd of 94,339, the Buckeyes built up a 21-10 lead at halftime, and were never seriously threatened in the last two quarters. The loss snapped Michigan's conference winning streak at 16. The fireworks started when tailback Michael Wiley followed his blocking to perfection, and sprinted 53 yards for a touchdown on Ohio State's second possession of the afternoon.

The Buckeyes' punt return unit—known as the "score team"—played a huge role in the victory. On the Wolverines' possession following Wiley's touchdown, OSU's Kevin Griffin forced punter Jason Vinson into a minus-yardage kick after Vinson had mishandled the snap from center. Ohio State took over at the Michigan 16-yard line. From there Joe Germaine heaved a scoring toss to Dee Miller, and it was 14-0.

In the second period, Derek Ross broke through to block one of Vinson's punts, and Jonathan Wells recovered for the Buckeyes at the Michigan 20-yard line. After a 15-yard penalty against OSU, Germaine and David Boston connected on their first of two scoring passes, this one for 30 yards. The two hooked up for another score on a 43-yarder over the middle, following Jerry Rudzinski's interception early in the third period. Dan Stultz provided the Buckeyes' last points with a 39-yard field goal early in the final quarter.

Ohio State's defense completely eliminated Michigan's running game, forcing

All-American split end David Boston

quarterback Tom Brady to throw 56 times. Brady connected on 31 for 375 yards and his team's only touchdown, a three-yard toss to Tai Streets just 25 seconds before the half. Jay Feely kicked field goals of 27, 34, and 30-yards. The Wolverines finished with a net four yards rushing.

The two teams combined for the highest passing total in any of the 95 games in this intense rivalry. Germaine's 330 yards were the most ever by a Buckeye in this series, Brady's 375 were the most ever by a Wolverine. Boston's 217 receiving yards (10 catches) were the highest ever against Michigan by a Buckeye, Street's 118 yards (nine catches) were the highest ever by a Wolverine against Ohio State.

It was a very thorough victory for the Buckeyes, who now were Big Ten co-champions with Michigan and Wisconsin. While OSU was defeating UM, the Badgers handled Penn State, 24-3, at Madison to secure a trip to the Rose Bowl. Both Ohio State and Michi-

gan had appeared in Pasadena more recently than Wisconsin.

Sugar Bowl Closes Excellent Season

The Buckeyes capped one of their most successful seasons with a 24-14 Sugar Bowl victory over eighth-ranked Texas A & M. Ohio State took control early with a 21-7 first-quarter lead, then relied on its defense to control all but one Aggie scoring threat in the second half.

After spotting A & M an early 7-0 lead, OSU scored three touchdowns within the next seven minutes to take command. Reggie Germany took an 18-yard TD toss from Germaine, Joe Montgomery ran one in from 10 yards out, and Kevin Griffin returned a blocked punt (by Derek Ross) 16 yards for the third six-pointer. David Boston, who battled a badly sprained ankle all week in practice, claimed 11 receptions for 105 yards and was named the game's MVP.

The following Monday, January 4, 1999, Tennessee claimed the undisputed national title with a 23-16 Fiesta Bowl win over Florida State. The Volunteers (13-0) were the only major college team to go undefeated. Ohio State finished second with a record of 11-1. It was the second time in three years the Buckeyes would close their season as the nation's number-two ranked team. It also marked the fifth time in the last six seasons Ohio State finished in the top ten of the country.

Honors Galore!

Antoine Winfield repeated as an All-American and received the Thorpe Award as college football's top defensive back. Rob Murphy also repeated as an All-American, and was joined by Damon Moore and David Boston. Joe Germaine, who established numerous passing records, was chosen the Big Ten Conference's MVP. So, what has been Ohio State's greatest team? Paul Brown's '42 squad, Woody Hayes' '54, '68, '69, or '73 teams, John Cooper's '96 or '98 units, or even Dr. John Wilce's 1916 team, which was the first Ohio State squad to go undefeated-untied? There clearly is no way to answer this question to everyone's satisfaction. But the 1998 Buckeyes, who outscored their opponents, 430-144, clearly established themselves as one of the finest Ohio State teams ever assembled.

1998				
September 5	at West Virginia	W	34	17
September 12	Toledo	W	49	0
September 19	Missouri	W	35	14
October 3	Penn State	W	28	9
October 10	at Illinois	W	41	0
October 17	Minnesota (HC)	W	45	15
October 24	at Northwestern	W	36	10
October 31	at Indiana	W	38	7
November 7	Michigan State	L	24	28
November 14	at Iowa	W	45	14
November 21	Michigan	W	31	16
January 1	Texas A & M *	W	24	14
Total Points			430	144
* Sugar Bowl				

**Season Record: 11-1
Big Ten Co-Champion**

1999

The Buckeyes approached 1999 with expectations of contending for the Big Ten title and a possible high national ranking, even with the loss of ten starters from the previous year, including five All-Americans. There appeared to be plenty of veteran players who could create another excellent season. But the year turned out to be a disappointment, at least by Ohio State standards. The Buckeyes finished the campaign at 6-6, failing to post a winning record for the first

Coach Cooper signs autographs and discusses the Buckeyes' 1998 season at the June, 1999, John Cooper Football Camp in Canton.

Photo courtesy of Gallery Studio

time since John Cooper's first Ohio State season in 1988.

OSU entered fall practice in search of a starting quarterback to replace talented Joe Germaine. The two prime candidates were Austin Moherman, a third-year sophomore who saw limited action in four games in '98, and sophomore Steve Bellisari, who was impressive his freshman season on special teams and as a reserve defensive safety. Moherman won the starting role for the August 29 Kickoff Classic season opener against the Miami Hurricanes.

Unhappy Beginning

Twelfth-ranked Miami upset ninth-rated Ohio State, 23-12, to hand the Buckeyes their first season-opening loss since a 16-10 setback to Alabama in the 1986 Kickoff Classic. The Hurricanes' biggest play was a 67-yard touchdown pass from quarterback Kenny Kelly to Santana Moss, just eight seconds

Nothing Beats a Day with Buckeye Tailgaters!

Chris Corbellini, a reporter for ABC's College Football, called it one of the largest tailgate parties he had ever covered. More than 1,000 Buckeye fanatics gathered outside Giants Stadium prior to OSU's opening game against the Miami Hurricanes in the Kickoff Classic. The gala event, which was three months in the planning, was hosted by John Porentas and friends from the O-Zone Website (TheOzone.net). A volunteer crew of 40 served 600 bratwurst, 1,200 hot dogs, 70 cases of soda, 500 jello shots, 17 trays of chicken wings, and 10 trays of potato salad.

ABC tagged its story with, "This is no fish out of water tale! This makeshift embassy from Columbus, Ohio, is complete with enough bratwurst to feed Staten Island!"

Fullback Matt Keller

Five Straight at Home

It was 13 days before Ohio State played its second game, defeating UCLA in the home opener on Saturday evening, September 11, 42-20. It was the Buckeyes' 21st straight home-opening victory, increasing their home-opener record to 97-9-4 through 110 years of action. OSU had not been defeated in a home opener since losing to Penn State, 19-0, on September 16, 1978.

Steve Bellisari came off the bench in relief of starter Austin Moherman to rally the 13th-ranked Buckeyes over the 14th-rated Bruins, in just the fourth night game in Ohio Stadium history. Bellisari was good on 11 of 16 passes for 159 yards and two of his team's six touchdowns (both to Ken-Yon Rambo). He also ran for 50 yards on three quarterback draws. Michael Wiley was the game's leading runner with 119 yards in 22 tries. The Buckeyes led in first downs, 27-18, and in yards gained, 507-365.

Ohio State increased its record to 3-1 with home victories the next two Saturdays

before halftime, pushing Miami's lead to 23-9. Neither Moherman nor Bellisari was overly impressive at quarterback, and Cooper was particularly disturbed with all of his team's mistakes. OSU lost two fumbles, threw two interceptions, incurred seven penalties, and allowed three sacks. It was Cooper's first season-opening loss in his 12 years at Ohio State.

over Ohio University and Cincinnati. It marked the first season OSU had faced two opponents from Ohio in 70 years, since defeating Wittenberg University (19-0) and Kenyon College (54-0) in 1929. The Buckeyes won over the Bobcats, 40-16, after being tied at halftime, 10-10. Bellisari got his first start at quarterback, and Rambo sparked Ohio State's second-half surge, finishing with seven catches for 181 yards and two touchdowns. OU coach Jim Grobe was very proud of his squad, indicating that he couldn't have asked them to have played any harder.

The lethargic Buckeyes defeated Cincinnati, 34-20, after trailing the Bearcats midway through the second quarter, 17-3. UC was still riding the momentum of a 17-12 upset over Wisconsin the previous Saturday. Cincinnati embarrassed the OSU defense, leading in first downs, 26-19, and total offensive yards, 525-496.

Ohio State opened its Big Ten schedule with home games against Wisconsin and Purdue, two teams the Buckeyes had not faced since 1996. The Badgers stunned OSU, 42-17, after the seven-point favored Buckeyes led 17-0 midway through the second quarter. It was Ohio State's worst loss at home since being shellacked by Purdue in 1967, 41-6. The Badgers' 42 straight points were the most consecutive points scored by an opponent in Ohio Stadium since Michigan ran off 58 in a row in 1946.

The 21st-ranked Buckeyes played much better against 17th-rated Purdue, edging the Boilermakers, 25-22. The lead changed hands five times in a game that was played most of the afternoon in a steady rain. For the second straight week, Bellisari was OSU's leading passer and runner, this time throwing for 174 yards and gaining 96 yards on the ground. Defensive end Brent Johnson made one of the afternoon's biggest plays, blocking a 29-yard field-goal attempt by Purdue's Travis Dorsch with 53 seconds remaining. A successful kick would likely have forced an overtime.

No Offense

Second-ranked Penn State scored in each quarter to upend Ohio State, 23-10, in front

---

"Big Ten Dean" Hits Century Mark

The Buckeyes' win over Cincinnati was John Cooper's 100th victory at Ohio State. Four games into his 12th OSU season, Cooper's record stood at 100-33-4, as he became just the ninth coach in Big Ten history to guide his conference school to 100 or more triumphs. Cooper became the "Dean" of the Big Ten in 1999, having coached in the league longer than any of the other ten head coaches.

of a crowd of 97,007 at Beaver Stadium. The win was the 314th for coach Joe Paterno, tying him for third with Amos Alonzo Stagg in major college victories. The Buckeye offense could muster only 143 yards of offense, including a meager six yards in the third period. It was the lowest single-game total in John Cooper's 12 Ohio State seasons. OSU scored its lone touchdown when Gary Berry recovered quarterback Kevin Thompson's fumble in the end zone. Cooper told reporters, "If you can't block in this league, and you can't tackle in this league, you're not going to beat the good football teams. That's what happened today!"

After the lead switched five times, Ohio State emerged from the Minneapolis Metrodome with a thrilling 20-17 victory over 24th-ranked Minnesota. With OSU's offensive line showing signs of improvement, tailback Michael Wiley wound up with 118 yards rushing, two touchdowns, and a key 28-yard halfback option pass completion to Steve Bellisari in the fourth quarter. John Cooper awarded the game ball to Dan Stultz, after Stultz

kicked field goals of 43 and 40 yards for the only points scored by either team in the final period.

Austin Moherman, seeing his first significant action since the UCLA game, led a key touchdown drive midway through the third period. Freshman Michael Doss, who had been impressive all season on specialty teams, saw his first significant action at strong safety with the defensive unit. It was Ohio State's 16th consecutive victory over Minnesota.

Happy Homecoming

The Buckeyes ran their season record to 6-3 with an impressive October 30 homecoming victory over Iowa, 41-11. After spotting the Hawkeyes eight points, Ohio State scored in each quarter to register a good solid victory with fine play from both the offensive and defensive units. OSU used seven different ball carriers and seven separate receivers to total a season-high 534 yards of offense.

Tackle Mike Collins (98) sacks Minnesota quarterback Billy Cockerham (5). Pictured are linebacker Na'il Diggs (32), end Brent Johnson (60), and safety Gary Berry (1).

Steve Bellisari threw for 240 yards and two touchdowns, and ran for another six points on an 18-yard quarterback draw just 12 seconds into the second period. One of Bellisari's scoring tosses went three yards to

tight end Kevin Houser, for Houser's first collegiate TD. Austin Moherman was four-for-four for 77 yards, including a 41-yard toss to split end Vaness Provitt for the afternoon's final touchdown.

Bad November

The Buckeye offense hit a new low for the season, registering just 79 yards (79 passing, zero rushing) during a 23-7 loss at Michigan State. It was Ohio State's lowest since gaining a net 63 yards during a 27-0 loss to Penn State in 1963. OSU had only four first downs the entire afternoon, with three of them coming on the opening drive. Dan Stultz punted 10 times for an average of 32.9 yards-per-punt.

It was Archie's day
For the first time, Ohio State retires a number

Columbus Dispatch
Sunday, October 31, 1999

Archie's Day

Archie Griffin's jersey #45 was officially retired during the homecoming halftime ceremonies. The surprised Griffin, who received one of the most thunderous ovations in the 78-year history of Ohio Stadium, was on the field with his 1974 teammates who were celebrating the 25th anniversary of their Big Ten title. It was a perfect afternoon for the only two-time winner of the Heisman Trophy, as Archie's son, Andre, entered the game at tailback and carried the ball three times in the fourth period. Also honored at halftime were three other glory teams from the past—1949 Rose Bowl Champions, 1954 National Champions, and 1979 Big Ten Champions.

At home the following Saturday, November 13, Illinois scored in each quarter and rolled past OSU, 46-20. The Illini took a 29-7 lead at halftime, scoring 10 points in the last 34 seconds of the second quarter. It was the most points scored in Ohio Stadium by an opponent since Michigan humiliated the Buckeyes in 1946, 58-6. The 26-point margin of defeat was the worst at home since losing by 35 points to Purdue in 1967, 41-6.

Ohio State finished the season, going zero-for-three in November, with a 24-17 setback at Michigan. This loss was not because of a lack of effort or desire. The Buckeyes gave it all they had, but were unable to overcome three second-half turnovers and 12 penalties (Michigan had one) throughout the afternoon. OSU had a decided edge in total offense, 368 yards to 252.

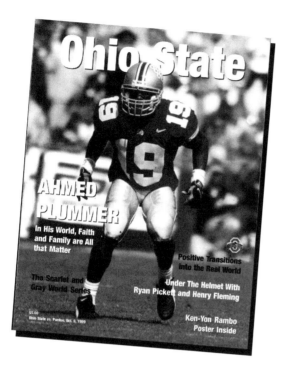

All-American linebacker Na'il Diggs

The game's telling play was likely UM's Todd Wells tripping up Jonathan Wells from behind at the UM six-yard line, forcing Wells to settle for a beautifully executed 76-yard sprint down the right sideline. With Ohio State leading, 17-10, the lead would have been 24-10 if Wells had scored. Instead, the Buckeyes finished the possession with a missed 30-yard field goal after the center snap was mishandled, allowing the Wolverines to stay just seven points behind.

Ohio State finished the campaign at 6-6, being denied the opportunity to play in a postseason bowl for the first season since 1988. The Buckeyes were narrowly outscored by their opponents, 287-285. Cornerback Ahmed Plummer was chosen the team MVP. Plummer also was awarded a graduate school scholarship by the National Football Foundation for his excellent standing as a scholar-athlete. Senior defensive end James Cotton was picked as the team's top defensive lineman, and freshman strong safety Michael Doss was selected the top first-year player on defense.

1999				
August 29	Miami (Florida)#	L	12	23
September 11	UCLA	W	42	20
September 18	Ohio University	W	40	16
September 25	Cincinnati	W	34	20
October 2	Wisconsin	L	17	42
October 9	Purdue	W	25	22
October 16	at Penn State	L	10	23
October 23	at Minnesota	W	20	17
October 30	Iowa (HC)	W	41	11
November 6	at Michigan State	L	7	23
November 13	Illinois	L	20	46
November 20	at Michigan	L	17	24
Total Points			285	287
# Kickoff Classic				

Season Record: 6-6
Conference: 8th Place (Tie)

2000

Wide receiver Chad Cacchio was often Ohio State's "go to" receiver. Cacchio finished the season with four touchdown receptions.

The Ohio State team and coaching staff entered the season confident that the Buckeyes could contend for the league title after finishing with a very uncharacteristic 6-6 record the previous season. John Cooper made several coaching changes. Fred Pagac was elevated to assistant head coach, John Tenuta became the new defensive coordinator, and Chuck Stobart took over as offensive coordinator. Cooper hired two new assistants —George Belu to handle the offensive line and Brian Williams to tutor the linebackers.

The 2000 season marked the second year in the three-year Ohio Stadium renovation project, and there were many eye-catching changes. The playing field had been lowered 14' 6", and 10 new rows of seats were added around the lower bowl. Nineteen new rows were added to the east side of "C" deck, permanent south stands had been erected, and a new scoreboard with instant replay capabilities had been installed.

Defense Takes Center Stage

The Buckeyes opened September 2 with a 43-10 triumph over Fresno State, before a record home crowd of 96,583. The defense (which had surrendered 287 points in '99) was outstanding, forcing six turnovers and scoring a school-record four touchdowns. Late in the first quarter, safety Michael Doss recovered an FSU fumble in the end zone for the season's first touchdown. Twenty-one seconds later, cornerback David Mitchell brought back a fumble 34 yards for another six points. Two other defensive TDs resulted from second-half interception returns, 51 yards by Mitchell and 25 yards by linebacker Matt Wilhelm.

Wide receiver Chad Cacchio scored his first career touchdown with a 23-yard strike from quarterback Steve Bellisari. Reserve quarterback Scott McMullen passed 44 yards to flanker Ricky Bryant for the final score very late in the game. It was McMullen's first collegiate pass and Bryant's first collegiate reception.

The following weekend Ohio State made its very first trip to Tucson to face the Arizona Wildcats in a Saturday night game. After a very ragged first half, which found OSU trailing 17-10, the Buckeyes outscored Arizona 17-0 in the final two quarters to win, 27-17. The Scarlet and Gray defense again dominated the game, holding Arizona to just

Defensive end Rodney Bailey

John Cooper was pleased that his team accumulated 467 yards in total offense, as tailbacks Derek Combs (142) and Jonathan Wells (113) each rushed for more than 100 yards. But he was very concerned about several dropped passes, nine penalties, and a blocked field goal attempt. Miami quarterback Mike Bath was very impressive, running for 105 yards and passing for 236 yards and two touchdowns.

Record Margin Against Joe Paterno

Ohio State opened conference play September 23, walloping Penn State, 45-6. The 39-point margin of defeat was the largest during Joe Paterno's 35 seasons as head coach, surpassing 38-point losses to Nebraska in 1983 (44-6) and UCLA (49-11) in 1966. Heavy thunderstorms and lightning forced the opening kickoff to be delayed 20 minutes. OSU led 17-0 at halftime and finished the afternoon with a distinct advantage in total offensive yards, 397 to 213.

Season's Finest Showing

After an idle weekend, the eighth-ranked Buckeyes dominated Wisconsin, 23-7, before a stunned Camp Randall Stadium gathering of 79,045. Still smarting from their

194 yards in total offense while making 16 tackles for losses.

The Buckeyes returned home September 16 to defeat Miami, 27-16, in the first meeting between the two Ohio schools since 1911. The 58-degree temperature was a pleasant contrast with Tucson's 95-degree reading the previous weekend. Buckeye greats Ollie Cline, Keith Byars, and Chris Spielman were introduced as the most recent former football players to be inducted into the Ohio State Athletic Hall of Fame.

Buckeyes sock it to Badgers

Combs' 80-yard run without shoe, dominant defense fuel win

Cleveland Plain Dealer
Sunday, October 8, 2000

humbling 42-17 thrashing in '99, OSU's relentless defense recorded 17 tackles for losses. Ohio State was now 5-0 on the season.

Derek Combs led the offensive assault with two galvanizing touchdown runs in the game's first nine minutes. Combs sprinted 80 yards on an isolation play for his first TD, even after losing his right shoe near the line of scrimmage, then capped a five-play 80-yard march with a 21-yard scoring dash. Both plays were executed perfectly. Combs went untouched for his second six-pointer behind excellent blocks by guard Mike Gurr and fullback Jamar Martin.

Tailback Derek
Combs, team MVP

Third-Down Efficiency Keys Gopher Upset

Unranked Minnesota knocked fifth-ranked Ohio State from the ranks of the unbeaten, 29-17, before a shocked homecoming crowd of 98,120. The Golden Gophers had lost 16 straight to Ohio State since posting their last series victory at old Memorial Stadium in 1981, 35-31. Coach Glen Mason's squad led 17-3 after one quarter and scored on their first five possessions.

Flanker Ron Johnson had a field day against the Buckeye defense, snagging five first-quarter passes for 105 yards and one touchdown. Johnson finished the day with eight receptions and 163 yards. Quarterback Travis Cole was equally effective, completing all five of his third-down passes in the first period.

The Buckeyes took to the road the next two weeks, winning at Iowa, 38-10, but losing a 31-27 heartbreaker at Purdue. Quarterback Steve Bellisari had a career day against

the Hawkeyes, hitting on 17 of 29 passes for 315 yards and three of his team's five touchdowns. At one stage in the first half, Bellisari completed 10 consecutive tosses. Senior receivers Reggie Germany and Ken-Yon Rambo

First Triumph at Horseshoe in 51 seasons

Minnesota's victory was its first at Ohio Stadium since coach Bernie Bierman's Golden Gophers defeated coach Wes Fesler's Buckeyes, 27-0, on October 15, 1949.

each caught their first touchdown passes of the season.

The game at West Lafayette was one of the most nerve-racking in many seasons, with the lead changing hands six times. Following is the scoring by quarters:

	1	2	3	4	Final
Ohio State	0	3	17	7	27
Purdue	0	7	3	21	31

The Buckeyes intercepted Boilermaker quarterback Drew Brees four times, but Brees came through with three fourth-quarter scoring tosses including a 64-yard game-winner to wide-open Seth Morales with just 1:55 left to play. Morales's touchdown came just 21 seconds after tailback Jerry Westbrooks swept two yards around right end to put Ohio State on top, 27-24.

Nate Clements scored in the third period with an electrifying 83-yard punt return, third longest in OSU history. Dan Stultz booted field goals of 35 and 45 yards to set a school career record of 51 field goals, two more than the prior high of 49 held by Tim Williams (1990-93). Purdue led in first downs, 25-12, total offensive yards, 486 to 278, and time of possession, 34:36 to 25:24.

Safety Michael Doss led the Buckeye defense in 2000 with 94 tackles.

#31 and #40

Jersey #31 of Vic Janowicz and #40 of Hopalong Cassady were officially retired in 2000. Janowicz, winner of the 1950 Heisman Trophy, was honored posthumously at halftime of the September 23 Penn State game. Cassady, who captured the Heisman Trophy in 1955, was saluted November 18 during halftime of the Michigan game.

Buckeyes Rebound

Ohio State got back on track with a 27-13 victory over Michigan State, after trailing the Spartans 13-3 in the first period. It was just OSU's second game at home in six weeks. The Buckeyes scored 17 points off of turnovers, and relied heavily on their running game in the second half to improve their season record to 7-2. Derek Combs rushed for a career-high 153 yards and one touchdown, Chad Cacchio had a career-high five receptions for 62 yards.

At Champaign on November 11, the 13th-ranked Buckeyes came from behind to edge underdog Illinois, 24-21, before a Memorial Stadium crowd of 61,207. With the contest tied 21-21 as the game clock ticked down to zero, Dan Stultz booted a 34-yard field goal inside the right upright to provide his team with the three-point victory. It was his fourth three-pointer of the afternoon. Tight end Darnell Sanders scored OSU's two touchdowns on short tosses of one and seven yards from Steve Bellisari.

Tailback Jonathan Wells was the driving force behind OSU's second-half comeback, finishing the afternoon with 131 yards on 27 carries and grabbing five passes for 50 yards. While the Buckeyes were defeating the Fighting Illini, they received good news from Iowa City and East Lansing. Iowa upset Northwestern, 27-17, and Michigan State toppled Purdue, 30-10, allowing Ohio State to move into a four-way tie for first place in the Big Ten with Michigan, Northwestern, and Purdue.

Wolverines Again!

The Buckeyes' opportunity to earn at least a share of the conference championship was erased November 18 with a 38-26 loss to Michigan, before a record Ohio Stadium crowd of 98,568. OSU led early, 9-0, but couldn't sustain the needed effort. The loss left Ohio State with just seven wins over their arch-rival in their last 25 meetings.

Michigan outscored the Buckeyes 17-0 in the third quarter to increase their lead to 31-12 heading into the final 15 minutes of play. OSU rallied for two touchdowns to tighten things up at 31-26 with 7:03 to play. The Buckeyes regained possession of the ball and were soon faced with a fourth-and-one at the UM 18-yard line. But a power play into the middle of the line came up short, and the Wolverines took possession of the ball with just 3:08 remaining. Ohio State's lack

of success in short yardage situations had been a problem all season.

With a regular-season record of 8-3, the Buckeyes accepted a January 1 invitation to face South Carolina in the Outback Bowl. Coach Lou Holtz's Gamecocks were the surprise of 2000, putting together a 7-4 regular season record after going 0-11 in 1999, the year Holtz took charge of the USC program. The Raymond James Stadium sellout crowd totaled 65,229, primarily because South Carolina quickly sold out its allotment of nearly 30,000 tickets. Fans were anxious to see their team play in their first bowl since 1995.

The fired-up Gamecocks flattened the favored Buckeyes, 24-7, after leading 3-0 at halftime. Guard Mike Gurr scored OSU's only touchdown, pouncing on a fumble in the end zone. Ironically, the game MVP was USC sophomore tailback Ryan Brewer, a native of Troy, Ohio, who normally played flanker. He scored all three of his team's touchdowns and accounted for 214 all-purpose yards. Brewer had been Ohio's "Mr. Football" coming out of high school in 1998, but had not been recruited by Ohio State, possibly because he was considered too small.

The Buckeyes finished the season at 8-4, winning six of their first seven but only two of their final five games. Tailback Derek Combs, OSU's leading rusher with 888 yards, was chosen the team's MVP. Dan Stultz was the leading scorer with 91 points, bringing his career total to 342 points, second highest in Ohio State history. Rodney Bailey was selected by the coaching staff as the recipient of the Most Outstanding Defensive Player Award.

On Tuesday, January 2, 2001, just one day after the Outback Bowl, Athletic Director Andy Geiger announced that John Cooper had been relieved of his duties as head coach. Geiger cited what he considered a deterioration in the football program, indicating it was time for a change. He also stated that Ohio State would buy out the remaining three years of Cooper's current five-year contract.

Cooper addressed the media the evening of January 2, indicating he was shocked by the action, but that he respected Andy Geiger's decision. With his family by his side to offer support, the dean of the Big Ten coaches stated he would have liked to have coached at least one more season. Cooper pledged complete support for the next Ohio State coach, and made it very clear that he will always be a Buckeye.

John Cooper completed his 13 Ohio State seasons with an impressive overall record of 111-43-4. Cooper is one of only nine coaches in the 105-year history of the Big Ten to win 100 or more games while coaching at a conference school. He led Ohio State to three Big Ten co-titles, and to the brink of national championships in 1996 and 1998, when the Buckeyes finished second in each of those final Associated Press Polls. Cooper's 24-year head coaching record is 193-83-6.

2000

September 2	Fresno State	W	43	10
September 9	at Arizona	W	27	17
September 16	Miami (Ohio)	W	27	16
September 23	Penn State	W	45	6
October 7	at Wisconsin	W	23	7
October 14	Minnesota (HC)	L	17	29
October 21	at Iowa	W	38	10
October 28	at Purdue	L	27	31
November 4	Michigan State	W	27	13
November 11	at Illinois	W	24	21
November 18	Michigan	L	26	38
January 1	South Carolina*	L	7	24

Total Points   331 222
* Outback Bowl

Season Record: 8-4
Conference: 4th Place

CHAPTER FIFTEEN

THE VOICE OF THE BUCKEYES

The thrill and excitement of Ohio State football is conveyed throughout the Buckeye state by The Ohio State Football Radio Network. Each season "The Voice of the Buckeyes" provides the color and pageantry of this great spectacle for all of Ohio through a network of 79 stations. Sports Radio 1460 The Fan (WBNS-AM) in Columbus has been the network's flagship station since 1984.

Veteran sportscaster Paul Keels has called the play-by-play action of Buckeye football since 1998. Keels's vivid portrayal of each play allows listeners to envision the activity as it develops on the playing field. Former OSU All-American guard Jim Lachey, who be-

came an All-Pro with the Washington Redskins, provides color commentary and insights about the flow of the game and the teams' strategies. Jim Karsatos, former Buckeye quarterback and co-captain, is the network's sideline reporter. Karsatos offers

The Ohio State Football Radio Network broadcast team of Jim Karsatos, Paul Keels, and Jim Lachey.

Dave Van Stone, Vice President and General Manager, Sports Radio 1460 The Fan.

Head coach Jim Tressel is joined by Keels and Lachey for the "Jim Tressel Call-In Show" each Tuesday evening. Listeners throughout Ohio gain the coach's perspective on the previous week's game and a preview of Ohio State's upcoming opponent.

Two network daily features are the "Jim Tressel Daily Show" and the "Buckeye Flashback with Jack Park." With host Paul Keels, Tressel keeps listeners abreast of the team's progress, position changes, and all current developments. Park's "Buckeye Flashback" allows fans to relive some of the finest achievements and most exciting moments in Ohio State football history.

Affiliate stations supplement the network's pregame, halftime, and postgame analyses with local programming, which of-

an informative view directly from the field, including game plan changes and injury updates.

Saturday's play-by-play descriptions are complemented by daily and weekly programming that provides fascinating and colorful behind-the-scene insights. "Buckeye Roundtable" is a unique program that originates each Monday evening from an affiliated station around the state. Hosted by Paul Keels, Jim Lachey, and Kirk Herbstreit, "Roundtable" is a lively and entertaining exchange of ideas and perceptions with listeners throughout the state. There is no other college football radio program of this type anywhere in the country.

Skip Mosic, Affiliate Relations Manager and Executive Producer of The Ohio State Football Radio Network.

Mark Wyant and Ryan Miller hosting the Buckeye Tailgate Party outside Ohio Stadium on Sports Radio 1460 The Fan.

Network affiliate WHBC (AM 1480) in Canton hosts the Ohio State Football Radio Network and the Ohio State Department of Athletics.

Kirk Herbstreit co-hosts "Herbstreit and Fitzsimmons," each weekday afternoon with Ian Fitzsimmons on Sports Radio 1460 The Fan.

ten runs from Saturday morning through Saturday evening. Ohio State football is also a frequent topic each day on radio talk shows throughout the state. While listeners are very familiar with the on-air personalities, it is the tireless efforts of many behind-the-scenes producers, program directors, engineers, sales people, promotions staffs, and other support people that make the network so successful.

Many of Ohio State's most enthusiastic fans have never been inside Ohio Stadium, but they have "attended" many games through the articulate and expressive programming of The Ohio State Football Radio Network.

Chris Spielman hosts a daily program, "Spielman on Sports," on Sports Radio 1460 The Fan.

Program Director Jeff Austin, Sports Radio 1460 The Fan.

Reporter Dom Tiberi and producer Paul "Moose" Spohn cover Ohio State football each season for WBNS-TV10 in Columbus.

Mike Greene, Sports Director at WMFD-TV in Mansfield, hosts a weekly Sports Talk program.

Reporter/producer Eric Kaelin, Sports Radio 1460 The Fan.

Producer Tony Pollina, Sports Radio 1460 The Fan.

Ian Fitzsimmons joins Kirk Herbstreit for "Herbstreit & Fitzsimmons" each weekday afternoon on Sports Radio 1460 The Fan.

Producer Bob Taylor, Sports Radio 1460 The Fan.

Producer Ted Holbrook, Sports Radio 1460 The Fan.

Reporter/Statistician
D.R. Railsback (right),
Sports Radio 1460
The Fan.

Former Sports Radio 1460 The Fan staffers
Tom Hamilton and Sue Stanton. Hamilton is
now the play-by-play voice of the Cleveland
Indians.

Vince Koza (left) and
Todd Walker of network
affiliate WIMA (AM 1150)
in Lima host pregame
activities outside Ohio
Stadium each Saturday.

Sports Anchor Jeff Hogan of
WBNS-TV10 and Coach Jim Tressel.

Ralph Guarnieri, Jr., of network affiliate WKKI (FM 94.3) in Celina hosts Buckeye Roundtable
with Jim Lachey and Kirk Herbstreit.

Stories are often shared with the opponent's radio network, especially during the week of the Ohio State-Michigan game. Paul W. Smith of WJR Radio in Detroit is joined by Jack Park, who has interviewed with WJR each season since 1986.

The late John "Big John" Wharff (right) during an early year with network affiliate WMOA (AM 1490) in Marietta.

Left: Former Buckeye co-captain Greg Lashutka (top) and Terry Smith called the play-by-play of Ohio State football from 1986 through 1990.

Chris Fowler, Lee Corso, and Kirk Herbstreit bring ESPN's College Gameday to Columbus.

APPENDIX

ALL-TIME RECORDS, STATISTICS, HONORS, FOOTBALL LETTERWINNERS

Results by Decade 1890-2000

Decade	Won	Lost	Tied	Total Games	Win %	OSU Points	Opp. Points	Point Diff.
1890-1899	40	39	5	84	50.6%	1,138	1,126	12
1900-1909	69	26	7	102	71.1%	1,812	722	1,090
1910-1919	55	16	8	79	74.7%	1,702	398	1,304
1920-1929	44	27	7	78	60.9%	1,079	547	532
1930-1939	57	19	5	81	73.5%	1,681	453	1,228
1940-1949	57	27	6	90	66.7%	1,850	1,224	626
1950-1959	63	24	5	92	71.2%	1,916	1,089	827
1960-1969	68	21	2	91	75.8%	2,006	1,053	953
1970-1979	91	20	3	114	81.1%	3,405	1,317	2,088
1980-1989	82	35	2	119	69.7%	3,387	2,200	1,187
1990-1999	91	29	3	123	75.2%	3,623	1,921	1,702
2000	8	4		12	66.7%	331	222	109
Totals	725	287	53	1,065	70.6%	23,390	12,272	11,658

Sid Gillman, Paul Brown, and Woody Hayes. Gillman, an Ohio State All-American in 1932, became one of professional football's most innovative coaches; Brown led Ohio State to its first national title in 1942; and Hayes compiled a 28-year Ohio State record of 205-61-10 from 1951 through 1978.

Results by Year
1890-2000

Year	Won	Lost	Tied	Total Games	OSU Points	Opp. Points	Point Diff.
1890	1	3		4	30	110	(80)
1891	2	2		4	20	80	(60)
1892	5	3		8	260	144	116
1893	4	5		9	202	178	24
1894	6	5		11	160	114	46
1895	4	4	2	10	62	102	(40)
1896	5	5	1	11	122	104	18
1897	1	7	1	9	18	168	(150)
1898	3	5		8	80	121	(41)
1899	9	0	1	10	184	5	179
1900	8	1	1	10	213	26	187
1901	5	3	1	9	94	56	38
1902	6	2	2	10	172	136	36
1903	8	3		11	265	87	178
1904	6	5		11	219	123	96
1905	8	2	2	12	199	63	136
1906	8	1		9	153	14	139
1907	7	2	1	10	160	49	111
1908	6	4		10	118	92	26
1909	7	3		10	219	76	143
1910	6	1	3	10	182	27	155
1911	5	3	2	10	47	40	7
1912	6	3		9	246	122	124
1913	4	2	1	7	154	27	127
1914	5	2		7	108	55	53
1915	5	1	1	7	105	39	66
1916	7	0		7	258	29	229
1917	8	0	1	9	292	6	286
1918	3	3		6	134	41	93
1919	6	1		7	176	12	164
1920	7	1		8	150	48	102
1921	5	2		7	110	14	96
1922	3	4		7	43	57	(14)
1923	3	4	1	8	124	99	25
1924	2	3	3	8	40	45	(5)
1925	4	3	1	8	55	45	10
1926	7	1		8	196	43	153
1927	4	4		8	131	92	39
1928	5	2	1	8	135	35	100

Results by Year (Continued)

Year	Won	Lost	Tied	Total Games	OSU Points	Opp. Points	Point Diff.
1929	4	3	1	8	95	69	26
1930	5	2	1	8	139	48	91
1931	6	3		9	194	68	126
1932	4	1	3	8	90	41	49
1933	7	1		8	161	26	135
1934	7	1		8	267	34	233
1935	7	1		8	237	57	180
1936	5	3		8	160	27	133
1937	6	2		8	125	23	102
1938	4	3	1	8	119	65	54
1939	6	2		8	189	64	125
1940	4	4		8	99	113	(14)
1941	6	1	1	8	167	110	57
1942	9	1		10	337	114	223
1943	3	6		9	149	187	(38)
1944	9	0		9	287	79	208
1945	7	2		9	194	71	123
1946	4	3	2	9	166	170	(4)
1947	2	6	1	9	60	150	(90)
1948	6	3		9	184	94	90
1949	7	1	2	10	207	136	71
1950	6	3		9	286	111	175
1951	4	3	2	9	109	104	5
1952	6	3		9	197	119	78
1953	6	3		9	182	164	18
1954	10	0		10	249	75	174
1955	7	2		9	201	97	104
1956	6	3		9	160	81	79
1957	9	1		10	267	92	175
1958	6	1	2	9	182	132	50
1959	3	5	1	9	83	114	(31)
1960	7	2		9	209	90	119
1961	8	0	1	9	221	83	138
1962	6	3		9	205	98	107
1963	5	3	1	9	110	102	8
1964	7	2		9	146	76	70
1965	7	2		9	156	118	38
1966	4	5		9	108	123	(15)
1967	6	3		9	145	120	25
1968	10	0		10	323	150	173
1969	8	1		9	383	93	290
1970	9	1		10	290	120	170
1971	6	4		10	224	120	104
1972	9	2		11	280	171	109
1973	10	0	1	11	413	64	349
1974	10	2		12	437	129	308

Results by Year (Continued)

Year	Won	Lost	Tied	Total Games	OSU Points	Opp. Points	Point Diff.
1975	11	1		12	384	102	282
1976	9	2	1	12	305	149	156
1977	9	3		12	343	120	223
1978	7	4	1	12	339	216	123
1979	11	1		12	390	126	264
1980	9	3		12	387	181	206
1981	9	3		12	387	253	134
1982	9	3		12	348	208	140
1983	9	3		12	410	206	204
1984	9	3		12	391	200	191
1985	9	3		12	325	212	113
1986	10	3		13	347	179	168
1987	6	4	1	11	224	181	43
1988	4	6	1	11	229	283	(54)
1989	8	4		12	339	297	42
1990	7	4	1	12	349	220	129
1991	8	4		12	277	187	90
1992	8	3	1	12	271	158	113
1993	10	1	1	12	351	193	158
1994	9	4		13	336	211	125
1995	11	2		13	475	220	255
1996	11	1		12	455	131	324
1997	10	3		13	394	170	224
1998	11	1		12	430	144	286
1999	6	6		12	285	287	(2)
2000	8	4		12	331	222	109
Totals	725	287	53	1,065	23,930	12,272	11,658

Les Horvath, 1944 Heisman Trophy winner; Archie Griffin, two-time Heisman Trophy winner in 1974-1975; Howard "Hopalong" Cassady, 1955 Heisman Trophy winner; and Vic Janowicz, 1950 Heisman Trophy winner. Not pictured is Eddie George, 1995 Heisman Trophy winner.

Results by Opponents
1890-2000

Opponent	OSU Won	OSU Lost	Tied	First Game	Last Game	Opponent	OSU Won	OSU Lost	Tied	First Game	Last Game
Air Force	0	1	0	1990	1990	Minnesota	35	7	0	1921	2000
Akron	4	1	0	1891	1895	Missouri	10	1	1	1939	1998
Alabama	0	3	0	1977	1994	Mount Union	1	0	0	1930	1930
Antioch	1	0	0	1894	1894	Muskingum	7	0	0	1899	1928
Arizona	3	1	0	1967	2000	Navy	3	0	0	1930	1981
Arizona State	2	0	0	1980	1996	Nebraska	2	0	0	1955	1956
Auburn	0	1	1	1917	1989	N.Y. University	2	0	0	1936	1938
Baylor	2	0	0	1978	1982	North Carolina	3	1	0	1962	1975
Boston College	3	0	0	1989	1995	Northwestern	52	13	1	1913	1998
Bowling Green	2	0	0	1992	1997	Notre Dame	2	2	0	1935	1996
Brigham Young	3	0	0	1982	1993	Oberlin	13	9	3	1892	1922
California	5	1	0	1920	1972	Ohio Medical	5	2	1	1896	1906
Camp Sherman	1	0	0	1917	1917	Ohio	5	0	0	1899	1999
Carlisle Indians	0	1	0	1904	1904	Ohio Wesleyan	26	2	1	1890	1932
Case	11	10	2	1894	1918	Oklahoma	1	1	0	1977	1983
Central Ky.	0	1	0	1895	1895	Oklahoma State	1	0	0	1989	1989
Chicago	10	2	2	1920	1939	Oregon	7	0	0	1957	1987
Cincinnati	10	2	0	1893	1999	Oregon State	2	0	0	1974	1984
Clemson	0	1	0	1978	1978	Otterbein	13	2	3	1893	1912
Colgate	1	0	1	1923	1934	Pennsylvania	3	0	0	1932	1953
Colorado	3	1	0	1971	1986	Penn State	7	9	0	1912	2000
Columbia	2	0	0	1925	1926	Pittsburgh	19	5	1	1929	1996
Col. Barracks	2	1	0	1894	1897	Princeton	0	1	1	1927	1928
Cornell	0	2	0	1939	1940	Purdue	32	11	2	1919	2000
Dayton YMCA	1	0	0	1892	1892	Rice	2	0	0	1993	1996
Denison	14	1	2	1890	1927	17th Regiment	1	0	0	1894	1894
DePauw	1	0	0	1905	1905	S. California	9	11	1	1937	1990
Drake	1	0	0	1935	1935	S. Carolina	0	1	0	2000	2000
Duke	3	1	0	1955	1981	S. Methodist	7	1	1	1950	1978
Florida State	0	3	0	1981	1997	Stanford	2	3	0	1955	1982
Fort Knox	1	0	0	1942	1942	Syracuse	4	2	0	1911	1992
Fresno State	2	0	0	1994	2000	Tennessee	0	1	0	1995	1995
Georgia	0	1	0	1992	1992	Texas A&M	4	0	0	1963	1998
Great Lakes	1	1	0	1943	1944	Texas Christian	4	1	1	1937	1973
Heidelberg	3	0	0	1898	1907	Texas Tech	1	0	0	1990	1990
Houston	1	0	0	1994	1994	Toledo	1	0	0	1998	1998
Illinois	57	28	4	1902	2000	UCLA	4	3	1	1961	1999
Indiana	59	12	5	1901	1998	Utah	1	0	0	1986	1986
Iowa	41	13	3	1922	2000	Vanderbilt	3	1	0	1908	1933
Iowa Seahawks	1	1	0	1942	1943	Virginia	1	0	0	1933	1933
Kentucky	3	0	0	1895	1935	Washington	6	3	0	1957	1995
Kenyon	17	6	0	1890	1929	Washington St.	7	0	0	1952	1991
Louisiana State	1	0	1	1987	1988	Western Res.	5	6	1	1891	1934
Louisville	2	0	0	1991	1992	West Virginia	5	1	0	1897	1998
Marietta	6	2	0	1892	1902	Wilmington	1	0	0	1926	1926
Miami (Fla.)	1	1	0	1977	1999	Wisconsin	49	14	5	1913	2000
Miami (O.)	3	0	0	1904	2000	Wittenberg	12	3	0	1893	1929
Michigan	35	56	6	1897	2000	Wooster	4	2	2	1890	1925
Michigan State	21	12	0	1912	2000	Wyoming	1	0	0	1997	1997
						Totals	725	287	53		

654

All-Time Coaching Records 1890-2000

Head Coach	Period	Number of Years	Won	Lost	Tied	Total Games	Win %
Alexander Lilley	1890-1891	2	3	5		8	37.5%
Jack Ryder	1892-'95,'98	5	22	22	2	46	50.0%
Charles Hickey	1896	1	5	5	1	11	50.0%
David Edwards	1897	1	1	7	1	9	16.7%
John Eckstorm	1899-1901	3	22	4	3	29	81.0%
Perry Hale	1902-1903	2	14	5	2	21	71.4%
E. R. Sweetland	1904-1905	2	14	7	2	23	65.2%
A. E. Herrnstein	1906-1909	4	28	10	1	39	73.1%
Howard Jones	1910	1	6	1	3	10	75.0%
Harry Vaughn	1911	1	5	3	2	10	60.0%
John Richards	1912	1	6	3		9	66.7%
John Wilce	1913-1928	16	78	33	9	120	68.8%
Sam Willaman	1929-1933	5	26	10	5	41	69.5%
Francis Schmidt	1934-1940	7	39	16	1	56	70.5%
Paul Brown	1941-1943	3	18	8	1	27	68.5%
Carroll Widdoes	1944-1945	2	16	2		18	88.9%
Paul Bixler	1946	1	4	3	2	9	55.6%
Wes Fesler	1947-1950	4	21	13	3	37	60.8%
Woody Hayes	1951-1978	28	205	61	10	276	76.1%
Earle Bruce	1979-1987	9	81	26	1	108	75.5%
John Cooper	1988-2000	13	111	43	4	158	71.5%
Totals	1890-2000	111	725	287	53	1,065	70.6%

John Wilce

Woody Hayes

Rushing Records

Rushing Yards—Game

314	Eddie George-36 att.	Illinois	1995
274	Keith Byars-39 att.	Illinois	1984
246	Archie Griffin-30 att.	Iowa	1973
239	Archie Griffin-27 att.	North Carolina	1972
235	Raymont Harris-39 att.	vs. BYU	1993
229	Ollie Cline-32 att.	at Pittsburgh	1945
224	Calvin Murray-35 att.	Indiana	1980
219	Eddie George-29 att.	at Michigan St.	1994
212	Eddie George-36 att.	Washington	1995
209	Michael Wiley-24 att.	Missouri	1998
209	Bob White-33 att.	at Iowa	1958
207	Eddie George-32 att.	Notre Dame	1995

Rushing Yards—Season

1,927	Eddie George	328 att.	1995
1,764	Keith Byars	336 att.	1984
1,695	Archie Griffin	256 att.	1974
1,577	Archie Griffin	247 att.	1973
1,538	Tim Spencer	273 att.	1982
1,484	Pepe Pearson	299 att.	1996
1,450	Archie Griffin	262 att.	1975
1,442	Eddie George	276 att.	1994
1,344	Raymont Harris	273 att.	1993
1,267	Calvin Murray	195 att.	1980
1,248	Jeff Logan	218 att.	1976
1,235	Michael Wiley	198 att.	1998
1,217	Tim Spencer	226 att.	1981
1,199	Keith Byars	222 att.	1983
1,166	Ron Springs	200 att.	1977

Rushing Yards—Career

5,589	Archie Griffin	924 att.	1972-75
3,668	Eddie George	683 att.	1992-95
3,553	Tim Spencer	644 att.	1979-82
3,200	Keith Byars	619 att.	1982-85
3,121	Pepe Pearson	659 att.	1994-97
2,974	Carlos Snow	610 att.	1987-89, 91
2,951	Michael Wiley	509 att.	1996-99
2,649	Raymont Harris	574 att.	1990-93
2,576	Calvin Murray	438 att.	1977-80
2,542	Jim Otis	585 att.	1967-69
2,466	Howard Cassady	435 att.	1952-55
2,308	Pete Johnson	534 att.	1973-76
2,162	Bob Ferguson	423 att.	1959-61
2,140	Ron Springs	396 att.	1976-78
2,116	Don Clark	385 att.	1956-58

Year-by-Year Leaders

Year	Name	Yards	Att.
2000	Derek Combs	888	175
1999	Michael Wiley	952	183
1998	Michael Wiley	1,235	198
1997	Pepe Pearson	869	192
1996	Pepe Pearson	1,484	299
1995	Eddie George	1,927	328
1994	Eddie George	1,442	276
1993	Raymont Harris	1,344	273
1992	Robert Smith	819	247
1991	Carlos Snow	828	169
1990	Robert Smith	1,126	177
1989	Carlos Snow	990	190
1988	Carlos Snow	775	152
1987	Vince Workman	470	118
1986	Vince Workman	1,030	210
1985	John Wooldridge	820	174
1984	Keith Byars	1,764	336
1983	Keith Byars	1,199	222
1982	Tim Spencer	1,538	273
1981	Tim Spencer	1,217	226
1980	Calvin Murray	1,267	195
1979	Calvin Murray	872	173
1978	Paul Campbell	591	142
1977	Ron Springs	1,166	200
1976	Jeff Logan	1,248	218
1975	Archie Griffin	1,450	262
1974	Archie Griffin	1,695	256
1973	Archie Griffin	1,577	247
1972	Archie Griffin	867	159
1971	Rick Galbos	540	141
1970	John Brockington	1,142	261
1969	Jim Otis	1,027	219
1968	Jim Otis	985	141
1967	Jim Otis	530	103
1966	Bo Rein	456	139
1965	Tom Barrington	554	139
1964	Willard Sander	626	147
1963	Matt Snell	491	134
1962	David Francis	624	119
1961	Bob Ferguson	938	202
1960	Bob Ferguson	853	160
1959	Bob Ferguson	271	61
1958	Bob White	859	218
1957	Don Clark	737	132
1956	Don Clark	797	139
1955	Howard Cassady	958	161
1954	Howard Cassady	609	102
1953	Bobby Watkins	875	153
1952	John Hlay	535	133
1951	Vic Janowicz	376	106
1950	Walt Klevay	520	66
1949	Gerald Krall	606	126
1948	Joe Whisler	579	132
1947	Ollie Cline	332	80

Rushing Touchdowns—Game

5	Keith Byars	Illinois	1984
5	Pete Johnson	North Carolina	1975
4	(14 tied)		

Rushing Touchdowns—Season

25	Pete Johnson	1975
24	Eddie George	1995
22	Keith Byars	1984
20	Keith Byars	1983
20	Champ Henson	1972

Rushing Touchdowns—Career

56	Pete Johnson	1973-76
46	Keith Byars	1982-85
44	Eddie George	1992-95
36	Tim Spencer	1979-82
36	Champ Henson	1972-74

Pete Johnson

Single-Game Rushing Records

Date	Name	Opponent	Yards	Att.	TDs
11/11/95	Eddie George	Illinois	314	36	2
10/13/84	Keith Byars	Illinois	274	39	5
11/17/73	Archie Griffin	Iowa	246	30	1
9/30/72	Archie Griffin	North Carolina	239	27	1
12/30/93	Raymont Harris	vs. Brigham Young	235	39	3
11/10/45	Ollie Cline	at Pittsburgh	229	32	1
10/18/80	Calvin Murray	Indiana	224	35	2
10/15/94	Eddie George	at Michigan State	219	29	1
9/16/95	Eddie George	Washington	212	36	2
9/19/98	Michael Wiley	Missouri	209	24	2
11/15/58	Bob White	at Iowa	209	33	3
9/30/95	Eddie George	Notre Dame	207	32	2
10/1/94	Eddie George	at Northwestern	206	39	1
10/5/74	Archie Griffin	at Washington State	196	21	1
10/14/72	Archie Griffin	Illinois	192	27	0
10/6/84	Keith Byars	at Purdue	191	30	2
11/13/82	Tim Spencer	at Northwestern	190	26	1
9/7/91	Butler By'not'e	Arizona	189	26	1
10/17/70	John Brockington	Minnesota	187	28	2
10/23/82	Tim Spencer	at Indiana	187	33	2
11/24/62	David Francis	Michigan	186	31	2
10/24/81	Jimmy Gayle	Indiana	186	29	0
11/15/80	Calvin Murray	at Iowa	183	25	0
9/8/84	Keith Byars	Oregon State	182	34	2

Passing Records

Passing Yards—Game

458	Art Schlichter	31-52	Florida State	1981
378	Joe Germaine	29-43	at Penn State	1997
362	Greg Frey	20-31	at Minnesota	1989
354	Bobby Hoying	24-35	at Penn State	1995
351	Joe Germaine	31-45	at Indiana	1998
342	Joe Germaine	19-35	at N'western	1998
339	Joe Germaine	27-39	Minnesota	1998
336	Art Schlichter	19-33	at Purdue	1981
330	Joe Germaine	16-28	Michigan	1998
319	Joe Germaine	18-30	at Iowa	1998
315	Steve Bellisari	17-29	at Iowa	2000
312	John Borton	15-17	Washington St.	1952
307	Joe Germaine	17-28	at Illinois	1998
304	Bobby Hoying	20-24	Purdue	1994

Passing Yards–Season

3,330	Joe Germaine	230-384	1998
3,269	Bobby Hoying	211-341	1995
2,551	Art Schlichter	183-350	1981
2,335	Bobby Hoying	170-301	1994
2,319	Steve Bellisari	163-310	2000
2,311	Jim Karsatos	177-289	1985
2,132	Greg Frey	144-246	1989
2,122	Jim Karsatos	145-272	1986
2,062	Greg Frey	139-276	1990
2,028	Greg Frey	152-293	1988
1,952	Mike Tomczak	145-244	1984
1,942	Mike Tomczak	131-237	1983
1,930	Art Schlichter	122-226	1980
1,904	Kirk Herbstreit	155-264	1992
1,847	Joe Germaine	129-210	1997

Passing Yards–Career

7,547	Art Schlichter	497-951	1978-81
7,232	Bobby Hoying	498-858	1992-95
6,370	Joe Germaine	439-741	1996-98
6,316	Greg Frey	443-835	1987-90
5,569	Mike Tomczak	376-675	1981-84
5,089	Jim Karsatos	359-629	1983-86
3,959	Steve Bellisari	267-539	1998-00
2,660	Stanley Jackson	194-353	1994-97
2,518	Don Unverferth	220-468	1963-65
2,444	Rex Kern	188-364	1968-70
2,437	Kirk Herbstreit	197-349	1989-92

Year-by-Year Leaders

Year	Name	Yards	Att.	Comp.
2000	Steve Bellisari	2,319	310	163
1999	Steve Bellisari	1,616	224	101
1998	Joe Germaine	3,330	384	230
1997	Joe Germaine	1,847	210	129
1996	Stanley Jackson	1,298	165	87
1995	Bobby Hoying	3,269	341	211
1994	Bobby Hoying	2,335	301	170
1993	Bobby Hoying	1,570	202	109
1992	Kirk Herbstreit	1,904	264	155
1991	Kent Graham	1,018	153	79
1990	Greg Frey	2,062	276	139
1989	Greg Frey	2,132	246	144
1988	Greg Frey	2,028	293	152
1987	Tom Tupa	1,786	242	134
1986	Jim Karsatos	2,122	272	145
1985	Jim Karsatos	2,311	289	177
1984	Mike Tomczak	1,952	244	145
1983	Mike Tomczak	1,942	237	131
1982	Mike Tomczak	1,602	187	96
1981	Art Schlichter	2,551	350	183
1980	Art Schlichter	1,930	226	122
1979	Art Schlichter	1,816	200	105
1978	Art Schlichter	1,250	175	87
1977	Rod Gerald	1,016	114	67
1976	Jim Pacenta	404	54	28
1975	Cornelius Greene	1,066	121	68
1974	Cornelius Greene	939	97	58
1973	Cornelius Greene	343	46	20
1972	Greg Hare	815	111	55
1971	Don Lamka	718	107	54
1970	Rex Kern	470	98	45
1969	Rex Kern	1,002	135	68
1968	Rex Kern	972	131	75
1967	Bill Long	563	102	44
1966	Bill Long	1,180	192	106
1965	Don Unverferth	1,061	191	99
1964	Don Unverferth	871	160	73
1963	Don Unverferth	586	117	48
1962	Joe Sparma	288	71	30
1961	Joe Sparma	341	38	16
1960	Tom Matte	737	95	50
1959	Tom Matte	439	51	28
1958	Frank Kremblas	281	42	16
1957	Frank Kremblas	337	47	20
1956	Don Clark	88	7	3
1955	Frank Ellwood	60	23	9
1954	Dave Leggett	578	95	46
1953	John Borton	522	86	45
1952	John Borton	1,555	196	115
1951	Tony Curcillo	912	133	58
1950	Vic Janowicz	561	77	32
1949	Pandel Savic	581	84	35
1948	Pandel Savic	486	69	36
1947	Dick Slager	236	69	19

2,348	Cornelius Greene	146-265	1972-75
2,252	Tom Tupa	171-304	1984-87
2,129	John Borton	167-293	1952-54
1,768	Bill Long	154-208	1966-68
1,338	Greg Hare	91-200	1971-73

Touchdown Passes—Game

5	Bobby Hoying	at Pittsburgh	1995
5	Bobby Hoying	Purdue	1994
5	John Borton	Washington State	1952
4	Bobby Hoying	Notre Dame	1995
4	Vic Janowicz	Pittsburgh	1950
4	Vic Janowicz	Iowa	1950
4	Tony Curcillo	Iowa	1951
4	Art Schlichter	Illinois	1980
4	Mike Tomczak	Oregon	1983

Bobby Hoying

Touchdown Passes—Season

29	Bobby Hoying	1995
25	Joe Germaine	1998
19	Bobby Hoying	1994
19	Jim Karsatos	1985
17	Art Schlitchter	1981
16	Joe Germaine	1997
16	Greg Frey	1990

Touchdown Passes—Career

57	Bobby Hoying	1992-95
56	Joe Germaine	1996-98
50	Art Schlichter	1978-81
37	Greg Frey	1987-90
36	Jim Karsatos	1983-86
32	Mike Tomczak	1981-84

Single-Game Passing Records

Date	Name	Opponent	Yards	Att.	Comp.	TDs
10/3/81	Art Schlichter	Florida State	458	52	31	2
10/11/97	Joe Germaine	Penn State	378	43	29	2
10/28/89	Greg Frey	at Minnesota	362	31	20	3
10/7/95	Bobby Hoying	at Penn State	354	35	24	3
10/31/98	Joe Germaine	at Indiana	351	45	31	3
10/24/98	Joe Germaine	at Northwestern	342	35	19	3
10/17/98	Joe Germaine	Minnesota	339	39	27	2
10/31/81	Art Schlichter	at Purdue	336	33	19	3
10/21/98	Joe Germaine	Michigan	330	28	16	3
11/14/98	Joe Germaine	at Iowa	319	30	18	3
10/21/00	Steve Bellisari	at Iowa	315	29	17	3
10/18/52	John Borton	Washington State	312	17	15	5
10/10/98	Joe Germaine	at Illinois	307	28	17	3
10/22/94	Bobby Hoying	Purdue	304	24	20	5
12/26/80	Art Schlichter	vs. Penn State	302	35	20	3
9/5/98	Joe Germaine	West Virginia	301	32	18	2
11/19/83	Mike Tomczak	at Michigan	298	40	21	1
1/1/80	Art Schlichter	vs. Southern California	297	21	11	1

Receiving Records

Pass Reception Yards—Game

253	Terry Glenn	at Pittsburgh	1995
220	Gary Williams	Florida State	1981
217	David Boston	Michigan	1998
199	Dimitrious Stanley	Wisconsin	1996
191	David Boston	Minnesota	1998
187	Bob Grimes	Washington State	1952

Pass Reception Yards—Season

1,435	David Boston	85 receptions	1998
1,411	Terry Glenn	64 receptions	1995
1,127	Cris Carter	69 receptions	1986
981	Dee Miller	58 receptions	1997
970	David Boston	73 receptions	1997
950	Cris Carter	58 receptions	1985

Pass Reception Yards—Career

2,855	David Boston	191 receptions	1996-98
2,792	Gary Williams	154 receptions	1979-82
2,725	Cris Carter	168 receptions	1984-86
2,252	Doug Donley	106 receptions	1977-80
2,090	Dee Miller	132 receptions	1995-98
1,894	Joey Galloway	108 receptions	1991-94

Touchdown Receptions—Game

4	Terry Glenn	at Pittsburgh	1995
4	Bob Grimes	Washington State	1952
3	Joey Galloway	Purdue	1994
3	Joey Galloway	Michigan State	1993
3	Alex Verdova	Wisconsin	1948

Touchdown Receptions—Season

17	Terry Glenn	1995
14	David Boston	1997
13	David Boston	1998
11	Joey Galloway	1993
11	Cris Carter	1986
9	Bob Middleton	1962

Touchdown Receptions—Career

34	David Boston	1996-98
27	Cris Carter	1984-86
19	Joey Galloway	1991-94
17	Terry Glenn	1993-95
16	Gary Williams	1979-82
16	Doug Donley	1977-80

Year-by-Year Leaders

Year	Name	Receptions	Yards
2000	Ken-Yon Rambo	53	794
1999	Reggie Germany	43	656
1998	David Boston	85	1,435
1997	Dee Miller	58	981
1996	Dimitrious Stanley	43	829
1995	Terry Glenn	64	1,411
1994	Joey Galloway	44	669
1993	Joey Galloway	47	946
1992	Brian Stablein	53	643
1991	Bernard Edwards	27	381
1990	Bobby Olive	41	652
1989	Jeff Graham	32	608
1988	Jeff Ellis	40	492
1987	Everett Ross	29	585
1986	Cris Carter	69	1,127
1985	Cris Carter	58	950
1984	Keith Byars	42	479
1983	John Frank	45	641
1982	Gary Williams	40	690
1981	Gary Williams	50	941
1980	Doug Donley	43	887
1979	Doug Donley	37	800
1978	Doug Donley	24	510
1977	Ron Springs	16	90
1976	James Harrell	14	288
1975	Brian Baschnagel	24	362
1974	Brian Baschnagel	19	244
1973	Fred Pagac	9	159
1972	Rick Galbos	11	235
1971	Dick Wakefield	31	432
1970	Jan White	17	171
1969	Bruce Jankowski	23	404
	Jan White	23	308
1968	Bruce Jankowski	31	328
1967	Billy Anders	28	403
1966	Billy Anders	55	671
1965	Bo Rein	29	328
1964	Bo Rein	22	320
1963	Paul Warfield	22	266
1962	Paul Warfield	8	139
1961	Chuck Bryant	15	270
1960	Chuck Bryant	17	336
1959	Chuck Bryant	11	153
	Jim Houston	11	214
1958	Dick LeBeau	8	110
	Donald Clark	8	110
1957	Leo Brown	7	83
	Dick LeBeau	7	91
1956	Leo Brown	8	151
1955	Bill Michael	4	50
1954	Howard Cassady	12	137
1953	Thomas Hague	19	275
1952	Bob Grimes	39	534
1951	Bob Joslin	18	281

Scoring Records

Points—Game

30	Keith Byars	Illinois	1984
30	Pete Johnson	North Carolina	1975
26	Terry Glenn	at Pittsburgh	1995
26	Joel Payton	Purdue	1977
24	(16 tied)		

Points—Season

156	Pete Johnson	1975
152	Eddie George	1995
144	Keith Byars	1984
132	Keith Byars	1983
120	Champ Henson	1972
114	Pete Johnson	1976
104	Terry Glenn	1995
102	Pepe Pearson	1996

Points—Career

348	Pete Johnson	58 TDs	1973-76
342	Dan Stultz	165 XP, 59 FGs	1996-00
300	Keith Byars	50 TDs	1982-85
295	Vlade Janakievski	172 XP, 41 FGs	1977-80
294	Rich Spangler	177 XP, 39 FGs	1982-85
291	Tim Williams	143 XP, 49 FGs	1990-93
272	Eddie George	45 TDs, 1 2 PT	1992-95
254	Josh Jackson	146 XP, 36 FGs	1993-96

Touchdowns—Game

5	Keith Byars (Illinois)	1995
5	Pete Johnson (North Carolina)	1975
4	(18 tied)	

Touchdowns—Season

26	Pete Johnson	1975
25	Eddie George	1995
24	Keith Byars	1984
22	Keith Byars	1983
20	Champ Henson	1972

Touchdown—Career

58	Pete Johnson	1973-76
50	Keith Byars	1982-85
45	Eddie George	1992-95
37	Tim Spencer	1979-82
37	Hopalong Cassady	1952-55

Year-by-Year Leaders

Year	Name	Points	TD	XP	FG
2000	Dan Stultz	91	0	34	19
1999	Michael Wiley	68	11	1	0
1998	Dan Stultz	92	0	53	13
1997	Dan Stultz	92	0	47	15
1996	Pepe Pearson	102	17	0	0
1995	Eddie George	152	25	1	0
1994	Josh Jackson	73	0	31	14
1993	Joey Galloway	78	13	0	0
1992	Tim Williams	79	0	31	16
1991	Tim Williams	63	0	33	10
1990	Tim Williams	79	0	40	13
1989	Carlos Snow	80	13	1	0
1988	Pat O'Morrow	77	0	23	18
1987	Matt Frantz	56	0	26	10
1986	Matt Frantz	71	0	26	15
1985	Rich Spangler	77	0	38	13
1984	Keith Byars	144	24	0	0
1983	Keith Byars	132	22	0	0
1982	Tim Spencer	90	15	0	0
1981	Bob Atha	88	1	43	13
1980	Vlade Janakievski	90	0	45	15
1979	Vlade Janakievski	97	0	43	18
1978	Art Schlichter	78	13	0	0
1977	Joel Payton	80	13	1	0
1976	Pete Johnson	114	19	0	0
1975	Pete Johnson	156	26	0	0
1974	Tom Klaban	79	0	52	9
1973	Bruce Elia	84	14	0	0
1972	Champ Henson	120	20	0	0
1971	Don Lamka	48	8	0	0
	Fred Schram	48	0	27	7
1970	John Brockington	102	17	0	0
1969	Jim Otis	96	16	0	0
1968	Jim Otis	102	17	0	0
1967	Bill Long	30	5	0	0
1966	Paul Hudson	36	6	0	0
1965	Willard Sander	48	8	0	0
1964	Willard Sander	42	7	0	0
1963	Dick Van Raaphorst	34	0	10	8
1962	David Francis	42	7	0	0
1961	Bob Ferguson	68	11	1	0
1960	Bob Ferguson	78	13	0	0
1959	David Kilgore	19	0	7	4
1958	Bob White	72	12	0	0
1957	Frank Kremblas	55	8	7	0
1956	Don Clark	42	7	0	0
	Jim Roseboro	42	7	0	0
1955	Hopalong Cassady	90	15	0	0
1954	Bob Watkins	57	9	3	0
1953	Bob Watkins	66	11	0	0
1952	Hopalong Cassady	36	6	0	0
	Fred Bruney	36	6	0	0
	Bob Grimes	36	6	0	0

Kicking and Punting Records

Extra Points—Game

10	Vic Janowicz	Iowa	1950
9	Rich Spangler	Minnesota	1983
9	Vlade Janakievski	at Northwestern	1980
9	Vlade Janakievski	Northwestern	1978
8	(7 tied)		

Extra Points—Season

57	Josh Jackson	60 att.	1995
53	Dan Stultz	54 att	1998
53	Rich Spangler	54 att.	1983
52	Josh Jackson	56 att.	1996
52	Tom Klaban	53 att.	1974
47	Dan Stultz	48 att.	1997
46	Tom Klaban	48 att.	1975
45	Rich Spangler	47 att.	1984
45	Vlade Janakievski	46 att.	1980
45	Blair Conway	55 att.	1973

Extra Points—Career

177	Rich Spangler	184 att.	1983-86
172	Vlade Janakievski	179 att.	1977-80
165	Dan Stultz	173 att.	1996-00
146	Josh Jackson	158 att.	1993-96
143	Tim Williams	145 att.	1990-93
100	Tom Klaban	104 att.	1972-75

Field Goal Records
Field Goals Made—Game

5	Bob Atha	Indiana	1981
4	Dan Stultz	at Illinois	2000
4	Pat O'Morrow	Syracuse	1988
4	Matt Frantz	at Purdue	1986
4	Vlade Janakeivski	Minnesota	1980
4	Tom Klaban	Michigan	1974

Field Goals Made—Season

19	Dan Stultz	24 att.	2000
18	Pat O'Morrow	23 att.	1988
18	Vlade Janakievski	21 att.	1979
16	Tim Williams	29 att.	1992
15	Dan Stultz	25 att.	1997
15	Vlade Janakievski	22 att.	1980
15	Matt Frantz	20 att.	1986

Field Goals Made—Career

59	Dan Stultz	91 att.	1996-00
49	Tim Williams	77 att.	1990-93
41	Vlade Janakievski	61 att.	1977-80
40	Dan Stultz	67 att.	1996-99
39	Rich Spangler	63 att.	1982-85
36	Josh Jackson	49 att.	1993-96
30	Pat O'Morrow	47 att.	1986, 88-89

Longest Field Goal—Game

59	Tom Skladany	at Illinois	1975
55	Dan Stultz	Indiana	1997
55	Gary Cairns	at Illinois	1966
53	Bob Atha	at Purdue	1981
52	Tim Williams	at Illinois	1992
52	Tim Williams	at Boston College	1990
52	Rich Spangler	vs S. California	1985

Punting Average—Season

47.1	Tom Tupa	45-2,118	1984
47.0	Tom Tupa	63-2,963	1987
46.8	Tom Skladany	41-1,918	1975
45.7	Tom Skladany	31-1,416	1974
45.2	Brent Bartholomew	72-3,252	1997

Punting Average—Career

44.7	Tom Tupa	214-9,564	1984-87
42.7	Tom Skladany	160-6,838	1973-76
41.9	Brent Bartholomew	237-9,927	1995-98
41.8	Tom Orosz	162-6,767	1977-80
40.6	Brent Bartholomew	107-4,340	1995-96
40.2	Jeff Bohlman	142-5,702	1988-90
40.1	Karl Edwards	101-4,046	1981-83

Return Records

Punt Return Records

Punt Return Yards—Game

170	Neal Colzie	Michigan State	1973
166	Tom Campana	at Michigan	1971
161	Garcia Lane	Purdue	1983
131	Nate Clements	at Purdue	2000
126	Jeff Graham	at Wisconsin	1990
105	Neal Colzie	Minnesota	1973

Punt Return Yards—Season

679	Neal Colzie	40 att.	1973
513	Nate Clements	39 att.	2000
447	Tom Campana	37 att.	1971
431	Larry Zelina	23 att.	1969
411	Garcia Lane	40 att.	1982
392	David Boston	47 att.	1997

Punt Return Yards—Career

959	David Boston	98 att.	1996-98
895	Garcia Lane	89 att.	1980-83
855	Neal Colzie	60 att.	1972-74
751	Mike Guess	73 att.	1977-79
695	Nate Clements	58 att.	1998-00
535	Tom Campana	50 att.	1969-71

Bob Klein

Kickoff Return Records

Kickoff Return Yards—Game

213	Carlos Snow	at Pittsburgh	1988
156	Ken-Yon Rambo	Minnesota	2000
148	Hopalong Cassady	Illinois	1953
147	Carlos Snow	vs. Syracuse	1992
136	Joey Galloway	at Indiana	1994
136	Bob Klein	Northwestern	1962

Kickoff Return Yards—Season

653	Ken-Yon Rambo	31 att.	1999
513	Carlos Snow	19 att.	1991
503	Jamie Holland	24 att.	1986
480	Tom Barrington	14 att.	1965
478	Ken-Yon Rambo	17 att.	2000
462	Joey Galloway	18 att.	1994
420	Lenny Willis	16 att.	1974

Kickoff Return Yards—Career

1,468	Ken-Yon Rambo	64 att.	1997-00
1,380	Carlos Snow	58 att.	1987-89, 91
981	Hopalong Cassady	42 att.	1952-55
730	Tom Barrington	24 att.	1963-65
702	Paul Warfield	29 att.	1961-63
696	Dante Lee	36 att.	1989-91

Tackle Records

Total Tackles—Game

29	Chris Spielman	Michigan	1986
29	Tom Cousineau	Penn State	1978
28	Tom Cousineau	SMU	1978
24	David Adkins	Oklahoma	1977
24	Arnie Jones	Michigan	1972
23	Tom Cousineau	Baylor	1978
23	Tom Cousineau	Indiana	1975
22	Chris Spielman	at Washington	1986
22	Tom Cousineau	Michigan	1976
22	Randy Gradishar	Wash. St.	1973
21	Marcus Marek	Michigan	1982
21	Tom Cousineau	Michigan	1978
21	Ed Thompson	Michigan	1976
21	Vic Koegel	Northwestern	1971

Total Tackles—Season (Solos–Assists)

211	Tom Cousineau	101-110	1978
205	Chris Spielman	105-100	1986
178	Marcus Marek	78-100	1982
172	David Adkins	98-74	1977
156	Chris Spielman	78-78	1987
156	Rowland Tatum	75-81	1983
149	Ed Thompson	74-75	1976
148	Marcus Marek	66-82	1981
147	Tom Cousineau	70-77	1976
146	Alvin Washington	70-76	1978
144	Bruce Elia	74-70	1974
143	Glen Cobb	71-72	1982
141	Pepper Johnson	74-67	1985
141	Tom Cousineau	62-79	1977
140	Chris Spielman	76-64	1985
140	Pepper Johnson	77-63	1984
140	Marcus Marek	58-82	1980

Total Tackles—Career (Solos–Assists)

572	Marcus Marek	256-316	1979-82
569	Tom Cousineau	259-310	1975-78
546	Chris Spielman	283-263	1984-87
408	Steve Tovar	239-169	1989-92
379	Pepper Johnson	190-189	1982-85
345	Alvin Washington	178-167	1977-80
338	Ed Thompson	163-175	1974-76
336	Glen Cobb	163-173	1979-82
320	Randy Gradishar	155-165	1971-73
316	Kelton Dansler	178-138	1975-78
314	Aaron Brown	173-141	1974-77
290	Jerome Foster	168-122	1979-82
282	Lorenzo Styles	184-98	1992-94
280	Nick Buonamici	122-158	1973-76
269	Eddie Beamon	131-138	1974-77

Year-by-Year Leaders

Year	Name	Total	Solos	Assists
2000	Mike Doss	94	73	21
1999	Na'il Diggs	94	64	30
1998	Damon Moore	81	62	19
1997	Antoine Winfield	100	82	18
1996	Damon Moore	89	61	28
1995	Greg Bellisari	98	54	44
1994	Lorenzo Styles	132	76	56
1993	Lorenzo Styles	117	84	33
1992	Steve Tovar	128	73	55
1991	Steve Tovar	97	61	36
1990	Steve Tovar	125	78	47
1988	Derek Isaman	88	45	43
1988	John Sullivan	88	38	50
1987	Chris Spielman	156	78	78
1986	Chris Spielman	205	105	100
1985	Pepper Johnson	141	74	67
1984	Pepper Johnson	140	77	63
1983	Rowland Tatum	156	75	81
1982	Marcus Marek	178	78	100
1981	Marcus Marek	148	66	82
1980	Marcus Marek	140	58	82
1979	Alvin Washington	120	69	51
1978	Tom Cousineau	244	142	102
1977	David Adkins	172	98	74
1976	Tom Cousineau	184	102	82
1975	Ed Thompson	126	59	67

Interception Records

Interceptions—Game

3	Damon Moore	at Iowa	1996
3	William White	West Virginia	1987
3	Mike Guess	at SMU	1977
3	Craig Cassady	at Michigan St.	1975
3	Bruce Ruhl	Wisconsin	1974
3	Ted Provost	at N'western	1967
3	Arnie Chonko	Indiana	1964
3	Fred Bruney	Michigan	1952
3	Fred Bruney	Illinois	1951

Interceptions—Season

9	Craig Cassady	105 yds	1975
9	Mike Sensibaugh	125 yds	1969
8	Neal Colzie	80 yds	1974
8	Mike Sensibaugh	40 yds	1970

Interceptions—Career

22	Mike Sensibaugh	248 yds	1968-70
17	Fred Bruney	212 yds	1950-52
16	William White	153 yds	1984-87
16	Ted Provost	124 yds	1967-69
15	Neal Colzie	205 yds	1972-74

Interception Yards—Game

100	Marlon Kerner	at Purdue	1993
100	David Brown	at Purdue	1986
81	Ed Thompson	Illinois	1976
75	Neal Colzie	at Indiana	1973
73	Ray Griffin	at Indiana	1976

Mike Sensibaugh

Interception Yards—Season

166	Gary Berry	5 returns	1997
125	Mike Sensibaugh	9 returns	1969
124	Fred Bruney	7 returns	1952
118	Chris Spielman	6 returns	1986
117	David Brown	4 returns	1986

Interception Yards—Career

248	Mike Sensibaugh	22 returns	1968-70
230	Hopalong Cassady	10 returns	1952-55
218	David Brown	12 returns	1986-89
212	Fred Bruney	17 returns	1950-52
212	Vince Skillings	13 returns	1978-80

Longest Plays and Highest Scores

Ohio State
Rushing
89	Gene Fekete	Pittsburgh	1942
88	Morris Bradshaw	Wisconsin	1971
87	Eddie George	at Minnesota	1995
82	Tim Spencer	Duke	1981
80	Joe Montgomery	at Iowa	1998

Passing
86	A. Schlichter-C. Murray	Wash. St.	1979
82	Bob Hoying-Terry Glenn	Notre Dame	1995
80	Greg Frey-Jeff Graham	Bost. Col.	1989
80	Joe Sparma-Bob Klein	at Michigan	1961
79	Tom Tupa-Everett Ross	Michigan St.	1987
79	Rod Gerald-Jim Harrell	Wisconsin	1977

Field Goals
59	Tom Skladany	at Illinois	1975
55	Dan Stultz	Indiana	1997
55	Gary Cairns	at Illinois	1966
53	Bob Atha	at Purdue	1981
52	Tim Williams	at Illinois	1993
52	Tim Williams	at Boston College	1990
52	Rich Spangler	vs. USC*	1984

* Rose Bowl

Punts
87	Karl Edwards	at Illinois	1983
80	Gary Lago	at Michigan State	1972
78	Joseph Whisler	at Illinois	1948
78	Howard Wedebrook	Michigan	1936
75	Tom Tupa	Illinois	1986
75	Jerry Fields	at Wisconsin	1959

Most Points Scored
128	Oberlin	1916
85	Drake	1935
83	Iowa	1950
80	Miami	1904
80	Marietta	1892
76	at Western Reserve	1934

Opponent
Rushing
91	Larry Ferguson	at Iowa	1960
88	Levi Jackson	at Michigan State	1974
80	Clinton Jones	at Michigan State	1965
80	O. J. Simpson	Southern California*	1968
79	Edward Cody	Purdue	1946

* Rose Bowl

Passing
90	Rick Trefzger-Craig Allen	Purdue	1994
90	M. Taliaferro-M. Yavorski	at Illinois	1962
86	John Reeves-Isaac Jones	at Purdue	1996
87	T. Marinovich-J. Jackson	at USC	1989
82	M. Lawson-K. Gibson	Mich. St.	1976

Field Goals
63	Morten Anderson	Michigan State	1981
56	Mike Gillette	Michigan	1988
55	Chris Bahr	Penn State	1975
52	Steve Goldberg	at Minnesota	1974
52	Mike Redina	Flordia State	1981
52	Sam Valenzisi	at Northwestern	1994

Punts
86	Dwight Eddleman	at Illinois	1948
82	Phil Vierneisel	Illinois	1974
77	Phil Vierneisel	Illinois	1974
76	Michael Friede	at Indiana	1978
74	Daniel Zarlingo	at Indiana	1976

Most Points Scored
86	at Michigan	1902
64	Wooster	1890
63	at Penn State	1994
58	Michigan	1946
50	Western Reserve	1891
50	Oberlin	1892

Heisman Trophy Winners and Top-Ten Finishers

Year	OSU Player	Position	Place	Heisman Winner
1942	Gene Fekete	FB	8th	Frank Sinkwich—Georgia
1944	LES HORVATH	QB	1st	
1945	Warren Amling	G	7th	Doc Blanchard—Army
1950	VIC JANOWICZ	HB	1st	
1954	Howard Cassady	HB	3rd	Alan Ameche—Wisconsin
1955	HOWARD CASSADY	HB	1st	
1956	Jim Parker	G	8th	Paul Hornung—Notre Dame
1958	Bob White	FB	4th	Pete Dawkins—Army
1960	Tom Matte	QB	7th	Joe Bellino—Navy
1961	Bob Ferguson	FB	2nd	Ernie Davis—Syracuse
1969	Rex Kern	QB	3rd	Steve Owens—Oklahoma
1969	Jim Otis	FB	7th	Steve Owens—Oklahoma
1969	Jack Tatum	DB	10th	Steve Owens—Oklahoma
1970	Rex Kern	QB	5th	Jim Plunkett—Stanford
1970	Jack Tatum	DB	7th	Jim Plunkett—Stanford
1973	John Hicks	T	2nd	John Cappelletti—Penn State
1973	Archie Griffin	TB	5th	John Cappelletti—Penn State
1973	Randy Gradishar	LB	6th	John Cappelletti—Penn State
1974	ARCHIE GRIFFIN	TB	1st	
1975	ARCHIE GRIFFIN	TB	1st	
1979	Art Schlichter	QB	4th	Charles White—Southern Cal
1980	Art Schlichter	QB	6th	George Rogers—South Carolina
1981	Art Schlichter	QB	5th	Marcus Allen—Southern Cal
1984	Keith Byars	TB	2nd	Doug Flutie—Boston College
1986	Chris Spielman	LB	10th	Vinny Testaverde—Miami (Fl)
1987	Chris Spielman	LB	6th	Tim Brown—Notre Dame
1995	EDDIE GEORGE	TB	1st	
1995	Bobby Hoying	QB	10th	Eddie George—Ohio State
1996	Orlando Pace	T	4th	Danny Wuerffel—Florida
1998	Joe Germaine	QB	9th	Ricky Williams—Texas

Major Awards Winners

Outland Trophy
Jim Parker—1956
Jim Stillwagon—1970
John Hicks—1973
Orlando Pace—1996

Lombardi Award
Jim Stillwagon—1970
John Hicks—1973
Chris Spielman—1987
Orlando Pace—1995
Orlando Pace—1996

Biletnikoff Award
Terry Glenn—1995

Butkus Award
Andy Katzenmoyer—1997

Thorpe Award
Antoine Winfield—1998

National Coach of the Year
Carroll Widdoes—1944
Woody Hayes—1957
Woody Hayes—1968
Woody Hayes—1975
Earle Bruce—1979
John Cooper (ASU)—1986

All-Americans

Year	Player	Pos.
1914	Boyd Cherry	E
1916	Chic Harley	B
	Robert Karch	T
1917	Charles Bolen	E
	Harold Courtney	T
	Chic Harley	B
	Kelley Van Dyne	C
1918	Clarence MacDonald	E
1919	Chic Harley	B
	Gaylord Stinchcomb	B
1920	Iolas Huffman	G
	Gaylord Stinchcomb	B
1921	Iolas Huffman	T
	Cyril Myers	E
1923	Harry Workman	QB
1924	Harold Cunningham	E
1925	Edwin Hess	G
1926	Edwin Hess	G
	Martin Karow	HB
	Leo Raskowski	T
1927	Leo Raskowski	T
1928	Wesley Fesler	E
1929	Wesley Fesler	E
1930	Wesley Fesler	E
	Lew Hinchman	HB
1931	Carl Cramer	QB
	Lew Hinchman	HB
1932	Joseph Gailus	G
	Sid Gillman	E
	Lew Hinchman	HB
	Ted Rosequist	T
1933	Joseph Gailus	G
1934	Regis Monahan	G
	Merle Wendt	E
1935	Gomer Jones	C
	Merle Wendt	E
1936	Charles Hamrick	T
	Inwood Smith	G
	Merle Wendt	E
1937	Carl Kaplanoff	T
	Jim McDonald	QB
	Ralph Wolf	C
	Gust Zarnas	G
1939	Vic Marino	G
	Esco Sarkkinen	E
	Donald Scott	HB
1940	Donald Scott	HB
1942	Robert Shaw	E
	Charles Csuri	T
	Lindell Houston	G
	Paul Sarringhaus	HB
	Gene Fekete	FB

Year	Player	Pos.
1943	Bill Willis	T
1944	Jack Dugger	E
	Bill Willis	T
	William Hackett	G
	Les Horvath	QB/HB
1945	Warren Amling	G
	Ollie Cline	FB
	Russell Thomas	T
1946	Warren Amling	T
	Cecil Souders	E
1950	Robert Momsen	T
	Robert McCullough	C
	Vic Janowicz	HB
1952	Mike Takacs	G
1954	Dean Dugger	E
	Howard Cassady	HB
	Jim Reichenbach	G
1955	Jim Parker	G
	Howard Cassady	HB
1956	Jim Parker	G
1957	Aurealius Thomas	G
1958	Jim Houston	E
	Jim Marshall	T
	Bob White	FB
1959	Jim Houston	E
1960	Bob Ferguson	FB
1961	Bob Ferguson	FB
1964	Jim Davidson	T
	Ike Kelley	LB
	Arnie Chonko	DB
1965	Douglas Van Horn	G
	Ike Kelley	LB
1966	Ray Pryor	C
1968	David Foley	OT
	Rufus Mayes	OT
1969	Jim Stillwagon	MG
	Rex Kern	QB
	Jim Otis	FB
	Ted Provost	CB
	Jack Tatum	CB
1970	Jan White	TE
	Jim Stillwagon	MG
	John Brockington	FB
	Jack Tatum	CB
	Mike Sensibaugh	S
	Tim Anderson	CB
1971	Tom DeLeone	C
1972	John Hicks	OT
	Randy Gradishar	LB
1973	Van Ness DeCree	DE
	John Hicks	OT
	Randy Gradishar	LB
	Archie Griffin	TB

Year	Player	Pos.
1974	Van Ness DeCree	DE
	Kurt Schumacher	OT
	Pete Cusick	DT
	Steve Myers	C
	Archie Griffin	TB
	Neal Colzie	CB
	Tom Skladany	P
1975	Ted Smith	OG
	Archie Griffin	TB
	Tim Fox	S
	Tom Skladany	P
1976	Bob Brudzinski	DE
	Chris Ward	OT
	Tom Skladany	P
1977	Chris Ward	OT
	Aaron Brown	NG
	Tom Cousineau	LB
	Ray Griffin	S
1978	Tom Cousineau	LB
1979	Ken Fritz	OG
	Art Schlichter	QB
1982	Marcus Marek	LB
1984	James Lachey	OG
	Keith Byars	TB
1985	Thomas Johnson	LB
1986	Cris Carter	SE
	Chris Spielman	LB
1987	Chris Spielman	LB
	Tom Tupa	P
1988	Jeff Uhlenhake	C
1991	Steve Tovar	LB
1992	Steve Tovar	LB
1993	Korey Stringer	OT
	Dan Wilkinson	DT
1994	Korey Stringer	OT
1995	Eddie George	TB
	Terry Glenn	FL
	Orlando Pace	OT
	Mike Vrabel	DE
1996	Orlando Pace	OT
	Shawn Springs	CB
	Mike Vrabel	DE
1997	Andy Katzenmoyer	LB
	Rob Murphy	OG
	Antoine Winfield	CB
1998	David Boston	SE
	Damon Moore	SS
	Rob Murphy	OG
	Antoine Winfield	CB
1999	Na'il Diggs	LB
2000	Mike Doss	SS
2001	LeCharles Bentley	C
	Mike Doss	SS

Most Valuable Players

Year	Player	Pos.
1930	Wes Fesler	E
1931	Robert Haubrich	T
1932	Lew Hinchman	HB
1933	Michael Vuchinich	C
1934	Gomer Jones	C
1935	Gomer Jones	C
1936	Ralph Wolf	C
1937	Ralph Wolf	C
1938	Jim Langhurst	FB
1939	Stephen Andrako	C
1940	Claude White	C
1941	Jack Graf	FB
1942	Charles Csuri	T
1943	Gordon Appleby	C
1944	Les Horvath	QB-HB
1945	Ollie Cline	FB
1946	Cecil Souders	E
1947	Dave Templeton	G
1948	Joseph Whisler	FB
1949	Jack Lininger	C
1950	Vic Janowicz	HB
1951	Vic Janowicz	HB
1952	Fred Bruney	HB
1953	George Jacoby	T
1954	Hopalong Cassady	HB
1955	Hopalong Cassady	HB
1956	Jim Parker	G
1957	Bill Jobko	G
1958	Jim Houston	E
1959	Jim Houston	E
1960	Tom Matte	QB
1961	Bob Ferguson	FB
1962	Bill Armstrong	C
1963	Matt Snell	FB
1964	Ed Orazen	T
1965	Doug Van Horn	G
1966	Ray Pryor	C
1967	Dirk Worden	LB
1968	Mark Stier	LB
1969	Jim Otis	FB
1970	Jim Stillwagon	MG
1971	Tom DeLeone	C
1972	George Hasenohrl	DT
1973	Archie Griffin	TB

Year	Player	Pos.
1974	Archie Griffin	TB
1975	Cornelius Greene	QB
1976	Bob Brudzinski	DE
1977	Dave Adkins	LB
1978	Tom Cousineau	LB
1979	Jim Laughlin	OLB
1980	Calvin Murray	TB
1981	Art Schlichter	QB
1982	Tim Spencer	TB
1983	John Frank	TE
1984	Keith Byars	TB
1985	Jim Karsatos	QB
1986	Cris Carter	SE
1987	Chris Spielman	LB
1988	Jeff Uhlenhake	C
1989	Derek Isaman	LB
1990	Jeff Graham	FL
1991	Carlos Snow	TB
1992	Kirk Herbstreit	QB
1993	Raymont Harris	TB
1994	Korey Stringer	OT
1995	Eddie George	TB
1996	Orlando Pace	OT
1997	Antoine Winfield	CB
1998	Joe Germaine	QB
1999	Ahmed Plummer	CB
2000	Derek Combs	TB
2001	Jonathan Wells	TB

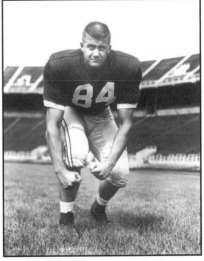

Jim Houston

Captains

Year	Captains	Year	Captains	Year	Captains
1890	Jesse L. Jones	1929	Alan M. Holman	1961	Thomas Perdue
	Paul M. Lincoln	1930	Wesley E. Fesler		Michael Ingram
1891	Richard T. Ellis	1931	Stuart K. Holcomb	1962	Gary Moeller
1892	Richard T. Ellis	1932	Lewis G. Hinchman		Bob Vogel
1893	A.P. Gillen	1933	Joseph T. Gailus	1963	Ormonde Ricketts
1894	W.G. Nagel		Sidney Gillman		Matt Snell
1895	Renick W. Dunlap	1934	J. Regis Monahan	1964	Jim Davidson
1896	Edward H. French	1935	Gomer T. Jones		Bill Spahr
	William A. Reed	1936	Merle E. Wendt		Tom Kiehfuss
1897	Harry C. Hawkins	1937	Ralph C. Wolf	1965	Ike Kelley
1898	John Segrist		James A. McDonald		GregLashutka
1899	D.B. Sayers	1938	Michael Kabealo	1966	John Fill
1900	J.H.Tilton		Carl G. Kaplanoff		Mike Current
1901	J.M. Kittle	1939	Steven F. Andrako		Ray Pryor
1902	W.F. Coover	1940	Jim Langhurst	1967	Bill Ray Anders
1903	James R. Marker	1941	Jack W. Stephenson		Samuel Elliott
1904	John D. Thrower	1942	George M. Lynn	1968	Dave Foley
1905	Ralph W. Hoyer	1943	Jack R. Dugger		Dirk Worden
1906	James F. Lincoln		Charles A. Csuri	1969	Dave Whitfield
1907	H.J. Schory	1944	Gordon Appleby		Alan Jack
1908	W.D. Barrington	1945	William C. Hackett	1970	Rex Kern
1909	Thomas H. Jones	1946	Warren Amling		Jan White
1910	Leslie R. Wells	1947	Robert O. Jabbusch		Jim Stillwagon
1911	Frank P. Markley	1948	David I. Templeton		Doug Adams
1912	Don B. Barricklow	1949	A. Jack Wilson	1971	Harry Howard
1913	W. Irving Geissman	1950	Henry Bill Trautwein		Tom DeLeone
1914	Campbell J. Graf	1951	Robert C. Heid	1972	Richard Galbos
1915	Ivan B. Boughton	1952	Bernie G. Skvarka		George Hasenohrl
1916	Frank Sorensen	1953	Robert V. Joslin	1973	Greg Hare
1917	Harold J. Courtney		George Jacoby		Richard Middleton
	Howard Courtney	1954	Dick Brubaker	1974	Steve Myers
1918	Clarence A. MacDonald		John R. Borton		Archie Griffin
1919	Charles W. Harley	1955	Frank C. Machinsky		Arnold Jones
1920	Iolas M. Huffman		Kenneth W. Vargo		Neal Colzie
1921	Cyril E. Myers	1956	Frank Ellwood		Pete Cusick
1922	Lloyd A. Pixley		Bill Michael	1975	Archie Griffin
1923	Boni Petcoff	1957	Galen B. Cisco		Brian Baschnagel
1924	Francis D. Young		Leo M. Brown		Tim Fox
1925	Harold B. Cunningham	1958	Frank Kremblas		Ken Kuhn
1926	Marty G. Karow		Dick Schafrath	1976	Bill Lukens
1927	Theodore R. Meyer	1959	Jim Houston		Ed Thompson
1928	Leo Raskowski	1960	Jim Tyrer		Tom Skladany
			Jim Herbstreit		

Dave Foley

Year	Captains
1977	Chris Ward
	Jeff Logan
	Aaron Brown
	Ray Griffin
1978	Ron Springs
	Tim Vogler
	Tom Cousineau
	Byron Cato
1979	Jim Laughlin
	Mike Guess
	Ken Fritz
	Tom Waugh
1980	Doug Donley
	Calvin Murray
	Ray Ellis
	Keith Ferguson
1981	Art Schlichter
	Glen Cobb
1982	Marcus Marek
	Glen Cobb
	Joe Lukens
	Jerome Foster
	Gary Williams
	Tim Spencer

Year	Captains
1983	John Frank
	Bill Roberts
	Rowland Tatum
	Garcia Lane
1984	Kirk Lowdermilk
	Mike Tomczak
	Mark Krerowicz
	Pepper Johnson
1985	Keith Byars
	Mike Lanese
	Pepper Johnson
1986	Jim Karsatos
	Sonny Gordon
1987	Chris Spielman
	Eric Krumerow
	William White
	Tom Tupa
1988	Jeff Uhlenhake
	Vince Workman
	Mike Sullivan
	Michael McCray
1989	Joe Staysniak
	Jeff Davidson
	Zack Dumas
	David Brown
	Derek Isaman
1990	Jeff Graham
	Dan Beatty
	Mark Pelini
	Vinnie Clark
	Greg Frey
1991	Carlos Snow
	Scottie Graham
	John Kacherski
1992	Kirk Herbstreit
	Steve Tovar
1993	Alan Kline
	Cedric Saunders
	Jason Simmons
	Chico Nelson
1994	Joey Galloway
	Marlon Kerner
1995	Matt Bonhaus
	Eddie George
	Bobby Hoying

Year	Captains
1996	Juan Porter
	Greg Bellisari
1997	Winfield Garnett
	Stan Jackson
1998	Jerry Rudzinski
	Antoine Winfield
	Joe Germaine
1999	Matt Keller
	Ahmed Plummer
2000	Rodney Bailey
	Steve Bellisari
	Joe Cooper
	Ken-Yon Rambo
2001	Steve Bellisari
	Mike Collins
	Joe Cooper
	Jamar Martin

Matt Snell

All-Time Attendance Records Since Dedication of Ohio Stadium in 1922

Year	Home Games	Home Atten.	Home Average	Total Games	All-time Total Atten.
1922	5	162,500	32,500	7	212,500
1923	5	148,113	29,622	8	236,113
1924	6	196,072	32,678	8	246,078
1925	6	201,445	33,574	8	276,945
1926	5	183,578	36,715	8	277,116
1927	5	188,776	37,755	8	323,776
1928	5	232,256	46,451	8	305,756
1929	6	213,941	35,657	8	354,941
1930	5	189,334	37,867	8	279,334
1931	5	163,356	32,671	9	301,278
1932	5	113,718	22,743	8	167,218
1933	5	139,065	27,813	8	264,573
1934	5	205,095	41,019	8	262,475
1935	5	252,950	50,590	8	353,314
1936	5	282,575	56,515	8	391,375
1937	5	274,432	54,886	8	399,683
1938	5	314,893	62,978	8	392,893
1939	5	250,885	50,177	8	386,362
1940	5	300,947	60,189	8	392,018
1941	5	287,715	57,543	8	486,468
1942	7	307,509	43,930	10	465,165
1943	5	150,071	30,014	9	288,580
1944	7	336,802	48,114	9	460,429
1945	6	378,327	63,054	9	544,567
1946	5	371,017	74,203	9	603,600
1947	6	428,436	71,406	9	603,591
1948	6	420,930	70,155	9	566,662
1949	5	382,146	76,429	10	743,154
1950	5	368,053	73,610	9	570,287
1951	6	455,737	75,956	9	636,484
1952	6	453,911	75,652	9	593,647
1953	5	398,890	79,578	9	630,042
1954	6	480,340	80,057	10	739,748
1955	6	490,477	81,477	9	669,375
1956	6	494,575	82,629	9	651,554
1957	6	484,118	80,686	10	770,372
1958	6	499,119	83,186	9	659,280
1959	6	495,556	82,589	9	690,681
1960	5	413,583	82,716	9	665,406
1961	5	414,712	82,942	9	623,934
1962	6	481,480	80,247	9	644,410
1963	5	416,623	83,324	9	622,545
1964	7	583,740	83,391	9	713,667
1965	5	416,232	83,244	9	687,022
1966	6	488,399	81,400	9	633,634
1967	5	383,502	76,700	9	591,693
1968	6	482,564	80,427	10	725,904
1969	5	431,175	86,235	9	687,858
1970	5	432,451	86,490	10	798,924
1971	6	506,699	84,449	10	751,463
1972	6	509,420	84,903	11	850,741

Year	Home Games	Home Atten.	Home Average	Total Games	All-time Total Atten.
1973	6	532,369	87,228	11	925,162
1974	6	525,260	87,543	12	897,062
1975	6	527,141	87,857	12	1,010,755
1976	6	526,216	87,703	12	885,858
1977	6	525,535	87,589	12	916,926
1978	7	614,880	87,840	12	939,036
1979	7	611,794	87,399	12	962,599
1980	7	615,476	87,925	12	927,885
1981	6	521,764	86,960	12	938,818
1982	7	623,042	89,006	12	904,660
1983	6	534,110	89,018	12	972,482
1984	6	536,691	89,448	12	937,915
1985	6	538,546	89,757	12	909,865
1986	6	538,497	89,750	13	992,090
1987	6	537,992	89,665	11	926,027
1988	6	541,795	90,299	11	839,460
1989	6	535,609	89,268	12	985,428
1990	6	536,297	89,383	12	828,238
1991	7	654,500	93,500	12	993,545
1992	6	555,900	92,650	12	929,561
1993	6	558,683	93,114	12	942,161
1994	6	558,619	93,103	13	980,277
1995	6	561,057	93,510	13	1,078,350
1996	6	564,167	94,028	12	958,119
1997	7	643,772	91,967	13	1,096,816
1998	6	561,014	93,502	12	920,967
1999	7	654,192	93,456	12	1,044,646
2000	6	586,542	97,757	12	978,551
Totals	455	33,715,370	74,100	785	52,857,337

All-Time Average, 785 games—67,114

Largest Total Attendance

	Year	G.	Total	Home	Away	Average
1.	1995	13	1,078,350	561,057	517,293	82,950
2.	1975	12	1,010,755	527,141	483,614	84,229
3.	1997	13	1,096,816	643,772	453,044	84,370
3.	1991	12	993,545	654,500	339,045	82,795
4.	1986	13	992,090	538,497	453,593	76,314
5.	1989	12	985,428	535,609	359,819	82,119
6.	2000	12	978,551	586,542	392,009	81,546
7.	1983	12	972,482	534,110	438,372	81,040
8.	1979	12	962,599	611,794	350,805	80,216
9.	1996	12	958,129	564,167	293,327	79,844
10.	1993	12	942,161	558,683	383,478	78,513
11.	1978	12	939,036	614,880	324,156	78,253
12.	1981	12	938,818	521,764	417,054	78,234
13.	1984	12	937,915	536,691	401,224	78,159

When Ranked Number One

When Ohio State Is Ranked Number One (51-8-1)

OSU	Opp.	Loc.	Opponent	Date	Result	Score
1	nr	H	Purdue	10/17/42	W	26-0
1	nr	A	Northwestern	10/24/42	W	20-6
1	6	A	Wisconsin	10/31/42	L	7-17
1	8	A	Illinois	11/18/50	L	7-14
1	nr	A	Northwestern	10/30/54	W	14-7
1	12	H	Michigan	11/20/54	W	21-7
1	17	N	Southern California	1/1/55	W	20-7
1	20	H	Southern Methodist	9/27/58	W	23-20
1	nr	A	UCLA	10/6/62	L	7-9
1	nr	H	Wisconsin	10/24/64	W	28-3
1	nr	A	Iowa	10/31/64	W	21-19
1	2	N	Southern California	1/1/69	W	27-16
1	nr	H	Texas Christian	9/27/69	W	62-0
1	nr	A	Washington	10/4/69	W	41-14
1	19	H	Michigan State	10/11/69	W	54-21
1	nr	A	Minnesota	10/18/69	W	34-7
1	nr	H	Illinois	10/25/69	W	41-0
1	nr	A	Northwestern	11/1/69	W	35-6
1	nr	H	Wisconsin	11/8/69	W	62-7
1	10	H	Purdue	11/15/69	W	42-14
1	12	A	Michigan	11/22/69	L	12-24
1	nr	H	Texas A&M	9/26/70	W	56-13
1	nr	H	Duke	10/3/70	W	34-10
1	nr	A	Michigan State	10/10/70	W	29-0
1	nr	H	Minnesota	10/17/70	W	28-8
1	nr	A	Illinois	10/24/70	W	48-29
1	nr	H	Washington State	10/6/73	W	27-3
1	nr	A	Wisconsin	10/13/73	W	24-0
1	nr	A	Indiana	10/20/73	W	37-7
1	nr	H	Northwestern	10/27/73	W	60-0
1	nr	A	Illinois	11/3/73	W	30-0
1	nr	H	Michigan State	11/10/73	W	35-0
1	nr	H	Iowa	11/17/73	W	55-13
1	4	A	Michigan	11/24/73	T	10-10
1	nr	H	Southern Methodist	9/28/74	W	28-9
1	nr	A	Washington State	10/5/74	W	42-7
1	13	H	Wisconsin	10/12/74	W	52-7
1	nr	H	Indiana	10/19/74	W	49-9
1	nr	A	Northwestern	10/26/74	W	55-7
1	nr	H	Illinois	11/2/74	W	49-7
1	nr	A	Michigan State	11/9/74	L	13-16
1	nr	H	Iowa	10/11/75	W	49-0
1	nr	H	Wisconsin	10/18/75	W	56-0
1	nr	A	Purdue	10/25/75	W	35-6
1	nr	H	Indiana	11/1/75	W	24-14
1	nr	A	Illinois	11/8/75	W	40-3
1	nr	H	Minnesota	11/15/75	W	38-6
1	4	H	Michigan	11/22/75	W	21-14
1	11	N	UCLA	1/1/76	L	10-23
1	3	N	Southern California	1/1/80	L	16-17
1	nr	H	Syracuse	9/13/80	W	31-21
1	11	A	West Virginia	9/5/98	W	34-17
1	nr	H	Toledo	9/12/98	W	49-0
1	21	H	Missouri	9/19/98	W	35-14
1	7	H	Penn State	10/3/98	W	28-9
1	nr	A	Illinois	10/10/98	W	41-0
1	nr	H	Minnesota	10/17/98	W	45-15
1	nr	A	Northwestern	10/24/98	W	36-10
1	nr	A	Indiana	10/31/98	W	38-7
1	nr	H	Michigan State	11/7/98	L	24-28

When Opponent is Ranked Number One (3-8)

Oct. 26, 1940, Ithaca, N.Y.

No. 1 Cornell	21
Ohio State	7

Nov. 22, 1947, Ann Arbor, Mich.

Ohio State	0
No. 1 Michigan	21

Nov. 20, 1948, Columbus, Ohio

No. 1 Michigan	13
No. 18 Ohio State	3

Oct. 6, 1951, Columbus, Ohio

No. 1 Michigan State	24
No. 7 Ohio State	20

Oct. 11, 1952, Columbus, Ohio

No. 1 Wisconsin	14
Ohio State	23

Oct. 15, 1966, Columbus, Ohio

No. 1 Michigan State	11
Ohio State	8

Oct. 12, 1968, Columbus, Ohio

No. 1 Purdue	0
No. 4 Ohio State	13

Jan. 1, 1973, Pasadena, Calif.

No. 1 Southern California	42
No. 3 Ohio State	17

Nov. 2, 1985, Columbus, Ohio

No. 1 Iowa	13
No. 8 Ohio State	22

Oct. 29, 1994, State College, Pa.

No. 1 Penn State	63
No. 21 Ohio State	14

Nov. 22, 1997, Ann Arbor, Mich.

No. 1 Michigan	20
No. 4 Ohio State	14

All-time Football Letterwinners

A

Abbott, Albert G.	1898
Ackerman, Cornelius	1925-26-27
Adamle, Anthony	1946
Adams, Douglas O.	1968-69-70
Adams, J. J.	1900
Adderly, Nelson W.	1965
Addison, Evert	1918-22
Adkins, David	1974-75-76-77
Adulewicz, Casimir T.	1959
Alber, George H.	1926-27-28
Alders, Gary	1981-82-84
Aleskus, Joseph P.	1937-38
Allegro, Joe	1975-76-77
Allen, Paul	1983
Allen, Robert M.	1932
Allen, Willie	2000
Amlin, George P.	1966
Amling, Warren E.	1944-45-46
Anders, Billy J.	1965-66-67
Anderson, Charles C.	1939-40
Anderson, Cedric	1980-81-82-83
Anderson, Kim	1964-65-66
Anderson, Richard L.	1964-65
Anderson, Richard	1952
Anderson, Thomas L.	1964
Anderson, Tim	2000
Anderson, William T.	1968-69-70
Andrako, Steven F.	1938-39
Andrews, Bill	1981-82
Andrews, Lawrence F.	1951
Andria, Ernest	1975-77-78-79
Andrick, Theodore K.	1964-65
Antenucci, Frank L.	1934-35-36
Anthony, Thomas	1981-82
Appleby, Gordon E.	1942-43-44
Applegate, Richard	1974-75
Arledge, Richard	1951
Armstrong, Billy J.	1960-61-62
Armstrong, Ralph A.	1949-50-51
Arnold, Dirtho	1957-58-59
Arnold, George A.	1907
Aston, Daniel B.	1969
Atha, Robert	1978-79-80-81
Auer, John J.	1953
Augenstein, Jack G.	1953
Ayers, Ronald	1974-75-76

B

Baas, James W.	1965-66
Bach, Terry	1977-78
Bachman, Stanley	1908-09-10
Backhus, Tom A.	1967-68-69
Backus, Clark	1982-83
Bahin, Michael	1895
Bailey, Ralph	1958
Bailey, Rodney	1997-98-99-00
Baird, Charles H.	1893

Baird, Steve	1995
Baker, Ray G.	1945
Baldacci, Thomas G.	1955-56-57
Balen, Alan,	1981
Ballmer, Paul E.	1958
Bargerstock, Douglas	1974
Barnes, Robert L.	1890
Barnett, Orlando T.	1963-64-65
Barratt, Fred W.	1928-29
Barre, Bjorn	2000
Barricklow, Donald B.	1910-11-12
Barrington, Thomas G.	1963-64-65
Barrington, Walter D.	1905-06-07-08
Bartley, Thomas A.	1967-68
Bartholomew, Brent	1995-96-97-98
Bartoszek, Mike	1972-73-74
Bartschy, Ross D.	1937-38-39
Barwig, Ronald	1977-78-79-80
Baschnagel, Brian	1972-73-74-75
Bates, John	2000
Bates, Roman	1983-84
Battista, Thomas	1971
Baumgarten, Eugene H.	1930-31
Baxa, Thomas L.	1972
Beatty, Dan	1987-89-90
Beatty, Greg	1989-92
Beatty, Hobart	1890
Beatty, Hugh G.	1909-10
Beam, William D.	1959
Beamon, Eddie	1974-75-76-77
Bear, C. L.	1911
Bechtel, Earl R.	1952
Beckman, Pete	1992-93-94
Beecroft, Charles	1971-72
Beekley, Marts E.	1951-52
Beerman, Raymond O.	1957
Beetham, Rupert R.	1899
Belgrave, Earl	1972
Bell, Farley	1975-76
Bell, Frederick J.	1917-18
Bell, Jimmie	1996-97
Bell, Kelvin	1981-82-83
Bell, Robert R.	1925-26-27
Bell, Robin A.	1925-26-27
Bell, Sean	1985-87
Bell, Todd	1977-78-79-80
Bell, William M.	1929-30-31
Bellisari, Greg	1993-94-95-96
Bellisari, Steve	1998-99-00
Belmer, Cliff	1978-79
Beltz, Richard H.	1934-35
Bender, Edward A.	1968
Benedict, Charles Y.	1897
Benio, Brian	1987-88
Benis, Joe V.	1930-31
Benis, Michael K.	1960
Bentley, LeCharles	1998-99-00
Berger, Jon	1991
Berner, Joseph	1981
Berry, Gary	1996-97-98-99

Bettridge, John W.	1934-35-36
Betz, Wayne O.	1961-62
Biel, William J.	1945
Bilkie, Edward R.	1950
Biltz, John W.	1949-50
Birdseye, Claude H.	1901
Blaine, Ernest D.	1910-11
Blair, Howard H.	1920-21-22
Blair, Kenneth	1984
Blanchard, Bruce J.	1925
Bledsoe, John	1971-72
Bliss, Harry W.	1919-20
Bliss, Keith H.	1937-38
Blinco, Thomas	1976-77-79
Blose, M. L.	1896-97
Bobo, Hubert L.	1954
Boddie, Chris	1987
Bodenbender, David G.	1964
Boesel, Richard	1915-16-17
Boesel, Stephen W.	1909-10
Bohlman, Jeff	1988-89-90
Bolen, Charles W.	1915-16-17
Bolin, Stuart R.	1895
Bolser, Harvey J.	1938
Bombach, Jaren D.	1967
Bompiedi, Carl J.	1933
Bond, Robert J.	1952-53-54-55
Bonhaus, Matt	1992-93-95
Bonica, Charles	1970-71-72
Bonnie, Dale B.	1947
Bonnie, David M.	1946-47
Boone, Chelsea A.	1909
Booth, William A.	1953-54-55
Booth, William R.	1936
Boothman, Dale M.	1900-01
Borchers, James	1990-91-92-93
Borton, John R.	1951-52-53-54
Boston, David	1996-97-98
Boucher, Arthur F.	1934-35
Boughner, Richard J.	1937-38
Boughton, Ivan B.	1913-14-15
Bowermaster, Russell L.	1956-57-58
Bowers, Brian	1973-74
Bowman, Howard	1890
Bowsher, Gerald J.	1959
Boxwell, Kenneth E.	1944
Boynton, A. J.	1893-94
Bradley, Robert T.	1925
Bradshaw, Morris	1971-72-73
Braun, Don	1982
Breed, Paul	1997
Breehl, Edward L.	1957
Breese, Clarence	1899-00
Bridge, Brooklyn B.	1912
Briggs, Maurice	1912-13
Brindle, Arthur B.	1905
Britton, Bobby	2000
Broadnax, Vaughn	1980-81-82-83
Brockington, John S.	1968-69-70
Bronson, A. P.	1890

Brophy, James F.	1897-98	Carson, James	1981-82-83	Cope, James	1972-73-74
Brown, Aaron	1974-75-76-77	Carson, Samuel K.	1893-94	Cornell, Fred A.	1902
Brown, Bernard	1979	Carter, Cris	1984-85-86	Cory, Lincoln T.	1927-28
Brown, David	1986-87-88-89	Carter, David W.	1928-29	Cothran, Jeff	1991-92-93
Brown, Deron	1992	Carter, DeWayne	1993-94-95	Cott, Richard S.	1919-20-21
Brown, G. W.	1902	Carter, Drew	2000	Cottrell, Ernest E.	1944
Brown, Henry	1983-85-86-87	Carver, Rolly J.	1904	Cotton, James	1998-99
Brown, Jeff	1972	Case, Claude H.	1902-03	Courtney, Harold J.	1915-16-17
Brown, Joe	1997-98-99-00	Cassady, Craig	1973-74-75	Courtney, Howard G.	1915-16-17
Brown, Leo M.	1955-56-57	Cassady, Howard	1952-53-54-55	Cousineau, Tom	1975-76-77-78
Brown, Matthew	1943-44-45	Castignola, Gregory	1977-78-79	Cox, Garth	1974-76-77
Brown, Randall	1992-93-94	Cato, Byron	1975-76-77-78	Cox, Joseph E.	1926-27-28
Brown, Stanley	1902	Cheatwood, Tim	1998-99-00	Cox, Joseph F.	1909-10-11
Brown, Timothy	1978-79	Cheney, David A.	1968-69-70	Cox, Melvin B.	1934
Brubaker, Carl R.	1953-54	Cheroke, George	1941	Cowman, Randy	1972
Bruckner, Edwin	1940-41	Cherry, Boyd V.	1912-13-14	Craig, Orlondo	1987-88-89
Brudzinski, Robert	1973-74-75-76	Chonko, Arnie	1962-63-64	Cramer, Carl F.	1931-32-33
Brugge, Robert S.	1944-46-47	Chrissinger, Warren O.	1936-37	Cramer, William E.	1917
Bruney, Fred K.	1950-51-52	Cicero, Chris	1983	Crane, Jameson	1945-46-47
Bruney, Robert O.	1962-63	Cisco, Galen	1955-56-57	Crapser, Steven R.	1969
Brungard, David A.	1967-68	Cisco, Jeff	1981-82	Crawford, Albert K.	1956-57-58
Brungard, George	1935	Claflin, Walter N.	1906-07-08	Crawford, Thomas E.	1957
Bryant, Charles S.	1959-60-61	Claggett, Edward F.	1904-06-07	Crecelius, David	1981-82-83-84
Bryant, Ché	1995-96	Clair, Frank J.	1938-39-40	Crecilius, Arthur W.	1894-95
Bryant, Jaymes	1986-87-88-89	Clare, Robert L.	1909-10	Crooks, Duane	1999
Bryant, Ricky	2000	Clark, James	1947-48-49	Crosby, Curtis	2000
Bryce, Chalmers K.	1906-07-08	Clark, David B.	1902-03-04	Crow, Fred.	1936-37
Bugel, Thomas E.	1963-64-65	Clark, Donald	1956-57-58	Csuri, Charles A.	1941-42-46
Bulen, Elwood J.	1900-01	Clark, Eugene L.	1943	Culbertson, Claude L.	1897
Bullard, Courtland	1997, 99-00	Clark, Myers A.	1924-25-26	Cumiskey, Frank S.	1934-35-36
Bullock, William M.	1938	Clark, Shane	1995-96	Cummings, John	1972
Buonamici, Nicholas	1973-74-75-76	Clark, Vinnie	1988-89-90	Cummings, William G.	1956
Burden, Mike	1996	Clarke, Adrien	2000	Cunningham, Charles	1971
Burgett, Richard K.	1941	Cleary, Thomas J.	1942	Cunningham, Harold B.	1923-24-25
Burgin, Asbury L.	1965-66	Clements, Nate	1998-99-00	Cunningham, John F.	1896
Burke, Timothy	1978-79	Clift, Gary	1987	Cunningham, Leo	1943
Burris, Brooks	1995-96-97-98	Cline, Oliver M.	1944-45-47	Cupe, Tony	1987
Burris, Scott	1978-79-80	Cline, W. D.	1895	Curcillo, Anthony	1950-51-52
Burrows, Norman	1978-79-80	Closson, Tony	1989	Curren, Michael F.	1904
Burrows, Roger W.	1970	Clotz, Dennis R.	1961	Curtis, Clarence	1981-82-83
Burton, Arthur F.	1967-68-69	Cobb, Glen	1979-80-81-82	Current, Michael	1965-66
Busich, Sam	1934-35	Coburn, James A.	1970	Curto, Patrick	1973-74-75
Buss, Charles	1891	Cochran, Kenneth L.	1931	Cusick, Martin	1977
Butts, Robert W.	1960-62	Cochran, Terrence A.	1965	Cusick, Peter	1972-73-74
Butcher, Fred E.	1895-96-97-00	Coffee, Charles B.	1927-28-29	Cutillo, Dan	1971-72-73
Byars, Keith	1982-83-84-85	Cole, George N.	1891	Czyzynski, Richard	1981-82-83
By'not'e, Butler	1990-91-92-93	Cole, Robert	1956		
Byrne, Edward G.	1903-04	Coleman, Ken	1987-88-89-90		
		Coles, Karl	1986-87-89	**D**	
		Collins, Mike	1998-99-00		
C		Collmar, William J.	1954-55	Dale, Michael D.	1970
		Colson, Dan	1994-95-96	D'Andrea, Michael	1979-80-81
Cacchio, Chad	1998-99-00	Colzie, Cornelius	1972-73-74	Daniell, James L.	1939-40-41
Cairns, Gary L.	1966-67	Combs, Derek	1997-98-99-00	Daniels, LeShun	1994-95-96
Calhoun, Matt	1993-94-95-96	Conley, William N.	1970-71	Dannelley, Scott	1972-73-74-75
Calkins, George H.	1894-95	Conlin, Ray	1984	Dansler, Kelton	1975-76-77-78
Cameron, George D.	1924	Connery, Will	1995	Darst, Lester D.	1907-11
Campana, Thomas	1969-70-71	Connor, Daniel D.	1961	Datish, Michael	1975
Campanella, Joseph A.	1950	Conrad, Frederick B.	1931-32-33	Daugherty, Harold R.	1945
Campbell, Paul	1976-77-78-79	Conroy, James	1969	Daughters, Charles G.	1916
Cannavino, Joseph P.	1955-56-57	Conway, Blair	1972-73	Davidson, James	1963-64
Cannavino, Michael L.	1946-47-48	Cooke, Clement C.	1910	Davidson, James Jr.	1985
Cappell, Richard A.	1969-70-71	Cook, Bryan	1989-90-91-92	Davidson, Jeff	1986-87-88-89
Cargile, Jeff	1983-84	Cook, Ronald L.	1955-57	Davies, Thomas C.	1918-19
Carlin, Earl V.	1939-40	Cooper, George	1984-85-86-87	Davis, Jeff	1971-72-73
Carlin, Oscar E.	1927-29	Cooper, Joe	1998-99-00	Davis, Jerome	1973-74
Carroll, Paul B.	1911-12	Coover, Winifred F.	1900-01-02	Davis, Paul J.	1943
Carroll, William M.	1930-31-32	Cope, Harry	1898	Davis, Robert	1995

Davis, Vernon H.	1898	Dwelle, Brad	1979-80-81-82	Fertig, Dwight L.	1967
Dawdy, Donald A.	1953	Dwyer, Donald W.	1965-66-67	Fesler, Wesley E.	1928-29-30
Dawson, Dino	1984	Dwyer, R. E.	1898	Fickell, Luke	1993-94-95-96
Dawson, Jack S.	1948	Dye, William H.	1934-35-36	Fields, Jerry E.	1958-59
Day, John	1995-96-97			Fiers, Alan	1959-60
Dean, C. A.	1902			Fill, John M.	1964-65-66
Dean, Hal S.	1941-42-46	**E**		Finkes, Matt	1993-94-95-96
Debevc, Mark C.	1968-69-70			Fioretti, Anthony R.	1922-23
DeCree, Van	1972-73-74	Eachus, William N.	1965-66	Fisch, Frank	1933-34-35
DeGraffenreid, Allen	1990-91-92	Eagleson, John H.	1898	Fischer, Louis C.	1950-51
Delaney, Kevin	1985	Early, Ellis T.	1921	Fisher, Richard	1939-40-41-45
DeLeone, James	1979-80-81	Eberle, John J.	1908-09	Fitz, Thomas	1964
DeLeone, Thomas D.	1969-70-71	Eberts, Mark	1981	Flanagan, Richard E.	1944
Delich, Peter D.	1931-32-33	Ebinger, Elbert C.	1955	Fleming, Henry	1997-98-99-00
DeLong, A. Z.	1895-96	Eby, Byron	1926-27-28	Fletcher, Kevin	1970-71-72
Demmel, Robert C.	1947-50	Echols, Reginald	1979-80	Flowers, James T.	1919
Dendiu, Traian T.	1944-46	Edwards, Bernard	1988-89-90-91	Foley, David	1966-67-68
Denker, Irv	1952	Edwards, Karl	1981-82-83	Foley, W. J.	1893
Denman, Edgar	1894	Edwards, William R.	1949	Fontaine, Lawton L.	1929
Detrick, Roger	1959-60	Egbert, Archie D.	1910	Fontes, Arnold P.	1965-66
DeVoe, Keith E.	1923-24-25	Ehrensberger, Carl H.	1930	Fontes, Leonard J.	1958-59
Diehl, William	1932	Ehrsam, Gerald R.	1966-67-68	Fordham, Forrest P.	1937-38
Diggs, Na'il	1997-98-99	Ehrsam, John H.	1944-45	Fortney, Harrison	1963
Dike, Ed	1904	Eisenhard, Tony	1997-98-99	Foster, Derrick	1989-90-91-92
Dill, M. R.	1928-29	Elder, Walter W.	1901-02	Foster, Jerome	1979-80-81-82
Dill, Raymond	1901	Elford, Drew	1996-97-98-99	Foster, Rodney	1961-62
Dillman, Thomas M.	1954-55-56	Elgin, Edward G.	1922	Foster, Thomas B.	1905
Dillon, Daniel D.	1966	Elia, Bruce	1972-73-74	Foss, Clarence M.	1902-03-04-05
Diltz, Charles R.	1901-02-03-04	Elliott, Samuel	1965-66-67	Foss, Earl D.	1910-11
DiPierro, Ramon F.	1944-46-47-48	Ellis, Jeff	1987-88-90-91	Fouch, George E.	1927-28-29
Disher, Larry L.	1957	Ellis, Ray	1977-78-79-80	Foulk, Charles W.	1890-91-92
Dixon, Joe	1975-76-77	Ellis, Richard T.	1890-91-92	Fout, James E.	1945
Dixon, Ken	1970-71	Ellison, Leon	1980	Fox, Samuel S.	1940-41
Dixon, Thornton D.	1939-40-41-45	Ellwood, Franklin D.	1955-56	Fox, Tim	1972-73-74-75
Doig, Hal F.	1920-21	Ellwood, Richard P.	1949-50	France, Doug	1972-73-74
Doll, John	1972	Endres, George J.	1950	France, Steve	1989
Donley, Douglas	1977-78-79-80	Endres, Robert L.	1951	Francis, David L.	1960-62
Donley, Fred	1908	Engensperger, Albert	1896-97	Frank, John	1980-81-82-83
Donovan, Brian P.	1968-69-70	Englebeck, Amos	1904-06	Frantz, Matthew	1986-87
Dooley, Joseph	1981-82-83	Epitropoulos, John	1978-79-80	Frayer, Leo A.	1894
Doolittle, Francis W.	1946-47	Ernst, L. C.	1891-92	Frechtling, Arthur G.	1899-00
Dorris, Victor	1937	Ervin, Terry L.	1966-67	French, Edward H.	1893-94-95
Dorsey, Robert S.	1947-48	Espy, Bennie E.	1962-63	Frey, Greg	1987-88-89-90
Doss, Mike	1999-00	Ewalt, Dwight S.	1913	Fried, Lawrence L.	1930
Douglas, Ivan	2000	Ewart, Kenneth L.	1917-19	Friedman, Max	1918
Dove, Robert E.	1944-45	Ewing, Harry E.	1905	Frimel, Rich	1988-89-90-91
Doyle, Richard A.	1950-52	Ezzo, Billy	1972-73-74	Fritz, Kenneth	1976-77-78-79
Drake, Phillip B.	1942			Fronk, Daniel A.	1957-58
Drakulich, Samuel	1933			Frye, Robert H.	1941-42
Dreffer, Stephan D.	1962-63-64	**F**		Fuller, Mark A.	1919
Drenik, Douglas J.	1962-63-64			Fulton, William S.	1899
Dreyer, Carl A.	1924	Facchine, Richard	1955	Funk, Robert	1964-65
Dreyer, Virgil O.	1915-16	Faehl, Paul J.	1950	Funkhauser, Samuel K.	1908-12
DuBois, Wilbur L.	1900	Fair, Robert F.	1963	Furrey, Mike	1996
Dudley, Rickey	1994-95	Farcasin, Constantine J.	1918-19-22		
Dugger, Dean	1952-53-54	Ferrall, Junius B.	1930-31-32		
Dugger, John R.	1942-43-44	Farrell, John R.	1960	**G**	
Dulin, Gary	1976-77-78-79	Fay, Sherman	1899-00-01-02		
Dully, Mike	1993-94	Fazio, Charles A.	1945-46-47-48	Gaffney, Mike	1972
Dumas, Zack	1986-87-88-89	Fedderson, Jerold V.	1943	Gage, Ralph G.	1958
Dunlap, John H.	1895-96	Federle, Tom	1963-64	Gailus, Joseph T.	1931-32-33
Dunlap, Nelson H.	1921-22-23	Fekete, Eugene	1942	Galbos, Richard	1971-72
Dunlap, Renick W.	1891-93-94-95	Feldwisch, Henry W.	1911	Gales, Charles P.	1935-36-38
Dunn, Craig	1981-82	Fender, Paul E.	1967	Gales, Richard	1971-72
Dunsford, Jan H.	1904-05	Ferguson, Keith	1978-79-80	Galloway, Joey	1991-93-94
Duncan, Howard D.	1946-47	Ferguson, Robert E.	1959-60-61	Gandee, Charles F.	1945-49-50
Dupree, Roedell	1995	Ferko, Richard	1970-71	Gandee, Sherwin K.	1948-50-51
Durtschi, William R.	1942	Ferrelli, Jeffrey	1975-76	Garber, Joseph	1986

Garcia, Mark	1997-98	Griffith, William N.	1924	Hefflinger, Ronald D.	1943
Garnett, Winfield	1995-96-97	Griggs, Anthony	1981	Heid, Robert C.	1949-50-51
Gaudio, Angelo R.	1946	Grim, Fred	1925-26-27	Henderson, Herbert R.	1920
Gayle, James	1979-80-81-82	Grimes, Robert L.	1950-51-52	Henry, Joseph P.	1949
Gayle, Shaun	1980-81-82-83	Griswold, Francis H.	1927	Henson, Harold	1972-73-74
Geib, J.R.	1911-12	Groza, Judd	1982-83-84	Henson, Luther	1977-78-79-80
Geissman, W. I.	1911-12-13	Grundies, Arthur J.	1938-40	Herbstreit, James H.	1958-59-60
Gentile, Jim M.	1968-69-70	Guess, Michael	1976-77-78-79	Herbstreit, Kirk	1990-91-92
George, August	1935	Gurd, Andy	1987-91	Herman, Judah	1988-89-90-91
George, Eddie	1992-93-94-95	Gurr, Mike	1997-98-99-00	Herrmann, Harvey J.	1959
Gerald, Rod	1975-76-77-78	Guthrie, George P.	1951-52	Herron, Kendall	1944
Germaine, Joe	1996-97-98	Guy, Richard S.	1954-55-56	Hershberger, Peter J.	1940-41
German, William	1959-60	Guzik, Frank A.	1953	Hess, Albert F.	1928-29
Germany, Reggie	1997-98-99-00	Gwinn, Anthony	1993-94-95-96	Hess, Edwin A.	1924-25-26
Gibbs, George C.	1893	Gwinn, Jayson	1993	Hess, William W.	1960-61-62
Gibbs, Jack G.	1954			Hicks, John	1970-72-73
Gibson, Millard F.	1906-07-08			Hicks, Tyrone	1978-79
Giessen, Carl	1894-95			Hicks, Marc	1988
Gilbert, Benjamin	1996-97-98-99	**H**		Hieronymous, Ted W.	1925-27-28
Gilbert, Charles R.	1948-49	Hackett, William G.	1942-43-44-45	Hietikko, James L.	1950-51
Gill, Arthur G.	1904	Hackett, William J.	1967-69	Higdon, Alex	1984-85-86-87
Gillam, Neal	1918-21	Haddad, George A.	1937	Hilinski, Richard	1953-54
Gillard, James H.	1905-06	Haer, Archie H.	1967	Hill, Douglas	1981-82-83
Gillian Lonnie R.	1967-68-69	Hague, Leslie J.	1947-48-49	Hill, Steve	1983-84-85
Gilliam, Neil,	1918-21	Hague, Thomas R.	1952-53	Himes, Richard D.	1965-66-67
Gillie, George W.	1905-06-07	Hall, Robert H.	1943	Hinchman, Lewis G.	1930-31-32
Gillis, Clarence	1901	Hallabrin, John D.	1939-40-41	Hlay, John	1950-51
Gillman, Sidney	1931-32-33	Haller, Tim	1986	Hoak, Frank	1987
Gilmore, James	1981-83-84-85	Hamilton, Forrest R.	1945-46-47	Hobt, Watt A.	1912-13-14
Ginn, Dwight G.	1914-15	Hamilton, Ian B.	1922	Hocevar, Mark	1982
Giuliani, Anthony	1983-84	Hamilton, Mardo M.	1944	Hoffer, Joe R.	1931
Givens, Dan O.	1971	Hamilton, Ray L.	1949-50-51	Hofmayer, Edward I.	1938
Glasser, Chester F.	1928-29	Hamlin, Stanley A.	1965	Holcolmb, Stuart K.	1929-30-31
Glenn, Terrance	1993-94-95	Hamrick, Charles E.	1934-35-36	Holland, Jay	1983-84
Godfrey, Ernest R.	1914	Hansley, Terence	1959	Holland, Jamie	1986
Gohlstin, Eric	1995-96-97	Hardman, von Allen	1961	Holliman, Ray	1984-85-87
Goings, Nick	1997	Hare, Gregory	1971-72-73	Holloway, Ralph B.	1968-69-70
Gordon, D. "Sonny"	1983-84-85-86	Hargreaves, William B.	1937	Holman, Alan M.	1928-29
Goodsell, Douglas R.	1951-52	Harkins, Donald L.	1962-63-64	Holtkamp, Ferdinand	1916-19
Gordon, George D.	1944	Harkrader, Jerry	1953-54-55	Holycross, Tim	1972-73-74
Gordon, Les	1975	Harley, Charles W.	1916-17-19	Honaker, Frank C.	1921-22-23
Gorby, Herbert L.	1945	Harman, Timothy A.	1970	Horn, Robert L.	1928-29-30
Gorley, Rodney	1979-80-83	Harper, Roger	1990-91-92	Homa, Randy	1997-98-99
Gorrill, Charles V.	1923-24-25	Harre, Gilbert A.	1934-35	Hornik, Joe	1975-76-77-78
Gottron, Jeff	1982	Harrell, James	1975-76-77	Hopkins, Tam	1997-98-99-00
Gradishar, Randy	1971-72-73	Harris, Jimmie L.	1969-70-71	Horvath, Leslie	1940-41-42-44
Grady, Robert J.	1929-30-31	Harris, Nate	1985-86	Houk, Ronald	1959-60
Graf, Campbell J.	1912-13-14	Harris, Raymont	1990-91-92-93	Houser, Bob	1993-94-95-96
Graf, Campbell R.	1939	Harris, Tyrone	1974-75-77	Houser, Kevin	1996-97-98-99
Graf, Jack R.	1939-40-41	Harrison, Preston	1994	Houston Sr., James	1957-58-59
Graf, Lawrence	1973	Harrison, Tyrone	1989-90	Houston Jr., James	1978
Graham, Jeff	1988-89-90	Hart, Randall J.	1967-68-69	Houston, Lindell L.	1941-42
Graham, Kent	1990-91	Hartman, Gabriel C.	1958-59-60	Houston, William	1990-92-93
Graham, Scottie	1988-89-90-91	Hartman, Leonard	1990-91-92	Howard, Fritz	1939-40-41
Grant, Cie	1999-00	Hartsock, Benjamin	2000	Howard, Harry C.	1914
Graves, Reggie	1986	Harvey, William	1984	Howard, Harry	1969-70-71
Graves, Rory	1983-84-85	Hasenohrl, George	1970-71-72	Howard, Tyrone	1993-94-95-96
Greenberg, Jack Z.	1931-32	Haubrich, Robert C.	1929-30-31	Howe, Frank H.	1940
Greene, Cornelius	1973-74-75	Hauer, Oscar A.	1958-59-60	Howell, Carroll	1952-53-54
Greene, Horatius A.	1969	Haupt, Richard A.	1961	Hoyer, Ralph W.	1903-04-05
Griffey, Craig	1990	Havens, William F.	1914-15	Hoying, Robert	1993-94-95
Griffin, André	2000	Hawkins, Harry C.	1897	Hoying, Tom	1996-97
Griffin, Archie	1972-73-74-75	Hayden, Leophus	1968-69-70	Hubbard, Rudy	1965-66-67
Griffin, Duncan	1975-76-77-78	Hazel, David	1972-73-74	Huddleston, Mike	1990
Griffin, Kevin	1995-96-97-98	Hecker, Robert H.	1943	Hudson, Addison, N.	1930
Griffin, Ray	1974-75-76-77	Hecker, Robert R.	1943	Hudson, Paul	1964-65-66
Griffith, A. G.	1892	Heckninger, Robert W.	1941	Hueston, Dennis	1983
Griffith, William A.	1928-29-30	Heekin, Richard J.	1933-34-35	Huff, Paul	1967-68

Huffman, Iolas M.	1918-19-20-21	Johnson, Robert T.	1965-66	Kirk, Chris	1996-97-98
Huffman, Rich	1988-89-90	Johnson, Thomas	1982-83-84-85	Kirk, Roy E.	1963
Hughes, John	1970-72-73	Jones, Ben	1960	Kittle, James M.	1899-00-01
Hunt, William P.	1924-25-26	Jones, Darrell (D.J.)	1992-93-94-96	Klaban, Tom	1974-75
Hunter, Charles	1977-78-79	Jones, David L.	1934	Klee, Ollie	1922-23-24
Hurm, Paul W.	1916	Jones, Edward S.	1933	Klein, Alex W.	1922-25-26
Huston, Arthur C.	1927-28-29	Jones, Arnold A.	1972-73-74	Klein, Robert J.	1960-61-62
Hutchings, John	1978-79-80	Jones, Gomer	1934-35	Kleinhans, John L.	1936
Hutchison, Charles	1967-68-69	Jones, Herbert M.	1956-57	Klevay, Walter S.	1949-50-51
Hutchison, John	1984-85-86	Jones, Herman	1975-76-77	Klie, Walter	1902
Hyatt, Bob	1974-76	Jones, Thomas H.	1909	Kline, Alan	1990-91-92-93
Hyme, Kevin	1995	Jones, W. C.	1903	Knisely, Heath	1996
		Joslin, Robert V.	1951-52-53	Knoll, Elmer P.	1902
		Judy, Lawrence E.	1922-23	Koch, Jay	1987-88-89-90

I

Iams, Alvin L.	1931			Koegel, Vic	1971-72-73
Idle, Ralph H.	1928			Koegle, Donald W.	1935
Ingram, Robert M.	1959-60-61	**K**		Koepnick, Robert E.	1950-51-52
Ireland, Kenneth D.	1962	Kabealo, John	1933-34-35	Kohut, William W.	1964
Isabel, Wilmer E.	1920-21-22	Kabealo, Michael	1936-37-38	Kolic, Larry	1982-84-85
Isaman, Derek	1985-86-87-89	Kacherski, John	1987-88-91	Kotterman, Larry	1985-86
		Kain, Lawrence	1973-74-75	Kozar, Jason	1997
		Kaplanoff, Carl G.	1936-37-38	Krall, Gerald	1945-46-48-49
		Kaplo, Edward	1922	Kregel, James	1971-72-73
J		Karch, Robert	1915-16-17	Kreglow, James J.	1924
Jabbusch, Robert O.	1942-46-47	Karcher, James N.	1934-35	Kremblas, Francis T.	1956-57-58
Jack, Alan R.	1967-68-69	Karow, Martin G.	1924-25-26	Krenzel, Craig	2000
Jackson, James	1901	Karsatos, James	1983-84-85-86	Krerowicz, Mark	1982-83-84
Jackson, Jermon	1995-96	Kasunic, Gerald S.	1963-64	Kreuzer, Dean	1995
Jackson, Josh	1994-95-96	Katzenmoyer, Andy	1996-97-98	Krisher, Gerald Glenn	1951-52-53-54
Jackson, Matthew	1976	Katterhenrich, David L.	1960-61-62	Kriss, Frederick C.	1954-55-56
Jackson, Paul	1901	Kay, Donald F.	1943	Kriss, Howard E.	1927-28
Jackson, Ray	1984-85-86-87	Kaylor, Ronald L.	1964	Krstolic, Raymond C.	1961-62
Jackson, Stanley	1995-96-97	Keane, Thomas L.	1944	Krumm, R. E.	1891-92
Jackson, Richard S.	1944-45	Kee, Michael	1983-85-86	Kruskamp, Harold W.	1926-28
Jackson, William F.	1904	Keefe, Thomas C.	1931-32	Kuhn, Richard	1968-69-70
Jackson, William M.	1921	Keenan, Charles	1987	Kuhn, Kenneth W.	1972-73-74-75
Jaco, William	1976-77-79	Keeton, Mike	1973	Kuhnhein, Scott	2000
Jacobs, Matt	1995	Keiser, Thomas L.	1890	Kumerow, Eric	1984-85-86-87
Jacobs, Mike	2000	Keith, Randal T.	1971-72	Kumler, Karl W.	1962
Jacoby, George R.	1951-52-53	Keller, Matt	1996-97-98-99	Kuri, Mike	1988-89
James, Daniel A.	1956-57-58	Kelley, Dwight A. (Ike)	1963-64-65	Kurz, Theodore R.	1968-69
James, Kenneth L.	1932	Kelley, Jefferson	1997	Kuszmaul, Greg	1995
James, Thomas L.	1942-46	Kelley, John L.	1966-67	Kutler, Rudolph J.	1922-23-24
Janakievski, Vlade	1977-78-79-80	Kellough, F. C.	1902		
Janecko, Gene K.	1944	Kelly, Rob	1993-94-95-96		
Jankowski, Bruce D.	1968-69-70	Kelly, Robert	1971	**L**	
Janowicz, Victor F.	1949-50-51	Kelsey, Ray T.	1945		
Jeannot, Fred G.	1903	Kennedy, Arthur	1890-91-92	LaVrar, Matt	1996-97-98-99
Jemison, Thad	1981-82-83	Kern, Carl	1972-73	Lachey, James	1981-82-83-84
Jenkins, Joseph	1967	Kern, Rex W.	1968-69-70	Lachey, Ron	1989
Jenkins, Joseph K.	1984-86	Kerner, Marlon	1991-92-93-94	Lacksen, Frank J.	1925-26
Jenkins, Michael	2000	Kessel, Joel	1992	Lago, Gary M.	1970-71-72
Jenkins, Thomas G.	1961-62-63	Kessler, Carlton G.	1943-45	Lambert, Howard L.	1961
Jenkins, William	1924-25	Keuchler, Lamar	1981-82	Lamka, Donald	1969-70-71
Jennings, Jack W.	1947-48-49	Kiefer, Arthur S.	1912-13-14	Landacre, Walter A.	1890
Jentes, Charles A.	1960	Kiehfuss, Thomas C.	1962-63-64	Lane, Garcia	1981-82-83
Jesty, James B.	1970	Kile, Eugene	1930-31	Lanese, Mike	1982-83-84-85
Jobko, William K.	1954-55-56	Kile, Robert J.	1897	Lang, Mark	1974-75-76-77
Johnson, Brent	1989-90-91-92	Kilgore, David S.	1958-59	Langenkamp, Max	1994
Johnson, Brent	1998-99-00	Kimball, Philip J.	1915	Langhurst, Earl J.	1938-39-40
Johnson, Earl F.	1933	King, Gerald L.	1970	Langley, Victor	1981
Johnson, Ernest Y.	1920	King, Percy	1997-98-99	Lantry, L. L.	1905
Johnson, Kenneth E.	1960-61	King, Robert J.	1897	Lapp, Harry R.	1916
Johnson, Kevin	1995-97	Kinkade, Thomas J.	1939-40-41	Large, Joseph H.	1890
Johnson, Ricky	1977-78-80	Kinsey, Marvin C.	1971	Larkins, Charles R.	1928-29-30
Johnson, Pete	1973-74-75-76	Kirby, R. E.	1905	Lashutka, Gregory S.	1963-64-65
		Kirk, Brenton S.	1947-48	Laskoski, Richard D.	1961
				Laughlin, James	1977-78-79

Lawrence, Paul C.	1910
Lawrence, Wilbert W.	1903-04-05
Lavelli, Dante B.	1942
Laybourne, Paul C.	1910
Leach, Scott	1984-85-86
Lease, Tom	1989-90-91-92
LeBeau, Charles R.	1956-57-58
Lee, Ben	1978-79-80-81
Lee, Byron	1982-83-84-85
Lee, Dante	1989-90
Lee, Darryl	1983-84-85-86
Leggett, William D.	1952-53-54
Lehman, Ernest	1943
Leonard, Judson C.	1905
Leonard, W. T.	1897
Levenick, Thomas	1979
Lewis, Darrell	1989
Lewis, Donald B.	1955
Lewis, Doyle	1979-82
Lickovitch, Gary	1987-88-90
Liggins, Leandre	1998
Lincoln, James F.	1901-03-05-06
Lincoln, Paul M.	1890-91
Lindner, James E.	1959-60
Lindsay, Kelton	1999
Lindsey, Kelvin	1982-83
Lindsey, William L.	1964
Lininger, Raymond J.	1946-47-48-49
Lipaj, Cyril M.	1942
Lippert, Elmer H.	1971-72-73
Lishewski, Richard	1986
Lister, Robert C.	1961
Livingston, Brian	1965
Lloyd, Erastus G.	1899-00-01
Loadman, Kevin	1998
Locke, Tony	1999-00
Logan, Jeff	1974-75-76-77
Logan, Richard L.	1950-51
Lohr, Wendell	1937-38
Long, David W.	1971
Long, Herbert	1910
Long, Paris	1999
Long, Paul	1991-92
Long, Thomas N.	1922-23
Long, William E.	1966-67-68
Longer, Robert M.	1964
Lonjak, William A.	1943
Lord, John C.	1958
Louis, Jason	1992-93-94
Loveberry, Clarence	1896
Lowdermilk, Kirk	1981-82-83-84
Lowe, Clifton D.	1909
Lowry, Orlando	1981-82-83
Luckay, Raymond J.	1951
Ludwig, Paul L.	1952-53-54
Luke, Steven N.	1972-73-74
Lukens, Joseph	1979-80-81-82
Lukens, William	1974-75-76
Lukz, Frank M.	1932
Lumpkin, John	1996-97-98
Luttner, Ken	1969-70-71
Lykes, Robert L.	1965
Lynch, Scott	1994
Lynn, George M.	1941-42
Lyons, James D.	1963

M

Maag, Charles	1938-39-40
Maag, Dennis	1993-94
MacCready, Derek	1987-88
MacDonald, Clarence	1916-18-19
Machinsky, Francis C.	1953-54-55
Maciejowski, Ronald J.	1968-69-70
Mack, Richard W.	1972-73-74
Mackey, Frederick C.	1924-25-26
Mackey, J. E.	1897
Mackie, Douglas	1976-77
Madro, Joseph C.	1939
Maggied, Sol	1935-36-37
Maggs, Robert	1983-84-85-86
Mahaffey, William W.	1932
Maldonado, Sammy	2000
Malfatt, Mike	1994-95
Maltinsky, Paul R.	1943-44-45
Mamula, Charles	1962-63
Mandula, George E.	1930
Mangiamelle, Richard C.	1962
Mann, George T.	1930
Manning, Ernest P.	1907
Manyak, John N.	1952
Manz, Jerry V.	1948-49-50
Marendt, Thomas L.	1971-72
Marek, Elmer F.	1925-26-27
Marek, Marcus	1979-80-81-82
Marino, Victor I.	1937-38-39
Marker, James B.	1901-02-03-04
Markley, Frank P.	1910-11
Marquardt, William B.	1902-04
Marsh, George C.	1929
Marsh, James R.	1970
Marshall, Clyde	1945
Marshall, James	1957-58
Marshall, W. D.	1890
Martin, Edwin D.	1890
Martin, Harold P.	1952
Martin, Jamar	1998-99-00
Martin, John C.	1955-56-57
Martin, Paul D.	1959
Marts, Raymond J.	1923
Martz, Valorus	1914
Mascio, Joseph	1944
Mason, Glen	1970
Matheny, Oliver S.	1918
Mathers, John H.	1892-93-94
Mathis, Almond L.	1971-72-73
Matlock, Bill	1987-88
Matte, Thomas R.	1958-59-60
Mattey, George J.	1948-49
Matz, James F.	1958-59-60
Maxwell, Earl P.	1912
Maxwell, John R.	1962
Mayer, Robert E.	1944
Mayes, Rufus L.	1966-67-68
Maynard, Lee H.	1903
McAfee, John N.	1933-34
McCafferty, Donald W.	1941-42
McCallister, H. A.	1898-07-08
McCarthy, Timothy J.	1924-25
McCarty, L. B.	1908-09
McClain, W. B.	1909-10
McClellion, Central	1995-96-97-98

McClure, Donald L.	1927-28-29
McClure, James A.	1912
McConagha, Arthur B.	1905
McConnell, Arden L.	1928-29
McCormick, Robert W.	1942
McCoy, John	1964-65-66
McCoy, Matt	1992
McCoy, Walter E.	1911
McCray, Michael	1986-87-88
McCullough, Bob	1949-50
McCune, J. H.	1918
McDonald, James A.	1935-36-37
McDonald, Paul A.	1905-06
McElheny, Norman E.	1944
McGinnis, Robert E.	1944-45-46
McGuire, Timothy A.	1966
McKee, David	1977
McLaren, James W.	1900-01-02
McMullen, Scott	2000
McNeal, Laird C.	1967
McNutt, Richard	2000
McQuade, Robert P.	1943
McQuigg, William G.	1936
Meade, John	1978
Means, John W.	1906
Medich, David	1980-81
Megaro, Anthony	1977-78-79-80
Meindering, Wesley	1965-66
Merrell, James	1951
Metzger, Joseph	1990-91-92
Metzger, Walter E.	1916-17
Meyer, Theodore R.	1925-26-27
Meyers, Russell L.	1917
Michael, Paul	1954-55-56
Michael, Richard J.	1958-59
Michaels, Alton C.	1922
Middleton, Richard R.	1971-72-73
Middleton, Robert L.	1960-61-62
Midlam, Max	1974-75-76
Miller, Carl J.	1894-95-96
Miller, Charles E.	1953
Miller, Dee	1995-96-97-98
Miller, Gary A.	1964-65-66
Miller, James R.	1937
Miller, Luke E.	1920
Miller, Nick	1980-81
Miller, Norman	1995
Miller, Ronald	1980
Miller, Robert N.	1935
Miller, Ryan	1993-94-95-96
Miller, Walter H.	1890
Miller, William G.	1943
Miller, William M.	1948-49-50
Milligan, Fred J.	1927
Mills, Leonard	1975-76-77-78
Minshall, William E.	1896-97-98
Mirick, Chester W.	1961-62-63
Mitchell, Essex David	1997-98-99-00
Mitchell, H. Jordan	1925
Mobley, Benjamin A.	1964
Moeller, Gary O.	1960-61-62
Moldea, Emil	1947
Moler, William A.	1927
Molls, Larry	1976
Moherman, Austin	1999

Moore, Damon	1995
Momsen, Robert E.	1950
Monahan, John Regis	1932-33-34
Monahan, Thomas	1937
Monnot, Dave	1990-91-92-93
Montgomery, Joe	1996-98
Moore, Anthony	1990
Moore, Damon	1995-96-97-98
Moore, Jimmy	1975-76-77-78
Moore, Thomas	1985-86-87-88
Moorehead, Lewis S.	1921-22
Morgan, Tommy Joe	1956-57
Morrey, Charles B.	1890-91-92
Morrill, David	1982-83-84
Morrisey, Edward L.	1911-12-13
Morrison, Fred L.	1946-47-48-49
Morrison, Steven A.	1972-74
Motejzik, John J.	1944
Mott, William H.	1953
Mountz, Gregory L.	1971
Moxley, Tim	1986-87-88-89
Moyer, Bruce M.	1967
Mrukowski, William	1960-61-62
Muhlbach, John L.	1966-67-68
Mullay, Patrick L.	1893
Mummey, John	1960-61-62
Murphy, Kurt	1996-97-98-99
Murphy, Rob	1996-97-98
Murphy, Robert	1978-79-80
Murray, Calvin	1977-78-79-80
Myers, Cyril E.	1919-20-21
Myers, Ord	1894
Myers, Raymond	1980-81-82
Myers, Robert C.	1952
Myers, Russell L.	1917
Myers, Steven	1972-73-74

N

Nagel, William G.	1892-93-94
Nagy, Alex	1957
Nardi, Richard L	1937
Nasman, Bert H.	1930-31-32
Navin, James J.	1920
Neal, George V.	1934
Neff, George E.	1943-44
Neff, Robert L.	1958
Neff, Scott	1982
Nein, James R.	1964-66-67
Nelms, Spencer	1981-82-83
Nelson, Willie (Chico)	1990-91-92-93
Nemecek, Andrew J.	1919-20
Nesser, John P.	1927-28
Nesser, William H.	1928-29
Newell, William F.	1947-48-49
Newlin, John M.	1940
Nichols, John H.	1923-24-25
Nichols, Roy	1989-90
Nickey, Donnie	1999-00
Nicols, Frank B.	1893-94-95-96
Nielsen, William B.	1967-68-69
Niesz, Dale E.	1960
Nixon, Thomas W.	1970-71-72
Norton, Elisha S.	1893
Norton, Frederick W.	1915-16
Nosker, William C.	1938-39-40

Nosky, Richard E.	1953
Novotny, George K.	1937

O

Oates, James G.	1965
Oberlin, Russell W.	1922-23
O'Cain, Timothy	1981
O'Dea, Stephen H.	1945
Odom, Timothy	1984
Offenbecher, Brent	1982
O'Hanlon, Richard M.	1946-47-48-49
Ohsner, Clarence S.	1927
Okulovich, Andrew J.	1A
Olds, Benjamin H.	1909-10
Oliphant, Marshall T.	1931-32-33
Olive, Bobby	1987-88-89-90
Olivea, Shane	2000
Oliver, Glenn F.	1943
Oliver, Robert H.	1901-02-03-04
O'Morrow, Patrick	1986-87-88-89
O'Neill, Pat	2000
Onrubia, Lorenzo R.	1907
Openlander, Gerald P.	1925
Oppermann, James D.	1968-70
Orazen, Edward J.	1962-64
Orosz, Thomas	1977-78-79-80
O'Rourke, Larry	1974
O'Shaughnessy, Joseph	1928-29
Ost, Dave	1993
Otis, James L.	1967-68-69
Ott, Jason	1998-99

P

Pace, Orlando	1994-95-96
Pacenta, James	1975-76
Padlow, Max	1932-33
Pack, Craig	1981-82
Pagac, Fred	1971-72-73
Pagac Jr., Fred	1999
Painter, William E.	1968
Palahnuk, Michael	1981-82
Palmer, James F.	1949
Palmer, James	1988-89
Palmer, James A.	1982-83
Palmer, John V.	1964-66
Palmer, Richard R.	1941-42-46
Pargo, Corey	1990
Parker, Albert E.	1962
Parker, James	1954-55-56
Parks, Ernest	1943-46
Parmele, G. W.	1909
Parsons, Richard	1972-73-74
Patchell, James H.	1922
Patillo, Tim	1991-93-94
Patterson, F. D.	1891-92-93
Paul, Tito	1991-92-93-94
Paulk, Foster	1989-90-91
Pauley, Douglas	1980
Pauley, Kenneth H.	1921-22
Paulsen, Ron	1985
Pavey, Robert M.	1910-11-12
Payne, Marvin	2000
Payton, Joel	1977-78

Peabody, Dwight V.	1915-16-17
Pearce, George D.	1891-92-93
Pearson, Pepe	1994-95-96-97
Peel, Jim	1987-88-89-90
Pelini, Mark	1987-88-89-90
Penn, Trent,	1982
Penny, Sean	1997-98
Peppe, Louis, J.	1931
Perdue, Thomas H.	1959-60-61
Perez, Marcus	1999-00
Perini, E. Pete	1946-47-48-49
Perry, William A.	1905-09
Petcoff, Boni	1922-23
Peterson, John	1987-90
Peterson, Kenny	2000
Peterson, Martin B.	1951
Peterson, William J.	1952
Pfister, Mark	1983-84
Pflaumer, Dale R.	1956
Phillips, Thomas G.	1946-47
Phillips, Thomas W.	1937
Piccinini, James A.	1939-40
Pickerel, Louis E.	1913-14
Picket, Ryan	1998-99-00
Pietrini, Louis	1974-75-76
Pincura, Stanley	1933-34-35
Pisanelli, Fred	1971
Pitstick, Anthony	1971
Pixley, Lloyd A.	1918-19-21-22
Placas, John G.	1941
Plank, Ernest V.	1943
Plank, Doug	1972-73-74
Plummer, Ahmed	1996-97-98-99
Polaski, Don M.	1967-68-69
Pollitt, Harry W.	1968-69
Poole, Loren W.	1898-99
Pope, Brad	1992
Popp, Milton F.	1928
Porretta, Daniel J.	1962-63-64
Porter, Juan	1993-94-95-96
Porter, Douglas	1974-75-76-77
Portsmouth, Thomas	1965-66-67
Portz, Grover C.	1909
Potter, Frank D.	1895
Potthoff, William J.	1924
Powell, Charles S.	1891-92
Powell, Craig	1992-93-94
Powell, Harold P.	1908-09-10
Powell, J. E.	1901-03
Powell, Scott	1986-87-88
Powell, Theodore	1972-73
Powers, Bret	1993
Price, Lance	1987-89-90
Priday, Paul	1942-45
Provenza, Russell D.	1957
Provitt, Vanness	1997-00
Provost, Ted R.	1967-68-69
Pryor, Ray Von	1964-65-66
Pulliam, Chad	1996
Purdy, David B.	1972-73-74
Purdy, Ross C.	1897

Q

Queen, Heath.	1998-99-00

R

Rabb, John P.	1936-37-39
Rabenstein, Howard P.	1930-31
Radtke, Michael	1967-68-69
Rainey, Cecil D.	1909
Rambo, Ken-Yon	1997-98-99-00
Rane, Frank W.	1890
Ranney, Arch E.	1902
Raskowski, Leo	1926-27-28
Rath, Thomas L.	1950-51
Raymond, Arthur W.	1910-11-12
Ream, Charles D.	1935-36-37
Reboulet, LaVerne B.	1928
Redd, John G.	1944-45
Redmond, Jimmy	1997-98
Reed, Malcolm	1926
Reed, William A.	1892-93-96
Reed, William H.	1925-26
Reemsnyder, R. C.	1904-05
Rees, James R.	1942
Rees, Trevor J.	1933-34-35
Reese, Wayne G.	1961
Reichenbach, James	1951-52-53-54
Rein, Robert E.	1964-65-66
Renner, Charles	1944-47-48
Reynolds, Robert	2000
Rhodes, Gordon M.	1916
Rich, Rocco J.	1971-72-73
Richards, Charles J.	1897
Richards, David P.	1955
Richardson, Hamilton H.	1890-91-92
Richardson, Kevin	1982-83-84
Richey, Lazerne A.	1896
Richley, Richard C.	1965
Richt, Fred H.	1894-95-96
Ricketts, Karl	1901
Ricketts, Ormonde B.	1961-62-63
Ridder, Fred	1984-85-86-87
Ridder, William E.	1963-64-65
Riddle, Abner E.	1901-02
Riehm, Christopher	1979-80-81-82
Rife, Roy E.	1918
Rigby, Richard R.	1909
Riggs, David R.	1926
Rightmire, Robert	1898-00-01
Riticher, Raymond J.	1952
Rittman, Walter F.	1903
Roach, Woodrow	1973-74-75
Roberts, Jack C.	1961
Roberts, Robert L.	1952-53
Roberts, Stanley	1911
Roberts, William	1980-81-82-83
Robinson, Philip	1956-57
Robinson, Joseph	1975-76-77-78
Roche, Tom	1974-76-77
Rodriguez, Alex	1992-93-94
Rodriquez, Camilo A.	1901
Roe, John E.	1944-45
Roemer, Wellington	1929
Rogan, Greg	1984-85-86-87
Rogan, Pat	1988
Roman, James T.	1966-67-68
Roman, Nicholas G.	1966-67-69
Ronemus, Thor	1950-51
Roseboro, James A.	1954-55-56
Rosen, Andy	1939-40
Rosen, John	1941
Rosequist, Theodore A.	1932-33

Ross, Derek	1998-00
Ross, Everett	1986-87
Ross, Paul	1976-77-78
Ross, Richard L.	1960
Rosso, George A	1951-52-53
Rothrock, Phillip	1904-05-06
Roush, Ernest J.	1934-35
Roush, Gary S.	1968
Rowan, Everett L.	1925-26-27
Rowland, James H.	1959
Rudge, William H.	1893-94
Rudin, Walter M.	1934
Rudzinski, Jerry	1995-96-97-98
Ruehl, James J.	1952
Ruhl, Bruce	1973-74-75-76
Rusnak, Kevin G.	1967-68-69
Rutan, Hiram E.	1890
Rutherford, William A.	1966
Rutkay, Nicholas G.	1937
Ruzich, Stephen	1950-51
Ryan, Lee E.	1912

S

Sack, Irving, A.	1928
Salvaterra, Joseph	1932
Sander, B.J.	2000
Sander, Willard F.	1963-64-65
Sanders, Chris	1992-93-94
Sanders, Darnell	1999-00
Sanders, Daryl T.	1960-61-62
Sanzenbacher, Walter O.	1906-07-08
Sarkkinen, Eino	1940
Sarkkinen, Esco	1937-38-39
Sarringhaus, Paul H.	1941-42-45
Saunders, Cedric	1990-91-92-93
Saunders, Keith	1977
Savic, Pandel	1947-48-49
Savoca, James	1974-75-76-78
Sawicki, Tim	1976-79
Saxbe, Harry M.	1897
Sayer, Delbert B.	1898-99
Scannell, Michael P.	1971-72
Schabo, Andrew	2000
Schachtel, Sol H.	1906-07-08
Schad, Albert F.	1913
Schaeffer, George O.	1890
Schaeffer, John F.	1908-09
Schafrath, Richard P.	1956-57-58
Schear, Herbert	1927
Scheiber, Arthur L.	1909-10
Schiller, Richard T.	1952
Schlichter, Arthur	1978-79-80-81
Schmidlin, Paul R.	1967-68-69
Schneider, Michael	1977
Schneider, Wilbur H.	1942-46
Schnittker, Max A.	1945-46
Schnittker, Richard D.	1949
Schoenbaum, Alexander	1936-37-38
Schoenbaum, Leon H.	1941
Schorv, Herbert J.	1904-05-06-07
Schram, Fred	1971
Schreiber, John M.	1897-98
Schulist, Bernard H.	1922-23-24
Schumacher, James W.	1952-53
Schumacher, Kurt	1972-73-74
Schwartz, Brian	1976-77-78-79

Schwartz, Gerald	1952
Schwartz, Robert M.	1915
Schweitzer, Fred L.	1915
Scott, Cyrus E.	1899-1900
Scott, Dan	1971-73
Scott, Darrion	2000
Scott, Don E.	1938-39-40
Scott, Dudley	1899-1900
Scott, Herbert	1891
Scott, James H.	1934
Scott, Robert M.	1962
Scott, Walter S.	1899-1900
Secrist, Fred M.	1905-06-07-08
Seddon, Charles E.	1916-17
Sedor, William J.	1942
Segrist, Charles F.	1897-98-99-00-01
Segrist, John L.	1897-98-99-00-01
Seifert, Rick E.	1970-72
Seiffer, Ralph E.	1924
Seilkop, Kenneth	1959
Selby, Samuel	1928-29-30
Sensanbaugher, Dean S.	1943-47
Sensibaugh, Mike	1968-69-70
Sexton, James R.	1938-39-40
Shaffer, Jay	1986-87
Shafor, Ralph W.	1911-12
Shannon, Larry R.	1947
Shavers, Alonzo	1994-95
Shaw, Robert	1941-42
Shedd, Jan W.	1955
Sheldon, Charles T.	1904-06
Sherman, John K.	1900
Shifflette, Donald F.	1925
Shoaf, Mick	1989-90-91
Showalter, Michael	1986-87-89
Simindinger, Scott	1997
Simione, John R.	1939-40
Simmons, Jason	1990-91-92-93
Simon, Richard E.	1969-70-71
Simon, Charles	1974
Skillings, Vincent	1977-78-79-80
Skladany, Thomas	1973-74-75-76
Skvarka, Bernie G.	1950-51
Slager, Richard F.	1947-48
Slough, Herbert	1925-27
Slough, Ralph E.	1943
Slusser, George C.	1942
Slyker, William V.	1918-19-20-21
Smith, A. G.	1950-51
Smith, Bruce R.	1970
Smith, Carroll J.	1950-51
Smith, Douglas	1984-85
Smith, Dwight	1987-88
Smith, Eric	2000
Smith, Frank P.	1938
Smith, Gregory	1990-91-92
Smith, Herbert S.	1904
Smith, Huston R.	1966-67
Smith, Inwood	1934-35-36
Smith, Jack E.	1933-34
Smith, J. H.	1905
Smith, Joseph	1979-80-81-82
Smith, Larry W.	1965
Smith, L.C.	1911
Smith, Leonard J.	1910-11
Smith, Richard S.	1930-31-32
Smith, Robert G.	1967-68-69
Smith, Robert P.	1968

Smith, Robert S.	1990-92
Smith, Rod	1990-91-93
Smith, Ted	1973-74-75
Smith, Will	2000
Smith, Jr., Harley W.	1945-46
Smurda, John R.	1972-73
Smythe, John J.	1910
Sneddon, Elvadore R.	1918
Snedecker, W. A.	1893-94
Snell, Matthew	1961-62-63
Snow, Carlos	1987-88-89-91
Snyder, A. J.	1896
Snyder, Charles R.	1912-13-14
Snyder, Laurence N.	1923
Snyder, Thomas L.	1944-47
Sobolewski, John J.	1966-68
Soltis, Edward	1985
Sommer, Karl W.	1956
Sorenson, Frank G.	1914-15-16
Souders, Cecil B.	1942-43-44-46
Southern, Clarence H.	1923
Spahr, William H.	1962-63-64
Spangler, Rich	1982-83-84-85
Sparma, Joseph B.	1961-62
Spears, Jeremiah G.	1938-39
Spears, Thomas R.	1953-54-55
Spellman, Alonzo	1989-90-91
Spencer, George E.	1946-47
Spencer, Timothy	1979-80-81-82
Spielman, Chris	1984-85-86-87
Spiers, Robert H.	1919-20-21
Springer, George E.	1914
Springs, Ron	1976-77-78
Springs, Shawn	1994-95-96
Spychalski, Ernest T.	1956-57-58
Stablein, Brian	1989-90-91-92
Stablein, Chris	1989-90
Stackhouse, Raymond L.	1943
Staker, Loren J.	1942
Stamp, Andy	1996
Stanley, Bernie D.	1963
Stanley, Dimitrious	1993-94-95-96
Stark, Samuel	1898
Staysniak, Joseph	1986-87-88-89
Stead, Nate	2000
Steel, Harry D.	1922-23
Steele, Rolland	1997
Steinberg, Donald	1942-45
Steinle, Charles E.	1897
Stepanovich, Alex	2000
Stephens, Larry P.	1959-60-61
Stephens, Tim	1983
Stephenson, Jack W.	1939-40-41
Stevens, Jacob F.	1896
Stier, Mark H.	1966-67-68
Stillwagon, James R.	1968-69-70
Stillwell, Obie	1994-95
Stimson, George W.	1898
Stinchcomb, Gaylord R.	1917-19-20
St. John, Lynn W.	1900
Stock, Robert H.	1964
Stoeckel, Donald C.	1953-54-55
Stolp, W. J.	1905-06
Stora, Joseph	1943
Storer, Greg	1975-76-77
Stottlemyer, Victor R.	1966-67-68
Stoughton, Brian	1995

Stover, Byron E.	1911-12
Stowe, John H.	1968
Strahine, Michael	1977
Straka, Mark	1973
Stranges, Tony J.	1944
Strausbaugh, James E.	1938-39-40
Strickland, Philip S.	1968-69-70
Stringer, Korey	1992-93-94
Strong, Terry	1970
Stuart, John D.	1921
Stultz, Daniel	1997-98-99-00
Stungis, John J.	1943-46
Sturrup, Fred	2000
Sturtz, Karl L.	1949-50
Styles, Lorenzo	1992-93-94
Sualua, Nicky	1994-95
Sullivan, John	1984
Sullivan, John K.	1916
Sullivan, John L.	1985-86-87-88
Sullivan, Mark	1975-76-77-78
Sullivan, Mark P.	1979-80
Sullivan, Michael F.	1985-86-87-88
Summers, Merl G.	1908-09-10
Sumner, Jamie	1994-95
Surface, Frank M.	1902-03-04-05
Surington, Cyril T.	1927-28
Sutherin, Donald P.	1955-56-57
Swan, Earl G.	1902-03-04
Swartz, Donald C.	1952-53-54
Swartzbaugh, Charles B.	1913
Swartzbaugh, John D.	1943
Swinehart, Rodney E.	1946-47-48-49
Sykes, W. E.	1897

T

Taggart, Ed	1983-84-85-86
Takacs, Michael J.	1951-52-53
Tangeman, T. H.	1899-1900-01-05
Tanski, Victor T.	1932
Tarbill, John W.	1899
Tatum, Jack D.	1968-69-70
Tatum, Rowland	1981-82-83
Taylor, Alvin	1978
Taylor, Charles A.	1919-20-21
Taylor, John L.	1920
Taylor, Russell E.	1928-29
Taylor, Walter	1991-92-93
Teague, Willie "Merv".	1970-71-72
Teifke, Howard A.	1943-46-47-48
Templeton, David I.	1946-47-48
Terna, Scott	1993-94
Ternent, William A.	1952
Theis, Franklyn B.	1955
Thies, Wilfred L.	1933
Thom, Leonard	1939-40
Thomas, Aurealius	1955-56-57
Thomas, George B.	1905
Thomas, James	1949
Thomas, John R.	1943-44-45
Thomas, Joseph R.	1933
Thomas, Pat	1987-88-89
Thomas, Richard J.	1951-52
Thomas, Will C.	1965-66
Thompson, Ed	1974-75-76
Thompson, Kenneth	1955

Thompson, R. E.	1905-07
Thompson, Rollin H.	1892
Thornton, Robert F.	1952-53-54
Thrower, John D.	1900-02-03-04
Thrush, Jack	1990-92-93
Thurman, A. G.	1893-95
Tidmore, Samuel E.	1960-61
Tillman, Micheal (Buster)	1993-94-95-96
Tillman, J. H.	1901-02
Tilton, Josephus H.	1898-99-00-01
Tingley, David R.	1959-61
Titus, Clarence H.	1896
Tobik, Andy Bill	1940
Tolford, George K.	1959-60-61
Tomczak, Michael	1981-82-83-84
Toneff, George	1944-48-49
Tovar, Steve	1989-90-91-92
Tracy, William P.	1906
Trapuzzano, Robert	1969
Trautman, George M.	1911-12-13
Trautwein, Henry Bill	1948-49-50
Treat, W. G.	1910
Trivisonno, Joseph J.	1955-57
Troha, Richard J.	1969
Trott, Dean W.	1919-20-21
Turner, E. C.	1902
Turner, Irwin	1916
Tucci, Amel	1939
Tupa, Thomas	1984-85-86-87
Tyler, Julius B.	1896
Tyrer, James E.	1958-59-60

U

Uhlenhake, Jeff	1985-86-87-88
Ujhelyi, Joseph A.	1928-29
Ullery, Jack C.	1925-27
Ulmer, Edward	1960-61
Unverferth, Donald V.	1963-64-65
Updegraff, Winston R.	1922
Urban, Harry N.	1897
Urbanik, William J.	1967-68-69
Uridil, Leo R.	1925-26-27

V

Van Blaricom, Robert P.	1932
Van Buskirk, Lear H.	1907-08
Van Dyne, Kelley	1916-17
Van Horn, Douglas C.	1963-64-65
Van Raaphorst, R. W.	1961-62-63
Vanscoy, Norman J.	1960
Vargo, Kenneth W.	1953-54-55
Vargo, Thomas W.	1965
Varner, Martin D.	1930-31-32
Varner, Thomas A.	1960
Vavroch, William B.	1952
Vecanski, Milan	1970-71
Verdova, Alex S.	1945-46-47-48
Vickroy, William E.	1941-42
Vicic, Donald J.	1954-55-56
Vogel, Robert L.	1960-61-62
Vogelgesang, Donald A.	1960
Vogler, Terry	1977-78
Vogler, Tim	1975-76-77-78

Volley, Ricardo	1977-78-79
Volzer, Donald H.	1920
Von Schmidt, Walter G.	1927
Von Swearingen, Fiske	1909
Vrabel, Mike	1993-94-95-96
Vuchinich, Michael N.	1931-32-33

W

Wagner, Jack, W.	1950-51
Wagoner, John	1987
Wakefield, Richard	1969-70-71
Walden, Robert L.	1964-65-66
Waldon, Larry	1996-97
Walker, Barry	1983-84-85-86
Walker, Dow R.	1902-03-04
Walker, Gordon H.	1928
Walker, Jack E.	1960
Walker, Stephen E.	1971
Wallace, Robert H.	1944
Walter, Tyson	1997-98-99
Walther, Richard E.	1950-51
Walton, Tim	1990-91-92-93
Wandke, Richard A.	1944
Ward, Chris	1974-75-76-77
Ward, Grant P.	1912
Warden, Leonard G.	1894
Warfield, Paul D.	1961-62-63
Warner, Duane A.	1960
Warner, Geoff	1986-90
Warner, Stormy	1988
Warnke, Darik	1997-98-99
Warren, Lee G.	1905
Warwick, Herbert S.	1904
Washington, Alvin	1977-78-79-80
Wassmund, James A.	1956
Wasson, Harold	1922
Wasson, Richard	1963
Wasson, Robert E.	1895-96-97
Wasylik, Nicholas	1935-36-37
Waters, E. C.	1904
Watkins, Jene	1959
Watkins, Robert A.	1952-53-54
Watson, Otha	1978
Watson, Thomas G.	1945-48-49-50
Watts, Robert S.	1922-23-24
Waugh, Charles A.	1970
Waugh, Thomas	1976-77-78-79
Way, Rex D.	1907
Wayne, Clinton	1997-98-99-00
Wears, Leland H.	1934
Weaver, C. Robert	1920-21
Weaver, David A.	1953-54-55
Weaver, J. Edward	1970
Webb, Ashanti	1998
Weber, Fred C.	1898-99-00
Wedebrook, Howard N.	1936-37-39
Weed, Thurlow	1952-53-54
Welbaum, Thomas A.	1938-39
Welch, John W.	1947
Welever, Arthur W.	1931
Wells, Jonathan	1998-99-00
Wells, Leslie R.	1908-09-10

Wendler, Harold	1923-24-25
Wendt, Merle E.	1934-35-36
Wentz, Burke B.	1925
Wentz, William A.	1959-60
Wersel, Timothy	1972
Wertz, George P.	1948-49
West, Edward F.	1936
Westbrooks, Jerry	1999-00
Westwater, James G.	1896-99-00-01
Wetzel, Charles J.	1908
Wetzel, Damon H.	1932-33-34
Wharton, Homer F.	1898-99-00
Wheeler, T. L.	1902
Whetstone, Robert E.	1953-55
Whipple, Charles A.	1905-06-07
Whisler, Joseph G.	1946-47-49
Whitacre, J.H.	1890
White, C. C.	1892
White, Claude	1938-40
White, Jan	1968-69-70
White, John T.	1942
White, Loren R.	1957-58-59
White, Stanley R.	1969-70-71
White, Terry	1984-85
White, William	1984-85-86-87
Whitehead, Stuart F.	1938-39
Whitfield, David A.	1967-68-69
Whitmer, Doug	1982-83-84
Wible, Calvin D.	1945
Widdoes, Richard D.	1948-49-50
Wieche, Robert	1917-19-20
Wiggins, Larry	1972
Wilder, Thurlow C.	1920
Wiles, A. O.	1902
Wiley, Michael	1996-97-98-99
Wilhelm, Matthew	1999-00
Wilkerson, Keith	1993
Wilkins, Dwight	1972
Wilkinson, Dan	1992-93
Wilks, William C.	1951
Willaman, Frank R.	1917-19-20
Willaman, Samuel S.	1911-13
Willard, Robert	1973
Williams, Albert C.	1943
Williams, David M.	1953-54
Williams, Donald W.	1939
Williams, Gary	1979-80-81-82
Williams, Joe J.	1935-36
Williams, Lee E.	1955-58
Williams, Mark	1990-91-92-93
Williams, Robert D.	1968
Williams, Timothy	1990-91-92-93
Williams, Shad	1970-71-72
Willott, Louis	1974-75
Willis, Leonard	1974-75
Willis, Marcel	1995-97
Willis, William K.	1942-43-44
Wilson, Andrew J.	1946-47-48-49
Wilson, C. R.	1899
Wilson, Donald A.	1932-33
Wilson, Jeff	1995-96-97
Wilson, John B.	1922-23-24
Winfield, Antoine	1995-96-97-98
Wingert, Albert C.	1930

Winrow, Jason	1990-91-92-93
Winters, Harold A.	1915
Winters, Sam C.	1945
Wiper, Donald W.	1920-21
Wiper, Harold A.	1917-18-20
Wisniewski, Steve	1996-97-98-99
Withoft, Clarence	1891-92
Wittman, Julius W.	1949-50-51
Wittmer, Charles G.	1959-60-61
Wolery, Scott	1974
Wolf, Ralph C.	1936-37
Wolfe, Russell H.	1946
Wood, Charles L.	1892
Wood, Michael	1984-85
Woodbury, Chester	1905
Wooldridge, John	1983-84-85-86
Worden, Dirk J.	1966-67-68
Workman, Harry H.	1920-22-23
Workman, Noel	1920-21
Workman, Vince	1985-86-87
Wortman, Robert C.	1964
Wright, David W.	1970
Wright, Ernest H.	1958
Wright, Ward	1945
Wright, William E.	1909-10-11
Wuellner, Richard W.	1938-39

Y

Yards, Ludwig	1932-33-34
Yassenoff, Leo	1914-15
Yassenoff, Sol	1913-14
Yerges Sr., Howard F.	1915-16-17
Yerges Jr., Howard F.	1943
Yingling, Walter E.	1928
Yonclas, Nicholas	1963-64
Yost, Benjamin P.	1898
Young, Donald G.	1958-59-60
Young, Francis D.	1921-23-24
Young, Louis C.	1938
Young, Richard A.	1953-54
Young, William G.	1925-27-28

Z

Zackeroff, Greg	1985-86-87-88
Zadworney, Frank S.	1937-38-39
Zalenski, Scott	1981-82-83-84
Zangara, Donald	1945
Zarnas, Gust C.	1935-36-37
Zavis, George J.	1941
Zavistoske, George	1941
Zawacki, Charles E.	1955
Zelina, Lawrence P.	1968-69-70
Ziegler, Randall K.	1963
Zima, Albert J.	1962
Zimmer, Frank E.	1931
Zincke, Clarence F.	1929
Zinsmaster, John L.	1930
Zizakovic, Srecko	1986-88-89